TO MY WIFE

The increased industrial power of labour – and, it must be added, of employers too – has made the ordinary legislative procedure inadequate. . . . the supreme legislative assembly in these matters becomes merely a body for registering decisions arrived at outside itself.

D. J. SHACKLETON, *Ministry of Labour, 21 May 1919*[1]

Politics in Industrial Society

Politics in Industrial Society

The experience of the British system since 1911

KEITH MIDDLEMAS

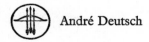 André Deutsch

First published 1979 by
André Deutsch Limited
105 Great Russell Street London WC1

Copyright © 1979 by Keith Middlemas
All rights reserved

Printed in Great Britain by
Ebenezer Baylis & Son Limited
The Trinity Press, Worcester, and London.

British Library Cataloguing in Publication Data

Middlemas, Keith
  Politics in industrial society
  1. Industrial relations – Great Britain – History
  – 20th century 2. Industry and state – Great
  Britain – History – 20th century
  I. Title
  331'.0941   HD8390

  ISBN 0-233-97129-7

CONTENTS

ACKNOWLEDGMENTS

A historian's indebtedness to his mentors and sources increases with time. Fully to acknowledge the advice and encouragement of colleagues and the criticism of fellow researchers and students which produce his amalgam of opinion in a book which has evolved over a number of years is impossible. But I would like to thank in particular Andrew Hardman, Patrick McGuire and Anthony Lerman: discussion of their research work was as valuable for me as I hope my comments were for them. Also I am grateful to Alan Cawson and to Brian McCormick who read the manuscript and made several helpful suggestions.

I acknowledge with gratitude the support of the Social Science Research Council whose grant enabled me to undertake the greater part of the research in public and private archives; and of the Nuffield Foundation Small Grants Scheme which facilitated its conclusion. I am also most grateful for permission to consult and quote from archives and manuscripts: to Her Majesty the Queen for her gracious permission to quote from papers in the Royal Archives at Windsor; to the Comptroller of HM Stationery Office for permission to quote from the State papers deposited in the Public Records Office; and to the following librarians and holders of private collections:

The Syndics of Cambridge University Library: Baldwin and Templewood collections; The Librarian, Churchill College, Cambridge: Bevin, Cunliffe-Lister, Halifax, Hankey, Margesson and Weir collections; The Conservative Research Department and Mr Geoffrey Block: Bayford papers; Conservative Agents' archive; Conservative Party archives; The Librarian, Transport House: Labour Party archives and the J. S. Middleton collection; The Librarian, London School of Economics: Beveridge Collection; The Librarian, Confederation of British Industries: the NCEO and BEC archives; The Librarian, Beaverbrook Library: Beaverbrook, Bonar Law, Davidson, Lloyd George and Younger collections; The Librarian, Federation of Engineering Employers: EEF archives; The Librarian, National Library of Scotland: Haldane collection; Mr Len Murray: The TUC archives, Congress House; Mrs R. M. Stafford, and the Scottish Record Office: the Steel-Maitland collection; Lady Eirene White and Mr Tristan Jones: Thomas Jones collection.

9

Acknowledgments

Finally, I acknowledge the permission of the various authors and publishers to quote from those works cited in the text, of which they have the copyright; that they are too numerous to detail here in no way diminishes this obligation.

NOTE ON REFERENCES

Footnotes which add materially to, or qualify, this text have been placed at the bottom of each page throughout. References and other notes will be found at the end. Archive collections are identified by initial letters, thus; RA – Royal Archives; LG – Lloyd George; JCCD – Davidson; SM – Steel-Maitland. For the public archives, normal notations are used: WC – War Cabinet; ADM – Admiralty; CAB – Cabinet, etc. A list of acronyms precedes the index.

INTRODUCTION

What is the system of modern British government? If, as a great deal of recent practical experience suggests, the accepted version of the working of the constitution, recodified from time to time in the textbooks of law and history, has become inadequate or erroneous, is it possible to discover a hidden code which explains more fully the behaviour of political parties, other institutions and government?

The limits of descriptive method scarcely need to be underlined. Political institutions, like all human organisations, are intangible entities, in constant flux. Evidence, even about the recent past, is necessarily fragmented or inadequate, and often simply not available because of official restrictions. Historians and political analysts habitually deal with sectors of national experience, parties, parliament, regional or local politics, or the politics of economic and strategic issues, chosen according to their expertise and the material available. The concept of totality or system is elusive, when it is not the product of dogmatic assertion of general theory; yet without theory, a system attained by cumulative description may be tautological.

Twentieth-century studies have, admittedly, been so overwhelmed with archival material during the last ten years (after the restriction on British government documents was reduced from fifty to thirty years, but also because of the increased availability and ordering of private archives) that it has become very difficult to study politics except in compartments. But as Konrad Lorenz suggested in his essay *The Fashionable Fallacy of Dispensing with Description*, anything so complicated as a living organism must contain elements which cannot be measured and quantified by scientific or mathematical methods, yet can only be understood if its functioning is studied as a whole, rather than as isolated aspects. What is true of experimental psychology is no less valid for the history of human institutions. The excuse that we must wait until all the groundwork of a new historical revision has been done is to ignore the ancient compulsion to form patterns and derive general theories in order to understand what we observe. Without that, groundwork remains mere accumulation.

Recent British historiography has suffered from a double bias: towards study of parties, almost to the exclusion of other institutions, and towards the history of Labour and Liberal parties rather than the long dominance of the Conservatives from 1916 to 1964. An approach to totality is made even harder by the lack of studies satisfactorily linking what, in the new jargon, is called 'high politics' at Westminster and structural developments in the constituencies or on the shop floor. Between the two lies a gulf both of method and understanding. If we ask how did political leadership affect 'grassroots' opinion, or how did that opinion condition the emergence of a certain type of party leadership, we fall back on assumptions about the influence of individual party leaders and the nature of the parliamentary system which are at present unverifiable or unsatisfactory. The vision of politics as an intelligible, regulated and orderly set of relationships, culminating in a coherent if complicated whole, cannot easily be sustained because institutions are not nation states, existing in a definable world, fortified with concepts of sovereignty and territory, and upheld by internationally recognised agreements. They are not, in their early stages of growth, constitutionally even legitimate. At what point, then, when institutions such as political parties, trade unions and employers' associations acquire formal, legal quantities, can their relationships be studied, measured and construed as a system? For Marxist historians, as for religious fundamentalists, the answer is less difficult than for those to whom theory comes hard, and who recognise the dangers of applying deductive reasoning in a fundamentalist way.

The point was made, pungently, by Professor Ralph Miliband in his inaugural lecture in 1975, when he castigated some of the trends of recent political analysis:

Political studies in Britain have been very weak in theory and in theorising capacity. The obverse of this coin is a crass empiricism, based on the pathetic fallacy that the more facts that one is able to accumulate, say about the mechanism of a political system or institution, the more one knows about the purposes it serves and the functions it fulfils.[1]

But it follows that what he calls

the attempt to see the political element as an integral yet distinct part of a totality which encompasses specific historical, economic, social and cultural elements; and to try to understand the functions which political institutions and ideas perform in the conflicts that constantly proceed between classes and other social groups rests on a predetermined viewpoint about the objective nature of conflict in society. Historians with different ideological presumptions will not agree – though they may concur on the importance of class struggle, for as Marx himself recognised, class analysis has never been the prerogative of the Left,[2] and many sound British Conservatives, Disraeli, Salisbury and Baldwin among them, used their insights into class conflict to pursue their own targets of avoiding crisis and harmonising clashing interests.

A transformation in the presentation of economic issues in the mid-twentieth century, however, makes it increasingly difficult to fit events into the classical exposition of class conflict, at least in industrially advanced societies. Writers as far apart as Galbraith and the epigoni of the Frankfurt school have shown that the corporate role of the state, inspired by an underlying aim of preventing crisis and conflict by arranging a continuous series of compromises between oligarchic interest groups, has led not only to a diminution in the power of individuals and electorates to control or limit the activity of politicians and bureaucracies, but to the blurring of ancient sources of class conflict particularly in the fields of wage-bargaining and unemployment provision. Many of the most significant conflicts of the last twenty years have lain between individuals and the institutions which, traditionally, represented their class interests.

This is not to say, however, that the system can be depicted by the mechanical quantification characteristic of much American political science in the 1960s, when it was claimed that late (sometimes called 'post') capitalist societies had entered a phase where managerial science and economic management had combined to resolve, or at least reduce to a minimum, the ancient sources of class conflict. Forecasts of an 'end of ideology' inside continuously more affluent societies have a distinctly dated look today, after the successive shocks of the late 1960s and early 70s to world economic and political stability. One must start with the assumption that power relationships are not naturally compatible, before studying the means by which conflict has been resolved in modern society.

A book begun in the very different circumstances of the late sixties as an attempt to explain the apparent incompetence, since 1900, of successive British governments faced with problems of political and industrial change has obviously been affected by contemporary debates over the last ten years. Every historian has to accept that his preoccupations about the past are so conditioned and this need not be any reason for apology. Without constant revision of the questions asked of it, history itself becomes repetitious; conversely, without the historical and comparative dimension, it would be hard to expect an answer to new questions, such as whether the scope of parliamentary democracy in Britain has diminished in recent years, and whether institutions such as trade unions and employers' associations have acquired corporate political power. Given the range of evidence made available since the opening of government archives in 1968, such questions can, however, be answered in a sufficiently continuous and dense* fashion to establish a theory not just about the behaviour of governments but of British 'governance' in the first half of the twentieth century, with definite contemporary implications and possibilities of comparison with other modern industrial societies where similar developments have occurred, though not necessarily at the same time.

It would have been folly to try to describe more than the dominant trends since the formative crisis of the First World War. I have taken as the essential minimum the evolving relationship between government, trade unions and employers' associations from the turn of the century to 1945; and, allowing for the changing nature of evidence, prolonged it to the early 1970s. This time-scale is logical: during the First World War, the relationship between the state and its citizens, between the 'political nation' and the real nation, altered profoundly. The implicit contract between them was sharply redefined in circumstances of extreme crisis as, in order to avoid defeat in war, the government imposed first military conscription and then industrial discipline of unprecedented severity. Over and above the venerable debates about the nature of compulsion in society, the political nation was faced with a distinct conflict between its conception of the national interest and what it discovered public opinion desired; and, to avoid political breakdown, was consequently forced to find ways of maintaining its authority, and the national interest which that implied, by fresh compromises.

By 1918 concessions had been made to newly enfranchised political institutions which were not to be found in textbooks like Dicey's *Law of the Constitution* or Anson's *Constitutional Law*. There followed a period of nearly half a century in which, by comparison with other industrial countries of Europe, Britain enjoyed remarkable stability and domestic peace. When political disruption did occur, in the later 1960s, it was at first seen as a series of economic disasters, a deterioration

---

*In the sense used by Henry James: 'Morally and physiologically' he wrote of England, 'it is a *denser* air than ours. We [Americans] seem loosely hung together at home, compared with the English.' (*English Hours*, Heinemann, 1905, p. 60.)

in the balance of payments, in Britain's relative performance, and rate of inflation. But by the measure of long-term economic performance, a satisfactory balance had been held for, at most, five good years in the early 1950s; whereas the political harmony that had been lost ran back through the war years to the early 1920s, a continuum almost without precedent in post-Reformation history. Thus the chronological half-century defines the study of the distribution and redistribution of power.

The importance of the British – or rather English* – example is not self-evident. In the sum of modern political science, studies of British models now rank low in Europe and have long been subordinate to those of the United States. This may be a reasonable standpoint, since Britain's century-long relative decline has encouraged a belief in her concomitant political decadence. But some of the patterns of most interest in the analysis of late-capitalist societies emerged in Britain thirty or forty years earlier than in Western Europe or the United States, and the apparent breakdown of the late 1960s ought perhaps to be seen as something singular, distinct from the European experience since 1968.

English history since 1918 has only recently been subjected to close structural analysis by economic and social historians and their demure disputes about aspects of the inter-war years have, understandably, a limited interest to European historians, preoccupied with the more spectacular conflicts between Fascism and Communism. Moreover the English have been content that it should be so: the operation of the fifty- then thirty-year rule against availability of any but official publication of government archives, and the steadily increasing stringency of official secrecy since the 1930s, has worked to the advantage of empirical rather than theoretical inquiries. The parliamentary democratic mode was inevitably most often reproduced – first admired, and later, on recent performance, disparaged by foreign observers.

Paradoxically, the post-1945 generation of English historians and their European and American counterparts tended to emphasise the flexibility of a political system which had evolved since the armed crisis of the seventeenth century without revolutionary explosion. They described what, by comparison with European examples, seemed the sensitivity of the political élite to the demands of important interest

*London-centred government, the Civil Service and institutions such as the TUC and CBI, whilst not exclusively English, tended in this period to behave according to the habits of an English-dominated political culture. The role of the Scottish TUC, for example, would form an interesting variant but is beyond the scope of this book.

groups in each decade, and the finely judged alternative use of coercion which, together, averted crisis. When set against the failure of popular insurrection in the 1790s and 1810s, the dissolution of Chartism and, much later, the waning of industrial discontent in the 1920s, flash-points such as Peterloo, Bloody Sunday in Trafalgar Square, the civil unrest of 1912–14, and the General Strike of 1926, counted as nine days' wonders, temporary lesions in the generally harmonious brokerage between state and people.

Such conclusions about the English tradition appealed, for different reasons, to commentators in America in the 1950s, still concerned to point up the ageing relationship with England, and in Germany where the Allied powers had a strong interest in the recreation of a parlia-mentary democracy, though not in France, already suffering the indignities of imperial collapse. They survived so long as foreign observers believed that England had something positive to contribute to the political form of the European Community, and it is a tribute to their persistence that, when optimism finally vanished, the consequence was incomprehension mixed with pity, rather than anger at betrayal. But the first idea jettisoned was that modern England might hold an example of value.

The generic weakness of this concept of the English tradition was exposed as soon as historians directed the light away from Westminster and Whitehall onto the regions and those groups excluded from 'high politics'. A radical tradition, exemplified earlier in R. H. Tawney's studies of the sixteenth and seventeenth centuries, more recently in Christopher Hill's analysis of the England of the Civil War, or Edward Thompson's exposure of the alternative political culture of a previously unchartered early nineteenth-century working class, argued that the political system had survived the conflict of classes only because of its firm grounding in economic power and its use of outright repression – and that this reinterpretation of the past might itself facilitate radical change in the future.

The 'Whig interpretation' of history nevertheless survived, as if a state of equilibrium were natural in society, achieved at times in the past and temporarily lost since by incompetence or mismanagement. Praise or blame might be allotted to Prime Ministers and Cabinets, and later to the whole apparatus of the state, according to their ability to maintain, reform and hand on the system without disruption. This cyclical and fundamentally Conservative view* seems an implausible

---

*Exemplified in a speech by Stanley Baldwin in 1925: 'How often has mankind travelled on the circumference of a wheel, working its way to a point that you could

vehicle to explain continuous multiple change in society and the process by which stability was recreated over time. Yet even the radical historians concentrated on periods of crisis, leaving relatively undamaged the assumption that the political system did survive because of its inherent flexibility and the skills of its élite, as if all wisdom were summed up in Lord Salisbury's reassurance to his colleagues that the landed interest would survive the passing of the Local Government Bill of 1888, because they would still rule the new County Councils, the more secure for having won their seats by democratic election.

After all, the worst had not happened. In his retrospective assault on Edwardian myopia and complacency, George Bernard Shaw made Captain Shotover declare, in *Heartbreak House*, as the bombing began: 'The captain is in his bunk, drinking bottled ditchwater, and the crew is gambling in the forecastle. The ship will strike and sink and split. Do you think the laws of God will be suspended in favour of England because you were born in it?' The bombs missed: but we need not postulate the existence of divine law to ask why England should largely have been exempted from the successive European crises of this century, the collapse of the nineteenth-century political system, the worst of the 'scorching effect' – as E. L. Woodward described it – of war itself, the efflorescence of Fascism, Nazi domination and the totalitarian face of Communism. What happened to the palpable class warfare of 1911–14? Why did the troop mutinies of 1919, the strikes of 1921 and 1926, the political crisis of 1931, the deep social lesions of the 1930s, or the crisis of the Second World War in 1940, not lead to revolutionary change, as similar occasions did across the Channel?

Total war in 1914–18 brought about large alterations in the nature of English politics which seemed to radical contemporaries as far apart as Tawney and John Maclean only the prelude to the collapse of capitalism. Others saw in the emergence of Lloyd George, as St Simonian superman, a new era of coalition, beyond party faction, buttressed by cooperative institutions and served by neutral experts better fitted to govern than the feeble instruments of the old system. Then in the 1930s, in the middle of appalling unemployment, at a time when disparity between the contented easy-going middle-class south and east of England, and the derelict, industrial, working-class remainder was still growing, many political commentators feared – or hoped – that the country would succumb to Fascist organisation, or

---

call democracy. Go but a little further and democracy becomes licence, licence becomes anarchy, and then the wheel goes full circle and anarchy comes back to tyranny and man has to fight his way back out of tyranny once again.'

that the National Government, with its overwhelming parliamentary majority, would erect an authoritarian state. George Orwell talked of 'the gentlemanly semi-Fascism' of the Conservative Party and G. D. H. Cole deplored the confusion only too evident after the fragmentation of the political left in 1931.

Plausible in their day, these diagnoses were incorrect. Parliamentary democracy appeared to survive – though England was not spared internal tensions and popular dissent during the First World War similar to those which grievously damaged France's political system and led in Germany to the abortive revolution of 1918, in Russia to the real revolution of 1917, and in Italy to the triumph of Mussolini in 1922. England was not then as isolated from European culture and experience as she became in the inter-war years.

But according to fashionable interpretation, British governments of the inter-war years were slothful in planning or weak in the execution of policies which were, in any case, futile in the face of great problems of economic decline. Rather than give them credit for the maintenance of political stability, this latter view invokes the 'English tradition' as an explanation, concentrates on the genius of Lloyd George, stigmatises the years 1922–40, and takes up, in 1940, the picture of a reunited nation under Winston Churchill, followed by the wise reformism of the Attlee government after 1945.

I argue the opposite: that a new form of harmony in the political system was established with great difficulty in the decade 1916–26; and that it lasted at least until the mid-sixties when the much-vaunted 'consensus' was seriously, if not fatally, disrupted. Is it unreasonable to assume that, earlier than in any other industrial country, British governments began to make the avoidance of crises their first priority? That even before the era of full suffrage they had discovered how to exercise the arts of public management, extending the state's powers to assess, educate, bargain with, appease or constrain the demands of the electorate, raising to a sort of parity with the state the various competing interests and institutions to which voters owed allegiance? That they sought to avoid, by compromise, crises in sensitive areas like wages and conditions, public order, immigration, unemployment, or the position of women, abolishing Hobbes' 'natural anarchy of competing wills' not by invoking authority (at a time of declining faith and deference) but by the alternate gratification and cancelling out of the desires of large, well-organised, collective groups to the detriment of individuals, minorities and deviants? That they created in Britain a political *Gleichschaltung*, subtle and loose enough to be resented only by those deviants and minorities; in which, despite the appearance of crises in 1922, 1931 and 1940, Party and Parliament declined in governing importance, while supposedly intractable economic conflicts were diffused, and the challenges of Conservatism and Socialism were alike dispersed in a common reformist policy justified by an unreal assessment of historical tradition?

To try to test this hypothesis, I began by studying the crisis of the First World War, when for the first time a British government was forced to bargain for national public support in order to fulfil the inordinate demand for munitions and manpower which, according to its military advisers, were necessary for victory. Thereafter the governance of the country changed, qualitatively as well as quantitatively, even though the vast extension of its scope masked the fact that it depended in the last resort on popular acceptance – as indicated in a handful of cases in the inter-war years where governments failed to obtain consent and were forced to abandon their policies.

But how were acceptable limits between government, institutions and popular opinion established? For lack of sound evidence about mass opinion, except at election time, one has to rely on detailed studies of the genesis of particular policies, especially on contentious issues where governments might be expected to have listened to the public voice, or to have tried to discover and interpret it. It is possible by this sort of accumulation to establish what successive governments (whose illusions that national opinion automatically corresponded to their concept of the national interest had been shattered in 1915–17) imagined public opinion to be, how they set out to measure it, what agencies they used, how they evaluated the result and incorporated it in their policy, and to what extent they embarked on programmes of public education, propaganda or coercion to ensure their acceptance by the majority of the population.

Governments, however, devoted themselves not simply to winning the lowest common measure of agreement, but to the management of opinion as an unending process, using the full educative and coercive power of the state. Propaganda agencies, techniques of persuasion were largely, though not entirely, the creation of the First World War emergency. During the Lloyd George Coalition government they were not abandoned. Opinion management sometimes failed to work; large groups even refused to follow and Sinn Féin in Ireland repudiated both the state's authority and its right of coercion. But with this exception, actual revolt was rare, short-lived and usually unsuccessful (in contrast to civil disloyalty in Weimar Germany, or France of the Third Republic). Over the twenty-five years after 1921, the crude methods of the wartime Ministry of Propaganda developed into the informal (and highly immoral) methods used during the Coalition; in due course these were transmuted into an increasingly formal network of information-gathering and use essential to the functioning of an interventionist state authority, and grounded increasingly in the assumption that the process was actually neutral – a curious outcome, reinforced by the apparatus of control which ensured secrecy about what government believed the public should not know.

But brokerage of this sort alone could not ensure harmony. The line of greatest social conflict, like the earthquake fault between continental plates, lay through industrial politics. Here the triangular pattern of cooperation between government and the two sides of industry, which is the main theme of this book, led to the elevation of trade unions and employers' associations to a new sort of status: from interest groups they became 'governing institutions'. Arnold Toynbee once observed that institutionalisation is the price of durability; what happened in Britain in the 1930s and 40s, however, went further. Equilibrium was maintained because the governing institutions came to share some of the political power and attributes of the state, itself avid to admit representative bodies to its orbit rather than face a free-for-all with a host of individual claimants. I have called this process *corporate bias*, but it should not be confused with the corporate state of classical Fascism, nor the somewhat naive corporatism from time to time advocated by industrial theorists in the 1930s and 40s in Britain, which centred on the National Industrial Council or industrial parliament, and would have shackled industry formally to government without in itself resolving the economic and social tensions fundamental to industrial life.

The experience of 1914–18, and the widely disseminated industrial conflict before and after the war showed that the nineteenth-century British political system had broken down under the weight of antagonisms in industrial society. The wartime Coalition government was, however, strong enough to resist the temptation to assume authoritarian powers taken, for example, in Germany in 1916 by Hindenburg and Ludendorff; and to fend off demands by the Labour movement for what it considered wholly unacceptable changes in social and economic organisation. By 1922 it had become clear that a sufficient number of union and employers' leaders had accepted the need of formal political collaboration with the state. TUC and employers' organisations crossed a threshold which had not even existed before the war, and behaved thereafter in some degree as estates of the realm, to the detriment of more ancient, obsolete estates, the municipalities, the churches, the 'colleges' of professional men, and the panoply of voluntary bodies, so important in the political system of the nineteenth century.

But the claims of governing institutions to a share of state power and enhanced status rested on their acceptance of fundamental national aims and their abandonment in practice (though not on the public platform) of the ideology of class conflict. Thus there grew up a new range of conflicts between them and their constituencies. In spite of a long attempt to impose more central control, TUC and employers' organisations failed to make their institutions fully representative according to the models obligingly preferred by corporate theorists, and because their association with the state remained vulnerable to revolt from below, they took care to veil it as far as possible. All partners to this political contract had a vested interest in secrecy; none was able to dispense with political education and the manipulation of opinion in its own sphere, because each feared the power of opposition from within its own organisation.

To say this is to begin with a conclusion. It would be quite wrong to imagine that the First World War produced a grand design, later incorporated into the structure of government. Indeed, there is little evidence that the War Cabinet were able to see far beyond the dictates of short-term survival on the war and domestic fronts. For a short time, from 1918 to 1919, a synoptic view prevailed, until the mists of industrial unrest, economic crisis, and civil war in Ireland closed down. Even so, few of Lloyd George's colleagues were able to share his vision. Not for nothing did he hang over his bed a piously worked sampler bearing a text from the Book of Job: 'There is a path which no fowl knoweth, and which the eye of the vulture hath not seen.'[3] The pattern has to be wrung from the evidence of day-to-day bargaining and political horsetrading. Managerial collective government is, after all, usually dated from the years 1941–43, with the introduction of manpower budgeting, the Beveridge Report, and legally enforced industrial arbitration.

But because it grew from day to day, flexibly, according to the exigencies of the time, institutional collaboration supplemented the party parliamentary system and produced a measure of harmony in the inter-war years. Secrecy about its workings, the survival of a deferential and uncritical tradition towards the governing process, and the generally Conservative trend of political commentators in the BBC and the national press, ensured that it was only rarely opened to public discussion. Survival into the 1950s of political and institutional leaders who had worked within the system helped to prolong the period of equilibrium. Not until a younger generation succeeded those party leaders like Clement Attlee or Harold Macmillan, and trade unionists like Arthur Deakin, Tom Williamson, and Will Lowther, was there a break in transmission of the doctrine that it was the prior aim of government to prevent crisis and class confrontation, and of the institutions to assist. One part of the explanation of the conflicts of the late 1960s may be found in the countervailing doctrine of economic rather than political management, and the decisions of the Labour government of 1964–9, and the subsequent Conservative administration to run counter to the inherited habits and political wisdom of the previous half-century by imposing self-destroying tasks on the institutions and appealing, at the same time, over their heads to the nation at large.

During these fifty years, the function of parties changed and the importance of ideology in party warfare steadily declined, so that election and inter-election propaganda either avoided ideological debate or relegated it to matters of marginal importance advanced by minority groups on centrally stage-managed occasions like party conferences. The admission of the Labour movement to the wartime coalition in 1940, far from being the quietus of inter-war collaborationism, represented a significant victory of inter-party harmony. The common struggle against an external enemy provoked in both Labour and Conservative Parties acceptance of the ideas of a mixed economy, a modified imperial role, a welfare state and the perpetuation of institutional consensus.

Long before 1945, Parliament had ceased to be the supreme governing body, and became instead the electoral source of the majority which provided the party element in government. The strength or weakness of that majority, its competence according to the standards used in the electoral battle, and the calibre of its leaders, of course affected party tenure. But the more that great economic, financial and strategic issues were taken out of political debate in the 1930s and 40s, the more parties and Parliament subordinated themselves to the administrative and managerial powers of the state apparatus. The electoral cycle itself ceased to correspond in any precise sense to the interactions of government and public on long-term political problems such as unemployment or industrial relations.

The role of the so-called 'neutral' element in the state apparatus also changed. Quintessentially late Victorian, the theory of public service reached its apogee in the last quarter of the nineteenth century. Constitutional historians took for granted that men in government service – the 'fit and proper persons' – were classless (in the sense of remaining impartial in all conflicts) and conscious of party, if at all, only in their private lives. Modified to meet twentieth-century requirements, this belief extended to cover experts and advisers to government, the staffs and boards of state corporations and, after 1945, of the nationalised industries. It survives, largely unimpaired. Yet if Parliament and parliamentary decisions were no longer the only or even the most direct source of power, the theory became a tautology: neutrality could be defined as congruence with the aims of the state, as perceived and defined by the same experts and public servants.

Although MacDonald and Baldwin, the party leaders in the inter-war years, repudiated what they regarded as Lloyd George's blurring of the lines of responsibility between civil service and elected politicians, they were both later constrained to accept the increasingly managerial function of the state; while others, like Steel-Maitland, Snowden, Sir John Simon, and Neville Chamberlain, positively welcomed the change. The disparity between the 'constitutional' view of Parliament as source of authority for a governing party and the functionalist approach to the actual running of the machine by an integrated team of party leaders, heads of departments, outside experts and powerful interest groups, was not reconciled by the brief era of the 'true party men' who destroyed the Coalition in 1922; it increased, to the detriment of party, after 1931, and culminated during Chamberlain's own administration after 1937.

These propositions have an importance not only for modern Britain, but most Western industrialised societies. The study of the historical period 1916 to 1945 stands by itself, but I have tried therefore to extend it into the province where 'contemporary history' meets political science and to discuss the nature of the contemporary system, its tendencies towards corporatism, and to make comparisons of value to present-day discussion.

University of Sussex
October 1978

PART ONE

PART ONE

I THE EDWARDIAN STRUCTURE

An undergraduate educated at one of England's ancient universities before the First World War, who found time in his courses to escape from the ubiquitous study of the classics, might have been taught about the relationship of the individual to the state, and the question of political obligation, using the contrast between Colonel Rainboro's classic statement of the individual case for manhood suffrage (during the debates held between representatives of the army and the generals at Putney in 1647) – 'I think the poorest he that is in England hath a life to live as the richest he; and therefore, truly, Sir, I think it clear that every man that is to live under a government ought, first, *by his own consent*, to put himself under that government' – and General Ireton's equally well-known rejoinder, that only the man of property truly had a stake in the country and a right to join in its rule.

Yet if he had asked about the relationship between the theory of government and popular consent and the practical evidence of class conflict in the society he entered after graduating, answers would have been harder to find. He would have been schooled on stereotyped descriptions of British politics, and perhaps of some foreign systems such as France or the United States (but not on a comparative basis); in the history of political ideas, in a grand hierarchy from Plato's *Republic*, via Aristotle and Aquinas, to Hobbes and Locke, Hume and Rousseau; and in the philosophy of a handful of concepts like sovereignty and rights. But this simplicity masked real obscurities and the fundamental doubt implied in Cromwell's quizzical remark, 'I am as much for government by consent as any man, but if you ask me how it is to be done, I confess I do not know.' If he had suspected that the accepted version was not congruent with the political experience of the nation as a whole, if he had asked questions about the actual distribution and use of political power in contemporary society, he would have been hard put to pierce through the formal descriptive screen of Crown and Parliament, legislature, executive and judiciary. The prolonged struggle between the House of Commons and the Lords, culminating in 1911, would have taught him more about how England was actually governed; yet he still might have concluded his inquiry, like the Liberal MP and writer, Charles Masterman, in agnostic despair, confronted with 'the appearance of a complicated machine which has escaped the control of all human volition and is progressing towards no intelligible goal; of some black windmill, with gigantic sails, rotating untended under the huge span of night.'[1]

Apart from the minority whom the Fabians strove to educate as the future political élite, an absence of critical theory to a great extent distinguished non-Marxist British political scientists from the European schools in Vienna, Berlin or Paris. The few lights among 'the insular and unanalytical people', like J. H. Green and F. D. Maurice, took almost for granted popular consent to the law of the constitution, while the theory of sovereignty put forward by J. L. Austen, corroborated by the findings of *The New Leviathan*, provided an antithesis to Hobbes' view of the law as a necessary set of rules imposed on recalcitrant individual wills. Where they failed to explain either how government constituted a continuous dynamic process, or how popular consent was mobilised and rendered effective other than at election time, the gap was filled by the work of constitutional lawyers and historians, recreating the past through the intellectual framework of nineteenth-century Liberalism. A certain type of parliamentary reformism was thus given the status of a national tradition.

Disparagement and resentment of foreign thinking* had their source as much in the deep unease prevalent among the late Edwardian political élite about Britain's declining achievements compared with those of Germany and the United States, as in the fact, noticed by Collingwood, that the English 'were always contemptuous of foreigners'. It was Scotland at the turn of the century which remained open to radical ideology. The dominant European sociologists of the 1890s and 1900s, Max Weber, Durkheim and Tönnies were, as yet, little read in an England where Freud was bowdlerised or ignored, even among psychologists, until his work found practical application in the treatment of shell-shock cases in the First World War. Thus Tönnies' distinction between *gemeinschaft* (the community based on real consent, which had once existed but had in recent times been lost) and *gesellschaft* (the formal association, embodying enforced assent conditioned by the

*The Times Educational Supplement review of one of John Dewey's books found it necessary, even in 1916, to state – presumably to an educated audience – 'We cannot wholly exclude the influence of foreign ideas. . . . If we repulse a direct attack, the stream flows in on us by the backwater of our Dominions.' (4 January 1916.)

28

economic and social organisation of modern society) scarcely influenced the debate about political consent and the rights of interest groups and minorities.

Because of what Maitland called the 'long troughs and hollows of history', and the enormous overlap in different sections of a densely layered society, many of Bagehot's deductions about the power of deference in stabilising the relationship between state, parliament and political parties, remained valid. But when it came to accounting for, and consequently legitimising, change, the Edwardian undergraduate would have turned for explanation to modern commentators like Dicey, who had revised his *Law of the Constitution* in half a dozen editions before 1911. Dicey's exposition of the growth of collectivism rested on examples taken from the 1890s,[2] while his analysis of the influence of Benthamite thinking in state policy-making shows that what he meant by 'public opinion' was no more than a reflection of the intellectual climate of the élite surrounding politicians of the day. Even so, in questioning the accepted wisdom that the political system could be defined simply as party-based competition for mass support, with the resultant parliamentary majority conveying the prize of office, Dicey came closer to an understanding of changing institutional relationships than his contemporary Ostrogorski, whose fear that the party caucuses would learn how to swamp voters with propaganda and rule West-minster with bands of subordinate hacks, seemed to give sombre point to the party crisis over the Parliament Act of 1911.

By 1911 the power of the state apparatus, as distinct from party administrations, *was* increasing, but in negative and often haphazard ways. There could be no reversal of the powers acquired in the second half of the nineteenth century as a result of continuity of administration, which G. M. Young observed in the field of education: 'Over all those late Victorian years soars the airy and graceful figure of the school inspector, ingeminating *porro unum est necessarium*: organise your secondary education,'[3] assisted by the accumulation of knowledge and scientific technology. Yet even in the minds of the Webbs, relentlessly searching for their legions of 'unassuming experts', this tendency could not compare with the centralised bureaucracies of Germany or France. The Civil Service as a whole did not act as a countervailing factor on its political masters: even in the high tide of the Liberal reformist period, the groups around Lloyd George and Churchill were divided among themselves. Politicians' use of patronage survived, and its corollary, the fleeting tenure and amateurish contributions indicated in the biographies of many Edwardian officials, so that even in 1912

Sir Lewis Selby-Bigge was to be found pleading with the MacDonnell Commission on the Civil Service for a more rigorous definition of expertise.

Among the older departments of state, it is true, established civil servants managed to influence the making of policy: in the Colonial Office, for example, during Joseph Chamberlain's tenure in the 1890s, and again after 1907. Yet there was scarcely any scope for development of a coherent line of policy: 'The staff did not have the leisure to speculate on the future of the Empire; they rarely had the opportunity of consciously moulding developments. Nor, perhaps, would they have welcomed such responsibility.'[4] Senior Foreign Office staff like Lewis Mallet, Charles Hardinge, Eyre Crowe and William Tyrrell did have this chance – and exercised it, until the outbreak of war and the triumph of Lloyd George in 1916 curtailed them; but their status remained a product of personal friendship rather than official usage. Grey may have 'enjoyed discussing questions of policy with his senior men and even encouraged debate and contention . . . [but] Grey was as much the master of his office as Salisbury.'[5] The influence of Admiralty and War Office in the planning of grand strategy needs no pointing up: but access to ministers remained the prerogative of a handful of charismatic senior officers – Admirals Fisher and Beresford and Generals Roberts, Kitchener and Haig; officials in the Service departments scarcely counted where policy was concerned, unless like Colonel Maurice Hankey, Secretary of the Committee of Imperial Defence, they were a part of the military establishment in their own right.

The only agency with power over and against party government was the Treasury, not so much because of its continuity and expertise in fiscal matters, as through its growing control over the remainder of the state apparatus. As Sir Robert Chalmers suggested in evidence to the MacDonnell Commission, greater conformity of practice, organisation and administration had been laid down in Treasury circulars over two decades before the First World War, and largely accepted by other departments. The Treasury was becoming the central coordinating department and thus defining the assumptions on which much of Whitehall activity was based. But Chalmers added that Treasury control rested on the willingness of central government to back it up; and the Royal Commission felt it necessary to report that, 'whatever may be its indirect influence, the Treasury does not, in practice, exercise a sufficiently effective control over the organisation of departments, unless a question of finance is involved.'[6] It was not to be given formal oversight of the Civil Service until 1919 and the real measure of its failure to develop the concept of a national economic policy can be seen in its helplessness in face of wartime exigencies and the demands for unfettered activity by War Office and Ministry of Munitions.

With the possible exception of the Labour Department of the Board of Trade no single office possessed a departmental opinion, nor the sort of creative capacity unleashed by Lloyd George's introduction of the Cabinet Office in 1916.[7] The collective influence of civil servants may even have counted for less than that of the political constellations of outsiders, whether Fabians or ex-members of Milner's 'Kinder-garten'. Indeed lines of demarcation scarcely existed: unofficial groups such as 'The Family', or those who attended the luncheons at the Authors' Club, included senior civil servants like Sir H. Llewellyn Smith of the Board of Trade, as well as writers, journalists and practising politicians.

For an inquiry as important as a Royal Commission, government could tap a remarkable range of talent: gifted editors such as C. P. Scott, J. A. Spender or A. G. Gardiner and writers like H. N. Brailsford, Clifford Sharp, W. S. G. Adams, H. Massingham, J. A. Hobson and L. T. Hobhouse, whose advice was showered on depart-ments as well as government. But these outsiders remained isolated from the forces of mass opinion, for the late nineteenth-century ideal of an informing and progressive press had largely been destroyed by the efflorescence of popular commercial journalism;[8] even in the heyday of the Liberal Radicals, the fourth estate's power over government rested on an illusion. Although the full nature of the transition to a popular Press with large capital investment and high profit margins did not be-come evident until after 1916 (when Asquith, Lloyd George, Bonar Law and Baldwin all had to come to terms with the phenomenon of the press lords, and their overweening political ambitions) the returns on Spender's or Scott's advice, for example, declined sharply after the crisis of 1911.

More important, as representatives of change, were the 'statisticians' like Rowntree, Boyd Orr and Bowley, who as influences on government would, in the long run, replace even such remarkable *hommes de confiance* as Lords Haldane and Esher. Haldane himself gave an epitaph on his own and Esher's influence to Beatrice Webb when he declared:

He believed more than we [the Webbs] did in the existing government order: in the great personages of Court, Cabinet and City. [In contrast] we staked our hopes on the organised working class, served and guided, it is true, by an elite of unassuming experts who could make no claim to superior social status, but content themselves with exercising the power inherent in superior knowledge and larger administrative experience.[9]

31

The 'unassuming experts' would dominate Civil Service opinion after 1916; but were not, as yet, aggregated in a 'visible college'.

On the fringe of government, older institutions which had once shared some of the powers and functions of the state, and still seemed to occupy as major a place in the constitution as they had done when Disraeli, in his 1872 Crystal Palace speech, called the Conservative Party to the defence of institutions, empire and people, had entered on their long decline. Evanescent regional power carried with it the vested interests of universities and boroughs alike, just as the new functions of government departments, bestowed by Liberal reforms, relegated professional colleges like the General Medical Council or the Law Society to positions of narrower sovereignty; with power only over their own members' initiation as graduates, physicians, priests or barristers.

Whatever conflicts Queen Victoria had entered into with her Ministers, Edward VII exhibited punctilious regard for constitutional propriety, and never sought to revive lost powers such as his nephew Wilhelm II enjoyed in Germany. The military and naval establishments certainly involved Ministers in their disputes over grand strategy and their warring factions carried argument as far as the monarch; but without exercising the hegemony of the officer castes of France or Germany. While the judiciary's scope of decision widened in tune with the increasing ambit of statute law into openly political preoccupations with the preservation of economic and social order, parliamentary reversal of the House of Lords' impolitic judgment in the Taff Vale case, 1902 (that trade unions were liable for actions done in their name) by enacting the Trades Disputes Act four years later, showed where ultimate political responsibility lay. Insofar as judicial influence did grow, it lay with the dissemination of nineteenth-century concepts about the rule of law, embodied in Sir Henry Maine's famous dictum that the progress of mankind stemmed from the transition between status and contract – origin of a rather different strand in industrial legislation from the blunt instrument of Taff Vale.

The last notable political battle fought by the non-conformist churches had been against the 1902 Education Act, and although their political influence lasted for many years, it was never again to be mobilised in the same way. There were (according to the *British Weekly*) eight million nonconformists in 1907 – nearly all Liberal supporters: nevertheless, what counted in a pressure group before women's suffrage had been won was not total numbers but male voters. The campaign for prohibition waned after 1905; the old unity disappeared; of 200

Liberal MPs perhaps less than half evinced a strong religious commitment in public life – although the sabbatarian lobby was still able to
enforce the law on Sunday observance, even in the munitions industry
in the First World War. Many nonconformists discovered deep
ambiguity in the doctrine of obedience and respect for authority when
confronted with the requirements of working-class loyalty to trade
unions and collective action on class lines.

The Anglican Church revived in the same period, according to
statistics of church attendance, and the Catholic Church greatly
increased its numbers, but neither went out of its way to intervene in
political conflict as Cardinal Manning had done by his celebrated
intervention in the 1889 London dock strike; the Anglican community
in particular put its energies into missionary work in the great cities
and shunned radical challenge to the existing order. Probably the most
contentious act of the Catholic hierarchy was the seal of approval
given in 1911 by Archbishop McGuire of Glasgow to the Independent
Labour Party's Catholic Socialist Society.

There is no need to point up the long decline of municipal power
and pride. In 1902 *The Times*, in a series of articles on British cities,
had extolled the virtues of what it called 'municipal socialism', but the
centralising process and government financial control were well under
way by 1911; and were soon to be accompanied by the effects of
standardisation and the application of quite novel government powers
in wartime. A similar decline had begun to afflict the voluntary bodies,
like the Charity Organisation Society. Their influence lingered on
into the 1920s to condition much social legislation and policy-making;
but already functions were being deliberately transferred under the
1911 National Insurance Act to trade unions, acting as Friendly
Societies.

If these changes had been the only ones noticeable in the late 1900s,
England might have been set for a long period of decorous administrative reform. But the new political forces were not simply mutations of
the old. Even if the newly-formed Labour Party had not yet outgrown
its Liberal parliamentary tutelage, the trade union movement was
beginning to compete aggressively for recognition in the political as well
as the industrial sense. The phenomenon of the organised working class
could neither be transmuted into conventional theory of parliamentary
consent, nor resisted with jeremiads about the dangers of democracy
derived from J. S. Mill, de Tocqueville and Robert Lowe's opposition
to the Suffrage Bill of 1866.

Naturally, opinion about how to accommodate the political desires

B

of the unrepresented real nation preoccupied politicians, civil servants and members of the political élite. Sharing a common cultural and intellectual background and a common concern with the continuance of stable government, they could hardly refuse to acknowledge an increased concern with the standards of working-class life, whether or not they drew radical or conservative conclusions. Now the social surveys of Booth, Rowntree and Bowley provided a new means of quantifying the problems of poverty: income, health, diet, housing. The ponderous concern of government was made explicit in a series of Royal Commissions, reflecting anxieties similar to those of the compilers of Parliamentary Blue Books in the mid-nineteenth century, while a growing academic awareness was reflected in the founding of the *Sociological Review* in 1908. By the time of the main Liberal welfare legislation, in particular the innovations of the National Insurance Act in 1911, scholarly definitions about social stratification and the political response of the working class had turned into commonplaces of parliamentary discussion.

At the time it was widely assumed that there existed a national class structure, with standard, regional variations. The Tory view of an organic society with deep political linkages across class was dismissed, for example, by the sociologist F. G. d'Aeth as 'mere romanticism' on the part of the old landed gentry.[10] Upper-class observers, like C. F. G. Masterman in *The Condition of England*, tended to take for granted rigid class divisions, as did the authors of the handful of examples of contemporary working-class literature.[11] So did J. A. Hobson in his analysis of the first General Election of 1910, when he postulated the existence of two Englands, the north with its heavy industry and robust proletarian character, and the south with its consumer economy, rentiers, and servile working class.*

To contemporaries, the social immobility of the working class appeared well documented. 'It was, by the eve of the First World War, a commonplace of informed social observation that manual workers were compartmentalised and ranked by notions of respectability as important for them as they were for non-manual workers.'[12] Between the strata, there was only restricted movement: hence d'Aeth's model of the complex hierarchy of status groups, with the 'old' working class at the base. A degree of nineteenth-century social mobility survived

---

*Sociological Review, June 1910. Historians only later sought reasons for the loss of Liberal working-class allegiance in the degree of diversity and fragmentation *within* the various strata, pointing out in the 1910 elections an extraordinary variation in support for, or resentment against, the political system. Cf. Neal Blewett, *The General Elections of 1910: the peers, the party and the people* (Macmillan 1972).

in trades such as building and textiles, but the rapid introduction after 1900 of mechanisation and new technology in the capital-intensive industries favoured stratification. In 1914 a French observer highlighted the phenomenon of working-class élites; skilled artisans' earnings might amount to three times those of the 'round about a pound a week' family, and the gulf between skilled and unskilled workers had barely narrowed in fifty years.[13]

Because these assessments were based on measurable quantities like housing, health, size of family, patterns of leisure, politicians seeking the means to accommodate working-class ambitions not unreasonably assumed that they would hold good for analysis of political consciousness. Certainly, the history of unskilled trade organisations and the 'new unionism' of the 1880s and 90s revealed constant tensions between them and the older craft and artisan unions, which refused to help organise or, in some cases, such as the Boilermakers and Spinners, even to recognise their unskilled auxiliaries. But even in the nineties, under the impact of technical change and mechanisation and the long growth of distributive and service industries, tension had increased between groups of workers divided by criteria of status yet approaching each other in actual spending power. After the slump of 1908, which seriously affected skilled workers in engineering and shipbuilding, general (or unskilled) unions attracted more recruits and even a body as hierarchical as the Engineers' Union was forced to accept non-apprenticed men as members.

This change in working-class organisation was reflected in debates about the type of political education and propaganda prescribed by parties: a comparison between 1900 and 1914 suggests that the impressionistic, often fearful and sentimental picture, derived from Mayhew and Booth, had given way to a more informed distinction between the 'respectable working class', and paupers, slum-dwellers and others within Rowntree's 'submerged tenth'. Discussion focused first on how to differentiate between the categories of the able-bodied poor, the casualties of society, and the 'unemployable' (which led some Liberals to seek welfare provision for the unfit, while retaining the rigours of the Poor Law for the 'unemployable'), and then on how to accommodate the aspirations to higher status of those in the 'respectable' category. The degree to which an individual sought betterment was seen as the key to the former: the difficulty came with the admission of *collective* political or industrial activity.*

*Clerks, for example, were not expected to form trade unions: as George Simkins, retiring President of the National Union of Clerks, remarked in 1907, 'We have not

Such distinctions were, however, confused by events during the bitter conflicts of 1909–14. The growth of a parliamentary Labour Party, and of large, well-organised trade unions, seemed to contradict the division between the hardworking, uncomplaining poor on one side – 'their aspirations are modest, to be respected by their fellows, to see their families growing up and making their way in the world, to die without debt and without sin'[15] – and syndicalists, socialists and subversive elements on the other. On two important issues opinion divided and not always on strict party lines: first, on whether political organisation among the working class represented a threat to the social fabric, or whether incorporation of properly motivated trade unionists should be seen as a stabilising influence; and, secondly, whether Britain's relative decline – the apocalyptic nightmare of the decade before 1914 – would be hastened or redeemed by such incorporation.

The educational system which had developed in the last quarter of the nineteenth century proved remarkably resistant to efforts to extend the full equipment of citizenship to the mass of voters. The theory that a classically educated élite should naturally assume the duty of political leadership was not seriously challenged except by a handful of radicals like R. H. Tawney and his co-founders of the Workers' Educational Association. Even the Webbs wished only to substitute professional qualification, not egalitarian entry. As well as opening up secondary education to the suitably qualified, the 1902 Act deprived many old-established endowed schools of the title 'public', at a time when the majority of public schools were developing the exclusive elements of boarding and organisation in the Headmasters' Conference, and achieving, with the universities, remarkable numerical success among the middle classes.*

In contrast, under the guiding Act of 1870, both church and state schools had been moulded during the 1880s by the Education Department in a way very different from the development of public and grammar schools. Expenditure on anything more than the essentials in

---

progressed [despite union with the National Clerks' Association] quite so rapidly as some think we should have done. The main reason is to be found in the environment of the class we are seeking to organise. As a rule clerks come from the middle class, a class opposed to trade unionism.'[14]

*University student numbers rose from 20,000 in 1900 to 42,000 in 1920 (·8 to 1·5% of the population). Public school members also increased dramatically up to 1914, partly because of the foundation of new schools, and partly because of all-round expansion and the erection of new buildings. Many now catered for 400–500 boys, and fees remained, in real terms, at the levels of 1860: Eton £167 a year, Charterhouse £116 a year.

higher elementary schools had been judged *ultra vires* and by the 1890s, Matthew Arnold's dictum 'the education of each class in society has, or ought to have, its ideal determined by the wants of that class and by its destination,'[16] had gained substantial acceptance. Advancement for working-class children still depended in the 1900s on individual merit and narrow entry to the exiguous state-aided secondary system. The dreary, narrow-minded world thus assigned to the great remaining mass of working-class children comprised reading, writing, and a religion backed by the remote figure of the rector, handing down daily and on Sundays the judgment that to keep one's station in life was the greatest Christian good.[17] A few maps might hang on the walls, mysterious and unexplained, or a little history intrude, but the system seemed calculated to enforce submission, the lowly status of women, and deference towards the superior, governing class. D. H. Lawrence, who had gone through it in the 1890s, depicted the horror of urban spiritual and material impoverishment, the classes of fifty or sixty, the noise, dirt and pitiful returns from children short of food and sleep; above all the pressures to cut education short, to go out and earn.

Slowly, under the influence of reformers like John Morley and Lyon Playfair,* and later Lord Haldane, Sir William Ashley and Tawney himself, and influenced by the alarmed outcry of the national efficiency lobby, warning that technical and scientific inadequacy would lead to strategic weakness in the face of Germany, the question of class destination came forward.† After 1907, the Board of Education began to implement a policy of admitting working-class children to 25 per cent of places in state-aided secondary schools, with the declared aim of increasing national literacy and technical skills; and a counter-attack at once developed, from the parents of middle and lower middle-class children who could not afford public school fees and had trusted the heirs of Arnold to preserve his exclusive principles. It was declared dangerous to tamper with the social pyramid.[19] Yet the actual numbers of 12- to 14-year-olds in grant-aided secondary schools in 1911 was only 89,000; among 15- to 18-year-olds, the total was a mere 33,000.[20] There was nothing here to suggest a reversal of the process by which a

---

*Playfair wrote in 1872 that primary education 'had only produced readers who do not read, writers who do not write and arithmeticians who do not count. . . . We have brought the complex tools of education and given them to the working classes but we have not taught them how to use the tools.'[18]

†Thus, the comments of the *Oxford Review*, 11 March 1899, on the proposal to found Ruskin College: working men might take up education 'as a hobby'; but a year at Oxford would make them discontented with their lot, prone to Socialism, 'and so increase more than ever the political difficulties of the country.'

working-class child could only climb the ladder by a process of selection into a world where success rested on conformity with middle-class attitudes.

It is scarcely a coincidence that a virulent debate raged over the limits of official censorship, whether of plays or literature, in the years up to 1911, and over acceptable changes in social behaviour, divorce and the sexual code. As Samuel Hynes showed in *The Edwardian Turn of Mind* (Oxford University Press 1968), resistance to reform took ground equally in defence of traditional morals and political postures against what was conceived to be the spread to a mass audience of insurgent and pernicious freethinking. Thus in the belief that salacity was a solvent of morality rather than an opiate of the people, limited editions of Freud or Havelock Ellis were seen as permissible (under a spurious medical justification) where cheap editions were banned.

But just as the Board of Education sought to open up secondary education, so in the years after 1909–11, censorship of drama and literature was relaxed, as if in admission that open discussion enhanced rather than threatened social harmony. In very broad cultural terms, attitudes towards working-class political literature were changing. Nevertheless, it would be premature to see any overt haste to provide in the state schools forms of modern civic and political education. From the 1870s onwards, the Education Department had slowly been imposing its values on primary and secondary schools by laying down rules for the selection and training of teachers, but contentious questions about the quality of life and distribution of power in society – if touched on at all – had been left largely in the hands of the churches. Officials were not yet to be encouraged to write into the curriculum a secular set of explanations of how the constitution was believed to work.

That remained the prerogative of the political parties: a duty enhanced by the evident decline in radical authority of nonconformist education, and the prevalence of mild reformism among leaders of the Anglican Church and the school of 'Christian Sociologists'.[21] Given the outbreak of dissent, at political and industrial level after 1909, it was hardly surprising that the parties responded, seeking not only votes (in the two elections of 1910) but incorporation of the organised working class, in order to ensure their future access to permanent power. Against a background of national and imperial crisis, protest in Ireland, economic decline and threats from suffragettes or trade unionists, Conservative and Liberal central organisations sought, via political education and propaganda, a new contract between themselves and the mass of the working class. For practical reasons, they came much nearer than the educationalists to the reality of politics; and because the Conservatives were in opposition, preparing for the hypothetical election of 1914 or 1915, their response is perhaps more interesting than that of the Liberals who, in the toils of government, had less scope for reappraising party organisation.

Even before their catastrophic defeat in 1906, the Conservatives had been considering a reform of party structure, not in an attempt to appease the traditional middle-class centres in the constituencies by delegation of powers, but by extending and improving the central party machine, as a preliminary to winning votes beyond the late nineteenth-century Tory Party limits. Thus the so-called 'Newcastle Resolution' of 1905 which envisaged the creation of 'a popular representative element in close touch with the constituencies', and the consequent claims of the National Union for greater control were relegated by the Central Office in the Concordat of 1906.[22] Gradually, the activities of the National Union were subordinated until it lost any chance of recapturing the position it had held in the palmy days of Lord Randolph Churchill.

The National Union had already been instructed in the need for mass working-class political propaganda at the time of the 1909 Budget,[23] and after Balfour had been replaced, in 1911, by the pre-eminently managerial figure of Andrew Bonar Law, Central Office merged with the National Union on its own terms, virtually without discussion. The Chairman of the National Union meekly accepted the change: 'They hoped . . . to form a businesslike organisation . . . like a railway company with a board of directors.'[24] The business corporation analogy suited the theme of national efficiency and contrasted happily with the 'extravagant' welfare schemes of Asquith's government and the supposedly damaging effect of Lloyd George's budget on the country's economic performance.

Although Law's influence was important, reform of the party machine owed more to the overriding need to win working-class votes from Liberals and an apparently stagnant Labour Party. Significantly, in their directives, party leaders tended to see these votes in terms of the class pyramid, and to imply that labour, formally organised in trade unions, could properly be seen as a contributor to social stability and national recovery. In 1905, Joseph Chamberlain declared, during his later tariff campaign: 'The question of employment, believe me, has now become the most important question of our time.' Taff Vale had been sloughed off. However much Conservatives might grumble, then and later, that the 1906 Trades Disputes Act set up unions as privileged corporations, they let the Bill pass through the Lords almost unscathed. A Conservative administration had already passed the Unemployed Workmen's Act in 1905, with Liberal support, against a Tory minority and this cross-party alignment survived during the passage of the Workmen's Compensation Act, the Trade Boards, and the rest of the Liberals' specifically working-class programme – even the second part of the contentious National Insurance Act in 1911. Just at the moment when trade unions appeared to betray the trust put in them by Liberal radicals, the Conservatives restaked their historic claim to the allegiance of the Tory working man.

The earlier Reorganisation Committee had envisaged a highly centralised authority,[25] but in June 1911, after unusually careful consultations, the next Committee came down in favour of decentralisation of certain functions, not to restore regional autonomy but to provide Central Office with an effective means of assessing public opinion and a propaganda machine.[26] Central control was perpetuated, discipline reinforced. Meanwhile, Conservative clubs were encouraged to act as 'forums for training working-class speakers' and the dissemination of propaganda.

If Central Office was to be a business, its trading policy was the manipulation of a mass electorate, and it needed professional agencies. Far in advance of Liberal or Labour thinking, secret intelligence departments were set up in each area, with a press bureau to maintain regular liaison with journalists and editors. Finance, candidates and agents had already been taken over by Central Office; in 1907 'literature' and 'speakers' were added. By 1911, the central party apparatus could accurately measure constituency opinion* and in turn use the constituency apparatus to influence public opinion. To complete the system, Sir Arthur Steel-Maitland, the Party chairman (who was also the head of Central Office, ranking second after Bonar Law) went out of his way to upgrade the humble constituency agents, formerly little more than low-paid hacks, to the status of voting members, the 'eyes and ears' of the party.[27]

The size of their majority in 1906, followed by the stresses of government after 1909, seem to have prevented a similar recasting of the Liberal Party machine. The MacDonald-Gladstone compact appeared, for a decade, to have diverted the immediate threat from the Labour Representation Committee/Labour Party. Despite his age and ill-health, Sir Henry Campbell-Bannerman remained the shrewdest of

---

*The 1911 Committee held 43 meetings, and received 108 witnesses and 289 written submissions.

party managers and committee men; but his successor, H. H. Asquith, spent less time in these essential pursuits. Open to serious dangers in parliament, where a large majority always undermines discipline, the party suffered in the constituencies as a result of the policy of the Liberal radicals: their reforms, such as employers' liability and unemployment benefit, damaged Liberal unity during their long parliamentary gestation and antagonised ancient sources of support.

Some historians have seen the programme of the Liberal Radicals as an attempt to outbid the socialist wing of the Labour Party and Independent Labour Party, whilst bestowing economic and social security on the working class, via the trade union movement. Others have argued that they were forced, by the tactics and by-election successes of the Tory opposition, continually to run ahead. Whatever the reason, the reformers' momentum weakened during the constitutional crisis and the conflicts over Ireland after 1912. The party could not, in the long run, hold real radicals like C. P. Trevelyan (who defected to Labour in 1915) nor, despite the 1906 Trade Disputes Act, could its conduct of industrial policy ensure any permanent concordat with the trade union movement after the great wave of strikes began in 1911. The unions themselves failed to back up the social radicals as the latter, somewhat naively, expected: the Trades Union Congress was not yet an institution confident enough to play one party against another.

But the Liberals failed also to make the necessary structural changes. Faced during their decade of government with resistance to social policies from powerful local business groups, and at Westminster with a lack of consistent party discipline, Liberal headquarters was unable to mobilise sufficient support to sustain the parliamentary party in the two elections of 1910; which left it dependent for a majority on Irish votes. Change came too late. John Gulland, the Chief Whip, and his inadequate staff were overburdened with the questions of finance and organisation so carefully delineated by the Tories; and delayed until 1912 a proposal to hand over constituency matters to a 'serious organiser'. Attempts to induce local associations to select more working-class candidates met with almost total failure. 'Perhaps the Liberal Party was inherently incapable of transforming its amalgam of interests and idealists into a disciplined phalanx capable of effective competition on national terms.'[28]

Whether or not they were successful in mobilising the working-class vote which appeared to lie at the upper end of the stratified class pyramid, the social policy of both parties was increasingly shaped in accordance with the known desires of working-class organisations (trade unions and trades councils) whose existence could, as a corollary, be recognised as part of the changing political system. This rivalry for common electoral ground continued, in spite of the elaborate charade of the Lords and Commons dispute and the breakdown over Ireland, as both parties invested in modest but increasingly interventionist policies. Indeed, party competition can be said largely to have created the crisis between Lords and Commons. The Conservatives were determined not just to impede Liberal policy, but to assert what they conceived to be their rights over the introduction and administration of social and industrial policy – with all the consequences and electoral advantages. Far from being indefensible, A. J. Balfour's strategy was sound according to Conservative definitions of the political system:* it was the Liberals who were initially out of tune, with H. H. Asquith's appeal to a constitution unborn before the trial of strength in 1911.

In this warfare, the parties reached out beyond dependence on any theory of deference: central party organisation and propaganda now took for granted the legitimacy of working-class demands. Neither party had become egalitarian; both, however, responded to the intrinsic challenge of socialism. The nascent Labour Party was thus caught in a complicated dilemma and reduced, after its spectacular success in winning twenty-nine seats in 1906 (largely as a result of the MacDonald-Gladstone pact), to a period of stagnation and inactivity.

For the largest of its creators, the trade union movement, the Labour Party provided an important legal and propaganda recourse; but despite ultimate affiliation to the TUC of formerly Liberal trade unions like the miners, intrinsic identification with the parliamentary process developed very slowly. When the largest unions opted for strike action in 1911–13, the parliamentary party was, in effect, excluded. So long as it remained, in Henry Pelling's phrase, 'a minority party content to press trade union claims', its existence was not threatened. But it remained vulnerable to the appeal of Liberal or Conservative reforms aimed at the incorporation of the trade union movement *qua* institution, as in the 1906 Act, even if such reforms had not then carried general party acceptance. Hence the choice put by the ILP MP, Victor Grayson, between competing, hopelessly as it appeared at the time, in the

*The divisions over unemployment relief, for example, had little effect either on party alignments or on the eventual form of the legislation on the statute book. (José Harris, *Unemployment and Politics: a study in English social policy 1886–1914*, Clarendon Press, 1972.)

parliamentary arena, or embarking on a programme of full-blooded Socialism. The previous twenty years' experience in England (unlike the examples of the Socialist parties in Germany and France) offered no encouragement to the latter course, while the ultimate step, of extra-parliamentary activity, attracted the hostility of the predominantly middle-class leadership of the ILP and the Parliamentary Labour Party (PLP) alike. But both might profitably have remembered William Morris's warning, uttered in 1885, of the strength of the old system and the tendency to over-optimism among Fabians about the ability of 'urban democracy, the study of political economy, and socialism' to make any impression:

They very much underrate the strength of the tremendous organisation under which we live. Nothing but a tremendous force can deal with this force; it will not suffer itself to be dismembered, nor to lose anything which really is its essence without putting forth all its force in resistance; rather than lose anything which it considers of importance, it will pull the roof of the world down upon its head.[29]

Unless it was a class party, Labour could not yet be distinctive; but if it called itself one, it could never hope to win a parliamentary majority. This dilemma lay behind the evolutionary approach, and the attempt gradually to supersede the Liberals, outlined in Ramsay MacDonald's pre-war writings, and Labour's attempted centralisation of party activity, to the long-term detriment of regional centres of power once dominated by the ILP and local organisations like Trades Councils.

Contemporary evidence about the responsiveness of working-class political behaviour to these various trends produces only ambiguous indications. Strong antagonism to the Boer War, for example, among Liberal radicals did not evoke much public response. Few members of the working class seem to have related the moral and political questions to their own experience, and it may be anachronistic even to ask the question since it presupposes an intellectual framework of reference which may not then even have existed,[30] as well as a purely hypothetical readiness on the part of the radicals to organise and lead a mass movement.

But if issues of foreign and imperial policy had no continuous impact on working-class opinion (apart from outbreaks of jingoism associated with disaster or military triumph) what of those which had immediate impact? The cases of temperance reform and women's suffrage suggest that where leadership was provided by middle-class pressure groups, and where the conflict took place outside 'natural' party divisions, working-class opinion lacked coherence and consequently offered no foundation for party advantage. Had the Women's Social and Political Union (WSPU) in its violent period after 1908 managed to aggregate an important body of working-class support, then it is hard to imagine that their case would have been so contemptuously and brutally dismissed. But both Liberals and Conservatives drew strength from the assumption that male working-class voters disapproved. Rowland Kenney (Annie Kenney's brother) was not the only one to notice that meetings were attended mainly 'by leisured suffragettes, as the music halls are frequented on a Monday afternoon by a certain type of person – and for much the same reason – it is the thing to go.' Few of the WSPU were prepared to follow Rebecca West, who broke away from the Pankhursts in 1913, and wrote a series of disillusioned articles for the *Daily Herald* and Blatchford's *Clarion*, suggesting that, rather than insult Asquith, the movement ought to rouse working women in offices and factories.

As the WSPU moved into its 'impossibilist' phase, abandoning public meetings as impracticable and refusing to argue a case that, as H. G. Wells saw, 'took too much explanation', the authorities were able to assume the mantle of *public* outrage. Well aware of the suffragettes' lack of mass support, the government responded, as in 1886 and even 1848, in defence of law and order, property, decorum and the constitution – free from the risk of party division. Cross-party agreement ensured the suffragettes' defeat, just as the Coalition government in 1917–18 finally endorsed the vote for women over thirty as part of a general settlement for wartime sacrifices.

Pressure groups like the temperance societies and the WSPU were unable without mass support to assume the institutional power which was already draining away from the churches and the long-established professional colleges and associations. But the sensitivity of the parties to working-class opinion *as a whole* can be gauged from their response to pressure for legislation against immigration.

The long nineteenth-century tradition of offering refuge to political outcasts (which embraced both Karl Marx and Prince Kropotkin) stood, in marked contrast to police methods in Europe, until the Aliens Act was passed in 1905. Until then, fears of anarchist conspiracy, like *Daily Mail* or *Boys' Own Paper* caricatures about lesser breeds, and racist theories about the 'virus in the body politic', could be brushed off; in 1900 Lord Salisbury rejected Queen Victoria's plea for legislation, following the murder of the Empress Elizabeth, by citing the general opposition of Liberal and Tory backbenchers.[31] But the experience of substantial immigration of Jews from the ghettos of Russia and Poland, after the terrible pogroms of the 1880s and 1890s, aroused quite different forces of opinion. A combination of heightened political violence in Europe (including the assassination of the King of Portugal), the activity of anti-alien groups like the British Brothers' League (which elicited 45,000 signatures in favour of exclusion, from the Borough of Tower Hamlets alone), and fears of racial decline not dissimilar to those prevalent in Germany and France in the 1900s, combined with working-class antagonisms to Jewish immigrants and their reluctance to integrate, to produce the Aliens Act.

Popular discontent probably declined before the issue passed the political threshold, and the Act itself owed something to the militant populism of a group of Tory MPs led by the Chesterton brothers and Arnold Wilson.[32] Nevertheless, immigration raised far more intractable questions than drink or votes for women. Defining citizenship tested deep assumptions in a conservative and stratified society, conscious of serious decline. If the Englishman on poor relief, and the shop assistant in the servile conditions of 'living-in', were to be denied such a basic citizens' right as the vote, under existing law, what of the immigrant, who appeared to contribute nothing to the national welfare? Working-class employment, housing and conditions were major considerations: Joseph Chamberlain campaigned against the threat to British employment from foreign sweated labour, and Balfour, in a letter to the King in June 1905, admitted that the Aliens Bill 'sought to keep out destitute and other undesirable aliens who should become a burden on the State and a charge on the rates.'[33]

However responsive each of the main parties had been to working-class opinion in legislating to counteract the effects of immigration or of the Taff Vale judgment, developments over the Irish question had, by 1911, thrown very grave doubt on the political system's capacity to contain irreconcilable conflict between them. Given Asquith's proposed intention to carry Home Rule, and Bonar Law's approval of Ulster's fight for its status by any means including civil war, breakdown appeared inevitable if, as seemed likely, the Liberal Bill passed in 1915, after the Lords' veto had finally run out. Under those conditions it is significant that both parties began to consider strategies to win popular consent quite distinct from the constitutional party-parliamentary mode (to which Asquith had appealed, in order to defeat the House of Lords). Backed by the authority of Dicey, the Conservatives proposed a referendum, and claimed to have discovered the 'national veto';*

*Clifford Sharp, for the Labour Party, attacked Dicey's position in a famous

45

while the Liberals (duly acknowledging their faith in King, constitution and the 'commonsense of the British people'), nevertheless toyed with devolution, hoping to make Home Rule respectable by a sop to the latent nationalism of Scots and Welsh.[34]

It is most unlikely that either of these expedients would have guaranteed a political settlement at Westminster, any better than the abortive party meetings held, under the King's auspices, in 1913–14; it was as well for the political system that war intervened and that J. E. Redmond and the Irish Nationalists consented, in patriotic faith, to a temporary postponement of the Home Rule Bill. Awareness of imminent breakdown, however, had accelerated the search for a stronger basis of popular consent among the organised working class, even before the great wave of strikes began in 1911. Yet the trade union movement, like the employers' organisations, revealed itself curiously unprepared for a political role.

To explain why, it is necessary to recall the economic circumstances of the 1890s and the behaviour of the major employers. Awareness of Britain's relative decline in export markets and technological innovation led the majority of employers and managers to look enviously at the process of cartel formation and amalgamation in the United States and Germany. Alfred Mond modelled Amalgamated Anthracite on Rockefeller's Standard Oil; others in the construction business looked to the operations of Georg von Siemens or B. H. Strousberg, linking finance capital and public works on a national scale. Not many would have gone as far as Emil Rathenau in advocating the supremacy of an entrepreneurial class, working in the national interest, in close collaboration with the state; but they could openly envy the success of his company, AEG, which, with Siemens, had by 1900 captured more than a third of the world market in electrical equipment.

At the same time, increasing agitation among unskilled workers (the 'new unionism') had led to fears of growing political conflict across all British industry, and of a profound confrontation between socialist and capitalist creeds. Only these fears can explain the persistence, tendentiousness and frequent brutality of employers' opposition to trade union growth, and their attempts to reverse earlier trade union

---

pamphlet, declaring that the British response would be conservative and monstrously unfair to Ireland, compounded of ignorance and prejudice inflamed by Tory propaganda. He also pointed out the fragmented nature of working-class opinion. 'Nothing is more vital at the present moment to the continued advance of socialism than a clear realisation of the fact that the working classes of England are not yet socialists, that until they are, socialist legislation is impossible and undesirable; and that in the meantime no energy can be spared from the work of education . . .'

gains by taking advantage of opportunities such as the judgment in *Lyons vs. Wilkins* in 1896, which undermined the status of picketing, or the reinterpretation of the law on tort which was made explicit in the Taff Vale case in 1902.

But the 1890s also brought new formal organisations, more powerful than those of the 60s and 70s,* more easily able to deny recognition to trade unions. Shipowners formed the Shipping Federation and introduced their own register of seamen pledged not to refuse to work with non-union men. In 1896 came the Employers' Federation of Engineering Associations (EEF), whose formation was followed by a climatic battle with the Engineers' Union (ASE) in 1897-8. During this six months' lockout, the employers' chairman, Colonel Dyer, declared that his Federation intended 'to obtain the freedom to manage their own affairs which has proved so beneficial to American manufacturers . . .'[35] At a cost of nearly £500,000, the ASE was forced to give way and to accept a damaging and humiliating redefinition of their rights, drafted by the Federation's lawyers.[36] Meanwhile, the supply of blackleg labour had been organised, first for Hull shipowners in 1893, but later on a national basis by William Collinson's National Free Labour Association. A similar body, the Free Labour Protection Association, was formed in 1897 by a groups of major employers. A year later, the Engineering Employers ('the most powerful employers' organisation in Britain's history'[37]) remodelled its own Parliamentary Committee to meet its declared aim of opposing 'the movement towards state socialism . . . and the influence of the TUC in Parliament.'[38]

The alliance put together by the EEF in 1898 functioned in public only for a short time, chiefly because the employers had won nearly every battle by 1901; but its organisation was not dismantled and was revived in 1913. In close association, engineering employers, coalowners, railway companies, shipowners and shipbuilders turned from open action to lobbying Ministers with the aid of a group of well-organised, sympathetic MPs; while full-time officials of the various employers' federations met regularly to coordinate their strategy against legislation to remedy Taff Vale, or to give evidence to Royal Commissions, during the next fifteen years.[39] Yet in spite of propaganda activities (which included publications like W. J. Shaxby's pamphlet, *The Case Against Picketing*), employers' associations took care not to become overtly

---

*Such as the National Association of Federated Employers (1873), and the Association of British Chambers of Commerce (1860), a loose confederation of business and industrial interests which never achieved much influence with the Board of Trade, nor internal coherence on major political issues like the tariff and trade union legislation.

political bodies, partly from a persistent fear of being held, legally, to be 'associations in restraint of trade', and partly because they assumed that publicity about their anti-union work would be too unfavourable. Apart from the EEF, whose hostility had always been clear* particularly after Allan Smith became Secretary in 1908, their metamorphosis came later, after industrial issues had been further politicised between 1911 and 1916.

Employers' activity reflected that of trade unions and in turn affected trade unions' own strategy and organisation. Being indissolubly linked by the fundamental circumstances of industrial life, the two sides' political evolution ran parallel. The militance of new unionism inspired the owners to accumulate reserves of blackleg labour; the growth of employers' associations and their parliamentary leverage led the TUC to seek influence among Liberal Radicals, and other unions to create the General Federation of Trade Unions (GFTU) in 1898 – to say nothing of union support for the formation of the Labour Representation Committee. Yet, like the employers' associations, TUC and GFTU avoided too much political responsibility.

Since the 1870s, the TUC's Parliamentary Committee had tended to criticise or promote legislation, without claiming representative rights to do so. From time to time, it took some part at General Elections, subjecting, for example, parliamentary candidates in 1874 to the 'Ten Questions Test'; but hampered by lack of staff, and without any clear mandate to intervene in the inter-union disputes of the late seventies and eighties, the Committee retained its narrow role and avoided new commitments either to unskilled unions or women workers. In 1893–4, under the influence of the miners' and metalworkers' unions, the majority were able to resist the demands of the Socialist societies and unskilled unions for better representation and parliamentary candidates pledged 'to the collective ownership and control of the means of production, distribution and exchange'; and in 1895 Trades Council representatives were excluded from the TUC, thus estranging much rank-and-file opinion from the policy-making organisation.

The conflicts of the late nineties made such a position untenable. Defeat of the engineers in 1898 inspired the founding of the GFTU, a federation of unions created for mutual financial support. Small

---

*During the 1897 strike, the EEF declared its intention to win complete freedom to manage their own business: yet added that they 'had no desire to encroach on the reasonable functions of trade unions' (EEF Minutes, October 1897). How narrowly the EEF defined these limits can be seen from its opposition to the Labour Party's proposed Bill in 1906 and any other legislation 'which would further increase the power of the trade unions'.

though it was in comparison to the TUC, the GFTU was for a time able to play a more independent hand. But divisions between individual unions, the 'Labourism' endemic in the Parliamentary Committee, and the slow adjustment to the LRC-Labour Party of unions with predominantly Liberal membership, made joint action difficult, even in reply to the Taff Vale judgment. The Labour Party's spectacular success at the 1906 General Election (when it returned twenty-nine MPs accompanied by twenty-five Lib-Labs) owed far more to the secret MacDonald-Gladstone electoral pact than the artificial 'concordat' patched together between Party, TUC and GFTU at Caxton Hall in 1905.

Deep disagreements about the future role of the trade union movement were exposed when the Royal Commission on Trade Unions set a conundrum by recommending, not legal immunity from prosecution for torts (as the Committee had asked, following Taff Vale), but statutory recognition as legal entities. Unions were to become, overnight, 'professional' corporations, with provision for the separation of benefit money from strike funds, so that their mutual insurance function would not be damaged as a result of legal action. The Committee baulked at the Liberal Bill and asked instead for a return to the old immunity. It was a strange but crucial decision inspired by a deep reluctance to take on the unknown responsibilities and constraints inherent in statutory existence, and by a preference for the purely industrial role which their leaders understood.

In subsequent years, the Committee sought little more than the right to advise Liberal Ministers on the drafting of Liberal reforms, a pusillanimity more striking because membership rose steadily – from 1.6 million in 1911 to 2.6 million in 1913. They also remained uneasy about political compromise with the Liberal Radicals, fearing that government might already have encroached too far, with its assumption of responsibility for minimum wages, Trade Boards and female labour, albeit in the poorly organised, 'sweated-labour' field. To be strengthened against the employers might not be sufficient recompense for loss of autonomy. This dilemma embroiled the TUC and GFTU in a good deal of sterile conflict with Ministers over demarcation without much corresponding gain. In spite of an overwhelming vote at the 1910 TUC in favour of legislation to remedy the Osborne judgment (which declared trade union contributions to political parties illegal) the government, preoccupied elsewhere, did not respond for nearly three years, and then in a manner which, by allowing contracting out, weakened the trade union position. A Labour Party, rent with faction and subject to attrition at by-elections, offered only an unsatisfactory parliamentary recourse. Yet the Committee remained content to be a post box during the militant years after 1911. Even in 1913, it spent months of discussion before launching on its members a simple questionnaire about the eight-hour day.

The Parliamentary Committee had, of course, to represent a political range from anarcho-syndicalist miners to highly conservative small craft unions, without any powers of coercion and with a minute staff. In 1908, for example, it asked the TUC for permission to publish a quarterly (rather than an annual) report: this modest piece of empire building passed only because the Miners' Federation (MFGB) delegate, who opposed it, had mislaid his card, with its 500,000 members. Although perhaps no worse off than individual unions like MFGB and ASE, with their underpaid officials and out of date constitutions, the Committee lacked any means to avoid the growing conflict of jurisdiction between Labour Party, TUC and GFTU. Meetings of the so-called Joint Board only led to repetition of disagreements; nor did the trade union bodies share the Labour Party's commitment to international solidarity. 'Foreigners could be forgiven if they found it difficult to work out whether there was any national authority at the head of the uniquely strong trade union movement in the most advanced industrialised country in the world.'[40]

As yet, conditions did not exist sufficient to change either employers' or trade union organisations' deep-rooted distrust of the political stage. In spite of the Conservative Party's conversion to the concept of party organised on business lines, employers were content to lobby government in private; in spite of the oblique suggestions of the Liberal Radicals, TUC and GFTU evidently considered the Labour Party adequate for the purposes for which it had (according to them) been founded. Nowhere in the Committee records is there any indication that the trade union movement as such claimed political representation. The political system might be in ruins; the crisis might resemble the breakdown threatened in Germany and France; but the British problem of the political assimilation of working-class power could not be resolved without the extraneous stimulus of war.

2 INDUSTRIAL CRISIS, 1911–14

The intractable position taken up by each side in Britain over the question of Irish Home Rule seemed to prove beyond question the failure of the classical two-party political system. The residual power of national institutions which had, in the end, surmounted the Lords and Commons crisis could do no more than postpone the likely civil war; surveying the evidence of breakdown, the wave of enormous strikes and the explosion of feminist discontent, in a brilliant essay written forty years ago, George Dangerfield asserted that Liberal England's death predated by several years the outbreak of the 1914 war.[1] More recently, historians have revised this theory, showing how different was the nature of these conflicts and how, in the case of industrial politics, Liberals and Conservatives acted with a common aim of furthering their electoral advantage.

But the ancient parties did not *welcome* the arrival of an organised working class. The rise to power of Lloyd George, Churchill and the Liberal Radicals and the slow infusion of social-imperialist thinking, put the Liberals in a position where accommodation to a Socialist Party (as distinct from the docile Labour Parliamentary group) or to aggressive trade unionism became progressively more difficult; and this tendency seems to have inspired the idea of coalition, even before the war, as an answer to political breakdown.[2] Uninterested in coalition, the Conservatives nevertheless avoided any precipitate commitment to bodies like the TUC or the General Federation of Trades Unions (GFTU), couching their appeal to working-class interests in very general terms, and emphasising both the importance of retaining the votes of the 'Tory working man', and the undesirable nature of the status given to trade unions by the 1906 Act. 'It makes a trade union a privileged body exempt from the ordinary law of the land. No such privileged body has ever been deliberately created by an English parliament,' wrote Dicey, so often a front runner for the party.[3] Anti-union tendencies and the urge to revise the law survived undiminished until the General Strike allowed sections of the party to bring in the 1927

Trades Disputes Act and alter the system of contracting out of the trade union political levy; as Sir George Younger, the Conservative Party chairman, wrote in March 1925, 'there are tens of thousands of votes of the men who form everywhere the nucleus of our working-class organisations in the constituencies. They exercise a very great influence on their fellows and will be antagonised fatally if the liberty they demand be not granted.'[4]

Similarly, trends appeared on both sides of industry: taking the form of carefully rationalised mistrust of the parties and the parliamentary system, as trade unions dissociated themselves from too close supervision by the Labour Party, and employers from Liberal extensions of the state's role as industrial conciliator. Each also evinced an intense antagonism towards the other, which was the product of five years of economic decline, and the feeling that both were preparing themselves for a struggle à *l'outrance* like 1897. Relationships had been especially inflamed in industries most affected by technological change, or by the effects of the slump of 1908–9 which had particularly disturbed the assumptions and expectations of skilled workers in shipbuilding and engineering. It scarcely needed a Marxist diagnosis to point out the renewed impact of American and German cartelisation, nor to forecast another onslaught by the employers, armed with newly-defined legal powers: the American Federation of Labour was already beleagured and trade unionism in Germany had to face an increasingly formal association between employers and the state. Yet in spite of the claims of left-wingers like Victor Grayson, the ILP and the Labour Party refused to reopen the question raised by the Social Democratic Federation (SDF), during the drafting of the constitution of the infant Labour Party, whether it should be 'a distinct party, based upon the recognition of the class war, having for its ultimate object the socialisation of the means of production, distribution and exchange.'

After 1911 many middle-of-the-road trade unionists, confronted with the apparent bias of the courts[5] and the outrageous conduct of employers in the London docks, the building trades and the Dublin transport system, came to accept the position once held only by doctrinaire Marxists. At the same time, among employers, primed with evidence of working-class discontent in France, Germany, Austria, Russia, Spain and Italy, to say nothing of the proliferation of the Second International to which the Labour Party had affiliated in 1908, there grew an acute fear of what the Liberal reformers were doing. Collectively, the employers had felt themselves weakened since the 1890s, partly by the 1906 Trade Disputes Act, partly because of internal divisions between individual exponents of employers' divine right, like Lord Devonport and Lord Penhryn, and bodies like the Mineowners' Association, the Port of London Authority, and the Railway Boards (who could still assert that 'the companies must remain untrammelled by the coercion and tyranny of an outside irresponsible body'), and on the other hand more far-sighted, flexible employers like Alfred Mond, David Davies or Alfred Baldwin, who were prepared to concede full trade union recognition and even to discuss the miners' or railwaymen's demand for a national minimum wage.

Although the Engineering Employers retained their harsh confidence in public, they too seem to have been willing to reappraise the role of trade unions, if for no other reason than that by 1911, industry could no longer afford the price of prolonged strikes like that of 1897. These tendencies scarcely amounted to a split in the employers' front: but they were reflected among trade unions, in a distinction between public language (such as Ben Tillett's celebrated injunction 'May God strike Lord Devonport dead') and private readiness to compromise, and between those unions which had suffered most in the 1890s, the miners, railwaymen and engineers, and others in the TUC with less need to re-establish their rights to employers' recognition.

To some extent, the appearance of naked class warfare which so greatly impressed Edwardian commentators came either from ultra-montane publicists outside, or from factious interests within industry. It did not require the publication of an explicitly élitist theory of politics, like W. H. Mallock's *The Limits of Pure Democracy* (1918), to exacerbate feelings of class tension: *The Times*, for example, ran a series of articles in 1901 on 'The Crisis in British Industry', in which it blamed Britain's economic decline almost wholly on strikes and restrictive practices, using information supplied by the Liberty and Property Defence League. The LPDL, itself, under the leadership of Lord Wemyss, and with funds subscribed by various employers' federations[6] devoted itself to producing lurid publicity against all collective forms of working-class organisation. The tendentious nature of much popular journalism, aimed at the middle-class market, also reinforced overt prejudice against radical working-class politics and activities. Ralph Blumenfeld, then editor of Max Aitken's *Daily Express*, became a founder member of the Anti-Socialist League and did not scruple to publicise his views: 'In every society, there exist the unsuccessful, the unfortunate, the discontented and the lazy; and these, together with the ill-balanced dreamer of dreams, are the material out of which Socialist parties are formed.'[7]

The economic imperative for trade union activity was clear enough. The real cost of living had risen roughly 5 per cent between 1902 and 1908, and rose again more sharply to 9 per cent over the years 1908–13. More and more men joined trade unions* and pressed wage claims, especially during the favourable trade conditions after 1910. But behind the cost of living lay a vast geography of socio-political unrest. Altered patterns of jobs and mechanisation had worked in many industries to the detriment of established hierarchies of labour and individual family. Thus the introduction of coal-cutting machinery upset the traditional pattern in which time-keeping among miners derived from the pace of the coal-face cutter, while the beginning of three-shift working and the eight-hour day involved disruption of many miners' social life. These, rather than wages, were responsible for the strikes in Durham and Northumberland in 1910.

As Edwardian sociologists had already noticed, mobility between the strata of working-class society had diminished. Consequent discontent and frustration took various forms: there followed an increase in white-collar unionism after 1911, among shop assistants, for example, campaigning against the degrading conditions of the 'living-in' system, and a profound unease among skilled artisans, enhanced by the slump of 1908–9, when men who had not known insecurity for a generation were put out of work for twelve to eighteen months.[8] Yet unions behaved in diverse ways. Previous antagonisms between craft and unskilled unions were sometimes softened, but in other cases not: among railway unions, the strongly hierarchical ASLEF and Railway Clerks always refused to join with the ASRS to form a National Union of Railwaymen. Over a third of all trade unionists belonged to bodies not affiliated to the TUC, and some evidence suggests that roughly 15 per cent of TUC affiliates chose to contract out from the political levy, after the Osborne judgment had been remedied by the 1913 Act.

Given its heterogeneous nature, the obvious strategy for the trade unions was to engage the employers directly and make recognition the main issue before economic circumstances, employers' cartelisation, or the attrition of the not unsympathetic Liberal government, made action even more difficult. No struggle was more bitterly contested than that over recognition. It underlay the ASRS claims for a general wage in-

*Numbers of Trade Union members affiliated to the TUC – that is, roughly 65% of the total of trade union membership:

1900	1905	1910	1911	1912	1913	1914
1·2m	1·5m	1·6m	2m	2·2m	2·4m	2·7m

(B. R. Mitchell and P. Deane, *Abstract of British Historical Statistics*, Cambridge University Press, 1962.)

crease in 1907, since none of the railway companies except the North Eastern had yet recognised the unions; and the famous strike of 1912 in the London docks, between the newly-reorganised Port of London Authority under its tough, unyielding, anti-union chairman, Lord Devonport, and the National Transport Workers Federation, combining dockers and seamen, led by Tom Mann, Ben Tillett and Havelock Wilson. The PLA's refusal to employ only union labour (and its practice of bringing in blacklegs to beat strikes) were endorsed for many years when the strike collapsed.

An absolute need to win acceptance of union rights inspired almost all trade union activity until the early part of the First World War, but while it was often combined with straightforward wage claims, it also engendered syndicalist forms of mass organisation and tactics: a far more difficult matter for political parties to adjust to, because it set up industrial organisation on a separate plane from political-parliamentary government. Liberals and Conservatives, who had readily accepted the wage-bargaining role of trade unions that certain employers still denied, found common ground with older trade unionists and craft unions in opposition to syndicalist or guild socialist ideas about working-class control of self-governing industries (expressed, for example, in the 1910 strike of miners against the Cambrian Combine, when the younger men demanded a guaranteed minimum wage to offset the fall in output caused by working thinner seams at greater depth, and rejected both the compromise formula of the Conciliation Board, and the advice of their leaders).

In these developments, the Parliamentary Labour Party took no part. Unable to outflank the Liberals on industrial policy, and fearful of bringing down the government by outright opposition, the majority of the PLP accepted the refuge offered by MacDonald's skilfully centralist leadership – 'We are too fond of imagining there are only two sides to a dispute,' he told the House of Commons in February 1912. 'There is the side of capital, there is the side of labour, and there is the side of the general community: and the general community has no business to allow capital and labour, fighting their battles, to elbow them out of consideration.'[9]

But the politics of accommodation and a faith in Labour's ultimate victory over the Liberals could not disguise the Party's subordinate position. In 1910 MacDonald welcomed Lloyd George's suggestion for a three-party coalition, with two minor offices granted to Labour men (an idea scotched by Arthur Henderson); but the PLP was not invited to the Constitutional Conference in 1910 nor to the Buckingham

Palace conference on Ireland in July 1914. The TUC claimed, single-handed, to have created it;* yet in the period of massive strikes, 1911–14, they tacitly denied it a political mandate. In contrast, the secessionist groups from the SDF, the Socialist Labour Party (SLP) and British Socialist Party (BSP), immersed themselves in industrial politics, aided, at the level of educational propaganda, by the Plebs League and the Labour College, formed in 1908 after a schism at Ruskin College.

These groups, though organisationally disunited, expounded theories of direct action, some acquired from France or the IWW (International Workers of the World) and Daniel de Leon in the United States, others, like Guild Socialism, with its rejection of any claim to a political dictatorship of the proletariat, home-grown. All were based on the common premise of industrial, rather than craft, unionism, and on acknowledgment that class conflict was a fundamental part of industrial society. Personalities, however, confused ideological simplicity. Industrial syndicalism clearly shaped the National Transport Workers' Federation, yet the far from docile railwaymen refused to join. Older militants, like Will Thorne of the Glassworker's Union, had to run fast to keep pace and sustain former reputations; while general unions, content for a generation with leaders of the artisan class such as Ben Tillett, Will Thorne, J. R. Clynes and even Tom Mann himself, began to be swayed by younger, aggressively proletarian claimants, forerunners of the shop stewards' movement of the First World War. As George Askwith, the Government's chief industrial conciliator wrote, in 1909: 'Official leaders could not maintain their authority. Often there was more difference between the men and their leaders than between the latter and their employers.'[10]

Rooted in factory and community, these groups shared a common political strategy. Although, overall, they were most successful in the West of Scotland, an unofficial railwaymen's organisation existed in Liverpool and a branch of the IWW, the International Workers of Great Britain (IWGB), at Camell Laird's.[11] In South Wales, the Plebs League took a significant part in the genesis of *The Miners' Next Step*, the first statement endorsed by a major union advocating elimination of the employer and full workers' democratic control of the industry; while in Dublin, James Larkin and James Connolly organised the transport workers on the basis of industrial unionism and direct action for

*'That party is the creation of the TUC. The unions were forced into politics and into the organisation of their own political party by the failure of the other political parties . . . to do anything to meet the unions' claims, even for remedial legislation.' Citrine to Beaverbrook, 31 March 1933. (Beaverbrook papers, Box C93.)

socialist aims. More generally, Trades Councils offered a geographical forum for syndicalist activity by men who attempted to recapture their responsibility on the TUC which they had lost in 1895.*

Repudiated by MacDonald, the Liberal Radicals, and the government's own Labour Department, industrial unionism (or anarcho-syndicalism as it ought properly to be described, to fit in with European developments) never amounted to more than a minority opinion. The National Transport Workers failed to call a general strike in 1912, the building trades' unions refused to amalgamate on such a platform, the Miners' Federation remained divided by regional patterns of behaviour, and class militancy among the strongest of skilled unions, the Engineers, gradually declined.[12] Nevertheless, the frustration arising from increasing stratification of working-class society and the conflicts between union hierarchies and the shop floor illustrate the range and intensity of forces in pre-1914 industrial society. They were factors which the state and the political parties could not ignore.

After twenty years' experience of industrial conciliation, and fully aware of the disastrous consequences of prolonged damage to production and industrial harmony at a time of worsening diplomatic relations with Germany, the government had a vested interest in promoting peace. This was revealed clearly during the Agadir crisis in July 1911 when Lloyd George appealed publicly to the patriotism of railwaymen and railway companies. Organised working-class dissent appeared to be not only a hindrance to industrial production but a threat to the political order, more serious because of the Labour Party's patent failure to restrain the extreme fringes of the working-class movement to the defence of that parliamentary democracy whose preservation, with working-class support, had been a potent reason for the offer of an electoral compact with the Labour Party in 1903 by Herbert Gladstone, the Liberal Chief Whip.

But how was government to intervene? Opinions divided, though not on traditional party lines. For those committed to the nineteenth-century two-party system, there could be no easy way to admit a new estate – other than a political party – to power. Diehards on both sides regarded the trade unions as lacking historic authority and legitimacy,

*To whom Trades Councils were 'the only ground on which the general problems of labour may be discussed, without the narrowness of view which, in the individual unions, is apt to permit only the immediate selfish interests of each craft to be discussed.' (Guy Bowman, 'The National Federation of Trades Councils', *The Syndicalist*, February 1912; quoted in R. Holton, *British Syndicalism 1900–14: myths and realities*, Pluto Press, p. 63.)

even to the extent of the pretensions to defend the national economic interest put forward by employers' associations; and might have opposed government action or conciliation in the words of the Permanent Secretary of the Home Office used during the ribbon weavers' strike in 1860, when answering an urgent plea for a Commission of Inquiry from the Lord Lieutenant of Warwickshire: 'What right has the government to interfere in this matter, except to keep the peace?'[13] In default of a theory of political adaptation, other than the electoral and franchise reform which had served in 1832, 1867 and 1885, the traditionalists perforce fell back on the antithesis between order and disorder, legal restraint and anarchy.

But the law had changed: it had been interpreted by the courts and amended in Parliament and might be amended again. The King could advise Asquith in 1911: 'To devise a scheme to prevent strikes as far as possible from even occurring, especially sympathetic strikes, and legislation to put an end to peaceful picketing,'[14] but the 'public opinion' he cited lacked political substance, and was politely ignored. Indeed, Churchill could declare in 1911:

'It is not good for trade unions that they should be brought in contact with the courts, and it is not good for the courts. . . . Where class issues are involved, it is impossible to pretend that the courts command the same degree of general confidence. On the contrary, they do not, and a very large number of our population has been led to the opinion that they are, unconsciously no doubt, biased.'[15]

Instead the diehards vented their spleen in the columns of the *Morning Post*, put money into the strike-breaking organisations, and built up on the backbenches a continuing case for the revision of trade union law and restraint of the immunity given by the 1906 Act.

Advocates of state conciliation, on the other hand, could point to the tradition built up by the Board of Trade's Labour Department since its foundation by A. J. Mundella, President of the Board of Trade in Gladstone's last government. The principles of government-sponsored conciliation and publication of labour statistics and material relating to industrial disputes had been established in the mid-1890s, even though the hopes of Liberal Radicals and Fabians for a separate Ministry of Labour had been denied. Under a series of gifted civil servants like Llewellyn Smith, Vaughan Nash and Arthur Acland, and labour correspondents and investigators with a wide range of trade union experience, the Labour Department soon established a reputation for radicalism and pugnacity. After 1900, however, in a climate unfavourable to trade union aspirations, it had to tone down its reports to avoid charges of bias brought by other interested government departments, and the employers' federations, for whom the Department represented the acme of socialist interventionism.

By virtue of its expertise, scientific approach and 'almost irreversible collectivist momentum'[16] the Labour Department gradually outweighed both Home Office and Local Government Board as the source of industrial relations policy. Assignment of the new Trade Boards to the Board of Trade in 1909 showed the political importance both of Churchill, as Minister, and of the tradition of investigation so painstakingly built up in the face of employers' lack of cooperation. Well before the conflicts of 1911–14, a body of opinion had been created, favourable to government attempts to ameliorate some of the disadvantages suffered by trade unions in industrial bargaining; and in the process a considerable amount of information had been accumulated about the weakness of legal sanctions, and the difficulty of applying in England legal precepts evolved in Canada (the Lemieux Act, 1903), the USA, Germany or Australia.

The Labour Department had refused to entertain ideas of compulsory arbitration, even when this was recommended by the Royal Commission on Labour in 1894; and it built up instead a continuing tradition of conciliation, much more to the taste of trade unions. The 1896 Conciliation Act had made a clear distinction between disputes of right (over the interpretation of agreements, soluble at law) and disputes of interest, over conditions, wages, terms of employment, etc., for which it prescribed an extension of the system of joint boards – voluntary groupings which would, ideally, have been based on strong employers' federations and strong trade unions. Thus it was hoped that only the few, major disputes (which the Webbs compared to modern warfare after diplomacy had broken down) would break out beyond the boards' province into the political arena.

Such developments encouraged visions of an institutional framework of industrial relations, even before 1900.* But government lacked a prescriptive right to interfere: nothing could happen without a request from industry itself. The Department had to its credit a series of conciliation successes in the nineties, yet the employers' counter attack in 1897–8 proved their ability to defy government intervention and reject out of hand a proposal for a National Conciliation Board. Ten years of

*Such as the formation of the National Union of Employers and Employed in 1894 by such men as Jowett and Seebohm Rowntree 'to promote and maintain between employers and employed a feeling of common interest'.

comparatively cautious activity followed, in which the Department seems to have been careful to appoint neutral outsiders as arbitrators and to avoid arousing employers' and Conservative Party fears 'of inviting the aid of state officials thought to have a distinct bias in favour of trade unionism'.* In what became the test case of the period, the Engineering Employers' Federation established a system of 'employer conciliation' which lasted in effect until 1971, while South Wales mine-owners refused in 1898 to recognise in any way the conciliator appointed by the Board of Trade. These restrictive conditions were only just coming to an end in the years 1909–11.

Both major parties showed themselves interested in 'respectable' trade union activity, and, implicitly, in the formation of powerful formal bodies on both sides of industry. But while the small group of Liberal Radicals or the Conservative, Joseph Chamberlain, could try to inculcate such ideas in the mass of party activists,† electoral strategy, the leverage of interest groups and political imagery, usually worked to prevent an enlightened bureaucracy taking industrial relations out of politics or the hands of politicians.

In the years before 1914, almost every variant of arbitration, conciliation, and intervention was attempted by Liberal Ministers, in strikes too large, or too significant to government, to be left to the Labour Department's officials. Almost at the beginning of the period, in 1907, Lloyd George, then President of the Board of Trade, had appointed Sir George Askwith, a barrister with considerable experience of industrial disputes, as a non-departmental conciliator in the service of the government. Askwith's personality remains enigmatic: he showed no great sympathy for the labour leaders with whom he dealt, and, in spite of his reiterated aim to set up a more permanent means of conciliation, he remained personally aloof, mistrustful equally of civil servants and politicians. A lawyer by training, product of a conventional

---

The Times, 24 January 1902. J. E. Gorst (Chief Conservative Organiser) had complained in 1893 about the Department officials: 'their appointment is a method of subsidising agitators and paying them for going about the country, propagating opinions in favour of the Government, not for giving reliable information on the conditions of labour.' (E. Wigham, *Trade Unions and the State*, p. 6.) In 1897 Lord Penrhyn denounced intervention, on the grounds that acceptance 'would establish a precedent for outside interference in the management of my private affairs.' (Wigham, p. 13.)

†As early as 1896 Chamberlain declared: 'What insurance will wealth find to its advantage to provide against the risks to which it is undoubtedly subject? If the rich want their rights to be respected as they ought to be, they are bound in turn to respect the rights of their less fortunate brethren.' (E. E. Gulley, *Joseph Chamberlain and English Social Politics*, Columbia University Press, New York, 1926, p. 213.)

Victorian education, he did not seek a legal framework for industrial relations but instead relied on his skill as a negotiator to build up an unrivalled reputation, as if the cult of his personality alone could prepare the way of peace; claiming always to take neutral ground, he strenuously opposed intervention by individual ministers or governments.

Askwith's early successes in the Belfast transport strike and the threatened railway strike in 1907, were not repeated in the slump conditions of the next two years when employers were forcing wages down. But after a brief foray by Churchill (who had replaced Lloyd George at the Board of Trade) into the question of legislation to give government power to set up courts of inquiry, with the setting up of the new Trade Boards, intervention by Ministers lapsed and the Department's scope broadened.

By the time that the great wave of strikes broke out, three separate but overlapping approaches to industrial conciliation existed: associated, in turn, with Cabinet, civil servants and 'impartial' outsiders. Askwith achieved some success in the National Transport Workers' (NTWF) strikes in many English dockyards between June and August 1911, but the railway strike which paralysed the north of England, and threatened disruption of food supplies, brought in Lloyd George, by now Chancellor of the Exchequer. In party terms, the crisis was acute: 'The government are bound at all costs to protect the public from the dangers and miseries which famine and a general unrest of industry will entail.'[17] Yet Asquith and Churchill, also for party reasons, sought a fight to the finish, using troops to keep supplies going. In this case Lloyd George triumphed, waving the patriotic, anti-German card (at the time of the Agadir crisis, July 1911) to force the railway companies to meet the men and thus at last to concede recognition.

But these methods had been haphazard, almost uncoordinated. In the middle of predictions for worse strife in 1912, Sir Charles Macara (a former president of the Cotton Spinners' Federation, who had been appalled at the effect of the 1911 disputes on Manchester) proposed the appointment of a joint body of men and owners to act as arbitrators in future strikes. Under pressure from the press and from the Labour Department, the government set up a National Industrial Council (NIC), with Askwith as chairman. But despite his grandiose new title of Chief Industrial Conciliator, this development isolated Askwith from the Board of Trade, without in any way diminishing the authority and capacity to interfere of the Cabinet Committee on Industrial Unrest.

1912 brought less violence than 1911 but much more time lost.

Worse, experience showed that so long as unions thought it possible to appeal to the Cabinet if the owners ignored them, they would do so at the price of ignoring the Industrial Council. The coal strike over the national minimum wage alone cost thirty million working days. Since recognition, in its widest sense, lay behind the miners' demand for a statutory minimum wage, and since the mineowners refused to discuss it, in February 1912, the Cabinet was constrained to put through an Act providing for district minima. Angrily, Askwith pointed out that existing machinery had been ignored. Yet the Cabinet, driven on by the Liberal Radicals, who sought state powers over essential industries and even the sanction of nationalisation to force recalcitrant owners to pay progressive wage-scales, went on to set up their own inquiry into the causes of industrial unrest.

If this was the new Liberal industrial concordat with labour, it was almost diametrically opposed to the Conservative vision of a harmony between employers and employed only remotely indebted to the state. Disagreement within government over the means of conciliation ran parallel to a party-political conflict over the fundamental nature of industrial politics; and perhaps out of fear of the logical outcome (in the face of a weak parliamentary majority, Irish troubles and German strategic ambitions) the Cabinet abated its claims. In the next trial of strength, the London dock strike (where both sides had rejected the recommendations of a committee set up by Lloyd George and Sidney Buxton in 1911), the Cabinet first referred the dispute to the Industrial Council, and then, as the NTWF began to collapse, disengaged altogether. Askwith was delighted: 'The present difficulty will cease to be mixed up with politics and ministers; temporary and panicky legislation may be avoided and the subject considered by persons conversant with industry.'[18] It was an end, he hoped, to what he called 'the degradation of government', and a blow to future sympathetic strikes. But the NIC was also discredited. Having tasted blood, the employers would talk only to Cabinet, and before Lord Devonport would consent to see Harry Gosling and his dock-workers, the Cabinet had to come back into the arena, to promise an inquiry as a means to get the men back to work.

By 1913 the inherent defects of all three modes of conciliation had been made obvious. Ministers were seen, publicly, to break ranks, while both Askwith, the NIC and the Labour Department suffered from the employers' prolonged offensive. When the new President of the Board of Trade, Sidney Buxton, proclaimed the need for compulsory powers to delay strikes and set up arbitration, the Tories, in Bonar

Law's words, grew adamant for 'complete detachment'. Government, they declared, had no part in judicial determination; and the extent of Conservative dominance on this issue can be gauged from the fact that although Lloyd George voted for a Commons' motion, moved by the Liberal MP, James O'Grady, to authorise compulsory conciliation in cases where the national interest was threatened, he did not even bother to speak, betraying, according to Askwith, his belief in 'the recognition of the *public* as the third party in trade disputes.'[19] Personal antagonism, as a result, deeply and permanently divided Lloyd George and Asquith; and, as Lloyd George fought on sporadically against the twin enemies of Toryism and the financial/industrial community, their differences weakened the Liberal Party.

These years vindicated no one but Askwith, and his personal, apparently apolitical, establishment of collective bargaining machinery, through which industrial disputes could be institutionalised; a system endorsed (before that body finally disintegrated) in the NIC's report for 1913. Strong employers, strong unions and a *habitual* form of bargaining, comprised, in his eyes, the best recognition of the 'rights of the public' and guarantee of the exclusion of 'bishops, mayors and local MPs, all hopelessly ignorant negotiators'.[20] Yet after a great success in the Midland metalworkers' strikes in 1913, even Askwith admitted defeat in the Dublin transport workers' strike. Sympathetic strikes exposed the limits of his methods; rather than envisage employers and unions of all trades as entities with as much interest in the affairs of one sector as another, he condemned the practice out of hand: 'No community could exist if resort to sympathetic strikes became a general policy of trade unionism.' The King (with whom Askwith had been in correspondence since 1910) and all the parties concurred. Speaking at the 1913 Conference, G. H. Roberts, President of the Parliamentary Labour Party, repudiated 'the harsh and violent criticism of those who claim to be, but are not, in uniformity with the Labour and socialist movement. . . . Direct activists affect to repudiate the representative government of modern democracy, and have aroused the suspicion that they favour violence rather than reason.'[21] Lines of battle, which were not to be broken until 1921, had been drawn up with the traditional political institutions (of which the Labour Party already formed part) on one side, and on the other, the newly-formed Triple Alliance (miners, railwaymen and transport workers) aiming at concerted action in support of any one of the three.

Before the outbreak of war it might have seemed that very little had been learned as a result of three years' unprecedented industrial strife.

The prognostication for industry and the political system itself in 1914 and 1915 could only be gloomy. Yet the Cabinet, the administrators, Askwith, and the political parties had all seen that future hope rested in the creation of formal processes of bargaining by institutions. Under what aegis and rules remained in dispute until the prior question of recognition had been settled. But even if industrial politics had not as yet been circumscribed by statute, the existence of state rights and a public interest had been perceived by politicians (according to their individual party ideologies); and the naïve belief that the state could remain neutral had been abandoned. The network of conciliation procedures had been widened, the Department of Labour had greatly extended its operations, and after 1909 the number of Joint Boards had increased rapidly, to 325 by 1913. On the other hand, neither employers nor unions were prepared to accept or even envisage giving up the de facto rights they had established, as a result of the strike wave, to force even Cabinet to mediate their quarrels; certainly not in favour of a system of legally constituted institutions, bound down to agreements made under the competence of the state bureaucracy.

At this period unions and employers did not possess a clear, comprehensive understanding of their collective power, nor of how it could be directed into the political field to guarantee industrial advantage. On the union side that deficiency might have been made good by the Triple Alliance (born in June 1914, but untried before 1919), with its aims of workers' control of self-governing industries. But although the Alliance with its anarcho-syndicalist overtones constituted a terrible warning to the political parties, its existence only increased the tendency for government to intervene to safeguard the parliamentary system by promoting industrial and class harmony. However revolutionary the sentiments expressed in *The Miners' Next Step* or unofficial railway committees' resolutions might be, the larger the union audience to which they were addressed, the less was their effective weight: and this fact, more than most, encouraged government and the parties to build up the TUC as an alternative. Moreover, 1912 had tested some limits of direct action; and although it was possible to imagine that a general strike planned by the Triple Alliance might succeed, the practical difficulties of organisation that had been revealed in its postponement of action until 1915 argued the other way.

Unfortunately for the government, the TUC had failed to make itself an institution representative of the whole trade union movement. Numerically, it outweighed the GFTU; but politically it had made no progress since 1910 other than to defend itself against Labour Party

64

encroachment. The Parliamentary Committee remained a post-box for resolutions; the TUC, with a tiny staff, remained unable to influence powerful unions, or do more than control the sessions of Congress. The Joint Committee still resembled a discount house for competing claims to status, ignored by Cabinet in most of the great strikes. Askwith and the Labour Department took the TUC at its own limited valuation, not least because it had always rejected recognition as a legal corporation, able to sue or be sued. In turn, the TUC had been content to ride on the strike wave, and to seem militant in 1911–12,* while in 1913–14 meekly accepting MacDonald's claim that the field on which the national struggle had to be fought was 'the state and not the workshop; the weapon is to be the ballot box, the Act of Parliament, not collective bargaining'.[22] Fortunately for its failing parliamentary position, the Labour Party found a not unwilling adjunct in a Parliamentary Committee threatened by the alarming enthusiasm of the Triple Alliance and exhausted by the preceding three years. It seemed as if the Committee would baulk at the question of whether to wait on the long growth of a parliamentary majority or look to the consolidation of the TUC's own political strength, and be content to agree to anodyne resolutions, designed to hold the Labour movement together, like 'Permanent improvement among the ranks of the workers can only be fully effected by joint action on trade union and independent political lines.'[23]

But Labour might never win such a majority. MacDonald declared in 1914 that in return for concessions Labour could offer government its cooperation over the Irish question; 'Irrespective of its name, and irrespective of other proposals it might make, the Labour Party would be bound to do its best to give that Party a chance for being responsible for the politics of this country.'[24] This was scarcely the tone of a party contemplating office in the next decade. It was not, therefore, surprising that the Parliamentary Committee refused entirely to trust politics to the 'political wing'. In June 1913, when on behalf of the Labour Party Arthur Henderson complained that TUC claims to a relationship with government entrenched on the parliamentary province, Bowerman replied: 'It was very difficult to say what was a political and what was an industrial question. Moreover they [the Parliamentary Committee] must retain a certain amount of political influence . . . to force the government to listen to their demands.'[25]

The *political* distinction between an institutionalised trade movement

---

*It rejected, for example, an attempt by Arthur Henderson to bring in a bill to make strikes illegal without a month's notice – a bill which probably had the support of many Labour Party leaders (TUC ARC 1911, pp. 230–37).

represented by the TUC and the anarcho-syndicalist tendency which the creation of the Triple Alliance emphasised, soon began to affect relationships between sections of the employers and like-minded groups in the Conservative Party. Early in 1913 Bonar Law came under pressure from several younger MPs[26] and the party managers[27] to encourage the political evolution of trade unions and the detachment of Labour from the Liberal Party, and although he did not give way (and indeed advocated the classic Conservative industrial solution of a return to piecework, with higher wages in return for higher productivity[28]) it became clear in the House of Commons and at the 1913 Party Conference that the Conservatives chose not to associate themselves with the attitudes of the victorious employers – an attitude easier to sustain since Lords Penrhyn and Devonport so clearly rejected *any* state interference or political advance on the status quo of 1897.

For their part, more moderate employers did not ignore political developments. Generally, the tone of their statements and continued anti-union propaganda conveyed the message that in future they expected governments to stand clear of industrial politics.[29] But while each Federation concentrated on building up its strength, the employers generally took care also to distinguish, in their propaganda attacks, between manifestations of syndicalist thinking and the activities of the Triple Alliance on one hand and respectable trade unionism on the other – tacitly therefore, encouraging the TUC to aspire to a larger role.

Like similar tendencies in the parties and government, this attitude contributed to the creation of representative bodies within industry with whom government could negotiate. Lloyd George himself, once the proponent of non-intervention,[30] became an ardent supporter, seeing in the establishment of industrial harmony a priceless electoral asset. Just as he had advocated party coalition in August 1910 and again in 1912–13, to abolish 'remediable poverty' on common political grounds, so he saw that if industrial, and hence class, antagonisms could largely be taken out of politics, socialism and syndicalism would be permanently restrained and parliamentary Labour made safe for the Liberal Party. By 1912, like some Conservatives, he was prepared to envisage plans for state compulsory arbitration: 'I agree we are tending that way and may have state interference within a comparatively short time.'[31]

But Lloyd George had as yet no coherent theory, no new *system* in view. Partly because of his background, his experience of exploitation by landlords but his relative ignorance of business and industry, he still listened to the authority of financial rather than industrial pressure groups.[32] He was not then, perhaps was never, the man to redress the balance between the two classes of capitalists and labour. The war compelled him to attempt a compromise, and in the process a new system did evolve, but neither he nor the Liberal Party inherited power as a result.

3 THE NECESSITIES OF WAR, 1914–16

Bound by their insularity and self-confidence, Edwardian political analysts rarely made comparison with European systems except in the fields of social services and education, where among a small but influential group of lobbyists, headed by Lord Haldane, the model of Wilhelmine Germany aroused feelings of positive admiration. Yet in Germany and France, the relationships between government, parties and institutions could have suggested many insights, even before the years 1915–17, when both suffered a crisis of war production and morale strikingly similar to that in Britain.

Because of her immensely rapid and recent industrialisation, and relatively short parliamentary tradition, Germany, in the early years of the century, lacked a close or constant link between trade unions and political parties. Trade union liberties, in so far as they existed, had been recognised by government in Bismarck's day, and syndicalist ideas of industrial self-government were in the 1910s much less prevalent than in England. In spite of being the largest party in the Reichstag, with 4·5 million votes and 110 seats after the election of 1912, the Socialist Party (SPD) suffered from the fact that the Reichstag itself had acquired only limited powers of control over the bureaucracy or the Chancellor. Acting in concert, the parties might demolish Chancellor von Bülow in 1909 but the SPD could not then form a substantive coalition, nor obtain reforms to meet working-class demands.

Political isolation of the working class in Germany, far more pronounced than in England, had been compounded by the aping of the aristocracy by a middle class prone to dreams of a conservative reaction against the evil effects of modern industrial transformation. The state machine remained under the archaic domination of an outworn landed class and the influence of large-scale industrialists, twin mainstays of the authoritarian system; and it seemed unable to resolve industrial and economic problems without direction from above. In these circumstances – legacy of Bismarck's contrived balance in society – the parties operated in a void, the SPD expounding doctrines of class warfare and revolution to a working class cut off from political and economic power. As Jean Jaurés pointed out sardonically in 1904, its doctrinaire socialism was matched only by its political incapacity.

Yet in the 1900s its subjection to the demands of trade unions helped to produce the conflict between theory and practice which Eduard Bernstein set out to appease by his doctrine of evolutionary socialism. The subsequent opposition of the vigorous Marxist section, headed by Karl Liebknecht and Rosa Luxemburg, and their outspokenly revolutionary language, aroused suspicion among the political élite about their wholesale alienation from the state. In the Kaiser's phrase, the Left became *Vaterlandslöse gesellen*; and this led Chancellor and government to seek what had been rejected in England – industrial collaboration between state, employers and the as yet less-politicised trade union movement.

Meanwhile, employers divided on political as well as functional lines. Representatives of heavy industry, dominating the Central Association of German Industrialists whose principal aim of cartelisation had been largely achieved in the period 1900–10, believed in creating a 'cartel of producing estates' which should incorporate agricultural producers, white-collar workers and other craft unions; on the other hand, the League of German Industrialists, representing, particularly, chemicals and electricity, and led by Emil Rathenau, favoured the creation of a high technology, mixed economy, based on close collaboration between state, management and industrial unions.

In theory, such organisation had proceeded further than in Britain, in spite of Germany's relative recent arrival on the industrial scene. As G. D. Feldman points out, 'however loosely held together, these combinations of interest groups demonstrated a tendency to form secondary systems of political power, alongside the bureaucracy and the political parties.'[1] But in practice, although the Central Association and the League developed their own employers' associations,[2] and even merged them in 1913, great differences of opinion remained on basic matters like the right of the state to intervene in industrial disputes.

In spite of their division into three federations,[3] trade unions consolidated their own position, particularly with smaller employers who had mostly conceded collective wage-bargaining before 1914. The Free Trade Union movement, led by Carl Legien, remained almost free of the 'craft versus general union' antagonism so characteristic of Britain; and although SPD members probably amounted to a majority, it tended inevitably towards reformism, frequently cooperating with other parties, particularly in local and regional government. Its General

Commission opposed not only political strikes, but the revolutionary language of the SPD for fear of endangering the industrial gains of the previous decade. 'Labourism', as Triple Alliance militants might have called their attitude, was seen as the means to win full recognition from employers and the state; unlike British unions, the FTU and CTU sought status as legal corporations, capable of making binding collective agreements *(Tarifvertrage)*.

Government and League (though not heavy industry) found this form of evolution not unattractive.[4] As Bismarck's attempt to buy working-class acquiescence with paternalistic reform receded into the past, it seemed increasingly important to wean the organised (trade unionised) working class away from the SPD. Hence the provision of reforms inimical to many employers in the 1900s, such as industrial courts, the extension of social insurance, factory inspectorate and housing schemes. Yet because of the opposition from vested interests and heavy industry, the state failed to create an effective industrial parliament or *Arbeitskammer* where employers and unions could discuss industrial questions; and it failed also to free the unions from police surveillance. Reluctant to recognise them as estates in the same sense as employers' associations, especially after the massive strikes of 1912, the government lost any chance of neutralising the movement – yet its reforms, as Krupp warned the Emperor, inevitably encouraged demands for political as well as legal parity.

For reasons quite different from the German SPD case, the French Socialist Party failed to unify itself until the 1904 conference of the Second International at Amsterdam, where the parliamentary socialists, Jaurés, A. Briand and Alexandre Millerand succumbed to the Guesdist (and SPD) principle of non-cooperation with bourgeois parties and condemned the French Socialist Party (SFIO), despite its 1·4 million votes and 103 seats won in the 1914 election, to permanent opposition. There existed a strong anarcho-syndicalist tradition (as in Italy, Spain and Portugal) side by side with the politically directed Guesdist movement, and trade unionism followed the anarcho-syndicalist pattern, under leaders schooled in the tenets of de Leon, the International Workers of the World (IWW) and Georges Sorel, who looked to the collapse of bourgeois society when confronted with the massive strength of the proletariat. Large sections drifted into the impossibilist argument that the millennium would arrive even without use of the climactic general strike.

The strike waves in France before 1914 were, however, due less to the theories of Sorel than to the attempts of trade unionists generally, lacking the support of a governing party, to legitimise their activity, to win recognition on a national scale, and to have a share in the ultimate take-over of political power.[5] The results resembled the limited gains in recognition won in Britain and Germany at the same period; but because in France the Confédération Générale du Travail (CGT) had so clearly been seen to direct and coordinate the political campaign, its membership swelled phenomenally. Its numbers (and percentage of French workers actually unionised) remained small in comparison with Britain and Germany; but the degree of coherence (and the concomitant growth in power of the Patronat, or employers' confederation) encouraged the growth of ideas about industrial cooperation.

In a very general sense, political and economic developments in Germany and France, as in Britain, led to tentative efforts by government to set up alternative political systems appropriate to modern industry, and to take the industrial question out of parliamentary politics. In the process, trade union federations were accepted, usually by employers in the newer industries, as having a function beyond that of pressure or interest groups. But in Britain before 1914 the entrenched opposition in Conservative and Liberal parties, and the heavy industrial sector, prevented formal collaboration in practice; while deep ideological disputes developed over the strategy to be employed as they reached the threshold of government. In contrast to the faith in working-class capacity to prevent war, prevalent among members of the Second International, the approach of war was sometimes seen by governments or employers in Germany and France as a stimulant to national harmony. In fact, for each of these countries, the first stage of the war, down to 1916, brought almost unmitigated conflict between the three parties to that hypothetical industrial entente.

Treating the unpleasant phenomenon like a malignant tumour whose frightened victim refuses to acknowledge its existence, the government avoided recognising the extent of working-class discontent in Britain during the early months of the First World War. Askwith, after all, had observed in July 1914 that Department of Labour machinery for settling disputes was working better than in the previous five years; with the exception of the engineering industry, 'trade after trade was gradually being organised on a basis of good relationships so far as the leaders of both sides were concerned. A network of associated employers and federated trade unions was spreading over the country.'[6]

As in France and Germany, the war brought about an unexpected surge of central authority which was, to a very large extent, supported by trade unions and parties. The former pursued a straightforward, simple argument – though one not necessarily endorsed by all those who had invested political and emotional capital in the high hopes of avoiding war by general strike. The Joint Board (TUC, GFTU and Labour Party) met on 24 August, 1914, to urge all unions and employers to end industrial action: 'Whenever new points of difference arise during the war period, a serious attempt should be made by all concerned to reach an amicable settlement, before resorting to a strike or lockout.'

No machinery as yet existed to enforce this exhortation; but the Parliamentary Committee approved the government's recruiting campaign, and the Labour Party followed suit, having seen MacDonald go into exile on the main issue of opposition to the war. As a whole, the Party never seriously entertained opposition after the German invasion of Belgium, and with an electoral truce in operation, Keir Hardie let it be seen that there could be no half measures: 'A nation at war must be united . . . the lads who have gone forth to fight their country's battles must not be disheartened by any discordant notes at home'[7] – sentiments echoed by the majority of the Executive of the rapidly disintegrating Second International.

Agreement on the war effort (with the exception of the ILP, SDF and SLP) did not prevent the Labour movement from pressing for fair treatment or from setting up the War Emergency National Committee (WENC) with representatives of the Labour Party, TUC, socialist societies, women's organisations and cooperatives. In due course the WENC qualified as a successor to the weak Joint Board, for Arthur Henderson, who had succeeded MacDonald, shrewdly saw that it could be the means to exclude the GFTU and submit the rest of the movement to an agreed division of labour: political questions for the Party, industrial for the TUC.[8]

Employers reacted differently. It is hard to avoid the conclusion that in the first months of war, when only a short struggle was envisaged, and while unemployment rose sharply in non-essential industries, some federations saw the chance of regaining the ground lost to the unions in the previous decade.[9] In December 1914, on the pretext of increasing war production, the Engineering Federation demanded that unions associated with munitions work should, unilaterally, surrender their rights to restrictive practices.[10] A deputation of Glasgow employers blandly asked for what Addison called 'all sorts of powers over workmen – a sort of martial law which they themselves might administer',[11] while the Mineowners' Association required withdrawal of the Eight

Hours Act.[12] These were, of course, the employers who had shown most hostility to unions in the past. But the advent of full employment, followed by a labour shortage, reversed the balance and such blatant manœuvres ceased. By 1915 employers' federations had, generally, postponed the long struggle over recognition for the duration and adopted a stance similar to that of the TUC in which patriotism blended nicely with self-interest. Their temporising attitude did not, however, prevent them from taking full advantage of later government proposals for relaxing restrictive practices, while resisting any serious attempt to tax their own enhanced war profits.

For its part, the Liberal Government entered the war without composite plans to regulate the economy or control the supply of raw materials, volume of production and allocation of manpower. Voluntary enlistment and the free market in labour, which depleted vital industries haphazardly, were allowed to run on, like the inflation which spiralled upwards from the first day, rising 22 per cent in the first six months. Time and again 'Lloyd George and his successors at the Treasury listened far more to financial groups than they did to others such as industrialists'[13] and showed a curiously business-oriented sensitivity on the question of profits, the money market and the admissibility of high wartime taxation. (In January 1915, Askwith noticed, in spite of the continued patriotic fervour, a strong current of opinion 'against middle-class contractors who are making money out of the war', and an equally strong union resistance to relaxation of restrictive practices.[14]) Even at this stage there was evidence of the danger of government 'appearing as the mouthpiece of the employers'.[15]

In that free state, the first wave of industrial disputes hit Clydeside in February 1915, when for two weeks nearly 10,000 engineers came out on strike, pressing for an extra 2d. an hour to meet the rising cost of living. The Clyde Labour Withholding Committee, forerunner of the Clyde Workers' Committee (CWC) made its appearance and, in a uniformly hostile climate, pressed the claim that the war in France should take second place to the class struggle at home.

Responsibility for industrial relations had already devolved on to the Board of Trade, since the government could rely neither on the ad hoc solutions nor the ministerial interventions of the pre-war period. On 4 February the Cabinet set up the Committee of Production, with Askwith in the chair, assisted by members of the Admiralty and War Office and Horace Wilson (later Permanent Under Secretary at the Ministry of Labour), to try to avoid strikes impairing vital industries. The free labour market had already collapsed, and Askwith found himself, in a

73

characteristic phrase, 'dealing with very complicated problems, the ignorance and prejudice of the masses, the obstinacy and prejudice of employers, and a general mess.'[16]

The Committee's first report recommended government to put an end to industrial stoppages on all official war work as well as to abandon restrictive practices, in return for a promise of their restoration at the war's end, and the resolution of all disputes by an impartial arbitration tribunal. Although these were harsh cuts at trade unions' substantive achievements since the 1870s, some progress was made in the engineering industry with the Agreement over production of shells and fuses, in which dilution (replacement of skilled men by less or unskilled men and women) was successfully bargained against the long-term restoration of job reservation. But the engineering shop stewards on Clydeside demanded that future dilution should be controlled locally rather than nationally; insistence on national settlements by the Engineering Employers, and capitulation by the engineers' union (ASE), entrenched a growing division between union leadership and its local members; and simmering discontent on the Clyde led the Chancellor of the Exchequer, Lloyd George, to seek a more comprehensive concordat.

On 11 March he invited the TUC, Parliamentary Committee and leaders of thirty-six individual unions concerned in war production to a conference at the Treasury. Later, like the stage-managed pre-war confrontations, he depicted the scene dramatically as he persuaded 'those stalwart artisans, leaning against the throne of the dead Queen [in the Treasury boardroom] and on equal terms negotiating with the government of the day' to endorse the Committee of Production's recommendations.[17]

Well aware of the contrary feelings of their rank and file, the miners refused to agree and the engineers (ASE) delayed until June, holding out for better terms and taxation of profits. Both were unpalatable signs for the government for they involved questions outside war production and indicated that bargains made in Whitehall might not stick in the provinces. In spite of permanent institution of the Committee of Production as an arbitration tribunal, some Ministers had reservations about its capacity to enforce government policy. Walter Runciman (President of the Board of Trade) argued that the Treasury Agreement lacked authority even in munitions and shipyard work, and feared that the patriotic card would soon diminish in value,[18] while Askwith (duly noting that 'workpeople are wonderfully obedient to strenuous telegrams') and Llewellyn Smith, Sir Frederick Black and William

Beveridge of the Labour Department pressed for legislation.[19] Trenchant criticism of the unions from shipbuilding employers, and by the Armaments Committee for the North-East, encouraged hostile views among officials and Cabinet Ministers.[20]

The government crisis of May 1915, which led to the first Coalition and the Munitions of War Act, had its origins in the shell-shortage crisis on the Western Front demonstrated by the second Battle of Ypres and the failure of the British advance at Festubert; and in the surge of opinion whipped up by the Northcliffe press against administrative incompetence, after Colonel Repington's famous attack on the government published in *The Times* on 14 May. In these circumstances, some sort of legislation would probably have been accepted by the majority of those trade union leaders who had signed the Treasury Agreement only to see their power ebbing away to shop stewards and works committees; but the actual Bill drafted by Lloyd George (now Minister of Munitions) with the advice of the National Labour Advisory Council and Arthur Henderson (brought into the Coalition as a junior Minister and the Government's unofficial labour relations advisor) ranged far beyond the vague commitments of the Agreement.

The Act forced the unions to abandon the right to strike and their restrictive practices, and to accept government arbitration, dilution by women, girls and young unskilled men, relaxation of the Factory Acts, restrictions on overtime and Sunday working regulations.* Prohibition of strikes could, by Royal Proclamation, be extended to any industry, regardless of the fact that the Treasury Agreement had been limited to munitions and engineering. In addition, it brought in the highly unpopular 'leaving certificate', without which a man could not give up work in munitions, and which seemed to many to be the first intimation of industrial conscription. In return, the government pledged itself to limit war profits to 20 per cent excess over 1914 (a surprisingly generous concession to employers, for whom 1914 had been a good year), and 'to use its efforts to secure the restoration of pre-war conditions in every case after the war'. But these pledges lacked legal clarity: and no mutually agreed record was made of what had been given up.[21]

Trade unionists faced a difficult choice. When set against the still rising cost of living,[22] employers' sacrifices seemed small, especially in view of their stiff resistance to wage claims. Lloyd George indeed had privately reassured Sir Vincent Caillard of Vickers Ltd that 'the Ministry had no desire to interfere with the conduct of their business'.[23] Unions found their members engulfed in a spiral of rent increases, housing

*This was later restored, after pressure by the Sabbath Observance societies.

shortages in munitions areas, and a climate of widespread anti-working-class propaganda carried on in the popular press. The government asked much and promised little. Lloyd George told the TUC in December 1915 that dilution depended 'on the unions exerting all their force to remove suspicions [of the employers] and to encourage the men and, indeed, as far as they can, *I will not say coerce, but* bring every influence to bear upon them under the stress of this great national necessity.'[24] Yet the TUC was to have no higher role than 'consultation' in determining government policy. Further legislation was held in reserve as a threat should they fail;[25] and when the ASE asked for representation on one of the boards set up to administer the Defence of the Realm Act, they were ignored. Nevertheless, to Committee members like J. H. Thomas, who genuinely deplored strikes in wartime, it seemed preferable to cooperate, rather than have the stringent Defence of the Realm (DORA) provisions used, as Runciman wanted.[26] A measure of involvement in the political process, however small, was better than exclusion.

This degree of collaboration imposed a fearful strain on unions' coherence as institutions; but the decay of rank and file allegiance did not show up, publicly and unequivocally, until the coal strike in South Wales in July 1915, the first substantive test of the Munitions of War Act. Like most deeply contentious disputes, this strike grew out of a variety of grievances and local factors: the 1910 agreement was due for re-negotiation; while cost-of-living increases angered communities with a history of pre-war militancy and syndicalism. After Askwith's initial attempt at settlement had been rejected by the owners, who refused to pay higher rates, Runciman called a conference of both sides for July 15. The Miners' South Wales Area had, however, been building up evidence of high war profits made by the owners, and set its sights on a minimum wage which would tide its men through the slump which they expected to follow the war's end. Despite a national appeal from their own union, the Miners' Federation (MFGB), to go on working, they voted down Askwith's proposals by 1,894 to 1,037.

Angrily and precipitately, Runciman invoked the Royal Proclamation procedure. Ignoring a further appeal from the MFGB, 209,000 men came out on strike, illegally, on 15 July. With Conservative support, Runciman and the Prime Minister stood firmly by the Proclamation and proposed, not to imprison the men (which would have been impossible), but to fine each of the 200,000 £5 or disfranchise them for five years.[27] But the MFGB secretary, Clement Edwards, ran to Lloyd George, who promptly chartered a special train and left for Cardiff with

Runciman and Henderson. With tactics reminiscent of his 1912 mediation, Lloyd George got a form of agreement by simply conceding the men's principal demands. Later, he and Runciman made speeches carefully tailored for public consumption, emphasising the gravity of the crisis and the 'cooperation and patriotism' of miners and owners.

Analysing the affair afterwards, Sir Arthur Steel-Maitland (a former chairman of the Conservative Party, with a close interest in industrial relations) was prepared to justify the miners' claims on cost-of-living grounds, in spite of their defiance of the MFGB and government. The owners had gained in public esteem by conceding, when, had they done so earlier, the strike could have been settled in the first place; he strongly deprecated the argument put by the owners, on the first of many occasions, that their supposed public-spiritedness should be rewarded by a government promise that the wage increases should be regarded as temporary, renegotiable in peacetime.[28] Steel-Maitland concluded that it would be hard to enforce the Act again: 'The last case in which it should have been first tried was in a peculiarly difficult area like South Wales, under somewhat difficult circumstances.'

Although Runciman still held faith in 'the strength of patriotic responsibility realised by both sides',[29] this sort of appeal diminished rapidly in value when confronted by the owners' hard-headedness and a stubborn local miners' federation, tied by a delegates' conference mandate. The Government had been seen to give way, the task of the MFGB and of men like J. H. Thomas of the Railwaymen (NUR) had been made harder[30] and, as Askwith gloomily declared, Section 1 of the Munitions of War Act had been impaired: 'The so-called settlement did more to cause unrest during the succeeding years than almost any other factor, and to lessen hopes of establishing a sane method for the settlement of disputes.'[31]

Government control of coal-mining in 1916 took that sector out of the dangerous political arena of the 'free' labour market. Elsewhere, Askwith and his Committee of Production tried to make a distinction between formal conciliation and government political intervention. The Committee settled a number of strikes by arbitration in 1915, in Scots mines and Lancashire cotton mills, and began to establish regular procedures, the better to cope with dilution and demarcation questions. Nevertheless, as Askwith foresaw, huge profits and inflation caused troubles 'which will blow the Munitions Act to the winds'.[32]

There had been no legal check on wages in industry outside the controlled trades, so that unions used awards in one to further claims in another, to the detriment of munitions workers, deprived of the right to strike. Leap-frogging led to animosity and local militancy and in November 1915 in his Fourth Report to the Committee Askwith suggested that the government should take over all firms concerned with munitions in order to limit profits and improve efficiency. 'Labour demands are not likely to be foregone unless it is made clear that there is no opportunity to employers to make undue profits. Rightly or wrongly, the steps which have been taken are not appreciated by labour and are not believed to be adequate.'[33] But however clearly the Committee of Production envisaged a future political contract, it lacked political influence with the Cabinet.

The questions of equity and working-class obligation in wartime had already been pointed up by the vigorous shop stewards' movement on the Clyde, where a rent strike early in 1915 had been rewarded by the rapid passage of a Rent Restriction Act. During the next eighteen months the Clyde Workers' Committee and similar groups of shop stewards in Sheffield, Coventry, Liverpool and Birmingham, led campaigns to remedy grievances over inadequate housing and poor conditions for munitions workers, as well as the high cost of living. The importance of these issues for the mass of working-class families can be gauged from the fact that the bulk of WENC work concentrated on them, leaving only matters arising from the Munitions Act to the TUC, whose rather passive approach to government in the first half of 1915 seems curious, given intense competition from the shop stewards' movement for the mandate of popular defence.[34] Too often for the credit of the TUC, the case against government and employers went by default.

From its beginning, the shop stewards' movement contained an ambiguity: its numerical support rested chiefly on its popular championship of working-class grievances against high profits, high prices, bad conditions and loss of union rights, in contrast to a union leadership, tied down by acceptance of the Munitions Act, which seemed to have abrogated responsibility; yet the organisation which facilitated success depended on a much smaller, political element involved in populist demands for workers' participation and the destruction of the capitalist system.[35] Whatever their politics, most individual shop stewards tended to take up ideological positions, while at the same time members of the SLP and the newly created British Socialist Party (BSP) moved into the front line with demands for workers' control and a negotiated peace.

In its long campaign in the second half of 1915 against dilution and the leaving certificate, the Clyde Workers' Committee succeeded in blending these dual elements; and the appearance of an alternative war policy in the West of Scotland, areas of South Wales, Tyneside and the Midland engineering shops, drove Lloyd George and Henderson to organise a counter-propaganda tour of factories in the munitions industry in December 1915. During the angry confrontation which took place in Glasgow, John Muir, Socialist Labour Party Chairman of the Clyde Workers' Committee, presented the shop stewards' case, in the face of what he stigmatised as government's capitulation to the employers: 'All industries and national resources must be taken over by the government; not merely "controlled" but taken over completely; and organised labour should be vested with the right to take part directly and equally with the present managers in the management and administration in every department of industry.'*

These were not sentiments to which Lloyd George could listen. The TUC had already effectively conceded all that the Ministry of Munitions had required, at its special conference in September 1915, by making a list of amendments to the Act – to which the government gave full effect in January 1916. Six months' close contact with the TUC representatives had been enough for Lloyd George to expel *individual* unions from the government ambit of consultation. Thus he conceded TUC requests for amendments to the Act concerning wages of dilutees and the leaving certificate scheme – but those to set up joint worker/employer boards to administer the Act, which had been proposed separately by the ASE, under pressure from shop stewards, were rejected out of hand.[36]

But this apparent harmony between government and official Labour (endorsed at the Labour Party's own emergency conference at Bristol in January 1916) ignored the national growth of the shop stewards' movement and the fear possessing Ministers that a small revolutionary group, led from Clydeside, might 'delude the vastly greater body of patriotic and loyal trade unionists by misrepresentation of the facts into expressing sympathy with the violent minority, believing them to be unjustly treated'.[37]

In the past, Lloyd George had often shown himself prone to hasty and harsh reactions, just the reverse of what he seems to have expected from the trade union movement. He had employed scarcely veiled threats to use DORA provisions for industrial conscription,[38] and later was to discuss both military discipline for munitions workers and the use of dockers' battalions to enforce the Derby conscription scheme. Possibly because of his early lack of industrial experience, Lloyd George never

History of the Ministry of Munitions, vol. 4, part 4, p. 104. The similarity of language to much of the TUC evidence to the Bullock Committee in 1976 should be noted.

understood the politics of industry as he did that of agriculture.[39] With profound misunderstanding, he imagined that trade unions and the TUC were bodies capable of making bargains and enforcing them, if necessary, against their members' opposition. 'What is the use of coming to terms with the leaders of the ASE,' he wrote angrily in June 1915, 'when the men behind them also insist on being consulted?'[40] Some months later he treated the TUC to a hectoring lecture for breaches of union agreements – and provoked from Ernest Bevin, the dockers' representative, a diatribe against 'the sinister crowd of civil servants who put those charges into his mouth. . . . Every employer with whom it was necessary to negotiate throws these charges in the teeth of the unions.'[41] As later evidence shows, the words might, fairly, have been aimed at the Minister himself.

For all his reforming ambitions and genuine sympathy for working-class aspirations, Lloyd George remained profoundly mistrustful of popular democracy, unable or perhaps unwilling to understand the limits on action imposed on its leaders by the composition of the British trade union movement. Detesting socialist and syndicalistic theories, he made far too sharp a distinction between the legitimacy of officials and the illegality of the shop floor leadership. The reason can be found in his fear of resurgence in wartime of that socialist dissent which his brand of liberalism had failed, in pre-war crises, to contain. Hence his harsh response to the outburst of discontent on Clydeside and the disruption of his campaign of political education at the climactic meeting in St Andrew's Hall on 25 December 1915. Contemporaries accused Lloyd George of over-reacting to a personal affront; in fact Muir and the Clyde Workers' Committee had called in question his whole conception of the political system.

A successful policy of 'thorough' followed, in which Lloyd George relied on the advice of a prominent industrialist, Sir William Weir.[42] *Forward* (the ILP newspaper which reported the St Andrew's meeting) and the SLP *Vanguard*, which Lloyd George regarded as more subversive, were suppressed. Muir, John Bell and John Maclean were prosecuted; the Ministry accepted a scheme for dilution devised by Wheatley and Kirkwood and then used it to break up the Clyde Workers' front; and finally, after a further strike by engineering workers in March 1916, the majority of the shop stewards were deported and held in Edinburgh jail. Further trials and imprisonments in April completed the temporary disintegration of the shop stewards' movement on the Clyde.

Demands for workers' control fell away. Experience suggested that it was possible to detach the political wing and its revolutionary ambitions from the popular movement and its economic grievances. The government seem to have concluded that future changes in industry should not be imposed without some consultation, not only with the TUC but also with factory workers. In Coventry, for example, the Ministry of Munitions actually pressed employers to recognise the local shop stewards' committees, to make dilution easier.[43] Lloyd George and his officials were beginning to see that sections of working-class opposition could be brought into contact with government by a process of institutionalisation similar to that already used for the TUC. But the incorporation of shop stewards' committees was accepted neither by the TUC nor by employers' federations, and official recognition of the committees remained open to the objection that it would compound problems of industrial relations after the war.

Even at the end of 1915 the Coalition government lacked a coherent industrial policy on more general questions. Civil servants and outside advisers argued over whether to set up a Ministry of Labour to replace the Department, now discredited in the eyes of TUC and Labour Party by its eagerness to speed up the procedures of the Munitions Act and to seek fresh powers to crush the Clyde Workers.[44] Llewellyn Smith argued (as he had done ever since the 1890s) that it would be a major strategic error to create a Ministry which would be seen to be so close to the unions as the Board of Trade already was to the employers. Weir and his fellow industrialists continued to advocate the use of commissions, like the one in Glasgow headed by the lawyer, Sir Thomas Munro, which had by-passed the shop stewards and made direct contact with the men – a policy vindicated by a Labour Department report in February that 'the *men* are in the main solid on the war and willing to make any sacrifice necessary'.[45] Given this weight of prejudice, the scepticism of the ASE is understandable, when told that the Ministry of Munitions saw itself as an impartial authority – dealing harshly but equally between management and unions.[46] 'General Consent', to use a phrase from a contemporary Labour Party questionnaire, had not been established, either by kicks or kindness.

The conscription issue now joined that of munitions production to create the greatest civil political crisis of the war. During the pre-war debate about national efficiency and the state of Britain's manpower in comparison with Germany, opinions had always divided on deep and traditional lines.[47] Tories had been accused of espousing continental patterns of militarism, and had responded with charges of Liberal negligence towards national security. Labour Party and TUC strongly opposed conscription, on the grounds of diminished individual liberty and the likelihood of its extension to civilian industry. The voluntary recruiting principle survived until early 1915, and for a long time Liberal Ministers evaded the issue. Lord Grey indeed wrote that 'conscription in the early days of the war was impossible; public opinion was not ready for it; it would have been resisted. . . . There would have been division of opinion, and resentment; the country might even have foundered in political difficulties.'[48]

But by 1915 the poor progress of the war made it impossible to dodge the issue and after the formation of the first Coalition on 19 May 1915, the Asquith government began, tentatively and rather deviously, by introducing a Registration Bill in June, accompanied by unwise public promises and disingenuous disclaimers in Cabinet about its future use as a basis for conscription. During the prolonged and conscience-stricken discussions, Balfour, chairman of the Committee of Imperial Defence, took issue with Churchill (then First Lord of the Admiralty) who wanted to introduce his own stringent proposals empowering government to direct anyone, anywhere, and at any time, with the reminder that, while conscription ought to concern everyone, including women, it would actually only hit particular occupational groups, like engineers and agricultural workers. 'If they prove recalcitrant,' he asked *'how are they going to be coerced?'*

The very name of 'enforced labour' the *corvée*, is odious to British ears, and it is useless here to quote the analogy of army discipline. . . . This is not the way in which Englishmen can be got either to feel or to think. Everybody recognises that in the army discipline is necessary and cowardice disgraceful. But it requires great imagination and originality to see that for an artisan to be drunk on Monday morning is as bad as for a soldier to disobey orders; or that going to a race meeting may be as bad as bolting from the trenches. If this, or anything like this, be true, we shall assuredly find that a certain proportion of our workmen refuse to obey; and they will invoke in defence of their refusal all the familiar commonplaces about the sacredness of personal liberty. If we fine or imprison them they will become martyrs; and martyrdom may engender a feeling of sullen opposition among their brother workers which will be far more disastrous to the cause of national production . . .[49]

The Cabinet subsequently followed these practical arguments rather than the moral protests which later surrounded the grim and unpopular struggle of conscientious objectors to avoid the charge of desertion. Balfour's question 'if they prove recalcitrant?' dogged Ministers first in England and then in Ireland for the remainder of the war, and forced them to come to terms with its elusive corollary: what did 'public opinion' want and what would it accept?

In order to test the case, put by the Tory conscriptionists, that there existed 'a strong and persistent demand throughout the country for a better organisation of the nation's resources', Henderson was asked what the Labour movement thought; for the first time he was permitted to cast himself in the role of honest broker. He replied that, in a meeting with Labour leaders on 8 June, Lloyd George had stated the need for the unions to co-operate and increase production; in return, the Government must accept that the 'established position' of working men must not be prejudiced, and must pledge itself to eliminate 'excessive profits or exorbitant prices of the necessities of life'.[50] Henderson went on to suggest a whole series of conditions designed to reduce to a minimum existing grievances in the munitions industry – conditions which were endorsed by the TUC by sixty-two votes to seven at a meeting with Lloyd George at the Board of Trade on 10 June.

This preliminary bargain scarcely amounted to a contract on the question of manpower, but the decorous, almost deferential, attitude of Labour leaders inspired a somewhat ambiguous resolution at the TUC's Conference in September 1915. Unions would oppose outright conscription, but facilitate in every way voluntary and quasi-voluntary recruiting; and Asquith and the Cabinet, in an attempt to avoid Liberal resignations, sought to appease Lord Kitchener's imperious demands for men by relying on trade union machinery rather than instituting a new, time-wasting system for registration; and they turned away thankfully from compulsion to ransack the armoury of moral blackmail.

The TUC's conciliatory stance established a much greater degree of political bargaining power than its involvement in the Treasury Agreement and the Munitions Act. But the voice of compulsion, represented in Cabinet by Walter Long and Lords Curzon and Lansdowne, was not silenced. Wholly convinced by War Office arguments that without droves of recruits the progress of the war would be grossly hampered, the Conservatives tried to make the bargain over the voluntary principle conditional on immediate trade union action. Austen Chamberlain told the Cabinet on 16 June, 'I believe the country to be not only prepared but eager for drastic action of this kind. It would be far more acceptable to the people immediately concerned, if the action were universal in this sense, that we asserted the right of the state to claim the services of any citizen.'[51]

In one week of debate, political expediency had confronted constitutional rights; 'public opinion' and 'feelings of the Empire' stood in the wings, while the Court circle, represented by Lord Esher, advocated outright conscription. Yet 'opinion' remained undefined; some of the conscriptionists' sources of opinion were no more representative than the Lord Provost of Glasgow's Conference – a body composed almost wholly of employers, concerned to condemn 'squandering' of their increased wages by work people, and to prescribe 'military law and discipline' on the shop floor.[52] Other government sources, cited by Liberal members of the Cabinet, pointed up very clear manifestations of working-class discontent and practical objections to the imposition of new obligations.*

The Liberal wing continued firmly in opposition; Runciman confided to his wife in August 1915: 'Even if Kitchener and Asquith together declare conscription to be necessary, the organised labour of Great Britain would have none of it. These two powerful names might get it through Parliament; no names, however powerful, can get it through the violent suspicions, hatred and determination of labour.'[53] During the summer, however, Lloyd George undermined the precarious unity which Asquith had managed to sustain in Cabinet. Ever sensitive to the press and the opinion of Tory ministers, Lloyd George

*Of considerable prophetic interest is a remarkable memorandum of 1 July (CAB 37/131/1) retailing the experience of the Insurance Department of the Board of Trade, which laid down, in the course of a discussion about aids for registration, something very close to the conditions for mobilising popular consent.

'(1) That it is impossible to secure the performance of any new duty by the individual member of the population unless the particular act of fulfilment is closely linked up with the personal self-interest of the individual, or with the action which he would normally take in his own self-interest;

(2) That legal sanctions as to penalties are powerless to secure the general performance by members of the population of any such duties if divorced from self-interested motives or actions; it is impossible to prosecute the whole population;

(3) That the use of legal sanctions to enforce the performance of any duty only becomes effective if the persons upon whom the duty is placed are limited in number and responsible in character, the more limited the number and responsible their character, the more effective being the sanction.'

The memorandum concluded: 'The most radical fallacy [of the Registration Bill] is the assumption that the individual number of the population can be brought to perform even the simplest operation by being subjected to a legal obligation to do so.' The author (S V [?]) held it impossible even to communicate such obligations to the public, citing the experience of the 1911 National Insurance Act. 'No system of legal obligation and penalties, even if the individual were aware of them, will induce or compel the general population to take steps which from their point of view are difficult and complicated, and the point and importance of which they cannot realise. This is not due to any lack of patriotism or of respect for law, but has its cause deep down in the genius of the nation, the freedom of its private life from bureaucratic incursions, its unfamiliarity with and distaste for formalities of procedure and "red tape". Such a system could only be successful when enforced, as in Germany, by a rigorous and ubiquitous police system upon a nation accustomed to be regulated in all the minor matters of life. Any system of registration which is intended to operate successfully in this country must be based upon different principles.'

made a speech to the War Policy Committee on 18 August in which he put the case for and against conscription in such a way as to convey his own acceptance of Kitchener's magisterial declaration that conscription would be necessary before the middle of 1916.[54]

Aware of this trend, and probably aware that several Labour leaders were privately ready to endorse conscription if the government declared it necessary,[55] Henderson made a new offer: the unions would help recruit another half million men, and only if they failed would they discuss compulsion. Like Grey, he claimed the existence of national political divisions and skilfully hinted that only a general election, with universal suffrage, could give Parliament the authority to legislate conscription. Even then, 'guarantees' about taxation of profits would be necessary to offset working-class opposition. And with some cunning, Henderson took care to organise protests from TUC and GFTU, and a deputation to Asquith 'to strengthen the PM's hands against the Cabinet conscriptionists'.[56]

Between them, Asquith, Grey and Balfour held the Coalition together. But as Balfour, a former Chief Secretary, had seen, such arguments could not be applied to Ireland. For security reasons that country could not be included, but to exempt it would be to accuse the Irish of disloyalty. Fearful of the effect of indecision on 'national unity' and of the possibility of a general election, the Cabinet vacillated, as if waiting for Kitchener's hammer to strike the anvil of public disquiet about the conduct of the war. Only the programme of education of the TUC continued. In a most secret session, which Henderson arranged, Parliamentary Committee, GFTU and Labour Party representatives listened to Kitchener and Asquith outline the emergency.[57] It did not require Henderson to point out what political status this invitation conferred on the Labour movement.

Lord Derby was appointed Director-General of Recruiting in October 1915, to head what one historian has called 'a gigantic engine of fraud . . . but a very astute piece of political tactics'.[58] But at the end of this year, Derby's report on his work as Director-General of Recruiting came as no relief. Paradoxically, his only real trouble had been in rural areas where many men had slipped on to the exemption list in advance. He confirmed 'abundant evidence of a determination to see the war through to a successful conclusion'[59] and paid tribute to the recruiting efforts of the TUC. But roughly 400,000 single men had refused to enlist. In December, intending to put moral pressure on the unmarried (since the Cabinet expected a public outcry if Derby turned to married men), Asquith had pledged freedom from attesting until single men had contributed fully. The single men's refusal to 'volunteer' therefore put the whole Cabinet compromise in jeopardy.

Asquith refused to prepare a measure of compulsion, in case it destroyed what was left of the Derby scheme, but the majority of Ministers, spurred on by Lloyd George, accepted the need both to coerce single men and to let the anti-conscriptionist members of the Cabinet resign. The division over the subsequent draft Military Service Bill, with Lloyd George and the Conservatives facing Asquith, Grey, John Simon, Runciman and R. McKenna, brought to a head the question of what kind of war the Coalition wished to fight; and it was repeated in the debates of 28 December 1915 to 1 January 1916 on the seventy-division army, which Asquith and the Liberal minority opposed on grounds of cost. McKenna, the Chancellor, claimed that the nation could afford only fifty divisions – a proposition which would neatly have put an end to War Office demands for manpower.*

A compromise was patched up, with some help from the King, and in the end only Simon resigned. But the manpower crisis confirmed beyond question what Robert Smillie, the miners' leader and strong opponent of the Military Service Bill, had declared: 'The attitude of Labour is the deciding factor. If the trade unions stand firmly by the resolution of their recent Congress, no government can disregard their decision.'[60] Unfortunately, the ambiguity of that resolution seems to have eluded him. Asquith put up a very shrewd defence: on 11 January, Henderson was called to the Cabinet to receive 'a harmonious and hearty tribute to his loyalty and courage', and the next day Asquith saw leaders of the PLP to remove 'misapprehensions' and to urge them 'to take action which would make the retirement of Henderson and his colleagues unnecessary'.[61] In the confused events of January 1916, Henderson's personal position in the Government became, for Liberal ministers, a guarantee against the dominance of Lloyd George, and for the Labour movement the only insurance against the rigours of industrial conscription.

Henderson himself played an extremely cautious hand, seeking to safeguard against the hard line of Lloyd George, and the well-publicised objections to compulsion of the Triple Alliance and Engineers, the authority built up by Labour Party and TUC in the first eighteen

---

*Asquith reported to the King that, on McKenna's figures, a seventy-division army would involve recruiting 300,000 men at once, followed by 130,000 a month. In fact only 80,000 a month, two-thirds of the total, could be spared. In any case, according to McKenna, the Treasury faced a deficit of £600 million by March 1916, and £2,000 million by March 1917, and could countenance no more increases. (CAB 41/37, 1 January 1916.)

months of war, as well as the unity of Asquith's not unsympathetic Cabinet.[62] His work suffered from the contortions of the Labour Party Conference at Bristol, where the joint executive (PLP, TUC and National Executive Committee) allowed membership and the platform to diverge sharply, after a free vote against the Military Service Bill – whose results the PLP chose, for political reasons, to disregard. As Henderson rather miserably reported to the Cabinet, Labour had no clear war aims apart from its abhorrence of the threat to industrial liberty; but he insisted that nothing but continuation of the present compact could convey the support of the working-class – 'the only party in the state which has it in its power to make dissent effective'.*

Asquith's Cabinet made a careful show of appeasing the grievances mentioned at Bristol, attending to rumours that civil servants were escaping call-up and that single men were escaping down the mines. Offers were made of a moratorium on rents, mortgages, hire purchase and life insurance, to help married men; finally, on 12 January, the Prime Minister met the NEC and PLP and gave a further pledge against industrial conscription and calls on married men. Satisfied, the Party conference gave its permission for Henderson to remain in the government, while reaffirming its (now purely technical) objections to the Bill.

During the winter, the call-up of single men proceeded under the new Act. Then in March 1916 came a new and vast demand for recruits from the War Office, entrenching on married men and prejudicing the whole fragile political compromise. The government moved with extreme delicacy, particularly after a speech by Asquith had been unfavourably received in the House of Commons on 19 April. A rather feeble, compromise Bill was produced, which satisfied no one and was later withdrawn. But in the background the heavy brigades were mobilised once more. TUC, PLP, GFTU and the key unions – transport workers and engineers – were invited on 26 April to hear from Asquith, Law and Kitchener the ultimatum: 'produce recruits or face compulsion'. At first the Parliamentary Committee tried to reject a responsibility 'too great for the Committee itself to accept',[63] but in three successive votes, 5–5, 6–3 and finally 8–1 in favour of the Government,

---

*CAB 37/140/17. The power of working-class dissent was carefully itemised by the WENC in a letter headed 'Absence of General Consent' to Lloyd George, pointing out the declared opposition of MFGB and NUR, the majority of the TUC, the Scottish Labour Party, the CWC and shop stewards of Liverpool and London, ASLEF and the majority of Trades Councils (WENC 5/2/3/8). An interesting attempt was also made to test public opinion by a questionnaire sent out through Trades Councils (WENC 5/2/3/42).

they overturned the TUC's earlier resolution (of September 1915) on the grounds that the Government had proved its case.

This surrender reflected the disastrous state of the war and the impact on English public feeling of the Easter Rising in Dublin. Asquith had admitted to the Parliamentary Committee, as he did to the King, that there was no alternative.[64] The second Military Service Bill passed into law in July. In August, C. A. McCurdy, the War Office Adjutant-General, began to report 'wonderful results': five months' conscription of single men and one month of marrieds had raised 700,000 men.

Yet Lloyd George had not really been right to declare that Henderson's and Runciman's 'fears and forebodings were exaggerated', and the dissent quantified in Labour's 'The Absence of General Consent' had not faded away. Henderson and the Labour movement had given in to Kitchener's immense authority as the Cabinet itself had done, and to the War Policy Committee. Secretive, unwilling to pin himself down to exact figures, grandly assertive, expecting total compliance, and never for a moment conceding the possibility that his assumptions about victory depending on numbers might be erroneous, Kitchener had simply confronted government with the incontrovertible fact of his personal prestige in the press and public mind.

In these circumstances, it was not easy for the Labour movement to draw up a profit and loss account of its first encounter with government. The Parliamentary Party could weigh the inclusion of Labour MPs in government against the disruption caused by reneging on its own conference resolution. Yet the Party had not made much impression on the Conservative side of the Coalition: Bonar Law disparaged even its claim to represent the working class.[65] On the other hand, Henderson's insistence on the Party's responsibility for *political* questions had been established within the movement and on the Joint Committees, effectively emasculating the TUC in the debates of January 1916 and ensuring Party dominance of the WENC for the rest of the war.[66] But that too was an equivocal development, since Henderson appears to have seen neither the electoral advantages of Labour Party association with government, nor the danger of linking the party to future, unspecified, coalition commitments.

Endorsement of the War Office case, however unwillingly made, put Asquith's Government in pawn not only to its military advisors but to the Conservative members of the Coalition, who, having suffered a great deal of rancour from Party members for giving assistance to the Liberals in 1915, watched uneasily the ascendancy of Lloyd George and the rantings of the Tory press. Unconvinced that a general election would return his Party with a sound majority, or be anything but dangerous in wartime, Bonar Law found himself attacked on three sides in the spring of 1916, by the press lords, Beaverbrook and Northcliffe, the Court circle, and his own party officials, all urging him to coerce the Liberals into taking married men, and to prosecute the war efficiently. Early in April, before the Easter Rising, Law decided to accept the advice of Kitchener and the Army Council,[67] and on 17 April he threatened resignation. Until then, he told Asquith, his Party had made all the sacrifices of principle; the Liberals had to accept their share: 'I think it easier for you to carry your supporters in favour of conscription than it is for us to obtain the support of our Party against it.'[68]

In these circumstances it may be asked why the TUC did not take a more outspoken line or attempt to build up a political counterweight to the conscriptionists in Cabinet. Until then it might have seemed that the TUC had been little more than the government's unpaid agent; the implementing of registration, the supply of information about wages and rents, and operation of the Derby scheme, had brought few rewards. Writing after the war, the Webbs affected to despise trade union pusillanimity, for pitching its claims too low, when it had such an advantageous ground for bargaining.[69] But by 1916, the TUC had also become the government's only lasting insurance against the shop stewards' movement and the terrifying combination of industrial and political unrest in wartime, clearly visible in Germany, Italy and France. In this light, Ministry of Munitions' policy appeared much more conciliatory than its Ministers' public pronouncements, since it involved trade unions in consultation without actually conceding them the formal representation which would have alienated employers, and led on to dealing directly with the TUC (as Lloyd George, Asquith and Kitchener had done at moments of military necessity) in terms of parity very different from the timid position taken up by Henderson earlier, in November 1915, when he had suggested that 'the important thing [in relation to the Treasury Agreement] is not to refuse wage claims but to stop them, or rather to create in the labour world a public opinion adverse to the making of further demands on capital during the war.'[70]

In these very early stages the triangular relationship between government, unions and employers seems ephemeral. But individual members of the TUC such as C. W. Bowerman, H. Gosling, J. H. Thomas and W. A. Appleton, had been raised to the level of national figures, and the Parliamentary Committee itself had matured sufficiently to take its own decisions on conscription in April 1916, acting as representatives of the whole working-class movement – an act as significant for trade union status as the PLP's refusal to implement the resolution of the Bristol Conference. The Webbs misjudged the attitude of government to trade union power.* The TUC's limited demands did not imply lack of energy, but careful trimming to the contradictory winds of employers' hostility and government initiative; for, in its now obvious desire to bolster the TUC, as against the shop stewards, government risked antagonising the former. Several of the District Armaments Boards, for example, criticised the Ministry of Munitions' use of unions as agents for consultation and control of production.† But many employers *did* prove responsive. By the middle of 1916 a new conception of trade unionism was becoming current in England in which responsible and representative leadership was seen to merit a role in the country's political life.

This status was, however, denied the unofficial movement, and the double standard applied to shop stewards illustrates Lloyd George's views about 'extremists' and the need to isolate them not only by coercion but by working up public opinion through a national propaganda campaign. War-weariness at home and the physical losses on the Western Front had long since discredited the optimistic assumption that the national interest would attract loyalty from the entire population. Two years' experience of industrial and social discontent indicated that consent could no longer be bought by patriotic appeals, nor – despite the efforts of the TUC – by government's protestations about fairness of sacrifice, consultation, or conciliation by the Committee of Production under the Munitions Act. The open unrest associated with the Shop Stewards' Movement on Clydeside, Liverpool and the Midlands indicated that for very many workers 'fairness' included the redressing of grievances outside the sphere of the munitions industry.

During 1916 the government moved from selective repression to a more general denunciation of 'unpatriotic activity' closely following the dictates of the popular press. The war emergency justified crude propaganda and a range of misinformation bordering on outright falsity – of

---

*Significantly, the PLP found it necessary in June 1916 to try and mend its fences with the PC.

†The East Anglian Armaments Board complained that 'the workman's interests are paramount, and the master's interests are entirely neglected.' A very general complaint was 'The Ministry is always shoving it down our throats – "consult your workpeople, do not make changes until you consult".' (Manchester and District Armaments Output Committee, 29 December 1915, quoted in Patrick McGuire, 'Unofficial Trade Union Movements and Industrial Politics 1915–22', D. Phil. thesis, Sussex University, 1979.)

which Lloyd George's post-mortem on the South Wales coal strike is a good example. Unrivalled as a propagandist, Lloyd George found use in strange instruments, in bards who might revive 'the old Welsh spirit' and in the denunciation of the Union of Democratic Control by Welsh ministers;[71] and it is scarcely surprising that the WENC complained of almost universal misrepresentation of the anti-conscription campaign.[72] Among the upper class, especially among officers at the front, judgments seem to have been vindictive and ignorant; conveyed in a crude satire aimed equally at 'base-wallahs' and 'conshies', 'the Hun' and the 'agitator'.[73] Lord Esher, for example, wrote from France in April 1915: 'Here if a man refused to work, drumhead courtmartial and a firing squad. Public opinion is so strong that if this were not done a shirker would be torn to pieces by his comrades.'[74]

Opinions of this sort underpinned the government's strict censorship, the deportations and trials for sedition – though it should be added that, apart from the vindictive campaign against John Maclean, its measures were both lighter and more discriminating than in Germany. The propaganda machine turned sometimes against employers' intransigence and war profits and bolstered trade union efforts,[75] and Lloyd George took great care to choose a suitable moment for the deportations,* but generally it worked to the detriment of working-class opinion: when Askwith, in a memorandum to the Cabinet, set out considerations of the high cost of living, urging the need to take steps over excessive profits and the privately-owned munitions industry which Labour would really understand,[76] he was ignored.

Nevertheless, in seeking, by the use of propaganda instead of concession, to create a climate in which wage demands could not be made, Ministers' accurate measurement of public opinion became a matter of great importance. In the first two years of war, they had relied on much second-hand gossip and prejudiced assertion. One measure of how seriously the Cabinet began to take working-class opinion is that these sources were supplemented during 1916 by material collected by trade unions themselves – such as the 'Absence of General Consent'. Even when disagreeing with the result, Bonar Law was prepared to acknowledge its value.† But such analysis did not provide a convincing answer

---

*J. Patterson (Secretary of the Glasgow and West of Scotland Armaments Committee) told Beveridge in January 1916 to prepare the ground for deportation carefully – 'A very much clearer issue would be a strike against the enforcement of dilution of labour'. (Beveridge III, 16.)

†Conservative Central Office had already refined its analysis of the press as the collection of cuttings, etc., accumulated by Steel-Maitland on the 1915 South Wales coal strike shows.

to the question: was working-class unrest merely the sporadic outcome of remediable economic and social evils, or the first symptom of a new, potentially revolutionary, political consciousness?

The shop stewards' movement extended far beyond the war sphere of munitions and engineering, into Lancashire textiles, the railways (especially in the Liverpool depots with their pre-war history of syndicalist thinking) and tramways where the 'stay-in-strike' was first developed.[77] Clydeside was not the only region where militancy became a passport to influence, and where shop stewards took on a non-industrial role in demanding rent control, lower food prices and the conscription of riches.[78] Yet the movement retained a very close link with individual industries, so that shop stewards on the railways in Liverpool, for example, made no effort to join the national organisation, while in Sheffield the engineers made few contacts with other trades, ignoring J. T. Murphy's rhetoric about a 'Workers' National Committee'.[79] A large part of their activity was directed, not at achieving workers' control in the pre-war, syndicalist, sense, but at remedying the impotence of their union officials, tied hand and foot by the Treasury Agreement and the Munitions Act. Their unelected status, in that sense, rested on a truer and more functional democracy, as William McLaine, leader of the Manchester shop stewards and a prominent member of the SLP, protested to Addison at a later stage of the war:

We have no desire and no intention of undermining the authority of our trade unions; on the contrary, we are out for this specific purpose of backing up our trade unions. The actions of you and your colleagues – that is to say the government – have placed our unions in such a position that they can no longer function as trade unions should.[80]

Government and employers failed to assimilate this challenge in 1916. Given existing propaganda resources, and the techniques already employed of by-passing the shop stewards' movement and bolstering officials, the policy of kicks and kindness served. Looking back from the standpoint of 1918, Lloyd George was to claim that repression had succeeded: 'That policy [of deportation and prosecution] destroyed the nerve of the Clyde Workers movement, and Glasgow has been comparatively quiet since.'[81]

Asquith baulked at the implications. 'I loathe the necessities which seem to confront us', he wrote to Lord Haldane in 1915, 'but we must put aside everything for which we care personally, to bring the main thing through.'[82] When it came to the point he proved irresolute over coercion and the manipulation of public opinion. Leo Amery had observed bitterly in July 1914 that 'for twenty years he has held a season ticket on the line of least resistance . . .', and his latest biographer compares his position at the end of 1916 to Captain McWhirr (in Joseph Conrad's *Typhoon*) sailing blindly to disaster: 'Omens were as nothing to him, and he was unable to discover the message of a prophecy till the fulfilment had brought it home to his very door. . . . Having just enough imagination to carry him through each successive day, and no more, he remained tranquilly sure of himself.'

Being neither a demagogue nor a democrat, Asquith was vulnerable to Lloyd George, whose stage repertoire embraced both roles. At the end of May 1916 Lloyd George drafted a letter to the Prime Minister warning him of what was coming.

The nation could endure [the disastrous performance of the War Office] and a good deal more, if they knew everything was being done that human effort and foresight could compass to insure final victory, but their confidence has been unduly shaken . . . The friendly press is showing marked symptoms of mutiny . . . Press and public could be moved [if the full story of the Dardenelles expedition came out] before the party politician, but in the end he will follow public opinion. There is only one answer that can satisfy the public, and that is that you have already made an end of the futile regime . . .[83]

The government had helped create the bogey and whether it was real or existed only in the minds of newspaper editors it seemed necessary to appease it. It serves no purpose to ask whether the Asquith Coalition, fortified by its links with employers and official Labour, might have survived if it had not jibbed at a public opinion which, in the hands of Lloyd George and the Tories, demanded more sacrifices than Asquith and his party could afford.

4 NATIONAL DISUNITY, 1916–18

After prolonged horse-trading between the leaders of the Coalition at the end of 1916, Asquith's Government collapsed. Chief casualty of the struggle, Asquith was replaced as Prime Minister by Lloyd George, since Bonar Law found himself unwilling or unable to form an alternative administration; and the unravelling by historians of those five knotted weeks, from the moment in early November when the Coalition began to break apart, until Asquith resigned on 5 December, has filled thousands of detailed pages. According to the traditionally accepted view, Lloyd George's overweening ambition, and Asquith's patent failure to run a war cabinet efficiently, provide sufficient explanation; more recently, the light had been directed on to the complexities of Cabinet allegiances, and Law's responsiveness to the problems of the Conservative Party.[1] To see any single personality as the prime mover in such a crisis must, inherently, be illogical: each represented interests and views in and beyond Cabinet, and each was responsive to the wider problems of war production and manpower shortages which created a similar crisis in France and Germany and led to the assumption by Hindenburg and Ludendorff of effective control over the German economy and the politicians.

If all the waverings of the Ministers (like Lloyd George who early in November agreed with Law to retain the Coalition and seek a General Election, then later considered resignation and only at the end, faced with Asquith's foxy stubbornness, pushed his demands right through) are taken into account, together with the encircling problems of war strategy, food supply, overseas credit, manpower and lack of public enthusiasm, the crisis can be seen as one not merely of personalities but of direction of the war and of the political system itself. Far more serious in its consequences than 1911, it inspired a form of panic, because after the inconclusive, catastrophically debilitating Battle of the Somme, the possibility of military defeat had to be acknowledged.

In the months before, the Cabinet had seemed unaware of the

accumulation of evil omens. Apparently contented with the uncontentious passage of the Military Service Bill and the planning of the Somme offensive for July, Ministers acknowledged compliments from their Allies; Lord Esher quoted Aristide Briand's remark: 'We are amazed at the skill with which Mr. Asquith had managed Parliament so as to engineer [conscription] in law without a disruption of national unity.'[2] This ignored not only the demands for even greater numbers of recruits by the Army Council in the months after Lord Kitchener had been drowned in the *Hampshire* on his mission to Russia, but the growing decay of French morale, the seemingly inexhaustible resources of the German war machine, war-weariness at home, and working-class discontent filtering through to the troops.*

Industrial unrest spread across the Midlands in the last quarter of 1916 and brought renewed political violence to South Wales and Clydeside. Once-moderate union leaders demanded wage increases as if their only mandate lay in vying with the shop stewards; and these rises set off complaints from pieceworkers in engineering and shipbuilding. The coming winter – the third of the war – threatened worse disorder, and Askwith, distinguishing between 'factious political demands' (put by shop stewards in South Wales and Liverpool) and the 'genuine cases' of Scotland, the North-East, Yorkshire, the Midlands and London, lamented: 'If only the government could deal with the cost of living! I do not say that they could, but they should show more interest in it and explain why they can't, if they can't, to the plain person, and what the plain person should do to obviate the result.'[3] In September, under heavy pressure from the railway depots, the National Union of Railwaymen (NUR) put forward a claim for 10s. a week, which Runciman was forced to admit was just, though he tried to keep the government out of the actual negotiation. Then in November, after the machinery of arbitration had failed, the Board of Trade had to take over the South Wales pits and settle miners' wages by district agreements rather than on the lines laid down in the Munitions Act.

Widening discontent provided a gloomy backcloth to an appalling manpower problem. As the Asquith Cabinet tried to retain a voluntary element in recruiting, looking desperately for panaceas like the use of Irish or coloured labour in the building trades, the War Office

*As early as March 1916 the High Command found it expedient to call Richard Tawney and other Fabians serving as private soldiers to an extraordinary conference at GHQ in St Omer to discuss with General Geddes 'what action the Government should take in view of labour troubles on the Clyde' (Jones, *Whitehall Diary*, vol. I, p. 24). They drafted an appeal 'from trade unionists at the front to trade unionists at home' but it was never transmitted.

quarrelled with the Manpower Board and began to harass unions in the munitions industries by indiscriminate recruiting. In October 1916 in order to buy time the Cabinet offered the unions yet another bargain, the 'trade card' scheme, which conceded skilled men exemption from military service, provided they worked in approved occupations. Launched by Lord Derby and Auckland Geddes in a meeting with the TUC and Labour Party in November, the scheme had an immediate appeal for the ASE who were to have the privilege of administering it. But the engineers' leaders could not prevent shop stewards and J. T. Murphy's Workers' Committee, on strike at Sheffield, from claiming much of the credit; and in due course other unions asked for and won the same privilege.

At the end of November, after the terrible casualties of the Somme battle, the Army Council broke through the polite veneer of ministerial discussions and issued a *démarche*, calling on the government to override the compromises made with trade unions not only in 1915–16 but in the new trade card scheme.[4] The Council required 50,000 men in two months and another 50,000 a month thereafter, all to be found from men under thirty-one in the reserved occupations. Without an apology for their profligate wastage of skilled men in the early stages of the war, the Army Council announced that these men must forthwith be 'debadged' and that the overall age of conscription must be raised to forty-one – thus challenging the entire existing structure of Government-TUC cooperation. Having talked of staving off defeat, Haig and Robertson would not hazard a final figure on the manpower totals needed actually to *win* the war; and on 30 November the Army Council went on to issue the government with final notice to introduce compulsory national service for everyone, with military conscription of all men up to fifty-five, or risk strategic decline as early as April 1917.

Under such pressure, Ministers reacted violently: Lord Lansdowne talked of a negotiated peace; Lord Robert Cecil of rationing, equality of sacrifice, taxation of wealth and closure of the London clubs; while Bonar Law and Lloyd George proposed extreme measures, to raise a million men by conscription up to sixty years of age (as in France) and putting older men to work on the land. In the end, confronted with further bad news from the Western Front, the German invasion of Romania, and capture of the Ploesti oil-wells, the *levée en masse* and the draft of labour from German occupied territories in Eastern Europe, and an announcement that the New York Reserve Bank might refuse to grant Britain the further loans on which both the French and Russian war efforts largely depended, they were all stampeded into introducing National Service and the principle of debadging skilled men, with only slight guarantee that those debadged would not actually be required to fight.

Since this call on married men meant abandonment of all his pledges, without parliamentary consent, Asquith's premiership was in effect terminated three weeks before the climactic political manoeuvres of December 1916. In his defence it can be argued that he tried not to betray the contract so laboriously built up with the Labour movement; a position which had much less appeal to the 'boldly and brutally interventionist'[5] Lloyd George. Yet the repercussions of debadging would not simply go away. The new Directorate of National Service was given a separate, civilian department, 'to allay any suspicion that the adoption of National Service for civil purposes could bring the person affected under military control';[6] and, in response to pleas from Henderson, a bid was made to recover TUC support by a promise that the voluntary system would continue, so long as numbers were sustained.[7] The composition of the new government also reflected Labour's continuing importance. Disappearance of the Asquith Liberals gave Lloyd George space to bring Henderson into the War Cabinet. J. Hodge went to the newly-created Ministry of Labour and G. N. Barnes of the ASE, to the Ministry of Pensions. The Labour Ministry, created largely at the request of TUC and Labour Party, represented a substantial concession at the expense of the Board of Trade and employers' opinion; and Lloyd George, master of presentation and public relations, hastened to proffer a new and more grandiloquent contract between the politicians and the real nation.[8] Some of his promises – on lower food prices, better distribution of supplies, industrial controls, and a share for Labour in the deliberations of the eventual Peace Conference – came very close to what the WENC had been asking for ever since 1915.

At first, the Labour movement seemed content to record its intense disapproval of the 'vile conspiracy'[9] Lloyd George and Bonar Law had used to oust Asquith. But as Henderson, who had found Asquith congenial and distrusted the 'men of action', admitted, 'the national interest, and the possibility of Labour securing a greater opportunity to mould policy and exercise executive authority in important administrative positions could not be ignored.'[10] At the 1917 Conference the Labour Party declared itself dedicated to the thesis of total victory by 1,800,000 votes against the 300,000 who supported a negotiated peace; and in spite of the obvious likelihood that the government would introduce total conscription, the TUC followed the lead Henderson had given, much as they had deferred to his authority and experience

D

of government during the manpower debates in 1916. Paradoxically, the division between political and industrial matters grew more rigid, as the TUC's role in the Joint Committee on 'Labour after the War' was subordinated to that of the Party; and even on the crucial *industrial* question of setting up the Directorate of National Service, the Parliamentary Committee accepted its role, content, apparently, to endorse the Government's proposal for 'collective transfer of men from non-essential to essential trades by collective agreement, with the unions controlling the class of labour required.'[11]

The TUC took up this meek position in spite of the greater numerical weight given to it in the Government, because of disunity in its ranks. The shop stewards' movement took no part in the political compromises and the more the TUC collaborated, the more its local leaders felt impelled to organise the direct defence of rank and file members' interests on such crucial matters as trade cards, dilution, transfers, cost of living. Gradually the movement took on a quasi-national structure, abandoning earlier, vulnerable essays in regional action like the Clyde Workers' Committee: and at the national level, experienced BSP (British Socialist Party) and SLP men reasserted themselves. The events of 1917, the October Revolution in Russia, and the Stockholm Peace Conference, gave the Shop Stewards' Movement the chance to declaim a political alternative to the Government's policy of total war. Hence, industrial discontent and opposition to military service had to be counted, by government, as subversive and possibly revolutionary, even when couched in modest and democratic language. When the call for establishment of Soldiers' and Workers' Councils on Soviet lines, and for dictatorship of the proletariat, was supported by middle-of-the-road ILP leaders like Ramsay MacDonald and Philip Snowden, at the extraordinarily fervid Leeds Conference, the War Cabinet might be forgiven for failing to distinguish between blind euphoria and the sustained beliefs of the (equally amazed) BSP and SLP delegates.*

From the moment he became Prime Minister, Lloyd George made two assumptions: that the TUC rather than the shop stewards represented, and could control, the mass working-class movement, and that the Parliamentary Labour Party could withstand the enthusiasm of the socialists outside, who comprised a large percentage of the party's most active members. Henderson's loyalty and willingness to cooperate

---

*Not least because of the wide support for the Conference, from normally moderate NUR branches; and the number of resolutions in favour of worker-soldier collaboration under the aegis of Trades Councils, and a negotiated peace (McGuire, *op. cit*).

thus became far more important than Lloyd George recognised or was prepared later to admit. But the allegiance of Labour leaders had other connotations. The hasty changes in government machinery which took place early in 1917 barely touched the lower administrative reaches. The Ministry of Labour, in particular, suffered from the rearguard actions waged by the Board of Trade, and other departments which retained a vested interest in labour as a 'political' question. Just as the War Cabinet itself claimed the right to act ruthlessly against strikers,* Munitions, the Directorate of National Service, the War Office, and the Admiralty all claimed rights to plunder the few remaining reserves of manpower, harshly and without regard to national long-term needs. At the same time, these departments used their recruits wastefully (the War Office and the Admiralty being the worst offenders) and insisted on buying peace and productivity by making separate wage awards which were quite unrelated to each other or to civilian trade differentials. As Beatrice Webb remarked in another context, Lloyd George had handed over the Departments to interest groups for short-term advantage.

To some degree, the loyalty of the TUC and the Labour Party protected the Government from the worst consequences of these conflicts and the clashes of personality which followed the dispersal of the young Turks from the Department of Labour, to confront each other as Whitehall mandarins: Llewellyn Smith representing labour interests at Munitions, Beveridge at the Ministry of Food (where he quarrelled with Lord Devonport, the Food Controller) and Shackleton at Labour itself, where he watched mournfully the prolonged in-fighting between John Hodge, his elderly hidebound Minister, and Askwith, now Chief Industrial Conciliator. Lethargic, yet over-impatient with unofficial strikers, Hodge made a poor showing, lasting only eight months before his obsessive patriotism (which had caused him to be chosen, in place of the far more suitable J. H. Thomas) and hasty temperament made him a serious liability. But until he was replaced by G. H. Roberts, the Ministry had little chance of establishing itself in industrial politics against Munitions, let alone against the War Cabinet; and internecine struggles continued on such a scale that the two Ministries prepared entirely different versions of the May 1917 engineering strike for the Official History of the War.

Askwith managed to impose some harmony early in 1917 with a

*A strike of boilermakers in Liverpool in December 1916, was broken by a joint declaration from Hodge (Labour) and Churchill (Munitions) that the ringleaders would be arrested and the local police reinforced to provide protection for blacklegs (WC 8/10).

national wage agreement in the engineering industry, and the Committee of Production began to meet three times a year to review and arbitrate nationally on wages in relation to the cost of living. Askwith called this system, somewhat immodestly, 'the most far-reaching which has ever been made or obtained force between employers and employed in this or indeed any country', and took the chance of a favourite crack at Cabinet interference: 'Quiet local pressure seems to answer better than agreements which look well on paper but are not practically couched.'[12] Meanwhile Sir Daniel Shackleton induced the Federation of Engineering Employers to recognise shop stewards' committees for certain purposes;[13] and by the end of 1917 national wage-bargaining had become widespread – though national *rates* remained elusive.

In spite of administrative disorders, the first months of toughness towards shop stewards or strikers and blandness towards the official union leadership produced good results. The Director-General of National Service, Neville Chamberlain, reckoned to raise 450,000 men by early March 1917 by withdrawing certain general exemptions, in spite of entrenching on the sensitive matter of trade cards; and his second report discussed the even more drastic possibility of abolishing appeals to Tribunals – though he was careful to emphasise the need for ASE consent.[14] Ministers' assessment of the balance between kicks and kindness and of the continuing need for popular consent shows clearly in an exchange at 10 Downing Street on 13 February, during a conference called to reassure Haig about the Government's support:

CIGS   Is everyone working hard?

PM   No. But you can't say so.
    Only chance is (1) to cut down liquor 30–20 per cent
              (2) piecework. Hodge says if
                 they won't, they must.
    – Will ca' canny? [go-slow]

AG   Give them to me.

D(erby)   Troubles most talked of, least happen.

PM   Next week, order will be made.   *On Rationing*
    Clyde to the devil.   CIGS Germany?
    So are the submarines.   PM   1/3 beer, no fat,
                                     1/3 our meat.
                                     ?Our people stand
                                           it?

D   But we believe the men are there.

PM   Will put an amendment to the MSA.
    If H of C won't take it, go to country.[15]

By April 1917, however, the Government was being driven harder than ever as a result of Russian weakness on the eastern front and the onslaught of German submarine warfare in the Atlantic. Skilled unions might struggle to retain the trade cards scheme, but the army required another 550,000 men between April and July. Lord Rhondda, Director of Manpower, told the War Cabinet that he could produce only half that number. He set out three possibilities: to let the army run down, avoiding casualties by a defensive campaign; to raise the age of conscription, fill jobs with old men, and send the young to the front; or to admit an overriding need to conscript exempted skilled men for essential work.[16] Fearful of the consequences of compulsion, and of being seen to break so many parliamentary pledges, the War Cabinet settled for the old Asquith tactic of delay, presenting its most persuasive front to the Labour movement and setting the threat of industrial conscription as a penalty for failure in the self-imposed task of recruitment and production.

Lloyd George regarded the trade card system as Asquith's worst surrender, a view bolstered by Conservative MPs' frequent attacks on the privileged position it granted to the ASE. Yet the new Prime Minister approached the skilled unions cautiously, well aware of the constraints which their power imposed. He talked softly to a Triple Alliance delegation in January 1917 and did not demur when Robert Williams defined, in quite formal terms, the compact between unions and government.[17] To an ILP delegation concerned with labour problems, land taxes and nationalisation he declared: 'I believe that the settlement after the war will succeed in proportion to its audacity';[18] and in March, in discussion with the Labour NEC, he concluded a brilliant argument for the emergency powers of the state by emphasising that he did not want industrial conscription if the Labour movement could do the work voluntarily. In spite of his natural bent towards coercion, Lloyd George was prisoner of past concessions. 'Having regard to the strong feeling existing in the country on the subject . . . it was impossible to proceed with any scheme until it had been demonstrated by experience that voluntary enrolment, reinforced by restriction of less important industries . . . was incapable of yielding the necessary supplies.'[19]

Negotiations with the unions began early in April 1917 against a background of further War Cabinet disagreement: and the Service ministers pressed for military service up to forty-five or even fifty years of age, and for the introduction of dilution on non-government work, while Hodge unwisely assured his colleagues that the trade cards scheme could be withdrawn with impunity. As Henderson forecast, he was quite wrong. Withdrawal brought skilled and unskilled workers closer together and led directly to an engineers' strike at the Vickers factory at Barrow-in-Furness, and talk by the Shop Stewards' Movement of a general strike. On 6 April Lloyd George advised the War Cabinet 'of a very considerable and highly organised labour movement with seditious tendencies which was developing in many industrial centres. At bottom, these appeared to be genuine and legitimate grievances, but there was a danger of them being exploited by violent anarchists'* – an alarming deduction which received some corroboration when Henderson reported discouragingly on his talks with the ASE at the end of April. 'The tone of the Conference had been very menacing. The delegates had demanded that the trade card scheme should be continued, and threats of an immediate stoppage throughout the country had been used. There was undoubtedly grave unrest, which had been deepened by the Russian Revolution. . . .'[20] Prudently, the War Cabinet deferred implementing abolition by a week, until after the May Day processions.

The engineers' strike began on 2 May in Manchester,[21] and although Henderson and Addison skilfully detached some groups, such as shipwrights, from support of the Workers' Committee, it spread to Coventry, Sheffield, Derby, Luton, Birkenhead, Liverpool, Bristol, Southampton and London, as well as to Barrow. Deprecating the retribution urged by the King and the Army Council, and the Sheffield employers – who advocated wholesale arrest of the ringleaders – the government rode out the storm and waited until the shop stewards overreached themselves by demanding Cabinet recognition. Only then, on 11 May, did the government proscribe the strike; and when men began to drift back to work they arrested a mere eight 'agitators', who were freed after a settlement had been reached, jointly, with the ASE and a shop stewards' delegation.

The May strike tested Askwith's machinery to the limit and forced him to tour all the districts in his search for conciliation, with promises that dilution would not be continued after the war.[22] As far as the Ministry of Labour was concerned, it led to the setting up of an Industrial Intelligence Department, to provide better information than that which had led to Hodge's absurdly over-optimistic forecast. But it also forced the War Cabinet to recognise that its alliance with the

---

*WC 115/9. He offered evidence (obtained by Special Branch) of Triple Alliance support for the No Conscription Fellowship and the Union of Democratic Control.

TUC had been found inadequate in the face of a powerful shop stewards' movement. In the heat of the strike, and to meet War Office needs, the government had not only forced the hand of the more ultramontane employers[23] but had conceded the shop stewards a sort of negative recognition, and thus weakened the official ASE and the Munitions Act itself, a poor legacy for subsequent implementation of the 'comb-out' and the leaving certificate.

In a characteristically dramatic gesture, Lloyd George replaced Addison at Munitions with Churchill and set up the Industrial Unrest Commissions (see below, Chapter 5) 'to remove justifiable reason for unrest'.[24] When the IUCs revealed the unsurprising fact that working-class grievances were based not, as Milner suspected, on 'subversive political elements' but instead on high food prices, low wages and unfairness of the call-up, the War Cabinet fixed the price of essential foods in July to prevent a further spiral of wage claims and strikes; and concluded categorically: 'For the vigorous prosecution of the war, a contented working class is indispensable.'[25]

But if this was the lesson of the May 1917 strikes for the War Cabinet, Departments remained prone to taking the easy way out; it was not until G. H. Roberts took over the Ministry of Labour from Hodge that a more vigorous and intelligent industrial relations policy could be put into effect, using the whole national and local conciliation apparatus which had been evolved since 1916. Roberts wrested labour functions from Munitions (whose incompetence under Addison had been clearly exposed) and asked the War Cabinet for overall control of wages to prevent unjustified wage claims, and the consequent leap-frogging between rival unions. Even then, although Roberts defeated one of the railway unions' claims for an eight-hour day, the Cabinet (as so often in crises) chose not to face up to the miners when the MFGB claimed 10s. a week extra in September 1917. Primed with expert advice that the miners were out of hand and could bring muni-tions work to a halt in ten days, regardless of the impact on other industries, they concluded that 'the government could not embark on a conflict with the miners when they were not certain to bring it to a victorious issue ... A great strike *would be equivalent to a military defeat.*'[26]

Lacking confidence in its propaganda, the government paid its Dane-geld – an outcome probably foregone since Lloyd George's personal settlement of the South Wales miners' strike two years earlier. The surrender was followed by Churchill's sanctioning of further piece-work in munitions supply, in spite of Ministry of Labour denunciations and an only partly successful reconstitution of the Committee of Production with final responsibility for wage control in October 1917. Chaotic squabbles immediately arose from the 12½ per cent award to all time-workers (which had been intended to restore the balance with pieceworkers), lasting until the end of 1917. Yet most Ministers had long accepted that the case for coordinating wages policy was unanswerable. As Bonar Law realised, if leap-frogging continued, and if the 12½ per cent award were extended haphazardly to private industry, government would have set itself up against the employers. On 1 January 1918 in an extraordinary prophetic statement he declared: 'Once the workpeople got the notion that they were dealing with the Treasury and not with the employers, there could be no end to their demands, and future strikes would be against the government.'[27] This issue divided the War Cabinet itself – for in order to justify a policy of wage control, Churchill and Geddes had opened up a new attack on the employers, asking for 100 per cent war profits tax, which Lloyd George and Bonar Law (as ever, open to employers' protests) opposed.*

The wages formula put forward, against Treasury objections, by G. N. Barnes on 7 January, certainly satisfied employers' susceptibilities. The Ministry of Labour was henceforward to be responsible for all wage claims, delegating them to the Committee of Production and its Coordinating Committee; employers and unions were assured of dealing with a single department. But this expedient by no means solved the wages question, and subsequent strikes among electricians revealed how little control the union leaders retained, and how flaccid the War Cabinet's resolve had become. Another miners' claim in June 1918 found Ministers again prepared to admit that 'the coal position today does not admit of stoppage';[28] and when a final cycle of wage claims erupted in September 1918, on the railways, over the whole issue of differentials and cost of living, it was only resolved by the curiously modern expedient of a threshold agreement based on the cost of living index.

The war ended with statutory wages policy discredited and an absence of coherent government policy, of which the shop stewards' movement had taken considerable advantage. Despite higher wages, losses of production had been far more serious than in the first half of

*Lloyd George replied that the government must consult with the employers; a fair enough statement, perhaps, if it had not been for his long history of inaction over war profits, and his close consultation with George Terrell, MP, representative of the Federation of British Industries. (WC 310/1.)

the war.* Faced with the long series of piecemeal settlements, and the reiterated backsliding of a War Cabinet unable to prevent a major strike and unwilling to coerce in the manner of 1916, employers countered with a sort of passive resistance, amassing evidence for the case that these wage settlements amounted to inadmissible government interference with the course of industry, to be remedied in peace-time. Those like Weir and Allan Smith, however, who had worked closely with government, realised that wage control had to a great extent been sacrificed deliberately in the interests of saving the political status of the trade union movement; for the government chose, not unjustifiably, to concern itself with political rather than industrial unrest. Phenomena such as organised resistance to the 'comb-out' in South Wales in October 1917 or the anti-war crusade led by John Maclean on Clydeside, led to plans for strike-breaking, and prosecution for sedition.[30]

But the government did not repeat the repressive campaign of 1915–16. Anxiety about the size of the 1918 May Day parade in Glasgow combined with employers' resistance to workers' representation on Production Committees, 'lest they raise political questions',[31] to encourage Churchill to think of extreme measures, such as conscripting shop stewards, and his ignorance of trade union susceptibilities certainly caused serious unrest in July 1918 in the final stages of dilution.[32] Nevertheless, Weir, Roberts and the other Ministers responsible for industrial politics opted for compromise, and Lloyd George, after a brief justification of earlier repression, came down on the side of the majority of workers, education of public opinion, and the necessary distinction between a trade dispute and an attack on the state. In that crucial confrontation in July 1918 at the time of the Coventry strike, the War Cabinet traded on its contract with the TUC: Churchill made his threats but left the TUC Advisory Committee to do the work of strike-breaking.[33] A similar threat sufficed in the September railway strike, in spite of Bonar Law's and Chamberlain's provocative talk of martial law.[34] But for the future, Conservative Ministers had come to a large measure of agreement for setting up a committee to coordinate

*		Disputes	Nos. involved (directly and indirectly)	Days lost
	1915	672	448,000	2,953,000
	1916	532	276,000	2,446,000
	1917	730	872,000	5,647,000
	1918	1165	1,116,000	5,875,000

(A. H. Halsey, *Trends in British Society*, p. 127.[29])

anti-strike activity in 'political' cases (such as Coventry) – a poor omen for peace-time.

On 19 June 1917, Lloyd George outlined his long-term policy to the General Staff, represented by Robertson and Haig, assembled in the War Policy Committee; and linked directly industrial harmony, production and the supply of recruits:

Every time we scraped any men in there was trouble in the House of Commons or a strike. The last strike, which had been due to calling up men from munition works, had lasted three weeks and had seriously put back the output of Sir Douglas Haig's guns. Then we had ordered a medical re-examination of rejected men. The result of this was that on Thursday in the House of Commons there would be the severest attack on the War Office that had yet been delivered. If we dip in one place for recruits they said: No, these are agricultural men; and so it was everywhere. All the newspapers without regard to party joined in the agitation. There was no place from which we could take men in large quantities without facing a serious trouble.[35]

Having paid tribute to Haig's personal susceptibilities, Lloyd George used the manpower shortage to deprecate talk of further offensives in 1917–18, and urged the generals to wait until the untried American divisions were fully trained and the 'unsettling effect' of the Russian Revolution had passed. 'It was very important not to break this country. . . . He did not want to face a Peace Conference some day with our country weakened while America was still overwhelmingly strong, and Russia had perhaps revived her strength.'

This view, with its strong chauvinistic overtones, was repeated in a very secret conversation with Sir Maurice Hankey, the Cabinet Secretary, at breakfast on 15 October. Lloyd George intended to win a total, not compromise, victory, which should leave the British army, unlike the French and Russian, one of the strongest in the world. Since there could be no outright victory in 1918 without the full use of American contingents, Britain must wait to make its great effort in 1919.[36] This 'extra year' concept explains the strategy both of the war and of industrial production; yet it led to extreme tension between the twin aims of sustaining the front line in 1918 and building up the hypothetical reserve for 1919. Where were these men to be found?

In spite of Lloyd George's foreboding, this manpower crisis was not foreseen, partly because of an obvious temptation to rely on trade union recruiting help, and partly because of a feeling that the War Office had habitually overstated its case. Even after the Easter Rising, it was argued, more men could always be found by conscripting them in Ireland.* Such facile assumptions could not survive the reappraisal made in December 1917 after the final collapse of Russia, the reverses at Cambrai, and the Italian catastrophe at Caporetto which, for the first time, brought home to Ministers the cost of the previous eight months' trench assaults (including the Battle of Passchendaele) in which three British had been killed for every two Germans. Far from creating a reserve army the War Office seemed to have no chance of holding on until American troops were ready. Haig's figures, confirmed by Lord Derby, indicated that by March 1918 the army would be depleted by 45 per cent and could scarcely prevent a German break-through. 1½ million men were needed; as far as the departments were concerned, something close to manpower budgeting (as it developed in 1941) was to be introduced; and Auckland Geddes offered no alternative to a wide extension of the call-up and conscription for Ireland.[37] The Government was being asked, at best, to choose between breaking its contract with the TUC or risking further revolt in Ireland; and in either case to face a storm in the House of Commons from Asquith's Liberals and the Labour Party. Hankey put it concisely: 'The problem is to avert a military catastrophe without plunging us into an economic catastrophe equally fatal to the cause of the Allies.'[38]

The War Cabinet Manpower Committee gave enormous weight to the government's obligations to popular feeling ('the war-weary people of this country') and to the TUC, admitting frankly their dependence 'on obtaining release from the trade unions from the pledges which

*This in spite of Asquith's warnings and the results of a survey of Irish opinion conducted by Neville Chamberlain in May 1916 which showed nationwide sympathy for the rebels – except in Ulster – after they had been executed (CAB 37/150/4). After the Rising, voluntary recruiting fell off sharply, accompanied by a rise in affiliation to Sinn Féin. General Sir John Maxwell reported in October 1916 that it would be hopeless to recruit further without support from Redmond and the Nationalists – the reason, indeed, for Lloyd George's peace mission, and 'concessions to rebels' in the summer, which had greatly angered the Tories (CAB 137/155/40; 41/37/2/24). Both Asquith and the Chief Secretary, Duke, recommended against conscription in spite of the depleted state of the Irish Divisions, and with a sop to the Tories on the 'right to conscript' (LG F30/2/8) the question was put aside. In March 1917, faced with a revived Sinn Féin and a press campaign in England against Irish 'evasion o sacrifice', the War Cabinet discussed whether it was possible to speed up Home Rule, with Dominion assistance; a bill was prepared leaving Ulster the option of staying out. This led on to the ill-fated Convention of 1917 and an attempt to put the onus on the Irish 'to settle their constitutional differences themselves' (WC 141/77). It was a fairly desperate gambit, given the size of army needed to coerce the country, if the Convention failed; but the hawks in the War Cabinet saw the chance of linking Home Rule and conscription and flushing out a large number of young men they believed to be available in Ireland (WC 175 and 186, July 1917).

were given them earlier in the war'. Logically, if harshly, they judged that Ireland should pay, if the Irish were to expect anything from post-war reconstruction. On the other hand, in a rebellion,

the Irish would probably rally to them not only the pacifists but others whose pacifism is at present veiled. It is understood that the trade unions would not desire to force conscription on Ireland. The effects of violent scenes in the House of Commons would not only reduce the prestige of this country in Europe, but might react in a highly detrimental manner in the USA and the Dominions. Moreover all prospect of a successful issue to the Irish Convention would be removed.[39]

This dilemma grew no easier with time. Torn between offending the TUC and handing Ireland over irrevocably to Sinn Féin, the government delayed until the German offensive in March 1918 forced it to choose. Lloyd George feared 'a seething mass of ferocity – for over seven hundred years Irish men had been unwilling partners in what was essentially a British show', and Ministers busily looked for alternatives, either by consultation with the TUC, as Milner and Roberts advised, or, in Churchill's phrase, 'by turning the flank of the trade unions'.[40] So heavily did Ireland weigh on an imperially-minded War Cabinet that the Military Service Bill of January 1918 actually omitted Irishmen living in Britain; but in spite of Henderson's apparent acquiesence the tenor of opinion at the Labour Conference at Nottingham suggested that party workers and trade unionists were by no means convinced of the need for a further 'comb-out'.

This absence of consent needs little explanation. Trade unions' own internal discipline and coherence suffered much more from their role as executors of government policy in the 'comb-out', with its manifestly unfair and arbitrary distinctions between one group of workers and another, than from the withdrawal of trade cards in the munitions industry. Between January and March 1918 the ASE, afraid both of losing political status and being undercut by the shop stewards, rejected the 'comb-out', relying on Henderson's reputation and bargaining skills (despite his dismissal (see below, p. 114) from the War Cabinet); while Henderson in turn used his new, detached, position to threaten wholesale withdrawal of Labour movement support for the war.[41]

For a short time these manoeuvres forced the War Cabinet to desist and to seek more roundabout means of recreating trade union allegiance. But Ludendorff's great offensive on the Western Front, and the likelihood of a breakdown of the Irish Convention, put an end to Henderson's tactics abruptly in March 1918. Emergency conveyed its own legitimacy. On 24 March the War Cabinet agreed to conscript men up to fifty in Britain *and* Ireland, to use conscientious objectors and ministers of religion on service overseas, to reduce the call-up notice to seven days, and to comb out still more men from the pits and dockyards. All pledges had been abandoned and Lloyd George turned desperately to President Wilson to commit the American levies of General Pershing – even if they were not fully trained.[42]

Evidently these new recruits were not intended for immediate service; after training, they would replace the reserves already committed to holding the German breakthrough. Thus the choice fell between alienating Ireland or the engineering unions. With complete unanimity the Cabinet's Irish advisers rejected the former. Not only would the Convention be prejudiced; according to all sources[43] conscription would be followed by rebellion, uniting Catholics and Nationalists against the imperial power. The Catholic Church would take sides, the Irish Executive would resign, the recruits themselves would join Sinn Féin and subvert the British army, and the Irish overseas, in the Empire and the United States, would damage the British cause irremediably.[44]

Early in April Lloyd George did consider conscripting men in Ireland, assured of support from the English Labour movement and the majority of the Convention,* But the ancient party divisions opened at once, as they had done in 1914, and Bonar Law led a harsh and unperceptive debate in the War Cabinet with a proposal to conscript even the Irish priests.[45] Instead of proceeding towards Home Rule (which Dublin Castle considered would win voluntary recruits) Lloyd George had to balance the factions and prevent the Conservatives from turning on him as they had turned on Asquith, while at the same time retaining Barnes, a fervent conscriptionist and Home Ruler, and the last major Labour representative in the Government.[46] Meanwhile in the parliamentary wings, ready to attack the unpopular call-up bill, stood Asquith and his Liberal following, still representative of nearly a third of the electorate.

President Wilson's decision to commit the American divisions let the British off the hook and the Irish question was devolved to a Committee, chaired by Walter Long, where federalism for the various sections of the United Kingdom was discussed as a sop to Ulster's defiance of Home Rule. The limits of coercion in Ireland had been

*The Convention voted 44–29 for Home Rule: the moderate centre, Southern Irish Nationalists and Unionists being opposed by an unholy alliance of Catholic Bishops, Sinn Féin and Ulstermen!

reached,* and since Lloyd George could not win party consensus,† the Conservatives were constrained to accept that without Home Rule there could be no conscription either. On that unsatisfactory but fortunately not too public basis conscription for Ireland was abandoned, 'until the new Administration had established itself': and that, understandably, had not been done before the Armistice.

Surprisingly, 20,000 Irish volunteers came forward: a figure which Lloyd George wished to falsify to 50,000 to appease opinion in England.[47] Secrecy and evasion shrouded the parliamentary debates while Long pursued the federalist chimera. The Cabinet never admitted failure. 'To do so,' Lloyd George declared rather archaically, 'would mean that the British government surrendered to the challenge of the Church on the question of supremacy of the British Parliament'; in the War Cabinet, on 29 July, he even denied that the double strategy had ever existed.[48] But it had, and the surrender occurred.

Conservative Ministers' claims for the sacrosanct principles of Unionism were thus treated more respectfully than the brave talk of national unity. When Auckland Geddes ventured to point out that a demand for 450,000 men would arouse dissent in industrial and agricultural areas, and that the public would not accept a conscription age of fifty and abolition of Tribunals without a quid pro quo in Ireland, Lloyd George replied that the choice was simply victory or defeat.[49] In spite of the laboriously created political contract, the English and Scottish trade union movement was called on to provide the sacrifice instead.

Imposition of the Ministry of National Service's new powers, and a 'clean-cut' for the 18–23 age group in all industries, 'in order to secure the proper psychological effect in the country'[50] did work for a short time in the late spring of 1918; and the War Munitions Volunteer scheme came very close to Labour's spectre of full industrial conscription. But in the process, Lloyd George's 'army of 1919' vanished, and the limits of popular tolerance, as well as the whole system of recruiting

*WC 397/6. Lord French considered that to apply conscription would require the use of 30,000 troops, two squadrons of aircraft, five cyclist brigades, and two battalions of artillery (CAB 1/26/12). (Devolution was not abandoned in peace-time but continued, *pari passu* with the collapse of Ireland into civil war. The Devolution Conference of 1919, under Speaker Lowther, went as far as proposing separate, federal units for Scotland and Wales as well as Ireland, but divided on whether England should form one unit or two.)

†F. Guest, the Liberal Chief Whip, told Lloyd George that 150 official Liberals, 100 Tories, 25 LG Liberals, and 18–20 Labour MPs, would support federalism if the Conscription Bill was postponed. Another 20 Scots MPs and 25 Welsh might be counted as Home Rulers. But it was hardly a coalition on which to base a government (LG F21/2/20, 3 May).

and production, became overstrained. For many months the public response to government propaganda had depended on the aggregate of individual appreciations of the state of emergency; and the news of a slackening in the German offensive in May 1918 was followed by rapid and cumulative shortfalls in recruiting and industrial production. Futile attempts to restore munitions supply by the use of Defence of Realm Act powers only exacerbated the Coventry strike, while Churchill's well-publicised plans to conscript strikers and mobilise the Trade Union Advisory Committee against shop stewards produced the antithesis of what he wanted.[51] Far from planning to utilise the army of 1919, the Cabinet gloomily predicted reductions in manpower and in munitions supply for Italy and France.[52]

The sudden collapse of German morale in October and November, after naval mutiny and in the middle of abortive revolution, took the allies by surprise. For nine months the British government had done little more than exercise its will to survive, pressing into use its exiguous credit with parliament, employers and the trade union movement. It seemed as if the political system had survived; but an inordinate number of conflicting commitments and illusory promises had been made, whose legacy went far to embitter any peace-time settlement. In the process, the participants who had made the bargains had themselves changed, so that the words 'trade unions', 'employers', 'Parties' and 'the state', conveyed not merely different assumptions and standpoints from those of 1914 but a different essence.

In the middle stages of the war, many employers' associations had reacted passively or defensively to the government's alternate exhortations and threats. Apart from their long, successful rearguard action against higher taxation of profits, they seemed content to exclude trade unionists where possible from anything but a token place in the actual running of wartime industry, while building up the case that the wage increases of 1916–17 were to be regarded as government-imposed, unrelated to the real profitability of industries, and open to revision after the war's end. Such views can be found represented among most of the District Armaments Committees, which were chiefly responsible for the control of production. Thus the East Anglian Board complained angrily of government bias towards the unions: 'The workmen's interests are paramount, and the masters' entirely neglected.'[53]

By 1918, however, the wages question had become paramount, forcing the federations to reconsider their role in politics. Overriding the immediate problems of conversion to peace-time production, employers feared the onset of a post-war slump. On the union side, miners, transport workers and railwaymen made no secret of the size of their post-war claims, based on war-time service to the nation, and their view that nationalisation had become imperative. As in the 1890s and 1910s, each body's awareness of the other enhanced their mutual antagonism: in 1916–17 the newly-formed Federation of British Industries had launched a propaganda campaign against nationalisation, sponsored a body intended to attack the Triple Alliance, called the National Alliance of Employers and Employed, and sub-sidised heavily publicity organisations opposing both nationalisation and the array of government controls.* As a District Armaments Committee meeting at Manchester in December 1918 claimed, 'we should have the right and power to manage our own businesses as soon as possible.'[54]

A more cooperative outlook had, however, always existed in certain areas. Soon after its creation in 1916, the FBI itself considered appoint-ing trade union representatives to its board, to ensure that its discussions reflected the balance within industry, and later even discussed opening its records to TUC inspection, to scotch rumours of anti-union bias. In the north-east region, trade union representatives had early on been admitted to certain armaments committees,[55] and while the Mineowners' Association or Sir Vincent Caillard, chairman of Vickers and a close associate of Lloyd George, might consider that all wartime strikes were the result of 'revolutionary and anti-patriotic bodies',[56] the FBI collectively came to the conclusion in 1918 that conditions and 'the absence of any human touch' in industry were to blame.[57] 'In future,' the FBI agreed, 'work people would expect to be consulted on a number of questions that had previously been dealt with by employers.'[58]

This façade of reasonableness concealed the employers' growing awareness of the need to increase their political power in the second half of the war and to recover the ground lost to government and TUC in 1915–16. In spite of the partiality shown by government towards employers (see below p. 132),† in particular the banking and financial community, in such general questions as financing the war largely by borrowing rather than high taxation, and the fiscal aim of a return to

*The FBI paid £5,000 in 1919 to an anonymous organisation (probably the British Commonwealth Union) providing counter-revolutionary propaganda in industry (FBI/C/19).

†'Abolition of profiteering and conscription of capital' were regarded by Lloyd George as tantamount to instituting the 'equalitarian state'. (Jones, *Whitehall Diary*, vol. II, p. 45.)

the gold standard at the pre-war parity, the employers had failed to become a representative body negotiating with government, and lacked regular access to Ministers in the manner achieved by the TUC. For this reason, as well as to build up a counter-weight to the TUC, the Government encouraged the formation of the FBI, to the extent of seconding two senior Foreign Office officials to assist it and to ensure that its trade promotion policy did not diverge from its own.[59]

Nevertheless, many employers found themselves at a disadvantage *vis-à-vis* the trade unions because normal wage-bargaining had been suspended, leaving them without a counter-weight in strikes, open on the one side to government-imposed wages settlements and on the other to the effective power of shop stewards' committees. It is hardly surprising that some employers in the munitions industry tried to involve official union leaders in production matters, in order to isolate the shop stewards,[60] while the Engineering Employers' Federation sought to integrate the latter, to bring them back under union discipline.[61]

As in the 1900s, the EEF emerged as the Federation with most political significance, creating a variety of informal relationships with shop stewards' committees which involved practical recognition, and at times – with the Huddersfield Association, for example – regular formal encounters.[62] Originally, under EEF pressure, the FBI had been forced to adopt a self-denying ordinance that as a public body it should not engage in politics over labour questions, but treat only of industry and commerce; because the EEF looked with considerable suspicion on the 'quasi-syndicalist' ideas of some FBI Council members.[63] In practice, as with the Labour Party and TUC, the distinction between political and industrial matters could not be sustained when economic management, financial priorities, taxation and investment had become inextricably mixed; and the attempt led to a long battle which was only resolved by the (EEF-inspired) creation of the National Confederation of Employers' Organisations (NCEO) in 1919. Meanwhile, the polarisation within government, which Llewellyn Smith had predicted, occurred during 1918, as the employers developed personal affinity for the Conservative Stanley at the Board of Trade, in contrast to trade unionists' sympathies for Roberts at the Ministry of Labour.

Individually, employers had been summoned to aid the government on a far greater scale than trade unionists or Labour MPs. Lord Weir, a senior member of the FBI, and Allan Smith of the Federation of Engineering Employers, were made advisers on production, Lord

Cowdray, Air Minister; Lord Rhonddha, Food Controller; Lord Devonport, Shipping Controller; while the press lords, Northcliffe, Beaverbrook (Minister of Information, 1918) and Rothermere (Air Ministry 1917-18) took on political responsibility in addition to their function as moulders of public opinion. To an extent which has never been fully documented, employers at the local level actually *ran* the war effort, the District Armaments Committees, like the one in Manchester, being composed wholly of members of the largest engineering firms, with only exiguous representation by the Ministry of Munitions.[64] Thus the business community reached to the centre of government in an unprecedented fashion – paralleled only in Germany – and promulgated a theory of government by and for economic interest groups which had previously, in spite of Lloyd George's sympathies, failed to gain political acceptance.

Circumstances led the employers from passive resistance to lobbying and finally formal embodiment in a representative institution. On the trade union side, the events of 1917-18 also imposed a profound reappraisal of structure and function in political life. Under attack by the Shop Stewards' Movement and unable freely to resort to strikes in defence of members' interests, officials lost much authority and status. Acceptance by government and many employers of the need to incorporate shop stewards' committees rendered old patterns of hierarchy obsolete; and even if the shop stewards had not wished to bring this about, the success of their campaigns prevented restoration of the *status quo* ante 1916, at least in engineering, textiles and transport. At the same time, the unions of the old Triple Alliance began to promulgate post-war claims; the miners had already succeeded in excluding the GFTU and its conservative leadership from the Joint Board in 1916, thus preparing the way for radicalising the whole trade union movement.

Almost fortuitously, the TUC found support for a different route back into politics, in the wake of Henderson's resignation from the government in August 1917. Whether the Conservatives forced Lloyd George to sack him, whether Lloyd George made a serious miscalculation in the haste and confusion after Henderson's return from Russia, or whether Henderson himself wanted a showdown, is not wholly clear: he had been sent by the War Cabinet to assess the position of Kerensky's government after the March revolution, and to find out Russian opinion about the proposed conference of socialist parties at Stockholm. Hostile at first, he returned convinced that Stockholm offered the possibility of a negotiated peace, or at least the promulgation of war aims; but his proposed journey, with the outcast MacDonald, to France, to concert Labour Party tactics with the French Socialists, antagonised the War Cabinet who felt he should have reported first to them. Conflict between the various loyalties grew rapidly in July. On August 10 Henderson carried the Labour Party Conference in favour of Stockholm and that night (in the 'doormat' incident) Lloyd George abused him and told him to choose between party and his duty to the nation. Yet despite this treatment, Henderson at first refused to resign; later he told Thomas Jones 'he would do all he could for the war, but would try to develop some form of criticism of the Government policy, and, after the war, attempt to recast Labour representation in such a way as to bring in a larger infusion of the non-trade unionists . . . the younger intellectuals who are keenly sympathetic with Labour.'[65]

Lloyd George may well have feared that Henderson's conversion would lead to creation of a socialist front, made up of MacDonald and the ILP, the No Conscription Fellowship, Union of Democratic Control and the Shop Stewards' Movement, on a programme including a negotiated peace. The effect on French morale, after the Army mutinies of 1917 and Kerensky's failure to revive the Russian war effort, would have been grievous. But however urgent Henderson's exclusion may have been for the Conservatives, Lloyd George underestimated the very power within the Labour movement* which had made his inclusion in the War Cabinet originally necessary, as well as his capacity for political organisation outside.

In the wilderness, Henderson moved away from the modest position outlined to Jones, capitalising on the joint needs of TUC and Labour Party. For some time the Parliamentary Committee had wished to play more part in foreign policy[66] and its support for a negotiated peace was skilfully woven into Labour's Declaration of War Aims in January 1918 – which helped to force the government to enunciate its own peace terms and, by implication, abandon the concept of 'total victory'. In opposition, Henderson was prepared to concede to the TUC that equal responsibility in 'political' questions he had previously denied them. At the same time, he worked to align the TUC with the Fabian group in the drafting of Labour's new policy – quite distinct from that of the Liberal party – *Labour and the New Social Order*. At the TUC Conference in September 1917 even the pacifist and GFTU wings appeared to be united, and Thomas Jones recorded an

---

*A power demonstrated as recently as the discussion on excess profits tax in May 1917 when in the name of the TUC he had demanded a 90 per cent rather than an 80 per cent duty and got 87 per cent (WC 128/17).

unprecedented meeting between Henderson, trade unionists, party organisers and intellectuals, to discuss party reorganisation on a constituency basis, using cooperators and unions, and effectively downgrading the importance of Trades Councils and ILP. 'Henderson thought that it should be possible to run about 200 candidates and to steal the Government's reconstruction thunder.'[67]

Although the TUC remained in practice the junior partner in the Joint Executive, docile to the requirements of Henderson's strategy, its direct involvement in party strategy for the first time since the foundation of the Labour Representation Committee in 1901 led to an administrative revolution in the Parliamentary Committee. The new secretary, Harry Gosling, acquired a larger staff, more money, and an International Bureau, which made possible later contacts with the European movements and the International Labor Organisation. The GFTU consequently faded away, although for a time it maintained links with Sam Gompers and the American Federation of Labor.

Meanwhile, joint research committees, founded by TUC and Labour Party, involved unionists for the next seven years in political policy-making in an almost novel way, until the rupture in 1925; and joint collaboration in due course led on to the new Constitution, with its aim for the nationalisation of the means of production and distribution – a document sufficiently radical for the Triple Alliance to endorse. A coherent financial and industrial programme set the Labour Party up in contradistinction not only to the Coalition and the handful of Labour MPs, led by G. N. Barnes, who stood by the Government, but also to the Shop Stewards' Movement, for the espousal of socialism was not accompanied by any sympathy for workers' control or popular democracy. From its inception, the TUC-Labour Party consortium aimed at capturing parliamentary power in a very different sense from the limited aspirations of the 1900s and defined itself as a competitor for government within the political system as Henderson and Sidney Webb understood it, not that of British Socialist Party and Socialist Labour Party shop stewards, with their concepts of direct action and industrial self-government.

In reply to this realignment of the Labour movement, the government evolved its own strategy, seeking to rationalise its heterogeneous nature and bind Liberals and Conservatives to a common programme. As early as 11 August 1917 the War Cabinet debated the need for a General Election to restore its popular mandate,[68] while Lloyd George's conception of a future coalition was in due course made evident in the share-out of the 150-odd 'coupons' for Liberals at the post-war

General Election, originally mooted in Addison's committee of prominent Liberals in July 1918.[69]

Lloyd George could offer much to a post-war coalition between Liberals he chose to bring with him and the Conservative Party: his unrivalled prestige, personal political skills and an incomparable secretariat, together with the known favour of the business community, and his vested interest in a reconstruction programme in which social welfare did not imply the planned socialism of what had now to be seen (in default of Asquith's following) as the intellectual parliamentary Opposition. Alone, all this might not have been enough to retain Conservative support for the Coalition and restrain Tory party managers from a return to two-party politics. But the managerial concept of government, which Lloyd George embodied, proved irresistible to Bonar Law and his colleagues, in spite of the often unattractive men around the Prime Minister, and their even less attractive methods. Secondly, the more the Labour movement turned towards socialism, the more Conservatives found comfort in an anti-socialist alliance in politics, and a tripartite harmony of government, business and unions as a bulwark against repetition of the breakdown of 1911–14. Hence the importance for them of containing the TUC on one hand by the public appeal of the reconstruction programme, and on the other by a joint Liberal-Conservative propaganda campaign and the stimulation of anti-socialist trade union groups.*

What is not so well-documented is that a case for a continued coalition from the *Conservative* side was being made at the end of 1916 – before the fall of Asquith or the accumulation of hostility in Ireland added yet another reason for preventing party warfare on the pattern of 1914. A number of informal discussions took place between Conservative and Liberal Party managers, whose agreements (on matters such as state control of vital commodities in peace-time, minimum prices and wages in agriculture, tax reform and the defensive use of tariffs) were sufficiently notable for Steel-Maitland to draft a preliminary document.[70] The groups failed to concur on plans to harmonise the relations of 'Capital and Labour', but went so far as proposing, first, a form of self-arbitration in industry, in which consent to a settlement by two-thirds

*Apart from the National Alliance of Employers and Employed, the main vehicle used was the British Workers' League, headed by a number of Conservative trade unionists, including Victor Fisher and W. Seddon. A sort of electoral pact was reached in February 1917 between the Conservatives and the BWL, under which the latter were to have a free hand in the next election in such seats as Blackburn, Leicester, Oldham, Newcastle and Durham – with the express intention of disabling ILP and Socialist candidates. (SM GD 193/99/2.)

of employers and workers in a district would be made legally binding on the minority; and secondly, the provision of state assistance to industries in need of protection during their infancy or defence against foreign dumping.

The importance of the Conservative position lies not so much in a revival of the tariff argument, but in the recognition given to the fears on both sides of industry: of the effect of trade union restrictive practices on profits, and of the effect on wages and conditions of 'Taylorism' or management-inspired essays in increasing productivity. Steel-Maitland sought to inspire his colleagues with a vision of 'a visible and automatic community of interest between masters and men, and of making the latter feel that they are a corporate part of a mutually beneficent organisation'. Such sentiments did not, of course, become official Conservative policy in the era of Bonar Law, nor could they resolve the contradiction between sponsorship of the British Workers' League and the appeal to members of the TUC, but they encouraged the belief that a coalition under the supreme managerial skills of Lloyd George could safeguard at once the Party's historic interest in the Tory working man and its vulnerability to the ideological attack on Capital, renewed in 1917–18 by the Labour movement as a whole. With far greater urgency than in 1911, Conservatives had to consider the validity of their ancient cross-class appeal; and this unease showed itself strongly during the Party Conference called in November 1917, ostensibly to reaffirm war aims and to deplore the negotiations for peace heralded by Lansdowne's letter and the Stockholm Conference.

Answering attacks on the Coalition's hesitancy about applying conscription equally and unwaveringly to Ireland, Bonar Law argued that there was no choice but to support Lloyd George and create a fresh alignment of political forces. To survive, Conservatism had to capture the votes of moderate trade unionists and those of the Labour Party who remained loyal to the Coalition.[71] He admitted quite openly that the Party would pay a high price, and suffer division, but threatened his resignation if they revoked membership of the Coalition. Disagreement among delegates came from the Ulster group and the diehard opponents of women's suffrage, rather than on labour matters; indeed one speaker argued that, with the new franchise, there could be no doubt that the Party was committed to winning a large share of working men's – and working women's – votes if it was to remain in power. 'We shall certainly not win the war unless we win peace at home. . . . *They* [the working class] are sending their sons to fight.'[72] The conference seems to have accepted that allegiance to Lloyd George was acceptable so long as it did not impair the party's hold on its own natural constituency. As part of a long transformation, begun with the organisation reforms of 1906 and 1911, the Conservatives pledged themselves to a coalition – but set on its existence and its reconstruction programme the overriding condition of success in economic and industrial affairs.

Among a mass of confused tendencies at the end of the war, the search for a new, stable political system became an obsession among Ministers, disoriented and dismayed by the collapse of central government in the majority of European nations. On 2 January 1918, in the middle of the manpower crisis, Hankey sent Lloyd George a paper on working-class opinion prepared by a young Conservative MP, William Ormsby-Gore (then Assistant Secretary to the War Cabinet) which linked war-weariness and anti-war feeling with the need for a declaration of war aims, compulsory rationing, and full taxation of war profits. In the Shop Stewards' Movement the author saw echoes of the Dublin strike of 1913 and the shadow of Bolshevism:

The essence of this movement is, of course, the new form of Marxian syndicalism, revolutionary in its aims and methods, aiming at the overthrow of the existing social and economic order by direct action; its leaders welcome unrest and strikes in any form and for whatever cause, they are the true, up-to-date revolutionaries, who seem to be appearing in every country in the world, and whether it is Petrograd, Chicago, the Belfast dockyards, the Clyde, or the West Riding of Yorkshire, it is all the same thing. It looks as if the Leaders, whether Jew or Irish, have this common feature, they are all men with dissatisfied national aspirations, embittered against society and bent on using the results of the War to overthrow the existing order of things.[73]

It was a message calculated to appeal to the prejudices and visions not only of the Prime Minister but all who dreamed of creating a centre bloc in national political life, sustained by the great institutions of the state.

5 LLOYD GEORGE'S CONTRACT, 1917–20

Ormsby-Gore's warning reverberated round the Cabinet room with each instalment of European disintegration, as revolution in Russia was succeeded by the economic collapse of Germany, dissolution of the Austria-Hungarian empire, revolt in Hungary, deep social unrest in Italy and Spain, and the withdrawal from European considerations of the United States, the only great power virtually unharmed by the war effort. A review of the state of Germany or France after 1917 must have suggested nothing but apocalyptic conclusions about the failure of political systems to survive the demands of total war on public consent, industrial production and the supply of manpower.

In Germany, in spite of the embodiment of popular enthusiasm in the *Burgfrieden*, old conflicts of interest survived, and the jealousies and ambitions of the heavy industry group and the Junkers were never tamed. The various sections of industrialists made their own terms with the state, approving the 1916 Hindenburg plan for total mobilisation of resources and the transfer of plant to essential industry only on condition that it interfered neither with their profit margins nor with the process of cartelisation. Trade union leaders, conscious of the debilitating effect of a persistent labour surplus, surrendered their privileges, including the right to strike, in return for the Auxiliary Service Law in December 1916: and found, as in Britain, that their side of the bargain needed constant reinforcement. The Labour movement made spectacular gains in industrial cities and in July 1917 was able to engineer the resignation of the Chancellor, Bethmann-Hollweg; yet his more sympathetic successor, Michaelis, fell a few months later, largely because Hindenburg and Ludendorff lacked the authority in civilian politics to defend the 1916 compromise against big business.[1]

Instead of attacking war profits, the High Command sought popular support by announcing a series of spiralling war aims, ever higher and less realistic, while the tangible links between army and industry, and industrialists and trade unions, weakened, and General Groener's self-styled 'alliance with Labour' fell rapidly into disrepute. Kaiser and Reichstag both failed to offer a truly national leadership after 1916 and working-class consent continued to be purchased by a series of compromises, following the Auxiliary Service Law, down to the long-delayed concession of full trade union bargaining rights in October 1918. A general comparison with Britain holds good: in its mixture of Bismarckian Bonapartism and Fascist dictatorship, the High Command strove to buy off revolution and even in defeat to safeguard the remnants of the nineteenth-century state.[2]

But the collaboration of army, industry and working class failed to sustain the war effort after Ludendorff's 1918 offensive. In sharp distinction to the British Labour Party, the SPD split, while politicians and the army failed to safeguard wages and conditions against inflation. Large sections of the lower-middle and working class had supported Erzberger's call for a negotiated peace in July 1917. Mass discontent fuelled the Spartacist movement and the great strikes of January 1918, and although the government tried to distinguish between moderate trade unions and the extreme Left by selective repression of certain strikes, like the one at Mercedes-Benz in Stuttgart, reform came too late to do more than ensure the defeat of the German revolution and the Soldiers' and Workers' Council of December 1918, by a strange alliance of army, big business and the SPD.

Five years passed before the revolutionary movement (embodied in the German Communist Party's attempted putsches in 1921 and 1923) was defeated. The resulting irreconcilable division of the political Left, between the Communist Party (KPD) and the Social Democratic Party, meant that the trade unions failed to profit politically from their inherent strength. The imbalances of industrial politics which had been evident before 1914 remained, so that the Weimar system had to be constructed on the assumption of continuing links between government and industry, and employers and unions, while industry and unions as interest groups themselves remained politically unrepresented.

Similar if less cataclysmic developments occurred in France. In spite of the 1914 political truce, the *Union Sacrée*, and the expressed willingness of Socialist and trade union leaders to cooperate in the war effort, successive governments betrayed an incapacity to impose on employers or industrial workers the full rigours of war taxation or rationing. After the initial loss of territory to Germany, French industry expanded rapidly, but because of its partial dependence on British loans and munitions supplies, and the divisions of control between departments, the government feared to tamper with the political balance. The sacrifices fell heaviest on agricultural areas which, in addition to providing France's food supply, had to find nearly half the levies to meet inordinate demands for manpower at the Front. After the collapse of General Nivelle's vaunted offensive on the Chemin des Dames in 1917, and the traumatic effect of the defence of Verdun (where more than two-thirds of the French army served at one time or another), came mutinies, unrest in rural areas, and demands that Britain should take over more of the line. The civilian government disintegrated after the quarrel between General Lyautey, Minister of War, with the Assembly, just as the *Union Sacrée* came to an end. The SFIO (Socialist Party) withdrew from government, avoiding implication in the political scandals of 1917–18, and took correspondingly no part in the 'stern Jacobin dictatorship' of Clemenceau. Pétain's military recovery, and the final patriotic outburst which Clemenceau helped to inspire after March 1918, carried France through to the Armistice; but profound anti-war sentiment showed itself in the support for Alphonse Merrheim and the abortive Zimmerwald Conference and the minority Socialist group's participation at the Stockholm Conference.

During the war the main union, the *Confédération Générale du Travail* (CGT) increased its bargaining power and its militancy. Post-war inflation, bureaucratic incompetence over demobilisation, all the difficulties of the reconstruction period, and the traditional suspicion of government, combined to inflate the reputation and size of the radical wing and that of the French Socialist Party. Immense strikes in 1919 led to fighting with police, and the 1920 railway strike came very close to realising the syndicalist dream of a climactic general strike; yet when the radicals failed to win parliamentary power in the election of November 1919 the reorganised employers mounted a successful counter-attack, with government support, and the aid of masses of blacklegs seeking job security. The *patronat* won, and as a result contributed to the secession of the Socialist Left in December 1920 and its affiliation to the Third International. For a time the CGT seemed closer to the new Communist Party but eventually it turned back with Léon Blum and the remainder of the SFIO; but even this Socialist–CGT grouping proved unable, and perhaps unwilling, to create a political relationship with the State in the sense that the Labour movement had achieved this in Britain by 1917; and after 1920 the CGT turned to *réorganisation économique*, and direct bargaining with individual employers and the *patronat*.

In France, as in Germany, big business emerged from the war with its influence over government enhanced, and the trade union movement lost its earlier degree of unified political representation. The parliamentary system in both countries had ceased to correspond to the politics of the real nation. Only in England did state, industry and labour movement successfully engage in the political dance outside as well as inside the traditional arena. This disharmony, as much as the example of the Russian Revolution, caused powerful Communist parties to emerge across Europe to challenge the strategy and legitimacy of the Socialist parties, dividing trade union movements themselves and ensuring that for nearly forty years European political systems would develop on different lines from that of Britain.

In reacting against the threat of revolution, to the extent of modifying ancient preoccupations about the political system, Britain developed its own distinctive form of triangular collaboration in the industrial sphere, between government, trade unions and the business class, just as in the field of parliamentary politics the Labour Party grew harmoniously to rival Conservatives and supersede the Liberals. Given the similarity of industrial experience and structural change in these three countries in wartime, the contrast between political stability on one hand, and instability and class conflict on the other, cannot be ascribed wholly to social or economic differentiation, and must be explained by developments in the political system, consciously willed and brought about.

During the formative years after the war when the patterns of political activity were set for the next decade, the recreation of stability in Britain depended on three closely integrated factors: emergence of powerful institutions enmeshed with political parties, on both sides of industry; deliberate choice by majority working-class organisations to work within the parliamentary political sphere; and successive governments' success in isolating the revolutionary movement. But in searching for a formal pattern of class cooperation, alternative to the inadequacies of European systems, the post-war Coalition Cabinet was confronted by a bewildering range of assessments about working-class opinion.

Although the decision had been taken to confer adult suffrage on all men and women over thirty as part of the wartime social pact, the vote could only serve as a preliminary. The predictable results of jingoistic propaganda in the 1918 Election scarcely answered the alarming question, rooted in previous discontent, of whether the trade union movement would abandon the generally 'constitutional' stand of the TUC or follow the shop stewards in a steadily more hostile and Marxist-inspired tide of radical demands. What the Shop Stewards' Movement signified

123

could not be answered as easily as questions about the position of the Labour Party in 1918, at a time when the Government could scarcely envisage the inhibiting effect of later mass unemployment.

Challenged by both TUC and Labour Party, the Shop Stewards' Movement had succeeded better than either in remedying certain basic working-class grievances; to contemporaries, the fact that the wage rates index came near to catching up with the cost of living in 1919 appeared largely to their credit, even if it actually derived from the work of Triple Alliance and TUC, and from the subsequent collapse of prices.* Drawing immense credit from their resistance to the war, BSP and SLP men like William Gallacher, A. McManus and J. T. Murphy, and the martyr-like figure of John Maclean, gave a sort of vivid unity to the movement which was, however, confused by the fact that in less publicised areas – on the railways and in textiles – shop stewards' leaders tended to be Labour Party members with greater influence in local government. Consequently many Trades Councils (which, in spite of the new local Labour Party organisations, still functioned as regional centres for the Labour movement) divided in their understanding of 'political' questions; at the same time, although shop stewards' activity tended to conform to patterns of particular industries, sections of large unions sometimes diverged. Thus railwaymen in Barrow considered joining the debilitated Shop Stewards' Movement as late as 1919 and textile workers retained an SSM link via the Herald League. Further complications in industrial allegiances followed the creation of the Communist Party – whose hustling tactics after 1921 produced political fusion and isolation of non-conformists in almost equal proportions.

Coalition Ministers tended, not unreasonably, to equate militancy with shop stewards and thus confuse the SSM with the Triple Alliance, identifying demands for workers' control or nationalisation with political ideology rather than contemporary strategy or habitual behaviour.[3] In fact, operating under a government control which could hardly be indefinitely prolonged, Triple Alliance leaders faced restoration of the authority of Railway Companies, transport employers and the Mineowners' Association, each of whom had a long record of anti-union prejudice to sustain their professed intention of reducing the higher wages won during the wartime emergency. For these unions, nationalisa-

*	1914	1916	1917	1918	1919	1920	1921	1922	1923
Cost of living index	63.6	91.3	113.9	130.1	140.8	170.9	126.8	115.0	112.8
Money wage rate index	52	61.0	72.0	93	121	162	130	101	100
(1930 = 100)									

(A. H. Halsey, *Trends in British Society*, tables 4.10 and 4.11.)

tion represented not only a principle (invoked at every Miners' Federation and National Union of Railwaymen Conference since 1911) but a practical means of safeguarding existing conditions* – a powerful argument which not only differentiated the Triple Alliance from the main concentration of shop stewards in engineering and shipbuilding (whose activity was soon cut back by heavy unemployment, with the decline of government munitions work) but also attracted support elsewhere across industry as a reliable means of enforcing minimum wages and conditions.†

At the time of the Industrial Unrest Commissions in 1917, government strategy had been based on the assumption that dissatisfaction and revolutionary subversion could be separated by careful inquiry. But in peacetime, it often became as difficult to generalise about the relationship between union officials and shop stewards as it was to distinguish the aims of TUC and Triple Alliance, because of diversity of practice in different industries and areas. During the forty-hour strike in Glasgow in 1919, official and unofficial members of the strike committee appeared indistinguishable; on the other hand, the fact that shop stewards had taken over many wartime functions, in engineering,‡ and attempted to capture important union positions in the NUR, gave leaders of the older generation like J. H. Thomas, R. Smillie and Tom Mann a severe (and in the case of G. N. Barnes, fatal) jolt. Those who took their places in the early 1920s, like Ernest Bevin, Walter Citrine, Harry Gosling and Arthur Pugh tended to work for a powerful, representative TUC, to the detriment both of the Triple Alliance and the Shop Stewards' Movement.

Recognition of the shop stewards' 'rights' (which Lloyd George urged on the Engineers' leaders during the Coventry and Birmingham strikes) had been given with extreme reluctance, and Dr Addison was

---

*J. T. Murphy described nationalisation, in retrospect, as 'a partisan effort to improve the position of Labour in the present, and ultimately assist in the abolition of the wage system'. (*Preparing for Power: a critical study of the history of the working-class movement*, Cape 1934, pp. 145–6.) Nationalisation also, of course, served as a defence against immediate redundancy in the face of lower requirements for coal and transport, and reviving European competition.

†In 1919–20, demands grew in the textile industry for an inquiry comparable to Sankey, to be followed by nationalisation, shorter hours, a guaranteed week, full employment, and wholesale unionisation. Among NUR branches, nationalisation was seen as the best way to enforce the closed shop (McGuire, *op. cit.*).

‡Where District Committees of the ASE often took the lead in setting up Shop Committees 'not to agitate or encourage friction or bad feeling between employer and employee, but rather to secure and maintain a good understanding between them' – as the President of the Leicester Committee put it in October 1917. (EEF Papers, Allan Smith Correspondence, 3 April 1919.)

probably right to conclude that the TUC had 'delighted' in the arrests after the 1917 May strikes. During the 1918 railway strike the NUR had plagiarised SSM proposals, while the TU Advisory Committee willingly propagated Churchill's threat to conscript strike leaders. Trade unionists, like their Labour Party colleagues, feared rather than welcomed the tide of popular democracy, especially when couched in anti-authoritarian terms. 'Vigilance Committees [railway equivalents of the shop floor committees] are not subservient to the rules and constitutions of the unions,' Edwards of the NUR wrote in March 1918. 'Their hands are free and unfettered. The only people they are responsible to are their constituents. Vigilance committees cannot go wrong; because they are formed on the basis of branch representation, they are simply a reflex of the district.'[4]

The adoption of an electoral majority strategy led necessarily to subordination of the Left, whether in the party or trade union movement; a marginalising process which can be seen equally in Henderson's denunciation of the SSM at the 1917 Labour Party Conference and the joint TUC-Labour Party attack on dissident Councils of Action in 1920 (below, p. 167). In so far as Lloyd George and his colleagues understood what was going on, the behaviour of individuals tended to reinforce the assumption that bargaining with a centralised parliamentary Labour movement was preferable to haphazard negotiations with unrepresentative factions.

In the two years after the war, however, the questions of nationalisation and workers' control outgrew their industrial context, to be debated by mentors of the Labour Party like R. H. Tawney (in *The Acquisitive Society*, 1920), G. D. H. Cole, or among influential policy advisers like J. J. Astor's Romney Street Group.[5] More important, patterns of industrial politics began to reflect the profound change which had occurred since 1914 in the composition of the trade union movement. Average figures disguise the fact that wages of unskilled men in wartime had risen markedly against those of skilled artisans.* Composition of all the regional wage differences which had been allowed to creep in after 1916, coming on top of dilution by female and unskilled labour, the loss of trade cards, and erosion of traditional differentials, created a relatively affluent class of semi-skilled workers towards whom many skilled men felt bitterness, mixed with the fear that government would continue to take advantage of them, not only in promoting scientific management,

---

*In building, 1914–18, labourers' wages rose threefold, bricklayers' $2\frac{1}{2}$ times. An engineering labourer getting only 50 per cent of a skilled fitter's wage in 1914, got 76 per cent in 1917, 80 per cent in 1920.

workshop discipline and time-keeping on the American model, but by altering the assumptions on which industrial differentials depended. As Stephenson Kent told Churchill in 1918,

the vaunted skill of the mechanic can be much more easily acquired than the mechanic had given the world to believe . . . the great number of dilutees who are capable of carrying on, from the employers' point of view, lessens the indispensability of the skilled mechanic.[6]

Skilled engineers already on the edge of unemployment might not necessarily turn to the more extreme fringes of the SSM, even when they felt that the TUC had failed them; but they had strong reason to make common cause with mass, unskilled unions: and to subscribe to the direct-action techniques of the Triple Alliance which they had tended to reject before 1912. In the same way, the disdain for militancy which the white-collar workers had once evinced, vanished, as railway and bank clerks, policemen and even civil servants, pressed for affiliation to the TUC.[7] Real rivalry existed within the trade union movement, not in some vague rhetorical sphere, but over the immediate and sensitive matter of restoration of trade union privileges and restrictive practices, and the campaign to sustain, and where possible improve on, the wages and conditions achieved in wartime; and the fact that majority demands came to be couched more and more in terms of nationalisation imposed a dual strain on the government, blurring the once simple distinction between responsible and revolutionary activity, and raising irreconcilable hostility among employers' federations, threatened with government expropriation.

With some justification, employers had watched in alarm the mass of competing, unrelated wage settlements handed down by different Ministers in the last months of the war. Yet the more farsighted of them had accepted an enormous extension of trade union functions – and even shop stewards' committees – in a way inconceivable in 1914. The stability of the political system in the 'revolutionary years' 1919–20 owes something to the majority who, unacknowledged by historians, had come to accept the Ministry of Labour view that formal sanctions against strikers, and non-recognition, had been proved unworkable as well as unacceptable. A hard-headed leader of the Engineers' Federation like Allan Smith, who sometimes referred to trade unionists as 'the enemy',[8] and had no intention of allowing the 'right to manage' to lapse,[9] could tell Vincent Caillard that shop stewards must be recognised, partly to support the official union hierarchy, and partly because they enjoyed *de facto* power;[10] and a very wide acceptance of the need for a new system of industrial relations among employers must be set against the better-known, splenetic opinions of mineowners and railway directors, facing nationalisation.

A functional distinction not unlike the pre-war division between the League and the Association of German Employers has to be made between the behaviour of Federations in declining, staple industries and those in expanding, capital-intensive industries like motor cars and lorries, chemicals, electrical and civil engineering. In the depressed industries, such as mining, shipbuilding, textiles and heavy engineering, where wage-cutting became standard practice after 1920, each federation tended to act on the lowest common denominator of cautious hostility towards unions, and liberal mineowners like David Davies or Alfred Mond found themselves submerged, in tripartite negotiations, by the hard-line, narrow-minded Adam Nimmo and Evan Williams. The ideology of class conflict complemented economic decline and cooperative ideas survived only where prosperity allowed.

Effective proposals for industrial concord came, not so much from practical experience of joint boards, or Lord Robert Cecil's concept of 'co-partnership' and the examples of Quaker business families like the Rowntrees and Cadburys, or even from the old National Association of Employers and Employed (always very much a front for the operations of the Engineering Employers),[11] but from employers' confederations themselves. Ever since the mid-war crisis, the EEF had taken a realistic attitude, recognising power where it existed, even in shop stewards' committees, but combining this with an unyielding insistence on productivity of labour and the sanctity of employers' profits. Admission of trade union strength never encouraged emulation of the supposed 'softness' of the Federation of British Industries, formed in 1916, against whose relative tolerance* the EEF campaigned – ultimately to the extent of founding the National Confederation of Employers' Organisations (NCEO), in 1919, with a far more 'political' constitution; but it provided a better ground for bargaining than had existed before the war.[12] The FBI itself put up a scheme for a 'welfare state' to be run jointly by employers and unions, in which the latter were required to make concessions on productivity and over-manning,[13] and carefully tried to dispel the suspicion that Lloyd George had conceded them industrial hegemony.[14]

At the level of public debate, propaganda often supervened. Thomas Jones recorded a group of employers 'prophesying into Bonar Law's

*Until deterred by the EEF in 1918, the FBI gave quite wide approval to the institution of workshop committees in the munitions industry.

ear the commercial downfall of the country if superior beings like stationmasters and inferior beings like booking clerks were allowed to meet on the same (Union) platform',[15] but the view that shop-floor workers could be a stabilising influence can be found, for example, in trade periodicals. 'When an intelligent worker sits with his employer in council, he will soon come to measure his demands by a new standard', the *Engineering Review* declared in 1917, a judgment confirmed by a Ministry of Munitions inspector, citing the experience of Rolls-Royce at Derby: 'Extremists are sometimes elected as shop stewards [but] responsibility steadies them.'*

Borne along on this change of attitude, sustained by the reports of the Ministry of Labour, and over-optimistically putting aside the memory of the deportations and arrests in wartime, Ministers allowed themselves to suppose that an industrial concordat could be created in 1919 by methods broadly similar to those adopted in the later stages of the war – a belief sustained by the bulk of their information about working-class currents of opinion.

The quality of this information seemed greatly to have been improved. Since 1916, the traditional party agencies, Members of Parliament, Whips, agents and observers in the constituencies had been subjected to the critical demands of a central administration which had found itself frequently and embarrassingly out of touch; and in this more sensitive climate working-class opinion had measurably shaped munitions legislation, the various Manpower Bills, and even the declaration of war aims. Government methods had become less amateurish: even if Lloyd George relied heavily on the reports prepared, rather impressionistically, by Frederick Guest, the Liberal Chief Whip, and on individual contacts with MPs and editors like C. P. Scott of the *Manchester Guardian*, his private correspondence reflects the weight of industrial firms' intelligence about shop stewards' activities in their factories. More generally, the War Cabinet relied on wartime agencies of proven reliability, such as the Intelligence Department and regional conciliation officers of the Ministry of Labour and the home reports of Military Intelligence,† (many of whose reports were, in turn, relayed to Caillard and the

---

*Min. Labour, Industrial Reports No. 2, p. 57. He continued: 'it is only a matter of time for a National Council of Shop Stewards to enter the arena as a permanent factor in labour politics.'

†Lloyd George's statement about 'a very considerable and highly organised labour movement with seditious tendencies', for example, was derived from this source (WC 115/9, 6 April 1916). Later, in 1917–18, the Coalition government paid up to £1,000 a month to a variety of informants in return for the names of ex-servicemen, schoolmasters and others who might either provide information about subversive tendencies or help to counter them. (SM GD 194/389.)

National Association of Employers and Employed (NAEE).[16] The whole was supplemented by *ad hoc* inquiries such as the Industrial Unrest Commissions appointed by Lloyd George after the strikes of May 1917 had revealed the dual need to reassure public confidence in government and to win back the respect of the trade union movement.[17]

Never 'public' in the normal sense, the work of these Commissions had extended beyond immediate grievances into future planning. Each of the eight Commissions held between ten and thirty meetings and interviewed up to two hundred witnesses – a remarkable (and, judging from the lists, genuinely representative) coverage, which gave all the more weight to their findings that the main grievances, the cost of living and profiteering, followed by the effects of dilution, conscription and administrative incompetence, were largely justified:

The want of confidence is a fundamental cause, of which many of the causes given are manifestations. It shows itself in the feeling that there has been inequality of sacrifice, that the Government have broken solemn pledges, that trade union officials are no longer to be relied on, and that there is woeful uncertainty as to the future. The Reports abound with instances of the prevailing feeling that pledges are *no longer observed as they were in pre-war days*. Allusions to 'scraps of paper' are painfully numerous.[18]

The speed at which a standstill on prices was imposed and the $12\frac{1}{2}$ per cent wages increase granted, together with abolition of the leaving certificate, and the high priority given to housing by the new Ministry of Reconstruction, indicates how sensitive the War Cabinet was to public opinion,* as the Government set out to improve its propaganda, if only to counter what Barnes called 'the feeling in the minds of workers that their conditions of work and destinies are being determined by a distant authority over which they have no influence.' Recognition of the line leading from the Commissions to the Ministry of Reconstruction, to promises of the 'land fit for heroes', and to the extension of the franchise, is essential to an understanding of Lloyd George's vision of the future political contract. But much of the effectiveness of these enquiries into the public mind was nullified because of his instinctive reluctance to tackle profiteering and injustices which were, themselves, reflected in the political composition of the War Cabinet and the state administration;[19] and to avoid this contradiction, the government superimposed

*WC 190/1, 19 July 1917. 'The War Cabinet were much influenced by the recent reports of the Commissions, who attributed much of the prevailing unrest directly to high food prices. . . . For the vigorous prosecution of the war, a contented working class was indispensable.'

another means of persuasion, seeking by the manipulation of public opinion a basis of consent sufficient to create peace-time harmony.

Lloyd's George's own publicity apparatus, run by the caterpillars of his private commonwealth, A. J. Sylvester, W. Sutton, and William Sutherland, had been supplemented and extended in the era of Lord Beaverbrook and the Ministry of Information, often with equivocal results and in the face of continued parliamentary hostility. As once-effective stimuli to the public mind weakened (the failure of the 'Peace Loan' provided a notorious example of the diminishing value of the patriotic card), the War Cabinet began to rely more and more on techniques of mass persuasion, and found their work well-rewarded in a period credulous enough to swallow the latter-day extravagances of a Northcliffe or a Horatio Bottomley. From 1917 onwards, references in War Cabinet to the value and use of the press became more frequent, together with evidence that large sums of money were being laid out to purchase favourable publicity.[20] Auckland Geddes used to prime editors of London newspapers, either with explanations of broken pledges to the Engineers, or his colleagues' answers to British Socialist Party (BSP) propaganda.[21] From this, it was only a short distance to smearing the Coventry strikers as anti-patriotic; during the railway strike in September 1918, Stanley met the press 'confident that their attitude would be in complete accord with Government policy' – and editors duly inserted reports suggesting that ex-servicemen were happily volunteering for strike duty.[22]

The government clearly intended to create a public distinction between good and bad trade union behaviour, in advance of the bargaining over post-war reconstruction. Supposed abuses of unemployment insurance, the fears of small investors, and the great mass of residual middle-class hostility to working-class aspirations, were all utilised in 1918–19 in one of the most tendentious (if, in the European context, understandable) campaigns since that of Home Secretary Dundas in the 1790s. Tory Ministers Chamberlain and Horne, could be found consulting with the FBI on how to present more tactfully the bitter question of profiteering, and asking editors to show their patriotism 'by refraining from attacks on the capitalist class'.[23]

It is hard to exaggerate the intensity or scope of such propaganda or its resources. Because no central propaganda agency existed, at the time of the paralysing railway strikes in 1919, capable of doing what he required, Lloyd George turned to more secret ways, setting up, under Sutherland's aegis, with Horne and the Coalition Chief Whips, Lord Talbot, Captain Guest and his friend Lord Riddell, an organisation 'concerned with Anti-Bolshevism and Increased Production Propaganda' intended to incite public hostility against the trade unions and political Left wing, and to encourage 'constitutional' as opposed to direct action. Sidney Walton, a former undercover agent and government fugleman was appointed to run it, with a fund of £100,000[24] subscribed, not from government funds, but industrial sources, chiefly members of the Engineering Employers' Federation, headed by Sir Vincent Caillard.* Walton took the main propaganda role from a variety of front organisations, set up during the war, such as the British Empire League, the British Workers' League, the National Democratic and Labour Party, and the National Unity Movement, all of whom had been in receipt of industrial subscriptions, and his 'information service' fed, without any restriction from the Official Secrets Act, on the government's most private sources of information, Special Branch and Secret Intelligence services.[25] Down to 1922, the network expanded, with MPs and journalists on the pay-roll, and a variety of notables including even the Lord Chancellor, until Walton claimed to be able to put 'authoritative signed articles' in *over 1,200* newspapers. The effect was prodigious and, even allowing for exaggeration, its returns can hardly be ignored.

Against the use of such methods and the impact of alarmist comments from Caillard on tired and sometimes panicky Ministers, or the long series of 'Reports on Revolutionary Organisations in the United Kingdom' assiduously prepared by Sir Basil Thomson (ex-head of MI5) and Special Branch, moderate men like Thomas Jones protested in vain that 'Bolshevik propaganda in this country is only dangerous in so far as it can lodge itself in the soil of genuine grievances.'[26] Ministers did

*Guest, the Liberal Chief Whip, described the process rather disingenuously: 'there are grave objections to the employment of taxpayers' money for this purpose, as many members of the Labour Party could justly claim that their own money was being used to overcome their political creeds.' Hence he and Talbot turned to 'those to whom a peaceful settlement of industry is a vital consideration' (LG F21/4/10). Caillard actually objected to the presence of the Chief Whips, fearing to give Walton's organisation 'political colour', and threatened that 'he and his friends embracing the very largest interests in the country, would not act upon the committee' (BL 98/1/8). The employers later went on to form their own body, called 'National Propaganda', in January 1920, under the chairmanship of Lord Inchcape (shipbuilding) with Sir Allan Smith (engineering), Lord Gainford (coalmining), Sir Hugh Ball (iron and steel), Lord Desborough (landowners), and Caillard and Admiral Reginald Hall (ex-head of Naval Intelligence) on its Central Council (EEF P/13/4): its aims were almost identical, being to counter nationalisation, revolutionary and extremist activities, to safeguard private enterprise and promote increased production; and its budget was £250,000 – roughly the same as the costs for the Conservative Party of the whole 1923 election. It should be added that Admiral Hall managed to make an agreement with the Inland Revenue in July 1920 whereby all such subscriptions were to be allowed 'as a trade expense' in computing firms' liability for tax!

not exactly deceive themselves, but by creating a machine for surveillance they highlighted the things they feared. Morbidly aware of the European revolutionary context, already inclined to interpret working-class unrest as subversion, they aroused in advance that trade union suspicion which wrecked the National Industrial Conference in 1919, and worse, not only programmed themselves to define the Triple Alliance and shop stewards as extremist organisations, but then set out to destroy them in a manner which ensured the downfall of industrial relations' reconstruction and of the Coalition itself.

Given the social and political composition of the Coalition Cabinet, a grand design of working-class appeasement could not conceivably have outbid the Labour Party–TUC programme of 1918. Yet, as Lord Milner and the South Wales Industrial Unrest Commissioners argued, a distinction had to be made between 'justifiable unrest' and 'deliberate agitation';* and to meet the former the government had to introduce some belated restraint on profiteering, some form of workers' participation in industry. Significantly, he advocated a deliberate move towards all-union shops and all-employer federations. As Seebohm Rowntree put it, in 1920, 'We have come to regard many conditions as intolerable which before had only seemed inevitable. . . . We have completely revised our notions as to what is possible or impossible.'[27] But could those whom the government were predisposed to regard as Marxists, bent on the destruction of capitalism, be induced to accept some form of better industrial management and working conditions in place of nationalisation and workers' control? And could a cooperative structure within industry be set up which would allow government to disengage from its wartime responsibilities?

Lloyd George's *intentions* are well enough documented. Early in 1919, Tom Jones noticed how far he stood ahead of his colleagues:

Several were drawing rather long faces and piling up the financial bogey and the PM forced the Minister to tell him how much they could spend in the next twelve months. The bill came to £71 million. He then asked: 'Supposing the war had lasted another year, could we not have raised somehow or other another £2,000 million?' It was blank nonsense to talk of a bagatelle like £71 million – a cheap insurance against Bolshevism.[28]

*LG F/38/2/5. In August 1917 Milner circulated a paper by Professor Arnold of Bangor, which argued that 'labour in revolt' actually comprised the better-paid, younger artisans, of the old industrial heartland, South Wales, the Clyde, Manchester and Sheffield. (GT 1849 WC 226/13.) The same point was made eighteen months later by G. D. H. Cole in a somewhat tendentious appendix to an NIC report on labour unrest. (GT 7057, Cmd. 501, Appendix I, p. xi.)

Such insights, however, cannot answer the questions of whether the aim was simply to buy off trouble or to recreate the consensus of 1914; and whether Lloyd George's emerging corporatism could accommodate the demands of the enlarged working-class electorate – or whether the unresolved dilemma of the pre-war Liberal Radicals would curse the reconstruction programme of 1917–20.

In a very well-known speech in March 1917, Lloyd George had replied to Labour Party demands for nationalisation and the conscription of wealth with a promise: 'I believe the settlement after the war will succeed in proportion to its audacity.'[29] But however well-meaning the work of Addison's Reconstruction Ministry, and of advisory bodies or Civil Service conferences organised to discuss state control of industrial monopolies,[30] it signified little when set against a governing mentality which, in the long run, acceded to the crisis elements of 1919 – industrial unrest, international debts, chaotic European exchanges and financial exigency at home.

Lloyd George's last attempt to institute synoptic planning took place at a conference of Ministers and civil servants held at Criccieth in July 1919, when his economic adviser, Professor Chapman, outlined a plan for industry, with the emphasis on state-inspired efficiency and investment in technology. At that stage, the Prime Minister was prepared to entertain such radical proposals as abandoning support of the exchange rate, fostering new industries, protection against foreign dumping, state investment in weak but essential industries like iron and steel, and control over electricity generation, standardisation and industrial research.[31] But what might have been the intellectual foundations of state capitalism in the early 1920s produced nothing beyond the abortive Electricity Bill of 1919 and two far-sighted but misused Acts governing Trade Facilities and Safeguarding of Industries.

On the political side, it is clear that Lloyd George understood that all the great questions of popular consent ran parallel to the lines of industrial politics. From Asquith's first tentative admission in 1916 that the vote would have to be granted to war-workers, to his later admission (February 1917) that a post-war Parliament must have 'a moral authority which you cannot obtain from what I may call a scratch, improvised and makeshift electorate',[32] to the final withdrawal of property qualifications in 1918, the history of suffrage extension confirms the relationship between working-class participation in the war and full political rights. More, the ambitious provisions of the 1918 Education Act suggest that, until the subsequent economy campaign, the state had accepted its duty to train citizens by public education to be equal alike to the demands of democracy and modern industry.* Educationalists like Tawney and Haldane even suggested that education should be seen as a twenty-year investment by the state: but such dreams fell to the exigencies of finance and the sheer inspissated ignorance and lack of concern on the parliamentary backbenches and in the town halls – a greater failure perhaps than the collapse of the over-ambitious, under-planned housing programme, which is usually taken as the measure of the failure of reconstruction.[33]

Yet housing is a fair indication of how financial interests were allowed to override reform. Although in the early days Bonar Law declared: 'If we did not make any effort to improve the conditions of the people, we should have a sullen, discontented and perhaps angry nation, which would be fatal in the last degree to trade, industry and credit',[34] the abandonment of building controls and of the whole state venture into housing followed naturally the priority given to preserving 'business confidence' and placating the business community in the supposed interests of industrial peace. Occasionally the government might stand up to 'a most extreme thing' (as Auckland Geddes called an FBI proposal that the state should compensate employers for *all* their wartime losses[35]) but it failed continually – despite all evidence from the Committee on Trusts – to check suppliers' price-fixing or manufacturers' and contractors' profiteering. Even the array of state munitions and aircraft factories, like the vast armaments complex at Gretna, was never used to produce building components because the Ministry of Munitions advised against alienating private industry.[36] Some levels of the state apparatus even sought constructively to build up employers' power, fearing that wartime circumstances had eroded its former superiority over the TUC.†

Partiality towards the business and banking community cannot wholly be explained either by civil servants' hopes of encouraging a trade revival or by Lloyd George's personal predilections, and must be blamed also on persistent Treasury advice that government should

*Haldane originally envisaged an enormous extension of secondary and further education including at least six hours a week, part-time, in day classes, for 14–17 year olds, together with new forms of technical instruction, and a reform of university fee structures to allow more working-class entrants. 'The Universities, like the Technical Schools, have been too little concerned with the industrial and commercial life of the country and too ignorant of the needs of the schools from which their students are drawn.' (TJ D1, 16 November 1916.) The words have a contemporary ring.

†I. Mitchell and Shackleton, 5 March 1918, speaking of the munitions industry, but by implication of employers as a whole. 'Consideration should be given to ascertaining whether an active opposition from the employers could not by some means be restored.' (LAB 2/228/A/486/18 quoted in McGuire, op. cit.)

disengage as rapidly as possible from its temporary industrial commitments. Lloyd George's ultimate failure to sustain the expectations of a large enough number of Liberal and Labour voters to keep the Coalition alive was foreshadowed by his failure to rally the Cabinet majority against FBI demands for *relaxation* of the excess profits tax in January 1918, and the fact that, of 4,000 complaints against profiteering in these years, only twenty-one came to court before 1921.[37]

It could hardly be denied that profiteering offended enormous numbers of working-class voters;[38] and in spite of Lloyd George's professed willingness to listen to the long-vested hopes of miners, railwaymen and transport workers and other unions, seeking to safeguard wartime benefits, the inability to carry any scheme of nationalisation suggests that the decision had been taken on grounds conforming to the party political balance of the Cabinet, and Treasury advice to abandon controls and leave industry to solve its own problems. Before the Sankey Commission on the coal industry was appointed in February 1919, Bonar Law took the field against a proposal by Horne, Minister of Labour, for government to discuss with the miners' union hours of work and nationalisation. Primed by the coalowners, Law suggested an 'appeal to public opinion' on the grounds that miners should not be given advantage at the expense of other trades; and Lloyd George backed him up: 'We will have to settle these immediate disputes [in the mines], and if we cannot, we shall have to fight the thing through. It may be a good thing, because labour is getting unreasonable in some respects.'[39]

Such statements vitiated in advance the Sankey Commission's brief resurrection of the hopes of 1917. But Horne (who was principally responsible for setting up the Commission) and Geddes also believed that Sankey would enunciate 'the basis on which the workers should participate in the control of conditions governing industrial life',[40] and it seems possible that, in addition to undermining the more extreme MFGB positions, the Cabinet hoped for a compromise over wages and conditions, falling short of actual nationalisation; which could later be extended to other industries,* thereby uniting moderates among employers and employed. Lloyd George and Bonar Law seem to have been agreed on seeking the growth of industrial institutions, interlinked under the general auspices of government conciliation procedures,

*WC 548/1. This fits with the Cabinet's acceptance of Sankey's interim report, in March 1919, containing recommendations for wage increases and the seven-hour day, and its effective postponement of debate on the main principle of nationalisation until July – by which time it was politically too late to implement. For a full discussion of the question see M. W. Kirby, *The British Coalmining Industry 1870–1946*, pp. 35–47.

buoyed up by increased productivity from the relaxation of restrictive practices and prosperity flowing from government-inspired techno- logical change* and trade facilities – a programme to some extent fore- shadowing that of the state corporatists of the 1930s.

A diverse but not unimportant range of supporters might have been found among Lord Robert Cecil's 'centre party' group, or the elder statesmen Balfour, Haldane and Lord Esher, accompanied by the whole scientific lobby, its political voice enhanced by wartime technological demands; and from such mixtures of civil servants, industrialists and academics as attended the Conference of Industrial Reconstruction Associations at Balliol in October 1919;[41] or the officials of the Board of Trade, who argued the case in terms of post-war economic policy,[42] and the small group of trade unionists who had been sucked up into the Lloyd George *apparat*, Stephen Welsh, a mining MP, Victor Fisher (ex-SDF), and Seddon of the British Workers National League.† But, quite simply, the economic recovery outlined at Criccieth failed. Standardisation, government research, safeguarding and trade facilities turned out to be very long-term investments. 'Rationalisation' in the later twenties and recovery in the mid-thirties rather than the Coalition's industrial policy were to benefit from what had been done. Harmony came therefore to depend on political expedients, the institution of Whitley Councils and the National Industrial Conference.

Originating in the Reconstruction sub-committee chaired by the Deputy Speaker, J. H. Whitley, in mid-1917, Whitley Councils, com- posed of representatives of employers and workers in each industry, were intended to discuss everything – not just wages and conditions, but participation, job security, technical education, and improvement of management – 'affecting the progress and well-being of the trade from the point of view of those engaged in it, as far as this is consonant with the general interest of the community'. Whitley certainly fitted with the long-term intention of successive Ministers of Labour to develop volun- tary arbitration agreements, codified and supervised by their depart- mental staff.[43] What Askwith had been striving for since 1911 had already been put on a formal basis with the creation of the Arbitra- tion Department in November 1918 and the national integration of

*Not however to the extent of interference: to the despair of the British Association and the growing sector of radical opinion among scientists, government's powers over DSIR were relaxed at the end of the war, while the £1 million research fund set up in June 1917 was administered in such a way as to encourage the self-help of employers rather than 'chaining them to government administration'.

†A group of younger Conservatives, with the approval of Neville Chamberlain and Milner, made overtures to the BWNL, and planned for an electoral pact with what they called the 'patriotic section' of the Labour Party (SM GD 193/99/2).

Conciliation Officers' work.* This in turn rested on the considerable degree of trust built up by officials amongst trade unions and employers over the preceding decade.

Unfortunately, the Councils received a rather lukewarm reception. The FBI appeared pleased that government was to withdraw from the field; but the TUC reacted uncertainly, and the most highly organised unions positively damned them, as a stratagem to circumvent collective bargaining: 'a complete identity of interests between capital and labour cannot thus be effected'.[44] The Government may not have expected more at that stage, and although the declining rate of instituting them seemed depressing,† it was argued that by 1921 $3\frac{1}{2}$ million workers had come within the Councils' scope. Within Whitehall the new framework of arbitration did much to reinforce the Ministry of Labour's work and defend it against the attacks of other Departments like the Board of Trade and Home Office, seeking the restoration of powers lost during the war.

Some of the blame may be put on Horne's reluctance to do more than exhort both sides to organise, though Whitley's first report had declared that the Councils' aims of higher production and enhanced status for labour 'can best be obtained by continuous cooperation between employers and employed in each industry, with the minimum of government interference'.[45] Ideological bias prevented more: in spite of pressure from within the Ministry of Labour, the Cabinet baulked at instituting local Labour Courts on the pattern developed in Germany after the war. A fair degree of consensus could be found in government, uniting Lloyd George, Bonar Law, the younger Conservatives and the senior civil servants of the Ministry of Labour, but only for the anodyne proposition, as Horne put it, that his Department should be seen as 'the Ministry of Munitions for Peace'. Defending it against the Geddes Committee economy cuts of 1921, he argued that Whitleyism and Labour conciliation now constituted the 'normal' mode of dealing with industrial disputes, and hence ranked with any other measure of social reform: 'It is not in the direction of repressing well-earned and promised assistance to men who have fought and

*Sadly for Askwith himself, industrial relations had become too central a preoccupation for government to suffer the foibles of one acerbic individual. Askwith was, in effect, dismissed by Lloyd George in order to give Horne a freer hand than Roberts had had. His reward was a peerage; and from the Lords he continued his jeremiads about the 'degradation of government' as Lloyd George wrangled with the railwaymen in 1919.

†Twenty were set up in 1918, 32 in 1919, 16 in 1920 and only 6 in 1921 – a tapering off explained by the fact that they worked well only in smaller industries, the Civil Service and local government.

suffered, that the public will expect economy'.[46] But in all abnormal situations, when the political element in big strikes surfaced, Horne had to concede the right of Prime Minister or Cabinet to intervene.[47] In that sense, nothing had changed since 1915; Ministers remained too jealous of power and too responsive to party pressures to allow the 'neutral' experts and the departmental machinery to supersede them.

Nevertheless, the Cabinet made one further essay in search of an industrial concordat. The National Industrial Conference originated in September 1917 as part of the discussion between Milner, Barnes and Roberts, about the growing political element in wartime strikes.[48] Roberts put to Cabinet a report on the employers' and unions' attitude towards Whitley, written after a careful survey of opinion in the press and industry,[49] which, taken together with the Industrial Unrest reports, suggested that the absence of workers' participation in the running of industry was a major cause of discontent. Recognising the need for both sides to be formally organised to a degree never envisaged by government before the war, and wishing to avoid overburdening Whitley Councils, Roberts promoted the idea of a national conference – supported by a quite remarkable propaganda effort during 1918, at home, and in France among the armed forces, setting out, among fairly obvious benefits like job security, now fashionable catch-phrases about technical training and technology, and advocating the complete collectivisation of industrial relations so that all employers and workmen should belong to closed shops.

Because the first post-war Conference led to a temporary moratorium on wartime wages and a measure of agreement on the restoration of trade union privileges, much political capital was subsequently invested in the idea. Many larger industries like cotton and shipbuilding already possessed joint boards; if smaller businesses and government and municipal service could be left to Whitley Councils, then something on the lines of an industrial parliament might satisfy the requirements of the highly unionised coal, iron and steel, railways and engineering sectors which remained. Horace Wilson of the Ministry of Labour, Horne and Auckland Geddes took this line early in 1919,[50] supported by the NAEE (acting on instructions from Lloyd George and Caillard); while the FBI made overtures to the TUC, asking for collaboration in advising government on trade questions at the Paris Peace Conference. The TUC hesitated at first but consented when pressed by Horne, and on 27 February the National Industrial Conference began.

Eight hundred delegates listened to Lloyd George's optimistic opening address, but in spite of the Prime Minister's bland hopes, many union leaders issued uncompromising statements; worst of all, the Triple Alliance and the ASE refused to attend. After recommending the setting up of a permanent NIC of 400 elected members, with a small steering committee to coordinate industrial relations and advise government generally on industrial matters, the Conference's momentum diminished, not least because its first report favoured two of the employers' *bêtes noires*, the forty-eight-hour week (following the 1919 Washington Convention) and the minimum wage. Lloyd George returned to Paris, and under the baneful influence of FBI and the financial crisis the recommendations foundered. When the Conference finally dissolved itself two years later, its three joint chairmen had good reason to protest that government had let them down.

Ernest Bevin claimed that the Conference had been merely another stratagem to divert trade unions from the struggle for better working conditions. Others have seen it as a corporatist attempt to introduce an alternative to Parliament itself. From preliminary Cabinet discussions it seems clear that it was intended to be a discussion forum for bodies fully representative of both sides of industry (which TUC and FBI could not then and never did claim to be) and 'the normal channel through which the opinion and experience of industry will be sought'. Beforehand, Lloyd George and Horne certainly made efforts to carry both FBI and the main body of Conservative opinion against Bonar Law's initial hesitancy.[51] Explaining the Prime Minister's despondency, Horace Wilson considered that 'he set very great store by it, and subsequently he never trusted those unions which had done so much to undermine it'.[52] Lloyd George had hoped that, given NIC, Ministry of Labour and Whitley, the State could draw back from the field occupied in wartime, leaving industry largely to govern itself. But having discovered the advantages of state intervention, neither side would let government do so, except at the price of concessions on wage-cutting or nationalisation which government politically could not afford. The invitation to industrial self-government resembled in a way the first Liberal proposal of 1906 to make trade unions a legally responsible estate. Like that, it was rejected – by both sides – and when the TUC or individual unions later proposed their own systems, the employers remained silent and passed responsibility on to Cabinet – just as the TUC was to try and do in the mineowners' lockout which precipitated the General Strike.

Lloyd George's design to raise up representative institutions, or estates, capable of resolving major industrial problems among themselves and of meeting government on political questions in the manner of corporations addressing themselves to the Crown, is the first overt attempt to create a formal, triangular relationship and utilise the tendency referred to here as 'corporate bias'. It failed, not just because of the aloofness of certain unions – whom Lloyd George then blamed – but also because the employers' openness and goodwill in public[53] and their collective understanding that a strong TUC was the best defence against rank and file indiscipline, were belied by their private acts, as industrial federations. The propaganda attack which government and employers subsequently directed against the Triple Alliance can also be seen as evidence that the NIC had been nothing but an elaborate charade designed to isolate those three unions from the rest of the movement; while the subsequent decline in the power of the Ministry of Labour, in the years 1920–5, and in the numbers of Whitley Councils, argue a lack of will in Cabinet to keep alive the spirit which the NIC had shown.

Interesting as these developments are in the context of the more permanent triangular harmony of the late 1920s, they did not much affect the main issues of 1919–20 which were settled by power-bargaining. In default of a new industrial concordat based on nationalisation, increasing prosperity, or contractual machinery, the government was forced back – albeit temporarily – on the brokerage between interest groups which had characterised the latter half of the war. Accepting reluctantly that the mass of overlapping wage settlements and claims in 1919 could not be resolved by Whitleyism because the main unions simply would not abandon collective bargaining, and that the outright constraints of wartime legislation could not be recreated, they had to rely on attrition, as economic circumstances weakened the militancy of certain unions like the railway clerks and white-collar workers after 1920 (most of whom then set up Whitley Councils which lasted for forty years, into the very different conditions of the 1960s). Elsewhere, the battles over restoration of trade union privileges and safeguarding or increases of wages reduced the government's aims to what was possible rather than what had seemed desirable in the flush of reconstruction, and set the pattern for the multiple realignments of political and industrial power down to 1922.

Even if, as they were forced to admit in private, the TUC had kept no proper record of the privileges surrendered in 1915,[54] they wanted restoration of collective bargaining, not in the pre-war sense, but on the basis of national agreements, nationally binding. This was bound to conflict with the rooted unwillingness of coal owners in particular to concede national wage negotiation terms; and certain members of the Cabinet, seeing a chance to break out of the vicious circle of competitive demands based on comparability and ancient differentials, challenged the doctrine that government was bound by its wartime pledge.

In October 1918 Churchill began to argue that the war emergency and conscription had altered the fundamental obligations of citizenship. Restoration of union privileges would work to the detriment of women and revive pre-war class confrontation;[55] and he attacked the Restrictive Practices Bill in words that might have been culled from Adam Smith: 'it would entrench a number of small and close corporations in restraint of trade.'[56] In echoing the nineteenth-century Constitution, he found support from the representatives of big business, Lord Rothermere and Lord Weir (who saw the idea as a means of increasing production, a sophisticated form of Taylorism) and a handful of high Tories around Austen Chamberlain. Against him were ranged Sir A. Stanley (Board of Trade), Horne, Roberts, Addison and Shackleton, all in fact who had direct dealings with the unions: 'The broad fact remains that whatever legal limitations may be placed on these promises, [they] were made in the hour of need . . . and have a definite and concrete meaning in the mind of the working class, which if not redeemed will be a source of grave trouble after the war'.[57]

On his return from France in November 1918 Lloyd George at first took Churchill's side but was later overborne by the weight of majority opinion and the likelihood that a refusal would only weaken trade union officials in the face of the shop stewards' movement.[58] The immediate outcome of restoration, however, justified Churchill's fear of a wave of strikes like 1911 and his mordant prediction that female employment would suffer as a result. Trade unions ignored the wartime expectations of most female and many unskilled workers who had taken the places of dilutees, and their understandable but ungenerous haste to restore male skilled employment on pre-war ratios set back for years the standards briefly achieved in low-paid and casual labour industries, to say nothing of the cause of equal pay, which Lloyd George and Churchill had shown some inclination to adopt.[59]

Surveying the chaos of overlapping wage claims, industrial disputes on the railways, among electricians and even in the Navy, at the end of September 1918 the War Cabinet decided to set up a committee to coordinate anti-strike activity. But their resolution soon wavered; when trouble erupted on the railways in December over the perennial demand for an eight-hour day, Lloyd George had to concede 'that it was a question, not whether the men could stand the strain of a longer day, but that the working class were entitled to the same sort of leisure as the middle class. The demand was for more human conditions . . . and it was a demand which, in view of public opinion, it would be difficult to resist.'[60] At a cost of £25 million a year, and fearful of similar claims elsewhere, the Cabinet gave way to 'public opinion'; and when the miners voted 6 to 1 in favour of a national strike for the six-hour day, nationalisation and 30 per cent wage increases, they stalled desperately with the expedient of a Royal Commission.

It was not safe to assume, however, that the government had conceded popular representation to the trade union movement. Lloyd George prudently avoided an immediate showdown with the miners; and Bonar Law warned the King that emergency conditions no longer applied: 'the struggle between workers and men will now have to be settled by arbitration or possibly public opinion'.[61] But just as he had bought time in South Wales in 1915 to turn on the munitions' shop stewards in Glasgow, Lloyd George used the miners' acceptance of the Sankey Commission as a reason for refusing to negotiate with the Clyde Workers' Committee (over the heads of ASE and shipbuilding officials) in the Forty-hour strike in the West of Scotland and Belfast in January 1919. As Austen Chamberlain pointed out, the government would no longer give in to blackmail:

Unfortunately in recent years there had been an increasing reliance placed on government as the ultimate arbiter in labour disputes, with the result that strikes were prolonged by the fact that neither side would say the least word as to what they were prepared to concede, as they expected the government to be called in at any moment.[62]

Law sent a curt telegram to the Lord Provost of Glasgow, refusing government intervention, and in a blunt repetition of wartime repression, troops and tanks occupied the city after a riot in George Square.

Evidence of a dual strategy of kicks for 'extremists' and kindness for 'responsible' workers can be found in the contrast between the Clyde Workers' Committee leaders' subsequent trial for sedition and Ministers' almost fervid desire to build up the status of the TUC. During the railway clerks' strike in February 1919 Churchill declared:

Trade union organisation was very important, and the more moderate its officials were, the less representative it was; but it was the only organisation with which the Government could deal. The curse of trade unionism was that *there was not enough of it*, and it was not highly enough developed to make its branch secretaries fall into line with the head office. With a powerful trade union, either peace or war could be made.[63]

Law went further, in a judgment remarkable for a Conservative leader: 'Trade union organisation was the only thing between us and anarchy.'[64]

Such acknowledgments should be distinguished from the Cabinet's fierce response to the police strikers and the London and Belfast electricians and its preparations to deny supplies of beer and luxuries to mining districts, for example, in the event of a coal stoppage.[65] The government probably overestimated the desire of 'moderates' like Thomas and Smillie for peace, but there was no doubt about their belief that most industrial unrest was caused by 'mutiny of the rank and file against the old-established leaders'.[66] Anything which imperilled law and order or bolstered the unofficial movement was anathematised and the rebirth of the Triple Alliance in March 1919 attracted threats of unprecedented severity: 'If such a struggle comes,' Law told the House of Commons, 'it can have only one end – or there is an end of government in this country.'

Seen from this angle, the Sankey Commission appears less a betrayal than a last obeisance to those trade unionists who had once looked with favour on the pre-war Liberal Radicals. But its deliberations also gave time to prepare to fight the Triple Alliance, and unroll a tissue of propaganda ('a good press was capable of influencing public opinion in favour of the government)'[67] which in no way diminished after the Government had accepted Sankey's interim report.

Eric Geddes took control of the organisation tentatively set up in the previous September, restyled the Cabinet Emergency Committee, and in the autumn of 1919 shaped it to meet the threatened rail strike. Its main functions – provision of information and intelligence, and maintenance of supplies and political propaganda – were given full backing from MI5, whose surveillance covered not only individual strike leaders, but the ILP, the NCCL and the Liberty League, and some Labour Party MPs.[68] The style may be gauged from a note from Hamar Greenwood: if rationing became necessary 'it might be advisable to reduce the ration in order that the strike may be brought home in the country, and the sympathy of the community alienated from the strikers.'[69]

Considering the effects of the 1919 police strike, especially in Liverpool, where looting lasted for three days, it is not surprising that the Cabinet relied on the military and intelligence services to enforce its policy. But even given their assumption that the TUC would react passively to an offensive directed against the Triple Alliance, doubts about the legality of such actions worried Ministers: in an answer to Law, the Chief of the Imperial General Staff had suggested that it would be illegal for the Army to run power stations; and when it was pointed out that soldiers had served on the railways in 1912, he added the devastating thought 'at that time we had a well-disciplined and ignorant Army, whereas now we have an Army, educated and ill-disciplined'.* So keenly did the Cabinet feel this threat that they asked Admiralty and War Office for legal opinions: and were duly disconcerted to find that the Services' legal advisers considered previous acts to have been *ultra vires* and that future orders were liable to be suspended by the courts.[70] Yet the emergency was so acute, and the government so afraid of arousing public debate,[71] that Kings' and Admiralty Regulations were not amended to allow strike-breaking until 1925; and use of troops and marines – including the 1924 Labour Government's preparation to bring naval stokers into power stations – continued on an unofficial and, indeed, illegal basis.

Uncertainty about reliance on the armed forces themselves evidently contributed to the government's near-panic early in 1919: in April, Lloyd George told Law that 'failure to win [against the threatened coal strike] would inevitably lead to a Soviet Republic – so that we ought to have our plans thoroughly worked out.'[72] For most of the war, Asquithian Liberals had combined with the Labour Party to present a unified front of parliamentary opposition; the Labour Party Conference in April 1919 voted for the 'unreserved use' of political and industrial power to restrain the government from intervention against the Bolshevik government, while the TUC itself set up its national 'Hands off Russia' campaign in September. Not, therefore, until the late summer of 1919 could Lloyd George say, truthfully, 'we can face a strike'.[73] But in default of military security, the Cabinet sustained its propaganda warfare against the disruptive left and the unions. As Balfour put it: 'The party that secures on its side either general opinion, or the opinion of the working class of the kingdom, must win'[74] – and a bizarre search developed for volunteer strike-breakers among supposedly 'loyal' classes like undergraduates, stockbrokers and 'members of the RAC'.

By the middle of 1919 it had become obvious that the reconstruction programme was in financial jeopardy, and misrepresentation took new forms, in order to compensate for the apparent failure of social reform. Bonar Law began to advise prosecutions for seditious speeches so as to

*WC 522/1. Rumours indicated unrest among troops whose demobilisation had been delayed; according to Col. Storr of the Cabinet Office, MI5 reports linked certain soldiers with extreme pro-Soviet groups (JCCD 745). The War Office even issued a circular to Commanding Officers (published in May 1919 by the *Daily Herald* to the government's embarrassment) asking how their troops might react to strike duty. Particular concern was voiced about skilled Army and RAF technicians, many of them staunch trade unionists, only recently drafted.

'impress public opinion with the revolutionary nature of present agitation', while Chamberlain suggested that the Home Office should select only the most violent left-wing speeches for publication.[75] When Sankey's inquiry aroused great public sympathy for the miners, Lloyd George particularly urged Law to increase the intensity of propaganda, in advance of the Commission's final report. 'It must be put solely on the ground that the miners have thrown over the appeal to reason in favour of recourse to brute force; that no well-ordered community could possibly permit such procedure . . . It is essential that the press should be on the side of government. . . .'[76] Meanwhile, the Emergency Committee's publicity side set itself to counter the miners' case for nationalisation; Eric Geddes wrote to Lloyd George during the Yorkshire miners' strike in July 1919: 'We must get public opinion in this district properly worked up to the gravity of the situation. I think that the public have had so much of strikes and government intervention that they are now apathetic. . . .'[77]

In this emergency the government seems to have lost sight of the vision of industrial harmony which had inspired its earlier overtures to trade unions and employers. Behind the flux of panic, revolutionary talk, and the tiny core of actual revolutionary planning, however, forces originating in the wartime imbalance of power began to take shape in a new industrial pattern. The government's almost irresistible drive to destroy trade union political militancy – and hence the Triple Alliance and the shop stewards' movement – happened to coincide with a hardening of opinion amongst employers. But that owed less to the surrealist manifestations of discontent in 1919 than long-considered evaluation of the roles of individual employers' federations and the FBI. Within a year of its inception in 1916 the FBI had been dismissed as 'soft' by the most powerful federation, the Engineering Employers, who attempted thereafter to deny it any sway over labour policy and confine it to far less politically contentious trade questions, appropriate only to dealings with the Board of Trade. Although the FBI's incompetent behaviour at the 1919 NIC, when confronted with the TUC's sound organisation and prepared statements, gave Allan Smith and the EEF an excuse to set up an alternative body, the National Confederation of Employers' Organisations (NCEO) had been envisaged much earlier, and was actually sketched out in an EEF Shipbuilders' and National Employers' Federation document in February 1918[78] whose preamble

Various commercial, financial and parliamentary interests were moving in regard to the formation of an organisation to line up *for the purpose of parliamentary action* [my italics] bodies of employers dealing with labour questions, manufacturers' organisations dealing with commercial questions [the NABM] 'city interests', [Associated Chambers of Commerce] and a Parliamentary party [the Conservatives] which would have for its object the development and maintenance of the British Industrial and Commercial interests

made it clear that action was being planned in relation to the growth of the Labour Party, the relationship between trade unions and government, and the government's professed intention to introduce reconstruction.

Having regard to the possible effect of recent events on the Continent and the possibility of maximalist theories taking root in countries not yet definitely affected, it appears necessary that the employers as a whole should consider what steps they should take to ensure a satisfactory and continuing cooperation. . . .[79]

At the time of the NIC, these groups made a clear distinction, very similar to the government's own, between 'normal' labour unrest, with which employers and unions could deal, and revolutionary phenomena, which they considered due 'to a state of indiscipline (1) of the workpeople to their trade unions, (2) of the workpeople generally towards the government, and (3) to objections which are felt by a section of the community to the present state of society'.[80] With this the employers had no part, and indeed evidently feared to deal because of the danger of class conflict. Instead they pinned responsibility on government, proposing a sort of functional cooperation of unions and employers, under Lloyd George's personal aegis. When the latter let them down, the NCEO gradually developed its political activity as a group interest, all the while denying any desire to infringe on the constitutional role of government and parliamentary sovereignty – a contradiction which ensured that its activity remained secret by comparison with that of the TUC.

Nevertheless, behind its daily work of mutual support in strikes, and anti-nationalisation propaganda,* the NCEO's more farsighted members set their aim higher than countering the TUC's supposed influence over government, and began to evolve the theory of an institutional link dependent on their own representative capacity[81] – a theory which had a remarkable appeal to Ministers who, by mid-1919, had largely capitulated to the exigencies of the financial crisis and abandoned the grand design of 1917.†

*Weir 4/1–3. The NCEO, together with FBI, Associated Chambers of Commerce 'and 300 MPs', took some credit for the victory of the Coal Association against Sankey in 1919.

†Lloyd George had, for example, rejected the idea of nationalising the coal industry 'on a Post Office basis' at the conference held at Criccieth, 17 July 1919. (Jones, *Whitehall Diary*, vol. I, p. 91.)

For a time, the coincidence of employers' short-term aims and the government's determination to destroy extremism seemed to prove that the two were engaged in an unholy alliance to destroy the working-class movement by a mixture of propaganda, military repression and economic deflation. While there is much truth in the first charge, and some in the second, deflation, undertaken in the second half of 1919, must be attributed rather to contemporary economic argument, the unanimity of evidence presented to the Cunliffe Committee on monetary policy and the gold standard, the state of overseas debts, and the chaos of world trade and foreign exchanges, rather than malignancy towards trade unions. There is no evidence that members of Government or Treasury officials welcomed the sudden slump at the end of 1920, the rise of mass structural unemployment, and the consequent transformation of industrial politics in the mid-1920s. But deflationary policy did coincide with a sudden harshness in government strategy. Freed from concentration on Ireland by a temporary lull in Sinn Féin activity, secure in the peace settlement signed at Versailles, with restored faith in the army and police, Ministers felt able to take issue with the largest unions outside the NIC on the main political questions of nationalisation and workers' control.

Their timing appears to have been very careful. In July 1919, when he invited the opinions of seventeen Coalition MPs, selected by Guest, on a wide range of problems,* Lloyd George still seemed concerned with the causes of working-class discontent. In Cabinet, he argued persuasively that TUC actions in preceding months showed a growing division between moderates and an extreme, largely Triple Alliance, minority which, led by the miners, was trying to blackmail both Labour Party and TUC into calling a general strike, not merely to force the government to nationalise mines and railways, but to cease military intervention in Russia; and he pointed out that Labour's national committees had been unable to hold back the Triple Alliance at the special conference in June, held after the final, divided report of the Sankey Commission. For two months Horne had been warning that the coming clash between unions and employers was likely to make the political system redundant, and turn the House of Commons into a shadowy organisation, validating decisions made elsewhere.[82] Fearing that the TUC would support the Triple Alliance on the grounds that nationalisation (unlike the question of Russia) was an industrial matter,

*LG F21/4/7–8, 21–22 July. They responded in favour of nationalisation of the mines (though not the railways), reduction in profiteering, and some workers' representation in coalmining management.

148

the Ministry of Labour advised the Cabinet to take a dramatic stand against profiteering, to undermine, in advance, the appeal of a general strike.[83]

In the Cabinet debate on 21 July, against the advice of Stanley (Board of Trade), Lloyd George temporised, citing the views of his seventeen MPs; a week later Churchill announced the withdrawal of troops from Russia, and other concessions to the Labour Party; and on 5 August, Lloyd George presented a complex judgment, based on nine months' experience since the Armistice.

Britain, he declared, was a debtor nation, profoundly changed since 1914, prone to strikes, falling output, and consequent loss of credit and competitiveness abroad. Its workmen worked less hard than in the USA or even France. First, then, they must recapture the public mind, and counter 'that formidable body of young men whose aim it is to destroy the present industrial and parliamentary system and replace it by a workers' state' – and whose advocacy of Soviet government drew strength from popular impatience with the parliamentary mode of government. Grievances, principally profiteering, must therefore be met: 'the making of money had become a craze, like an alcoholic craving, which could not be resisted. But it had got to be stopped. The working classes would not tolerate it. . . .'[84]

High-sounding though this argument was, it disguised another instalment of the plan to split the Triple Alliance from the main body of trade unions, (which accelerated after 25 July when the Triple Alliance decided to go ahead without the support of the full Labour movement, by setting for August a ballot on the question of a general strike). Of the three possible solutions for the coal industry, Lloyd George evidently preferred the least radical,[85] and his remedies for profiteering continued to fall so far short of minimum public expectations that they can hardly be described as a bid for national consent.[86] Churchill, whose sympathies had been stirred, wished to go further, but the rest endorsed Lloyd George's programme. Within days the Yorkshire miners' strike collapsed and Lloyd George, encouraged by the Triple Alliance's discomfiture, announced the government's rejection of Sankey's main recommendations.

Faced with the complete betrayal of what the miners believed they had been promised, the Triple Alliance hesitated. While the TUC discussed whether to offer support to a strike for nationalisation, the railwaymen, whose pay talks had broken down, unilaterally called a national strike for 26 September, relying on their capacity to bring the country to a complete standstill. A note of hysteria entered the debate,* as Lloyd George threatened to use emergency labour to run the trains. 'The strike really amounted to civil war. Never before had the entire railway system been deranged and the government had to fight. . . . The country', he reassured the Cabinet, 'was sufficiently disciplined to endure the rigours, so long as there was no starvation.'[87] But reports coming in from regional Intelligence Commissioners indicated a certain public hostility towards a policy of repression. Unnerved by the skilful propaganda put out by the NUR, Stanley wavered, and as soon as the strike began to spread to the docks and among other transport workers, Lloyd George changed course and sought a way out in personal negotiation with J. H. Thomas.

The railway strike, which might, if prolonged, have caused real distress and starvation in large cities, ended after nine days, and for a time the most serious threat passed away. Bevin achieved his well-known settlement for the dockers without involving government, and a renewed campaign for nationalisation by the miners in December 1919 was simply ignored – wisely, from the Government's point of view, since in March the miners suffered TUC defeat by 3·7 million to 1 million votes on a proposal for a general strike. But the test had only been postponed. Lloyd George could exhibit Thomas, Gosling and Tillett as moderates, interested only in wage-bargaining; but behind this, he still believed, there lurked men interested only 'in a complete change in the social order' – like Robert Williams of the MFGB and Cramp of the NUR.[88] This was the version which coloured Cabinet decisions during the next two years, until the Triple Alliance, and then the Coalition, destroyed themselves.

Nevertheless, by the end of 1919, a new form of political activity was growing up, as yet only half understood, but radically different from the pre-war system. Hopes of the great contract had dissolved, but there now existed formal, powerful, employers' institutions, a fully fledged Ministry of Labour, and a TUC increasingly accustomed to dealing in

---

*CAB 27/60 *passim*, where the use of Walton's agency was discussed, as well as the attachment of trade union funds and reduction in unemployment benefit unless the men opted for 'public service'. A shaky note in Lloyd George's hand, dated 3 October, shows how the dual strain of the peace negotiations in France, and maintaining order in Britain had affected his judgment:

'1 Meeting of Mayors to urge formation of Civic Guards.

2 Supplies of domestic coal should strike last a long time.

3 Special meeting of Parliament if all TUs come out.

4 Protection of blacklegs.

5 Prepare newspapers that men working railways would become permanent and places would not be kept open for strikers.'

(TJ C5/77.)

the political arena, wedded to a major political party which, almost alone in Europe, encompassed the majority of the non-Conservative working class. At the same time, the government's apparatus for manipulating public opinion had grown inordinately, enabling it – on its own estimate – to confront the spectre of Bolshevism and survive. Lloyd George himself, searching always for a middle way in politics, had shifted away from Liberal radicalism towards a corporatism best described as the creation in Parliamentary politics of a *staatspartei*, composed of Liberals and mainstream Conservatives (leaving a fringe Right wing and a much larger, but powerless Labour Left); complemented in industrial politics by a triangular collaboration in which employers' organisations and TUC should make themselves representative of their members and in return receive recognition as *estates* by government.

Whatever line individual Ministers took while Lloyd George was away in Paris, they aligned themselves behind him in the crucial decisions of July and September 1919; all, therefore, shared in the incipient devaluation of the party system, and of Parliament as the nucleus of political life which the evolution of a centre party and the elevation of the employers' organisations and the banking interest as pillars of the new Commonwealth implied. For a time it seemed as if the post-war years would witness the apotheosis of Lord Weir and Lord Kindersley – the engineer and the merchant banker – founding industrial consent in working-class affluence and managerial profit achieved by increased productivity and unrestricted competition. Liberal Radicalism might be dead but the creed of the late Victorian Liberal businessman survived.

But acceptable though this was to Lloyd George and Bonar Law, it increasingly offended the party men beneath them who, in relative isolation from Cabinet power, were faced with the rough job of sustaining their leaders' majority from among the votes of an increasingly alienated working class. So long as popular opinion could be manipulated and cajoled by success, they were not moved to question too deeply. But by 1920 they were beginning to see that success depended on a collaboration of estates which was, at that stage of history, inconceivable, because the TUC could not become representative, even if the Cabinet had not pursued its vendetta against the Triple Alliance. The balance between TUC and employers was not yet so level that trade union leaders could ignore the rudiments of the class struggle. In the battles of 1920–2, the nature of Coalition support from unions and Conservative party changed, vitiating the whole conception of a centre bloc.

6   LLOYD GEORGE'S PYRRHIC VICTORY, 1920–2

During the later years of the Coalition, as fear of revolution died away, and the harsher symptoms of discontent receded, Lloyd George's government slowly changed its strategy towards the Labour movement, although without lifting the propaganda barrage, or ceasing in public to stigmatise the modest creed of the Labour Party as 'bolshevism'. How little justified that term was can be gauged from the solid, undistinguished impression made by the parliamentary Labour Party after its gains in 1918* with spokesmen like J. R. Clynes and W. Adamson who in no way looked like the standard-bearers of a new age. Most of the (presumed) left-wingers of the ILP had been defeated, MacDonald and Snowden among them, and all but eleven of the sixty MPs carried trade union nomination. Indeed, privately, Lloyd George seems to have agreed: 'The real dangers to England do not emanate from Bolshevism,' he declared in 1920. 'Bolshevism is almost a safeguard to society, for it infects all classes with a horror of what may happen if the present organisation of society is overthrown.'[1]

The image of Bolshevism still recurred, of course, in the Cabinet debates of 1920–1, reflecting earlier obsessions. 'The ministers who have come over here seem to have the wind up to the most extraordinary extent, about the industrial situation,' Thomas Jones commented in January 1920. 'From a meeting yesterday I came away with my head fairly reeling. I felt I had been in Bedlam. Red revolution and blood and war at home and abroad!'[2] Jones's diaries, more vivid than the cold minutes, depict the full scale of military calculations, the forebodings of the General Staff, and the lurid reports of MI5 and Sir Basil Thomson. 'How many airmen are there available for the revolu-

---

*The Labour Party gained 22 per cent of the total vote in 1918 as against 7 per cent in 1910; 2.5m votes out of 11m. Many of these could be attributed to the extra numbers of seats contested. Municipal elections bore out a trend running strongly right through the period 1910–20; but the fact of trade union predominance remained: of 140 candidates, only 31 came from the Labour Party or ILP and 7 from local Labour Parties.

tion?' Lloyd George asked Air Marshal Trenchard, and on hearing that only a hundred machines could be kept going, 'presumed they could use machine-guns and drop bombs'.[3] It is hard to tell how seriously this was meant. Most members of the Cabinet would probably have settled, like Horne, for dropping leaflets instead. 'The great mass of working men,' Sir Basil Thomson told the Prime Minister, in much less lurid phrases than he used in his reports to Cabinet, 'are against violent revolution, but at the moment they are very sore about a number of minor [*sic*] points such as high prices, shortage of houses, and the impending rise of railway fares, grievances which the press might have done much to alleviate. . . .'[4]

Churchill, Horne and Bonar Law all gave credit to the press, and to Walton's skilful manipulation, which, they believed, had turned public opinion against the miners, 'who are regarded by their fellow trade unionists as already possessed of disproportionate privileges compared to the rest of the world';[5] and it is clear that government was shifting away from reliance on coercion to a much subtler concept of imposing its values by persuasion and political education. True, after the 1920 coal strike an Emergency Powers Act was introduced, giving wide powers to declare a state of emergency and bring in supplies, and the use of troops to break strikes was still debated;* but the main effort now went into the Supply and Transport Committee's organisation which had emerged, covertly, out of the old Cabinet Strike Committee at the end of 1919, and soon embraced supply, strike-breaking activities like pumping out coal mines, and propaganda.

Confined though it was to national, paralysing strikes, the Committee's scope was almost unlimited, professional advice being sought even from the United States; and its publicity sub-committee, under Sir Philip Lloyd-Greame, embraced the former activities of half a dozen government departments.[6] With an odd touch of sensitivity (reminiscent of Geddes' remark that 'public opinion might not be favourable to deliberate preparation by government for industrial war during a period which is superficially one of industrial peace'[7]), propaganda, as distinct from publicity, came under two secret departments, separately financed: one run by Admiral Hall, former Head of Naval Intelligence, and the other by the ubiquitous Sidney Walton. £100,000 *a week* was budgeted, if needed, for official and unofficial action, and the cost was

*Churchill finally admitted in November 1921 (CP 111) that illegal use of the Services had been made; but for several months no satisfactory alternative was found, in spite of protests from the CIGS and Director of Intelligence (CP 544). Churchill's suggestion of a 'citizen guard' found no favour with the professional soldiers.

carefully disguised among general departmental votes.[8] Both were linked with the NCEO, though funds for Hall's organisation were channelled through 'National Propaganda' (above, p. 132); but as far as other finance was concerned, Walton's money came from Coalition funds, Hall was paid by government.[9] The whole, with its separate Scottish and Welsh vernacular sections, had been completed by the beginning of 1921.

Apart from resolving the touchy argument over legality of the use of troops, the breadth of the Supply and Transport Committee's operations made a military reserve almost otiose; during the crisis in April 1921, *carte blanche* was given to the Committee's propaganda sections to spend as much money as its members considered justifiable.[10] But all this was aimed specifically at the Triple Alliance rather than other unions; when that had been defeated, the publicity section was actually closed down. Perhaps the clearest indication that the TUC was not the object of hostility can be found in the decision in August 1920 not to use secret intelligence information about financial support given by Soviet Russia to the *Daily Herald*, for fear of alienating moderate trade unionists and interfering with the government's main aim of 'uniting the other trade unions against the miners'.[11] In that, everything was fair, including surveillance of miners' leaders, telephone tapping, and the opening of mail – which, of course, in the unwary Theodore Rothstein-Sylvia Pankhurst correspondence gave the Intelligence Service what it had suspected all along.

The miners, railwaymen and transport workers who formed the Triple Alliance were less united than the authorities believed. Their strategy had to be attuned to each union's needs and to economic circumstances, such as the level of real wages,[12] and unemployment – which, after holding at the low level of 2 per cent in 1919–20, rose suddenly, as the post-war boom burst in the second half of 1920 to 12.9 per cent in 1921. Before the Alliance's precipitate loss of bargaining power in mid-1920, it had been possible to campaign for better wages or conditions; after, there could be only a long, defensive action against wage-cutting advocated equally by FBI, NCEO and Board of Trade, not on a short-term, cyclical basis, but as a strategic policy based on the need to cut production costs against a background of falling prices. The coal strike of October 1920 just caught the flood; that of April 1921 ran out on the ebb of government decontrol of the mines, and unemployment.

In spite of the impassioned objections of miners and railwaymen to a return to the sway of private companies, after four years of state control, the state rejected responsibility, and it did the unions no good to argue that it remained, effectively, their employer up to the moment the mines and railways were handed back.[13] After Sankey's final report had been rejected, other unions which had taken up the nationalisation theme as a way of establishing certain principles – such as the minimum wage, length of hours or factory conditions – began to abandon it, even as a secondary line of defence; nationalisation fell slowly into desuetude, stock-in-trade of MFGB conference resolutions over the next twenty-five years. Solidarity between unions also suffered from the return to sectional activity. Scarcely any organised opposition was offered, for example, to the crushing blow to agricultural workers' standard of living, either when the wheat subsidy was withdrawn in 1921 or during the long years of rural depression.

Government skilfully exploited inter-union (and in the case of the Miners' Federation, intra-union) divisions, utilising the timidity (or commonsense, depending on the point of view[14]) of J. H. Thomas in making its railway settlement in 1919, and relying on the predicted compliance of individual union leaders. The granting of almost 'personal' concessions in order to build up certain reputations[15] suggests that government hoped gradually to tame union behaviour in the manner sometimes put forward by Henderson during the war. Not until much later in the twenties was a Cabinet or Minister of Labour prepared even to consider that union representation could not adequately be expressed without including rank and file opinion.

The Triple Alliance's inherent weaknesses scarcely showed in October 1920 when the Miners' Federation took on the Government, alone,* and won a temporary increase in wages largely because of Lloyd George's fear that the strike could attract sympathy from the NUR, which had only recently been placated. Intervention disconcerted those who had hoped to see the miners weakened by attrition;[16] but against Conservative criticism that he had merely paid another instalment of Danegeld, Lloyd George argued the efficacy of a new policy, more in tune with the requirements of the NCEO, to bargain higher wages against union concessions on regular output and productivity.[17]

In the following months, however, the economic position worsened rapidly; increased production of coal became unnecessary in the face of over-stocked world markets and falling commodity prices. At the beginning of 1921 the Treasury began to put great pressure on the

*The MFGB called for support from the Triple Alliance, but was unwilling to accord the NUR any share in the conduct of the strike.

Cabinet to decontrol the mines earlier than had been announced, because the subsidy was already costing £5 million a month and was, in their forecast, likely to reach £40 million by the autumn. True to its tradition of subservience in financial questions, the Cabinet gave way, fixing 31 March as the date after which all state undertakings would lapse, and leaving owners and miners unprepared to consider two of the great problems of twentieth-century industry – the varying profitability of different regions, and the high cost of modernisation. Wholly unwilling to touch profit-sharing, and probably unable in the open market to raise capital for investment, the owners took the easiest way and announced heavy wage cuts on a district basis, a course which called in question deep principles of trade unionism yet which Frank Hodges, the MFGB secretary, admitted to have a certain logic, when he declared that, in the state of the mining industry, only a fresh government subsidy could cover both profits and existing wages.[18]

For government, the problem of dissociation from industrial disputes coincided with this culminating struggle of the Triple Alliance: watching the irreconcilable struggle of one million miners against the owners' lockout which followed decontrol, the Cabinet prepared to use all the resources available under the 1920 Emergency Powers Act. When flooding in the pits threatened permanently to impair production, Ministers argued urgently which battalions of troops could be spared – from Ireland, or from Silesia? After railwaymen and transport workers announced their support, the tone of debate momentarily renewed the hysteria of the worst days of 1919.[19]

What actually happened on 15 April, the day before Triple Alliance action was supposed to begin, is still not entirely clear; but it was as much the result of a crisis within each union in the Triple Alliance as between the three of them, since the NUR had already, on 7–8 April, changed tactics in relation to the miners; while many branches altered their opinions as the strike developed. In his later plea of justification Thomas was probably correct in alleging that the NUR's membership was divided. According to the government's own information, NUR and Transport workers had wanted the miners to go on talking,[20] while an intervention by the National Council of Labour seemed to indicate a measure of rivalry between TUC and Triple Alliance.

Commenting on the struggle for supreme authority, Lloyd George depicted Thomas as the man the Cabinet could rely on: 'He wants no revolution. He wants to be PM. He does not want to be a commissary for Bevin.'[21] With the Cabinet suitably persuaded, the Prime Minister capitalised skilfully on an injudicious remark about district agreements made by Hodges to a group of MPs on 15 April; and although Hodges at once challenged his interpretation, he was in turn disavowed by his own executive. While the three unions suffered from inadequate communication among their leaders, the government's publicity apparatus swamped the country with Lloyd George's brilliant but tendentious statements about the miners' 'attacks on the nation'.

Denied their claim to joint control of the strike, Thomas and Williams asked the miners to go back to work; and when this was refused they called off the strike. On Black Friday, unquestionably, the Triple Alliance died. Bevin drew the obvious deduction: joint action was impossible without joint control. But although Thomas and J. T. Cramp, representing the NUR, abandoned any hope of nationalisation (by the agreement to decontrol which they signed with government on 24 April), the syndicalist – even anarcho-syndicalist – tradition did not wither away at once, and the newly-formed Communist Party was able to make useful political capital by denouncing the 'betrayal' of the Triple Alliance, and the Government's only too obvious partiality towards the owners.*

Lloyd George's public popularity swelled as a result of the demonstration of government strength, and the Cabinet quickly concluded that their intention of retiring from the industrial arena altogether had been vindicated. But their victory owed less to the weight of public opinion than to collusion: at one moment, worried about the owners' inability to present their own case in public, the Cabinet offered them the assistance of Lloyd-Greame's propaganda section;[22] and when the FBI got cold feet and suggested, on 14 March, a temporary subsidy to stave off the crisis, Lloyd George refused to listen.[23] Edwin Montagu was the only Minister to complain that the owners' figures of war profits were fraudulent and their offer to the men despicable[24] – and being a junior, he was disregarded. During the strike deliberate restriction of essential supplies 'to bring public opinion to bear on the miners' leaders' was discussed – and approved, provided that it did not suggest that the government was in difficulty;[25] and awareness of this attitude (though the facts were kept largely secret) poisoned trade unionists' opinion of Lloyd George for years to come. Yet in the end the MFGB got better terms in June than they had been offered in March (including a profit-sharing agreement which greatly displeased the owners). The Triple Alliance being dead, Lloyd George could afford to be generous.

*Jones, vol. I, p. 141. Austen Chamberlain admitted that although Horne, on his own, could make no headway with the Mineowners' Association, the Cabinet did not wish 'to put the owners in the wrong'.

As Jones described it: 'The Strike Committee very sick. They had been waiting for two years to press the button . . . But Jim Thomas upset it all and despoiled Sir Hindenburg Geddes of the fruits of victory.'[26]

Thomas might, paradoxically, have claimed credit for the subsequent rundown of the Supply and Transport organisation and excused his inevitable implication in the collapse of the shop stewards' movement, for which historians have not been kind to him. Nationalisation and workers' control as matters of practical politics were shelved for twenty years. In retrospect, the proposition that the Triple Alliance could on its own have begun the transformation towards a socialist society is at best tendentious, and at worst, given the Alliance's highly sectional character, indefensible. But the conflation between the industrial aims of the Triple Alliance and the revolutionary preparations of a minority of the SSM, BSP, SLP and (after 1921) Communist Party of Great Britain (CPGB), which the government's propaganda had done a great deal to create, had one long-term, unforeseen effect: the enormous reserves of state power built up since 1919 were gradually dispelled, so that Black Friday may have helped to prevent Lloyd George from becoming a British Mussolini, served by men like Geddes and Lloyd-Greame, whose manipulation of the organs of publicity and coercion was becoming habitual and increasingly unquestioned.

By the standards of the *Employers' Year Book* for 1920, the period of 'co-partnership' appeared to be over: managers had reasserted their right to manage, and the engineering employers' lockout of 1922 put in irons those shop floor district committees which, on the basis of EEF recognition, had managed to establish a degree of real autonomy from the Engineers' union (ASE). Dr T. J. Macnamara, the new Minister of Labour, deliberately delayed setting up a court of inquiry into the lockout until the ASE itself was beaten, confirming the melancholy conclusions of Charles Reynolds (who had forecast an age of harmony only four years before) that Labour's 'new era' of joint councils had been replaced by a resurgent capitalism aiming 'by concessions to obtain satisfied workers and to consolidate industry on its present lines'.[27] What he deplored, Lloyd George extolled. As the shop stewards' power withered in the hostile political and economic climate, the danger of revolution, when the army had been 'weak and inexperienced', receded. 'The working man,' Lloyd George told a deputation of Conservative MPs, 'was getting away from this state of affairs and the extremists were not making the same impression on him

. . . the temper of the country was undoubtedly against the extremists.' And this 'was of more value than many Acts of Parliament.'[28]

Heavy, structural unemployment achieved more than manipulation of the press, although the Shop Stewards' Movement did not disappear entirely. But a Ministry of Labour official shrewdly argued the distinction between trade union behaviour and working-class political consciousness. Reporting on the SSM in February 1920, he noted 'the increasing tendency for the trade unionists of one shop works or small districts to act together, irrespective of their division into crafts or occupations. What is called "class consciousness" is obliterating the distinction between those who follow different occupations in the same works.'[29]

In its earliest days, the Communist Party attempted to capture this feeling and to organise not only those antagonistic to trade union bureaucracies but the ranks of others who, being newly unemployed, shared an even harsher common experience. But the CPGB probably overreached itself after Black Friday with its denunciation of 'betrayal' and calls for unofficial action, while the National Unemployed Workers' Movement (NUWM) encountered the same opposition from organised unionism as the CPGB did from the Labour Party in its prolonged, ambivalent struggle to affiliate to the Labour movement, following Lenin's tactics of infiltration. The National Conference of the SSM turned away in 1920 to an increasingly remote and visionary preoccupation with revolution; and the CPGB had, as J. T. Murphy complained, to begin again almost from scratch on the shop floor. Nevertheless, the very existence of the CPGB and the Minority Movement and NUWM, over which it exercised almost complete control at least until after 1926, prevented the rest of the Labour movement from accepting too hastily the pattern laid down in Lloyd George's dealings with individual union leaders, just as what was known of the government's links with employers gave the Left the basis for counter-propaganda.

It is not easy to draw up a balance sheet after Black Friday, or to judge whether real progress towards triangular cooperation had been achieved by the destruction of the Triple Alliance. Against the government's record on profiteering, and failure to introduce a Capital Levy in 1920, could be set the remnants of the grand design set out at Criccieth in 1919: financial help for the coal industry,[30] safeguarding of industries, and the Trade Facilities Act. Of equal importance, other sectors of the employers had recoiled at the inflexibility of the mineowners; before decontrol occurred, 'the FBI got cold feet, and came running to No. 10 with protests against the big wage cuts'.[31] An awareness had emerged, across the whole field of government, among Ministers and civil servants, of the need for formal organisation of industrial politics; Churchill and Bonar Law were not alone in believing that only the trade union movement stood between the State and anarchy.

In turn, the TUC became aware both of distinctions in attitude among employers[32] and the desire of government for more logical, bureaucratic structures (foreshadowed in Haldane's Machinery of Government Report 1918) which the TUC's institution of a formal General Council in 1921 seemed to accomplish. The symbiotic relationship between unions and employers, in which organisations and patterns of behaviour became increasingly interlinked, shows clearly in the definition of NCEO's supremacy over FBI which was written into the new NCEO constitution in December 1922.[33] 'The national welfare', according to a Council minute of July 1921, 'demands that there should be in this country as there is in many others, a central organisation for employers, well-informed and firmly established; an organisation which is not merely in a position to deal with difficulties as they arise, but which can act in anticipation of them.'[34]

Vestigial resistance from traditionalist Federations slowly gave way to an understanding that the complicated political repercussions of such questions as the new International Labour Organisation (ILO), set up under the Versailles settlement, and the Washington Forty-Eight-Hour Convention, could best be dealt with by politically trained bodies. The NCEO soon put forward a reasoned claim to speak direct to government;[35] and by 1922 Allan Smith could state: 'It is the NCEO and TUC which the Government applies to when it wishes the views of employers and workers *as a whole* on any labour question.'

Membership (measured on the somewhat arbitrary scale of number of workers employed by constituent Federations) rose from $2\frac{1}{2}$ million in 1919 to 5 million in 1922, and 7 million in 1925: and the NCEO usually added a further 3 million from the affiliated Trade Boards Employers' Consultative Committee, to give itself 60 per cent of all wage-earners in the country – a figure considerably higher than that of the TUC. Under the 1922 Constitution each Federation acquired individual representation on the Council. In spite of this quasi-democratic character, however, the NCEO operated in considerable secrecy during the 1920s, hoping to avoid attracting the hostility from trade unions experienced by the FBI.

On the question of principle, like the TUC itself the NCEO sought influence as a lobby, qualified to deal with government by virtue of its 'mass membership', rather than aspire to the political legitimacy implied in the 'industrial parliament' concept, discredited in 1919. Like the TUC it claimed the right to be party to policy decisions at the earliest stage, and it was so consulted over the Whitley Councils and the Industrial Courts Act 1919. Very early on, at the initiative of the Ministry of Labour, in Roberts' day, a procedure was developed in which all Bills concerning labour and industry were shown by Departments to the NCEO and the TUC, to be vetted before introduction to the House of Commons; and several were amended at this stage. Indeed the Ministry seems to have envisaged the regular formalities of deputations and consultation as another means of institutionalising industrial relations;[36] the existence of long-running disputes like that over the Washington Hours issue, or unemployment insurance, tended in themselves to increase regular liaison with government, more than sporadic lobbying.[37] The Ministry staff, headed by Sir Montagu Barlow, provided information equally for either side, and Macnamara's unemployment insurance scheme, promulgated in December 1922, owed much of its form to joint participation.

The early preponderance of heavy industrial Federations in the NCEO Council[38] began to disappear as other sectors claimed representation, and its President, Lord Weir, though an engineering employer, increasingly took up a position which, in the context of institutional cooperation, could be called progressive:

If the NCEO is to be regarded generally as voicing the agreed policy of employers on great national questions, arising out of and affecting the relations between employers and workers, [he declared in 1924] then we have to assume a very great responsibility. I am confident that in collecting and coordinating the views on specific subjects given to us by our constituent members, we will now bear in mind and give full weight to the legitimate aspirations of all workers. Only by this policy will we be in a position to claim that in the advice we give to Government Departments and others, our proposals are based on what we conscientiously believe to be the best for industry as a whole.[39]

An element of special pleading here cannot be ignored: yet this does not come from a public statement, and it marks a vast difference from the ultramontane attitudes of 1911 or even 1917. The NCEO, of course, maintained its old links with individual MPs and 'front groups' such as the Independent Parliamentary Group,[40] and it gave up little of its sympathy or financial support for strike-breaking before 1927. But underneath these habitual patterns, change did take place:

F

the very divergent philosophies of industrial reality held at the end of the war by NCEO and TUC tended, in the circumstances of the 1920s, and through the process of institutionalisation itself, to become increasingly compatible. Class conflict did not disappear on Black Friday; but organisations emerged which had a vested interest in its accommodation.

Under the direction of Horace Wilson, Permanent Under-Secretary from 1921–37, and Frederick Leggatt of the Industrial Relations Department, the Ministry of Labour staff encouraged this process, even stimulating the NCEO to rationalise its relations with the FBI and to introduce its Constitution in 1922.[41] Using as far as possible the apparatus of Conciliation Officers which had fortunately survived the economies of the Geddes Committee in 1920, it made very significant gains in the fields of conciliation* and cooperation† – in contrast to the relative failure of Whitley Councils to reach beyond discussion of wages and conditions. But, bedevilled by shortages of staff in the years before 1925, Macnamara and Barlow were unable to break out of the limitations set by the political parties' unwillingness to give up the prior right of central government to intervene when it chose; and the 'élite of unassuming experts' (in Beatrice Webb's phrase) had to wait, whatever their 'superior knowledge and larger administrative experience'.

The TUC made correspondingly rapid adjustment to political circumstances between 1919 and 1921 which was barely acknowledged in public and which coloured only very slowly the movement's public self-presentation. Economic circumstances imposed structural stress: membership fluctuated violently, rising to a peak of 7 million in 1920 and declining to 4.7 million two years later, when unemployment

---

*A crude correlation appears in the strike figures, if allowance is made for the fact that the single large disputes of 1921 and 1926 caused the greatest loss of working days.

	1919	1920	1921	1922	1923	1924	1925	1926
Strikes	1,352	1,607	763	576	628	716	603	323
Days lost (000s)	34,969	26,568	85,872	19,550	10,672	8,424	7,952	162,233
No. of workers directly involved (000s)	2,401	1,779	1,770	512	343	558	401	2,724

(Source: A. H. Halsey, *Trends in British Society*, table 4.14.)

†The railway settlement of 1921, for example, embodied a Central Negotiating Board, nominated by FBI, Associated Chambers of Commerce, and TUC/Cooperatives, while the Industrial Court developed in legal form the highly important principles of 'adequate livelihood' as a first charge on any industry, and comparability of wages between industry and the public service.

162

reached 14.3 per cent of the insured population.* Funds dropped sharply as did the percentage of unionised labour, from 54.5 to 37 per cent of the working population, creating a dangerous weakness *vis-à-vis* the NCEO.

But some union leaders had begun as early as 1918 to plan for a new central organisation, retaining the old parliamentary ambit but adding to it something of the industrial methods and flexibility in crisis of the Triple Alliance.[42] Harry Gosling, of the Transport Workers (whose 1919 Negotiating Committee served as an early model), and Ernest Bevin agreed on the need for a 'central directing body in future national crises'[43] and, with the Labour Party in mind, envisaged 'the development of the industrial side of the movement, as against the "deputising" or "political" conception'. After a careful programme of political education the idea was launched at a special TUC in December 1919 and formally approved in 1920.

At first, this successor to the Parliamentary Committee ran well behind the Triple Alliance, and in the coal strike in October 1920 had to submit to some fairly patronising remarks from Hodges and the MFGB.[44] As late as January 1921 it felt so unsure of its authority that it rejected an FBI invitation to discuss the industrial position. But its latent power showed clearly during the April 1921 strike. Ignoring the fact that its help had not been invited, the General Council summoned the Triple Alliance leaders to a joint conference on 14 April, to discuss a general strike in defence against wage cutting; and after the Black Friday débâcle, in May, its ambitions began to flower.

'Should not the [General Council] as the elected executive of the trade union movement assert itself to intervene?' Arthur Pugh asked C. W. Bowerman, the secretary. 'I feel that this is now expected by the majority of organised workers, and that despite opposition from any extreme sector, it must take the matter in hand, if its existence as a representative body is to be justified.'[45]

General Council minutes soon reflected a melancholy pleasure in the decay of its rival, the Triple Alliance, as the new body made requests beyond the imagination of the old Parliamentary Committee, asserting its right 'to initiate and take what steps are necessary to get

*	1918	1919	1920	1921	1922	1923	1924
TU membership (males 000s)	5,324	6,601	7,006	5,627	4,753	4,607	4,730
Percentage of working population (males)	41.8	51.6	54.5	43.6	38.5	37	37.7
Unemployment %	0.8	2.1	2.0	12.9	14.3	11.7	10.3

(Source: Halsey, *Trends*, table 4.12.)

momentous decisions strictly obeyed',[46] and to ask for cash subscriptions or the power to direct individual unions to strike in sympathy with others. With thirty members, this General Council (GC) was both larger and more representative, and although Gosling failed to persuade the more conservative unions to agree to a permanent Chairman (like a union General Secretary) a bureaucracy soon developed, capable, for the first time in British union history, of conducting formal relationships with European and American trade unions and the ILO.

In conformity with Henderson's Labour Party plans, joint research and policy-making departments were created which survived until the disillusioning experience of the first Labour Government in 1924. For a few uncomplicated years the TUC supplied a strong contingent to the National Executive and the parliamentary party, and an unprecedented amount of cash. Secure in the blanket provision of *Labour and the New Social Order* – a 'Fabian blueprint for a more advanced, more regulated form of capitalism'[47] – the GC saw no reason to indulge in ideological debate, preferring to wait on the proofs of parliamentary socialism in office, while 'framing a comprehensive Labour policy from Congress to Congress, serving as a lead to the trade union movement generally'.[48]

Men like Bevin, George Hicks and Gosling believed, quite simply, that strikes would diminish in relation to the growth of centralised trade union power. As conflicts with the GFTU or Triple Alliance died away, the burgeoning machine, guided by its brilliant young secretary, Walter Citrine, benefited from all the cumulative advantages of continuity and access to specialised information, and in turn inspired individual unions to further amalgamations and higher professional standards of administration, which only the MFGB – locked in its social and geographical isolation, and bound by its long history and constitution to a unique form of popular democracy – chose to ignore. Engineers and others amalgamated to form the AEU in 1921, followed by the General and Municipal Workers' Union, while dockers and carters set up the Transport and General Workers' Union, Bevin's home ground for another twenty years. If nothing else, this evolution made a revival of the Triple Alliance almost impossible.

Ministers of Labour naturally welcomed the change. Macnamara, for example, rejected in 1920 a proposal to introduce a strike ballot, on the grounds that any dispute serious enough to cause a major strike ought to be sorted out at once, rather than delayed and further embittered.[49] Lloyd George himself conferred specific political recognition when he invited members of the General Council to his confidential discussions on unemployment policy, held at Gairloch in October 1921. The General Council's opposition to his foreign policy at the time of the Chanak affair was treated as seriously as if it had actually been able to direct its members as categorically as it threatened – and in this sense, it inherited the historic advantage of the Council of Action's opposition to Russian intervention.[50]

Yet Lloyd George thought it too large a body to deal with, preferring to take the chair of a smaller policy-making group of half-a-dozen employers, bankers and trade unionists.[51] This was precisely what the General Council could not do, mistrustful as it was of being implicated in compromises by the political master who had undermined the Triple Alliance, and unwilling to venture so far without Labour Party guidance. But their lack of competence in binding individual member unions to any tripartite economic programme was not their only disadvantage: the TUC still had to come to terms with the challenge of the extra-parliamentary Left. The aftermath of Black Friday disoriented the shop stewards and remnants of the Triple Alliance without putting a term to the *political* influence wielded by the tiny left-wing parties – BSP and SLP and, after 1921, the Communist Party.

At the 1919 Labour Party Conference, fears of losing mass popular support (as the SPD risked in Germany and the Socialists (SFIO) in France, when confronted with industrial unrest and the Twenty-one points of the Third International) and of prejudicing the whole concept of parliamentary socialism, created profound divisions between the constituent bodies of the National Joint Council and the rank and file movement, between older trade union leaders and younger SSM delegates, between MFGB and the other members of the Triple Alliance, and between Clynes and William Adamson, defending the parliamentary Party on one side, and Herbert Morrison, representing the local organisations on the other. The Conference voted in favour of the highly contentious issue of direct action to enforce nationalisation; but Henderson put his immense prestige in the balance (as Hugh Gaitskell was to do over unilateral disarmament forty years later) and stalled the Labour movement, decisively: 'To force upon the country by illegitimate means the policy of a section, perhaps of a minority of the community, involves the abrogation of parliamentary government, establishes a dictatorship of the minority, and might easily destroy eventually all our constitutional liberties.'[52]

British political debate rarely exposes fundamentals in this way; but Henderson's declaration of belief in the immanence of the nineteenth-century constitution (and in the willingness of others to accept its rules) was not coincidental, because it permeated the whole history of the campaign against intervention in Russia, in 1920–1. True, Labour leaders were prepared to tolerate direct action in the *international* sphere, making the somewhat specious distinction that the Coalition government had no democratic mandate to smash the infant Russian state, but they were not prepared to do so at the dictates of the rank and file. When the BSP called for a general strike, after government had renewed its arms supply to Poland in April 1920 and London dockers had refused to load them on the cargo ship *Jolly George*, Labour Party and TUC reiterated the arguments for parliamentary action. Only in August, when the government came close to war in its efforts to rescue the retreating Polish army and force Russia to accept an armistice, did fear of the popular appeal of shop stewards, BSP and the rest, particularly in local Labour Parties and Trades Councils, induce Labour and TUC to approve extra-parliamentary resistance. Barely able to avoid the appearance of leading from behind, the official end of the Labour movement agreed to set up Councils of Action.

The real object of this demonstration disappeared before the design could be implemented, because Lloyd George at once reverted to conciliatory tactics, promised to send no British weapons and denied any warlike intentions. A Polish recovery along the line of the river Vistula, made his withdrawal easier. Even before Labour's National Conference (which in its enthusiasm echoed the Leeds Conference hysteria of 1917), the leadership was able to relax and indulge its immense propaganda victory, no longer worried by the nightmare of having to call a general strike. But the Councils of Action, buoyed up by an extraordinary wave of popular sentiment in favour of the Russian experiment,[53] would not go away. 350 of them, haphazardly set up, based largely on the still inchoate local Labour Parties, and on Trade Councils permeated by shop stewards' militancy, took on a life of their own, as their Controllers broadened the scope of demands to include *de facto* or even *de jure* recognition for Russia, a halt to the war against Sinn Féin in Ireland, and support for police strikers.

The Councils' links with French Socialists and their skilful propaganda led the Labour Party at first to welcome their 'permanent effect on the solidarity and efficiency of the Labour movement'.[54] But by September 1920, the three secretaries, J. S. Middleton (PLP), Fred Bramley (TUC) and J. Lindsay (NEC), had become gravely embarrassed by the threat to central policy-making of individual councils pushing upwards resolutions on controversial questions like the hunger strike of Terence McSwinney, Mayor of Cork. At the end of the year they concluded that some were wholly out of hand: Birmingham and the North-East Federation of Councils were demanding a National Convention of Councils of Action – something which looked like a takeover bid for the National Council of Labour itself. An attempt to defuse the Irish bomb by organising Labour's own Commission of Inquiry left Councils' autonomy, even anarchy, untouched and in January 1921 a majority of them decided to call a general strike against sending troops to Ireland and the government's inadequate policy on unemployment.[55]

Middleton declared that the Councils were controlled by Communists; and to break their power, Labour's own National Council called a special conference, where it was argued that the Councils of Action could not force the TUC to call a strike, nor expect individual unions to pay for it. Official deprecation of direct action provoked the North-East Federation to break away and proclaim a wholly independent National Convention, with Local Councils remaining 'permanently in session, as emergency committees through which all matters requiring action by local Labour Parties and Trades Councils can be dealt with.'[56] Such prescriptions for government by general assembly appealed only to a minority, however, and the breakaway groups eventually merged with the CPGB-dominated National Minority Movement.

Communist Party infiltration may have made official Labour's dissociation inevitable, but it would be too easy to accept at its face value Middleton's evidence or Henderson's statement that the Councils had been a 'spontaneous combination, of a temporary character, rather than a permanent feature of a well-thought out and clearly defined policy'.[57] Government investigation[58] bears out the conclusion that the Councils of Action represented, in tangible form, and on an issue of immense appeal, the last manifestation of that popular democracy which the shop stewards' movement had always claimed existed.

It is significant that the Councils of Action example recurred frequently during the tactical discussions on nationalisation, obliging Henderson to deplore the effect on moderate voters, and to insist that a general strike could not, as the syndicalists believed, be divorced from political considerations: 'A great disservice is being done to the interests of the workers by those who belittle the value of parliamentary government, and who seek to undermine the confidence of the workers in our political institutions. These things react against the Labour Party and against the interests of the workers when we have to resort to political action.'

The outcome of the General Strike as well as the post-1921 parliamentary tactics of every Socialist party in Europe could have been forecast at that moment. Wittingly or not, the Labour movement chose its future as an organisation for the capture of parliamentary power; a choice from which it would not be budged by the NUWM, the CPGB in its revolutionary phase, the Cook-Maxton campaign, nor the Hunger Marchers. Labour Party and TUC claimed, as much as employers or Conservative Party, a vested interest in preserving and enhancing the country's governing institutions; and while they could acknowledge in August 1920 'the enormous number of resolutions [favouring Councils of Action], letters, and expressions forwarded to our various offices, of the overwhelming majority of the 6 million organised trade unionists in this country',[59] that same enthusiasm, six months later, had to be damned as Communist-inspired and 'irresponsible' – in terms barely different from Lloyd George's definition of it as 'unconstitutional . . . I think that cuts very deep in a democratic country where suffrage is universal, because once that begins, there is no saying where it will end. I do not want to make an Ireland of this country.'[60]

Some of the philosophy and patterns of political organisation in factories and localities which encouraged the evolution of the Communist Party survived after 1921 within the Labour movement, but they had deliberately been made marginal and more or less permanently identified with Soviet-Russian affinities or affiliation. (Nevertheless, during the next thirty years and perhaps longer, the 'left-wing tendency' of Labour provided a fund of black propaganda for Conservatives and Liberals to use.) But although it is essential to an understanding of Labour Party history to recognise the existence of a policy of marginalisation, ostracising the Councils of Action did not blur the party's identity. Aided by the Fabian intellectuals with whom he had teamed up in 1918, Henderson continued to rely on the plain mathematical calculation that a predominantly working-class electorate must eventually vote Labour into power.

Nevertheless, an ambiguity was built into the Labour movement: the trade unions took up position as an estate of the realm, orienting themselves towards employers and government, while the Labour Party invested its capital in the two-party system and set itself to seize the central apparatus of the state by patient political education aimed at the mass electorate.* As Maurice Cowling has argued,[61] this made

*Some idea of the scope of the effort of the Labour Party joint research programme of 1920–4 can be found in the papers of J. S. Middleton. It is hard to overestimate

inevitable a Conservative resurgence and the fall of the Coalition; but it also brought about a steady and permanent diminution in the scope and power of parliament itself.

On its own, the Labour Party scarcely threatened the Coalition, nor its enormous Conservative preponderance: 338 out of 484 MPs. But in the summer of 1921, at a time when 76 Coalition Liberals had just abstained in an important division on economic policy, and when rising unemployment was leading Lloyd George, at Gairloch, to propose drastic and unpopular measures, Conservatives had to assess the long-term electoral support of continued Coalition, against the likelihood that industrial class warfare would polarise national politics. Loyalty to Lloyd George had been greatly strained by the Irish Truce: all the blandishments of Austen Chamberlain and Lord Birkenhead had been needed at the Party Conference to hold Tory delegates to the Coalition line. While they acquiesced, many of the rank and file never forgave this betrayal of Unionism, and, in their distrust of Lloyd George's state corporatist proposals for economic reorganisation of the service industries, swung steadily against the principle of coalition itself. Preoccupied with the loss of party identity, they could scarcely be expected to welcome the renewed vigour of the Labour movement. Corruption, in the sense of sale of honours, probably bulked less than a more general objection to press and public opinion manipulation and a sense that old decencies and conventions were being overridden by Liberal and Conservative Whips and Ministers alike. Behind that, seems to have been a clear, if impressionistic, feeling that the Coalition had slipped out of the control even of Bonar Law or the Tory majority, which came to a head during the Chanak affair, when, for trivial gains in the Eastern Mediterranean, Britain and the Dominions were almost pledged to war with Turkey.

Churchill's avid canvassing of a Centre Party, and Chamberlain's and Birkenhead's known support for fusion, suggested a future in which Lloyd George and Bonar Law would lead a grand army of MPs, flanked in the Commons by fringe Opposition groups, forever denied power. Conservatives like Colonel Gretton and Lord Lloyd had not

---

the effect, not just of published books like Tawney's *The Acquisitive Society* (Bell 1921) but the experience of joint activity, and the blend of effort by Labour MPs, civil servants and elder statesmen like Lord Haldane in drafting a coherent set of proposals for what to do when they came into office. The experience of government, later in 1924, should not detract from the fact that this gave depth to the simplistic analysis of *Labour and the New Social Order* and served, most usefully, to counter the Conservative's new programme in opposition, after their 1923 election defeat.

fought the 'socialist menace' to be relegated in this way;* and they attracted allies as the Coalition imperceptibly used up its reserves of success, order and efficiency (the bulwarks of the corporate mentality). None of the critics in Cabinet denied Lloyd George's ability: a future prime minister 'less experienced and skilful remained a nightmare when considering industrial unrest'.[62]

Yet anyone who looked back to the era of Disraeli had to view with horror the loss of votes among Tory working men, trade unionists themselves, which the tactics of the Supply and Transport Committee implied,[63] and the party managers grew less and less willing to endanger their success in holding roughly one-third of the working class since 1911, in pursuit of an evanescent and possibly untenable position. They drew support from Conservatives of very different backgrounds: Sir Arthur Griffith-Boscawen, W. C. Bridgeman, Edward Wood, representatives of the country gentry, and those with experience of late nineteenth-century industry, like Stanley Baldwin, who deprecated both the 'hard-faced men who looked as if they had done well out of the war' in the NCEO or the banking world, and the policy of deflation which they pursued.† Thus the party managers, Sir George Younger, Leslie Wilson and Sir Arthur Steel-Maitland, were joined by the stalwarts with a regional base.

Stanley Baldwin, the principal instigator (though not the decisive factor) put the case clearly enough – corruption, misuse of the Civil Service, the 'morally disintegrating effect' of coalition politics – although he carefully avoided casting the net of accusation too wide for fear of implicating Bonar Law.[64] But his supporters, particularly the party men, had feared also an intemperate election, called by Lloyd George without Conservative consent.[65] According to L. S. Amery, they were 'much closer in touch with the rank and file of the Party, in parliament and the constituencies, they knew how completely estranged their leaders had become from the prejudices, as well as the ideals, of their party'.[66] The crucial deputation to Austen Chamberlain (leader since

---

*A formal proposal for a Centre party was actually discussed by the principal Liberal and Conservative party managers in February 1920, but it ran into such opposition from the parliamentary parties that it died. Beaverbrook commented drily: 'The orthodox Tories appealed to the age-long traditions of a Party now caught fast in the house of semi-Liberal bondage'. (Lord Beaverbrook, *Decline and Fall of Lloyd George*, p. 190.)

†Baldwin was not then convinced, as he became in 1925–6, of the need for wage-cutting; his stance against Lloyd George ought not to be separated from his conversion to Protection, as a cure for unemployment less than a year later. Most of the rebels can be found associated with the planned electoral pact with 'the patriotic section of labour', inspired by Milner in 1917. (SM GD 193/99/2.)

Law's retirement) 'unanimously emphasised the importance of preserving the solidarity of the Conservative Party, and having a leader of our own who, though perhaps allied with some of the Liberals, would be more independent than at present of Lloyd George – and who might be PM if our number after the election justified it.'[67] Frigidly, Chamberlain turned down the only chance of preserving some aspects of the Coalition, and, personally, of ever becoming that Prime Minister.

It is reasonable to argue that in the eleven years of his leadership Bonar Law may have retarded the conscious move towards a policy aimed at the working-class electorate which can be discerned in the party reforms of 1906 and 1911; and on a long-term analysis this, as much as the controversial tariff, may explain the loss of the 1923 election. Yet the changed nature of the post-war electorate could not be denied: the rigid stratification of the Edwardian working class had been loosened, the pyramid flattened, as a result of narrowing differentials between skilled and unskilled workers, the increase of white-collar workers and mechanisation, lower population growth, greater social mobility, the impact of inflation, the unprecedented redistribution of wealth by war taxation, and the spread of a pungently anti-plutocratic ethic (to which Baldwin himself subscribed). All discussions of 'working-class consciousness' in the electoral dimension had to contend with the evidence that the Labour movement had established an ideologically attractive alternative.

Although the inarticulate far Right, represented by Sir Henry Wilson, might dream of a military coup to eliminate those politicians whom he regarded as traitors for dealing with Bolsheviks,[68] Central Office staff were politically too literate to be taken in by Coalition propaganda. The Society of Conservative Agents, often the source of new ideas, complained repeatedly about organisational weakness in the regions after 1919;[69] and they were backed up by a handful of constituency delegates at the 1920 Party Conference who specifically warned that working-class Tories would soon vote Socialist.[70] The 1921 Conference brought louder protests, against dismantling National Union branches in favour of Coalition organisations, and against over-hasty decontrol of mines and railways: 'gradual wage reductions would have met the case', without imperilling Tory votes.[71] The evidence is scattered, but bears out what Law said in December 1922: 'Long before the Carlton Club meeting, the Coalition had ceased to appeal both to the rank and file of the party, and to the country generally.'[72]

All this and the persuasion, even blackmail, of his friends, might not have brought Law out of retirement, to swing the Carlton Club meeting against Austen Chamberlain, if it had not been for the Central Office calculation that, on its own, the Conservatives could win an election by 25 seats[73] – in the event, a gross underestimate of Coalition decay. The 'true party men' could not yet offer a convincing substitute for Lloyd George's 'dynamic force',* being tied to an older political imagery, to Wood's archaic vision of rural interdependence, Robert Cecil's idealised co-partnership, or Baldwin's own vision of paternalistic industrial harmony; but they could agree on one thing: only in government could they offer an alternative to the corporate methods and centrist theory which six years of Lloyd George had almost canonised. It was not enough to attack Labour: as Baldwin saw, the Conservatives must face the challenge of socialism or go the same way as Asquith's Liberals.

That this tendency had not fully matured can be seen in the 1922 election, which has been called 'the most complex of the century',[74] as, sticking desperately by forgotten standards, candidates stood for whatever label they thought the public might recognise. Bewildering allegiances replaced the pattern painstakingly constructed since 1916; but since the politicians were only adapting to a situation they knew had already changed, the results were actually very simple. Asquith's group, who might theoretically have won, with Lloyd George, a bare majority, failed either to re-establish itself or defend Lloyd George against the devastating Tory attack; while the shadowy arrangements sought by Lord Grey, Robert Cecil and a number of Liberal and Coalition Labour MPs who could have been called social democrats, imprinted nothing on political debate.

The totals of votes are significant: Conservatives received $5\frac{1}{2}$ million; both groups of Liberals $4\frac{1}{2}$ million; Labour 4.2 million.† Clearly the Coalition could have won, had it held together; equally clearly, the Tories had retained their traditional vote. Labour made huge gains and the political side of the movement at last achieved representation by 57 non-trade union MPs, of whom 32 were sponsored by the ILP. Lloyd George fell because the political system he tried to create was anachronistic, more suited to the circumstances of the late 1930s than

*Lloyd George and the system he represented was, Baldwin declared at the Carlton Club meeting, a 'dynamic force . . . a very terrible thing: it may crush you but it is not necessarily right . . . It is owing to that dynamic force, and that remarkable personality, that the Liberal party, to which he formerly belonged, has been smashed to pieces; and it is my firm conviction that, in time, the same thing will happen to our party'. (*Baldwin*, p. 123.)

†In terms of seats: Conservatives 347, Labour 142, Asquithian Liberals 60, Lloyd George Liberals 57.

those of 1922 – which may explain why, to the end of his life and in many different schemes he scarcely varied its fundamentals. The density of British political life prevented him from carrying by such methods what he needed to win in a hurry, to prolong his run of success; and the instruments of coercion and propaganda, however novel and ingenious, were never actually used in an election because he had been deprived of them beforehand by his former allies.

During the years between the fall of the Coalition and the General Strike, out of more openly ideological conflict than had been seen since 1911, the Conservative Party rearranged itself almost spontaneously, drawing back Chamberlain and Churchill to tower over the 1925–9 administration, and throwing up, in the Baldwin-Steel-Maitland axis, an approach to industrial politics more in tune with Disraelian themes than with the style of Bonar Law's brief and inconclusive time as Prime Minister. In a curious way, the programme launched by Joseph Chamberlain in 1903 proved successful on reintroduction, despite loss of the 1923 Tariff election: creeping protection, industrial harmony, carefully costed welfare reforms, and a general withdrawal from financial orthodoxy towards rationalisation and intervention ensured the survival of the party in electoral terms, and its triumph in 1925. But the apparent rebirth of the two-party system at the Carlton Club meeting turned out to have been illusory: the prime issues so adroitly taken out of parliamentary politics during the Coalition era were not permanently reintroduced.

A shutter fell after the Armistice, which inhibited the free passage of ideas and cut Britain off from the rest of Europe for many years, so preventing close analysis or assimilation of similar political experiences. Yet European comparisons revealed, albeit indirectly, something about the British predicament in the 1920s. In Germany, state and industry became inextricably enmeshed, the former relying on the latter for support in its economic and industrial policy, and industry in turn looking for state acquiescence in a continuation of the long process of cartelisation – while both turned to the army to suppress the Communist and right-wing revolts of 1920 and 1923.

Because profound emotional and ideological divisions between Socialists and Communists, going back to the abortive revolution of 1919, prevented the emergence of a countervailing political power on the left, German trade unions had to resort to formal relationship with the employers and the state on the general pattern set by the Stinnes–Legien agreement. Article 165 of the Weimar Constitution embodied the idea of a Federal Economic Council – a concept derived partly from Bismarck's desire to create an industrial parliament to counterbalance the Reichstag, and partly from the Cohen–Kaliski plan put forward by the last Workers' and Soldiers' Congress in 1919. Given its explicit anti-parliamentary tone, it was hardly surprising that the SPD rejected the idea, as did the Communists, in favour of the Soviet system; but the German Federation of Trade Unions and the employers pressed so hard that in 1921 the government conceded, setting up a carefully balanced Economic Council with equal representation to each side.[1]

As a matter of right, this body was allowed to vet all legislation on economic or social questions, but it was denied equality with the Reichstag (envisaged by its trade union protagonists) and reduced to an advisory capacity. In spite of an over-large composition[2] it worked well, yet to some extent its style reflected that of the Reichstag, just as its members held many of the privileges of deputies, thus betraying the hope of Walter Rathenau that it could avoid rhetorical display. Most of its success came from the work of its sub-committees after 1923, not least because the politicians jealously cut down its budget; and in the 1920s its usefulness became confined to the supply of information and advice on legislation – matters on which in Britain TUC and NCEO had achieved their aims by much less formal methods.

In France, governments of the Third Republic, chronically short of state funds, remained wholly opposed to intervention in economic and industrial questions, impervious to protests from parties of the Left. The breakaway group, later the French Communist Party (PCF), was caught up in the difficult transition to a Leninist vanguard all through the sectarian period down to 1934, while the Socialists, led after the 1921 split by Léon Blum, took the parliamentary road, yet rejected any chance of office in a non-Socialist government, thus ensuring that there would be no substantial shift in the political balance before the mid-1930s.

The power of the French bourgeoisie, for all the economic and social changes and the psychological damage caused by the war, remained at least until the 1930s politically little different in structure from what it had been before the war. The rulers of the Third Republic, faced with the threat of revolution, had succeeded to a large extent in a conservative reconstruction of the old state and had found that the old constitutional methods had been adequate for their purpose.[3]

For this reason, ideas of an industrial parliament made no progress.

Pressure for workers' control existed in France after 1918, but government consistently rejected Communist trade union plans for a Council, representative of industry, until after the CGT had set up its own Economic Council, with neutral outsiders, in 1923. The Herriot Ministry finally accepted the principle of a body quite different from the German model, with only forty-six members drawn from Labour, capital and consumers, in which the state as such was not represented (or only by officials within other categories), and the 'Labour' section included both employers and workmen.[4] In order to allow for the expression of class interests, overall numbers gave exact parity between the two, but the Council was in no way allowed to entrench on the regulatory authority of central government: it reported to the Premier, not to the Assembly, in a purely advisory capacity, and it had no right of prior consultation over legislation. French employers, generally poorly organised compared to their German counterparts and temperamentally unwilling to seek state help, either for investment or trade facilities, made use of the Economic Council in default of something better as did the CGT, and the pre-war tradition of purely 'industrial' politics was therefore extended, producing an increasingly stylised pattern of confrontation and negotiation on starkly defined class lines.

French and German patterns of industrial political organisation thus echoed many of the trends experienced in Britain; but the far closer understanding between unions and Labour Party on the one hand and employers and Conservatives on the other (enhanced after the return to two-party parliamentary activity after 1922–3) encouraged the evolution of a much more flexible, subtle and inconspicuous system than the formal structures of Economic Councils or the abortive National Industrial Council of 1919 – even though, as late as 1927–9, Arthur Henderson and some of the 'Tory Corporatists' sought to revive them.

Yet this tendency can also be over-stressed: in the longer term, down to the 1930s, reversion to two-party politics created an apparent harmony between parliamentary and industrial/economic activity, an illusion which may have been binding on MacDonald, Baldwin and their colleagues, but which became increasingly transparent to employers and trade unionists. W. Milne-Bailey, of the TUC Research Department, argued the whole case carefully in December 1926, citing the failure of Whitley Councils to reflect the real balance of power in industrial politics and attacking the idea of a recreated NIC because of the traditional arguments that

Parliament represents the entire nation, producers and consumers alike, and therefore it is competent to decide all social and industrial, as well as political issues. The establishment of an industrial parliament is regarded as a menace to the supreme authority and prestige of the political Parliament and of the State itself. The Civil Service frequently dislikes the project too, as setting up yet another rival system of experience and knowledge. . . . The belief that industrial peace will be furthered by the setting up of such a body is very widely held and yet it is almost certainly illusory.[5]

Yet he went on to point out that Parliament itself was no better at representing the views of either side of industry. Its 'inadequate knowledge is very real and constitutes a genuine defect in any parliament elected on a territorial basis'; and expedients like advisory committees

do not in the least meet the demand of industry for *vocational* representation and authority. . . . The traditional method of Royal Commissions and government committees is no longer adequate. They get most of the expert advice, it is true, but they are only appointed for specific problems that have become too urgent and too controversial for treatment in any other way, whereas what is wanted is continuous work. . . . Parliament is essentially a place for rhetoric, for speeches that are going to be reported and will be read by constituents, and which are therefore verbose, unrealistic and unbusiness-like. Given the democratic form and method of election of Parliament, no reform in procedure will be of much avail in correcting this tendency.

Curious as it is to find sentiments normally associated with business-men being argued by trade unionists, it is only the measure of how far their institutions had come to resemble each other. Four years' experi-ence since the Carlton Club meeting had convinced them that the measures taken by the 'true party men' to destroy Lloyd George's system had done nothing to resolve the political tensions within industry.

In a different sense, also, Conservative and Labour politicians may have been perfectly sincere in their resolve to sweep away the Prime Minister's personal bureaucracy, the Garden Suburb, corruption and the sale of honours, and to impede Lloyd George's recovery – but that did not prevent them from considering his many overtures, in 1924, 1926, 1929 and 1934–5. The drift back to the centre began early in certain quarters. 'Our business,' Austen Chamberlain wrote in January 1924, 'is now to smash the Liberal Party. Two-thirds of it is already Labour in all but name. We might give a new meaning to Unionism by drawing over and eventually abolishing the other third.'[6] Nevertheless, the former coalitionists had discussed reviving the Coalition with Bonar Law, and Baldwin continued to fear this tendency in the party during the attacks on his leadership in 1925 and 1930, right down to its consummation in the formation of the National Government in 1931.

MacDonald's obsession with the need to show himself a party man in terms that could have been drawn from Dicey and Anson derived less from extra-parliamentary tendencies in his party than his concep-tion of a Labour style embodied in respectability, efficiency, 'the meti-culous observance of constitutional rules and procedures however trivial'.[7] Angry at the Clydesiders' rough Parliamentary tactics, deaf to the blandishments of the CPGB, contemptuous of the General Strike which he described in his diary as 'one of the most lamentable adventures in crowd self-leadership of our labour history',[8] he attracted even in 1924 the accusation of 'trying to turn the Labour Party from a party of the working class into a national party';[9] while the TUC found almost incomprehensible his opposition to the well-established practice by which government departments showed them (and the NCEO) legislative proposals before the Bills themselves went to the House of Commons. How little he responded to the claims of interest groups and institutions can be seen in his defence of proportional

177

representation: 'It will weaken the organisation, but strengthen reason; it will make Ministers more the instruments of the general will than the captains of the party horse.'[10]

However resistant Baldwin and MacDonald were, personally, to ideas of coalition, the period 1922–30 as a whole was marked by a profound though irregular shift towards institutional cooperation and the adoption of state corporatist ideas. This is not to say that corporatism triumphed: the Cabinet interested itself in the German and French examples, but concluded that their National Economic Councils possessed inadequate powers;[11] and the group of politicians and businessmen who showed some admiration for the direct relationship of Italian employers to the Fascist state, remained an unrepresentative minority.* But a steady *rapprochement* developed between those government departments dealing with industry, their official and unofficial advisors, the scientific lobby, large and increasingly coordinated groups of employers and, even before 1926, the majority of trade union leaders.

To quote Milne-Bailey again:

An Economic Council (the term seems preferable to "Industrial Parliament") merely seeks to do well what Parliament at present does badly, and in so doing achieves the full recognition, by the community, of the claims of vocational groups. The Trade Union movement is not satisfied with the way in which Parliament handles industrial problems. It has had to criticise severely not only anti-labour Governments but the Labour Cabinet of 1924 itself – and not only for its lack of industrial knowledge but – even more serious – for its assertion that a Government must *in all matters*, including industrial conditions, have rights superior to those of the organised workers ... Through [an Economic Council] they would exercise far greater influence on the economic and industrial affairs of the nation than they can possibly do at present.[12]

Similar views can be found expressed in contemporary NCEO Council meetings and in the resolutions of Chambers of Commerce; their legislative corollary is to be found in the Trade Facilities Act, widely accepted by the late 1920s among manufacturers seeking state investment, especially in the declining staple industries;[13] in the Safeguarding of Industries Act under which industries as large as Iron and Steel applied for tariff protection, and in the institution of state corporations like the Central Electricity Board in 1926, pushed through against Conservative Party opposition on the unchallengeable recommendation of Lord Weir. 'Only rationalisation can save us and get rid

*Churchill and the signatories of *Industry and the State* (1927), Oliver Stanley, Robert Boothby, Harold Macmillan, John Loder. (See L. P. Carpenter, 'Corporatism in Britain, 1930–45', *Journal of Contemporary History*, I, 1976.)

of unemployment,' Sir Basil Blackett wrote in 1929. 'It means for us essentially the getting rid of individualism in industry, cooperation, amalgamation, ruthless scrapping of out-of-date plant and out-of-date directors, and it can only be done if the banks come out boldly and face it . . .'[14]

American business methods (usually introduced through the American takeovers of companies followed by wholesale purges of their boards) vied with the homegrown technique called Mondism, after the founder of ICI which was itself the creation in 1926 of a merger of Brunner-Mond, Nobel Industries, British Dyestuffs and United Alkali. The period saw the rise of Lever Brothers, British Oxygen, the Association of British Machine Toolmakers, and the Metropolitan-Vickers combine, as well as the first moves towards cartelisation of the iron and steel industry, following the German model. In the era of Mond and Harry McGowan, ICI itself set up its own world-wide cartels and carved up the expanding world market in chemicals with IG Farben and Dupont.[15]

Government did its best to facilitate the rationalisation programme, instituting at Cabinet level the Committee of Civil Research (CCR), and later, in the second Labour government in 1929, MacDonald's far more ambitious 'Economic General Staff' – the Economic Advisory Council (EAC).[16] Misconceived demands by the politicians in the end negated the long-term effects of both bodies, but their very existence reveals a demand for an improved statistical basis for policy-making and the influence of men like Balfour, Haldane, and the scientific establishment, of which Sir Basil Blackett and Thomas Jones were active members. Some of their efforts may have been naïve: the search for 'neutral' information about profit margins, profiteering and division of total product ran, predictably, into the blank opposition of companies unwilling to admit detailed investigation of balance sheets; and the CCR had to abandon its attempt to write a 'new Domesday Book' of industry and corporate ownership.[17] On the other hand, the idea of a more productive and efficient sub-division of 'industry' reached the threshold of acceptance with the CCR's recommendation of 'two economists, three men of business experience, three of working-class experience, a banker and a lawyer', to the Macmillan Committee on Trade and Industry in 1929.[18]

Overrun by the 1931 crisis, weighed down by too many incompatible demands and the need to consider unemployment as a current rather than a structural problem, the EAC failed to rise above party industrial or economic politics; but the Balfour Committee, working away through the late 1920s, accomplished a great deal by tying political discussion down to specific industrial problems; as, patiently and largely unrecognised, did the joint Research Associations licensed by the Board of Trade, and linked with the Department of Scientific and Industrial Record. Weakened by the unfavourable economic climate, employers' lethargy and government's own underestimate of the cost and stimulus required, these Associations nevertheless emerged as pools of research for industry to tap, inculcating the concept of collaboration between government and private sector.

Meanwhile, a division grew up between this body of opinion wedded to structural reform of British industry, and the orthodox defenders of financial policy. Quite apart from their recurrent attacks on the Treasury, increasingly in the 1920s industrialists came to see the banks as retrograde, even malevolent, in their attachment to late nineteenth-century investment patterns. More direct involvement with industry, a characteristic of German or American banks ever since the 1860s, attracted British managers faced with intractable problems of falling productivity and declining competitiveness. Blackett in particular criticised the clearing banks for holding huge frozen deposits, unlike their European counterparts; while Sir Arthur Salter claimed later that rationalisation of the Iron and Steel Federation could be carried through without legislation, because so much of the industry was in the hands of the banks that if they only chose to cut their paper losses (in 1931), they 'would put inexorable pressure to come within any agreed scheme'.[19] Swayed by Cabinet pressure, the Bank of England did help to facilitate the Metropolitan-Vickers merger, and to set up the Bankers' Development Corporation in 1929, but the banks generally, and in particular the almost moribund merchant banks, can hardly be said to have taken the lead in industrial regeneration.

Evidence about shortages of investment is ambiguous: there is, as yet, no study of the capital market to show whether the operation of Stock Exchange new issues was inadequate, or if there was truth in Montagu Norman's assertion that high bank rate had no appreciable effect on corporate borrowing. That certain sectors experienced remarkable growth is not in dispute, although economic historians argue about its extent and distribution.[20] What is important here, however, is more the climate of opinion: the widely diffused antagonism between industrialists and bankers which forced government for the first time seriously to examine its in-built prejudice in favour of the bankers,* and the equally

---

*In this the accountants took a significant (and almost unrecognised) part. Thus in 1928, Steel-Maitland told the Cabinet that Sir William McClintock, speaking for the accountancy profession, favoured industrial rationalisation, but that it would be necessary first to overcome the jealousies and 'individualism run riot' of the five main clearing banks (CP255/25, 23 September 1928).

significant common ground, on which employers, trade unionists and government could meet, confident in their belief that the future profitability of national industry could be considered separately, and at a different level, from wage-bargaining.

To say this may seem paradoxical, given the intransigence of mineowners and miners, the General Strike, and the ever-present factor of mass unemployment, with its accompanying decay of old industrial areas, as Britain, like a patient in the last stages of leprosy, atrophied at derelict extremities where no development corporation or finance house seeking an outlet for investment would ever look. The paradox was neatly embodied in the conclusions of the Samuel Report on the coal industry in 1925: on one hand the long-term promise of a reborn, profitable industry; on the other, immediate wage cuts and longer hours.

Two deeply contradictory tendencies existed side by side, and the system of the early 1920s proved incapable of harmonising them. One answer to the question of how a Conservative government could take over electricity supply in 1926 (in what amounted to an early case of nationalisation) yet in the same year could not give a government guarantee that Samuel's long-term proposals would in fact be imposed on the recalcitrant mineowners in return for miners' short-term sacrifices, can be found in economic history: since 1900, as mining trades became more settled, a new managerial class composed of fewer but more powerful owners had emerged,[21] whose insistence on standard wages and contracts was opposed on all points by an equally powerful Miners' Federation, seeking national agreements and a minimum wage – leading to the survival of twin dinosaurs whose social and geographical isolation led to habitual, sanguinary conflict.

The other reason is political: the realignment of parties in 1922–3 was accompanied by a consistent evasion of hard choices – particularly where these impinged on traditional party supporters and interests, so that the tendency towards cooperation between employers and unions was diminished by a failure of government to maintain the impetus of the Lloyd George period. For both these reasons, the General Strike – and its defeat – became a necessity.

To distinguish between general underlying trends and particular cases of conflict, and to emphasise that both TUC and employers' organisations were, in certain respects, prepared to collaborate under the aegis of government, is not to indulge in revisionism for its own sake. It would be as wrong to forget the influence of Whitley Councils, for example, in perpetuating an earlier style of collaboration* (even though by 1926 the TUC considered them inadequate to resolve the main problems of industrial politics) as to over-emphasise the authoritarian attitudes and ultimate success of the coal owners in the General Strike. But neither was central to collective industrial behaviour and an analysis of the 1920s must allow for the existence of two cycles, the short, normally violent activity concerned with wage-bargaining, and the longer and more tranquil one of approaches by employers and TUC to the common ground of structural change in industry between 1923 and 1931.

'The employers' ceased in the 'twenties to be an informative description. In the long debate amongst historians on the rise of the corporate economy, a sort of balance has now been struck between pre-1940 observations about monopoly power in companies on one hand, and the explanation centred on the power and role of the state; and the vast changes, the spread of large-scale production techniques and the altered pattern of ownership which stemmed from the reorganisation of the 1890s, and more particularly from the demands of the First World War, can now be seen in better political as well as economic proportion.[22]

Numerically, the majority of small and medium-sized businesses continued as family firms, rarely quoted on the Stock Exchange, content to raise money when necessary from the banks as they had done in the nineteenth and even eighteenth century. After 1920, however, a steady increase developed in the number going public as their owners sold out,[23] accompanied by amalgamation of medium and large concerns. Most firms by the 1920s belonged to the Trade Associations or Federations and the worse the structural decline of industry, the more individual employers tended to look to these organisations for support in wage-bargaining with the unions, while they sheltered behind their corporate relationship with government in such matters as price-fixing and cartels. The Federations in turn swelled the ranks of FBI and NCEO so that by 1928 the NCEO could claim a membership covering 60 per cent of the national workforce, and 57 per cent of gross national output.

The NCEO aimed at nothing less than a closed shop for all employers,[24] and while the Council still insisted publicly that it was no more than the mouthpiece of its members, in its actual proceedings, such as the collec-

---

*One official pointed out in 1927 that virtually no national strikes had taken place since 1919 in the fifty-four industries concerned. (Secretary of the Joint Committee on Flour Milling, November 1927, quoted in W. Milne-Bailey, *Trade Union Documents*, p. 496.)

tion of evidence for the Blanesburgh Committee on unemployment insurance, it tended to dictate to individual Federations the answers Lord Weir and his colleagues wanted. Thus, it had a status quite different from that of the National Association of Manufacturers, the lobby of the small firms, which never became a political institution. Like the TUC, it was dominated by a Council whose changing membership reflected accurately the diminishing importance of staple industry and the strength of the capital-intensive high-technology sector;[25] and by 1925 its dominant role as political wing of the employers' movement had been conceded by the FBI.*

Within the NCEO, however, it is possibly unwise to emphasise too much the arbitrary distinction between 'old' and 'new' industry, as far as political behaviour is concerned; the economic basis for such definition is far from clear, and all Federations in the inter-war years tended to settle where they could, in threatening economic conditions, for cartels, accompanied by entrenched opposition to the 48-hour week (Washington Hours Agreement) and any increase in their contributions towards social security payments. However negatively, these patterns created a habit of common action in relation to the opposition – the TUC – within a common context of government legislation and policy. But diversity could not easily be contained: the Iron and Steel Federation's repeated applications for a protective tariff forced every other industry to reappraise its attitudes to protection; just as the extreme behaviour of the Mineowners' Association before and after the General Strike offended large numbers of more enlightened – and economically more liberated – employers.

Nevertheless, to a very marked degree, the NCEO Council came to resemble the General Council of the TUC. Both lacked coercive powers over powerful individual members; both pursued a middle way between radical and conservative extremes; both assumed, correctly, that government would prefer to deal with a closed shop of employers or unions rather than a divided interest incapable of expressing an agreed view or partaking in joint negotiations. Where legislation was concerned, evidence to Royal Commissions or Cabinet, and nominations to government bodies, the NCEO conceded that 'the one is counterpart of the other'.[26]

*NC/463, 1611. Stephen Blank concedes that the FBI was never particularly successful as a pressure group, nor did it offer much 'leadership of industry' for fear of creating discord among different groups of its constituents. Indeed, it often subordinated itself to individual Federations such as the EEF and Iron and Steel, and by the later 1930s had become 'primarily a provider of services'. (*Industry and Government in Britain*, pp. 7, 30, 51.)

This did not mean that they ranked equally in political power: in spite of its secretive methods* (which made it difficult for government to grant public recognition) and low level of funds compared to Federations like the Engineers,† the NCEO dealt much more effectively than the TUC General Council with Civil Servants in the Ministry of Labour, Treasury, Health or Home Office,[27] whether they found them responsive, or whether they mounted attacks against their 'socialist tendencies', using something very close to blackmail (as against Steel-Maitland, the Minister of Labour, in 1926–7).‡ The NCEO's Research Department, organised by Weir and Andrew Duncan, managed to insert its figures into many of the unemployment debates in parliament, in contra-distinction to those of the TUC or Ministry of Labour and its *Report on Labour factors in the cost of production in the export industries* became one of the standard texts in the wage-cutting arguments of 1924–6.[28]

As the TUC's superior organisation during the National Industrial Conference in 1919 had stimulated employers to form the NCEO, so the NCEO's expertise at presenting evidence to Committees and Royal Commissions, and its claim to speak for industry as a whole, 'in the fullest possible knowledge of the facts', in turn spurred the TUC to institute its own Economic Committee in 1929. Apparent proof of the NCEO's argument that only a reasoned statement of their case would 'educate' Ministers[29] inaugurated an era of open competition centred on the two longest defensive actions of the period, the questions of the 48-hour week and unemployment insurance; and very gradually the claims of both bodies to institutional status began to preclude irresponsible or overtly sectional behaviour. Its experience during 1925–6 encouraged the NCEO to distance itself from the Conservative Party as the experience of 1924 helped to dissociate the TUC from Labour; a dual process at organisational level which in no way diminished the

---

*Moir explained the need for secrecy, in 1929: 'Our success as an organisation has been largely due to the fact that we have never broadcast our achievement. I have always felt that if government departments . . . had, at the backs of their minds, the fear that if they adopted our suggestions they would find us the next day in the newspapers claiming credit for it, they might well refuse to give effect to our arguments, even though we were right, just in order to avoid the possibility of the Labour Party accusing them of being in our pockets.' (Moir to Rivers-Fletcher, 24 April 1929, NC 2667.)

†In 1924, the Secretary, Forbes-Watson, sourly contrasted an NCEO deficit of £1,100 with the TUC's annual income of £142,000 (NC 886).

‡The FBI and NCEO were 'most tremendously disgusted at the attitude of his [Baldwin's] three main interfering departments, namely, Labour, Home Office, and Health, in their socialistically inclined attitude towards all employers' problems . . .' Lithgow to Baldwin, 25 June 1927 (SM GD 193/94/2).

interest of both in closer links with the state apparatus, state planning and finance.

Language itself changed: whatever might be said in private counsel before the General Strike, only Evan Williams and his colleagues of the Coal Owners' Association let the mask slip in public, because the NCEO baulked at giving the TUC gratuitous advantage. In 1925 the EEF actually opposed the MacQuisten Bill, which sought to alter the system of political levy contributions to trade union disadvantage; and Baldwin's courageous rejection of government support for the Bill, and his famous 'peace in our time' speech, evoked a rapturous welcome from the NCEO, in which the unlikely pair of Sir Eric Geddes and Sir Vernon Willey actually talked of a 'truce of God'.

However, until the General Strike, the employers were not prepared to initiate schemes for a revival of industry, except on the basis of wholesale wage-cutting to reduce costs. Where they did advocate an expansionist argument, it was couched in traditional terms of an increase in productivity, won by union cooperation in a return to piece-work and shop floor competition, which the unions simply could not accept.* Although such arguments resembled the recommendations of the Samuel Report, they left quite unguaranteed the question of investment and mechanisation on which real profits in the world market – and hence high wages – depended. As the MFGB were to argue in 1926, sheer production was not enough, since there was no point in working longer hours to produce more coal which could not be sold in export markets. Nor had the TUC then evolved the argument that in return for acceptance of modernisation, with its inevitable displacements and redundancies, union members might be entitled to a share in the benefits.[30] In default of an initiative which could only come from government, and which would have required far more of a guarantee than Samuel could provide, the TUC avoided a commitment which would have seemed a concession. Consequently, in tune with the unwillingness of the majority of employers to embark on such a risky and possibly unprofitable business, the NCEO and FBI rested their case on wage-cutting, citing the experience of Britain's main competitors, Japan and Germany.

The lines of this argument were fairly simple: the return to the Gold Standard had induced a recession in British exports;[31] hence to maintain

---

*Tom Jones wrote of Weir that, in spite of the accumulated evidence of past misdeeds, such as his part in the Clydeside deportations, 'it should be said that he is all out for production on American lines, against the stupid restrictions of the unions, and would be willing to pay high wages if he got the output.' (Jones, *Whitehall Diary*, vol. II, p. 4.)

the same level of export activity, production costs (of which wages were the largest item) must fall by the 10 per cent by which sterling had been overvalued. But this could not be done across the board because of what was delicately called 'rigidity', that is, trade union resistance and the ability of firms to pass on costs to the consumer in the 'sheltered' areas of the home market. Whatever politicians, even the Prime Minister, might say about cuts for everyone, the FBI and NCEO accepted that wage-cutting could only be carried out industry by industry. Aware of the potential disruption, they hedged their bets, leaving the coal owners determined to force down wages, unilaterally if need be. It is not an exaggeration to say that this strategy put the coal owners and miners in the front line. Collectively the rest of the employers stood to gain by dissociating themselves from the political odium bound to fall on the Coal Owners Association, while benefiting from the fall in the price of coal-based energy in the home manufacturing market, which they predicted, correctly, would follow the trial of strength between owners and miners.[32] In addition, the inevitable defeat of the MFGB would leave other unions exposed to piecemeal wage-cutting.

The dinosaurs in the coal industry were thus left to fight out their archaic battle in which both owners and miners could only, in the long run, lose; while the industrial institutions of which they were eccentric members gave what help political constraints allowed, before withdrawing to take up alternative positions on another field. It is not surprising that in the weeks before the General Strike, Lord Weir pressed on Baldwin the need to raise the miners' working day from seven to eight hours, while the NCEO gave full support to the owners: nor that, when the strike broke out, the NCEO retired discreetly to the shadows. Two years later Weir was prepared privately to admit that this policy had been carefully planned;[33] that the NCEO would have preferred to win hands down, but recognised that its political importance was too great to chance in the coal industry conflict, as the TUC (foolishly, by their standards) did. Evidently NCEO, like government, expected the TUC to play the same game and derive similar political benefits. Unwisely, even unjustifiably, they assumed that the TUC's opposition to the Triple Alliance in 1921 had been as dispassionate and logical as their own calculations, and that the TUC would, or could, pay the price of wage-cutting without a fight.

After four years of closer cooperation with the Labour Party than had been obtained at any time since 1900, the TUC reconsidered its relationship only with considerable reluctance. Nevertheless, disillusioned by the attitude of the Labour Cabinet in 1924, in particular by Mac-Donald's 'constitutionalist' opposition to their access to government departments and his evasion of their advice,* to say nothing of the government's attitude towards strikes and the existing strike-breaking machinery,[34] the TUC reacted harshly. If Labour Ministers wished to demonstrate themselves independent of TUC influence in order to impress their Tory and Liberal predecessors, if MacDonald was to accuse striking unions of 'disloyalty', then, as W. J. Brown told the TUC in 1925, 'even with a complete Labour majority in the House of Commons, and with a Labour government that was stable and secure, there would be a permanent difference in point of view between the government on the one hand and the trade unions on the other.'[35]

A degree of incompatibility had always existed between the party's need to win votes and the trade unions' obligation to defend members' interests; but the experience of 1924 was needed to point it up sufficiently clearly for the TUC to seek to alter the old division of labour within the movement laid down by Henderson in 1913. The TUC came to realise that 'Labour leaders . . . will always stand for the authority of the political Parliament over even the Trade Union movement. . . . To them the Unions are useful, even vital organisations for specific purposes, but those purposes and the organisations themselves must always remain subordinate to the political Government.'[36] But it lacked leverage: Bevin's resolution forbidding the party to take office again in a minority was defeated at the 1925 Scarborough TUC Congress, and on the Labour Party side no further rethinking of the relationship took place before 1931.

For its part, the TUC deliberately broke up the Joint Committees during 1925, accusing them of having become almost autonomous, under the domination of left-wing MPs. Henceforward, the TUC would develop its own research and policy-making organs. 'It was impossible,' the Functions Committee Inquiry concluded, 'for the work of the TUC adequately to be carried out by joint departments. The identity of the trade union and political labour movements [must be] kept entirely distinct, and while the closest collaboration is necessary, the work of each necessitates its own machinery'.[37] The General

*PREM 1/24. During a TUC deputation in April 1924, Bramley (Secretary of the General Council) complained that T. Shaw, Minister of Labour, had abrogated the well-established practice of departments showing Bills to the TUC and of indulging in confidential discussions. He gave specific examples of past cases where TUC amendments had been accepted; MacDonald and Henderson, however, defended Shaw on the grounds of the 'sovereignty of Parliament'. (See also CAB 204/24.)

Council's staff was increased; Walter Citrine, a brilliant organiser, took office as secretary in 1925 after the sudden death of Fred Bramley and gave an increased emphasis to the centralising process which Bramley and Gosling had begun in the early 1920s. Although the organisation department failed to establish any substantial control over individual unions (as the General Strike revealed) the General Council emerged in 1927 qualified as a policy-making machine.[38] The line runs clear on to the TUC's claim to parity with Labour's NEC on the National Joint Council in 1929, and its unsuccessful attempt to shape Labour Government policy in the crisis of August 1931.

However consistently this development of the theory of TUC autonomy from the Labour Party matched that of the NCEO from the Conservatives, its practice fluctuated widely. The annual turnover of members of the General Council, as much as changing circumstances, accounted for a rapid shift between militancy in 1925 and moderation in 1926. As the Ministry of Labour noticed, a membership of thirty-two was too large to be effective,[39] while on controversial questions, such as the family allowances proposed by the ILP in *Socialism in our time*, the General Council too often reflected the disagreements of its members, a weakness from which the NCEO rarely suffered. Only at the very end of the 1920s, with the setting up of the Economic Committee, could it give a clear lead to the movement on a major change of policy like the tariff – and even then only when cajoled by Bevin and the Transport and General Workers' Union.[40]

It could be argued that in periods of Labour government TUC pretensions suffered no more than those of the NCEO in its long struggle with Steel-Maitland and the Conservative Cabinet between 1925 and 1928 (see below pp. 191). But in the activity of the Communist Party and the various remnants of the Shop Stewards' Movement, the TUC had another impediment, much more damaging than, say, the stance of the Coal Owners was to the NCEO. The Labour Party could with impunity and the help of the TUC block vote demolish the CPGB's annual application for affiliation; but the trade union movement had to contend with Communist infiltration not only on the shop floor but in the National Unemployed Workers' Movement (NUWM) and in Trades Councils, where, as the General Council recognised early on, 'their propaganda value is – or could be – enormous.'[41]

On the ideological level, and because of their close association with the Minority Movement (successor to the Shop Stewards) and control of the NUWM, the Communist Party claimed a rightful position in the 'struggle to force the capitalists to relinquish their grip in industry' (in the words of a 1925 TUC resolution); inevitably this put the TUC on the defensive. As the Research Department complained, 'Communist sections try to discredit the Industrial Parliament project on the ground that it is a form of "class collaboration" '.[42]

Given CPGB assumptions, the charge was true: however diverse individual unions' practice had been in the early 1920s, the TUC had committed itself to national wage agreements, and collective bargaining *vis-à-vis* the employers, and a political relationship with government whether Labour or Conservative. In this sense – which extended into all its research and planning work – the General Council stood for gradual reform of the capitalist system rather than sudden transition to socialism: even the emergency programme drafted by the Economic Committee and put to the Labour Cabinet in the August crisis of 1931 amounted to little more than that finally introduced by the National Government in 1931–2.

When it came to organisation and strategy, the TUC's care not to alienate the unemployed by complete refusal to recognise the NUWM or the tactic of the hunger march did not disguise the fundamental conflict of interest between them and the Communist Party, nor the outright hostility which developed when the CPGB took up its United Front strategy early in 1924. Taken with the miners' proposal for a massive alliance of the Left in 1925, with its clear intention to revive the defunct Triple Alliance, this hostility seemed to be directed as a 'counterblast to the FBI' and the policy of wage-cutting. In a competitive situation only too reminiscent of 1917–21, the TUC could hardly afford to seem less militant,* especially since this battle was fought outside as well as inside the factories, and on Trades Councils which had in many cases given organisational focus to the errant Councils of Action in 1921–2.†

In the course of that campaign the General Council was forced to adopt many of the techniques of its opponents. It excluded CPGB members, prescribed model rules and finally imposed its own parallel structure on the Trades Councils after 1926;[43] but although the majority of Councils had been 'recovered' by the time the CPGB

---

*A point fully appreciated by government, *vide* Steel-Maitland's paper, CAB 239/25. One of the few sympathetic actions of the Labour Cabinet in 1924 had been that Clynes, the Home Secretary, passed on to the TUC secret information in order to help them exclude members of the CPGB from trade union office (CAB 273/24).

†The link between Councils of Action and the Communist-dominated National Federation of Trades Councils survived until 1924, despite an increase in syndicalist tendencies. But the TUC succeeded in imposing its own organisation, the Joint Consultative Council, in May 1924, staffed with staid, elderly nominees, thus pre-empting the CPGB's campaign for a united front.

abandoned the United Front in 1929, leftist tendencies were not erased, surviving into the era of renewed conflict after 1933; and the TUC was constrained to prevent direct affiliation even of those Trades Councils which its General Council 'recognised' as purged of the CP taint. Moreover, the years 1925–6 gave the Communists a unique advantage. A CP/Minority Movement resolution in favour of the United Front was carried by a majority of two to one at the 1925 TUC Congress; and for a few months it looked as if the industrial tactics of Cook and J. T. Murphy might succeed. The CPGB call for militant support of the miners before the General Strike, backed as it was by Trades Councils and Councils of Action bent on creating an alternative sphere of government, represented a persuasive alternative to the apparent vacillation of the TUC leaders – a challenge the General Council could not ignore* even though, in a way that has not been sufficiently emphasised, it also predisposed them against complete involvement with the miners long before the dramatic events of May 1926.

The deep inclination towards dissociation from the left-wing attitude to the General Strike derived as much from the 'cherished illusion' of parliamentarianism and the equally cherished right of individual member unions to dissent from the TUC as it did from the leaders' dilemma. The Communist Party's numerical weakness forced it to try and build up the General Council as a virtual dictatorship of the working-class movement,† which was more than the great bulk of trade unionists could stomach; and secondly, the CPGB's submissiveness to the external direction of the Comintern‡ turned it away from the United Front after the failure of the General Strike, towards the creation of a politically and industrially autonomous party, a course which greatly facilitated the triumph of reformism in TUC and Labour Party down to 1934.

The degree to which TUC and NCEO had become governing institutions can be measured, not by their offensive action (because the temporary unwillingness of government to take issue might produce an almost fortuitous triumph, like Red Friday in 1925) but by their capa-

---

* Particularly because of the skilful way the CPGB sought to blur the lines of demarcation. 'Consolidate your press *locally*,' the CPGB Executive advised members. 'Insist on the formation of the workers' alliance under the supreme authority of the General Council.' (*Workers' Weekly*, 9 October 1925.)

†The CPGB proposed more than the General Council ever dared to ask for: a power of financial levy and a power to summon individual unions to strike in sympathy. (Minority Movement 'Open Letter on the Capitalist Offensive', 1925.)

‡R. Palme Dutt had, of course, always opposed the United Front from within the CPGB.

city for sustained defence. The Washington Hours case illustrates the point for the NCEO; the wage-cutting issue, and hence the General Strike, for the TUC; and unemployment insurance legislation for both. All three issues touched on the basic institutional function of representation of grievances, and called in question the hold of either side over government itself.

Successive governments' prolonged refusal to ratify the 48-hour week, laid down by the Washington Convention of 1921, outraged a generation of trade unionists to whom British dilatoriness in the face of the European trade union federations and the ILO seemed inexcusable; especially since in 1925 the Conservatives actually conceded that what they did would influence working conditions as far away as India and Japan. In spite of the complaints of the small group of Tory radicals, however, government listened to the NCEO who, on the somewhat specious argument of the need for long hours in agriculture and transport work, fought what they publicly damned as 'proposals endangering British industry' backed by the 'political agitation' of the TUC.[44] More pertinently, they argued that British sovereignty would be infringed by ILO rules; and that refusal to ratify would facilitate wage-cutting in the 'sheltered' industries.[45]

When, in 1926, the Baldwin Government seemed ready to ratify, the NCEO mobilised large numbers of backbench MPs and conducted a press campaign comparable to the early activities of Sydney Walton,[46] which intimidated Steel-Maitland, Minister of Labour, and ensured that, when the Cabinet did decide to legislate, they tempered the Bill as much as possible, going so far as to consult not only the NCEO but individual employers who were shown confidential copies of the emasculated Bill.[47] So successful had the NCEO been in its own defence that it tried to avoid public odium: 'they did not wish to be put in the position of appearing to oppose reform',[48] Philip Cunliffe-Lister (who had changed his name from Lloyd-Greame) told his colleagues, and in due course Conservative Central Office had to produce an anodyne account of the episode for the forthcoming General Election.[49]

Not all employers opposed the Washington Hours: the FBI was prepared to accept the limit in exchange for productivity bargains,[50] and individual employers, many of them later members of the Mond group in 1928–9, took a softer line in private talks.[51] But they were not prepared to challenge the NCEO's predominance, at least until the TUC's position had been weakened after the General Strike. Some chased the chimera of 'non-political unionism'; but tacitly accepted the credit when the NCEO, in its recruiting campaign, claimed to have achieved *reductions* in workmen's compensation and in liabilities under previous Factory Act legislation;[52] and no one actually dissociated himself from the vindictive lobbying by the NCEO's Labour Investigating Committee during the genesis of the 1927 Trades Disputes Act.

NCEO and TUC took predictable courses over unemployment insurance legislation, seeking advantage according to whichever party was in power and entrenching themselves alternately in opposition. The TUC aimed for a comprehensive, non-contributory scheme; the NCEO for full insurance contributions. Yet, as in a formal dance, they agreed on certain conventions: that both were representative of their members, with views which had to be considered by government; and that, failing conclusive victory by either side, the state should apportion the cost equally, taking one-third itself. When the Conservative Government set up the Blanesburgh Committee in 1926, both institutions were invited to provide research material on wages and employment, and a detailed study of the preparation and submission of their evidence justifies their claims to 'vocational representation'.[53] When in the end, in spite of all the pressures on Churchill,[54] the Treasury baulked at the cost of increasing the state contribution to make up equal thirds, the NCEO, mournfully watching the bankruptcy of the Fund, deplored the result as much as did the TUC; though of course the latter could not sympathise with the NCEO's protest against renewed public borrowing, after 1928.

The NCEO's ideological attitudes in the late 1920s remained diametrically opposed to those of the TUC, and provided much of the intellectual background of the 1931 May Report, with its alarmist prediction of the effect of such borrowing on financial stability. Yet the 1929 Labour Government continued its predecessors' practice of relying equally on the two institutions for advice. Margaret Bondfield (Minister of Labour) set up an advisory committee on unemployment insurance anomalies with three NCEO, three TUC and two government members, and the NCEO duly appointed its top men.[55] Both sides had crossed the threshold which separates the lobby from the institution; both had access to likeminded MPs and the press;[56] both could make their anger felt if the government chose to ignore their status and rights. In spite of the natural predilection of Tories for employers, and Labour Ministers for trade unionists, a continuity had been created which rivalled that of government departments; although, up to the end of the 1920s, by private contact with civil servants like Horace Wilson and Warren Fisher as well as Ministers, the NCEO were still able more effectively to filter their assumptions intravenously into the state apparatus.*

Independent observers recognised them as estates of the realm. The Astor Group suggested, rather disingenuously, in 1927:

The trade union movement has reached a position in which many of its present tendencies are inconsistent with its co-existence in a democratic state. It has attained a status which should enable it, properly directed, to take a much more responsible share in the development of industry, and at the same time an acknowledged strength which renders unnecessary several of its privileges which were reasonable at the stage when it was essentially an organisation fighting against odds.[57]

The TUC put the emphasis slightly differently. Rejecting wholly the argument that they existed on sufferance 'by gracious permission of the state', they claimed origin in 'the needs of mankind under certain conditions; and their standing and authority are independent of the state and they should be supreme *in their own sphere*. . . .' Without deliberately endorsing the then fashionable philosophy of pluralism, the Research Department argued, as early as December 1926, that the trade union movement

has implicitly adopted those principles. It is developing a body of inter-union law and judicial machinery for interpreting it; it is developing its own hierarchy of government, its own civil service, its own sanctions, independently of the state; with employers it is creating codes regulating conditions of labour . . . it has even, at the request of the state, taken over important administrative functions.[58]

Governments' standpoints developed in harmony with these institutions in spite of the apparent withdrawal of parties to the political poles. Recognising where institutional power lay, Baldwin took care (as much as Lloyd George had in 1916) not to make appointments to his second Ministry which would antagonise union opinion.[59] Conversely, the 1924 Labour Government's 'constitutional' stance owed a great deal to its belief that it was necessary to convince big business and the banking world of its respectability; Tom Shaw's labour policy actually antagonised the Ministry of Labour officials because it resembled some of the worst features of Lloyd George's period in its approach to strikes and Communist Party infiltration,[60] to say nothing of devaluing the Inquiry

*For example, NCEO memoranda NC 1161 (4 March 1925) on social service contributions, NC 1430 on wage-cutting, and the attack on the 1930 Coal Mines Bill (Weir 4/20). It could be argued that the TUC had an equally effective vehicle in sympathisers like Thomas Jones, J. J. Mallon and Seebohm Rowntree.

procedure by setting up seven committees in nine months, thus taking the 'appeal to public opinion' to absurd lengths.

Unable to make progress with Shaw, for whom Wilson and Shackleton showed personal rancour, the Ministry staff put their hopes on the new man, Steel-Maitland, in 1925, correctly judging him to have Baldwin's confidence. Steel-Maitland has been somewhat underrated. Jones described him as

most industrious and has laboured hard to get up the subject, but distrusts himself, turns constantly to Horace Wilson at his elbow, apologises, protests that he is being frank and straight, which of course he is trying to be, but the total impression is of weakness and cloudiness.[61]

Faults of manner, however, could not disguise his intellectual power, persistence, and the fact that he had a synoptic vision of industrial policy.

His design evolved in two stages, separated by the crisis of 1925–6. 'I had hoped this spring,' Steel-Maitland told Robert Cecil in October 1926, 'to have got an agreement between employers and employed that was intended to go *pari passu* with the Convention [on Washington Hours]. That fell through, and instead of it there came the [General] Strike.'[62] The earlier plan was vitiated partly because he had assumed, wrongly, that NCEO and TUC were ready to bind themselves to an industrial concordat in a way previously unimaginable; and, consequently, he had to wait for the altered climate after 1927. But he was not wrong in sensing the existence of common ground, not only between NCEO and TUC, but between MacDonald's section of the Labour Party and the mainstream of Conservative thinking which Baldwin represented. By returning Labour with 151 seats against the Conservatives' 415 and virtually eliminating the Liberals (42), the 1924 Election had committed Labour irrevocably (as Milne-Bailey admitted) to capturing a popular vote beyond the strict confines of the working class.

On this basis, what Baldwin called (on the occasion of the 1925 Party Conference) 'a peace treaty for a limited time' could be amplified. In the first stage, Steel-Maitland held a series of private meetings with leading employers and trade unionists in March 1925,[63] in which he attempted first to trade employers' concessions against wage reductions, mainly in the sheltered trades, and secondly to see what measures of legislation on trade union practices might be acceptable, given Conservative Party demands for political levy amendment, secret ballot, registration and restrictions on picketing. Fortified by reports of these meetings, Baldwin destroyed the MacQuisten Bill (which would have altered the practice of contracting out of the political levy), confident that he could, in due course, bring in a better, more equitable form of amendment to the 1906 Act itself, steering between the diehards who wanted to return to Taff Vale and the few who desired no action at all.[64] Other factors in the 'peace treaty' included abrogation of mining royalties (by now an offence even to the opponents of coal nationalisation), schemes for co-partnership in the pits,[65] and continued subsidies for coal and shipbuilding.[66]

Steel-Maitland's scheme survived Red Friday and the government's warnings of what would be done to suppress a future general strike.[67] Even in March 1926, on the verge of the strike itself, a second series of very secret encounters with trade unionists and employers (including Evan Williams of the Coal Owners' Association) encouraged him to think that triangular cooperation could be achieved.* Citrine advised him that a *treaty* was premature: 'he had tried to get the General Council to think the thing out, but they were inclined to say, as was natural with simple men, and elderly, dealing with very technical questions of another trade, that that was for the unions to do, and tell them.'[68] But Citrine wished government to offer negotiations in the coal dispute as an earnest of what might happen after, and agreed to the idea that a small TUC delegation (Bevin, Pugh and Citrine) should meet the Cabinet and the Coal Owners' Association. Meanwhile, Horace Wilson discussed with Bevin how the TUC could convince the miners of the need for wage reductions, if a high-level bargain on the future of the coal industry were made between TUC and NCEO.[69]

This attempt to stifle the General Strike at birth failed; chiefly because it was impossible to induce either TUC or NCEO to detach themselves sufficiently from miners and owners (witness the pressure put on Baldwin himself by Weir to consider longer hours in the pits as more important than reduced wages). But Steel-Maitland had allowed for backsliding: for a big trade union Bill, 'much would depend on the moment chosen for its introduction; the most favourable time would be after a big strike'.[70] As a last resort, that strike was not unwelcome; the dinosaurs had to be rendered extinct, from the point of view of government, NCEO, and the TUC itself, if indeed the choice lay between class warfare and the collapse of capitalist society on one hand and industrial harmony on the other.

The distinction made by Baldwin and Steel-Maitland may have been

*SM GD 193/387. Many of his conclusions were substantiated by his private office's press research work and the reports presented by John Hilton (then an official of the Ministry of Health) on the unemployment question.

too tidy: Beatrice Webb observed accurately in September 1925: 'The Conservative government will go forward in one direction: exactly as the Labour government failed to go rapidly forward, so the Conservative government will find itself prevented from going backward. Public opinion will insist on the *middle* way – but it will be a collectivist middle way.'[71] Nevertheless, the Government's public presentation of its case, its apparent moderation up to the moment of rupture on 30 April, its determination to smash 'extremism', its insistence on the constitutional issue, were all designed to imprint that choice on trade unionists and the public mind – and the intensity of secret preparations for the strike throws doubt, not on Steel-Maitland's sincerity, but on the sincerity of his Cabinet colleagues.*

Steel-Maitland had to contend with Conservative enthusiasm for drastic amendments to the 1906 Trades Disputes Act, which had been simmering ever since Dicey protested at the unwarranted and unprecedented privileges it conferred on trade unions. As Prime Minister, however much he supported his colleague, Baldwin also found it hard to deflect Churchill's skilful argument (with which he had great sympathy), that unions' legal status should be counterbalanced by imposing the contractual responsibility which the TUC had shuffled off at the time of the Liberal Bill in 1906. It was scarcely easier to curb backbench demands for reform of the political levy,† in spite of the attitude of moderates in the NCEO; and although Baldwin won the support of the majority of the Cabinet when he destroyed MacQuisten's Bill, this

---

*The emergency organisation, run down after Black Friday, had been reinforced in 1922 (CAB 20/22/4) before being subsumed into the full Supply and Transport organisation, on lines recommended by Sir John Anderson in July 1923; and from then on Anderson, aided by the Chief Civil Commissioners and the Departments, prepared quite specifically to counter any general strike. (CAB 27/204: J. C. C. Davidson, *Memoirs of a Conservative*, pp. 179–80.) Kept alive, if not actually much used by the Labour Government, the apparatus was renewed in 1925. (CP 27/239 shows that Clynes (the Labour Home Secretary) used Special Branch to spy on Communists and open their mail, etc., and relied on the propaganda service to build up moderate trade union leaders at the expense of those 'extremists' with which the Government seems to have been obsessed.) (See also CAB 27/259, EC 24/3 for Wedgwood's view, in comparison with Davidson.) Davidson's *Memoirs* make clear that when Baldwin declared 'we were not ready', as an explanation of Red Friday, he meant ready in the sense of public opinion, not the technical state of government counter-measures. (Davidson 227–31; CAB 27/260–61.) The Supply and Transport organisation (covered discreetly by the purely civilian front called the Organisation for the Maintenance of Supplies) functioned as a professional, quasi-military arm of the state, far more efficiently than the old Emergency Committee under Geddes in 1921.

†A petition signed by 258 MPs had been presented to Chamberlain at the 1922 Party Conference, pointing out that 'there would be widespread and serious indignation among the *wage-earning* supporters of the Conservative Party if the present Bill were not supported officially'.

avoidance of a gratuitous attack on the unions set up antagonisms in the party which were strengthened both by the conspiracy theory of trade unionism avidly put forward by the Home Secretary, William Joynson-Hicks, and by the predictably extreme views of sections of the party organisation.* The fact that the desire not to 'strike the first blow' (as Baldwin told the 1925 Party Conference) was based on an estimate of the unreadiness of the nation at large for a struggle *à l'outrance* was not admitted by that narrow public opinion to which Party leaders must respond, which damned as weakness the offer of a renewed subsidy to the coal industry on Red Friday, in July 1925, and which stored up recrimination against the outbreak of a general strike.

The government was well aware that after the French withdrawal from the German coalfields of the Ruhr in 1924 and the consequent rapid fall in profits of those pits which exported English coal, a head-on clash in the coal industry could not be avoided. It was obvious that the coal owners would seek to force wages down, and that, to defend themselves against a policy of wage-cutting, other unions were virtually bound to support the miners; also that, to ensure a general saving in the price of basic energy and hence of industrial costs, the NCEO were bound to stand by the Coal Owners' Association. In itself, this logic justified the Supply and Transport Committee's preparations.

But the Government was unwilling to be seen to put state resources behind the employers in cutting working-class wages,† and resorted to a dual policy: a subsidy to tide the coal industry over nine months while the Samuel Commission investigated the basis of future profitability; and a campaign of mass political education. To answer the cry of 'who governs England', Baldwin announced that 'the public will know [in nine months] what it does not know now, the merits of the dispute and the necessity, if any, for a strike.'[72] Crude though some manifestations

*Labour Sub-Committee Reports to Conservative National Council 1921–5 advocated a fight on every possible issue – against the T and GWU amalgamation, the political levy, use of trade union funds to support the *Daily Herald*, and the Labour Colleges, etc. A fair sample of Conservative propaganda can be found in the programme of Philip Stott College for Political Education (Davidson papers). Central Office planned to set up an insurance company specifically for working-class members, to undercut trade union friendly society benefits (Admiral Hall to Davidson, 5 April 1923, BL 111/34/164). The Local Associations all supported MacQuisten's Bill (CAB 27/269, BL 25/4).

†'Public opinion is, to a considerable extent, on the miners' side,' Baldwin told the King on 25 July; even some Tory MPs were supporting their case for an inquiry. 'To put it bluntly, it was felt that public opinion would not be convinced that the miners were wholly in the wrong, and that, in those circumstances, it would not be justifiable to plunge the country into so dire a struggle.' (RA GV B2015/5–19.) (According to Hankey, these *political* considerations were not mentioned in the Cabinet minutes recording the decision to renew the subsidy. *Ibid.* /19.)

of this plan were (the Home Secretary obtained the conviction of twelve leading Communists under the 1795 Incitement to Mutiny Act) its effect was to emphasise the *national* nature of the problem and to set the TUC as a representative body against the 'factional' miners' union, Minority Movement, or Triple Alliance.

Far less effort went into detaching the NCEO, because of the intractable nature of the problems of the coal industry. With bitter memories of being forced by Lloyd George, especially over the Seven Hours Act in 1919, the coal owners stuck out obdurately for lower wages, longer hours, and district agreements, and never budged until they won all three at the end of 1926. Yet economic logic argued otherwise. Declining profits, worn-out seams, lack of mechanisation, led Samuel to the only possible conclusion short of nationalisation: that the industry must be reorganised, albeit on the basis of savings from reduced wages and longer hours.

There is some evidence that the MFGB could have accepted such a scheme of modernisation and rationalisation, in spite of the inevitable increase in unemployment, if the government had guaranteed the future investment on which profitability and higher wages depended.[73] But the owners blindly rejected any form of reorganisation, fearing that the majority of smaller pits would be forced out of business. No conceivable cuts in wages could have saved for long those depressed, under-capitalised and incompetent concerns; yet men like Adam Nimmo blandly assumed that government would back them up,[74] displaying an intransigence in discussion not unlike that of ruling élites on the verge of extinction in pre-revolutionary France or Russia.* As in 1790 and 1917, their attitudes helped to determine the tactics of the opposition; and the Government, unwilling for political reasons to coerce the owners, had to watch a struggle develop over hours and wages rather than over the terms recommended by Samuel which they preferred.

They also assumed that the NCEO would urge moderation on the coal owners even though the latter, vengeful against Baldwin's gift of the subsidy, utterly rejected Samuel's concept of 'equal sacrifice'. But in fact, knowing in advance how little influence even far-sighted owners like David Davies and Alfred Mond had, the NCEO barely tried.[75] The Cabinet accepted Samuel's report in April 1926, with the proviso that both parties did so as well; but the owners offered only trivial conces-

---

*'Nimmo's company pays 10 per cent; but the Coal Owners have always gone to the utmost limit of self-sacrifice, the question in debate is always fundamental, and always involves a vital principle on which the Owners cannot possibly carry compromise an inch further.' (T. Jones, *Whitehall Diary*, vol. II, p. 12.)

sions (a minimum wage comparable with that of 1921 for an eight-hour day which would have meant a reduction in most districts of 20 per cent), and the failure to guarantee future investment suggested a degree of bias on the part of government which completed the alienation of the TUC.*

The events of late April 1926 showed the miners' leaders, far from being the 'stupid men' of Birkenhead's famous jibe, as realists confronted with demands at least as harsh as the economic extinction against which the owners struggled. Herbert Smith and Arthur Cook could concede nothing, in default of the state guarantee which might conceivably have avoided the strike. Yet the TUC, divided between reformers and revolutionaries, constitutionalists and the advocates of resistance like John Wheatley ('We need 10,000 armed men to prevent Britain becoming a land of coolies') and the enthusiasts of the Scarborough Congress of 1925, was lamentably unprepared to take on a representative role. In the months before, the General Council's Special Industrial Committee (SIC) had ignored the known facts about the Supply and Transport organisation and had put the onus on the MFGB to set its own house in order,[76] recalling with a certain *schadenfreude* the miners' rejection of TUC advice in 1921. For procedural reasons only, the TUC had been spared an appeal by the MFGB to the reconstituted Triple Alliance in July 1925, so that the General Council's claim to the credit of Red Friday and the subsidy was inherently weak; Citrine's blunt declaration that there could be no question of a general strike unless the General Council were given full powers had been forgotten in the Scarborough tumult; and, embarrassed by the CPGB's unwelcome advice that it should take dictatorial control of the trade union movement, the TUC failed to establish agreement on the first principles of joint action.

On the other hand, after their preliminary meetings in February 1926, the MFGB did very little to keep the General Council informed and only approached the SIC five days before the strike began; while the disastrous ambiguity of Herbert Smith's phrase ('We have handed this thing over to you, of course, functioning in this business along with you')[77] indicated how little the miners themselves had progressed from the mistrustful couplings of the Triple Alliance. The SIC, in turn, rejected help from the Labour Party, and took the political stage itself

---

*'It is impossible', Tom Jones noticed, 'not to feel the contrast between the reception which Ministers give to a body of owners and a body of miners. Ministers are at ease at once with the former, they are friends jointly exploring a situation.' (Jones, *Whitehall Diary*, vol. II, p. 19.)

in a series of eight meetings with Baldwin and Steel-Maitland, in which they appeared inclined to accept the main principles of Samuel's report, thus building up in the Cabinet a rather unrealistic expectation of compromise.

It is obvious from TUC records[78] that Pugh (who even visited Baldwin in great secrecy at Chequers)[79] and the SIC tried their best to avoid the strike, and took reluctant control of a campaign in which they could not really believe: and their inability to make any bargain stick with the miners leaves their later tirades against government for its failure to coerce the coal owners more than disingenuous. The Cabinet also came close to duplicity in listening to the blandishments of Lord Weir and the SIC, and then blaming owners and miners for a hardening of attitude which they could perhaps have helped to avoid. It can be argued that the Government's defensive preparations confirm that they had foreseen the possibility of breakdown; yet this need not condemn as simply a diversionary tactic the attempt at a negotiated settlement with the TUC outlined in the Pugh–Baldwin conversations at Chequers. Historians may always argue whether the small negotiating teams came near agreement on the night of 1 May. The miners could not and would not share the General Council's wider anxieties, however, and the *Daily Mail* incident only completed a joint estrangement which became patent at the Cabinet meeting the following morning. Given the personal composition of the institutions concerned, and their political and economic predicament, it is very hard to see how any of them could have behaved otherwise.

During the nine days of the General Strike, 3–12 May, as the General Council was exposed to alternate praise, blackmail, patriotic appeals and finally execration, the NCEO bided its time and the FBI discreetly supported the emergency service,* welcoming in public the government's 'constitutional' stand. The government showed itself adept at mobilising public opinion, and Baldwin at rebutting the 'mistaken impression that this was a lawful exercise of the rights of the working class. It is nothing of the sort'.[80]

Meanwhile the coal owners obdurately resisted all attempts at mediation, and encouraged the formation of breakaway miners' unions. After the General Strike had collapsed, leaving the miners to struggle on alone, they reverted to district wages, and in June concentrated on

---

*Giving logistic aid, for example, to provide coal supplies to power stations and gas works then and during the six months miners' strike to keep industries from short-time and lay-offs.

forcing the government to put through an Eight Hours Bill, using all their powers as a lobby in the Lords, among backbench MPs, and in the press. Unwisely, the Cabinet gave them this Bill, as part of a 'gentleman's agreement' about a nation alminimum wage, which the owners later repudiated. Later, when the Cabinet offered a reorganisation scheme, and the long-promised financial aid which might, even then, have tempted the miners, the owners despatched it by refusing to issue a new scale of wages contingent on longer hours. They had probably never intended to play the government's game, merely using the chance to smash MFGB opposition – in which they amply succeeded.[81]

Baldwin salvaged something when the Cabinet coerced West Yorkshire owners into abandoning the worst of their catastrophic wage cuts; yet only Churchill, briefly, in September, actually instilled fear into the owners with a proposal for a special National Court. Then the NCEO, fearful for their cheap coal supplies, stirred up backbench discontent effectively enough to turn Baldwin and the majority of the Cabinet against the Chancellor.[82] Reviving in the Tory demonology the spectre of Lloyd George's wartime bargains, the NCEO argued: 'When the state is the third party, *with the final say*, negotiations between the other two parties, who are really responsible, become unreal and very largely ineffective.'[83] In practical politics, this had already become dubious doctrine; but on the 'true party men' who had broken up the Coalition it had its effect. In the last resort, confronted with party resistance, the Cabinet refused to contemplate the introduction of compulsory arbitration *which neither side might accept*: and were immensely relieved when the MFGB settled the point by vetoing any settlement containing longer hours or lower wages.[84]

The trade union movement appeared to lose on all fronts. However much their social environment and economic desperation justified the miners' actions, the fact remains that, after the collapse of their strike in December, the coal owners gained every point and MFGB bargaining power was broken for a generation. But for the miners' highly decentralised procedures, a better settlement might have been reached in late September – but it must be added that the miners' leaders gave no clear indication in public of what they felt, privately, to be the only way out.[85] Membership dropped, catastrophically at first and then more slowly down to the Second World War, and breakaway 'company unions' sprang up in Nottinghamshire and Yorkshire,[86] with Communist-led Miners' Industrial Unions in South Wales and Lancashire. The MFGB's collegiate structure had concealed deep divisions which were shrewdly exploited not only by owners, but by Conservatives seeking, as ever, the chimera of 'non-political unionism'. Baldwin set up a Conservative Party fund, administered by Waldron Smithers, which helped to finance the Spencer Union in Nottinghamshire, until about 1935;[87] Joynson-Hicks overhauled the Home Office procedure for controlling pickets, and Conservative Central Office raised its distribution of anti-union leaflets from the 6·8 million of 1926 to 18·8 million in 1927.[88]

A less dramatic fall in numbers took place among nearly all trade unions, attributable partly to disillusion, partly to the slow lessening of tension as employers generally abandoned the attempt to cut wages. Apparently less serious than in 1921, when the TUC had lost 600,000 members in one year, the prolonged slide had begun before 1926 and continued into the slump after 1929. But decline hit most acutely unions affiliated to the TUC; and the *density* of membership, a vital indication of union strength, dropped from 37 per cent in 1926 to a mere 29 per cent in 1931. Use of the strike weapon, not unnaturally, dropped by five-sixths from 1923.*

But the employers' federations also suffered a severe decline in membership at the same time† (although for different reasons, as firms saw less need for defence against trade unions); and although the long haemorrhage weakened formerly militant unions, it is both too simple and too harsh to suggest that 'the [1926] surrender immeasurably advanced the transformation of the workers' movement into a tame, disciplined trade union and electoral interest'.[89] The General Strike only completed a work begun long before, in which the leadership of the whole Labour movement detached itself from the persuasive doctrines of the shop stewards' movement and the Communist Party. Their curiously ambiguous defence mounted against the Trades Disputes Act in 1926–7, when the TUC's protests seemed much more a means of diverting blame from its 'guilt' in the collapse of the Strike than any concerted attack on those old demons, 'the powerful em-

*	1924	1925	1926	1927	1928
TUC membership		4.3m			3.6m
Stoppages	716	603	323	308	302
Total workers involved	613,000	441,000	2,734,000	108,000	124,000
Days lost, (000s)	8,424	7,952	162,233	1,174	1,388

†The EEF, for example:	1918	1921	1925	1927	1929	1931
Number of firms	1,469	2,600	2,389	2,175	2,069	1,968
Number of workpeople employed	439,000	448,000	624,000	533,000	540,000	405,000

(E. Wigham, *The Power to Manage*, p. 125.)

ployers' associations and reactionary class influences which control the Tory government',[90] suggests that the extra disabilities it imposed on the Left were not entirely unwelcome.

The Act itself marks another stage in the developing antithesis between governing institutions and the political parties. Badly drafted (as Lord Hailsham, the Lord Chancellor, admitted) its long-term effect was scarcely more than symbolic, apart from that section which enforced political levy contracting-in, to the detriment of Labour Party funds. Economic weakness provides a more convincing explanation for the lack of strikes after 1926 and previous estimates of the Act's restrictive force should be revised in the light of experience of resistance, albeit in very different circumstances, to the Industrial Relations Act after 1971. But the use of legislation as a means to regulate industrial politics derived from a long Conservative intellectual tradition, summed up in Sir Henry Maine's famous dictum that the future of humanity lay in progress from status to contract, and Baldwin's gloss that socialism implied the reverse.

Early in 1925 Churchill had raised the question of equity involved in contracting-out, suggesting in its place Exchequer subsidies for all parties' electoral expenses;* while Lord Birkenhead had envisaged something even more contentious, 'which will involve complete reconsideration of the exceptional legal status conceded to trade unions [in 1906] and which, they seem to me, under the influence of extremist elements, to have grossly abused.'[91] In Central Office the idea of legislation seems to have encompassed an alteration in the balance of political power;[92] and in the Conference resolutions in 1926, after the General Strike, it reached the point of retribution which finally shaped the statute itself. Conservative backbenchers had originally opposed legislation, according to a survey made by the Chief Whip,[93] but they succumbed to constituency pressures, after an uncommonly wide inquiry revealed the strength of Tory voters' opinion, especially in industrial areas.†

*Jones, *Whitehall Diary*, vol. I, pp. 3–11. Churchill (and later, Baldwin) committed themselves, on the basis of rather dubious evidence, to the proposition that 23 per cent of all trade unionists habitually took advantage of the contracting-out provisions. But CP 35/27 (February 1927) gives the precise figure of 111,000 contracted-out of those 111 unions (3.3 million members) who had a political levy. Only by adding to that the 1.1 million other unionists whose unions did not have a levy, could the 23 per cent figure be sustained! See also SM GD 193/4333, showing that since 1913 there had been only seventy appeals against victimisation, under the 1913 Act.

†This enquiry, covering 292 constituencies was the most thorough ever undertaken by Central Office. Highest priority among the recommendations fell on the secret ballot, reform of picketing and the political levy. Few cared about reforming the 1906 Act or reference to an Industrial Court (Neville Chamberlain's idea). The survey directly affected the scope of the final Bill (SB D 3.4).

Although Steel-Maitland and his officials emerged as protagonists of a moderate, farsighted line, avoiding legislation, and although the Cabinet Committee, led by Lord Cave, gave weight to many of the arguments against legislation later magisterially endorsed by the Donovan Commission in 1968, in the end, constituency opinion won:[94] the speakers at the Party Conference in October 1926 seemed unable to distinguish between General Council and Communist Party, and this blind unanimity led not only to the 1927 Act, but to the establishment of the Philip Stott College 'as a centre of political information and training' in combating socialism, and to a vigorous anti-Bolshevik campaign.

The victorious employers' associations, echoing the cautious attitude towards legislation expressed by civil servants and the Minister of Labour during the Strike itself, drew rather different conclusions about the future of trade unionism as an adjunct of government, and as a part of the political system. Taken aback by the remarkable solidarity of unions' sympathetic action, they sought to prevent its recurrence, but in their joint proposals to Cabinet for reforming the law on picketing and for a Royal Commission on the workings of the 1906 Act, FBI and NCEO showed themselves careful neither to hustle the government nor to be seen in a vindictive posture – thus tacitly dissociating themselves from the coal owners and the railway companies' victimisation of strikers. Such views were much closer to Steel-Maitland's; and the government, having paid its dues to the necessities of party propaganda, in a deliberately vague and imprecise way,[95] finally desisted from tampering with the 1906 Act.

The negative influence of the TUC can be gauged from Cave's admission that 'it is essential that legislation should be such as will demand the support of the great mass of public opinion *including that of moderate trade unionists.*'[96] And it is clear from what followed that the swingeing provisions of the Act only temporarily deterred a return to collaboration between government, employers and trade unions. Horace Wilson had already predicted 'a return to realism' for the autumn of 1926, and on 11 October Steel-Maitland told Baldwin that the time was ready for him cautiously to work towards a new concordat, using 'reliable men' in the Labour Party (Snowden rather than Mac-Donald), Pugh and Bevin on the General Council, and Herbert Morrison, because he had influence with Lord Weir.[97] During the passage of the Trades Disputes Bill, his main concern had been to increase the power of 'moderate' leaders against 'extremist' shop stewards. 'What is needed,' Steel-Maitland declared, 'is that the position of the leaders should be better safeguarded. . . .' The Government's best plan was to 'reform from within' by 'helping the unions build themselves up . . . with as much regard as possible to their deep-seated, if unreasonable, susceptibilities'.[98]

Such intentions suited an NCEO deeply worried about its declining membership, as well as Citrine and Bevin who were anxious to re-establish the status of the General Council; and in this sense, if no other, the Act served the intentions of Steel-Maitland's original 1925 plan, in edging collective bargaining away from the 'political' back towards the 'industrial' sphere. Ministers did not, however, revert to his former optimism that government could simply 'hold the ring': too much had happened to implicate it in industrial politics. In the long run towards the next election, the Conservative Party needed to take some initiative and emphasise new themes to counter the dazzling programme of regeneration inspired by Lloyd George.

Their proposals at times looked rather timid, probably because Steel-Maitland counted for less than Churchill or Chamberlain in the Cabinet pecking order. 'I want to try again,' he wrote to Robert Cecil in October 1926, concluding that if the TUC was to get anything like the Washington Hours, it could only be in return for a bargain on increased productivity. Weir replied, equally cautiously, 'an understanding between the leaders on each side, of certain general matters, is the next step, but it must be approached very carefully. Any insincerity would ruin it. . . .'[99]

Yet such thinking clearly envisaged TUC and NCEO or FBI as corners of a triangle whose apex was government; an association which an increasing number of employers was prepared to support. During the two years after the General Strike, majority opinion among employers changed; so that in spite of their victory, and largely because of their behaviour, the coal owners drifted into isolation – where they remained until their unlamented extinction twenty years later. As unemployment began, very slowly, to fall,[100] arguments in favour of rationalisation became acceptable, and a group of the more forward-looking members of the FBI (who had always been inclined to accept the Samuel Report), like Sir Peter Rylands (an ex-President) and Sir Alfred Mond, proposed schemes for the regrouping of the coal mines on the model adopted by the Rhenische-Westphalien syndicate.

The NCEO, having gained its cheap coal at the price of the 162 million working days lost in the General Strike, remained highly suspicious at this apparent breach of the demarcation line between the two bodies. Allan Smith and the EEF led the opposition to Mond inside the divided NCEO Council, threatening even to break it up.[101] Yet the ideas of other individuals on the Council, like Weir and Moir, resembled those of Mond; and firms such as Dunlop, Courtaulds, Richard Thomas, and Dorman Long seemed anxious to follow the lead given to rationalisation by the mergers which created ICI and British Oxygen. NCEO and FBI also shared a common and growing dislike of the influence held over government by financial interests. The deplorably inert attitude towards industry which had characterised British merchant banks during the 1920s was already changing,[102] but the hegemony of Lord Cunliffe and the Treasury knights, and the views of the Bank of England on high interest rates (later presented magisterially by Montagu Norman to the Macmillan Committee) survived unimpaired.

Banks and finance houses now appeared as scapegoats, prime obstacles to change; Keynes blamed them, in particular, for the General Strike. Steel-Maitland deliberately avoided them in his 1928–9 scheme for industrial reorganisation backed by government loans.[103] A sudden, sharp and unwelcome increase in bank rate in 1929 exacerbated the feeling that industry's interests were being continually subordinated to those of the City. Organised industry confronted the British banking system with the accusation that it was a closed corporation concerned with overseas capital markets rather than the home industry on which it had grown fat, and won powerful support from the TUC (in the Mond-Turner report) for its demand, first, that government should provide its own national credit policy, and secondly (in the appointment of the Macmillan Committee), a means to review the arcane operation of the Gold Standard itself.

The TUC jumped on this bandwagon with unusual speed. Rationalising their actions at the 1926 Congress, the General Council had already advanced the thesis that the Strike had been only a 'claim to something much deeper than the event. [It] reflected the growing discontent of the workers with the whole structure and policy of the industrial system and the determination to resist the traditional idea that bad trade can be made good, economic vitality and progress obtained, and industry placed in a healthy condition by the mere expedient of degrading the standard of life of the working class.'[104] As wage-cutting slowed down,* the TUC welcomed the opinions of like-minded employers, seeking shade from the heat under the magic umbrella of 'rationalisation'. In December 1926 Milne-Bailey foresaw, quite accu-

---

*Wage-cutting continued after the General Strike, for example, in the woollen trade, but despite the continuing theoretical debate between A. C. Pigou and Professor Henry Clay (in the *Economic Journal* 1927) it ceased to be a *concerted* policy, aimed at the 'sheltered trades'.

rately, both the onslaught against trade unions' legal privileges and the concomitant 'opportunity for claiming powers in another direction, as a *quid pro quo*, and the urgent need for those powers in order to counterbalance what could otherwise be a serious injury.'[105]

By 1928, convinced that the long-awaited trade revival had been permanently delayed, government was prepared to facilitate such cooperation. The genesis of the Macmillan Committee, the evolution of the Industrial Transference Board, the Five Counties coal-marketing scheme, and the Mond-Turner talks all belong in this context. In two consecutive Cabinet Papers Steel-Maitland can be found urging employers to facilitate transference, pressing for a tariff for the iron and steel industry as a weapon to enforce reorganisation, and trying to induce the five main clearing banks to combine to provide finance for industry.[106] But it was necessary first to overcome the collective suspicions of the TUC, and Conservative Party rancour made it impossible for Steel-Maitland or Baldwin to work openly. After some very tentative and secret overtures, Lord Weir chanced the idea of joint conversations in a House of Lords debate in December 1926. He spoke elliptically of 'a few men of good intent, not coming as delegates to voice an official policy dictated to them, but coming together as practical men to seek a solution to practical questions.' Early in January 1927, at Steel-Maitland's request,[107] a meeting was suggested with certain members of the General Council – Bevin, Kayler, Hicks and Pugh; but these declined, waiting for more positive rank and file support. Neither side saw the way clear since Ministers and NCEO still insisted on excluding the idea of a renewed National Industrial Council (advocated by Arthur Henderson and a handful of TUC leaders); while other trade unionists, like Bevin, argued that talks should build up between individual employers and union branches.[108]

In the autumn of 1927, however, after the passage of the Trades Disputes Bill, George Hicks, the TUC President, made a notable offer to the employers during the Edinburgh Congress, which elicited another from Baldwin about industrial peace, and a firm response from Mond. By twenty-four votes to three the General Council consented to discussions, and a committee was set up in January 1928. Mond's initiative did not in any way commit the NCEO where the EEF continued its rearguard action but, rather, those employers individually dissatisfied with the weight given by government to staple industries, and orthodox financial ideology.[109]

But the meetings took place on the basis of shared interests in industrial reorganisation and financial expansion; and Mond assumed, rightly, that the employers' organisations could not ignore his lead. What worried the Cabinet, and the mistrustful NCEO, was that Mond's committee might make 'damaging' concessions. Fearing the emotional response to issues like worker participation, compulsory publication of accounts, and the closed shop, which Mond considered open to debate, Steel-Maitland joined with Allan Smith in warning some of Mond's coadjutors, like Hugo Hirst, not to underestimate the capacity of Bevin or Citrine nor their own isolation from the mass of the business community.[110]

In these circumstances, the Cabinet, like the Henderson group, revived interest in the formal and more restricted Economic Councils operating in France and Germany; while at the opposite end of the spectrum, the Communist Party, the Independent Labour Party (now directed on very radical lines by James Maxton), and A. J. Cook of the MFGB wildly tried to destroy what they understood to be a cross-class collaboration. As a member of the TUC delegation, Cook assiduously leaked the secrets of the Mond-Turner deliberations, and published a derisive pamphlet called 'Mond Moonshine'; but he failed to disrupt the talks. The so-called Cook-Maxton Manifesto campaign petered out in half-empty halls. But the Mond–Turner report itself gained little real support, partly because its recommendation of yet another variant of Industrial Council rested on nothing more substantial than voluntary association, partly because its suggested machinery resembled the long-despised Lemieux Act. For lack of other comfort, the General Council voted in favour by eighteen votes to four, claiming to see in it 'the things that the trade union movement has been claiming for years to have a voice in, and for years it has been denied'; yet it is doubtful if they valued it as more than recognition that the hostilities of 1926-7 had been forgotten. Like NCEO and FBI, who rejected it out of hand, the TUC had no desire to be tied down to enforceable contracts.[111]

Given the TUC's response, their own desire to keep government out of industrial relations, and the very practical need to discuss the issue of redundancies with trade unions, severally and collectively, if they were to make any progress with rationalisation, the NCEO after a good deal of internal dissension, and without the support of the most powerful Federation, the EEF, took its own slow and pugnacious way. In February 1929 the NCEO proposed to the TUC a conference on matters of common interest, as a formal alternative to Mond-Turner;[112] and the General Council concurred, by eighteen votes to two. At the first tripartite meeting, in April, a conciliatory approach by Sir Ralph Wedgwood, NCEO representative, did something to diminish suspicion. Quite rapidly, all three agreed to abandon the openly corporatist themes associated with the Industrial Council project; and set themselves instead to build their own form of institutional cooperation – corporatist in a far more subtle and flexible form.[113] In the extraordinary mood of mutual felicity, the TUC learnt to its surprise that the NCEO and the FBI feared the same reaction from their members as it did, if they tried to impose central direction; and both sides agreed, not only to make discussions permanent (the Joint Sub-Committee), but to extend them to fundamental questions of industrial legislation, unemployment and national economic policy.

In contrast to the largely ineffective work of Mond-Turner, this tripartite body gave joint evidence to the Macmillan Committee in May 1930, and then took up the vast and contentious question of redundancy and retraining. In 1930–2, its work included even more important joint submissions to the 1931 Imperial Conference, and the 1932 Imperial Economic Conference held at Ottawa.[114] As the NCEO admitted, these were matters of enormous and irrevocable importance, for it had, at last, publicly identified itself as the employers' political representative.* In the same way (and to the employers' surprise) the TUC refused to be deflected from discussing legislation and government policy by the presence of a Labour Cabinet after 1929: a resolve enhanced by Labour Ministers' cavalier behaviour over repeal of the Trades Disputes Act. The General Council had declared in 1929: 'The movement can find more use for an efficient industry than a derelict one, and the unions can use their power to promote and guide the scientific reorganisation of industry, as well as to obtain material advantage from the reorganisation.'[115] Since then, the TGWU had become the Labour Party's landlord, and the *Daily Herald* passed into TUC hands, giving Bevin the major voice in editorial policy: a new relationship with the Party was developing in which the TUC was to challenge successfully the hallowed doctrine of separation of political and industrial functions enunciated by Arthur Henderson before the First World War.

In the aftermath of the General Strike, Steel-Maitland, Weir and Milne-Bailey, the chief exponents of cooperation theory, had each foreseen some form of grouping between employers and unions, independent of the political parties, under the benevolent, ill-defined auspices of government.[116] It came about organically, in response to deep economic needs and problems in British industry. No individual or group

*NC 3450. Even in March 1928 Weir had still preferred a policy of 'non-alignment', pointing the contrast between the NCEO's activity during the General Strike and the exposure of the General Council. Such an efficient instrument as the NCEO, he said, 'should not be used injudiciously' (NC 2435).

could claim sole credit, nor could the government long retain its dignified distance. In July 1927, in reply to a question of what would happen if a National Industrial Council asked for legislation and a government refused to introduce it, Steel-Maitland had elicited from the Cabinet the classic constitutional reply that no party politician would sign away the sovereignty of Parliament.[117] For nearly three years after the General Strike, Baldwin's government stuck on that hook: 'The outstanding feature [of policy towards coalmining] was the conflict between the perceived need for rationalisation and the political objections to any policy innovation which could be interpreted as a move towards public ownership.'[118]

Yet in 1929, in the last months of the government's life, Baldwin and Cunliffe-Lister were persuaded to legislate for the mining industry, and coerce the coal owners in a way they had rejected in 1926; Baldwin even hinted, years too late, at enforcing the Washington Hours—and, incredibly, instead of scouting the idea out of hand, Evan Williams offered to take it to the FBI/NCEO/TUC group for discussion.[119] In January 1930 as the chill of the depression settled Allan Smith himself implored government to finance, not only large industrial amalgamations, but the investment programme of *any* efficient firm in engineering: a remarkable turnabout for the proud EEF,* the sort of vision more akin to that once held by Walter Rathenau than anything British industry had previously known.

Something so recently cultivated, even on congruent economic interests, could hardly be expected to have survived the 1931 crisis unharmed. Former hardliners on nationalisation like Weir and Allan Smith might attempt to force some of the more obdurate owners like Lord Gainford and Lord Londonderry to moderate their attitudes towards the Labour Government's 1930 Coal Mines Act,[120] but, spurred by the EEF, the NCEO could not resist the temptation, and the pressure of many of its component Federations, to take up a belligerent position, by publishing a pamphlet in February 1931 advocating renewed wage-cutting as the best means to surmount the world depression.† The gesture was overtly political, designed to weaken the government (then in the throes of the censure debate which led to the setting up of the

---

*TJ C11/72. He envisaged a detailed programme, supported by government, unions, employers, and the banking system, to implement rationalisation from the factory level upwards, with national provision of finance and technology.

†This pamphlet, ostensibly concerned with the bankruptcy of the Unemployment Insurance Fund, closely resembled Conservative Party policy. It was published without giving notice to the Joint Sub-Committee of FBI/NCEO and TUC (GC F and GP Minutes, 19 February 1931. SM GD 193/77/3 April 1931).

May Committee on public expenditure) and to dissociate the NCEO from any taint of collaboration. But although it achieved the first aim – causing MacDonald to summon leaders of NCEO and TUC to separate meetings, at which he revealed to both sides wide incomprehension of the issues involved and actual ignorance of the joint body which existed[121] – the public antagonism it aroused did not upset the fundamental equilibrium between industrial institutions. In the meeting with MacDonald, Weir claimed great pride in the tripartite talks; there is even some evidence that the NCEO and the FBI, with at least the connivance of the TUC, were trying to jump the Labour Cabinet into imposing a protective tariff. 'Any agreement on national economic problems,' Weir wrote in February, 'come to between the TUC, NCEO and FBI, would weigh very powerfully with the government.'[122]

Open divergence on the political plane did not therefore preclude private collaboration (a paradox which recurred in the years 1944–5, as the wartime coalition began to break apart, and as TUC and British Employers' Confederation made their harmonious dispositions for the post-war world). But in 1931, as in 1926, the General Council could not wholly disengage from its party political allegiance. Until the final crisis it remained loyal to MacDonald, and Citrine, rather unhappily, had to decline an FBI request for a special meeting on 21 August, a week before the government fell: 'our people's views are so strong. . . .'[123] Nevertheless, the joint discussions continued – without the NCEO – through the rest of 1931 and 1932, and the Hirst–Citrine exchanges remained optimistic long after the Ottawa Conference had ended.

Indeed the NCEO's factious adoption of the Conservative line did it a good deal of harm, and exposed it to a certain amount of recrimination after the Conservative party joined the National Government. The subconscious affinity of FBI and TUC stood out in sharp contrast to the political hostility of Conservative and Labour parties. Whereas the NCEO in a sense broke ranks by temporarily abandoning the politics of industrial harmony, the TUC held firm, without in any way betraying its particular commitment to Labour ideology, but simply by asserting its right, as co-founder of the movement, to be heard – and respected – on matters of economic policy.

That the Labour government ignored it is not surprising, given the social composition of the Cabinet, the predominance of Philip Snowden, Chancellor of the Exchequer, and his rooted opposition both to protection for industry and to trade union interference with Ministers' sovereignty. For all the TUC's assistance in disposing of ILP pretensions to dictate policy in 1928–9, Labour Ministers' attitudes had not changed since MacDonald had first deplored the practice of government departments' consultation with TUC and NCEO on legislation, in 1924. By 1929 fewer Labour MPs owed their seats to trade union nomination and fewer came from the working class. Snowden had already rejected a number of TUC suggestions on coal and unemployment policy before he vetoed Henderson's proposal fully to consult the TUC during the August 1931 crisis.

Initiatives by the TUC's Economic Committee were similarly ignored. Their interesting, proto-Keynesian suggestions in March about increasing working-class purchasing power as an antidote to the depression, their plans for refinancing the Unemployment Fund, suspending the sinking fund and increasing taxation were all rejected, virtually without discussion; and the revenue tariff – a form of protection – was finally defeated by Snowden's threat to resign. Nor was the TUC granted benefit of consultation; apart from one very formal meeting with MacDonald and Snowden on 20 August, it found itself kept wholly in the dark during the climactic week.[124]

How great a mistake MacDonald and Snowden made can be seen from the sequel, as the TUC revealed its capacity to stiffen Henderson and the minority of Ministers against the cuts in unemployment benefit, which finally split the Cabinet; and in the way in which the TUC remoulded the party structure itself after 1931. The August crisis showed that the trade union movement could destroy a Labour government.[125] But the lesson went much further than that, further even than reinforcing the attitude of trade unions towards employers during the 1930s. Ineffective though the left wing was to change policy, it could see the real issues involved. *Power Loom*, the monthly paper of the Nelson Weavers' Association, declared in June 1930: 'Undoubtedly the most important issue now facing the working class is this question of *rationalisation*, involving as it does the sharp question of class struggle or class collaboration.'[126] The Labour Cabinet baulked at something of such economic and political significance; and Bevin and Citrine and the General Council collectively discovered their unsuitability as well as their incompetence, arriving, tacitly, at the point already reached by Weir, Moir and Allan Smith.

At the first tripartite meeting on 24 July 1929, Weir had declared: 'We have in the past depended on the government for such contact as there has been between us as central organisations. We have now got the job, today, of meeting by ourselves. We do not dispute the right of Parliament, but we do dispute the ability of politicians to handle industrial questions better than you, the GC, and ourselves can do.'[127] Three years earlier, in his research paper for the General Council, Milne-Bailey had written: 'A Parliament of the ordinary democratic kind, elected on a territorial basis, is largely ignorant, and is bound to be ignorant of industrial needs and problems, and to that extent is a very unsatisfactory authority for industrial regulation and legislation.'[128] In the long cycle of the 1930s both bodies would go on to challenge Parliament itself, acknowledging in their own way that Lloyd George had been right all along, only within the wrong party formation, and ten years before his time.

8 COMPROMISE AND HARMONY, 1931–9

The unique and politically violent events of 1931, the collapse of the second Labour Government, and the autumn election which appeared temporarily to destroy the parliamentary Left in British politics, imposed a dramatic break between the 1920s and 1930s which most accounts of the inter-war years have been content to perpetuate. This division, however, derives more substance from the history of party government, as the two-party system slid back into the abeyance of the Lloyd George era, than from the study of politics or economics in a wider sense. Speaking of the system as a whole, one can say that 1931 accomplished trends originating in 1916, just as the recovery which developed after 1933 owed its strength to factors already present in the late 1920s. Important as it is to point out the effect of the Depression on political behaviour, in enforcing extreme caution, deflation and conservatism in government and institutional policy, it needs also to be said that the years 1931–4 were exceptional and that thereafter other trends supervened.

In August 1931 the political crisis contributed to the long-term weakening of the party system. But long before the 'true party men', Baldwin and MacDonald, succumbed to each other's wishes and to the King's invitation to form a National Government, big business, trade unions and the state apparatus had acknowledged the importance of a peculiarly subtle and pervasive form of corporate interchange, less and less affected by party hostilities. The contempt for Labour's incapacity expressed in 1931 by both NCEO and General Council was only one symptom of wide dissociation between the party system and the behaviour of institutions. In the decade before Labour as a party returned to power in the 1940 coalition, organised labour settled down to live with organised management, both clinging to the state in a hostile economic environment, assisting it, willingly or not, in its aims of avoiding internal crisis, and pushing the political extremes, Right or Left, beyond the boundary of parliamentary politics.

The damage that employers and TUC suffered during the 1929–33 depression of course enforced greater caution than they had shown in the roaring twenties. Though less hard hit than in 1926, or 1921, the TUC continued to lose members.* Some unions, particularly the MFGB, wasted by the Spencer defections in Nottingham and Derby, and long-term reductions in manpower, entered an irreversible decline, falling from 804,236 in 1929 to 588,321 in 1939. But decline in numbers is not necessarily a sign of institutional collapse. Admittedly all unions suffered financially from diminishing dues; during the Depression they were able to offer only feeble resistance to sporadic wage-cutting for fear of exacerbating the unemployment which was the prime cause of reduced membership. But real wages had been rising steadily since the mid-1920s, as the price of primary products fell in the world market;† for those in work the 1930s turned out to be a period of steady, even complacent prosperity, and the unions only reflected their members' preoccupations when they gave priority to the defence of existing jobs and wages, rather than to the creation of new jobs or betterment of the conditions of the unemployed. Whatever was said in public, the movement tended to cling to the *status quo* achieved in 1929, waiting for the long-deferred trade revival, as governments had done in the early 1920s, and concentrating their energies, consolidating power in a highly conservative fashion.

As so often in the past, the employers' federations mirrored this pattern. They too lost members for a variety of reasons, sometimes as a result of amalgamation and changes in industry, sometimes because individual firms sought freedom to make their own wage settlements outside the ring. The Engineering Federation, for example, fell from the 2,600 member concerns of 1921 to 1,806 by 1935. Allan Smith's authority was challenged on the NCEO Council in 1933, as a result of this shift away from political militancy.[1] But the remainder, like the TUC, consolidated, seeking to strengthen their authority. Secure in state recognition of their status as equal participants on Royal Commissions

*	1925	1926	1927	1928	1929	1930	1931	1932
Actual membership of TUC (000s)	4,671	4,407	4,125	4,011	4,056	4,049	3,859	3,698
Density – %	37	34.6	32.1	31	31.1	30.8	29.1	27.8

	1933	1934	1935	1936	1937	1938		
	3,661	3,854	4,106	4,496	4,947	5,127		
	27.4	28.8	30.6	33.4	36.6	37.8		

† Cost of living	1920	1922–4	1927–9	1930	1931	1932	1933–4	1937
(1930 = 100)	170.9	115	105	100	92.4	90.3	89.2	100

and government committees, the FBI and the NCEO seemed content to sustain their position (particularly against smaller companies, prone to break ranks), citing in recruiting propaganda their success with the Ministry of Labour on questions such as unemployment insurance policy, and showing themselves as touchy as any ancient institution at derogation of their dignity.[2]

Their defensive posture reflected the habit of long reliance on latent support in the Conservative Party, which caused the NCEO after 1931 to claim much credit for the downfall of the Labour government and for the imposition of deflationary policies recommended by the May Committee.[3] Yet this had caused the NCEO at least to make a number of damaging miscalculations. During the uneasy period after the Conservatives lost the 1929 election, they had joined in the attacks on Baldwin's leadership, when they envisaged unseating him, not out of love for Beaverbrook or the Empire Free Traders, but in order to replace him with Neville Chamberlain, harbinger of the tariff and Imperial Preference. Their advocacy of an immense cartel to end cartels, a sort of Imperial Comecon, brought curiously varied support, from Tory corporatists and the so-called 'YMCA' radicals – Harold Macmillan, Robert Boothby, Terence O'Connor and Brendan Bracken;[4] allegiance which did them no good when Baldwin survived.

On the level of economic interest, employers' attacks on the financial system in the late 1920s alienated those sections of the Conservative Party which sympathised more closely with orthodox Treasury views and the pretensions to economic hegemony of central bankers like Montagu Norman; and yet, unlike the TUC, who set out to repair the 1931 damage by remodelling the Labour Party against a future election which would give a real majority, the employers collectively failed to bind to themselves dominant elements among Conservatives, or to develop a philosophical justification and practical means of organising the free enterprise system which they claimed to represent.

Individuals like Weir or Allan Smith could see the need to formalise relationships not with one party but with the state; the majority of their colleagues on a swollen Central Council with a shifting population ignored this important distinction, contenting themselves with bland statements of increasingly out-dated principles which no longer applied to those great questions of planning and state intervention which inextricably blended 'political' with 'economic' judgments. It is true that this tendency was enhanced by the ancient fear (absent, since 1906, from trade union deliberations) of being held 'in restraint of trade', in spite of government's incitements to form cartels.[5] But it owed a great deal more to changes in the business world: many of the new recruits to the NCEO Council, representatives of mass-production industry like motor car companies, turned out to be insular and anti-union, sheltered as they were from the slump by domestic demand. Lord Weir, symbol of rationalisation and cooperation, was to an extent displaced by Lord Nuffield, symbol of narrow-minded individualism: 'On the management side, there was insufficient understanding of the crucial link between efficiency and good labour relations; and perhaps most important, evidence of this can be found among the newest sections of industry, thus providing yet another reason for doubting the "old/new" dichotomy.'[6]

As a result, the balance between employers and TUC, *vis-à-vis* government, began to change, much as it had done in the later stages of the First World War. The TUC not only established its right to be heard in state policy-making, but habituated itself to dealing with complicated questions of industrial education and technology[7] (such as coal by-products research); whereas employers' organisations (though not individual employers), tended to remain impervious to the work of scientists and technologists until the Second World War, at least as far as investment decisions were concerned.

Instead of leading to a profound industrial revival, the impetus of rationalisation slowly dissolved, in a period characterised by over-cautious decision-making and increasing structural rigidities on both sides of industry, stultifying many of the hopes held before 1931. Although it should be added that the purpose of cartels in the staple industries, like coal-mining, was now to preserve employment as far as possible, maintain existing wages, and regulate trade in the interests of the national consumer rather than the short-sighted minority of owners,[8] the operation of the coal cartel in particular led to a marked reduction in output per man during the 1930s and an unwarranted resuscitation of many moribund pits.[9] Creative energies instead went into building up company structures and industrial institutions against the day when the world market and the British political system would open up again and the economy expand, allowing the political struggle between them to resume on a basis of prosperity, as it had in the years 1918–20 and 1927–30. But when that revival did occur, after 1934, the struggle was indefinitely postponed.

Something hopeful, even ebullient, had been destroyed by the failure of politicians in Britain, Europe and America to control the slump; confidence in the flexibility and capacity for renewal of the modern economic system had been impaired, far more seriously than in the troubled years after the First World War. For a short time in Britain, rationalisation had genuinely engaged the energies and creative ability of many of the best brains in management, labour and government. When the possibility of recovery opened up after 1934, faith lay dormant.

Physically, however, expansion took place in the mid-thirties, restoring the institutions almost to the numerical strengths of the 1920s. Unions' membership, and more important, density of affiliation, rose, in tune with economic recovery. An increased secretariat and new TUC buildings emphasised the professionalism of the General Council and the Economic Committee which had been Citrine's long-term aim. The Bevin-Citrine era, as it should properly be called, witnessed a flowering of administrative capacity, and the arrival of a new generation of leaders trained in the new style, like Arthur Deakin, who had followed Bevin upwards in the T & GWU and was to succeed him as General Secretary in 1940, Jack Lawson, Tom Williamson of the GMWU (General Secretary in 1946) and others, contemptuous of the 'carthorse' image perpetuated in the cartoons of David Low, schooled on the government's Economic Advisory Council and determined to better the contemporary achievements of French and (pre-1933) German union federations.

This 'new unionism' of the thirties spread across the South East and South of England and the Midlands: the AEU, who first admitted semi-skilled men in 1926, doubled its membership between 1933 and 1939, to 400,000, and won the forty-hour week and holidays with pay, well in advance of others; while the ETU also doubled in size (to 70,000); but the fastest growth was experienced by general unions, the T & GWU reaching 654,510 in 1937, at last surpassing the miners, while the GMWU rose from 269,357 (1934) to 467,318 in 1939. Despite its attrition, the MFGB itself was able in 1937 to challenge the breakaway Spencer Union and, by a long strike at Haworth Colliery, to force the government to intervene and induce the Nottinghamshire owners to bring the Spencer Union back into the National Federation.

At the same time, the control over the majority of Trades Councils, finally won against the Communist Party in the mid-1930s, helped the TUC to extend its influence in previously weak areas like casual labour, agriculture and even domestic service. Trades Councils, once purified of Communist affiliation, served as recruiting centres of immense value in such political campaigns as that against the Means Test, enabling the TUC also to win back from dangerous affiliation to the NUWM or Communist Party many of the unemployed, otherwise beyond trade unions' reach.[10] They channelled local information on economic conditions through to the TUC and could campaign against the employers on a matter like workmen's compensation without committing the TUC to head-on conflict with the NCEO. As instruments of local political power they maintained some influence over the Labour Party during the TUC's four-year struggle to remodel the political wing to its own design, and in turn, brought into the union hierarchy, and the General Council, a number of younger men experienced in local administration.[11]

Gradually, hesitantly, the TUC assumed the role of rule-maker and arbitrator for the movement – though never to the dogmatic extent once demanded by Lloyd George: the results tended to confirm historic differentials and demarcation lines in a profoundly conservative way because, as Bevin clearly realised, the TUC could only become an authority by accommodation to individual unions' historic idiosyncrasies. Thus the only formal measure of the period accepted by TUC members, the 'Bridlington Agreement' of 1939, regulated supposedly pernicious habits of inter-union poaching and recruitment in a most monopolistic way, serving to exclude new small unions (like the Chemical Workers) and preventing fragmentation of existing bodies, without, however, aggregating to the General Council any real power of policing or central authority.

The confident optimism about the TUC's role prevalent in the late 1920s was replaced by a sombre, realistic assessment of what employers and government could offer and what the TUC could in practice, and in adverse economic conditions, expect. Having gone furthest towards cooperation in the tripartite talks after 1929, the General Council could make it clear that it did not expect to be ignored as a policy-making body, by the National Government, as it had been by the Labour Government in 1931; but it became far harder to achieve genuine government recognition after 1937, in the era of Neville Chamberlain, than it was to win modest sops to TUC status: such as its right to equal representation with employers on state inquiries and the boards of new state corporations, or the conferring on Pugh and Citrine of knighthoods which placed them on the same footing as the Civil Service heads of departments and the chairmen of great companies.

As far as policy-making was concerned, the TUC had to be content consciously to prepare the position for a future Labour government, rather than influence Treasury or Cabinet during the 1930s.[12] Hence their conversion to the concept of physical planning, before 1931, with state enterprise envisaged as a means both of economic control and job creation, was followed by acceptance of protection, and a series of far-sighted statements on fiscal, industrial and world monetary policy. In 1932–3 a major debate developed on the scope and form of national-ised industry,[13] which exposed the fundamental choice between setting up state utility corporations on the pattern advocated by Herbert Morrison and regionally directed concerns with working-class rep-resentation. Confusing though the economic argument was, it could not conceal the political struggle, for the unions wished to retain a voice in the running of nationalised industries, without at the same time taking on responsibility towards an 'essential' state sector where strike action and collective bargaining would be hampered (as in 1924 and 1929–31) or forbidden by the state itself. This deeply ambiguous question was never really resolved in spite of the adoption of a com-promise formula at the 1933 Labour Party Conference.[14] Embodiment of the TUC's vision of nationalised industry as responsible not to 'the nation' but to the working class, in contradistinction to the private sector of the economy, had to wait for legislation in the 1940s and practical experience in the 1950s. Nevertheless, the TUC sustained its wider claims as an institution *vis-à-vis* government; continuing in its research papers to draw on the corporatist tradition evident before 1931.[15]

The TUC's Economic Committee, which had benefited substantially from the work done by Bevin on the Macmillan Committee in 1929–31, and from the standards of research set by the TGWU during the 1930s,[16] stimulated an outburst of creative work, including training programmes for union members and the institution of research depart-ments under John Price of Ruskin College in 1937. The TUC's inner institutions were moving away from simplistic ideas of nationalising the banking system to a far more sophisticated model of state control of credit much influenced by Keynes' own desire to salvage the capitalist system in the most humane way. At this stage they still acknowledged that fiscal matters, allocation of resources, and detailed planning fell within the ambit of government, of whatever party colour; but a claim to a voice in labour legislation, tariffs, financing of industry, and the value of the pound – in fact, planning for the mixed economy – was endorsed by a vast majority as early as the 1931 TUC, sweeping away the derisive votes for left-wing resolutions calling for immediate destruction of capitalism.

Numerical gains on both sides (for the British Employers' Confederation (BEC), as the NCEO began to call itself after 1934, completed its recruiting drive in that year with the claim to have enrolled firms employing 7 million workers, 60 per cent of the industrial population, more than all union members in or outside the TUC[17]) should be set against the paralysing loss of confidence in the political system which had taken place in the bleak years of the slump. The TUC's loss of faith in the Labour Party in 1931 was followed by employers' disillusion with the Conservative-dominated National Government.

Commenting on the British political situation in 1934,[18] and on whether the National Government could survive the forthcoming general election, or should be reinforced by a group of eminent leaders as an alternative to 'left-wing dictatorship', Weir deprecated both democracy and the two-party system. It was too late, he suggested, to create an 'educated electorate' in the manner Baldwin had always assumed possible, for party squabbles were bringing closer the free market economy's final confrontation with socialism and nationalisation. The only real cleavage in politics lay between that danger and 'sane, democratic evolution' – but the latter was not to be found in any party, not even among Conservatives, whose machine existed for the benefit of Tories, and which lacked 'the definite appeal that we are looking for. . . . Of course the solution would be the creation of an *effective* National Party embracing all existing machines, but towards this I believe very small progress is being made.'[19]

It would be wrong to cast this revival of Lloyd George's centre-party dream as the model to which every employer aspired in the 1930s – even though Weir himself believed that only for such an all-party crusade against socialism would the bankers and large companies subscribe. But after twenty years of brokerage between industry and government, Weir's representative importance cannot be ignored. His thinking encompassed the wish to create a more permanent link between government, industry and finance, and the feeling that party politics had become outmoded and inefficient. Acceptance of the need for corporate harmony did not, however, exclude the search for sectional advantage by subtler modes of restraint over labour demands. Trade unionists' vestigial suspicion about class collaboration showed clearly in a warning given by Bevin in his speech as Chairman of the TUC in 1937: 'The temptation to the trade unions as time goes on, from the other party granting concessions, is very real. The industrial policy of your opponents has changed. Do not be under any delusion. The old

221

bitter hostility which made the unions fight on the basis of the Taff Vale judgment and similar things had gone. It is a new technique which is being introduced.'[20]

Techniques, rather than the philosophical defence of free enterprise against socialism, engaged the theorists of the FBI Research Department, seeking answers to the exigencies of trading in a depressed world market, as they embraced standardisation, pricing agreements, Empire preference schemes, marketing boards, and even toyed with the legacies of Cecil's ephemeral co-partnership: profit-sharing schemes, model villages, and the panaceas of the Industrial Society, sponsored by the Duke of York. Most major companies responded to the depression by improving their financial skills and promoting finance men to their boards, a revolution in company structure led by the accountancy profession and its president, Sir William McLintock. At factory level, they investigated American systems of time and motion study and market research (the Hawthorne experiment) considering what could be learned from the behavioural sciences. Yet too often they discovered that benefits of amalgamation and rationalisation, so easily predicted in the 1920s, evaporated as cartels broke down, just when they seemed perfect, because the temptation to break out and undercut grew irresistible.[21] The remedy appeared to lie in yet further cartelisation: in collaboration with overseas competitors (as the ailing ICI and IG Farben parcelled out the Middle East); in the formation of the Iron and Steel Federation in 1934, or in the pit amalgamations carried out in Scotland by the Reorganisation Commission under the 1931 Act.

Whatever Bevin might say in public, the union-management talks of 1929–31 had shown that both sides had a vested interest in formalising their relations and raising the techniques of collective bargaining to the national level. The leverage these institutions could one day exert over government had been indicated when Sir James Lithgow warned MacDonald in February 1931 that the FBI and General Council were able to harmonise their views on tariffs, even if political circumstances and the government's ideological opposition made it inexpedient at that moment.[22] But throughout the 1930s this potential was grounded in the lowest common denominator of activity, as the history of the rearmament programme shows (see below, Chapter 9). Instead of using their joint bias towards cooperation to campaign in public for economic goals, both sides took refuge in secretiveness or bland statements like Citrine's claim: 'During the years of my secretaryship of the TUC, this association grew into a friendly intimacy and a confident relationship without any sacrifice of principles by any of the parties or any interference with the autonomy of the respective constituents.'[23] On the contrary, if the 'confident relationship' meant anything more than a platitude, then autonomy and principles *were* the price to be paid.

In determining their own constituencies' and civil servants' attitudes of mind, and hence the lineaments of policy in wartime, after 1940, management and union behaviour signified much more than the approach to 'planning' among the representatives of what Marwick calls 'middle opinion'.[24] Their 1920s attacks on the banking system and Treasury dominance of government's economic policy had also influenced the growth of a system of secondary banking in the thirties – investment trusts, credit finance, and the operations of building societies and insurance companies – at a time when narrowing overseas investment opportunities were turning the merchant banks themselves back towards the domestic market. Even if this investment followed profitable new lines, to the detriment of the social needs of the depressed areas, its very deficiencies encouraged institutional conversion to the idea of the planned economy, not primarily on the lines of short-term equilibrium and full employment of resources advocated by Keynes, but as a matter of long-term structural adjustment, in which the state provision of credit took a major part. And on the role of the state, FBI, NCEO and TUC had agreed since 1927.

They diverged, naturally enough, on political lines, over the means chosen to implement planning. The TUC envisaged state control exercised through a public sector at least partly responsible to the workers in each industry,* whereas the employers severally tended to favour some of the many brands of corporatism derived by the statists like Mond (now Lord Melchett), Sir Basil Blackett, Sir Arthur Salter and Roy Glenday, or the 'Tory Corporatists', among them Leo Amery, Hugh Sellon, Harold Macmillan, Oliver Stanley and Robert Boothby.[25] But these schemes would have required political dictatorship to impose them from above, or a basis of consent which could not conceivably have been created in the climate of opinion in the 1930s; however stimulating, they were excluded from the mainstream of political possibility until the very end of the decade.

Instead, the existence of practical collaboration on Empire preference

*The General Council/NEC Report, 1933, assigned the managerial function to neutral technocrats, on the assumption that government would appoint the men who actually ran state industry. This was to be the model in 1945; yet it ignored the 1933 Labour Conference and TUC Congress majority in favour of trade union participation, as constituency members of state boards.

and marketing boards,* on policy towards the special areas,† transport infrastructure and pricing,‡ and the requirements of research and technology (heritage of the Balfour Committee, CCR and EAC) indicate practical concerns absent from the formal schemes of the ideologues; just as Runciman rejected the Bill proposed in April 1935 by Melchett, Hugh Molson and Macmillan (which would have enabled industries to reorganise themselves and coerce recalcitrant minorities) with the declaration that reorganisation could never take place according to the precepts of 'any one cut-and-dried method'.[26] The 1937 Barlow Committee on the location of industry and population, for example, recognised the importance of specifically regional economic policy and based its recommendations on the assumption that trade unions and employers were ready to concur. Specific groups of employers followed suit: the National Farmers Union and the General Council (acting for the Agricultural Workers) in time developed a coherent policy towards Dominion marketing boards.

When it came actually to deflecting government financial policy, or challenging long-hallowed assumptions about industrial investment, employers and unions seemed to have advanced some way from 1929. Government and Bank of England gave an enticing lead with cheap money and easier credit – even if their significance was less than was claimed in the 1930s.[27] The Bank's skilful operation of the Exchange Equalisation Account, and the brilliant conduct by its permanent officials of the floating of the pound between 1931–3, provided further encouragement for industrial revival. But when it came to actual state investment, in particular to the pusillanimity of Treasury provision for the Depressed Areas, conventional wisdom, which Montagu Norman used to cite in his classic denial of the connection between high interest rates and lack of investment, supervened.

*In which a considerable part was played by multi-national corporations, Shell, ICI, Dorman Long, English Electric; by the group of tariff specialists in the Department of Overseas Trade; and by the General Council, which, for example, chose Commonwealth Preference rather than the Briand scheme for European federal union, in May 1930 (Bullock, *Bevin*, vol. I, pp. 440–4). The Milne-Bailey Report (1930) recommended an economic trading bloc, based on free trade inside a tariff wall, composed of Commonwealth nations, equally balanced between primary producers and manufacturers. Such thinking coincided with that of the FBI, and underpinned the joint delegation to Ottawa in 1932, and their similar attitudes towards the multi-national trading companies themselves.

†J. C. C. Davidson, Commissioner for West Cumberland, found much support for the idea of a Development Trust from employers, trade unions, local authorities and churches. (JCCD to Baldwin, 2 August 1934, SB D 2.3 (Unemployment).)

‡Bullock, vol. I, p. 612. Bevin's own ideas (appropriate to the General Secretary of the TGWU) were for a coordinated transport system, under a state corporation, without actual nationalisation of road haulage or buses, etc.

Against the overwhelming combination of Chamberlain and Fisher at the Treasury, TUC and FBI could only seek allies in other departments, Labour and Board of Trade, or back the suggestion of the *Next Five Years* group for a Ministry of Industry, without much hope that they could overcome the Chancellor's doctrine of balanced budgets or his hostility to the blandishments of Keynes:

'Look around the world today,' Chamberlain declared in 1933, 'and you see that badly balanced budgets are the rule rather than the exception . . . they do not produce those favourable results which it is claimed would happen to us. On the contrary, I find that Budget deficits repeated year after year may be accompanied by deepening depression and by a constantly falling price level. . . .'[28]

Sir Malcolm Stewart, Chairman of the Special Areas Commission, signified his conversion to a policy of industrial expansionism in his final report, 'No one will challenge the need to maintain the measures now employed, but these do not touch directly the problem of unemployment, which cannot be left to drift. A bold bid must be made to secure even a partial reduction.'[29] But, in spite of TUC encouragement, lacking organised support from BEC and FBI, he could do no more than resign, and in the prevailing climate, his resignation had little effect beyond a minor Amending Act of 1937. The furthest point to which government would go was with schemes for reorganisation of the cotton industry in 1936–9, and fishing industry Bills in 1935 and 1938; and in assessing how far employers and unions had crossed the threshold of political activity, one has to ask whether these very limited concessions on the part of the state were sufficient to rank them yet as governing institutions.

Employers and trade unionists' own claims to 'success' suggest that they believed it did. In its recruiting propaganda, with considerable justification, the BEC made much of its influence over the formation of Unemployment Assistance Boards,[30] and on the management of the UAB's finances down to at least 1939–40.[31] The TUC in turn claimed to have shaped legislation; on workmen's compensation in 1934,[32] and over the forty-hour week in government factories in 1936, when Citrine was able to convince Fisher (Treasury) and Wilson (Labour) to waive their contention that 'It is not the practice to recognise the General Council as competent to approach the Government directly on matters affecting the Civil Service.'[33] In February 1937 Bevin and Citrine actually offered Baldwin, the then Prime Minister, a bargain: union help with the difficulties of the rearmament programme

H

in return for a committee of investigation into the question of holidays with pay;[34] and in due course Bevin served on the Amulree Committee, and saw its report, covering eight million workers, pass into law in 1938.

Success depended on how powerful were countervailing pressures, not only from other interests, or conceptions of the national interest, but from within groups of employers or individual unions. The unsatisfactory history of the Iron and Steel Federation and the tariff, in spite of Sir Andrew Duncan's long fight to rationalise the industry, show how rebarbative contacts with government might become.[35] Unwilling to assign more public money than he had to, Neville Chamberlain ignored Bevin's offer in 1935 of full TUC support if the Treasury would only put up £20 million (rather than the derisory £2 million) backing for the Special Areas.[36] TUC efforts to lobby for extension of the forty-hour week were met by the polite evasion that it must be achieved industry by industry.

Personality also counted: labour movement protests against the imprisonment of Tom Mann and Wal Hannington after the 1932 Hunger March dented MacDonald's resolve to 'vindicate the law', not least because of what he called 'moderate public opinion', the feelings of National Labour supporters among the TUC and the possibility of creating a common grievance between TUC and Communist Party.[37] Seven years later, however, on the edge of war, the TUC got little change out of a Conservative Prime Minister, when Chamberlain treated them to a lecture on economics rather than concede a new committee on unemployment on the lines of the old EAC.[38] The fact that right of access to central government did not necessarily convey power needs to be underlined, as does the fundamental failing of employers or union central organisations to deliver bargains binding on their members – still in government eyes a bar to any reciprocal arrangement.

On the other hand, both institutions held government in a net whose meshes, if not strong, were at least numerous. The 1930s witnessed a remarkable proliferation of committees and bodies staffed by the same small groups of individuals: the long-lived Poo-Bahs of the state, Hankey, Fisher or Wilson were matched, by Weir, Moir or McLintock in a bewildering variety of guises, representing Chambers of Commerce, Associations and Federations, or Citrine, Hayday, and Bevin on National Joint Council (NJC), TUC, or General Council and the representative associations of Trades Councils. Knowing each other's foibles, habits and prejudices, they shaped their strategies accordingly; and from habitual contacts, the constituents of the triangle grew familiar to each other.

As Llewellyn Smith predicted in the 1900s, the notion of a Ministry of Labour led inevitably to the transposition of industrial conflict inside central government, as trade unions battened on to the sympathies of the new Ministry to obviate employers' traditional predominance in the mind of the Board of Trade. By the 1930s, however, both sides of industry tended to esteem Trade and Labour as well-wishers in contrast to an impervious, unthinking Treasury; and increasingly doubted the capacity not only of parties, as they then existed, but of the state apparatus itself to provide the help each so greatly needed.

Inheriting its tradition from Steel-Maitland and Margaret Bondfield (who had stood up consistently to her Cabinet colleagues in defence of the department) the Ministry of Labour continued slowly to rise in the government pecking order, using its influence as chief agent of industrial conciliation to alter work processes and attitudes.* After ten years as head of the department, Horace Wilson, who had become one of the more powerful of the great mandarins of the inter-war years and a frequent advisor to the government on economic questions, was succeeded by Sir Frederick Leggatt, equally industrious and influential; between them, they tided over the inadequacies of the Ministers who held office fitfully between Margaret Bondfield and the appointment of Ernest Brown in 1935.

As if in preparation for its apotheosis under Ernest Bevin in the 1940s, the Ministry had been geared up to the level of a major department of state; with undiminished sympathies for industrial modernisation carried through by joint agreement, and extension of trade union activity, particularly in the least coordinated and lowest-paid industries.[39] Utilising legislation and the work of its Conciliation Officers, the department had gone some way to institutionalise mutual contact of employers and unions, for which the TUC was duly grateful.[40] But when the Scottish TUC asked in 1931 that its Conciliation Officers be given powers to set up Conciliation Boards to force employers into negotiations, at a time when unemployment had invalidated the strike weapon, the Ministry declined: perhaps wisely, since its influence

*The Ministry played a considerable role in the cotton industry 1929–32, in the Midland Agreement and the eight-loom experiment in Lancashire, which occasioned the 1931 lockout (RA GVB 23/5/1–25); the Cotton Manufacturing Industry Act, 1934, gave the Ministry legal power to enforce negotiated rates – thus finally ending the employers' habit of cutting wages in defiance of collective bargaining. (See also TJ A6.)

depended on accretion, like the TUC's own slow progress towards the Bridlington Agreement, taking into account the myriad inconsistencies of historical reality.

The Labour movement was in no position to challenge the Treasury until 1940, when manpower budgeting was imposed. In all the great pitched battles over the allocation of resources and fiscal policy during the inter-war years – such as safeguarding of industries and the 'cruiser crisis' in the twenties, the unemployment fund in 1931, the Special Areas policy, and rearmament in the thirties – the Treasury won. Continuity, as much as possession of the most gifted recruits to Whitehall, gave it advantage over any other department. Insofar as a modern system of government had been constructed during and after the First World War, it had endorsed the Treasury system of financial surveillance over all other departments, which was then confirmed by the 1919 Minute making Sir Norman Fisher titular head of the Civil Service. Even before the return to the gold standard in 1925, it had become archaic to talk of separation of policy-making functions between Treasury, Bank of England, or even the clearing banks. Haldane's dream of complementary Ministries of Finance and Economics remained unfulfilled until the creation of the Department of Economic Affairs in 1966. As the complexity of government planning grew, invoking longer and longer-term budgetary commitments in social welfare, unemployment provision and defence contracts, and as the scope for radical change afforded to any incoming party administration diminished in direct proportion to the planned expenditure of its predecessor, the Treasury acquired an overview of the whole scope of government which was, in the nineteenth-century sense, unconstitutional. Treasury values replaced those of the once-autonomous departments of state, leading to a new hegemony – source of the twin theses of financial blindness and incompetence, beloved by historians of the inter-war years.

In default of a coherent history of Treasury control (which has, too often, been confined to single issues such as unemployment or regional policy), it is hard to judge whether this hegemony really crippled industrial growth or whether the financial world (taking government and the banking system in the broadest sense) was right to disparage demands for state assistance from incompetent, slothful and timorous entrepreneurs. After all, the main difference between the 'Treasury view' of industrial investment and that of employers and unions lay, not in controversy about the *need* for expansion and innovation, but the method. After 1932 the Treasury and the Bank

228

could congratulate themselves on the provision of cheap and easy credit without endorsing unproved incursions into the capital market by state agencies, either nationalised banks or Industrial Development Corporations. In the last resort, the argument about financial stability and the national interest revolved in the 1930s around propositions about foreign policy, and the economy as the 'fourth arm' of defence, as much as over the structural problems of decaying industries and regions.

To those in industry, however, the Treasury appeared to lack a coherent industrial policy: it opposed the additional powers to allocate state capital sought by the Special Areas Commissioner, Sir Malcolm Stewart, or Sir Ernest Gowers, Chairman of the Coal Commission, yet eagerly arrogated influence in fields far removed from its traditional ambit – such as Fisher's 1934–5 incursion into foreign policy in the Pacific, and Chamberlain's attempt to arbitrate on grand strategy by counterpointing limited liability in European defence and Far Eastern commitments.[41]

Much of this animus against the Treasury derived from uncertainty about the limits of the power established successively by Churchill, Snowden and Chamberlain over other less influential Cabinet Ministers, which, in turn, meant that competing demands from defence, welfare and industrial reorganisation were resolved by a form of inter-departmental brokerage, rather than under Cabinet authority. However effective, this brokerage could be disguised neither as high principle nor planning, and was consequently despised by the radicals among employers, management and unions almost as much as by the political critics, Oswald Mosley or Macmillan on one side, Stafford Cripps or John Strachey on the other. The most that can be said is that Treasury predominance enhanced conservative tendencies latent in British industry. Insofar as governments deliberately sought to institutionalise employers and trade unions as a means to improve political harmony during the inter-war years, they succeeded; but the price was paid in diminished innovation and hyper-cautious attitudes to capital invest-ment. As Adam Smith had forecast, in such situations the managers of firms or unions chose first to better their own members, and where government offered stimulus, traded in return – as the Iron and Steel Federation did for the tariff – the minimum response.

Price-fixing at one end, restrictive practices at the other, may have been no more widespread than in the 1920s or indeed the 1890s,[42] but they certainly received greater practical stimulus from the political environment. Despite the urgency of rearmament, aircraft manufacture was tailored, not to what the nation could afford, but to the speed dictated by the Society of British Aircraft Constructors, and the electrical and engineering unions, in order to avoid disrupting the industrial political harmony so painstakingly built up in the previous decade.[43] Outsiders' advice often reinforced such trends: Macmillan's Industrial Reorganisation Bill of 1935 aimed at providing, not only larger units of production but increased control of output and regulation of investment by the producers themselves, thus dispensing in the end with the market forces of supply and demand. For all the talk of 'managing the economy', the gap between politicians' advocacy of expansion and the cartelisation that actually went on grew rapidly: the price of avoidance of conflict turned out to be political compromise, industrial feather-bedding, and low overall growth.

Much of the talk about industrial self-government merely disguised the pattern of oligopoly of the 1930s, that 'competitive equilibrium'[44] which employers (and to a lesser extent unions in 'sheltered' trades) were content to enjoy, pending the distant future when an electoral shift would give a single party political power to indulge one at the expense of the other. Competitive equilibrium infused the political system as pervasively as it did the economy, and government exhibited a reluctance to coerce, out of fear of precipitating economic or social breakdown, civil disorder or renewed slump.

The deep strategy of crisis avoidance, natural in a complex modern industrial economy, which the Conservatives of 1922 had denounced in all Lloyd George's previous dealings with industry, developed and ramified after 1931 until it had become an essential part of the triangular harmony between institutions. Just as Chamberlain drew on the decay of France and the isolationism of the United States to justify his scheme for 'limited liability' in foreign policy, so his colleagues reassured themselves that in a profoundly hostile world Britain must cut domestic commitments to her capacity and to the willingness of industry and labour to provide. No balance sheet between government and governing institutions can be established, for both had become interdependent. The alternative was believed to be an intolerable level of disharmony, as the very few confrontations of the decade indicate.

For five days in February 1935 the balance was disrupted, on the ever-contentious issue of unemployment relief. Restoration of benefits to the level before the 1931 cuts, and universal equality of relief had long been government aims: progress on the first had been promised in April 1934, as a form of appeasement to the TUC in a particularly lean period.[45] The second aim involved the creation of the Unemployment Assistance Board (UAB), accompanied by new scales of benefit early in 1935; and Chamberlain himself, architect of administrative reform during the previous Conservative government, presided over the Committee drawing up the new regulations, making adjustments for rent and special circumstances, ending a mass of local anomalies, and for the first time separating public assistance from the old 'poor law taint'.[46]

The UAB's legislative principles, quintessentially in the Chamberlain tradition, had been superimposed on previous policy, including the recommendations of the 1930-1 Royal Commission, and their enactment exposed the Chancellor of the Exchequer personally to hostile criticism. As Wilson wrote to MacDonald, he 'had made all the running'.[47] The government, too, had committed its prestige, because the levelling-out of payments was politically a dangerous matter which 'will require very careful consideration by the Cabinet before they are submitted'.[48] Yet to meet local authorities' impatience to introduce the new scheme in 1935, the regulations were hastened through, against the advice of Henry Betterton, the Minister of Labour.

When published, the scales showed that in some areas, notably the Labour-controlled boroughs of South Wales and Durham which had long paid higher rates,[49] the unemployed would suffer severe cuts, while in big cities, like Glasgow and London, the amounts allowed for rent would be inadequate. Both questions had been raised by the National Labour members on the Committee, whose memories of the 1931 Cabinet crisis were still vivid: Chamberlain and the other Conservatives rejected their warnings on fiscal and political grounds, claiming that an overall increase of £3½ million should offset such individual hardship.[50] Behind MacDonald, timidly warning his Cabinet of public anger, stood J. H. Thomas and Ernest Bevin; while on the other side, BEC and FBI urged the advantages of administrative tidiness at the lowest possible cost to industry. In advance of the public announcement, the divisions of August 1931 reopened, predisposing the Conservative majority to override what they took to be the special pleading of the National Labour remnant.

MacDonald had suggested that 'public opinion was not so much concerned with the actual way in which the money was to be distributed as with the question whether the distribution was equitable and reasonable'.[51] Following on the spectacular Hunger March of January 1934, the NUWM's national campaign for repeal of the 1931 cuts, and a notable press and BBC investigation of the conditions of the unemployed,[52] the news that the most dismal and derelict parts of Britain were actually to lose £2 million a year loosed an unprecedented series of protests. At popular level, the NUWM and Communist-led Trades Councils renewed their outcry and staged a mass march from South Wales, while most national newspapers showed antipathy for what appeared patently to be the UAB's inequity.

Yet at first the Labour Party and TUC remained aloof, content to voice their anger in the House of Commons and the lobbies – a delay largely attributable to the involvement in the popular campaign of 'suspect' bodies such as the NUWM. It was not until 31 January 1935 (after a frenzied collation of regional reports), when the official Labour movement realised how far it had been upstaged by Communist Party strategy, that J. S. Middleton sent a circular letter on behalf of the National Council of Labour, pointing to the existence of 'a great and spontaneous wave of feelings . . . Huge and spirited demonstrations have been held; and Labour in parliament has accepted the first (sic) opportunity to take vigorous action.'[53] On 1 February, only just in time to catch the wave of militancy, the party and TUC launched a joint 'Appeal to the Public Conscience'; yet the NCL at once assumed the leadership, even of the South Wales deputation which, a fortnight late, it had discovered to be 'the most representative of trade unions, local Labour parties, trades councils and cooperative societies that had ever been held'.

This manoeuvre to dissociate popular feeling from the Communist Party succeeded as far as the public was concerned: NCL members accompanied the deputation to the Ministry of Labour and arranged for the BBC to give them a hearing: and Bevin was able to declaim, from the steps of Montague House, that, if the government ignored the plea, 'they must have the hearts of a Pharaoh'.[54] Having learned from the Councils of Action in 1921, TUC and Labour Party assimilated the popular wave, and safeguarded their own institutional supremacy. The employers, of course, faced no such crisis and contented themselves with ostentatious support of the UAB and its chairman, Lord Rushcliffe, and subsequently loudly deplored the Standstill Act as a 'serious check to administrative reform'.[55] The government, however, suffered the most severe legislative defeat of any of the inter-war years.

It is not easy to answer the question of why they gave way on a measure of such importance, so long prepared, and so closely associated with Chamberlain, the Chancellor. The minutes of the Cabinet Committee which on 31 January and 4 February took the decision to withdraw the scales, and then to bring in the Standstill Act, were taken in great secrecy and have since disappeared, and the actual

Cabinet record is a masterpiece of equivocation designed to ease Stanley's intolerable dilemma of responsibility for his predecessor's Act.[56] Labour Party and TUC naturally claimed credit, as did the NUWM and Communist Party. Uproar in the House of Commons may have had some impact, but on the evidence available, including the post-mortem after Stanley's inevitable resignation,[57] the two main reasons were discovery that the actuarial basis of the scales had been wildly wrong,* and the fear of very widespread popular unrest involving over one million of the unemployed. The decisive factor may have been the events of 5 February in Sheffield, when 10,000 demonstrators crowded into the main shopping streets outside the City Hall; the Riot Act was read, troops were assembled, and the revolutionary spectre of 1919 briefly reappeared.[58] Until then, Stanley and Chamberlain were inclined to fight; after, they accepted responsibility for the débâcle.[59]

A test case like this exposes the tolerance of the political system: in the fifteen years since 1919 the network of power relationships in society had been regulated to the point at which a breakdown, or reversion to open hostility between government and public had become unlikely, so long as the former took pains to tailor its policy to the limits of popular acceptance. In 1935 that calculation failed, and government wisely gave way. For another similar instance it is necessary to jump nearly forty years to the Industrial Relations Act, 1971. Proof of the Government's rediscovery of sensibility, and of the real impact of public opinion in February 1935, can be found later, with the carefully-planned, circuitous imposition of uniform scales, not, as before, in a single edict, but region by region, over more than two years, and at a higher level, 'at all times avoiding a large number of simultaneous reductions merely for the sake of bringing the allowances into conformity with the original figure'.† As the post-mortem showed, 'the strong feelings aroused by the original arrangements were almost immediately calmed by the Standstill Act'; and the government deduced that political equilibrium must never be disturbed again in this way. The case reinforced the long tendency towards crisis avoidance, even at the expense of important legislation, ministerial resignation and party outcry.[60] On TUC and Labour Party it reinforced the conclusions

---

*Instead of the 'handful' of special cases where reductions had been predicted, nearly half the unemployed lost – 750,000 on transitional benefit, 200,000 in other categories. Instead of the scheme providing an extra £3½ million, it worked out at £3 million less – a miscalculation of 15 per cent. (UAR 34/8.)

†CP 172/36. Under Ernest Brown's final scheme in June 1936 only 60,000 reductions occurred, 250,000 increases.

of 1921: instead of rethinking their relationship to the NUWM and Trades Councils or constituency party organisations, they at once mounted a campaign to obscure the fact that the popular movement had won the day.[61]

No British government with its electorate in mind could be seen to be lax in the preservation of law and order. In February 1935 the government mortgaged its legislation to preserve the façade of civil authority – and compounded the surrender by giving tacit consent to the Labour explanation that its cause had been institutional rather than mass protest. This curious conspiracy provides another example of the process of marginalisation as an element indivisible from the growth of institutional collaboration. Dissociation of extremes of Right or Left from legitimate claims to the political stage that had been begun deliberately during the second half of the First World War, was pursued avidly by Lloyd George, and continued during the 1920s in the attempts of successive governments to elevate formal institutions in industrial politics to the detriment of shop stewards, Minority Movement, Triple Alliance, or even, in 1925–6, the Coal Owners' Association. The pattern recurred at a lower level, in relations between the institutions themselves and the extremities: expressed in the long struggle between TUC and Communist Party and (more covertly) between the leaders of NCEO and FBI and the ultramontane right.

During the 1930s, under this powerful centripetal force, an area of 'respectable' political authority was defined, composed of the three main parliamentary parties (excluding Communist Party and British Union of Fascists (BUF)) and, at the industrial level, TUC, BEC and FBI, excluding the National Unemployed Workers' Movement or any other popular association. However small the actual mass support these fringes acquired, compared to their European counterparts, the centrist parties and institutions kept up a perpetual struggle to ostracise them completely and deny them any political validity.

Since government encouraged the process, it utilised the law, police and the agencies of mass persuasion to re-establish sound political activity and educate or persuade the electorate to content itself with traditional parliamentary standards. By European standards the effort was uniquely successful, and contributed substantially to that conservative insularity which was the 1930s' chief characteristic. So deep were the reasons of state involved that government barely allowed itself to be hampered by the opposition of dissident critics; and the newly-formed National Council for Civil Liberties often found itself lumped together, in official eyes, with the Communist Party. The coercive apparatus of the early twenties, like the Supply and Transport organisation, also survived, to be refurbished in 1932,[62] and two major and contentious statutes reinforced the existing law, the harsh Incitement to Disaffection Act, 1934, and the more carefully judged Public Order Act, 1936.

The potential appeal of Fascism to the mass of long-term unemployed in Britain worried Labour Party and TUC as much as intellectuals of the ILP or Communist Party, though the fear grew above all among trade unionists after the Nazi destruction of German unionism in 1933–4.[63] Under the stimulus of German and Italian intervention in the Spanish Civil War, awareness of the possibility of a peculiarly British form of semi-Fascism extended beyond the crude manifestations of the BUF to a diagnosis of something profoundly insidious by writers as diverse as George Orwell, G. D. H. Cole and Wal Hannington.[64]

For the Labour movement as a whole, an anti-Fascist campaign offered a relatively safe means of responding to the renewed overtures from the Communist Party which followed the *grand tournant* of the Comintern in 1935. Whether eliciting recruits for the International Brigade (the vast majority of whom were of working class, non-Communist background) or championing the victims of the Blackshirts, Labour Party and TUC competed effectively with the Communist Party, Labour MPs extracting, for example, significant concessions from the National Government by their eye-witness accounts of stewards' brutality at the BUF meeting at Olympia in 1934. *Fascism at Home and Abroad*, drafted by Citrine and published in February 1934, represented the first organised attempt to undermine the BUF at popular level, preceding the Labour Party's series of questionnaires about Fascist penetration and the National Joint Council's trenchant report, warning against the appeal of Rothermere's propaganda and prescribing legislation against 'movements subversive to the Constitution and the democratic system'.[65] Dread about quasi-military conflicts between Fascists and Communists underlay Citrine's denunciation of both to the TUC in September, and the resolution forbidding any union or Trades Council to admit members of either – origin of the more famous Black Circular of October 1934.[66]

Within the predominantly Conservative Cabinet, what might have been a debilitating argument over the merits of the BUF's claims to stand against 'world communism' disappeared after the Defence Requirements Committee Report in January 1934 defined Germany as the ultimate enemy against whom Britain should rearm. Disquiet about persecution of Jews and churchmen in Germany limited sympathy among Tory MPs to a narrow band of the extreme Right, almost devoid of party influence. The BUF itself failed to elicit official support on every occasion it offered aid to the state, most clearly when Baldwin derisively ignored it during the Abdication crisis.

The Conservative Party had, in fact, eliminated Sir Oswald Mosley himself as a potential candidate for power even before his break with the Labour Party in 1931. He was, Baldwin noticed then, aiming at 'a kind of veiled dictatorship' with himself at the top.[67] In spite of Mosley's attempts to provide the movement with an industrial programme, employers' associations showed little interest and paid no subscriptions to Fascist groups,[68] partly from fear of countervailing industrial disruption by the Left. What employers desired, as Weir had argued, was a 'truly National Government', not a Fascist clique supported by no more than a handful of individual employers, in their private capacity, like the coal owner, Lord Londonderry and the press magnate Lord Rothermere, or Arnold Wilson, backed by anti-semitic groups like the Britons.

The contrast with big business support for the Nazi party after 1929, Mussolini's *squadristi* in 1921, or *Action Française* in 1934, scarcely needs pointing. Business support of British parliamentarianism is, in its way, as remarkable a tribute to the fact that in the 1930s the political system still worked, as is the almost apolitical behaviour of the British Legion compared with ex-servicemen's associations elsewhere, the *Anciens Combattants*, the *Stalhelm* or the *Legião de Viriato* – which in turn may not be unrelated to the very limited ideological content of British youth movements and folk groups.[69] This is not to say that many of the ideas Mosley put out during his political career were not attractive: as early as 1920 he had spoken of an 'alternative consensus', when seeking to revive radical Toryism against the Coalitionists, and in *Revolution by Reason* (Leonard Parsons 1925) he and John Strachey had pre-empted some of Keynes's and Mond's ideas by criticising the City and the banks rather than attack capitalist society head-on. His 1931 Manifesto showed striking similarities to *The Next Five Years* programme, while the hierarchy of corporations and syndicates, together with the National Investment Board outlined in *The Greater Britain* (British Union of Fascists 1933), evoked sympathies among a heterogenous group of like minded Conservative MPs, civil servants and businessmen,[70] including Lord Melchett, Salter, Blackett and Glenday, economic adviser to the FBI. But like all other static schemes, its very precision alienated men who knew how slowly compromises were constructed in the practical world of industry.

The audience who sucked in the Fascist message eagerly in Germany, France or rural Ireland, small farmers, small businessmen, the *petits bourgeois*, in Britain lacked organisation above the level of ratepayers' associations. Their voice penetrated only at one remove, via the Association of Municipal Corporations and the Chambers of Commerce, both significantly less important than they had been in the 1900s. Above all, Fascist ideas failed the simple arithmetical test of the balance of power between employers and TUC: FBI and BEC were not in business to give the opposition gratuitous political ammunition, nor did they have any sympathy for the contrived tension and talk of crisis which were Mosley's standard justification for BUF accession to power.

By 1934, TUC and Labour Party had become conscious of an acute need to define the scope of legitimate activity within the broad conspectus of the Labour movement. Challenged by the extra-parliamentary Left and the Communist Party's appeal to shop-floor leadership and the unemployed, the rules of 1918 no longer served. Jointly, Labour Party and TUC coped with the ILP, first attacking, and then, at the 1927 and 1928 Conferences, suffocating, its attractive programme *Socialism in our Time*, whose principles of a minimum wage, family allowances and nationalisation of credit and productive industry conflicted with current policy.

General Council and NEC found an alternative manifesto for the 1929 election in *Labour and the Nation*. After the parliamentary scuffles which followed, and the failure of the Cook-Maxton campaign, the ILP developed a spontaneous fundamentalist approach, purging its membership and finally disaffiliating on what its leaders, James Maxton, John Paton and Fenner Brockway, conceived to be a programme of revolutionary socialism. Since the membership fell by 1934 to a mere 4,392, its influence almost ceased, though its former members remained a potential threat, within the Socialist League or the United Front. During the dispute, the Labour Party developed a disciplinary committee and an attitude towards free-thinking MPs, harsh by comparison with its tolerant past, while in certain regions like Glasgow, where the long war of attrition with the ILP continued, the local party became as monolithic and unreasoning as the worst of its competitors.

To a great extent, the ILP had destroyed itself. The Communist Party nearly followed suit. In the euphoria left over from the General Strike, the NUWM and National Left Wing Movement (the old

Minority Movement) Conference attracted fifty-four local Labour Party delegates in 1927. But there followed the internecine struggles of the industrial wing (J. T. Murphy and Arthur Cook) against the Leninists (Palme Dutt and Harry Pollitt); and the success of the latter, confirmed in 1929 by the Comintern, reduced the party to a tiny vanguard (5,400 in 1932), secure only in its revolutionary purity. With almost suicidal zeal, it dissolved the NUWM, greatly facilitating the TUC's efforts to purify Trades Councils and union branches, and to relegate the Unemployed Workers' Movement to a sort of limbo.[71]

But in 1933–4 the CPGB changed its strategy as Russia, threatened by the rise of Nazi Germany, abrogated its hostility to German socialism (which had materially contributed to the collapse of social democracy and outlawing of the German Communist Party) and sought allies in the West and membership of the League of Nations. The Labour Party suddenly ceased to be 'social fascist'. A renewed parliamentary offensive, supported by the United Front with the ILP, and infiltration at all levels of the Labour movement, led to a proliferation of unofficial strikes, greater popular support for the revived NUWM and hunger marchers, and heightened antipathy from official union leaders.

Doubly sensitive to this renewed appeal to shop-floor democracy, and to accusations that their understanding with employers and government had turned them into class traitors, the General Council reacted harshly. Analysing the meaning for British unions of what had happened in Germany, Italy *and Russia*, in a long memorandum in May 1933[72] linking Communist Party and BUF together, Citrine justified total opposition to Left or Right wing infiltration. He blamed totalitarianism, not on economic circumstances (as the Socialist League maintained) but on what he called 'confusion of thought' among Socialists: 'too many people have toyed with the idea of dictatorship', whether Mussolini's Italy or Stalin's Russia. In a foretaste of his later attack on the Russian state, he castigated fellow-travellers and their insidious propaganda: 'Many people do not perceive that the principle of dictatorship of the proletariat, like the dictatorship of Fascism or the Nazis, is a dictatorship of a political party.' Hence the need to outlaw such tendencies from the Labour movement, to fight state supremacy and the crisis techniques being employed against parliamentary democracy.

Two policy documents followed, in 1934, *War and Peace*, on foreign affairs,* and the so-called Black Circular, outlawing members of the

*To which Socialist League amendments were defeated by a majority of 10 to 1 at the Labour Party Conference. The 1934 TUC repudiated all forms of extra-parliamentary activity, Bevin's statement being particularly outspoken (Bullock, *Bevin*, vol. I, p. 553).

BUF or CPGB from any union or Trades Council administrative or elected office. TUC and Party worked hand in hand against any threat to the status of the National Council of Labour, in effect forcing the Socialist League, in its pursuit of revolutionary socialism, to seek alliance with the Communists, in what Miliband calls an 'artificial Leftism', which cut the League's throat and permanently discredited its theory of spontaneous working-class action.[73] Stafford Cripp's election to the NEC in 1934 exposed him personally, without strengthening the League, and he suffered grievously at the hands of Bevin who possessed

a much more organised theory of the role of Labour than Cripps on the Left, and than his trade union colleagues on the Right. At the core of that theory lay the notion of institutionalised cooperation between the trade unions, management and the state, to be supplemented by the parliamentary pressure of the Labour Party for legislation beneficial to the working class.[74]

The Socialist League could be nullified far more easily than the Communist Party, which benefited from European developments, sharing in the enthusiasm for the Popular Front in July 1936 in France and collaboration between Spanish Socialists and Communists which began later in the year. A defence of parliamentary socialism against dictatorship of the proletariat (in *Democracy and Dictatorship*, issued by the NJC in March 1933) and a declaration of 'incompatibility' of CP membership (*The Communist Solar System* (1933)) were not enough: the National Joint Council had to renew the campaign, putting the onus on the TUC to purge union branches and Trades Councils. Conditions had changed since the twenties: permeation of a whole union like the Miners' Federation being difficult (although the MFGB voted in favour of CP affiliation to the Labour Party in 1936) the CP had concentrated on key sectors, creating difficulties even in a tightly-run union like the TGWU. In ten years, Bevin was unable to eradicate Communist influence among London busmen. But on those Trades Councils which had formed the original rebellious Councils of Action, and best resisted TUC purging in the past, the full rigours of the Black Circular were applied: limitation of agendas, imposition of model rules and TUC procedures, and 'reorganisation' for those that would not submit.

In the end, even loyal Trades Councils were subordinated to the Trades Council Joint Consultative Committee, on which they became simply 'labour correspondents' for the TUC, channels for information and the distribution of instructions, their resolutions merely 'filed for future reference'; so that their slow decline as centres of regional power was completed by deliberate evisceration. The General Council won, using the methods of Tammany Hall more effectively than their opponents.* Not all dissent was silenced: foci of Communist influence survived, in places like East London and the West of Scotland, while CP membership rose slowly to 18,000 in 1939, sufficient to sustain the party through the equivocations of the Nazi-Soviet Pact, and swell it at the end of World War II.

But the Left, whether ILP, Socialist League, or Communist Party, lost the chance to develop an *effective* socialist alternative during the unprecedented economic crisis, just as it failed to make sufficient electoral capital out of the issues of peace and war at the general election of 1935. The TUC's strictures were applied to groups only too self-indulgent in 'symbolic' faction disputes, led by 'left wing leaders who shared a disastrous insensitivity to the realities of political power and influence'.[75] And afterwards, in the years immediately before the war, it became much easier to pick off the Socialist League, Cripps himself, and the Labour League of Youth, and undermine the effort to create a Popular Front in 1938.

The existence of the NUWM however, affected the TUC more subtly, for an organisation representing the unemployed – even under Communist dominance – could hardly be shrugged off as hostile to working-class interests, except on the grounds that a general industrial grouping weakened individual unions' capacity to restore jobs – a poor argument, given the conditions of the thirties and the unlikelihood of job creation. But Communist influence in the NUWM threatened the TUC's understanding with employers and government and pre-cipitated a deeper conflict over the nature of the economic organisation of society. After a deal of skirmishing at the time of the 1932 hunger march, the General Council attempted to break the NUWM from below by instructing Trades Councils to set up their own associations of unemployed. Less than a quarter responded, or obeyed TUC instructions to ignore the Jarrow March. In 1936 various attempts were made to coordinate action and the London Trades Council produced Wal Hannington and C. R. Attlee on the same platform.[76] But in spite of such temptations, and the alarming number of Trades Councils which admitted to paying lip-service to the TUC line while helping the NUWM on the side, the General Council refused full recognition,[77] even after the collapse of the Socialist League. 'Re-

*The General and Municipal Workers simply banned the election of any CP member to any union post.

'organisation' of Trade Councils continued down to 1941 in order to define the permissible centre of political life and as far as possible eradicate left-wing populism entirely, until the Communist Party became a legitimate if highly unwelcome ally, in the 'great patriotic struggle'.

The price of respectability, as Bevin had shrewdly guessed, amounted to less than the pessimists expected.[78] The Left polled only 331,000 votes at the Party Conference, in October 1937, after the Socialist League had been expelled. Thereafter, the General Council could concede more weight to the (purified) constituency organisations, at the expense of the TUC block vote, when the NEC amended the party constitution.* Bevin forced the Communist busmen in the TGWU into outright opposition, if not impotence, in the same year, making nonsense of United Front propaganda,[79] and in due course he and Arthur Deakin achieved their apotheosis, scattering the remaining pretensions of the Rank and File Movement, by 291 votes to 51.[80]

Government attitudes towards left-wing activity differed from these blunt attempts to drive dissent into isolation, because the state naturally desired mitigation, rather than to force dissension outside civil allegiance and create martyrs for converts to feed on. Given its Conservative composition, the National Government's anti-Communist stance is hardly surprising, nor the feeling that Fascist ideology represented a lesser threat to European stability than Soviet Russia.† For the Cabinet, choice between Republic and Franco's rebels in the Spanish Civil War raised a moral as well as strategic dilemma which could only be resolved by non-intervention. But these assessments of European events implied no special sympathy for Mosley's BUF and the occasional partiality of treatment between the two factions in the East End of London reflects Metropolitan police methods rather than government instructions.[81] The Cabinet summarily refused all BUF overtures and ordered the Special Constabulary to disband any BUF members who refused to resign.[82]

A more temperate opinion about the threat from extreme political activity emerged, between the rigorous provisions of the Incitement to Disaffection Act, 1934, and the Public Order Act, 1936. In that first uneasy year, the Government sought new and permanent police powers

---

*Ironically they elected Cripps and Laski – who within four years had returned safely to the bosom of the party.

†Baldwin told a deputation of privy councillors, led by Churchill, in July 1936, that 'if there is any fighting to be done in Europe, I should like to see the Bolsheviks and Nazis doing it.' (Baldwin, p. 947.) For Chamberlain's views see Middlemas, *Diplomacy of Illusion*, Chapter 2.

to combat the hunger marchers, and remedy what it regarded as the inadequacy of ancient, almost disused statutes[83] under which Tom Mann and Wal Hannington had been held after the hunger march in 1932. Even then, however, Baldwin and the government were prepared to accept advice from the National Council of Labour and amendments from both opposition parties, to ensure that the Bill did not offend too greatly established conventions about civil liberties;[84] and despite what Sir John Gilmour, the Home Secretary, and Lord Trenchard, head of the police service, said about 'organised disorder', the Cabinet would not tolerate police demands for power to control all open-air meetings, judging that to be an intolerable abrogation of traditional rights.

The degree to which government sought party and institutional consent can be seen from the fact that, although public opinion was reckoned to be amenable to legislation prohibiting the wearing of uniforms by Blackshirts in 1934, the Bill was postponed, pending Labour Party agreement.[85] For a time, the business community's hostility towards clashes between Communists and Fascists, and the General Council's urging of Chief Constables strenuously to enforce existing laws, went unrequited. It was not until the TUC induced the National Council of Labour to issue a memorandum, in March 1936, condemning private armies, uniforms, drilling and incitement to violence, that the government agreed to go ahead with the Public Order Act; and, even then, they took care to justify the prohibition of uniforms in terms of that public opinion which they had tried to educate over the previous four years:

There is no doubt at all that the resentment against the wearing of uniforms by the Fascists is immense. The practice is felt to be repugnant to British ideas and to suggest the assumptions of authority by a private army. People are very much alive to the fact that in Germany the wearing of black or brown uniforms led to the overthrow of liberties.[86]

The Bill was carefully calculated to infringe custom and behaviour as little as possible, to appease working-class opinion, and to preserve the appearance of impartiality between treatment of CP and BUF; and government remained sensitive to Liberal and Labour opinion as late as July 1937, when the new Home Secretary, Samuel Hoare, banned a march after a request from Herbert Morrison.[87] On the other hand, when Trenchard requested a complete prohibition of all marches for three months, he was refused:[88] political equilibrium counted for more than police advice.

Marginalisation ensured the exclusion of protest, dissent and extra-parliamentary political activity, beyond the limits of legitimacy set arbitrarily by government, parties and governing institutions, in spite of bleak economic conditions apparently favourable to their growth; and in the process, the change from a party system, offering genuine alternatives, to one in which parties competed for control of the state apparatus, was speeded up. Many economic problems which had seemed intractable in terms of party viewpoints in the 1920s changed their appearance, for as the governing institutions developed structures of cooperation, political necessity compelled them also to sublimate the more open manifestations of class warfare. As one member of a visiting American delegation in 1938 observed: 'While we in America have had increased strife in industry, the British have been blessed with little of this conflict between capital and labour.'[89]

This change had not been imposed from above, but had been brought about by the multiple responses to circumstances, and to each other, of the governing institutions. The state of equilibrium was not static but protean, continually transmuting itself into new forms. The corporate triangle between government, employers and unions was not a system, as the corporate theorists of the thirties defined systems, but a tendency, or bias, central to the evolution of modern government. So highly was equilibrium valued by its partners that all, even government, abrogated large parts of their autonomy to preserve it. Institutions which had grown up in this form, largely at the will of governments, in turn came to depend on the state, and the state found itself dependent on the compromises thereby achieved. The capacity of political parties in government to alter direction was thus steadily reduced, until in many of the most vital questions of policy they could do no more than avoid crisis – even in the emergency preceding the Second World War.

9 EMERGENCY, 1935–40

An institution's power can only satisfactorily be measured when its limits are questioned. In spite of the apparently unprecedented growth of state power, British governments in the First World War had been forced to react to emergency demands by seeking cooperation from industrial institutions to provide the munitions and manpower to fight a particular sort of war; thereafter, their successors attempted, with modest success, to incorporate what they hoped would become representative institutions in a more formal system. The spectre of political disorder which had threatened when nineteenth-century constitutional certainties became discredited after 1911 was chained down if not destroyed by the instauration of a new order. But like most new orders it reproduced many of the least attractive features of the old: in the 1930s, especially in the emergency conditions experienced after 1935, it came to resemble a close corporation, almost a conspiracy against the public, in the sense defined by Adam Smith.

When in 1934 the National Government accepted Germany as the prime enemy against whom it should rearm, and began to repair armaments deficiencies, it found itself again dependent on the practical cooperation of industry and labour to avoid military and strategic destitution. Sheer numbers of aircraft were made central to a policy, first of attempted deterrence, then, after 1937, of island defence; in both cases, production demands involved diversion of resources and manpower from civilian life. As Lord Weir gloomily warned the Cabinet in January 1936, air rearmament depended on the Society of British Aircraft Constructors (SBAC) and the engineering and electrical trade unions (AEU and ETU); to these, the politicians added their own third dimension – a public opinion far more hostile than in 1910–14 to the very idea of rearmament.

Some leading politicians inclined to ignore the third element. Churchill indeed deprecated it altogether in the early stages, reverting to a Lloyd George Coalitionist standpoint, seeing the Government's role as vanguard, leading popular opinion. In March 1934 he declared: 'He [Baldwin] has only to make up his mind, and Parliament will vote all the supplies. There need be no talk of working up public opinion. You must not go and ask the public what they think about this.'[1] Later, in his great philippics against the government, and in the Arms and the Covenant campaign in 1936, he appealed to the public, whose mood Baldwin had always held paramount in the long programme for public education. Public debate, however, the conversion of the Labour Party to support of rearmament, the wide impact of pacifist opinion, shown in the by-election disasters of 1933-4 when 20 to 25 per cent swings against the government on the issues of peace and armaments became commonplace, and the mood of caution which induced Baldwin to postpone seeking a mandate for rearmament until the General Election of 1935, because a Labour government would have given no rearmament at all, is secondary to a study of the relationship between industrial institutions and government.

Given its inherited experience of mobilising national resources and manpower during the First World War, and its huge parliamentary majority, the National Government should have had an easy run because calculations about public opinion and votes hardly applied to the SBAC or trade unions, who were not tied to the electoral cycle. But the speed of rearmament was, instead, affected by the Cabinet's own misgivings about the power of industrial institutions to impair the system's smooth functioning in the later 1930s. Even when considering the possibility that war *might* occur, avoidance of economic or social crisis ranked high during the preparatory stages of rearmament; a priority which explains why Ministers attempted (as they had done with earlier controversial decisions, such as the tariff, safeguarding, and setting up the electricity state corporation) to spread responsibility for decisions, farming out strategic questions to 'neutral' civil servants (like the members of the Defence Requirements Committee) or an employers' representative like Lord Weir, who became chief adviser on aircraft production in July 1935, and whose pronouncements moulded Cabinet debates and gave government an additional right to speak, *ex cathedra*, on matters where grand strategy impinged on industrial life.

The history of rearmament began with abrogation of the Ten-Year Rule in 1932 after the Japanese attacks on Shanghai; Britain's aim was set at air (rather than naval or military) parity with any potential enemy in March 1933, even before the end of the Disarmament Conference. In political terms, the next stage began with Baldwin's public

announcement of parity as a goal, in March 1934,* shortly after the very
secret Defence Requirements Committee (DRC) report which defined
Germany, rather than Japan, as the ultimate enemy against whom
rearmament should be directed.[2] The outcome of the defence debates
of mid-1934 (in which Chamberlain argued for a concentration on
purely British air defence, against Baldwin's advocacy of an effort
spread over all three Services in the context of the defence of North-
West Europe, Britain, France and the Empire, or at least the white
Dominions) laid especial emphasis on a balance between building
fighters for defence and bombers to provide a deterrent against German
aggression; but, since the deterrent failed to circumscribe Nazi territorial ambitions before Chamberlain became Prime Minister in 1937, it
was abandoned, fighter production instead becoming the one sector of
rearmament on which antagonistic groups in Cabinet, or the warring
Service departments and Treasury, could most easily agree.

The original DRC report proposed belated completion of the 1923
Fifty-Two squadron scheme, followed by further acceleration plans.
In July 1935 came the Defence Policy and Requirements Committee
(DPRC) (a purely political body intended to keep defence and foreign
policy in harmony, and bridge the gap between Cabinet, Service Chiefs
and Treasury[3]), and the DRC's second report, recommending strict
numerical parity with Germany by the approval of 1,500 front-line
aircraft. Six months later, the third report endorsed the Air Ministry's
Scheme F, consisting of a further 234 front-line machines with greatly
increased reserves, involving building a mass of new types, Hamp-
dens, Wellingtons, Hurricanes, Spitfires and Blenheims, and taking
great risks, as the first two were ordered in bulk before prototypes had
been fully tested, and the Bristol Beaufort was ordered straight off the
drawing-board.

Weir's catalogue to the DPRC in January 1936 of shortages of skilled
labour, machine tools and factory space shows how heavily these orders
strained existing production facilities. At the same time, the unsettled
disputes of 1934 concerning the balance between Services, and between
the cost of the total programme and the civil budget, divided the
Cabinet again, in advance of Baldwin's retirement and his replacement
by Neville Chamberlain. Advocates of unified planning demanded a
Ministry of Defence and were not mollified when Baldwin appointed
Sir Thomas Inskip, a distinguished lawyer, as Coordinator and un-

*'In air strength and air power, this country shall no longer be in a position inferior
to any country within striking distance of our shores.' (*Parliamentary Debates*, Commons, 5th series, vol. 286, col. 2078.)

acknowledged deputy Prime Minister, particularly since Inskip never managed to surmount inter-departmental rivalries over scarce resources.

The Defence White Paper of 1936[4] with its somewhat specious promise of no interference with the 'course of normal trade', deliberately disguised the existence of serious ministerial disagreements about industrial and political priorities. Even so, the increased Estimates raised a parliamentary storm which, in turn, facilitated Chamberlain's imposition of new ideas after he became Prime Minister in May 1937: fixed limits of expenditure, abandonment of the concept of deterrence, and concentration on home defence – the strategic setting for the isolationist foreign policy, and the strategy of appeasement, 1937–9. Roughly imposed, disastrous to Anglo-French understanding, and unravelled precipitately after the invasion of Czechoslovakia in March 1939, the rigorous logic of downgrading the Field Force in 1937–8, as Britain reneged on her military commitments to France in the six months before Munich, failed to resolve the problem of industrial production of fighter aircraft.

Despite rationing of the Services to £1,500 million in December 1937, the importance of large numbers of fighter aircraft increased remorselessly, in direct proportion to Chamberlain's ruthless argument that the Army would not need its five-division Field Force and Territorial Army because Britain was not going to fight a Continental war again. During 1937–8, the year of rationing, the Air Force was able consistently to evade the limits set by the Treasury and Inskip according to what the nation was believed to be able to afford;[5] and when increases became politically possible, after the *Anschluss* in March 1938, Chamberlain conceded the Air Ministry's Scheme K, amounting to 12,000 machines by May 1940 (in place of the 8,000 by May 1941 of Scheme F) – the increase to be achieved by a 30 per cent rise in productivity, with extra labour, working double shifts. Finally, Scheme L, adopted on 24 April 1938, gave the totals of K with increased reserves. Even in the most isolationist period of appeasement, when it seemed that the Chamberlain Government was preparing to envisage with equanimity German hegemony over Eastern and Central Europe, physical production of fighter aircraft remained essential to national defence.

Yet the Chamberlain Government, like its predecessor, chose to accept the conditions of production laid down by industry, rather than impose its own urgency and risk industrial or political unrest. It accepted as dogma the Treasury's pre-condition that rearmament financing should not interfere with normal economic conditions, swallowed employers' opposition to any state interference in the private sector and

247

with almost equal timidity allowed the unions in the aircraft industry to sustain restrictive practices nearly as flagrant as SBAC profiteering. In an interesting recent study, Robert Shay argues that 'the whole reorganisation of the defence programme was embarked upon, not out of concern for the adequacy of Britain's military preparations, but out of concern about the effect that the increasing cost of those preparations would have on the economy. . . . There was almost an implicit assumption that Britain and her social and economic order were identical, and that if that order were upset, not only could Britain no longer defend herself, but there would no longer be a Britain worth defending.'[6] The charge is not unreasonable, even if the wider political context diminishes its animus against the governing class.

Early in 1936, the Principal Supply Officers sub-committee* of the Committee of Imperial Defence became obsessed with the deficiencies in production capacity, bottlenecks and shortages of skilled labour. With Baldwin's concurrence, they brought in Lord Weir, Sir James Lithgow and Sir Arthur Balfour, none of whom was concerned directly with aircraft production, but who represented FBI/BEC opinion and had all long experience of working with government.† Their introduction to policy-making greatly facilitated, among other measures, the 'shadow factories' scheme of the Air Minister, Lord Swinton, but it also ensured that influential employers' ideas on the proper relationship of industry and government would be deeply imprinted on the manner of rearmament. Weir had already written to Baldwin in May 1935, suggesting that the aim should be 'not to turn industry upside down by creating a war spirit and practice . . . but quietly and very rapidly to find an effective British compromise solution'.[7] This position he continued vigorously to defend against Inskip's counter proposal to raise production, by talking of 'martial law in time of peace'.[8] Industry would work to Air Ministry targets, but only on its own terms.

Weir was only playing fugleman for his colleagues. In October 1935, the FBI, angered by a Conservative Party Conference resolution recommending 'the organisation of industry for speedy conversion to the purposes of defence if need be', presented its demands to the Cabinet who were represented, significantly, by the top team, Baldwin and Chamberlain, attended by Wilson: 'Industry ought to provide any organisation which was necessary from within, and not have it imposed

*Composed of the Civil Service heads of the War Office, Admiralty, Air Ministry, Board of Trade, Ministry of Labour, and the Chief Industrial Advisor, Sir Horace Wilson.

†Weir's advice to the DPRC had precipitated the whole Ministry of Defence debate in the spring of 1936.

on them from without.'⁹ The men and institutions were of 1936, but the tone recalled 1914. Like the TUC, and with equal fervour, the FBI rejected any hint of industrial compulsion and were almost wholly reassured by the reply – though Chamberlain did venture to warn them not to let prices rise, or they would create inflation, leading to excessive wage claims and industrial unrest.¹⁰ Baldwin made an equally modest point: let industry avoid the stigma of profiteering and government would not intervene. If not, the Government's Contracts Department might seek entry to SBAC books: 'it was in their interests to play the game, both as industrialists and as taxpayers'.

The dismal saga of attempts to control profiteering in and after the First World War ought to have dissuaded Ministers from offering a gentleman's agreement in the form of a political contract. The employers spurned contractual limits. In subsequent correspondence they defended the rights of private enterprise, even against a largely Conservative government, and hinted that they would not cooperate (i.e., fulfil aircraft orders) if the government tried compulsion.¹¹ During the production crisis, late in 1936, which gave rise to a Commons debate about the need for a Ministry of Supply, Weir declared that 'coercive interference' could only be imposed close to the outbreak of war.¹² He need not have worried. Baldwin gave the government's answer in September: 'Our plans assume contact and collaboration between government and industry, right up the scale. . . .'

Baldwin's view of political consent, fundamental to his conduct of national policy, involved the unpleasant corollary that a democracy must necessarily lag two years behind a dictatorship. When considering compulsion, traditional habits, rights and assumptions had to be set against the urgency of demand. To the House of Commons, he argued in favour of equality and temperance: 'nothing could be done which would menace organised labour or trade union standards'.¹³ But, in practice, the government went further to appease the aircraft industry than the unions, conceding, on the 1919 pattern, a modification of Treasury contract procedures,* guaranteeing against future cutback in armaments orders, either after a war or at the end of the emergency, together with safeguards for loss of profit and obsolete plant. They also accepted the SBAC's dubious argument that a fifteen-year guarantee would be cheaper (since plant would be written off more slowly), without

*When Weir argued (not unreasonably) that the Treasury Contracts Department simply could not cope with the technical aspects of aircraft design and costing in an age already into the 'technology spiral', the Cabinet set up an Emergency Expenditure Committee (later, the Treasury Inter-Services Committee) to vet contracts instead. (CAB 24/259; CP 26/36, Appendix C, 2 December 1936.)

apparently considering the alternative argument that exposure to commercial risk was more likely to inspire entrepreneurial skills, whereas guarantees might only bolster complacency.[14]

In spite of these favours the SBAC required more. As part of the process of shortening the production period, Swinton had forced the manufacturers to accept the principle that they should remedy deficiencies during the production run, rather than at prototype stage, at consequently greater expense. At the same time, the SBAC saw the long, potentially profitable runs of aircraft, ordered in the early thirties, disappear under successive waves of new models which gave little chance to amortise research and development costs. When, early in 1938, Swinton began to talk of further discipline, the SBAC conducted a press campaign against his Ministry and primed the Cadman Committee on Civil Aviation with material which, when published, gravely damaged Swinton's personal standing,* and provided the principal excuse for Chamberlain to sack him: at one time the Prime Minister was dealing direct with the SBAC over his head, using Horace Wilson as go-between,[15] rather as he was to do with Neville Henderson, before Eden's resignation as Foreign Secretary.

Chamberlain, in effect, helped the SBAC to bring down the one Minister with the political will to introduce compulsion into production, fearing the effects of Swinton's forthrightness on his own followers in Cabinet and on harmony in the aircraft industry. But this cosy liaison between government and manufacturers soon grew vulnerable to the risk of exposing politically unpalatable profits, obtained with government money, from defence contracts. It would hardly have been a popular parliamentary defence to restate the manufacturers' argument that high risks, the chance of error (the almost useless Boulton Paul Defiant, one of Churchill's favourites) or the remedial work necessary, for example, on early models of the Blenheim and Wellington, and the first undergunned Spitfires, required entrepreneurial courage which justified high profits elsewhere, and repudiation of the doctrine of the fair market price. Although the Labour Party had assisted, for distinct reasons, in the attack on Swinton, Chamberlain's Cabinet could not rely on them to abstain from parliamentary criticism; and they prepared to rebut attacks on profits rather than educate trade union opinion.

---

*CAB 27/643; CA 38/3. They also asserted that Swinton had not consulted them, despite his appointment of Sir M. Bruce-Gardner as liaison officer for the Ministry; and attacked him at the time of Weir's mission to Canada to buy aircraft in April 1938 (PREM 1/238, 21 April 1938).

Whether deliberately or unconsciously is not clear, the TUC allowed the scandal of excessive profits to pass by during the crucial years 1935-9. They had, after all, spent a great deal of time and energy coercing the Labour Party into a more realistic attitude on rearmament; *War and Peace* in 1934 frankly recognised that there might be circumstances in which Britain and the Labour movement would have to fight for collective security; and it jettisoned the anarchic idea that an outbreak of war could be prevented by a general strike.[16] The whole General Council attended the climactic meeting of the NCL on 21 May 1935 and set the tone for acceptance of air rearmament against Germany, which was followed by Bevin's crushing attack on Lansbury's pacifist leadership at the subsequent Labour Party Conference. (As G. D. H. Cole pointed out, the TUC had become 'a largely political assembly which, meeting only a few weeks before the Labour Party Conference, could define the trade union point of view and marshal the trade union battalions behind official policy. That done, the decisions made at the TUC could be re-registered at Conference, with the aid of the massed trade union vote'.[17])

Suspecting that Labour's electoral recovery at the 1935 General Election had actually taken place *circa* 1932-3, so that the party might well not improve its chances much before the next General Election in 1940,[18] the General Council set itself to safeguard what it had already gained, *vis-à-vis* government, rather than wait in the wings for a hypothetical future.* Rather than take up a position of hostility and endanger trade unions' hold over government, the TUC tended towards passivity, listening when Ministers asked for help with production, but not chancing their unwritten status by gratuitous interference with SBAC profits – which, after all, also sustained AEU and ETU wages and levels of employment. The fact that 'the trade union leaders were, and felt themselves to be, the living proof of the higher status of Labour within a capitalist system',[19] precluded violent opposition: the fury over non-intervention in Spain never led the General Council to consider action like that in support of Russia in 1920,† although, during the 1936 TUC, Bevin did speak of 'driving the government to defend democracy' if

---

*'More and more, the trade union leaders spoke and acted as the responsible heads of vast, highly centralised concerns, engaged, by means of well-tested and routinised processes of bargaining and compromise, in the hiring out of their members' labour, and deeply concerned to avoid any disturbance of industrial discipline.' (Miliband, *Parliamentary Socialism*, p. 236.)

†According to Dalton 'those who opposed non-intervention in 1936 had no clue in their minds as to the risks and the realities, for Britain, of a general war. Nor did they, even dimly, comprehend how unrepresentative they were, on this issue, of the great mass of their fellow countrymen.' (Dalton, *The Fateful Years*, p. 102.)

Czechoslovakia were attacked. The furthest that the TUC would go against the SBAC was to ask the Party to deprecate in the Commons the 1935 rise in share values of aircraft companies which had taken place on the forecast of large war contracts. But when Swinton put the argument of risk, research costs and continued harmony ('it is better to proceed by sound business agreements rather than by coercion, unless coercion is proved necessary'[20]) and refused to take on powers to inspect SBAC books to prevent profiteering, TUC and Labour Party let the charges lie.

Unfortunately, as Shay points out, the Air Ministry largely failed to proceed by 'sound business agreements' or to get a fair bargain in their negotiations with the SBAC on the initial agreements of 1936, on which all future contracts were based. Swinton, an industrialist himself, does not seem to have pressed very hard the car manufacturers Rootes and Nuffield (who were to run the 'shadow factories' until conversion to aircraft production); the Ministry team did better with Austin, giving him what Weir regarded as a very modest profit.[21] The SBAC proved even more obdurate and although the Air Ministry brought in the foremost accountant of the 1930s, Sir Thomas McLintock, he made virtually no headway against a well-organised cartel, consisting of the four manufacturers of aero engines and fifteen of airframes.

To be fair, the SBAC had an excellent record of research and development, as the results of the Schneider Trophy Race showed (without such a base, indeed, the development of Spitfires, Wellingtons, etc., would have been inconceivable); but its members had been starved of mass production until the combined expansion of military and civil aviation after 1936, and, having survived the Depression, they had every intention of doing well out of the golden years to come. Reassured on the civil side by the government's formation of the state corporation British Imperial Airways, the SBAC pressed for its guarantees on military aircraft, fearing that the vagaries of diplomacy might terminate the boom too soon;[22] and the government accepted rates of profit well above those permitted even to Rootes and Nuffield.

Chamberlain and Wilson showed themselves sensitive to the possibility of public outcry[23] and the Treasury argued long over whether the profit rate should be determined on the firms' own capital investment (which was small in comparison to the sums from government) or total turnover, as the SBAC naturally desired. But the Air Ministry needed the machines so greatly that Swinton deflected Treasury requirements, though without entirely letting the SBAC off McLintock's hook. BEC and FBI also tried to moderate the SBAC's more outrageous proposals much as they had done with the Coal Owners' Association in 1926, on the grounds that employers generally were being exposed to public odium:

'What do they want' (Weir wrote of a "stupid letter" from the SBAC), 'with threats which would at once provoke a grave political and industrial situation and open up the whole case of private munitions? To blackmail the State in emergency is a present to Socialism, Communism, and all evil movements. More than that, no sector of Private Enterprise can do this by itself, *risking all Private Enterprise*.'[24]

Like the aerospace industry after 1945, the SBAC ignored this warning and the likelihood of future retribution. McLintock won a sort of compromise in September 1936, in which government reserved the right to review profits, and demand repayment in excessive cases, but promised in return to compensate the SBAC for redundant capacity if and when the programme ceased; a compromise which remained the model of such contracts for more than thirty years, covering the Ferranti and De Havilland repayments of the 1950s and 60s. Other similar agreements were made in industries affected by military contracts, such as shipbuilding,[25] but only the SBAC won the main claims against Treasury opposition;[26] and Chamberlain's displeasure at Swinton's necessary complicity became another reason for his dismissal.

SBAC power depended, of course, as Swinton and Weir admitted, on the strategic emergency; and the trade unions involved utilised their advantage in a similarly defensive way, seeking safeguards for free collective bargaining and the right to negotiate production schedules with the SBAC, rather than under government supervision.[27] In one sector of the economy at least, metalworkers, engineers and electricians could look forward to good wages and renewed employment, provided no one talked of industrial conscription. As for the TUC, their line remained that of 1936: 'They are awaiting an approach from government on the question of labour in rearmament: but it was not up to the General Council to take the initiative.'[28] The General Council actually restrained militant unions like ASLEF from the embarrassing demand that government should consult them about the programme[29]—a hesitancy due as much to the sectional interest of the aircraft industry as to lack of unanimity about left-wing fears that armaments might be used by Conservative warmongers. (Bevin even told Francis Williams in 1936 that the trade unions could have been in a stronger political position if they had not been tied to the Labour Party.[30]) It was left to the AEU, the union most closely involved, to worry about the decay of collective security, and in particular the policy of non-intervention; its General Secretary, Jack Little, told the 1938 TUC that 'if the government would shift the embargo on the despatch of munitions of war to Spain, that would throw the doors wide open to dilution.'[31]

This bold gesture, reminiscent of the response to Stockholm in 1917 and the 1921 Councils of Action, caused government and TUC equally to shy away. The Cabinet viewed the skilled labour question and the possible need for compulsory transfer or dilution with far greater apprehension even than it did its harmony with manufacturers of essential armaments. Yet from the moment in 1936 when Weir introduced the figure of a shortage of 100–120,000 skilled men, it consistently avoided consultation with trade unions until shortly before the *Anschluss* in March 1938, fearing exactly the sort of 'blackmail' which the AEU *tentatif* implied.

The incompatibility of good industrial relations on one hand and a low rate of wage inflation on the other had been exposed as early as February 1936, when Ernest Brown, Minister of Labour, pointed out that employers were beginning to raise wages in competition for certain skilled grades.[32] The unions were unwilling to relax restrictions, particularly on skilled job qualification and entry requirements, fearing that an influx of new members would lead to redundancies at the end of the rearmament programme – in the same way as the SBAC dreaded excess capacity. Brown admitted that without skilled labour the programme would fail; and he sought to make the manpower question central to rearmament by giving the Ministry of Labour representation on the Committee of Imperial Defence, advocating, at the same time, a frank approach to the TUC, offering treatment equal to that of the employers, with equivalent guarantees against unemployment. 'The clock of industrial progress cannot be set back; improved procedures, when once introduced, have come to stay.'[33]

If Brown's thesis had been accepted, Britain would have escaped many of the manpower difficulties of 1937–40, and the great 1940 revolution of manpower budgeting might have been achieved in peacetime. The effect on trade union sentiment would have been considerable. But the Cabinet dared not upset industrial harmony by opening negotiations over dilution, new training schemes, or transfer of labour, which could be achieved only after lengthy bargaining and which, if unsuccessful, might have led to social and economic disruption similar to that of 1915–16. Instead, in concert with the SBAC and BEC (through Weir's agency) and by using labour exchanges and regional UABs, they tried unofficially to regulate the supply of labour to prevent bottlenecks and wage competition. Ministry of Labour officials compounded the evasion:

If the speed is such that the whole handling of the labour side of the situation can be left to the industries themselves, it will, from the point of view of the absence of labour troubles, be the best solution. The more the Government are directly involved, the more they will be put into the position of solving the employers' difficulties by buying off the Trade Unions.[34]

Ministers' political prejudices and assumptions about the likely impact of industrial unrest left them no choice but to reject Brown's overture. Inskip minuted in September 1936:

Direct action by the government with the object of securing dilution might well lead to very serious labour unrest apt to damage the export trade. I should anticipate that long before the need for such action arises, ample warning will be available, and there will be time to explore all avenues, and devise the least harmful solution.[35]

A clue to how procrastination could be justified can be found in Brown's diversion of several defence contracts to Merthyr Tydfil, to ease Welsh unemployment.[36] Still, it is remarkable that Cabinet hostility to TUC consultation survived so long unchallenged. Two years passed, in which the only real concession to working-class opinion, the National Defence Loan (which Chamberlain planned as a means to soak up excess profits and placate Labour*) was abandoned in the face of City and business opposition, before the Nazis marched into Austria in March 1938, destroying Chamberlain's hopes of a negotiated colonial settlement with Hitler. Then the door was opened very slightly. On 14 March, the three Service Ministers, Swinton, Duff Cooper and Leslie Hore-Belisha, asked for authority to meet the TUC, Cooper to urge the unions to work double shifts, and Swinton to seek the transfer of 70,000 men to aircraft factories.† Inskip (and the majority) disowned emergency tactics, afraid that, in response to requests for dilution, the TUC might try to impose conditions such as government agreement to take the Czechoslovak question to the League of Nations.[37] Instead, after a suggestion originally put up by Hankey with Chamberlain's agreement, Horace Wilson privately met Citrine to discuss the TUC's

*Chamberlain explained this to the BEC and FBI, warning that if they failed to contribute there could be strikes and rearmament delays: 'we might even end with such concessions to Labour as would very seriously handicap our competitive trades' (T 172/1856/5/13/37).

†He had already requested, in October 1936, authority to 'prick the eyes' out of non-essential factories, a proposal which turned the Cabinet wholly against him, even Brown suggesting that it was 'outside the sphere of practical politics' (CP 327/36).

attitude to a voluntary scheme for transfer of men to meet Swinton's requirements, in which the bargaining point was a guarantee against government interference either with collective bargaining or individual management.[38]

Under the private auspices of Prime Minister rather than Cabinet, a conference with the General Council took place on 23 and 28 March 1938, and a voluntary compact was worked out under which the TUC consented to expedite the movement of skilled workmen into defence industries, and accept a modest degree of job downgrading and dilution.[39] It was almost unpublicised, and – shades of the 1915 Treasury Agreement – was shortly afterwards criticised by the AEU on the grounds that the TUC had abrogated responsibility towards its own members.[40] Meanwhile the Cabinet at last demanded a quid pro quo from the employers: Inskip and Wilson met Sir Alexander Ramsey, NCEO President, on 16 March, and were offered assistance on terms similar to those of the TUC – which left wages, profits and management virtually untouched. The voluntary contract precluded compulsion on one hand, competitive bidding for skilled labour on the other; and the Air Ministry was told simply that the government had chosen 'to get the best it can out of a joint voluntary effort by the firms and trade unions'.

Until his enforced resignation in May 1938, Swinton never allowed the Cabinet to forget the price of consensus over the previous two years.[41] His colleagues, however, preferred the line of least resistance; and in their defence it can be argued that sheer quantitative expansion of the Air Force in 1936–7 might have given Britain numerical parity with Germany in 1938 (in the terms of Baldwin's 'parity pledge') at the cost of a mass of obsolescent machines. But that was not the reason given at the time; nor for the system of rationing and the concomitant appeasement of Germany which, at the price of Czechoslovakia and the stability of France, avoided war at Munich in September 1938. Even if Shay exaggerates his case by suggesting that the Conservative Party, which dominated the government, represented the interests of the class which stood to gain the greater economic benefits from continued industrial peace and profits, his chief contention, that government identified the preservation of equilibrium and the avoidance of crisis with national survival in peace or war, remains unanswerable.[42]

Triangular cooperation, for which the March 1938 agreement served as a model, provided armaments acceleration without tears – to the detriment principally of the unions, who got no real guarantees, and found themselves prevented from putting forward wage claims based on the scarcity of labour. In May 1938, the AEU actually challenged the General Council's right to make such binding agreements, claiming, very much in the style of the shop stewards in 1917–18, that industrial bargains should be made between individual unions and government, the workers and the real employers.[43] Citrine's authority was compromised for a time and Chamberlain debated with his private advisers how best to take advantage of the conflict.[44] In contrast, the SBAC only suffered the first small dent in its monopoly in June 1938, when forced to widen the list of sub-contractors (an action which achieved a remarkable increase in production and revealed how narrow the old monopoly had been).

On the institutional level, however, the TUC's voice began at last to be exercised within the curtilage of government. Its high-mindedness – which could be taken, either at its face value as reluctance to blackmail a government faced with European crisis, or as sheer pusillanimity – was rewarded with limited access to background strategic information. Chamberlain and Lord Halifax (the new Foreign Secretary) went this far 'so that they may give the necessary support, and give the lead to the individual unions',[45] evidently assuming that the TUC would influence the Labour Party in a favourable manner: instead, in April 1938, the General Council modestly put its objections to the government's policy towards Spain and Russia. Since this was exactly what Inskip and the rest of Chamberlain's inner Cabinet had always dreaded, they discussed what sort of machinery could be evolved to limit the TUC's capacity, without pledging government too closely. The model of the tripartite council of the building industry appealed to Ball and Wilson: others wanted TUC and NCEO representatives appointed on the Committee of Imperial Defence. But the latter idea, like Citrine's concept of a Council of State with TUC members, was dismissed by Chamberlain as a 'dangerous innovation'* and until 1939 the relationship remained voluntary and informal.

Labour shortages, combined with the crisis of foreign policy towards Germany in the summer of 1938, compelled the government to grant greater weight in practice to union power than it could conceivably admit to in the House of Commons. Yet away from Chamberlain's followers, among the Tory dissidents around Churchill and Eden, there was talk of more positive collaboration with the TUC; and within

---

*PREM 1/251, 27 June. J. S. Philips, of the Ministry of Labour, suggested that membership of the CID would 'enable both parties to get out of their responsibilities and place them on the government'.

the Cabinet itself, Lord Halifax, a sound *party* man, in the Baldwin sense, began to see that Labour leaders were beginning to speak 'the language of national resistance with growing fluency, leaving the majority Conservatives to speak of peace and conciliation'.[46]

In 1938, Chamberlain rejected Halifax's suggestion of a General Election, intended to restore the National Government's mandate, not only because the indecisive evidence of by-elections threw doubt on the supposed success of Munich,[47] but because it might stir up bitterness and prevent further industrial cooperation. Yet the government could only avoid explicit compromise with the TUC if its foreign policy succeeded; and the timid broadening of the Administration in November 1938 (still excluding the Churchill or Eden groups and Halifax's 'better Labour men'[48]) only postponed the issue. 'It may seem strange to you,' the Conservative Chairman, Sir Robert Hacking, told Collin Brooks, 'with your right-wing views, that we have to tolerate such a position that we cannot defend the nation against the will of the unions, but there it is. It is part of the price that we have to pay for this alleged democracy.'[49]

Intimidated a little by the possibility of an employers' counter-attack, morbidly conscious of the background of a million unemployed, and aware of the danger of a revival of shop floor militancy, the TUC held back from making substantive claims until the impact of war emergency in 1939–40.[50] Rather than consult them, or take individual Labour leaders into the Cabinet, Chamberlain's government delayed, almost to the point of folly, the introduction of crisis measures, hoping desperately in the interim to avoid war and preserve public confidence. And all that time, quite blatantly, the SBAC continued to make its profits, even when Chamberlain at last acknowledged the need to impress public opinion with evidence of equality of sacrifice. His pledge in April 1939 'to take profit out of the war' showed how little had been achieved since 1936;* and the level of excess profits tax, set at 60 per cent, or 20 per cent *less* than in 1917, indicates how over-riding had been the influence of the employers' cartel. Having won their battle to rate profits on turnover, rather than private capital invested, the SBAC had made huge sums from government money, to pay dividends which were, by any standards, exorbitant. After renewed public outcry, the very secret

---

*The machine tool industry, for example, formed a ring in 1937, and refused to let government see firms' accounts, daring them to take compulsory powers. Nothing happened, bar an ineffective Industrial Panel, until the introduction of the Ministry of Supply Bill, May 1939 (Shay, *British Rearmament*, pp. 248–9).

Murray Committee of Inquiry was set up in 1938; but Treasury witnesses did not scruple to deflect the House of Commons Estimates Committee, blandly covering up civil servants' inability to extract credible profit and loss figures from the aircraft companies.[51]

It was not until Hawker Siddeley declared a spectacular dividend in December 1938 that the Treasury induced the Inland Revenue to divulge figures which showed that the SBAC had made an *average* profit of 10 per cent on total capital, including government loans – that is, over 20 per cent on their *own* private invested capital – and that 1938 figures would be yet higher.[52] The Chancellor was not told until January 1939: even then, like the Murray Committee's outspoken condemnation of the McLintock agreement, the news was never allowed to reach Cabinet, the whole matter being surreptitiously disposed of by Treasury and Air Ministry officials. When the Air Minister asked for an immediate Excess Profits Duty, the Treasury refused, on the grounds of the 'shock to business confidence' (using, as evidence, City opposition to Chamberlain's previous National Defence Loan and the unlikely possibility that a recurrence would make Germany think Britain was on the verge of disintegration). The Air Minister, Kingsley Wood, was left on his own to confront the SBAC by threatening to publicise the Inland Revenue figures[53] – a bluff at once called by the SBAC, which refused to renegotiate the McLintock agreement, and hung on until, in the wake of the Ministry of Supply Bill in July 1939 and on the eve of war itself, they finally agreed to take a lower rate of profit, and return one-third of any excess to the state.

This was the price of the government's pertinacious attempts to avoid war. Chamberlain's unusual personal pliancy may be explained by the fact that he had suffered twice at the hands of the employers, first, at the meeting with the FBI in October 1934 when the industry's imperious conditions had been laid down, and secondly, with the humiliating defeat imposed on him in 1937 over his proposed National Defence Loan. On a wider scale, however, the argument that emergency legislation might frighten the public and the business world unnecessarily was allowed to impose wide constraints on policy-making, overriding practically every expression of national urgency. When it came to increasing taxation, in November 1938, the Treasury reacted as if the European emergency existed as part of a remote, theoretical syntax, mixing concern about the effect of higher taxes on enterprise with doubts about capacity for future borrowing. Sir Richard Hopkins declared:

It will be far more difficult to raise the money, as the investing world would certainly expect to be shown that the nation can easily handle the interest charges. I do not say that the City is right to argue this way, but that is the way they do argue, and we must humour them if we want their money.[54]

In the emergency debates in January 1939, when the government believed, wrongly, that German invasion of Holland was imminent, Treasury officials were still discussing whether British reserves and capacity to borrow sufficed for war.[55] The rules laid down in 1937, against the advice of Swinton, Cooper and Eden, about non-interference with 'normal trade', were maintained, like the principle of rationing of Service expenditure to a fixed cash sum, until the German invasion of Czechoslovakia in March 1939 forced radical revision of the strategy of appeasement. Even then, though a Civil Defence scheme was hastily evolved, the Ministry of Supply question and that of compulsion in the aircraft industry (where production failed to rise in the first half of 1939[56]) were again postponed. Samuel Hoare, at the Home Office, recorded a struggle with a tiny staff against the 'hostility, apathy and ignorance' of local authorities over Air Raid Precautions; yet of all forms of defence in the five months after Munich, ARP was reckoned to have been the most successful.[57]

At times and with a certain self-interest in mind, the employers' institutions pushed government, urging the need for contingency planning for war to insure production schedules against disruption.[58] But on the crucial issue of emergency organisation, FBI and BEC still averred that they could resolve all problems without government interference:[59] an attitude which may have strengthened Chamberlain in dismissing Inskip – together with Brown and Hore-Belisha, both persistent advocates of a Ministry of Supply. Even after the German occupation of Prague, in March 1939, Chamberlain avoided any commitment, setting up instead another Committee to advise government and refresh its contact with industry. When in May a Ministry of Supply became inevitable, in the face of demand from the House of Commons and the minority in Cabinet whom Chamberlain had never wholly silenced, the Government's Bill turned out to be the least stringent possible. And it was not until July 1939 that the Treasury finally opted for higher taxation, government direction of savings, and the rest of the paraphernalia of financial mobilisation.[60]

Afterwards, in the early months of the 'phoney war', Chamberlain tried to recover what was finally accepted as lost ground by issuing a circular to all departments requesting the utmost cooperation with trade unions.[61] But practice showed this to have been mere propaganda. Under the Ministry of Supply Bill, the advisory panel for industry contained only businessmen and no trade union representative. Nor, despite protests from the Labour movement after war had broken out, was the TUC given any responsibility for implementation of the government's industrial policy. The flagrant inability to instil a mood of urgency, or guarantee fair sharing of the burden, ensured that all the ancient faults of the First World War, poaching of skilled labour, leap-frogging wages, and disruption of production schedules, would continue, almost unabated, until the crisis of 1940.

As in 1916, the government approached conscription with even more forebodings than when it considered dilution or transfer of labour. In 1937 Chamberlain had renewed Baldwin's pledge (made two years previously in the very different context of pacifist sentiment) not to introduce conscription in peace-time; and the context of foreign policy and assumptions about public opinion explain the voluntary nature of the National Service scheme finally worked out by Ministry of Labour, BEC and TUC in December 1938, which provided for local committees in each district to organise volunteers and civil defence.

Neither BEC nor TUC was consulted about the most important question, the schedule of reserved occupations, however, and both sides pursued their own advantage, the BEC seeking to by-pass trade union influence by making reinstatement of men after their military training voluntary rather than automatic,[62] and the TUC attempting to trade cooperation for repeal of the 1927 Trades Disputes Act. On a more elevated level, NCEO, FBI and the Chambers of Commerce pledged support for Samuel Hoare's voluntary Civil Defence Scheme in July 1938, and the TUC achieved the principle of direct dealings with government on over-all industrial policy, leaving particular negotiations to each industry. This mildly defensive posture, reminiscent of the anti-compulsion stance of 1915–16, can be seen in Bevin's agreements in the docks, road haulage, construction and milling, on which his biographer comments:

He was not only seeking to defend his members and the union's interests; he was convinced that a democratic society could only develop its full resources if it drew on the capacity of its members for self-government and did not take the easier, but in his view less efficient, course of concentrating power in the hands of an overworked Civil Service.[63]

The Cabinet delayed a decision about conscription, on political grounds, through 1938–9, in spite of a plea from France after Munich for a gesture to inspire confidence in the supposedly common strategic effort. Like Asquith, Chamberlain allowed himself to be impressed by

Labour's hostility, without trying very hard to persuade the movements' leaders otherwise.* In February, after a meeting with the NCL, he assured the Cabinet that Labour would support his government on every issue but conscription, and that that would lead to strikes.[64] Because 'Labour was acting very helpfully and was turning a blind eye to a number of practices to which they would ordinarily raise objection', he rejected the idea, and settled for an increase in the Territorial Army to which, Arthur Greenwood assured him, the Party would not object.[65] At departmental level, however, after January 1939, Ernest Brown, who had been appalled by the failure to consult about reserved occupations, began to bring TUC leaders into Ministry of Labour discussions on matters like wartime regulation of wages and industrial disputes, which would be contingent on any general scheme of manpower mobilisation. To allay their suspicions, Sir John Anderson also gave an assurance that national service would not lead on to industrial conscription.

When emergency measures were at last introduced in May, in two separate bills for Military Training and Mobilisation, the inner Cabinet justified its earlier decisions and the secretiveness about preparations for conscription which were undertaken in March,[66] on the grounds of Labour Party opposition (accurately predicted from secret information supplied by Joseph Ball) and of Chamberlain's proposition that it would be necessary to wait for European events to sweep away Labour's sectional prejudices, making unnecessary such forms of appeasement as a wealth tax or an attack on employers' profits.[67] Yet the General Council, apparently docile, went out of its way to facilitate the bills behind the scenes, preventing Trades Councils from attacking conscription in public, and shunning Bevin's somewhat apocalyptic proposal for a grand alliance of peaceful trading nations against aggression, which he had proposed to a startled TUC in April 1939.[68]

Unlike the Labour Party, the TUC seems to have been primarily concerned to avoid a threat to union freedoms from a new Treasury Agreement, rather than to attack the government, and Chamberlain was evidently sufficiently aware of the distinction to argue privately with Sir Horace Wilson the case for closer understanding.[69] Nevertheless, the half-hearted approval given to voluntary national service by a special conference of trade union executives in May 1939, and fears of TUC demands for repeal of the 1927 Act, deterred him. When he met

*The EEF also remained unconvinced about the need for dilution. Ramsay was summoned to a meeting with Chamberlain in March 1938; but the Cabinet 'still left it up to the parties to work out the necessary steps'. (E. Wigham, *The Power to Manage*, p. 146.) A joint agreement on dilution between EEF and AEU was not secured until August 1939.

the General Council, on 26 July, to discuss unemployment, Chamberlain treated its members to a lecture on economics – a repudiation of their claims to right of consultation in complete contrast with the practice, not only of Brown, but of Hoare, the Home Secretary, who in preparing the new DORA regulations followed the old precedents and showed the Bill, before presentation to the Commons. 'The TUC were nervous about the Regulations being used to stop the threatened railway strike. They pressed for affirmative resolutions and a time limit. I agreed to the time limit.'[70]

Discrepancy of treatment continued even after the outbreak of war. After a joint meeting at the Ministry of Labour on 6 September, BEC and TUC created a joint committee on labour questions and put their organisations at government disposal.[71] But when Citrine asked for the TUC to be given full cooperation, he got a patchy response: Hoare replied, 'Where general principles of the employment of industrial workers in connexion with civil defence are concerned, the TUC should be consulted.' Brown declared 'Our view is that the TUC or the appropriate trade union should be consulted on *all* contemplated action which affects labour,' but the Board of Trade, Ministry of Supply and Treasury, all found collaboration uncongenial, and the Ministry of Food actively opposed it.[72] In sum, the departments would not grant the TUC more than an equal voice with the employers, without any of the appointments in the Ministry of Supply which BEC and FBI had already been given – the latter, it was suggested disingenuously, in their *executive* capacity.

Citrine's reply, written on 4 October, 'If the government wished to keep the goodwill of the trade union movement, it must have its proper place in the national effort', may have inspired the Chamberlain circular of 16 October, asking for departmental cooperation with the TUC. Until May 1940, however, the General Council kept up its complaint about lack of real consultation and in spite of palliatives to working-class opinion like the food subsidies introduced in January 1940 to limit cost of living increases, manifestly never gave full political allegiance to the government during the period of the phoney war.[73] The General Council gave Bevin solid support when in May 1939, he denounced the emergency measures as the work of the old gang, the bankers and the appeasers; and a year later, the only two members of Chamberlain's Cabinet to be given office under Churchill were Brown and Hoare, those who *had* listened to the TUC. But union leaders went no further than stating their case: Bevin restrained those members of the General Council who wanted to make a complete break over conscription, in case they should weaken the organisation against an employer-government front.[74]

Defensiveness owed much to historic memory, not only of 1915–16, but of NCEO behaviour down the years; and the fact that Bevin shocked the government's new advisers, Maynard Keynes and Sir Josiah Stamp, with his preoccupations about 'wages commensurate with the cost of living', when asked by Seebohm Rowntree to forego any improvement in living standards for the duration of the war, shows only that they failed, as did Chamberlain, to understand what Bevin meant when he wrote bitterly: 'No employer will make sacrifices unless he is compelled to. All the prices I have seen fixed, and the changes being made, indicate that taxation and everything else is included, and the employers rake off the top, and in this farcical state of society for one class to be trying to measure another upon a fodder basis is intolerable.'[75]

Largely because union-employer relations had been stabilised ten years earlier in terms which neither wanted to change, whatever temporary advantage each might try to gain, the pre-war months did not revive the open class struggles of 1915–16. The appearance of industrial equilibrium had barely changed since 1931. When government made the concessions necessary to retain harmony between the institutions over aircraft production and conscription, the SBAC won astonishing concessions unmatched by the largely negative gains made by trade unions. But Chamberlain could never bring himself to go so far with the TUC as with BEC or FBI: even in March 1940 he tended to patronise their contribution to the war, and loftily set the repeal of the 1927 Act as a prize for continued good conduct: it was 'controversial', and might impair 'harmony in the House of Commons'; instead, after the war, the TUC could return 'with their record of cooperation and urge their case'.[76]

But, ironically, the very fact that there could be no enduring bargain while Chamberlain remained Prime Minister showed how, underneath appearances, the power relationship had changed. While the SBAC got its golden years of profit, the TUC took all the main tricks – the postponement of emergency legislation and conscription and its eventual introduction largely on their terms – both signs of the government's tardy awakening to the strength of the organised working class. TUC and Labour Party combined to emasculate the Control of Employment Act in September 1939, in favour of Bevin's programme of industry by industry control, which had the additional advantage of extending trade unionism in previously weak areas.[77]

Confrontation with the unions ranked even above dismay at disastrous labour shortages: the government ignored the Wolfe Report in January 1940, with its forecast of 70 per cent deficiencies of manpower in certain key sectors, and postponed, until the final crisis in May 1940, measures for the control of wages and compulsory direction of labour.[78] Desperate though the rise in the cost of living was (6 per cent in the first three months) in the only serious labour dispute after the outbreak of war, caused by the miners' claim for an increased hourly wage in October 1939, the government ignored warnings of a wage spiral like that of 1917–18, and of inflation caused by high coal prices, from the Service Ministers, Churchill and Hore-Belisha, and the Chancellor of the Exchequer, Simon, and gave way, Chamberlain personally intervening with the Mines Department and the coal owners in order to avoid a Cabinet crisis.[79] Admission of the necessity of buying productivity and harmony in wartime by wage increases might be counted as the fruit of First World War experience, but it demeaned the voluntary appeal on which the government's previous strategy had been based, and opened up a host of competing claims from other powerful unions. Not surprisingly, having sold the pass, the Cabinet put all its efforts into propaganda and managed to ensure that the award (of 8*d.* a shift, or 25 per cent more than the owners had been prepared to grant) received scarcely any publicity.

Such conflicts between appearance and actual behaviour could not survive the exigencies of war. In the long run, rectification of the balance of power simply could not be delayed, and this, rather than any specifically Conservative betrayal in 1940 at the time of Chamberlain's fall,[80] produced, under Churchill, government which was truly a coalition between parties symbolising the inextricably entwined interests of industry and labour.

10 THE WARTIME TRIANGLE, 1941-5

Comparison of the effects of two world wars on society has become a favourite preoccupation of twentieth-century British economic historians in search of answers to questions such as how and why war stimulated economic innovation and social change; questions which can equally well be applied to changes in political structure. That the crisis of May 1940 changed the political landscape is not in dispute. But did its significance lie in the ending of Conservative hegemony, or the induction of Labour into that hegemony? Did the circumstances of the time create a new balance of forces or was an existing imbalance between the country's political institutions only remedied by the arrangements made after the fall of Chamberlain? Did the composition of the Coalition government, its programme, and its behaviour towards power groups and public, represent the implanting of a political contract, re-establishing previously informal understandings in a more open form than had been possible during the 1930s? And should the success of the war effort after 1940 be attributed to benefits of political harmony, after the self-inflicted disabilities of the Chamberlain years, rather than the once-fashionable single factor explanations of Churchill's leadership and the heroic public response to the disasters of 1940-1?

As Alan Milward has argued, it is relatively easy to answer these questions on financial and industrial grounds.[1] After eight years of the National Government's careful balancing of rearmament, financial resources, and public opinion, Britain was largely unfitted to respond to blitzkrieg strategy, except in the one defensive arm (the fighter and radar screen) on which effort had been most concentrated. On the other hand, and in contrast to Germany, her credit overseas was substantial, her price structure – despite early wage inflation – controllable, and her technological and productive possibilities substantial enough for a long war. The experience of 1939-43 is by no means an unmitigated condemnation of the previous government's industrial policy. After initial mistakes, and with a few exceptions of which the chief relate to the coal

266

industry, the industrial base inherited from the 1930s permitted the creation of an amazingly efficient total war machine – something which occurred partly in Germany, but at a later date, and not in France or Italy.

A similar judgment can be made about the political structure, given that an underlying symmetry of institutions enabled a relatively painless transition from the attitudes and compromises of the Chamberlain period which, as suggested above, had prevented efficient use of the power available.[2] The detritus of mutual mistrust which had accumulated during the autocratic rule of Chamberlain's inner Cabinet since 1937 impeded *rapprochement* with the trade union movement or Labour Party comparable to the 1914 truce, or the *union sacrée* and the *Burgfrieden*. A bland refusal to recognise the recurrence of old, First World War problems of rising cost of living, competing wage claims and excessive profits on war contracts, temporarily disguised their impact, but postponed, for example, solution of the conflicts between Treasury attempts to repress inflation and the effect of high prices on trade union wage demands. The National Joint Council, made up of equal numbers of BEC and TUC representatives appointed by the Minister of Labour, Ernest Brown, lacked power to arbitrate on national wages policy; yet the government feared to enforce Treasury policy (most obviously in the case of the coal industry, p. 265 above) because, as Walter Citrine told Sir John Simon, the Chancellor of the Exchequer, it could not be done without TUC assistance, and trade union leaders would be repudiated by their members if they tried.

Unwilling to offer a bargain to the TUC by control of prices and profits, and subsidies to offset the rapid rise in the cost of living, or to give executive power as the BEC demanded, the government avoided considering both the problem of TUC discipline – and hence of a renewed Shop Stewards' Movement – and BEC anxieties reminiscent of 1917–18 about long-term wage policy, inflation, and the impact of wartime settlements on their civil prosperity. Instead, it allowed them to divide among themselves on the Joint Council, while seeking a purely party settlement. The Labour Party, of course, unwilling to serve with him, Simon or men like Horace Wilson, head of the Treasury after Fisher's retirement,[3] refused Chamberlain's invitation. But Eden and Churchill accepted; a sign sufficient for Labour and Liberals to give tacit support in return for equally tacit and almost meaningless acknowledgement of their 'right' to behave as a responsible opposition. Stifled by an electoral truce arranged between the Chief Whips, afraid of prejudicing a future Labour Government with embarrassing compromises, the Labour Party was prevented from criticising or insisting on reform, in spite of brave public talk.[4] Attlee and his colleagues were reduced to diverting attention from their predicament by enthusiastic support for the Finns' struggle for independence against Russia in the winter war of 1939–40.*

Thus, apart from a handful of dissident MPs like the members of the all-party Action Group† and the ILP remnant, real opposition came from outside parliament, from the TUC, pressing for a bargain in return for wage restraint, and from the FBI, which demanded a single Ministry of Economic Planning.[5] Both were rejected, although Chamberlain responded more warmly to the latter by bringing Sir Andrew Duncan into the Board of Trade, and putting Lord Reith (a favourite of the BEC) into the Ministry of Information in January 1940.

For five months nothing more substantial occurred, apart from the Prime Minister's tentative proposal to sack the unpopular Simon and replace him with Lord Stamp. Chamberlain saw that his concept of waging war was at stake, as much as Asquith's had been in December 1916, and he fought at least as hard in its defence. In retrospect, even in the last letter he wrote before his death, he justified everything he had done, including the Munich settlement and 'limited liability', the little-England strategy of appeasement and the search for peace after 1939.‡ When it came to the May crisis, Labour's hyper-cautious attitude almost permitted him to survive as Prime Minister, for in spite of contacts with dissident Conservatives, and the knowledge that at least twenty Tories would vote for the motion of censure on Norway, the Parliamentary Party could not decide whether to oppose, in case they simply consolidated the government's majority.[6] But a deeply divided meeting finally came down in favour and in the event Labour was joined by forty Conservatives, with another forty abstaining.[7]

The whole conduct of the war being at issue rather than the Norway campaign, Chamberlain could only have survived thereafter by reconciling those Tory rebels who demanded a Coalition containing at least some Labour and Liberal Ministers. According to one source, Clement

---

*Even this occurred under TUC pressure, following Citrine's visit to Finland (although the NEC then issued a pungent condemnation of Russian imperialism, after the partition of Poland, which did something to purge the embarrassments of former members of the Socialist League after the Nazi-Soviet pact).

†Eleanor Rathbone, Bob Boothby, Clement Davies, supported by Lloyd George and some of the technocrats, Walter Layton, Robert Brand, Arthur Salter.

‡'Never for one single instant, have I doubted the rightness of what I did at Munich . . . I regret nothing in the past: I do regret that I should be cut off when I feel capable of doing much more, were it not for physical disability.' Chamberlain to Baldwin, October 1940. (Baldwin of Bewdley papers, Cambridge.)

Davies, Attlee and possibly Arthur Greenwood might have served with him, if Simon and Hoare had been sacked as a sign that appeasement had been repudiated;[8] but Attlee was argued out of it before his crucial meeting with Chamberlain, Halifax and Churchill at 6.30 pm on 9 May, and, quite correctly, begged time to consult his party. The next day, as Germany invaded France and the Low Countries, the NEC announced its refusal to collaborate.

An untidy debate in the special conference in Bournemouth reflected the fact that the NEC's reasoning was not simple. For nearly a decade, party and TUC had hated Chamberlain more than any subordinate member of the Treasury team before 1937 or the inner cabal which had ruled since; as David Margesson, for three years Chamberlain's Chief Whip, realised, they found his contempt impossible to stomach:

He engendered personal dislike among his opponents to an extent almost unbelievable . . . His cold intellect was too much for them, he beat them up in argument, and debunked their catch phrases. Those of us who have lived in country districts know how much a man whom they call 'sarcastic' is disliked. It's a form of mental superiority which produces hate.[9]

Yet, lacking a definite compact with government such as Arthur Henderson had negotiated in 1916, they dreaded a new, unknown Tory Cabinet, and a possible repetition of debilitating compromise followed by peace-time attrition like 1919–26. With a measure of blind faith, and under the stimulus of General Council spokesmen, Labour voted in defence of what had been gained since 1926, and in hope of what might be won from a coalition led by anyone else.[10]

Chamberlain duly resigned, destroyed by Labour's veto. What followed, as Addison points out, was not a case of the reconstituted Conservative Party asking Labour to join, as Asquith had asked Bonar Law in 1915, but something much more like December 1916, with the entry of Labour on terms of 'moral equality' after the collapse of the Chamberlain administration. Nevertheless, strict party equality was not achieved, even in the reshuffle in the autumn, and the Labour Party began at a disadvantage, having failed to commit itself to Churchill. Hugh Dalton, Herbert Morrison and Sir Stafford Cripps were not alone in supporting Lord Halifax, out of dread of Churchill, (the diehard of 1926 become Prime Minister and Minister of Defence, armed with authoritarian powers*). But their views could not bind the

---

*The King supported this view, out of admiration for Halifax, whose high personal reputation had not been overshadowed in popular imagination. (J. Wheeler- Bennett, *King George VI*, Macmillan, 1958, p. 443.)

Conservative leaders' meeting on 9 May, when Churchill timed his bid perfectly, and Halifax conceded that a Prime Minister could not hold office from the Lords.*

In the first stage of the Coalition, the Labour Party drew response appropriate to the context: a measure of equality in the War Cabinet (Attlee, Deputy Leader and Lord Privy Seal, and Greenwood, Minister without Portfolio, to match Chamberlain and Halifax, under Churchill) and outside, with Bevin (Minister of Labour), Morrison (Supply), Dalton (Economic Warfare) and A. V. Alexander (Admiralty); but, lower in the ranks, only sixteen junior ministers to fifty-two. Moreover, among the leaders themselves, Attlee made little impact, Morrison became enmeshed in problems of detail, and Greenwood increasingly incapacitated himself through drink. During the first stage, until Chamberlain's physical collapse in the autumn, only Bevin – a trade unionist not even yet an MP – influenced the management of the war itself.

Appropriately revealing the importance of personality in political life, photographs taken of the Cabinet on VE Day in 1945 show the King flanked by Churchill and Bevin – with Sir John Anderson in attendance, and the party politicians, with the Chiefs of Staff, standing discreetly at the rear.[11] Practically as well as symbolically, Bevin made himself the personal and political match of the Prime Minister, as no one else in wartime.[12] According to Lord Beaverbrook, Churchill instructed the setting up of a Committee of Public Safety, if the Germans invaded in 1940, composed simply of Churchill, Bevin and himself.[13] But Bevin's career in the War Cabinet, uninterrupted after November 1940, signifies much more: not only his capacity as Minister of Labour, but the culminating importance of Labour in wartime and its recognition by the war directorate – something which Arthur Henderson had urged, unavailingly, on Lloyd George. In the crucially important period 1940–2, before the Beveridge Report and planning for reconstruction, when defeat always seemed imminent and necessity drove Conservative ministers to decisions almost free of party ideology, Bevin was able to demand control over manpower (and fight for it against Beaverbrook's Ministry of Production), and then utilise the system of manpower budgeting, which was instituted in December 1942, to elevate his Ministry into the principal department of government.

The war emergency made labour the ultimate resource. Manpower

*Moreover, the moment at which Kingsley Wood, long a close supporter of Chamberlain, switched sides to Churchill, indicated a movement of party and popular opinion that the leaders could not ignore (Addison, p, 102, quoting Horace Wilson).

finally ranked above both finance and production, so that Bevin stood where no Cabinet Minister had previously done, rival to the Chancellor of the Exchequer himself. As he told Arthur Deakin in June 1940, he sought power to control conditions at the war's end, and to remedy what Henderson, for all the Labour Party's long-term gains, had lost in 1917: power over demobilisation, and control over industry, which would give 'the chance to lay down the conditions on which we shall start again'.[14] For that chance the TUC had waited since 1931, and it came about, not as a result of an election, but on the clear recognition of trade union power to determine, either way, supply, production, manpower and morale.

This radical change in the machinery of government was facilitated by the new line-up of the War Cabinet in November, when Morrison took the Home Office, Anderson became Lord President, and Kingsley Wood went to the Treasury, and by the public mood of combined panic and aggression at the end of 1940. Party and electoral considerations, and the fundamental shift to the Left among the electorate were to affect the reconstruction programme in 1942–3, on which Labour triumphed in 1945, much more than they did the decisions of the previous two years, when military disasters initiated in a few months changes which had taken four years to achieve in the First World War.

Although most emergency controls were imposed in response to immediate strategic considerations, their planning suggests the existence of a form of contractual thinking among members of the War Cabinet, long pre-dating the period of economic and social preparation for peace-time. Based on physical planning concepts, akin to the ideas expressed in the TUC Economic Committee's discussions, or those of PEP and the Next Five Years group in the 1930s, this policy was also governed by assumptions derived from Keynes about the possibilities implicit in financial and currency management, not only for future domestic welfare schemes and renewed, even full employment, but a new post-war trading system based on an international currency.[15] The Budget was used firmly as a regulating mechanism for the first time in April 1941, with a deliberate variety of aims; controlling wages and prices, and hence inflation, ordering industrial production and the supply of munitions, and creating a stable basis for future employment.

Social reform came later, after survival had been achieved. The settlement of 1940–1 was state-imposed, in the manner of corporatist systems of the inter-war years, rather than won through the medium of opinion, like the contract for peace-time envisaged in the Beveridge Report, or the promised reforms on which political parties prepared for

271

the post-war electoral campaign. The publicity given to Beveridge, the success of Ministry of Information, press, Army Education Corps, or Army Bureau of Current Affairs (ABCA) in raising and sustaining public expectation that the country would be a better place after the war, all *followed* the establishment of a political contract, during an emergency which wholly concentrated public and party opinion on the war effort and from which popular influence was almost wholly excluded. The diversity of opinion after 1943, and the widespread fear – to which parties responded – that the 'contract to reform' might not be performed, relate to increasing party divergences, leading up to the post-war election; and it is in this sense only that it is accurate to suggest that 1940 gives the key to post-war reform. Reconstruction, social welfare, town and country planning, education, counted little beside the issues of manpower and industrial production in the period following the fall of France.

Indeed, in its first eighteen months, the new War Cabinet failed to reach agreement on war aims and reconstruction largely because of the low priority allotted them. Party blueprints of the 1930s could not easily be harmonised just because their authors had taken on joint responsibilities; and although Churchill appointed a senior Labour Minister, Arthur Greenwood, to the Reconstruction Committee in January 1941, his increasing incapacity, and the irregular meetings of the Committee, meant that little had been achieved before he was dismissed a year later. The field was left open to those with fully-developed schemes for economic reorganisation, dating from the early 1930s, TUC, FBI, BEC and the technocrats, who could now launch them by skilful lobbying or ministerial influence. Thus it was Bevin's speech in January 1941 on social security after the war which Keynes cited in his memorandum on war aims, and G. D. H. Cole who attracted the support of Greenwood and Reith, and won Treasury financial help for the Nuffield College Reconstruction Survey in February 1941 (see below p. 295).

The full influence of collegiate opinion-makers, like PEP and the 1941 Committee – what H. G. Wells called the 'well meaning (but otherwise meaningless) miscellany of people earnestly and obstinately going in every direction under their vehement professions of unity'[16] – would take volumes to analyse: reconstruction plans usually attributed to the master designs of Beveridge and Keynes in fact owed much to the sedimentary intellectual deposits of academics, journalists and editors, and bodies like the Oxford Institute of Statistics and the National Institute of Social and Economic Research.

The genesis of Beveridge's Committee, for example, reveals both his debt to Liberal antecedents and the accidental pattern of influence over policy at the time. Pressure from a TUC deputation seeking, in February 1942, reforms in health insurance and unemployment benefit, inspired the Minister of Health, Malcolm MacDonald, to set up a more general study of the inter-connections of social security policy. Keen to exclude Beveridge from his own Ministry of Labour, where his arrogance was a constant source of conflict, Bevin asked for his appointment. Thereafter, with slight help from Greenwood, Beveridge made his own way;[17] and although it is inconceivable that Bevin was not generally aware of his ideas, his first outline, setting out in embryo the concepts of the national minimum wage, comprehensive health service, social insurance, family allowances, and the maintenance of full employment, which he drafted for the guidance of his officials on 11 December 1942, was considered by the Treasury so outrageous that Kingsley Wood insisted Beveridge alone should sign it, exonerating the civil servants from responsibility for its commitments.

It seems reasonable to argue that, if it had not been for the existence by 1942–3 of widespread popular radicalism, focused directedly on programmes of reform for the first time since the mid-1920s (and perhaps since the age of the Chartists), which the Labour Party utilised and the Conservatives could not ignore, then government might have relegated Beveridge and his report to a rosy but indefinite future, much as Churchill himself did with schemes for nationalisation in his declaration in October 1943: 'Everything for the war, whether controversial or not; and nothing controversial that is not needed for the war.'[18]

After the mid-war crisis, when it was clear that Britain would not lose against Germany, this radicalism shaped both the course of party politics and the methods adopted by government to sustain the apparatus of controls. But that was in 1943–4; earlier, state control was not established, as it had been in 1915–17, by a process of bargaining for consent. In 1940, the country could not afford the luxury of argument about voluntary obligation, and as a result, when more open debate began about the amelioration of poverty, unemployment and unfair distribution of wealth, it took place on the basis of two or three years' experience of state activity which had *already* profoundly changed the social relationship between classes. It was not party which benefited, but the image of government; government which had run, fairly and efficiently, if often without inspiration, such mundane areas of potential friction as food supply, evacuation and labour exchanges. Slowly but inevitably, the state came to be seen as something vaster and more beneficent than the political parties, under whose temporary management it rested, as the real guarantor of reform and reconstruction, which parties could do no more than pledge themselves to fulfil.

Labour and Conservatives adjusted themselves rapidly to the change of ground; but up to 1943 they contributed little, partly because of their common assumption that the Coalition would last for three years after the end of the war.[19] Party reconstruction committees were set up late, and worked ineffectively. Shinwell and Laski incorporated in the Labour document a theory of imminent capitalist collapse too radical for their Coalition leaders;[20] while Rowntree, for the Liberals, failed to renew the 1920s inheritance of reformism. Churchill, on the other hand, held back those Conservatives like Eden (who in May 1941 gave a faint spur towards new thinking), and forbade discussion of any controversial or costly commitment. As Addison says, 'Reconstruction could not come about through Churchill. But it gradually flowed around and past him, like a tide cutting off an island from the shore.'[21] But it was not a Tory tide: the clause in the Atlantic Charter (August 1941) concerning social welfare was inserted at Bevin's dictation, and later watered down by the War Cabinet. A Conservative Reconstruction Committee was not even set up until autumn 1941 and, even then, despite its able chairman, R. A. Butler, it remained tied to Central Office, concerning itself with public opinion, party propaganda, and reform conceived only with the post-war election campaign in mind.[22]

In spite of the classical formulation of the political contract suggested by the official historians of the war economy, linking popular sacrifice during the desperate years after Dunkirk with the genesis of social reform in 1942–3 and its subsequent implementation,* the primary contract in the first, catastrophic war years, when it seemed at least possible that Britain might lose, had to be established in the field of production, between government, employers and the industrial and agricultural labour force, represented by their unions. Assessing public morale, at almost the worst moment of the war, in September 1941, the head of the Ministry of Information's Home Intelligence, Stephen Taylor, concluded that material factors mattered more than ideals: food, warmth, rest, security of the home and safety of the family counted for more than belief in victory, equality of sacrifice, a just cause, or the

---

*'There existed, so to speak, an implicit contract between government and people; the people refused none of the sacrifices that the government demanded from them for the winning of the war. In return, they expected that the government should show imagination and seriousness in planning for the restoration and improvement of the nation's well-being when the war had been won. The plans for reconstruction were, therefore, a real part of the war effort.' (W. K. Hancock and M. M. Gowing *British War Economy*, History of the Second World War, UK Civil Services, HMSO, 1949, p. 541.)

integrity of national leadership. Such views could have been taken from the Industrial Unrest Commissioners of 1917. In complete contrast to later usage of the 'Dunkirk spirit', Taylor wrote: 'The public is unimaginative. It is unable, and has apparently no great wish, to picture the details of the post-war world. It speculates relatively little about the end of the war.'[23]

If Home Intelligence was correct, this is to say no more than that public planning for reconstruction could be afforded only when victory was in sight, distantly, sometime after the middle of 1942. Meanwhile, the issues settled in 1940 at the most fluid period, when almost any extension of power, or alteration of the pre-war system was possible, had determined the relationships of the political system; and the fact that incipient corporatism of government, industry and trade unions was reinforced, and set free of party entails and ideology, a full three years before the restoration of party warfare on any scale, explains the remarkable distinction between industrial and parliamentary politics up to the war's end and beyond.

The emergency of 1940 led to a ban on strikes and lockouts which lasted until 1951, the submission of trades disputes to compulsory arbitration, stringent penalties against unofficial strikers, and limitations on industrial freedom of speech – things never achieved by the most extreme advocates of coercion in 1916–18. Yet these powers were taken, not in the manner of Hindenburg and Ludendorff, nor as a result of any electoral mandate, but after the consent of the trade union movement, represented by 2,000 executive delegates at the Central Hall, Westminster, had been given to their representative, the Minister of Labour, on 25 May 1940.

'I have to ask you,' Bevin declared, 'virtually to place yourselves at the disposal of the state. We are Socialists and this is the test of our Socialism. It is the test whether we have meant the resolutions which we have so often passed . . . If our Movement and our class rise with all their energy now and save the people of this country from disaster, the country will always turn with confidence to the people who saved them . . . And the people are conscious at this moment that they are in danger.'[24]

Considering the TUC's response to Chamberlain only six months before, this unreserved surrender of privileges can be explained only by the change in political direction of the war effort. Until then, compulsion had not been a central question: Chamberlain's Cabinet had avoided insisting even on dilution, as Bevin found on taking office. Ernest Brown had got no further than the compromises on transfer of skilled men achieved in the aircraft industry in 1938, while the Mines Department had instituted a decentralised system of indirect control so lax that Army recruiting was allowed to take over 700,000 miners (admittedly, mostly then unemployed), to the grave detriment of coal production by 1941.

The assumption that trade unions would respond voluntarily to productivity appeals, if they were allowed to retain the right of wage-bargaining, had been defended by the TUC side on the National Joint Council, just as the BEC had claimed the right to offset the cost of higher wages with higher prices, as they did with coal, after the miners' settlement in October 1939 (above p. 265). In spite of Treasury horror at the impact of inflation on the country's financial base (which had been their chief preoccupation during the whole period of rearmament), and the appalling moral drawn by the inner Cabinet and their closest adviser, Horace Wilson, from the 1916–18 history of wages, prices and industrial unrest, the government refused to introduce compulsion. Unmanned by the bogy of working-class discontent which they had themselves helped to create, by concentrating on controlling wages to the exclusion of prices and profits, they assumed, despairingly, that compromise was impossible, citing such evidence as the TUC's response to Keynes' ingenious scheme for compulsory saving from a national minimum wage. Why, Bevin had asked belligerently, should the working class lend the government money for the war, with no guarantee of employment or improvement after?[25]

In May 1940, authority changed hands: the Ministry of Labour acquired power not only to mobilise and control manpower but, by implication, to determine wages over the heads of employers and prevent strikes. Under the Emergency Powers (Defence) Act, government possessed unprecedented powers which conferred on Bevin a role comparable in civil life to Churchill's in the direction of the war. He won his first battle with the Treasury on 22 May, the day the Emergency Powers Bill passed the Commons, when he raised the historically depressed wages of agricultural workers and railwaymen, in spite of jeremiads from Chamberlain and Kingsley Wood. He saw the Excess Profits taxes raised from the absurdly low 60 per cent to 100 per cent, extracted from the Home Office its traditional responsibility for factory inspection, which he then used (and widened under the Essential Work Order) to force employers, collectively and individually, to employ medical and welfare staff and to make some permanent contact with workers' opinion through personnel departments. Then he took control over the transfer of skilled labour, to prevent poaching, at the same time safeguarding union procedures by making it compulsory for employers to hire men via trade unions or labour exchanges.

Put baldly, the Minister of Labour's authority, *vis-à-vis* the Treasury, Board of Trade or the three Service Ministries, whether in the new Production Council, or War Cabinet, derived from the strategic fact that labour rather than machinery or capital had become the scarcest and most prized industrial commodity. Bevin's interpretation of this authority envisaged, from a trade union point of view, the possibility of an industrial concordat far more lasting and wider than that of 1915–18. But the benefits could only be drawn in return for an equally unprecedented industrial discipline. Enormous as the Ministry's powers were, they did not quite amount to industrial conscription,* and Bevin hoped that the Emergency Powers Act could be used sparingly, until, in the light of public understanding of national needs, it became otiose.

But the emergency powers' harshness was unequally distributed: out of the whole nation subjected to the Act (in 1943 conscription was extended to cover all men and women up to the age of 51) the impact was felt chiefly where labour shortages existed, by the skilled and best organised unions, engineers', electricians' and dockers', or those who had suffered worst from unemployment and low wages in the thirties, such as miners and shipbuilders. Like Lloyd George in 1915, Bevin found it hard to achieve dilution by agreement. The support enthusiastically pledged by delegates in May 1940 turned out to be illusory in the hard cases, among unions habitually resistant to TUC discipline and frequently unconcerned by the theoretically overwhelming legal powers of Order 1305 and the Restriction of Pre-war Practices Act, or the submissive example of the remainder of the six million workers covered by the law. Bullock describes as Bevin's worst job the rationalisation of shipbuilding labour practices; the dockers proved only slightly easier, despite their membership of his own TGWU.[26]

Beyond the scope of legal coercion, however, and under government auspices, management and unions took advantage of the new machinery for joint consultation at all levels of industry to recreate some of the hopes of industrial self-government prevalent in the late 1920s. On 22 May 1940, Bevin put a choice to the National Joint Council between submission to, or cooperation with, government direction:

We [the War Cabinet] came to the conclusion that, with the goodwill of the TUC and the unions, and the Employers' Federation, a little less democracy

---

*The National Association Tribunal resembled in some ways the 1915 Committee on Production. But unlike its predecessor it dealt satisfactorily with the great majority of cases under Regulation 1305, and extra powers proved unnecessary.

and a little more trust, in these difficulties we could maintain to a very large extent the peace-time arrangements, merely adjusting them to these extraordinary circumstances.[27]

At the bidding of the authentic voice of inter-war middle opinion, the over-large council reconstituted itself, into a seven-a-side Joint Consultative Council (JCC), meeting twice-monthly over the next eighteen months, usually with Bevin in the chair.

The JCC became in due course the primary instrument of government industrial policy. Within three days, in the first week in June, Bevin had reached agreement on dilution in the engineering industry, after talks with Alexander Ramsay of the EEF and Fred Smith of the AEU, drafted in terms that the tolerant Ramsay could enforce on the stubborn employees in Coventry. Its first serious conflict came, predictably, over wages, a matter postponed too long for temporary compromise, because the War Cabinet now realised that any broad settlement would be binding during and after the war and must, therefore, take into account all the tangled questions of relativities and the basic standard of life.

In May, in a White Paper on wages, the Treasury urged an immediate freeze, followed by four-monthly reviews. In Cabinet, the case was put by Greenwood, as well as Kingsley Wood, with Keynes' and Anderson's support, and reiterated during the next ten months. Rather than take on directly so much political clout, Bevin skilfully used the new JCC to set a precedent of lasting importance by offering employers and unions a choice between government determination of all industrial wages, equally, making special allowances only where it was persuaded they were necessary; or a continuation of normal collective bargaining, in which government held residual power of compulsory arbitration and prohibition of strikes. On 12 July he reached agreement, against Treasury and Cabinet advice, to retain collective bargaining but to ban, in advance, strikes or lockouts,* and this agreement became the basis for the Conditions of Employment and National Arbitration Order No. 1305, under the Defence Regulations – under which, formally, wages could be raised only if both sides agreed, or after compulsory arbitration.

The unions gained enormously in comparison with the one-sided Treasury Agreement of 1915, and in less direct ways, in the most contentious fields of industrial relations such as cotton and textiles, where

---

*'I asked them, *in the name of the Government*, to agree to the prohibition of strikes and lockouts, and to arbitration where other means of settlement had failed.' (Bevi 2/4: memo of 24 March 1943, p. 12.)

employers were at last bound by law to observe district collective bargaining. But although the balance had moved in the unions' favour, both sides benefited, for collective bargaining had long been in the interests of the better organised, more profitable trades who in the past had supported Weir's conception of a high-wage, high-production, economy.* Both sides certainly gained against government, for wages tribunals were required to judge on the merits of each case, ignoring wider comparisons, to the detriment of the national interest – as Lord Simons, the first Chairman of the main Tribunal, pointed out.[28] Above all, the Order vindicated its principal author: Bevin had always intended to ensure freedom for industry to resolve its own conditions, without government pretensions to intervene, believing that there could be no middle ground between that and total control, in the form either of a freeze or of government wage-fixing for each industry, both of which would have set the state against the unions, weakened the war effort, and resurrected the shop stewards movement of 1916–18. In this sense, May 1940 completed the business begun at the tripartite talks of 1929.

Afterwards, other means had to be found to control inflation. Defeated in the long argument, the Treasury developed an alternative strategy on the premise that if excessive profits and rising prices could be checked there would be no case for widespread wage increases; and Kingsley Wood's April 1941 budget, drafted on sound Keynesian principles, introduced the 100 per cent excess profits tax, 10s. income tax, price controls and clothes rationing, as a fiscal bargain to match the tripartite wages system. In complete contrast to World War I, the dual policy worked: prices were held while wages rose gently, and a vast, socially just, redistribution of income took place as a result of high war taxation. Comparing 1947 with 1938, national wage rates rose 18 per cent, salaries fell 21 per cent and the income from property fell 15 per cent;[29] although wage rates and prices kept parity, *actual* wage earnings (based on long wartime hours' overtime) increased rapidly,† giving

---

*After 1940 the EEF 'accepted it all as inevitable'. (Wigham, *The Power to Manage*, pp. 146–7.) The main agreement about Joint Production Committees was reached in March 1942, despite EEF fears about losing the right to manage.

†	1936	1937	1938	1939	1940	1941	1942	1943	1944	1945
Wage rates	100	104	106	106	119	128	137	144	153	159
Cost of living	94.5	100	98.9	101	114	124.7	132.3	138	140.6	145.7
Wage earnings	103	–	109	–	141	154	174	191	198	196

	1946	1947	1948	1951	
Wage rates	172	178	187	212.5	
Cost of living	150.8	159	169.8	197.1	(A. H. Halsey, *Trends in British*
Wage earnings	207	221	239	289.5	*Society*, tables 4.10, 4.11.)

rise to expectations which, after the war, led to the wage inflation that Beveridge had come to fear would be the inevitable corollary of full employment.

In political terms, these arrangements created something close to parity between unions and employers, and elevated their joint body, the JCC, to the status of an unofficial government department. Bevin himself virtually became Minister for Industry.[30] But being ill-tuned to party and parliamentary niceties, he made a poor showing and suffered harsh attacks in the House of Commons, where his Conservative critics had been angered by the generous wage settlements given to agricultural workers in 1941 and by the assistance to dilution in certain areas. His Labour critics were also scandalised by his threat to employ the Essential Work Order, 1941, to bring mobile battalions into the ports of Clyde and Mersey (the only two rivers safe from German submarines) to clear a huge backlog by unloading ships.[31] Neither was particularly mollified by his refusal to interfere with the balance of power between dock employers and workers, nor by his instructions to the former to work towards a guaranteed wage and the ending of casual labour, which in fact set the pattern of port employment, and later of the building trade, for the next thirty years. But the power of MPs to question industrial political settlements had declined steadily since 1931, and he survived unscathed, like Churchill against Cripps' and his allies' censure of grand strategy in 1942.

Wages and conditions, the substream of industrial relations, caused relatively little trouble outside the coal industry after 1941. With Order 1305 and the Essential Work Order in existence, official strikes ceased completely. Following the pattern of 1916–18, unofficial ones increased in number, but given the very different attitude of the Ministry of Labour, most were neither large nor prolonged. Bevin and his permanent Under Secretary, F. W. Leggett, tended to regard them as a safety valve, and few prosecutions took place. Against the often deliberately disingenuous questions put in the House of Commons (and the more serious complaints by lawyers, concerned at the existence of a law widely seen not to be enforced),[32] Bevin emphasised that Order 1305 had to be seen as a secondary line of defence: frequent prosecution would compromise the government's credit, and any imprisonment might degenerate into unseemly farce.[33]

The order has a substantial deterrent effect, but is an instrument which would probably be shown to be useless if any considerable body of workpeople chose to defy it. A large number of workpeople cannot be sent to prison, and it is undesirable to make martyrs by selecting a few for prosecution. It is therefore the policy of the Ministry of Labour to continue to deal with disputes on the basis of cooperation with the organisation in industry and to take legal action only in cases in which it can rely on the support of the constitutional elements among the workpeople. . . .[34]

But the state of the coal industry[35] soon forced the government to abandon this plausible doctrine, even at the risk of stirring up resistance. Hasty and unthinking army recruitment in the first months of war had drained the pool of unemployed miners which would otherwise have formed a reserve of labour for the demands of home industry in 1941–2, allowing the Miners' Federation, for the first time since 1924 to attack the mineowners from a position of strength. Since the Conservative element in the War Cabinet consistently rejected the principle of nationalisation, and opposed at first even such centralised state control as had been imposed in 1916, subsequent developments give an interesting insight on the balance of power between them, in comparison to their counterpart elsewhere in the reasonably harmonious wartime compact.

In tune with the patterns established under the 1930 Coal Mines Act, and to avoid any of the political embarrassments of 1916–21, the Mines Department had since 1938 instituted a highly decentralised scheme for wartime, whose indirect methods avoided any state interference with prices, profits or wages. Unfortunately, the total number of miners in work had fallen from 766,300 in 1939 to 697,600 in 1941, and when armaments production reached its peak in mid-1941, the industry proved quite inadequate to fuel it. In May, the Minister in charge, David Grenfell, forecast a serious shortage for the end of the year. The fact that nearly every European country was experiencing the same problem, with worn-out seams being worked by elderly miners, using second-rate equipment, did nothing to ameliorate the catastrophic 10 per cent fall in output. Despite wartime regulations absenteeism had risen, also by 10 per cent. Much of the explanation lies in the poorer seams of South Wales and the North-East, in fatigue, and the fact that fewer shifts were being worked at the coal face because of lack of men;[36] but many in the Conservative party, and particularly Lord Beaverbrook, urged Churchill to crack down on absenteeism as a clear case of industrial indiscipline.

At the end of 1941, with Cabinet approval but against Bevin's advice, Grenfell was ordered to prosecute at Betteshanger Colliery in Kent, a difficult pit which had been opened by Welsh miners in the 1920s. Against unwavering opposition from the MFGB, the prosecution ran into the sands, and the limits of state authority were exposed, as they had been in South Wales in May 1915. Only nine of the thousand miners charged ever paid their fines, and court officials were advised to desist from pursuing the remainder.

The Essential Work Order, under which the charges had been brought, was disliked by owners who lost their powers to hire or fire their men, but loathed by miners because of the inquisition into absenteeism and the prohibition on seeking more profitable wartime work elsewhere. Their claim for a national minimum wage of £4 had been rejected as inflationary; and in these frustrating conditions, productivity per man fell sharply. In April 1942 Sir John Anderson presented the War Cabinet with an alarming review, warning of worse shortages in 1942–3, and demanding the recruitment of 15,000 miners – half of whom would have to be retrieved from the army. He proposed that coal be rationed to the domestic market, and opened the great question of coal reorganisation, leaving the War Cabinet to face up to a series of unpalatable propositions, likely not only to debilitate the army but to estrange public opinion in a bad winter, and to revive the bitter debate on nationalisation.[37]

In other industries – even in the docks – where conditions were poor, security of employment, hours and work facilities had been improved, under the stimulus of the Ministry of Labour and the JCC, in lieu of higher wages; but the mineowners generally had refused to make similar improvements. Quasi-voluntary collaboration had manifestly failed, as Anderson found when seeking to mediate between the competing intransigence of owners and miners to produce a scheme for the War Cabinet, somewhere short of state control. On one side, Evan Williams defended the indirect system; on the other, the MFGB argued in favour of an ingenious plan drawn up by Bevin and Dalton,[38] for requisitioning the mines on 'compulsory leases' until the end of the war, with a rent related to the previous five years' profits – based on the belief, as Dalton admitted, that the owners would never regain control. Seeking to increase production and reduce absenteeism without either reinforcing legal sanctions or antagonising Conservative voters, Anderson recommended, instead of either, a system of dual control under which the miners would be given a wage increase, the owners would retain their rights (and thus avoid the Bevin trap), but the state would direct operations through the Board of Trade and in effect become responsible for all the difficult problems of productivity.[39]

In spite of Labour Party support for Bevin, the War Cabinet plumped for Anderson's recommendation, and to facilitate it went so far as to withdraw nearly 8,000 miners from the forces. The political disagreements which lay beneath much of the Cabinet's specious reasoning against extension of state authority had already been revealed, however, in the House of Commons on 7 May, when Dalton's plans for coal-rationing had run into fierce opposition from the Conservative 1922 Committee: a defence of householders' opinion and mineowners' prejudices that masked the party clash between Conservative backbenchers and a Labour President of the Board of Trade, which the official historians of war production called 'one of the biggest storms of the war in the sphere of domestic politics'.[40] Nevertheless, in public, Labour ministers presented dual control as a halfway house, giving the miners certain advantages;[41] and when the Ministry of Fuel and Power was set up in June with a Liberal, Gwilym Lloyd George, in charge, only the ILP divided the House.

The miners, however, treated the White Paper as a betrayal, and accused Bevin who, angry at the loss of his scheme but loyal to the War Cabinet decision, succeeded in mollifying their discontent only by substantial wage increases, in the basic wage and in shift pay, in August 1942. This lifted miners' earnings from 59th to 23rd in the industrial table, and was accepted by the owners in preference to a wave of unofficial strikes. But absenteeism and unofficial action continued until in March 1943 the Greene Committee recommended the creation of a new national conciliation board, giving parity to owners and miners, accompanied by a national tribunal. This represented recognition of the need for a formal, national method of industrial relations and set in motion a process of evolution so that, by 1945, the political conditions of the industry and the posture of both sides had changed substantially.

The War Cabinet, however, still baulked at altering the structure of authority. In October 1943 it rejected nationalisation either on MFGB terms or on the model suggested by Gwilym Lloyd George. Churchill personally scotched it in the Commons with his famous declaration (above, p. 273). For lack of a comprehensive reorganisation,* Bevin, Dalton and Lloyd George fell back on wages to appease the militancy that threatened to cut short supply yet again in the winter of 1943-4; but although the next review set out unprecedented terms, with a £6 minimum for coal-face workers, it fell short of miners' demands for piece-work rates, and ran into the apparently insuperable political

---

*At the time the labour shortage had become so serious that Bevin was directing men into the pits; Labour MPs argued that if the state of coal-mining was so bad, it had to be nationalised. (Kirby, p. 187.)

objection that, to pay it, government would have to override the existing, technically free, bargaining procedure.

Conservative Ministers had to choose between their principles and avoiding inflation on one hand and industrial harmony on the other; and by opting for the latter, they opened the gate to the creeping nationalisation they had staved off the year before. Harassed by Bevin and Lloyd George, and bewildered by the number of unofficial strikes in the first quarter of 1944, they gave way and allowed the Ministry of Fuel and Power to take responsibility.[42] Piece-rates were granted which brought the miners back from 41st place to 14th in the industrial wages table, accompanied for the first time by a guarantee lasting at least until December 1947 – a settlement which abolished for ever the fear of a return to district agreements.

Thus, despite their numerical disadvantage, Labour ministers achieved a great deal for the MFGB (or National Union of Mineworkers as it became in 1945), while the owners conceded more, perhaps, than Churchill or his colleagues understood. But if the triangular relationship, even in this politically backward area altered, accommodating itself in the long run to wartime realities of industrial and political power, short-term imbalances remained, arousing conflict infectious enough to hinder the smooth chronology of change. In particular, Bevin's personal position suffered directly from an outbreak of unrest and unofficial strikes while the new scale of miners' pay was delayed.

In the past, Bevin had carefully retained a buffer state of union officials between shop floor and government: cases of direct intervention, involving sanction, had been rare. Indeed, after the Betteshanger surrender, prosecution under Order 1305 and the Essential Work Order was abandoned, even for cases where Bevin claimed evidence of real subversion, such as the Clyde shipyards. But so important were the wider repercussions of apparent repudiation of a settlement by local miners' leaders, in the period before the November landings in 1944, that Bevin, infuriated, turned on them savagely, using the forum of the TUC and the whole range of the press (including the now highly patriotic *Daily Worker*) to defend his policy and blacken the strikers.

Agreement was reached on 20 April 1944; but, on the way, Bevin also put through Regulation 1AA, which conferred the drastic (and legally somewhat dubious*) power to prosecute those who invited strikes. Great recriminations ensued in the Labour Party and the House of Commons, mainly from those whom he most despised, like

---

*The Regulation was based on the 1797 Incitement to Mutiny Act and the law on conspiracy, then in a state of disuse.

Aneurin Bevan and Sidney Silverman, but also from middle-of-the-road MPs. Sixteen voted against the new Regulation, and ninety-three more abstained. The quarrel had ramifications outside, and *Tribune* charged Bevin with seeking a dictatorship, while the Left, so recently disorganised, and bewildered by the loss of Stafford Cripps, revived sufficiently to harness the latter-day surge of popular radicalism and harass Labour ministers for the rest of the war.

Regulation 1AA was politically too sensitive a matter, even without the incubus of War Cabinet support, for the NEC to do more than reprimand Bevan, leader of the dissidents; and the War Cabinet itself expeditiously revoked it in May 1945, before its scope could become an election issue. Bevin's reasons for pushing it through, however, are interesting as a comment both on his industrial priorities and on the General Council's continuing animus against the Communist Party, even when it had become, since the Nazi attack on Russia, a patriotic element. Actual evidence of subversion existed: from MI5 reports it seems clear that Communist influence* had revived rapidly within the MFGB, particularly in South Wales, after 1941; while Trotskyite activity on the Clyde and at Barrow appeared to be confirmed by two serious strikes at Rolls-Royce and Vickers-Armstrong.[43]

At the Labour Party Conference in 1943, the miners voted for Communist Party affiliation, and the General Council began to suspect a campaign to revive Communist influence, utilising the immensely popular example of Russia's war effort. At much the same time, in the early part of 1944, the War Cabinet was informed that the 'emergency mentality' which had sustained public tolerance of state powers had diminished.[44] In the period January–April 1944, 850,000 days were lost in South Wales, and another one million in the Yorkshire strike over 'home coal' allowances. Rather like the 1917 Industrial Unrest Commissions, Home Intelligence reports suggested that unofficial strike leaders held power only because they complained of local grievances, which were remediable; but Bevin, warned of infiltration by the MFGB leader, Ebby Evans, and aware of a Communist revival in his own TGWU, suspected political machination by the old Minority Movement and fortified his position with the sanctions of Regulation 1AA, taking care, however, to broaden his support by the traditional Ministry of Labour method of drafting it in consultation with the BEC.

In defiance of the libertarian language of the Left Wing, TUC and employers could combine with the War Cabinet to reinforce industrial

*The National Shop Stewards Committee was revived in 1940 but its activities were severely restricted by the Communist Party after Russia entered the war.

harmony at the expense of the tertiary level of industrial political activity, which they subsequently labelled as agitators and extremists. But by 1944 earlier tripartite understandings about the relationship between parliamentary coalition and the industrial sphere had become uncertain, their contractual premises weakened by Conservative opposition to postwar planning and, in particular, by the antagonisms aroused by the Beveridge Report. Party warfare renewed itself each time the War Cabinet drifted into discussion of future principles, although departmental planning still ran on the assumption that the Coalition would be prolonged for two or three years after the war. Bevin's personal position became steadily more ambiguous as his many responsibilities – to TUC, JCC, Labour Party and War Cabinet – slipped out of the once-uncomplicated pattern of 1940–2.

Bevin remained, of course, immensely powerful, having won the long-running skirmish with Lord Beaverbrook at the Ministry of Aircraft Production over rival claims on skilled manpower. Since September 1940 he had chaired the small Production Executive, which gave him a measure of control over the greater part of industrial production; while scheduling and registration of male and female workers had brought more than six million, in 30,000 factories, within the ambit of his Ministry. He had access to all information on the war effort, and to a supporting apparatus organised almost on military lines;* he could use both to enforce a degree of conformity previously unknown, insisting, for example, on truly joint consultation between employers and unions on national and regional Production Boards, as well as between BEC and TUC on the Joint Committee.

Yet the enthusiasm that created forty-six new Whitley Councils during the war in large industries like retail distribution, and reinforced the wages boards which incorporated $15\frac{1}{2}$ million workers by 1945, indicated a sense of common purpose far too wide for any department of state to claim authorship. The comment that 'the annual records of the General Council begin to read like the records of some special government department, responsible for coordinating policy in the social and industrial spheres',[45] is equally valid for the BEC; and if tripartite consultation at last gave the TUC its requirements of 1930, it also permitted the majority of employers to redress their old grievances

---

*Bevin's position resembled that of Commander-in-Chief, surrounded as it was by twelve Regional Controllers, and the periphery of Regional Industrial Relations Officers (the old CCOs). Leggett served as Chief Industrial Commissioner, bearing Askwith's old title but with none of his overweening independence; while Philips directed economic strategy. Other able subordinates like H. C. Emmerson and G. H. Ince, were to become Permanent Under Secretaries at the end of the war.

against the banking system. In 1944 the Bank of England finally responded to the criticisms put before the Macmillan Committee fifteen years before, with plans for long-term finance for small businesses (ICFC) and large companies' restructuring (FCI) which provided, amongst many other things, for the reorganisation of coal mines by a Central National Coal Board – a point at which the employers (though not yet the coal owners) may be said finally to have abandoned their defence against nationalisation.

Consequently, it became very hard to hold together the drifting continents of party and industrial institutions. In September 1941, when Citrine had attempted to stand up to Bevin's demands for total compliance from the General Council,[46] the leaders of the trade union movement had conceded. Three years later, with Laski's Labour Reconstruction Committee ploughing the sands, their eyes fixed on a hypothetical election some three years after the war had ended, a resumption of party politics still appeared undesirable and unnecessary. Yet the Labour Party seemed unable to induce the Conservative majority either to play fair with the Beveridge Report or mines' nationalisation, or to take care of the delicate equilibrium of the General Council, torn between its duty to the Coalition on the one hand and the requirements of local miners' leaders and shop stewards on the other. Over the Beveridge Report, like the future of coal-mining, and largely in defiance of the Conservative majority, a compromise was reached, sufficiently attractive to check the drift; but the more the parties quarrelled, the more TUC and employers tended to dissociate themselves from parties, seeking in the comfortable liaison of the Joint Committee an alternative to renewal of the sterile political arguments of the 1930s.

Both institutions gave evidence to Beveridge during 1942, much as they had done to Blanesburgh, accelerating a debate among themselves on rather different lines from the arguments between Labour and Conservatives. Earlier BEC criticism of Beveridge's ideas, based on their cost in terms of export prices,[47] and of Beveridge's hostility to 'the spider-web of interlocked big banks and big businessmen',[48] slowly gave way, under the influence of the paternalistic views expressed by the ICI men, Melchett and McGovern, and the 120 signatories of *A National Policy for Industry*, in favour of a welfare system including corporately-provided employees' housing, supplements to state pensions, and subsidies against unemployment – proposals more akin to Beveridge's original, insurance-based principles. After the Report had been published, according to a BIPO survey, few employers expected much benefit, but 75 per cent thought it should be adopted:[49] a fair

287

measure of consensus (with the opposition coming chiefly from textile manufacturers and the skirmishing troops of Aims of Industry, which had been formed in 1942), roughly comparable to the TUC's response, that much of it was unacceptable to the unions,* but that it would serve as a basis for bargaining.

Party warfare broke out, not so much on the Reconstruction Priorities Committee (where Morrison led for Beveridge against Kingsley Wood and the Treasury) as in the public sphere, largely as a result of the Labour Left's championing of popular fears that the Conservative majority and the employers might combine to dilute its recommendations. Attlee and Dalton, in fact, gave the Report a lukewarm reception, and found themselves not unwillingly united with their Conservative colleagues, in keeping wartime promises to a minimum, against the strivings of Labour backbenchers and the Tory Reform Group. Attlee even befogged discussion with the bromide statement that 'these changes have already taken place'.[50]

In party research groups and in the Services' education programmes a more radical approach questioned both the financial will to reform, and the very limited guarantees of the existing Coalition's political contract; but the initial reluctance of Bevin or the Labour Party leaders to challenge the Churchill/Treasury rule against detailed commitments in wartime,[51] (for example over the Utthwatt Report on town and country planning and land values), compared unfavourably with the apparent enthusiasm of the TUC, or indeed with the proposals of *A National Policy for Industry*.

It is hard to see how Labour Cabinet Ministers could have acted otherwise without rupturing the Coalition or placing themselves in jeopardy. But their compromises had a deleterious effect, not least on Bevin's personal status. The days when he could ignore criticism from the Left wing or ride full tilt against them with the accusation that they were seeking a socialist revolution in wartime, had passed. As a result of an unwise diatribe against what he saw as Left-wing factiousness, in February 1943 Bevin estranged himself from the Parliamentary Labour Party for an important eighteen months, while his enforced defence of Churchill's decision to destroy the Greek Communist rebellion in 1944-5 made later relations with the parliamentary Left uneasy. Nor was the correlation of political factors good enough for him to rely on institutional equilibrium to guarantee post-war reconstruction and prevent an intemperate decontrol like that of 1919, and restoration of

*Beveridge's part in Lloyd George's repression on Clydeside in 1915-16 was never forgotten.

the 'normalcy' of a pre-war era. The Conservatives in the Coalition owed Bevin no loyalty; Churchill denied him, as Chamberlain had, a pledge to repeal the Trades Disputes Act, yet required him to defend the War Cabinet's halting policy on Beveridge.

Speaking after the 1943 Labour Party Conference, Churchill made it clear that continued party cooperation depended on Labour's promise to sustain the Coalition. In default of an election (which Labour might easily lose, on 1943 estimates) or the Conservative endorsement of reform which Churchill had specifically denied, Bevin, whose own ideas about post-war reconstruction were very straightforward,* could see no alternative but to acquiesce. On 14 October 1943, (in the name of the trade union movement rather than the PLP), he put terms to a meeting of Ministers,[52] which, taken with his private memoranda of the time, suggest that he envisaged his own special position, and the existing state of industrial equilibrium, as an insurance policy for the future. It was not simply a question of restating the May 1940 pledge at Central Hall, nor extending emergency legislation like the Employment and Arbitration Order 'which was designed to meet conditions at a critical stage of the war' into a longer-term arrangement for the transition (or coalition) period after; but to recast them both and establish a more powerful system of government intervention in industry, intended to stimulate TUC-employer bargaining, and cover, as a reserve power, those cases where collective bargaining failed. Whether such incompatible intentions could have been composed under emergency conditions or not, Bevin certainly set himself further on in the continuing tradition of corporatism than any of his predecessors, Askwith, Lloyd George or Steel-Maitland, precisely because he foresaw the growing dominance of government, deriving from its power to effect economic decisions.[53]

Bevin was prepared to bargain, allowing advantage to the (predominantly Conservative) agricultural interest in return for government control of what he saw as public utilities, coal, electricity and water. In addition, he offered to persuade the TUC to accept certain restrictions on the freedom of labour and restrictive practices after the war, so long as the bargain was sealed by repeal of the 1927 Act.[54] But Churchill

*Fuller employment, fair shares between industrial profits and wages, a welfare state, education for all up to sixteen and 'a new conception of industrial relations beginning with better wages and conditions (to be secured by joint negotiation) and extending to something approaching a partnership on equal terms between management and workers [and] the extension of joint consultation with the unions and employees to the whole range of government economic and social policy.' (Bullock, *Bevin*, vol. 2, p. 191.)

would concede only that such a package should be enacted by a Coalition government *after* the war; and some members of the Labour Party, like Dalton and Morrison, who predicted a Conservative victory in a general election, concurred, preferring to campaign for a minimum three-party programme, and a percentage allocation of ministerial places.[55] Paradoxically, Halifax gave Bevin more support[56] than did Attlee who stuck to his line (as he had done in 1941 when composing the Bevin–Citrine quarrel) that the TUC–War Cabinet axis was essential, not only for the war effort, but for the future of the Labour Party.[57]

Since coalition is unkind to rank and file MPs' ambitions, Labour backbenchers showed no more enthusiasm for these schemes than Conservatives. Churchill temporised, and by the spring of 1944 the seams of coalition had begun to spring apart. Identified with centrism, Bevin came under fire, not only from the Labour Left – Aneurin Bevan attacked him in vituperative terms for corporatist ambitions, in April 1944 – but the Tory Right, using the mouthpiece of the *Economist*; and in his defence, he estranged himself further, insisting repeatedly that the Labour Party was the creation of the TUC, and that only the TUC had won or could win lasting gains for the working class.

By 1944, however, there could be no ignoring the great radical swing in public opinion, anti-fascist, libertarian, egalitarian, even utopian, blending belief in military victory with reform, equality of sacrifice with faith in models derived from Roosevelt's New Deal or Russia's socialist appearance.[58] Bevin was forced to argue his case for industrial equilibrium in front of the party or see it go by default. The October 1944 Labour Party Conference not only decided to fight the next election independently, but carried against the platform a resolution on nationalisation, which, as Addison suggests, was probably responsible for the addition of Iron and Steel to the 1945 Manifesto.[59]

Unable to ignore this divergence between institutional thinking and public feeling, transmitted as it was by every party and trade union agency, Labour MPs recoiled – as did their Conservative counterparts, for similar reasons. The 1944 TUC gave a half-hearted vote for retention of the Coalition, but leading trade unionists began to watch uneasily, fearing that Churchill might call a snap post-war election, and win a Tory majority which would exclude them from future policy-making and leave the unions exposed to an employers' counter-attack like that in 1921. In a letter to Attlee, written on 18 May 1944, Bevin said: 'The PM has taken the line that he will not agree to nationalise anything during the war. We must await a general election. Yet it looks as if Max

Beaverbrook and all the forces associated with him are attempting to denationalise what we have got. . . .'[60] Curiously, Churchill reacted in the same way to the accumulation of mistrust: having chosen the Labour members of the Reconstruction Committee, he watched their superior performance with an unease which turned to morbid suspicion in 1944–5. As plotting and quarrels increased between his hatchet men, Beaverbrook and Brendan Bracken, and Labour Ministers, Churchill increasingly leaned towards the advice of Conservative party managers against renewal of Coalition.

A few despairing attempts were made in 1944 to preserve the veneer of collaboration: Bevin was still to be found defending the idea as late as June 1944,[61] looking for a way out of the Trades Disputes Act impasse by 'taking it out of the political arena' with the aid of members of the Tory Reform Group.[62] But at the Party Conference in the autumn, to safeguard his own position he accepted the party line against continuation and in favour of broadside nationalisation. 'Political' questions like land development values or public ownership could not yet be divorced from party considerations – at least so long as public opinion appeared to be moving strongly in the radical direction.

As the party machines began to line up for the coming election campaign, with the War Cabinet dividing every time future policy was discussed, the contrast with industrial politics grew more marked. Bevin's joint authorship with Lord Woolton of the 1944 White Paper on Employment (the government's answer to Beveridge's skilful lobbying and his (unofficial) inquiry *Full Employment in a Free Society*) indicates the common ground that existed, not so much between parties as between like-minded groups, between Treasury and Reconstruction Committee, between Keynesians (especially Dalton) on the one hand and the structural approach to reorganisation advocated on the other by Hubert Henderson, together with the Tory corporatists and Conservative reformers and economists, led by Henry Brooke (spokesmen on industry), especially those with industrial links like Hugh Molson and Arnold Gridley.[63]

Very many employers now accepted the principles argued by the TUC Economic Committee in the mid-1930s, the positive virtue of state attempts to iron out the cycle of boom and slump and to plan financial developments with industrial activity (profits as well as employment) in mind. Their conversion represented the final surrender of nineteenth-century allegiances, and might have been delayed much longer but for wartime emergency conditions; but it ensured that the employers, collectively, would take a different attitude from those Tory backbenchers who opposed the White Paper, on the archaic grounds that unemployment could only be cured by a revival of trade (as if nothing had been learned since 1923); just as the TUC accepted the White Paper gladly, in contrast to the Labour Left, led by Aneurin Bevan, who attacked it because they sought the death, not the Keynesian transformation, of capitalism.[64]

Before 1945, therefore, it had ceased to matter greatly to TUC or employers that the Coalition would not survive the end of the war. In May 1945, against a background of world events, with victory over Japan in mind, Churchill made a last overture which the Labour movement refused. Their programme had been tailored to the requirements of a war-heightened electoral expectancy: retention of state power over the economy, controls on production, allocation of raw materials, and direction of labour; but nationalisation (on Morrison's model) had been limited to vital industries only. Indeed by March 1945 the trend was running so fast against Ian Mikardo's group, who had challenged the leaders in 1944, that the NEC rejected Morrison's scarcely revolutionary slogan 'Public versus Private Enterprise', and almost dropped iron and steel out of *Let Us Face the Future*.[65] As Addison points out, these compromises disgusted party militants and ensured that Attlee's government could not achieve much more than the plans sketched out in 1940–2. But those Labour leaders who looked outside the parliamentary field, especially Morrison, showed themselves keen, not just to brand the Conservative Party as doctrinaire and reactionary, wedded to belief in a primitive, outmoded capitalism, but also to reassure employers and other forward-looking capitalists that a Labour government intended nothing untoward.[66] Not for nothing had Morrison told a pre-war Party Conference that Labour's new public bodies could be appointed 'on business ability and nothing else.'[67] Wavell reported Bevin as saying, on 15 May, 'that he thought Labour would get into office very soon and would then hold power for twenty or thirty years. He professed optimism about Labour's attitude, about agreement with employers, about the standard of living, abolition of unemployment, etc.'[68]

Denied the consummation of immediate state ownership of staple industry, Bevin nevertheless achieved a considerable part of his ambition to extend state regulation over the private sector and establish something close to parity between trade unions and employers. But then his Ministry lost its wartime primacy as manpower demands lessened, as other departments like the Board of Trade entrenched themselves in labour matters, and as he himself grew preoccupied with foreign policy and the direction of the Labour Party. Nevertheless, trade unions entered the formal political and administrative system, having achieved recognition of what had previously been only implied by their privileged and regular access to Ministers and civil servants. Through TUC representatives on the NJC and Production Councils, they acquired formal as well as customary access to the employers' side, and benefited from a great variety of concessions enforced by the Ministry of Labour, such as working conditions in ill-organised areas like catering and retailing. Membership of unions rose consistently and in previously almost unknown trades, so that the 1946 total was 30 per cent above 1939, with the TGWU reaching over one million, the AEU 825,000 (in 1943), the General and Municipal 726,000. Meanwhile, strong new groupings were created among public service and ship workers.*

On the other hand, the 1946 figure of 7·1 million trade unionists failed to match the number of workers employed by the component Federations in the BEC, and only just surpassed the 1920 total. The ban on strikes contained in Order 1305 masked the fact that the TUC had achieved no greater control over union behaviour or inter-union demarcation disputes since the tenuous Bridlington Agreement of 1939 – a weakness which the 1944 Report avoided with a few discreet sentences on the virtues of amalgamation, and a puff by Citrine for the new, functional TUC building, with its superior offices and centralised bureaucracy. Congress House may have been able to look Tothill Street (where the offices of the FBI and BEC were) in the face; but the TUC – as distinct from Bevin himself – does seem to have flinched from defining long-term aims other than the search for equality, in all fields, with the employers.

This paucity of ambition may be explained because, at first, in their joint discussions, there seemed no reason to assume that employers would voluntarily refrain from an attempt to restore the *status quo ante*, as they had done in 1919. But after 1943, as BEC and FBI began to show a rather different face, the TUC's attitude changed, so that members of the General Council looked more and more to government

*Numbers and density of trade unionists

	Men	Density	Women	Density
	(000s)	(%)	(000s)	(%)
1939	5288	38·9	1010	16
1942	6151	44·9	1716	26·6
1945	6237	45·1	1638	25
1946	7186	51·8	1618	24·8

(Halsey, *Trends in British Society*, table 4.12.)

rather than to the political parties whose growing ideological rupture seemed likely to undermine – and, in default of a Labour victory, defeat – hopes for reconstruction, full employment and a welfare state. In this, union leaders only reflected the anxieties of their constituent members. In complete contrast to the latter days of 1918, therefore, they concentrated on securing the future for a return to free collective bargaining, while giving greater and more friendly acknowledgment to employers' associations than ever in the past, insisting on equal representation of workers and management on Industrial Boards without pretension to interfere in managerial functions.*

Such a minimalist programme contained very little that was offensive to 'progressive' industrialists who, after the middle of the war, worked on the same assumption that political coalition would continue, buttressing wartime industrial practices with renewed annual manpower budgeting and economic controls. Nor did they need to worry about TUC proposals for a National Investment Board (for which Allan Smith had implicitly declared, as early as 1931) or the submission of joint TUC–FBI advice on economic policy, which had already taken place at the Imperial Economic Conference at Ottawa. Members of the BEC and FBI had already taken out an insurance policy against the trap envisaged by Weir a decade earlier, in which they might have faced a majority Socialist government, bent on destroying private enterprise, by becoming the government's executives in the Ministry of Supply and on the whole hierarchy of Production Boards, Business Advisory Council, capacity clearing schemes, and the Export Groups who operated in more than two hundred industries. War emergency had brought the corporations wholesale into government service (as Unilever worked, for example, for the Ministry of Food), forcing change even among the diehards of the cotton spinners and mine-owners (although as late as 1944 both these could still be found opposing the Bevin–Woolton White Paper on Employment).

The substantive change seems to have occurred in 1942–3. The year before, when they produced a paper on *Reconstruction*, the FBI had still been concerned at the old danger of being held in 'restraint of trade', and spent its time justifying trade associations and cartels to the new Coalition, and dispensing propaganda against repeal of the 1927 Trades

---

*The TUC interim report *Postwar Reconstruction* (1944) envisaged a state-planned economy with trade unionists at all levels of industry and on the public corporations. These were not, however, to be seen as representatives, because unions would retain the right to take on the corporations in wage bargaining; 'industrial democracy' amounted to no more than the anodyne 'simple democratic right of work-people to have a voice in the determination of their industrial destinies'.

Disputes Act. In contrast, the BEC canvassed a number of self-government schemes, similar to the Amery–Glenday proposals of 1935, including a far-sighted booklet by Robert Boothby, *The New Economy* (Secker & Warburg 1943); later, one of its members, Sam Courtauld, took up the theme of co-partnership once advocated by Robert Cecil.[69] Meanwhile, the BEC's main efforts were concentrated on creating an industrial concordat while emergency conditions preserved their influence over government and with the TUC. The second generation of its leaders, headed by Sir Cecil Weir and Sir Samuel Beale, staffed the Export Groups' Central Committees; and provided many of the 120 signatories of *A National Policy for Industry* which, late in 1942, recommended the creation of a hierarchy of industrial asssociations under a central council.[70]

These developments explain the very interesting series of discussions at Oxford under the auspices of the Nuffield College Reconstruction Survey, an inquiry originally started by G. D. H. Cole and later funded officially by the government in April 1941. Publication of *Employment Policy and the Organisation of Industry after the War*, by members of Nuffield College in 1943, injected into the drafting of the Bevin–Woolton Employment White Paper the concept of industrial equilibrium as the basis for future bargaining between government, employers and unions. A remarkable and diverse number of participants, industrialists, economists, trade unionists, civil servants and politicians, took part; and at the culminating Eighth Conference in April 1943 G. D. H. Cole was able to point out that although each group had approached the idea of full employment 'according to the philosophy in their minds about the way in which society ought to be organised on its industrial side',[71] they had agreed to far more advanced propositions on industrial organisation and the attitude of the state towards monopoly power and public ownership, entrenching so deeply on 'political' matters, when considering the rights of private enterprise and the extent of state control, as to exceed Churchill's prohibition on post-war planning.

What had occurred amounted to the acceptance of socialism without tears; the employers admitted the necessity of extending the pre-war concept of the state corporation, by the use of Industrial Boards, through the transitional post-war years. Speaking for the BEC, Sir Cecil Weir accepted as 'uncontroversial' wide structural changes in industry designed to recover Britain's exports and prolong the 'cooperative understanding of men and management'. Weir and D. W. Coates (for the cotton spinners), Lord Melchett (ICI) and F. J. Osborne (building trades) might dispute details with J. J. Adams and George Chester, the TUC representatives; but Chester in turn pledged the TUC 'to fit into the new form of organisation proposed and to modify its regulations in such a way as to meet the new situation' – provided, first, that employers' cooperation was real, and, secondly, that Labour was 'accorded its full rights and position'.[72] Weir showed himself content to accept collective bargaining, even in nationalised industries, and in an almost lyrical passage set out to atone for the past:

It was necessary to get rid of the idea that there was a fundamental antagonism between employers and workers. Undoubtedly there had been a remarkable development during the war of the team spirit in many factories, particularly in those works where contact between the owners or managers and the workmen was constant and where the motive of service had taken precedence over the motive of profit. If we were to establish this incentive not only in war but in peace it would entail public supervision in order to guarantee the observance of explicit obligations without which that degree of self-government which should be exercised by employers, managers and workers, in every industry (whether publicly or privately owned) could not be obtained ... *Public ownership was not of itself the bogy which it had been. We had to ask whether a particular enterprise would work better under public or private ownership and it was clear that there were cases where the former could not be avoided.* [my italics] Where it was in the interests of the community, certain services should be publicly owned, but the control, administration and management should not be bureaucratic, and should be recruited from the right sources, under terms of remuneration which would attract the best men.[73]

Glenday (one of the corporatists of the thirties), and the economists (Roy Harrod, Harold Clay, Joan Robinson, Dudley Stamp, Nicholas Kaldor, D. H. Macgregor) all concurred; Sir Raymond Street even conceded that the Iron and Steel industry would require an Industrial Board if it failed to remedy the shortcomings it had shown during the 1930s; and Harold Clay, once the diehard opponent of state intervention, embraced the TUC on the closed shop, citing the cases of professional colleges like the British Medical Association and the Law Society.

The Nuffield exchanges showed that whatever each group had found disturbing in previous reconstruction schemes was now outweighed by mutual advantages in creating a new system of equilibrium. BEC and FBI could accept state control, even nationalisation, just as the TUC could envisage instauration of Keynes' humane capitalism, while the economists who had so lamentably failed to agree on MacDonald's

EAC in 1930 hailed an era of recovery and growth unimpeded by industrial conflict.*

April 1943 serves as a convenient moment to point, finally, the discredit of the pre-1931 'free market' approach to industrial politics, and the endorsement of equilibrium by the three main interests concerned. From then on industrial and parliamentary politics naturally drifted apart. But while acceptance of some form of mixed economy, to which BEC–FBI (and later the CBI) held throughout the post-war period, may be counted as imaginative by comparison with employers' attitudes after World War I, apparently historic admissions like Weir's, that 'public opinion would *demand* closer supervision of private enterprise',[74] did not signify a voluntary or, indeed substantive transfer of power. Whatever the future shape of state enterprise,† the employers' side stood to gain.

Weir's statement comprised recognition, not just of the facts of trade union power, but also of the aspirations of the new managerial élite, whose steady rise to the main boards of medium-sized and large companies since the 1930s had been greatly accelerated in wartime. These were concerned not with ownership but control, less with dividends than corporate growth. The state corporate sector was to be run by 'the best men', suitably paid for their skills, who would inevitably exercise greater sway over government's economic planning than the TUC's Economic Committee ever could, thus avoiding Beveridge's bogy of the 'evils of organised pressure groups' and recreating, in the reconstructed future, the old hegemony of entrepreneurial values. In cash terms, as Roy Harrod pointed out, post-war reconstruction alone could involve the investment of £600–700 million a year (or £1,000 million including plant replacement) which no sector of private enterprise nor the banking system could guarantee to raise or spend in a steady flow. Only a rudimentary understanding of economics was needed to see the

---

*The Conference Report was later published in order to prevent any attempt by the diehards to reimpose pre-war practices. (TJ C22, p. 9) Only one participant, Sir John Greenby, criticised the document for its political implications and its continuous invocation of government intervention – a viewpoint which was countered by Weir and Paul Cadbury, speaking specifically on behalf of 'the progressive industrialists'.

†For a time the model of the Export Groups structure may have been more attractive than Industrial Boards, since it involved fewer concessions to labour; and the Board of Trade, though not Dalton himself, seems to have preferred it. Carpenter (*JCH*, January 1976, p. 20) sees the Central Committee of Export Groups as a sort of Industrial Parliament, similar to the Industrial Advisory Council once advocated by Macmillan. But it was in fact confined largely to the FBI-Board of Trade axis, rather than the politically more important Ministry of Labour-NJC (TUC and BEC) of which the Nuffield Conference was an offshoot. Being a purely employers' grouping, it attracted no TUC support as a model for future industrial constitution.

multiplier effect of state spending on such a scale; above all when endorsed by the TUC. And the cast of mind exemplified by members of the General Council, in particular by Citrine,* may explain why even the coalowners came running to climb on the bandwagon before it was too late.

Their bid was pre-empted by the managers and higher executives of the largest and most efficient coal combines, whose representatives serving on the Technical Advisory Committee handed down in September 1955 a comprehensive indictment of the previous twenty years' inadequate investment, shortsighted planning, and unforgiveable lack of cooperation with the miners, recommending at the same time a programme of mergers under statutory authority which stopped just short of a complete state takeover.[75]

Undermined by what in private they saw as a betrayal by their own side, harried by the Miners' Union (Will Lowther declared in November 1944 that 'under private ownership it is impossible for any permanent solution of the problems connected with the industry to be secured'),[76] and finally cut off from their ancient political support when the Churchill government (after the Labour withdrawal in May 1945) accepted compulsory reorganisation in order 'to preserve the incentives of free enterprise while safeguarding the industry from political interference in its day to day management',[77] the mineowners first capitulated, then precipitately accepted compulsion and Emmanuel Shinwell's nationalisation scheme in 1945, with its surprisingly generous compensation terms. As Kirby remarks, 'to the protagonists of excessively tenacious individualism, it would hardly have been an attractive prospect to reassume the peace-time direction of one of the most tightly controlled and regulated British Federations.'[78]

They asked only that they might assist in the process; and for a time actually succeeded in emulating their counterparts in gas, electricity and the railway companies, because Labour was unready[79] and the NUM, thrust into a morass of conflicting loyalties, was no longer prepared to insist on workers' control or even participation. How tenacious the old system could be in its final stages can be gauged from the extremely centralised pyramid of authority that emerged in 1946,

*'We did not fear such a spiral if the Government could convince the men that, in the general pursuit of full employment, they were determined to take the necessary steps to control prices.' (Quoted in Wigham, *Strikes and the Government*, p. 95.) Beveridge, however, did not trust the TUC. Prophetically, he wrote 'If Trade Unions under full employment push wage claims unreasonably, maintenance of a stable price level will become impossible; wage determination will perforce become a function of the state.' But the dilemma of the inflationary effect of full employment was reserved for the 1960s.

organised on functional lines, which only the old, but newly-promoted managers themselves could operate with any degree of facility, and which had to be modified in 1950, after three years marked by bad labour relations and inter-departmental jealousies.[80]

In occupying a sort of middle ground, as the political parties drew apart, both employers and TUC General Council took great care to dissociate themselves from ideological warfare. In private, the employers repudiated the anti-socialist press barrage put out by Aims of Industry and the Society of Industrialists (led by Lord Perry (Ford Motors), Lord Leverhulme, and the publisher, Ernest Benn), while the BEC attempted to evade identification with anti-Beveridge, diehard Conservative MPs and the 'vested interests', pinpointed as the objects of public mistrust in Ministry of Information inquiries.[81] The factious opposition of 116 Conservative MPs (including members of the so-called National League for Freedom*) who broke the electoral truce to vote against Bevin's Catering Wages Bill in February 1943, showed what they were trying to avoid. The TUC, in turn, continued its long campaign to subdue the Left.

Certain unions, chiefly the Engineers, had been campaigning since 1941 for a measure of workers' participation in management as part of a bargain to increase output. Later, the demand had spread to nearly all shipyards and Ministry of Public Works construction sites, and roughly half the coal mines. But no mention of industrial democracy penetrated *Let Us Face the Future*; and, apart from the plaintive voices of a few Trades Councils, after 1943 little was heard of it in the TUC's annual meeting.

Communist Party tactics, however, caused real difficulty. Buoyed up on the manifest heroism of Russia's defence against Germany, and its own record of patriotic exhortation to increase productivity, the CPGB claimed a novel legitimacy which embarrassed Churchill and the Ministry of Information on one hand and the TUC on the other. Bevin did not hesitate to associate himself with Foreign Office attempts to distinguish, in the public mind, between enthusiasm for their Russian ally and subversion at home;[82] but not much came of this activity, and although the Cabinet actually organised a demonstration on behalf of Russia in 1942 ('to get in ahead of the CP', as Bracken told Eden[83]) the Communist Party grew steadily, from 12,000 at its 1941 nadir to 65,000 by September 1942.[84] Succumbing to popular opinion, the TUC

---

*Run by Sir Douglas Hacking, Sir Patrick Hannon and Waldron Smithers, all old Central Office men. The League dedicated itself to fighting 'the strong movement now on foot to continue unnecessary official control of trade, industry, business and private life after the war'. (*Daily Herald*, 17 April 1943.)

withdrew its Black Circular in 1943. To Bevin's fury, infiltration began again, not least in his own TGWU. In 1944 the miners voted for CPGB affiliation to the Labour Party, and a substantial minority opposed Bevin's Regulation 1AA (aimed at the CP). The leftward trend reached its peak after the war (below p. 414), but even before 1945 had already re-established itself in the historic regions of Clydeside,* South Wales and Durham, among the NUM (where the CP led the General Secretary, Ebby Edwards, by the nose in its campaign for nationalisation), on the old dissident Trades Councils, and among local organisations of tenants which, particularly in East London, became the base of the Communist Party's post-war electoral effort.

It was hard to combat this tendency in wartime. The Minority Movement had survived the 1930s at shop-floor level and in certain districts;[85] and some Trades Councils, especially those associated with the old Councils of Action, had established themselves as progenitors of local services and hospitals, rent reform, legal aid, citizens' advice, birth control and civil liberties, all of which proved attractive in the popular radical mood. In a sense they were to the TUC what the Socialist League had been to the Labour Party, and for a short time they were able to unravel the restrictions of the thirties and challenge the General Council and the NEC. But although the Communist Party's anti-capitalist propaganda affected to some extent Britain's relations with Russia, and future Foreign Secretary Bevin's personal prejudices, it scarcely threatened the institutional line-up of employers and unions which had already survived the rupture of the Coalition.

Between 1940 and 1945, the trade union movement achieved its fundamental aim of parity with the employers in the eyes of government. Against the odds, and the trend of electoral politics, the employers retained most of their pre-war political power while making shrewd accommodation to changed conditions. Neither, however, attempted to challenge the enormously swollen powers taken by government during the war and indeed both submitted themselves (as in 1916–18) as agents, on the assumption that thereby the system of triangular cooperation would be strengthened – an assumption that proved axiomatic in the immediate post-war years. Although in the remoter future it remained possible to envisage a return to an as yet undefined normality, the eventuality of an ideological struggle was seen as chronologically separate from the party contest of 1945.

*Of all the cases of prosecution under Regulation 1305, 72 occurred in Scotland, only 39 in England and Wales.

Both governing institutions took up moderate positions in relation to the popular radicalism which flowered after 1943. Apart from a handful of diehard employers, already discredited or soon to disappear with the advent of nationalisation, no one wished to return to the 1930s; and only a minority of individual union leaders sought to discuss the possibility of a fully Socialist economy. Later, their search for an acceptable theory of industrial society matched the change that took place in public opinion in the last months of the war, as expectations of Beveridgian reforms were suddenly chilled by fears of a Conservative triumph at the polls. As Mass Observation and Ministry of Information reporters both noticed, there was by then much less public demand for far-reaching measures than for calculated reforms, careful demobilisation, immediate *visible* justice for all groups, reinstatement, etc., which had formed the staple of discussion on Bevin's Joint Committee since 1943,[86] or the War Aims Committee, Reconstruction Committee, and all the unofficial bodies outside government. Addison concludes[87] that the public was content with what it was offered: reforms couched in the terminology of the old progressive centre, backed by a state guarantee; on which the Labour Party rode to victory in 1945 at the expense of the Conservative Party and the diehard and radical fringes, from whom unions and employers had skilfully disengaged.

Many of the politically contentious issues of the post-war Labour Government's policy were, therefore prejudged: the industrial institutions could find some basis for agreement in state ownership of transport and public services, while nationalisation of the Bank of England could be seen as a form of government commitment to provide the state investment of which the thirties had been starved. Apart from the Iron and Steel Bill, which the Attlee government left until 1949, Labour's programme contained little in principle in the industrial sphere to which the 120 signatories of *A National Policy for Industry* could object. In so far as that programme had been predetermined by institutional consensus, party political power was diminished and institutions and the managerial élite elevated – especially in the newly acquired public sector.

Ideological questions about the historic function of management or organised workers had been blurred to the point where those who insisted on the logic of the class struggle appeared to be reactionary or subversive; and once-clear economic cleavages in capitalist society appeared to be replaced by conceptions of the modern industrial state which predated, by ten years, the state of mind categorised by Daniel Bell in *The End of Ideology* (Free Press, Illinois, 1960). The idea of a managed, class-free, industrial society exercised enormous attraction in the latter half of the war, offering a basis for political reconstruction which had been absent from the abortive NIC in 1919; and if the price were the vestigial influence of shareholder and shop steward, then these, it was assumed by the protagonists at Nuffield, could look to material prosperity for recompense, because without industrial conflict national wealth could only grow.

But did this long-lasting immunisation against radical theology, and the Labour Party's consequent inability to progress beyond the commitments of 1940, encompass the corporate state, as Aneurin Bevan protested at the Labour Party Conference in 1944? In a somewhat anodyne conclusion, Bevin's biographer claims that:

'The organised working class represented by the trade unions was for the first time brought into a position of partnership in the national enterprise of war – a partnership on equal not inferior terms, as in the First World War, and one from which it has never since been dislodged, as it was after 1918.'[88]

Samuel Beer goes further, talking of the 'new social contract' implicit in trade union economic power.[89]

The marshalling of industrial institutions as agents of a managerial state, and the dissociation of dissenting groups, achieved in wartime many of the desiderata of the 1930s' corporatist thinkers and gives weight to Bevan's indictment. State hegemony, after all, rested on its technocrats as well as its institutions. Beveridge, like Beatrice Webb, overstated the neutrality of administration and administrators' reform, leaving behind him an unanswered question whether the élite of 'unassuming experts' was compatible with democratic freedom. But Beveridge's group, like Keynes, never underestimated the power of institutions. Full employment, wages and prices could only be held in equilibrium if the 'moral atmosphere' was right: 'If the workers feel that genuine progress towards social justice is being made it will not be hard to solve the [inflation] problem.'[90]

That judgment may not have seemed absurdly over-optimistic at the time of the victory celebrations of 1945. Labour and Conservative parties' retreat to polemical positions comparable with 1922 seemed to diminish the bias towards corporatism which had earlier been accentuated by the adoption of physical planning controls; but that, too, contained an element of illusion. The Conservatives had come a long way from Chamberlain's presuppositions: deeply influenced by employer's attitudes, by the lobbying of the Tory Reform Committee (led by Quintin Hogg and Lord Hinchingbrooke) and by the practical lessons of the coal industry, the party offered only muted opposition in public to nationalisation of service industries after 1945, reserving its fire for parliamentary filibustering and the climactic battle over the steel industry. Labour went further, assimilating in wartime not only the restricted Morrisonian concept of state enterprise, but commitments to European defence and Commonwealth which differed little from the Conservative position when Churchill resumed office in 1951.

To European observers, the British political system seemed to have survived, justifying in part a claim to parity on the world stage with Russia and the United States. Nearly twenty years would pass before economic attenuation revealed the limitations both of the neutral experts and of the control which workers' and employers' central organisations possessed over their wayward members. As the memory of wartime popular radicalism faded, they might have been forgiven for assuming that British democracy was as adaptive as its historians claimed, and for ignoring the 'unconstitutional' role of institutions which had made survival possible.

PART TWO

PART TWO

The fictions of parliamentary sovereignty came under assault long before their practical derogation during the years of the National Government after 1931. The 'agreement to differ' among Cabinet Ministers and the elimination of great areas of public policy from the parliamentary field were foreshadowed in 1927 by Lord Thomson, a future Labour Air Minister – 'I do so agree with you about keeping Air Policy out of party politics'.[1] A convention that had formerly been applied chiefly to foreign policy steadily engrossed other major areas of state policy such as industrial revival, and many affiliated to the National Government deplored the fact that Labour Party resistance in the thirties, or the Tory diehards, prevented its extension to rearmament and India. Others, like Lord Weir, went further, seeking to remedy Parliament's inadequacies and the distortions in policy continuity caused by two-party alternation by taking yet greater questions 'out of party politics'. W. Milne-Bailey, Secretary of the TUC Research Department, wrote in 1926:

Now that industrial topics take up more and more of Parliament's time, the serious shortcomings of Parliament in this direction are becoming more obvious. The traditional method of Royal Commissions and Government Committees is no longer adequate. They get most of the expert advice, it is true, but they are only appointed for specific problems that have become too urgent and too controversial for treatment in any other way, whereas what is wanted is continuous work of this kind. Further, being appointed by a Government of a definite political colour, such bodies are 'pacted', they are given a particular bias to start with and hence they command little or no confidence.[2]

In the most obvious sense, they had their reward: for fourteen years after 1931 Britain ceased to have a two-party system as that had been understood before 1915 or since 1922. But in what way was this different? Until 1945, twentieth-century government was often conducted by coalition, or by parties owing their position to the co-operation of others – as the Irish supported the Liberals in 1910–15, or Liberals upheld Labour in 1924 and 1929. It can be argued that with the sole exception of 1922, the ideological element of party contributed very little to the important crises, which led to redistribution of power and coalition in 1915–16, 1931 and 1940; and that the revival of party standpoints signified by the Carlton Club meeting petered out within five years.

A combination of obsession with the history of Labour and Liberal parties, working to the detriment of the Conservatives who held effective power for forty-six years out of the century's seventy-seven, and the exclusion of historians from central government archives for fifty years (until the reduction to thirty in 1969), has tended to obscure that aspect of party concerned with the state apparatus and institutions, emphasising instead parties' mutual interactions in the 'high politics' of Westminster, or, more recently, the 'grass roots' culture of the constituencies. Nevertheless, the deep change in the nature of government which took place during the First World War and inspired Lloyd George's attempt to create out of post-war coalition a permanent centre grouping, ensured that the traditional form of party politics was not recovered, in spite of the restoration of 'normal' party activity in 1922.

It was Bagehot who first observed the distinction between the real division of power and the dignified version of the constitution. Myths inevitably surround the formation of the National Government, the subsequent devaluation of the party system, the influence of industrial institutions, and the role of Parliament itself *vis-à-vis* the state apparatus in the 1930s and 40s, befogging textbooks, procedural manuals and contemporary debates about sovereignty inside Britain.* Yet in no complex modern society is it conceivable that present-day realities should instantaneously be reflected in continuous rehabilitation of traditional theory. In Britain especially (as Paul Johnson has pointed out in *The Offshore Islanders*, Weidenfeld 1972) it has been habitual to modernise the constitution by appeal to a remoter, purer and usually fictitious past, overlaid by recent abuses which may be remedied, rather than to advocate change – and this process is, inevitably, slow.

To assess the change in party politics since 1911, and the balance between strategy for government and ideological preoccupation is virtually impossible on a statistical basis or, for lack of sound evidence

---

*A survey conducted by the Hansard Society in the summer of 1977, for example, discovered that 49 per cent of the sample of secondary school leavers believed that the House of Commons made all important decisions about the running of the country. *The Times*, 17 August 1977.

about voters' opinions, from outside the system itself. The records inside – of party or institution – are necessarily biased and myopic and sometimes, where organisation is concerned, extremely dull. But they do reveal a calculating face rarely displayed in public, a mundane, even cynical, preoccupation with what Burke called 'interest', more valuable than the selective offerings of election time. In the light of such evidence, between 1911 and 1945, it can be said that parties had become more homogeneous, the range and variety of views they presented diminishing, like the number of manifestos, in proportion to increasing central direction; inter-party warfare became a matter of stereotyped abuse rather than the rational discussion whose decline Edwardian parliamentarians had already become accustomed to deplore.

Great areas of national policy tended to become the prerogative of ministers and civil servants, acting within the curtilage of 'government', rather than of political leaders and MPs in the House of Commons. Consequently, party strategy, organisation, finance and propaganda were devised for electoral conflicts which provided, not administrations in the broad, nineteenth-century sense, but the personnel of Cabinets, the mandate for a set of policies, and the House of Commons majority which ensured tenure of the state apparatus so long as the Prime Minister determined. Well before 1940, Parliament as distinct from government had lost the power of initiating policy or legislation, except on the narrow front reserved for 'private members'; while even its negative power of restraint over government expenditure had been seriously curtailed by administrative changes contingent on the presentation of complex Estimates and the weakness of its select committees in the face of departmental secrecy.

This view is now commonly accepted,* in a decade increasingly disillusioned with parliament after many years' devaluation of the language of political management. But it was not one which could decently be argued in public in the 1930s, even though the pattern of the 1931 crisis showed how far the 'true party' principles set out at the Carlton Club meeting had decayed. In retrospect, the destruction of the Lloyd George Coalition itself, painted by the participants and subsequent historians in dramatic colours, seems a rearguard action, like Napoleon's brilliant defence of France in 1814 – a retreat, nevertheless, into defeat. Asquith's distasteful attitude to coalition in May 1915 ('to seem to welcome into the intimacy of the political household

*As in Anthony Down's well-known hypothesis that electoral competition drives parties towards the ideological centre in an attempt to win the middle ground, and thus elections.

strange, alien, hitherto hostile figures, is a most intolerable test'³) had become archaic by 1918, though clearly many ministers and most backbenchers retained their dislike of combinations which effectively reduced by half the number of appointments available. The strong animus against coalition, which still infused Conservative policy-making and propaganda in 1924,⁴ had lessened five years later when party managers like Neville Chamberlain and Samuel Hoare, fearing a *bloc des gauches* of Labour and Lloyd George Liberals, could listen to the blandishments about a common front offered by MacDonald.⁵

Baldwin's authority was enough then to defend the distinctive merits of party, despite the loss of the 1929 General Election. But subsequent attacks on his leadership weakened his capacity to resist. The New Toryism which he had enunciated in a brilliant series of speeches, in opposition in June–July 1924, had run its course in legislative reforms and the industrial concordat of 1928–9, leaving afterwards a hiatus which the election post-mortem did little to remedy.

In two important aspects, the differences between Conservatives and the Labour Party were being eroded, whatever the leaders personally chose to represent as party policy. First, the explicitly anti-union and anti-socialist policies★ propounded by the Tory Labour Committee, symbolised in MacQuisten's aggressive attack on the trade union political levy in 1925, gave way to a certain sensitivity on labour issues, commensurate with the changing forms of union-employer discussions. Admittedly, such action often masked self-interest: in 1925 the party for the first time sent delegates to the ILO Conference at Geneva – to represent the NCEO case on Washington Hours. But the public aspect could not be dismissed. For some months after the General Strike, Central Office thinking on trade union legislation was affected by a report from the Principal Agent revealing Conservative working-class pressure, mainly from the Midlands, for reform (secret ballot, registration, etc.) rather than retribution.⁶ Later, after the Trades Disputes Act, the once-diehard Labour Committee abandoned the more vindictive aspects of its anti-union posture, while the newly-formed Bonar Law Memorial College at Ashridge set out to induct its students with a reasoned critique, more in line with the preoccupation of Tory trade unionists.⁷

By 1933 the Conservative Party Conference, previously almost wholly unsympathetic to union aspirations, could agree on a resolution that slum clearance and employment provision constituted the best

★Taught, for example, at the party college at Overstone Park; 500 students, mostly working class, attended these courses in 1923 (Labour Committee Minutes).

answer to socialism.[8] More surprising, at the 1935 and 1936 Conferences no attack was mounted against the government for its surrender to working-class protest over the UAB scales (above, p. 230). By the standards of 1922 (though not of 1911) the party had, for electoral reasons, renewed its former acceptance of trade union aspirations, even if it still chose to believe that they could be detached from socialism.*

Changes in Conservative organisation before 1931 indicate that, despite intense disapproval from many constituencies, the party eventually resumed the centralised direction necessary to the practice of coalition. For some years after 1922, and especially after Bonar Law's retirement, coalition remained a synonym for autocratic leadership and betrayal of principle. Younger, the chairman, wrote in 1925: 'no new organisation should be entrusted to those responsible for the old system. . . . That had absolutely broken down and become a by-word.'[9] Baldwin's sensitivity to constituency opinion can be gauged from the way he chose to launch his New Toryism in a series of country-wide speeches in 1924, and from his palpable sensitivity to Conference resolutions. In 1927–8, after reform of the Executive Committee, the local associations were strong enough to defeat proposals by J. C. C. Davidson, the Party Chairman, for limiting the size of Conference;[10] and although Davidson resisted a National Union Central Council proposal to vet the party's 1929 Manifesto – a request which he compared to 'the committee system in Russia'[11] – in the angry post-mortem after 1929 he was swept away and Central Office's personnel and role drastically pruned.† A vast volume of recrimination boiled up in the answers to a Central Office questionnaire about the state of the party in November 1929; 260 local associations sought to democratise the upper strata, and make the Leader responsible to the National Executive, and Baldwin barely survived the assault which followed, in 1930.

But this attempt to revive an almost mythical past, associated with Lord Randolph Churchill's Tory Democracy in the 1880s, was stalled at the special Conference in July 1930; the ill-organised majority of Provisional Divisions vacillated too long, allowing Central Office to reiterate the Leader's supreme authority.[12] Conservative conferences were not to resemble Labour ones. The prizes of decentralisation slipped away; and although a price was exacted behind the scenes in

*The 1937 Conference endorsed a campaign aimed at the 10 million voters either not unionised or belonging to unions not affiliated to the TUC.

†The Hoare Report on Organisation (1931) emphasised the failure of the Publicity Department to put out 'modern propaganda', and criticised Organisation, which had not supplied 'the necessary reports on constituency feeling and atmosphere'.

October 1930, when Sir Robert Topping instituted a new, federal scheme for Provisional Councils, and imposed heavy economies in Central Office, by the mid-1930s these new Councils had lapsed into the advisory semi-impotence of the old federations. Apart from what Central Office referred to as the 'independent areas', Kent, Sussex and Surrey, the rest succumbed to greater centralisation because their boundaries had been redrawn on the lines of economic rather than political geography.[13]

Baldwin continued faithfully to attend Executive meetings, following the 1930 precedent, but in matters of policy he and Chamberlain firmly controlled Conference. Meanwhile, changes in the method of conducting business, Chamberlain's single-minded work at the Research Department, and the complete overhaul of party machinery after the 1929 débâcle, inculcated a professionalism new to British politics,* that was matched by developments among the National Society of Agents, who in turn gave particular support to Chamberlain, the Party chairman, and whose influence seems to have been cast in favour of coalition in 1931.[14]

Deep divisions over the future of India, in 1933-4, forced the Conservative Party to define the rights of individual MPs in a similar, fundamental way. Baldwin took the line that the opposition, led by Henry Page-Croft and Churchill, were attacking the party *as government* rather than criticising its policy as a party, and his appeal to members' loyalty carried with it the threat that the Coalition Government might fall. In particular, Baldwin attacked Page-Croft's disingenuous appeal ('how absurd it is to suggest that we brother and sister Conservatives may not commune together as to whether [the Government of India Bill] should go forward'[15]) as fatal to the principles on which the National compromise had been erected; and in spite of the narrow majority at Bristol, in 1934, when the platform came closest to a major defeat in twentieth-century Conservative history,[16] he carried the final round in time for the autumn 1935 election and the new debates on imperial defence, where organised party factions faded away. By 1937 the process of centralisation was almost complete: Chamberlain paid scant notice to the views of Conference during his tenure of office and

*The Research Department owed its origin to the curious omission of the 1929 Manifesto drafting Committee actually to meet. The Party had to begin the campaign without policy guidance, and Hailsham and Stonehaven drafted a substitute the weekend after. (Research Department History, ORG File.) Bensons, who had first been used by the party in 1912, were blamed afterwards for the disastrous choice of slogan – 'Safety First' – but at the time, it seemed the height of professionalism to hire the services of an experienced advertising agency (SM GD 193/389).

the constituencies had to wait another decade to raise the question of their rights, if any, to influence a future Tory Cabinet.

In many respects, these structural changes, and the demotion of constituency influence after its apparent triumph in 1922, resemble the better-documented history of the Labour Party. In spite of the strict 'constitutional' stand taken by MacDonald during the first Labour government, which so offended TUC aspirations to parity of consultation, and caused left-wing MPs to complain that he was 'trying to turn the party from a party of the working class into a party of the nation',[17] the party failed during the 1920s to take account of rank-and-file opinion or to utilise still-vigorous Trades Councils and local Labour parties.*

Debilitating conflicts with the ILP after 1927 impaired attempts to take account of opinion outside the PLP. Under the dominance of MacDonald and Snowden, organisation grew more remote and autocratic than the originators of the 1918 constitution, Henderson and Webb, had imagined possible.† MacDonald's wish to make the party 'respectable' can be explained on the ground that to a believer in the nineteenth-century constitution (as his spurning of TUC influence in 1924 and 1931 indicates), parliamentary sovereignty mattered more than the concept of a 'Labour Movement'. Derogation of parliament implied in the contemptuous behaviour of Clydeside MPs, or the extra-parliamentary socialism of the ILP after 1931, was to be deplored. Even when leading the remnants of his party into coalition in 1931, MacDonald remained a parliamentarian and a party man in the classical sense, having evinced a mistrust as great as Baldwin's for Lloyd George's schemes for cross-party groupings in 1926 or 1929.[18] With such assumptions, it was not hard to explain rejection of the ILP's pretensions to being the conscience of the movement and their appeal to the verdict of the 1927 and 1928 Conferences over the heads of the Parliamentary Party, and to justify the creation of a disciplinary

---

*The history of the Advisory Committee, for example, between 1918 and 1929, suggests that party officials remained content to draw on information already processed by Fabian groups from press cuttings and Friendly Society reports, or sympathetic local authorities, rather than institute inquiries among local parties and Trades Councils which might conflict with existing pre-conceptions. (JSM/LG/16–117, *passim*; JMS/NH/1–22.)

†The 'Organisation of the Party' file in the Research Department contains, not, as one might expect, schemes for an Economic General Staff (which MacDonald kept to himself) but only a series of demarcation disputes between NEC and PLP, and acrimonious correspondence about attendance of MPs in debate. The party was evidently sensitive to criticisms such as Bevin's, in July 1928: 'in the opinion of my executive council, the Movement is entitled to better service from the Labour MPs than was apparently rendered in connection with this Bill'. (LP/PA/19.)

procedure, harsh by comparison with earlier tolerant attitudes towards dissenting tendencies within the party; especially when ILP votes threatened to bring the 1929 Labour Government down.

As Labour and Conservative Parties increased the power and scope of their central organisations, a certain degree of conflict with industrial institutions probably became inevitable. The Conservative Party had never depended on employers' organisations for supply of voluntary workers in constituencies where organisation was poor, as Labour did on the unions, nor could it be said of them, *mutatis mutandis*, that 'the Labour Party always needed the unions: the unions did not always need the Labour Party'.[19] Yet at least until the mid-1940s, the Conservative Party depended on the NCEO and FBI and their members, collectively and individually, for financial help. After the disaster of 1923, when, on the death of the eccentric and senile Lord Farquhar, the party had been found virtually bankrupt, Davidson and Sir George Younger had raised nearly £1 million in three months.[20] Waldron Smithers collected £250,000 for the 1929 election from one City group and the directors of two other companies.[21] Most Conservative leaders showed themselves prepared to listen to the advice of business interests, and Davidson probably typified party attitudes when in 1929 he advised the new Treasurer, Samuel Hoare, to talk to and respond to 'captains of industry . . . about what is actually going on in politics, and not of what was, ten or fifteen years ago'.[22]

In 1929–31, in Opposition, Conservative Party committees maintained their liaison with the NCEO on questions of industry and labour relations.[23] But industrialists could no longer expect the easy returns on their investment which had been obtained in the palmy Coalition days by men like Caillard and Allan Smith. The Conservative Government of the late 1920s sometimes treated NCEO and FBI with disdain: witness the employers' disapproval of Steel-Maitland's overtures to the TUC, Baldwin's attempt to prevent the General Strike or Churchill's sympathy with the miners during his brief time in charge of the coal strike negotiations in September 1926. The NCEO and Engineering Federation did not scruple to attack ministers personally, and used the Tory lobbies to reiterate ancient if disputed rights to party consultation. But beyond that – and their quite separate rights *vis-à-vis* government – they had no power in the period of the two-party system to do more than scheme, or dream, like Weir, of a truly 'national' party.

More surprisingly, given its historic, financial and organisational links, the TUC failed equally to establish its rights to participation in Labour government. Labour Party managers had scarcely reacted to the TUC secession from joint research committees in 1925, and in spite of the reliance on the unions' bloc vote to defeat the ILP's attempt to promote its fundamentalist programme, *Socialism in Our Time*, *schadenfreude* towards the TUC, its Economic Committee, and its association with the Macmillan Committee inquiry into the Gold Standard and the Bank of England's financial policy, go a long way to explain the lack of innovation during the years of opposition which so inhibited the second Labour Government's economic policy after 1929.

Dislike of the TUC's reminders that it had helped found the party concealed MacDonald and Snowden's deep aversion to a challenge to their concept of parliamentary sovereignty which, as early as 1926, had been implied in the claim for 'vocational representation for industry'.* (Speaking for its own members, the TUC Research Department indicated 'that Parliament of the ordinary democratic kind, elected on a territorial basis, is largely ignorant and is bound to be ignorant of industrial needs and problems, and to that extent is a very unsatisfactory authority for industrial regulation and legislation. . . . If vocational groups are to be given legal recognition for the purposes of abolishing some of their privileges [a reference to the argument preceding the 1927 Trades Disputes Bill] they must be given legal recognition for constructive purposes of government.'[24])

MacDonald's encounters with the TUC and NCEO in February 1931 (above, p. 211) suggest that as the crisis developed he was not unwilling to negotiate the terms of a tripartite political concordat, but only on party terms; and the Cabinet's almost contemptuous rejection of TUC claims to participate in solving the August crisis can be seen as the high point of party delineation against institutional power: a climax followed almost at once by the TUC's prolonged reshaping of policy and the structure of the Labour movement itself. But even before the institutions recaptured and added to their influence over the parties in the 1930s a paradox was developing: more centralised organisation and tighter discipline over constituency opinion were not being rewarded by an increase in the capacity of Cabinets to effect political change.

There are, of course, several explanations for the incapacity of the 1929–31 Labour Government: its domination by MacDonald and Snowden, whose rejection of social-democratic economists' remedies divided both Cabinet and Party; its tacit acceptance of Treasury and

*Snowden made explicit his denial of TUC rights to consultation in his *Autobiography*, vol. 2, Nicholson & Watson, 1934, p. 941.

Bank of England authority in questions of finance; and the consequent growth of cross-party thinking and practice. It is almost certainly unfair to saddle MacDonald with charges of conspiracy to sell the Labour Party out in advance of the crisis: his original proposal of a Council of State ('without in any way abandoning any of our party positions'[25]) must be seen in the context of his plans for an Economic General Staff, rather than a grand, inter-party congress; and the appearance of well-known economists, businessmen and trade unionists on the Economic Advisory Council in 1930, in preference to party men, places it well within the triangle of government, TUC and employers which had evolved in the late 1920s.[26]

Nevertheless, as Hoare noticed, transactions on India, electoral reform and disarmament took place in three-party conferences[27] and MacDonald subsequently attempted in 1930 to deploy policy for agriculture and unemployment in the same way. In June 1931 he proposed a tripartite committee on future legislation. Lloyd George was amenable; Baldwin was not, for, he said, what MacDonald asked amounted to 'a striking innovation in our constitutional procedure'.[28] Primed by Steel-Maitland, who suggested sardonically that 'a government only invites cooperation because it is in difficulties', Baldwin demanded in return a part in decision-making which MacDonald would not concede; even in the Lab-Lib talks he hung on to the Cabinet's sovereignty until the end. This problem was never solved. When MacDonald suggested cooperation over measures to meet the economic crisis early in 1931, when the May Committee was set up, he found Neville Chamberlain and Hoare not unsympathetic.[29] Yet when J. H. Thomas made a more open approach to the NCEO, suggesting that it was possible to take economic policy-making out of the party arena altogether, the employers gave the same answer as Baldwin; and the offer lapsed.

On a broader scale, apart from contributing to the legend of betrayal and the reserves of Central Office propaganda,[30] these ill-assorted overtures fortified the assumption that Britain's crisis was a mere facet of the world 'economic blizzard' (to use MacDonald's phrase at the 1930 Labour Party Conference), against which the best shelter lay in a revival of the party truce which had been made at the start of the Great War. The intellectual seedbed referred to under the heading 'Council of State' had already been planted by Lloyd George and the Liberal authors of *Britain's Industrial Future* (1928), whose proposals for structural reform of government and a Ministry and Council of Industry (like the recommendations of Mosley's celebrated 1930

Memorandum) would have entrenched on parliamentary and party functions, and taken most economic and industrial questions 'out of politics' – party politics, that is. Even though voters had not endorsed it in 1929, the Liberal programme had influenced Tawney in drafting Labour's manifesto, *Labour and the Nation*, and the Labour Conference in 1930 almost accepted Mosley's proposals against the Cabinet recommendation.

Searching for similar neutral ground, in a memorandum of June 1930, Hoare, the Conservative Party Treasurer, recommended that his party should accept a modest form of proportional representation, to appease the Liberals and prevent them from an accord with Labour; in return, they should ask for an elected second chamber, with powers (like the French Senate had) to control finance, and thus check any future socialist majority in the Commons.

We should really obtain security and the certainty that whatever policy was adopted by the new parliament would be a *continuous* policy on which all commercial and industrial interests might work as an established fact, and on which they might base their economic plans. . . .[31]

The party principles and ideological certainties of 1922 were being deliberately dulled in the interests of sound government and defence of the pound. Baldwin could still write to Chamberlain, just before the Government fell, 'I think in the long run it is all to the good that the Govt. have to look after their own chickens as they come home to roost, and get a lot of the dirt cleared up before we come in . . .'[32] But his belief in a purely Conservative triumph succumbed to the King's appeal on 23 August and the evident willingness of Chamberlain, Samuel and MacDonald to enter a National Government.[33]

Afterwards, out and out distinctions were not renewed in the old way. In the early months of the National Government, Conservative Ministers' attempts to redraft the Buckingham Palace agreement so as to give them clear preponderance in Cabinet were deflected, not least to prevent what many Ministers feared, a return by MacDonald and Thomas to Labour once the emergency had passed.[34] The worst clashes of the 1931 Election occurred between Labour Party and National Labour candidates;[35] and the Election result itself appeared both to castigate the failures of the previous government, and to discredit single-party administration.* At the same time it confirmed

*Labour seats fell from 209 (1929) to 52 (46 Labour, 5 ILP, 1 semi-independent). The PLP was reduced almost wholly to its trade union, mostly MFGB contingent, although even in ancient strongholds like County Durham and Northumberland it

the lesson Conservatives had drawn from their temporary disillusion with advertising and American market research techniques, that while good results might be obtained by promises and manifestos, seats were won primarily on voters' awareness of government performance, above all its managerial competence.

Crisis avoidance was not new; as a guiding principle it can be traced all through the history of unemployment insurance policy, the employer-union talks, and much of the industrial reorganisation of the late twenties. But the 1931 crisis enormously stimulated the tendency of Conservative Cabinets to give priority to avoiding political confrontation or ideological commitment. Fifteen years before the widespread acceptance of Keynesian theories which would enable – for a time – successful brokerage between political and economic requirements, policy questions involving the allocation of scarce resources, such as unemployment benefit, industrial assistance and social welfare, which were inherently political and had been previously closely contended, were subjected to brokerage between National Government, institutions and interest groups, to the gradual exclusion of purely party voices. Even though it involved him personally in abandoning his party position, MacDonald's Council of State initiative turned out to be more long-lived than he could have imagined.

Sustaining the National façade involved the Conservative Party in further compromise, even at the price of 'sacrifices' in its own constituencies. Rather than jettison the handful of National Labour MPs or the Samuelite Liberals, they put up with recriminations from below and suppressed claims that 'we have a National majority to put Tory policy through'.[36] In 1932–3, fearing a revival of the opposition and the confluence of Labour with Lloyd George and the Samuelites, which the accession of Sir John Simon and his thirty-five Liberal Nationals did little to diminish, Lord Stonehaven, the Party chairman, began to take seriously schemes for founding a National Party.[37] Quite apart from allowing substantive modernisation, it would, he thought, appeal to 'large numbers of non-Party voters who think that the only real dividing line between political schools of thought should be drawn between socialists and anti-socialists'.[38]

---

suffered (Morpeth swung from a Labour majority of 16,000 to a Tory one of 6,000, Gateshead 16,700 to 12,938 Tory). Overall, the party lost 1.7 million votes (8.3 million to 6.6 million) as something like 25 per cent of its adherents abstained or voted Conservative. Thomas Jones, lately Deputy Secretary of the Cabinet, and a life-long Labour supporter wrote: 'I voted Conservative for the first time in my life . . . Labour had to be beaten. We could not trust them with the Bank of England, not yet . . .' (*A Diary with Letters 1931–50* (Oxford University Press 1954) p. 20.)

A revival of the sort of centre party thinking abandoned in 1922 fitted closely with what Weir and his colleagues in the NCEO and FBI desired – a distinction between 'nationalisation on one side, and sane democratic evolution on the other. . . .'[39] In 1934 Weir believed that the Conservative party and its propaganda machine had come to stand only for 'the benefit of what is called Conservatism, something which has not the definite appeal we are looking for. Of course the solution would be the creation of an effective National party embracing all existing machines'. But he was right in thinking that 'very little progress is being made'; reluctantly, Stonehaven had to concede that the formal creation of a National Party would cause too much damage to the organisation at constituency level, even though, in that year, 100 Tory MPs signed a motion in favour; and in spite of the fact that the 1934 Central Office report forecast that the forthcoming election would in fact develop along the socialist/anti-socialist antithesis Weir had envisaged.[40]

Deeply concerned about national survival in the face of Germany's ambitions and Japan's economic and military growth, Baldwin as party leader sought instead to avoid both the bitterness of an election held on class lines and the creation of a centre party deliberately designed to drive moderate Labour from the Westminster stage, along the road already taken by the Mosleyites, ILP and Communist Party.* In contrast to Chamberlain and Weir, he assumed that another defeat would kill off 'socialism' for good, together with the 'quack doctrines' of Cole, Laski and Cripps, and so cast the 1935 election campaign in subdued colours which did not, like the naked anti-socialism desired by the party managers or the NCEO, exclude the revival of Labour as a future alternative government, acceptable to the majority of the electorate.[41] In this he judged shrewdly the Labour party leaders and those trade unionists who, as Miliband writes, 'were and felt themselves to be, the living proof of the higher status of Labour within a capitalist system. . . . They were not men to press more militant postures upon their parliamentary friends.'[42]

But the tide Baldwin resisted in front, crept in behind, leaving parliamentary landmarks cut off from the changing mainland contours of the political system. Preoccupied with the deepening crisis of European diplomacy, and the threat to Britain's fragile economic recovery from continuing world recession, the National Government began to make the avoidance of crisis central to its way of life. In public

*In 1931 Mosley's New Party polled a mere 36,377 votes in twenty-four constituencies, and the CPGB only 70,844.

order, or the treatment of the unemployed, ministers moderated their party prejudices to external requirements, just as they took a sort of dictation from the SBAC on aircraft production. Even Chamberlain's habitual aloofness from the General Council implied less a revival of the antipathy of the early 1920s than a carefully judged avoidance of their bargaining power, while the overtures to the TUC made by Churchill and the Tory dissidents in 1938–9, though unsuccessful, reveal an understanding that even party revolution could not succeed without institutional liaison. It was a Conservative party official who declared in 1938 'that we cannot defend the nation against the will of the unions. . . . It is part of the price we have to pay for this alleged democracy.'[43]

The price that the Conservative Party paid for ignoring the mis-givings of its traditionally-minded supporters differed from the simple pitfalls created by the record of SBAC cupidity (see Chapter 9) – although, in the crudest sense, the crisis of 1940 could be blamed on inadequate rearmament. The ideal partnership, in which employers and a Conservative Government had invested a good deal of political capital during the 1920s, came in the end to look like just another cartel, and the most debilitating result appeared, not in the forms of organisation nor in party rhetoric but in the retardation of Conservative industrial policy and, consequently, immaturity of Party philosophy.

The Conservative debate about the role of the state in modern industrial society, which had stirred fitfully in the days of Disraeli and Bonar Law, and seemed likely to win a significant audience in the Baldwin-Steel-Maitland era, was not continued in Baldwin's third term of office, nor during the leadership of his two successors. Lacking a truly modern answer to the challenge of socialism, to replace the old, free market defence and the stereotypes of the 1920s (which they themselves had weakened irrevocably by their interventionist policies during the 1930s), Conservative leaders instead tended to assume that economic recovery (and, after 1940, wartime victory) would fill the gap. By 1944 the Party managers could see something of the shape of disaster to come; but among their recommendations they did not suggest either repudiating the heavy heritage of the inter-war years or a whole-hearted endorsement of social reform.* Philosophical default

*In April 1944, Robert Topping, the Principal Agent, recommended a complete overhaul of the publicity machine, redrafting of post-war propaganda, a renewal of the youth movement, and endorsement of younger candidates; all to offset forecasts which revealed the radical turn of public opinion on such issues as the 'Russian experiment' (nationalisation), the welfare state and the attribution of blame for the 1930s (1944 Organisation Report, especially Appendix I).

under Chamberlain and Churchill contributed in great measure to the Tory rout in 1945; and it was left to the members of the Tory Reform Committee, led by Quintin Hogg and Lord Hinchingbrooke, to take up the lead already given by employers' institutions and draw political argument away from the old stereotypes of socialism and capitalism. On many questions, especially the future of the coal industry, Tory reformers shaped post-war industrial policy, but even the 'Miners' Charter'[44] came too late to offset immediate electoral retribution.

The practical desuetude of the two-party system during the long National Government years had an even more depressing effect on the aspirations of the Parliamentary Labour Party. Determined never again to be ignored, as it had been during the August crisis, and seeking to deny the Party its claim to be the sole fount of political ideology or imprint its own version of its origins, the TUC kept aloof from the electoral drama in 1931. Afterwards, on an impotent PLP composed mainly of elderly miners' MPs, led by the immensely popular but administratively incompetent George Lansbury, the General Council was able to instil a revisionist doctrine, blaming for catastrophe not only MacDonald and his National Labour fragment (whom the PLP supinely hoped might still return[45]) but

the manifest reluctance on the part of the late Labour Government to have contact with the General Council. That state of affairs must be righted. . . . The primary purpose of the creation of the party should not be forgotten. It was created by the Trade Union Movement to do those things in Parliament which the Trade Union Movement found ineffectively performed by the two-party system.[46]

Such historiography did not endear itself to the Socialist League, nor to G. D. H. Cole who, in his *History of the Labour Party from 1914*, pointed up the concomitant role of the socialist societies and the Fabians, and the theoretical importance of the 1918 Constitution. But the General Council went further, shaping to a very large extent the Party's administrative organs and policies. In November 1931 the Council demanded reconstruction of the National Joint Council, to provide equality of representation, not between PLP, NEC and TUC, but between General Council on one side and the others: 'The General Council should be regarded as having an integral right to initiate and participate in any political matter which it deems to be of direct concern to its constituents.'[47]

So much for the careful division of policy between 'industrial' and 'political' matters instituted by Henderson in 1913! Two years later, having gained 50 per cent of the NJC, they enforced wide limits on the Parliamentary Party's freedom: no future Labour government should be formed without consulting the NJC; the NJC might now discuss *all* new questions of policy; future Cabinet Ministers were to attend its debates; and Lansbury was constrained to call himself, not 'leader' but 'spokesman' of the Party.

The exercise culminated in Bevin's personal onslaught on Lansbury's leadership at Brighton in 1935, and the long shift of policy away from disarmament and pacifism. Bevin made no secret of General Council intentions, setting out the TUC's future political role quite explicitly to his own Transport and General Workers' Conference as early as November 1931.[48] To extend the campaign to political education, he subsidised the *Daily Herald* with union funds (until 1933 when its gifted editor, Joseph Elias, raised circulation to two million) and bought Blatchford's old weekly, *The Clarion*, in June 1932. For five years the General Council was to regard itself as vanguard of the movement, until in 1936, believing the process to be complete, it surrendered part of the representation it had won on the National Council of Labour (thus facilitating the election of Stafford Cripps and Harold Laski to official positions where their radicalism was frequently nullified, and at the same time appeasing demands for greater democracy from unrepresented constituency parties).

The TUC did not, of course, seek to run the Party's day-to-day affairs, and justified what one historian has called 'a form of tutelage which lasted for the remainder of the decade'[49] by recalling Arthur Henderson's invitation to do just that, in the aftermath of the 1931 crisis.* With the growth of Labour in local government, particularly after the capture of a majority of seats on the London County Council in 1934, the General Council had to concede on a number of local questions like that of future control of London passenger traffic. But it achieved at last the recognition denied by MacDonald between 1924 and 1931, as well as rights never made explicit in the Party's early parliamentary years, and the 1935 election result appeared to associate the Party's conversion from pacifism and extremism with its electoral rehabilitation.[50] How tutelage actually worked can be seen in a case like that of February 1936, when Bevin (T and GW) and Holmes (Secretary of the Agricultural Workers) complained that the Parlia-

---

*At the first meeting of the PLP after the collapse of the government, he invited the General Council to attend – probably to prevent the secession of more MPs which MacDonald still expected. (Dalton, *The Fateful Years*, vol. 1, entry 28 August 1931, also author's interview with Sir Frank Markham, September 1965.)

mentary Party had not approved an agricultural unemployment scheme, favoured by both unions and the TUC. The NEC jumped to order, and duly instructed Labour MPs to vote, even for a government Bill.[51]

More and more the trade union leaders spoke and acted as responsible heads of vast, highly centralised concerns, engaged, by means of well-tested and routinised processes of bargaining and compromise, in the hiring out of their members' labour, and deeply concerned to avoid any disturbance of industrial discipline. As Ernest Bevin told his Executive Council in December 1936, with reference to the 1920s: 'Those were the days of advocacy. Ours is the day of administration.'[52]

'The trade union movement,' Bevin told the 1937 TUC, 'has become an integral part of the state' – and earned a savage rebuke from Laski in the New York *Nation* for 'collaboration with Capitalism'.[53] That he could ignore: the Socialist League had been dissolved, the Labour Party was ready to accept rearmament, and it had adopted *Labour's Immediate Programme*, a manifesto almost entirely acceptable to the General Council. As Bevin's biographer points out, 'the Labour Party had been reformed, not on the pattern of the Socialist League or the ILP, nor on that of Lansbury and the pacifists, but by the centre group to which Bevin, as well as Attlee, Dalton and Morrison belonged.'[54]

These changes should of course be seen as part of the social democratic evolution implicit in the Labour tradition since its foundation;[55] only the subordination of parliamentary to union leadership was new, and the General Council's often naked insistence that the so-called 'anomaly' of MacDonaldism should be abrogated. Quite apart from TUC tutelage, however, the Party remained deeply deferential towards the theory of parliament, tacitly accepting Baldwin's doctrine of a place in the Commons reserved for 'responsible' Labour and rejecting, with increasing severity, the crisis analysis and proposals for rule by emergency decree advocated by the Socialist League, and in booklets like Laski's *The Crisis of the Constitution* (1937). Although with TUC assistance, the Party's organisation improved rapidly during the 1930s, until research capacity and techniques for assessing public opinion matched its opponents' resources,[56] Labour's *Immediate Programme* concentrated on questions of physical planning, and amelioration of the acerbities of existing conditions, to the detriment of debate about the future nature of socialist society. Exclusion of the Left from influence helped to ensure that no significant advances in political philosophy were made before the 1940 crisis brought the centre group into government.[57]

As for the Liberals, while it might be harsh to say that they had ceased to affect Britain's political culture by 1924, it had clearly become impossible for their leaders to do more than stomach electoral decline, contenting themselves, under Asquith, with dreams of past glory. Hoping to hold the balance in British politics, Lloyd George appealed in turn through the next decade with his fund and his Inquiries to each of the major parties; but in 1935 the Conservatives finally out-manoeuvred him, leaving him dangling in the arid air of a Cabinet Committee, having to endorse his friends' warnings that government-employer-union cooperation had vitiated his brightest schemes for British industry.[58] The illusion of fielding three hundred Lloyd George candidates vanished in the election of 1935. He had been right to assume that the businessmen who had supported him in the twenties would participate in corporatist politics, but wrong to think that they would remain Liberals; nor did he misjudge his own popularity, but only its parliamentary weight.

During the 1930s, the primacy of parties in the parliamentary political system suffered another form of subordination as outsiders entrenched on their monopoly of manifestos. Lloyd George's well-funded, ingenious Inquiries were intended to restore his centrist position by throwing doubt on long-established party antitheses. They were challenged not so much by official party programmes (the Conservatives failed even to produce a manifesto for the 1929 election, while *Labour and the Nation* merely updated the proposals of 1918) as by Mosley's Memorandum and the ILP's *Socialism in our time*, which were in turn followed by a series of group manifestos, all proclaiming the triumph of reason, sound inquiry and 'neutral' solutions, all owing intellectual lineage to Hobson, Keynes in his middle years, and the Mosley-Strachey essay, *Revolution by Reason* (1925).

In a characteristically Fabian manner, the heirs of the Webbs' 'unassuming experts' began to pontificate to a politically-educated audience, tired of the stereotyped attitudes and formal invective of party conflict. The sparkling schemes of those whom A. J. B. Marwick has called 'Middle Opinion' – the signatories of *The Next Five Years*, the founders of Political and Economic Planning (PEP), the Romney Street Group, and those corporatists who admired, without seeking directly to emulate, state corporatist models in Europe, helped to put traditional party policy-making in a dull, degraded light, just as their talk of a new National Industrial Council revived the critical attack on Parliament's inadequacies.[59]

324

Indeed the deduction that Parliament had 'failed' in 1931 is almost the sole common bond between their programmes, which ranged from Sir Arthur Salter's anti-union *Framework of an Ordered Society* (1933) (based on analysis of the relations between President Hoover and American industry) and Blackett and Glenday's aims of a highly controlled, centralised economy run by a rationalised state apparatus, to the productions of the Tory radicals, Macmillan, Stanley and Boothby, who showed themselves sympathetic to working-class aspirations – *Industry and the State* (1927), *Reconstruction* (1933) and *The Next Five Years* (1935). The last, probably the most successful in its appeal and signed by certainly the most representative collection of what would later have been called Establishment figures,[60] set out a middle way between parliamentary rule and corporatism, as was proper for those with a vestigial stake in party politics; but its proposal for an Economic General Staff, representative of interest groups, seems much closer to corporatist than parliamentary models.

All this public discussion had a certain effect on the National Government, as Stonehaven's consideration of the National Party idea suggests, and rather more on the FBI* and some areas of the Civil Service.†

But its main impact was felt later – after 1940. Few actually imagined that such schemes could be superimposed, readymade, on the complex subtleties of industrial and political organisation. But the more they were claimed as an alternative to a wasteful and ineffective two-party and parliamentary system, the more the old 1922 defence of party suffered and, with it, belief in the capacity of parliament to solve the profound questions of economic and social organisation or the avoidance of class conflict. The issues on which 'middle opinion' claimed to hold an answer were, after all, precisely those which it had become fashionable since 1929 to extract altogether from party politics.

But the most pervasive attack on the limitations of party politics resulted from the wholesale adoption after 1940 of welfare and economic management schemes which owed nothing to Labour or Conservative thinking. All Beveridge's plans derived from Liberal philosophy, while Keynes' theories of economic management had been rejected over more than a decade by governments of both main parties, whose

*Lord Melchett persuaded the FBI in 1934 to consider association with his Industrial Reorganisation League, but opposition from the iron and steel and electrical industries, as well as distrust among employers for Melchett himself, killed it off.

†In particular, the imperial theme was important, linking as it did the Conservative 'New Imperialists' (D. C. Watts's phrase) with the officials of the Dominion and Colonial offices and the Department of Overseas Trade, the TUC and the FBI (see p. 228 above).

conversion in wartime acknowledged the barrenness of their intellectual past. Even though Labour managed both to radicalise Beveridge and acquire a sort of post facto parentage for the system of manpower budgeting, public opinion in the second half of the war came, very generally, to expect legislative reform and economic betterment *from government*, expectations which the parties (if Labour) might only guarantee, or if Conservative, betray.*

That the scope of government increased dramatically between 1931 and 1945 is, of course, a truism, yet like all truisms, needs occasionally to be repeated. It would take a major study, of which the groundwork is scarcely begun, to measure the changing balance of effective power between the higher Civil Service and the parties which provided cabinets of the inter-war period – an analysis which would have to probe much more deeply into the social background of senior officials than the biographies of individual heads of departments like Maurice Hankey, Thomas Jones, Warren Fisher, Horace Wilson, or Robert Vansittart, who dominated Whitehall for a longer period of office than their predecessors or successors. A great deal has, quite legitimately, been attributed to their personal influence on the continuity of policy evolution;[61] but more inquiry needs to be devoted to the *practice of government*, codified over many years by perhaps two hundred senior civil servants, following the lines laid down by Hankey, in the so-called 'War Book' and the projected 'Peace Book' of 1919.†

It is not an exaggeration to say that as policy decisions and their execution over a period of years grew more complex, the system developed by government departments eventually compared with the semi-Victorian Whitehall of 1911 as the Ministry of Defence in 1945 did to the War Office of Kitchener. One crude way of expressing the change is to list the handful of Ministers who succeeded in pushing through, to legislative completion, *and execution*, policies of which their ministerial officials disapproved: John Wheatley's 1924 Housing

---

*P. Addison, *Road to 1945*, pp. 247–8, citing Home Intelligence and Ministry of Information surveys of public opinion. It is not entirely fanciful to link this phenomenon with the growth of the Common Wealth movement, in 1941–45, and its success in contesting a series of by-elections with the unconcealed aim of transforming society in wartime, and achieving a People's Peace thereafter. Extra- indeed anti-party by inclination, it heralded a very different, mass democratic criticism of the inter-war parliamentary system, in which bodies as opposed as the Communists and the Scottish Nationalists could combine.

†T. Jones, *Whitehall Diary*, vol. I, pp. 76, 123, 281. As early as 1925, Jones pointed out that the codification of practice involved in the 'Peace Book' inevitably entrenched on party politics, even on relatively uncontroversial questions like taxation, imperial affairs, devolution, and the protection of 'sheltered' trades.

Act is probably the only example in the inter-war years, whereas the records are littered with failures like Fisher's 1919 Education Act, J. H. Thomas' economic policy of 1929, or the Special Areas policy after 1934.

Blame has usually been put on the blanketing effect of Treasury control. Agonising arguments over reconstruction in 1919 already witness the fact that allocation of limited resources rather than discussion of first principles had become the prime function of Cabinet – a phenomenon angrily depicted forty-five years later by Richard Crossman in his *Diaries of a Cabinet Minister* (3 vols., 1975–7). While it would not be true to say that by 1965 nothing had changed, virtually every Cabinet division in the inter-war years originated in refusal by the Chancellor of the Exchequer to fund or acquiesce in other Ministers' policies: apart from the obvious case of the reconstruction programme, one can cite the cruiser crisis of 1925, safeguarding of the iron and steel industry in 1929, the tariff proposal in August 1931, and implementation of the Defence Requirements Committee Report in the summer of 1934. (On the last occasion, after weeks of Cabinet wrangling, Neville Chamberlain refused to concede to a majority decision, reserving his position with the words, 'in particular the Chancellor of the Exchequer does not bind himself or his successors to find the additional sums mentioned in the Report within five years, or within the particular year to which they are allotted'.[62])

The common criticism that Treasury deference to orthodox financial premises diverted or destroyed every progressive initiative in the inter-war years may have been greatly exaggerated by party politicians avid to excuse the deficiencies of party government; and a reasoned defence is long overdue. But the ability of parties in government to effect change does appear to have become more circumscribed than it had been in the 1900s, not, as some argued, because of class-based resistance to the Labour Party's timid social democracy, but because the state apparatus accumulated knowledge, expertise and hence *residual* power, most clearly in the economic and industrial Ministries (Treasury, Trade, Labour) where parties' ideology had been subordinated, as a function of their experiences in government, to policies of crisis avoidance.

Because the formal lineaments of party survived as matters of electoral practice and educational prescription, endorsed by the organs of mass communication, Parliament *appeared* still to be the home and parties the source of political power. Except among small numbers of political scientists, armed with Marxist analysis as a means to explain political culture, and the even smaller numbers who, before 1945, had even heard of Gramsci's concept of hegemony, there was no stimulus to investigate real changes in the distribution of power. If there had been, it would have encountered a dense resistance enhanced by the steadily increasing practice of administrative secrecy (discussed in Chapter 12).

Although after 1931, and even more rapidly after 1940, the parties transformed themselves into machines for winning votes and for projecting selected politicians into Cabinet, to the detriment of political debate, they continued to behave as if they represented deep interests or classes in the nation, and as if 'their' governments were in some umbilical sense tied to the general will which gave them being. A brief examination of the record of any government between 1924 and 1940 should show the error. But the illusion was sustained because the leadership, above all the persons holding office as Prime Minister and Chancellor, acquired a new function as intermediaries between the state apparatus (of which electoral victory gave them control) and the party whose exertions had placed them where they were, not wholly unlike that of the priest mediating between unseen authority and congregation, at once the accomplice of God and the representative of his people.

Again, it is hardly necessary to argue in detail the transformed political power of Prime Minister and Chancellor within Cabinet and Whitehall and over whatever coalition or single-party government took office after 1911. It explains the paradox of a Labour Party committed in theory to parliamentary socialism yet led until 1931 by MacDonald, a gradualist heir to the principles of Comte, and by Snowden, a philosophic Liberal, as well as that of a Conservative Party turned away by Baldwin, R. A. Butler and Harold Macmillan from the out-and-out free-market principles of Bonar Law to mild state interventionism and, later, acceptance of the welfare state and the mixed economy of the 1950s. As Chancellors of the Exchequer, Lloyd George, Baldwin, Snowden, Churchill and Neville Chamberlain engrossed areas of foreign and defence policy well beyond the scope of the Treasury as it had been understood before 1911. In short, since the accession of Lloyd George in 1916, the Prime Minister's functions had been incorporated, combining in a single individual the roles of leader of the governing party, commander of the state apparatus, and spokesman for the political life of the nation.

Naturally, in the early stages, party members, and sometimes party managers, rebelled: hence the attacks on the Coalition leadership in 1922, on MacDonald in 1924 and 1929, on Baldwin in 1923, 1930 and

1936. But backbench acrimony could be tempered by patronage, another aspect of Prime Ministerial power which expanded as ministries, governmental committees and state agencies grew, like amoebae, by division and subdivision. Also, because the process was slow and not constant, dependent on the variable qualities of individuals, it did not present an easy target. The first Prime Minister who could be described as having assimilated all these functions, *in peacetime*, may have been Baldwin, during the Abdication crisis in 1936, when for four months he became in reality broker of the Constitution, between King and Whitehall (because the heads of the Civil Service sought Edward VIII's exclusion), the parties, the established Church, the national institutions (including the TUC), and the Dominions, represented by their own Prime Ministers. During that crucial test of the political system, popular opinion and Parliament entered only at the last and least important stage.

The cult of leadership, always endemic in Conservative Party imagery, may have affected the self-perception of very many politicians of other parties during the inter-war years, as the twentieth-century obsession with political biography suggests. The composition of their photographs, newsreels of politicians in action at international conferences, the style of MPs' election addresses, or the sheer, deferential space accorded to them in the popular press, suggest that, in the inter-war years, British politicians inherited for a time something of the mystery and awe once reserved for kings, prelates and generals. Becoming statesmen did not necessarily drain them of party feelings, but it often implied adoption of a double standard of behaviour, between Cabinet and conference platform, which had not previously been so explicit, nor so likely to elevate duty to government over allegiance to party. It is not always necessary to look for innate élitism, or subservience to officials in order to explain why so many party leaders abandoned in government the programmes their Conferences had previously endorsed, or betrayed the political promises which had formerly been understood to symbolise the relationship of party to electorate.

Parliament (which in common language after 1911 meant the House of Commons) remained the geographical point where party and government activity merged, but the scope of its debates narrowed. It was still possible for a single member's speech to destroy legislation, as the Independent Labour MP Rosslyn Mitchell did with the Prayer Book Bill in 1928, and possible for party protest to hinder government, over the Unemployment Assistance scales in 1935, or the introduction of the Ministry of Supply in 1939. But the incompetence of parliamentary debate to develop effective criticism or control over the policy and finance of the governing majority was shown repeatedly through the 1930s, not least by Churchill's failure to mobilise Conservative MPs' opinion – or even their attendance in the Chamber – by sheer force of argument in his philippics on national defence. The climate of the decade proved equally unkind to the expression of minority political philosophy. In its attempt to criticise the wartime coalition, Common Wealth encountered the same procedural constraints as had the ILP contingent; while the 1936 campaign known as 'Arms and the Covenant', which was to have been Churchill's populist onslaught on the failure of rearmament, withered without public notice, despite its well-attended meetings, because the national press and the BBC ignored its existence.

The growth of consensus, or inter-party agreements on India, imperial economic policy, or, after 1940, on defence and wartime strategy, inhibited an ancient and still valuable function of the nineteenth-century parliament. Where dissent *did* occur, backed by enough votes to influence a government concerned for its majority, it tended to focus on the immediate symptoms of inequality or injustice, like the shadows in Plato's cave; on the Means Test rather than the root causes of unemployment. Even the main exception – Labour's long skirmishing against the National Government's foreign and defence policy – was to a very large extent a matter of unfinished business, rooted in the anti-armaments conclusions of the late 1920s' post-mortem on the First World War. Despite its public appeal, and the remarkable testament of the Peace Ballot, dissent had little influence on the evolution of government policy, except on the choice of an election date in 1935; and in spite of the temptation to revive the direct action groups of 1920–21, it was confined strictly to parliamentary channels.*

It is possible that the erosion of ideological differences between the main parties which preceded 'Butskellism' in the 1950s can be related to the well-documented decline of class bias in voters' preferences since the 1930s.[63] Although the parties opened up a new front in their electoral war, in local government (where Labour at last captured some of the principle urban centres, notably London in 1934), the extension did not intensify issues of principle between them; rather the contrary, since it took place against a much longer trend of the drain of power from local to central government. The more local authorities were dominated by men with party labels, the more they began to

---

*Bevin specifically repudiated the extra-parliamentary tactics of ILP and the Socialist League in 1934–7, and direct action over Spain in 1938. (Bullock, *Bevin*, vol. 1, p. 553.)

look like tinplate reproductions of Westminster, especially in Labour areas like Glasgow where the feud with the ILP ran deepest. Seeking to consolidate its control of local authorities, the Labour Party also veered away from Keir Hardie's old doctrine of 'Home Rule All Round' (with separate parliaments for England, as well as Wales, Scotland and Ireland) into a hostility towards all separatist ambitions, strikingly similar to Conservative Central Office feelings towards the 'independent Areas' in the late 1930s. The capture of central government and control of the incipient state corporatist economy required party dictatorship, even if, in remoter constituencies, discipline and acceptance of the party line were hard to enforce. Not until the late 1950s (and then unsuccessfully) would a Labour ex-minister echo John Wheatley's speech to the 1928 Conference:

> It is absolutely necessary, if you agree with us that Socialism is the only remedy . . . to give instructions to your Parliamentary Party more definitely as to the line they are to pursue when you place them in power. This Conference has been called to instruct me and every MP. Is the whole Labour movement to do no more than improve on the financial proposals placed on the statute book by Sir William Harcourt in the late nineteenth century?[64]

Churchill's plea (in 1930) that his party should face up to Labour on 'great imperial and historical issues' and 'identify itself with the majority of Britain as under Lord Beaconsfield and Lord Salisbury, and should not hesitate to face controversy, even though that might not immediately evoke a response from the nation', had to wait even longer for a revival.*

This is not to say that in their strategy for acquiring and holding power Labour and Conservative parties ceased to represent class interests altogether, only that as the logical consequences of representation were evaded in the search for a broader electoral base, so the rhetoric of class became confined to each party's transactions with its faithful militants, with diminishing effect on its actual policy in government or coalition. Inevitably, the nature of parties changed as self-interest propelled them along the road already travelled by the governing institutions; for in spite of the presumption that, if anywhere, class conflict was to be found in economic relations, they too had found in

---

*Churchill remained, of course, a political romantic, reared in the pre-1911 system: in *My Early Life* (Butterworth, 1930) he looked back to a golden age 'when we had a real political democracy, led by a hierarchy of statesmen, and not a fluid mass distracted by newspapers. There was a structure in which statesmen, electors and the Press all played their part. . . . All this was before the liquefaction of the British political system had set in' (p. 372). But if the sentiments were archaic the observation was accurate enough.

the patttern of collective bargaining a ritual which appeased the customary forms of class behaviour and protected the real interests of unions and management in cross-class collaboration. Screened by skilful presentation of their traditional roles, the party machines succeeded in keeping antique distinctions alive at election time, even after 1951, despite their lack of substantive disagreements, so that the dichotomy between real and formal behaviour survived almost unimpaired.

The process can be detected among Conservative ministers as early as 1927. Long before the triumph of crisis avoidance over party principles implicit in the Standstill Act on unemployment benefit scales in February 1935 (see above p. 230), Steel-Maitland told the Cabinet that, whatever the party thought about grants for relief work as wasteful, 'disguised subsidies' to the indigent, class interests could not be allowed to dictate policy. The grants gave 'tangible evidence of an effort to provide employment, and are probably effective in allaying unrest, where unemployment is severe, to a degree out of proportion to the numbers actually involved. We cannot close [them] down at present.'* A case even more indicative of how the lines were blurred is the Abdication crisis, when collusion between party leaders blanketed discussion, as the newspaper proprietors' collusion blanketed the press, until the risks of raising a King's party among MPs or reviving the republican agitation of the 1870s had passed. It is surely remarkable that the two *important* issues raised by Edward VIII's troubles, the question of the distribution of political authority in Britain and the Empire, and attitudes towards Nazi Germany (either of which could easily have been raised before the last, reverential Commons debate on 10 December 1936) should have failed to find parliamentary focus.

In government, Labour avoided disturbing the equilibrium of the 1940 coalition on any issue which did not have clear electoral repercussions. Leaving Beveridge, full employment and social reconstruction apart, therefore, Attlee and his colleagues subscribed to a foreign and imperial policy not unwelcome to Conservatives of a mildly radical tinge. It has been argued that Labour leaders effected a change in Conservative foreign policy in wartime, but the reverse seems more likely, as Attlee and Bevin (the future Foreign Secretary) acquired the 'new imperialist' habit of thinking, on such matters as the Second

---

*CP 46/27 February 1927. A similar compromise approach was applied to the bankrupt Unemployment Insurance Fund itself, despite the ideological dilemma involved for a Conservative Cabinet in increased state borrowing to balance current expenditure (CP 244/28 and CP 312/28).

Front and post-war reconstruction in Europe.[65] Cripps' 1938 Memorandum, in which he had argued for an international policy indistinguishable from that of the CPGB and the Popular Front, was soon forgotten; the Dalton-Morrison strategy based on *Labour's Immediate Programme* triumphed. Cripps himself had worked his passage home to the Party by 1943, the time that Attlee was arguing in terms which might have been borrowed from Lord Halifax, against the high Tories in the War Cabinet, Leo Amery and Lord Linlithgow, that India belonged to the Empire, not as a matter of brute force, but because Indians themselves accepted 'British principles of justice and liberty. . . . It is precisely this acceptance . . . which puts us in the position of being able to appeal to them to take part with us in a common struggle.'[66]

In *The Road to 1945*, Paul Addison argues that Labour's assumption of commitments in South-Eastern Europe (involving defeat of the Communist revolution in Greece), the Mediterranean, Africa and South-East Asia were no more than the counterpart of its domestic strategy. As far as economic management was concerned, the Labour Party led where before 1945 only the young Tory reformers dared follow. But their leaders took care not to outrun the limits set by the burgeoning consensus between unions and industrial management. While the NEC conceded defeat, temporarily, to the left wing at the 1944 Conference, by modifying their report recommending control and planning for strategic industries like steel,[67] and inserted into *Let Us Face the Future* (1945) proposals which went some way beyond what the BEC/FBI participants of the Nuffield Conference were prepared to accept, the Manifesto remained, in Miliband's words, 'a mild, circumspect document',[68] barely advancing on the proposals of 1937. Indeed, nationalisation of steel was almost withdrawn later and – far more significant – the banking and insurance systems were excluded. Most of its recommendations, except for iron and steel, could be accepted privately by Conservatives after the 1945 election, on grounds of the diminished efficiency and patent unprofitability of industries like coal and gas in private hands; and in this sense *Let Us Face the Future* appears like a survey of the geography of future accord. As it declared, in almost direct repudiation of the 1944 Mikardo resolution on workers' 'democratic control and operation' of nationalised industries: 'Socialism cannot come overnight, as the product of a weekend revolution. The members of the Labour Party, like the British people, are practical-minded men and women.'

With such antecedents, the distinction between the radical popular expectations of 1943–44 and the 1945 Labour Government's limited achievements is not surprising; writing in 1951, R. H. Tawney was not prepared to claim more than that they had accomplished the greater part of the 1918 programme.[69] The stimulus to fundamental change in society in the 1930s and 40s came from *outside* party altogether: from overseas events (the world depression, the rise of Hitler and the dominance of Europe by Nazi Germany), from the neutral experts, Keynes and Beveridge in 1940–3, and from public demand after the war crisis of 1940–2 had subsided. Both major parties absorbed the stimulus and reacted, albeit slowly, in order to survive; and Labour in due course derived electoral benefit in 1945.

Power lost or dissipated is not easily recoverable, given the vigour and tenacity of new institutions as they cross the threshold of government. As the parties contested for the votes of an increasingly fluid electorate, behind banners which bore less and less relevance to post-war realities, and on manifestos constructed of policies often so similar in essence that only the use of highly colourful imagery maintained distinction, governments tended to set their aims no higher than the avoidance of crisis, eschewing in practice the possibilities of change. To some this development may have been welcome: at Nuffield College, Sir Cecil Weir had bluntly declared common interest with the TUC when he made clear that in accepting the growth of a state sector, the employers would be subject neither to Whitehall nor to party politicians. He only echoed TUC claims dating from the mid-1920s when he declared:

We are not to weaken Parliamentary authority to create a corporate state or to sabotage democracy, but if the public were to exercise directional control over industry, as we all believed would be necessary and inevitable, there was a great deal to be said for the revision of the parliamentary medium in its dealings in the field of economic affairs. It might be wise to consider a system by which expert committees would be set up . . . Parliament as much as industry has to adapt its machinery and procedure.[70]

By 1911 standards, Weir and the economists like Sir Roy Harrod who supported him were endangering the roots of British democracy, and completing the betrayal already begun by the parties themselves; yet the TUC representatives let this assertion of managerial hegemony pass by default.

In 1941, David Margesson, Conservative Chief Whip, acknowledged what Baldwin had always denied – the inadequacy of party in crisis and the necessity of coalition: '*Party politics take people's minds off the essential of going out to win,* so no matter how big a majority we had in the fateful division [in the Norway debate, May 1940] or if the House had not divided at all, the result would have been the same, since a coalition was impossible under Neville.'[71] Eight years later, the Maxwell-Fyffe Report defined the Conservative party bluntly as 'an educative political force and a machine for winning elections'[72] – a clear statement of government-oriented thinking. Bevin described the complementary triangular system, in a speech in March 1945 on the part played by trade unions in wartime industrial cooperation:

Voluntary in its nature, democratic in its functioning, united by law and yet stronger than law because it rests on men's words, it stands stronger than anything else man has yet conceived . . . I believe, however much the political battle may rage, however much parties may divide, this great machinery of industrial relations which has stood us in such good stead during the years of war, will see us back to an orderly industrial society, at the end when victory is won.[73]

Such statements run counter to the assertion that the parties formed the wartime coalition to prevent effective power draining away from parliament.[74] Atrophy of the party-parliamentary system had begun before 1931, and its decline was not checked by the belated revival of Labour; two-party politics in the 1922 or pre-1914 sense were not restored, despite the end of coalition in 1945. During the years of the National Government, old Conservative economic and industrial principles had been laid aside, while Labour's choice of the parliamentary way to socialism had blurred once-clear positions about the distribution of wealth and power in society, and replaced them by acceptance of tenets of social democracy common to industrial management and progressive Conservatives.

For forty years after 1926 Parliament ceased to give sufficient space to ideological divisions in society, and for a time it appeared as if the divisions themselves had disappeared. Those who welcomed an 'end of ideology', however, either ignored or discounted the sheer good fortune which sustained the remarkable (indeed by historical standards unnatural) prosperity of the 1950s, just as they over-estimated the capacity of governments, civil servants and institutions to achieve compromise once profound economic disparities reappeared. So long as prosperity lasted, the illusion held good that the mass of people acquiesced in the politics of institutional collaboration. But Britain's post-war recovery produced vast changes in the balance between manufacturing and service industry, with repercussions on union and management organisation which put an intolerable strain on their arrangements with government, even before multiple forms of break-down emerged in the mid-1960s. By then the parties had become so debilitated that they proved incapable of giving a lead and had instead to respond hastily and ineffectively *in defence* of the triangular system – in the greatest possible contrast to the ideals of the 'true party men' of 1922.

12 CONTINUOUS CONTRACT

Over and above the relationships between party, industrial institutions and the mass electorate created by universal suffrage, British central government established, during and after the First World War, a direct link with public opinion, whose consequences were ultimately as significant as the expansion of suffrage itself. Such a change from the pre-1914 system, of course, ran counter to what nineteenth-century commentators had regarded as the democratic mandate. Confronted with an apparently new phenomenon, the Institute of Public Administration appointed a study group in 1931 to investigate what it considered to be the enormous problem of making public opinion heard against state power, given 'a rather marked failure of democratic institutions in all countries to become effective instruments of action at times when action is necessary'.[1] The Institute was, of course, concerned more to increase public influence over government than to investigate why new mechanisms of control had debilitated the rights they believed to have existed in an earlier golden age. They avoided asking the question as to whether government itself was guilty of manipulating national opinion and deliberately inculcating the supine attitudes the Institute deplored.

A traditional legal answer to such a question would probably have been that individuals had many modes of redress – as voters, taxpayers or ratepayers, as members of parties, trade unions, churches, professional bodies, and, in the last resort, by appeal to the courts of law. But discussion of redress of grievance, for individuals or interest groups slides past the point of the question: what influence in the intervening period, in moments of domestic or international crisis and in the long troughs and shallows between, did the real nation hold over the political nation?

Six years after the inconclusive second General Election of 1910, a coalition, whose composition and policies were almost entirely different from those of the peace-time Asquith government, had to face up to the munitions and manpower crisis and submit to some of the demands of those sections of the real nation involved in supplying shells and fighting men. Political bargains were struck on a basis of what was known about public opinion and what it was believed public opinion would swallow. Hurriedly and often amateurishly, government had to evolve techniques of opinion-testing and control, progressing from indiscriminate use of the patriotic appeal, and crude censorship of the press, to the institution of the Ministry of Information and more subtle methods of propaganda; a hidden history characterised by refinement of skills and increasingly formal agencies of mass persuasion.

Opinion-testing began at the level of empirical reliance on the subjective reports of civil servants, MPs, or sympathetic observers, which could still be found in the first War Cabinet's armoury, and culminated in an apparently methodical structure of information-collecting, based on government departments, and designed to filter out, at appropriate levels, anything extraneous to Cabinet decisions.* The formal system still incorporated amateurish elements: in the late 1930s Baldwin could be found consulting friends like Thomas Jones and Geoffrey Dawson about 'opinion', much as Lloyd George had done with C. P. Scott, Lord Riddell and Robertson Nicoll, and as subsequent Prime Ministers have done ever since. But it aspired to scientific accuracy, and assimilated the techniques of the infant social sciences,[2] as well as the methods of American market research, already a fashionable preoccupation with the Conservative Party, whose long association with Bensons had led to their handing over much of the 1929 election campaign to the epigoni of Madison Avenue. But apart from the development of Mass Observation by Charles Madge and Tom Harrisson, the approach to evidence, sampling and methodology remained naïve and often over-confident, lacking an antidote until G. H. Gallup himself began to analyse their complexities in his paper, 'The Quintemensional Plan of Question Design' (1947).

Untroubled by doubts about their findings, Ministers assumed that opinion-testing constituted a most necessary addition to the infrequent verdict of general elections and the often ambiguous results of by-elections. Modern government could hardly be run like a horse race from the uncertain impact of, say, the Newport by-election before the Carlton Club meeting, the St George's, Westminster, campaign of 1930, or even the apparently clear-cut result of East Fulham in 1934. Opinion-testing appeared to provide a precise, speedy, economical and,

---

*A good early case is to be found in the reports on the likely impact of conscription in Ireland, 1917–18 (above, p. 109).

above all, regular form of contact with the authentic voice of the people; and, in due course, Ministers and civil servants came to believe that without it they would lose touch with the vagaries of the mass electorate, and that voters whose specific grievances were not appeased would turn away from parliamentary politics altogether, in cynicism or disgust. Thus a paradox developed: to defend the parliamentary system in the era of complex modern government, political leaders disparaged the open, party forms of activity on which it had been based, in favour of a clandestine, state-inspired alternative.

Organised opinion polling did not develop in Britain until the late 1930s, at least twenty years after government had begun the regular process of assessing opinion, and for another decade the effect of polls was only to reinforce existing procedures rather than to encourage their revision. Cabinet Ministers, after all, were often concerned with questions far too sensitive to be trusted to public scrutiny, or too limited to specific interest groups, like employers' federations or trade unions, to permit the use of impartial sampling techniques. In these cases, they relied on well-tried methods, utilising individual investigators, government committees like the CCR, EAC or Committee of Scientific Research. Lord Haldane had emphasised the role of the advisory committee in the 'Research and Information' chapter of his 1918 Report on the Machinery of Government, and although his recommendation of a research and intelligence branch in each department of state was never fully implemented, it could be said, by 1936, that all 'post-war development had been in the direction of creating bodies on which persons representing organisations, interests, movements, and the *unorganised public,* have been assembled to advise departments and assist them with their work.'[3]

Ministers of course kept count of the press[4] and from the time of Lloyd George 10 Downing Street had its own Press Officer. Where security of the state was concerned, the Prime Minister turned to the unpublicised networks managed by Special Branch and the Secret Intelligence Services; and all Ministers were provided with departmental assessments of opinion, derived from diverse sources such as local trade boards or unemployment assistance offices. If one adds the research resources supplied at party level, private contacts and the pervasive influence on politicians of the press, the range of information passes beyond the capacity of historians to describe except in individual cases. But party and private sources seem, from the biographies of a number of inter-war Cabinet ministers, to have lagged a little way behind those of government, not least because of the superior resources of the state apparatus and its particular, urgent interest in continuity, as opposed to parties' entanglement in the long electoral cycle. Thus the *Conservative Agents' Journal* can be found discussing market research techniques and showing an interest in the sampling methods of the American Democratic Party in 1935, some ten years after the Ministry of Labour had begun similar studies of trade union opinion; and the prevalence of military intelligence analogies, which government departments had long outgrown, can still be found in J. C. C. Davidson's description of the Conservative Research Department in 1928:

The information service corresponds to the intelligence service of the Army. It then passes that information to the operations side for use. The first duty of the intelligence service is to survey the background (from constituency dossiers), establish the enemy's strength, ascertain the best points of attack, including the weakness of any of the opposing commanders and advise on the form of attack most likely to succeed.[5]

The Labour Party, of course, eschewed military models, but while relying on the greater range of sympathetic organisations like Trades Councils – as in the questionnaires on the spread of Fascism and attitudes to the Means Test (above, p. 235) – it, too, fell behind government in developing the technique of assessment and manipulation.

The effect of public opinion on government policy cannot easily be summed up in a single generalisation. As individuals, politicians in the inter-war years appear to have been obsessed with the importance of opinion-testing, yet in Cabinet and ministerial discussion they tended to play public opinion down (or at least this is the impression given by the British system of committee minuting).* In crises, however, possible public reactions usually bulked large, though they were often expressed in very imprecise forms, characteristic of the emotive jargon so frequently found in party committee rooms. Compared with these, civil service assessments made up in clarity and attempted objectivity what they lacked in pungency.

Among the few cases where opinion-testing erred, and public opinion ran counter to government predictions, that of the UAB scales of 1935 has already been described (above, p. 230). A long-planned administrative reform was precipitately abandoned in the face of militant opinion

---

*It should be remembered that minuting of Cabinet meetings varied considerably, being very full under Lloyd George, formal under Bonar Law and MacDonald, slightly fuller under Baldwin, Chamberlain and Churchill, and formal again after 1945. Discussion was, normally, attributed to individuals in Cabinet committees throughout the inter-war years, often in great detail; but almost invariably *party* matters, to do with electoral calculations, etc., were omitted. Thus a greater impression of political altruism is given than was often the case.

expressed variously by TUC and Labour Party, South Wales hunger-marchers, CPGB propaganda and Sheffield rioters. In retrospect it seems strange that in a case where as many as 110,000 South Wales and Durham men were to be disqualified from unemployment benefit, warnings like those of Steel-Maitland[6] or J. H. Thomas – 'very great care should be taken in the way the scheme was presented to parliament and the nation'[7] – should have been ignored. It may be unfair to blame Chamberlain's notorious intolerance of the ill-educated public for the disaster, however: Chamberlain himself foresaw considerable electoral benefit from freeing public assistance from the 'poor law taint';[8] and it was the Unemployment Assistance Board, and some of his own staff who showed a failure of political imagination, discounting the public relations aspect, with the statement, 'the Board are not making a new first-class social service of high political value whose benefits need to be rammed down the throats of the public'.[9]

Afterwards, the Board had to admit that the Standstill Act 'had shown the consequences of ignoring past history',[10] and the Government took nearly two years to reimpose its uniform assistance scales, with a deal of rather devious manoeuvring, district by district, to avoid aggravating public discontent again. Ernest Brown, who succeeded Oliver Stanley in the unenviable position of Minister of Labour, found himself caught between incompatible demands to restore the government's prestige while tempering UAB progress to 'previous local practice and the approval of local opinion'.[11] Even more embarrassing, the Cabinet had to draw up a formula to ease government candidates through the 1935 General Election ('it would be awkward for an old parliamentary hand, but quite intolerable for an inexperienced candidate'),[12] while maintaining silence about the appalling miscalculations of the number of unemployed affected, and the sums actually involved.[13]

Continuing sensitivity to opinion can be detected in the final Cabinet Committee scheme, in June 1936, for it scaled down some of the worst reductions, and hit hardest young unmarried unemployed men, who might be expected to attract least public sympathy. It was drafted under the injunction 'at all times to avoid a large number of simultaneous reductions merely for the sake of bringing the allowance into conformity with the regulation figure' – in spite of the fact that conformity had been the principal, if not the only, purpose of the original Act. Even then, the Scottish Ministers, with marginal Conservative seats in mind, jibbed at alienating working-class opinion yet further. 'As I have urged upon the Committee,' G. Collins, the Secretary of State for Scotland, wrote, candidly, 'the new regulations will be judged by public opinion [in Scotland where 70 per cent of the 'standstill' cases were] not purely on their abstract merits . . . but by reference to:

1 The final assessment as contrasted with the Standstill arrangements *now* in operation, and

2 The fidelity with which the government's election pledges have been honoured.'[14]

Even more bluntly, Walter Elliot argued that, on such figures, he would have lost his Scottish seat in 1935. Under the plain fear of public wrath, the gap between elderly and youthful Ministers, which was to be such a marked factor of Chamberlain's later administration, opened up. The time-scale for the cuts in scales of benefit was extended yet further, to March 1937, and their severity once more reduced.[15]

The tense first week of February 1935 taught the National Government one lesson about prediction and persuasion. That government could also be deflected by evidence from another quarter, can be seen from the Hoare–Laval débâcle only ten months later, in December 1935, when the considerable investment in collective security built up by Hoare's Geneva speech condemning the Italian invasion of Abyssinia was abruptly dissipated by exposure (due to French government leaks) of his plan with Pierre Laval to partition the unfortunate country and buy in return the peace that the League's sanctions could not achieve. However logical the plan seemed – even, in retrospect, reasonable – its *realpolitik* horrified the international relations' morality of the liberal establishment and the Labour Party, and attracted a barrage of biting and often brilliantly informed criticism (such as Geoffrey Dawson's famous editorial in *The Times* 'A corridor for camels'). A group of young Tory critics gathered around Austen Chamberlain and the Conservative Party foreign affairs committee, while fifty-nine National Government MPs signed a motion deploring the Pact. In its metropolitan intensity, this episode surpassed the Conservative revolt over India; yet as an expression of public opinion it seems to have been a chimera, compounded of outrage in the 'quality' press, and selective fury at Westminster. Nevertheless, the price was Hoare's head. Only once in this century has the Cabinet collectively demanded the resignation of a Foreign Secretary, and compelled a Prime Minister and Chancellor (Baldwin and Neville Chamberlain) to go, lugubriously, and enforce its will.[16]

The dimensions of state policy and public opinion are well illustrated over a long and complex period by the case of rearmament. Perhaps nowhere in the inter-war years was the dissociation between the two (deplored by the Institute of Public Administration), more evident than in the discrepancy between public opinion – or passion – over the growth of armaments and government policy in the critical year 1934; nor is there any other example of such pains being taken both to measure and educate the national electorate in subsequent years.

The twenties had seen belief in pacific action, rather than war, installed as the ark of the diplomatic covenant, sustained by all-party consensus about progressive reductions in the Service budgets, and the specific limitations reached at the Washington and London Naval Conferences. Public debate tended to centre on broadly anti-war lines, rather than to follow in detail the actual problems of international aggression which arose* – a trend encouraged by popularisation of World War I historians' diagnosis that great armaments led automatically to war. Quite apart from their own sensibility to the immensely influential portraits of the 1914–18 horror published by British, French and German writers in the late 1920s (which affected, for example, Neville Chamberlain's attitude to Britain's continental involvement), party politicians could not but be aware of electoral pressures,† and the popular appeal of Labour Party essays in collective security such as the Geneva Protocol and the Anglo-Soviet treaties.

The rise of Japanese militarism and Nazi power in Germany in the early 1930s exposed not only the contradictions of collective security but the contrast between the National Government's half-hearted public belief in disarmament and the growing conviction of the Service chiefs that a measure of rearmament was essential to British interests. Secretly, the Cabinet set up the Defence Requirements Committee in 1933 and followed its report through with contentious rearmament proposals, while in public talking variously of disarmament, 'remedying deficiencies', and only in July 1934, of actual *re*armament.‡ This careful trimming owed less to the very radical, unilateralist position taken up by the Labour Party after 1931[17] than to the electrons which surrounded that nucleus: perhaps sixty societies,[18] ranging from the rapidly growing League of Nations Union,§ led by Lord Robert Cecil, to small groups like the Association of Yorkshire Mayors, and distinguished individuals

---

*In February 1932, when he attended the sixty-nation Disarmament Conference at Geneva, General Temperley defined the problem: 'One felt almost a sense of shame that one was taking part in a colossal make-believe, that the public had not been told the truth, for nothing but a miracle could bring success.' (Major General A. C. Temperley, *The Whispering Gallery of Europe*, Collins, 1938, p. 168.)

†Thus, in 1924, Churchill told Baldwin that a future Conservative government must not increase armaments, or it would lose the next election. (SB D1, Naval.)

‡Significantly the Cabinet Committee on Disarmament did not change its name until July 1935, although for eighteen months it had talked of nothing but rearmament.

§200,000 members in 1929, nearly 1 million in 1933.

343

like Gilbert Murray and G. M. Trevelyan, who from time to time coalesced in common action (such as the joint statement issued in October 1933 by TUC, NUR and British Commonwealth League). These propagated assiduously damaging facts about war in all its aspects,* which at least until Germany's withdrawal in 1934 from the Disarmament Conference attracted almost universal press sympathy. In this period occurred the chief manifestations of public anxiety – the Oxford Union debate (repeated in most universities) and the Peace Ballot whose final result, in June 1935, seemed to represent an overwhelming repudiation of the very idea of war. For this public, even the Abyssinian war failed to expose the essential ambiguity of the Ballot or its corollary that in the last resort, imposing sanctions could mean war.†

Government being composed of party men, by-elections had their own significance, especially since they established what appeared to be a clear and frightening pattern in the run-up to the next general election after 1931. Modern methods of study enjoin a great deal more caution than was present in party headquarters in 1934–5;[19] but the figures did show a quite unusual correlation of results. An average swing of 17·6 per cent against the Government occurred in twelve by-elections in the second half of 1933 and another of 15·3 per cent in fourteen more during 1934. Given the revival of Labour (which in any case had sustained its basic working-class vote in 1931)[20] these were serious portents for a hypothetical general election in 1934.

After East Fulham, when the Conservative candidate lost a safe seat to Labour with a swing of 29·1 per cent, Baldwin asked Arthur Baker, a *Times* columnist to investigate – and Baker corroborated the emphasis on pacifism which had already become conventional party wisdom.[21] No wonder that at the end of 1933 Baldwin rebutted Vansittart's request for massive rearmament with a warning about what might happen in an election 'when you will have the socialists who would give you no rearmament at all, instead of me who gives you not enough',[22] nor that he postponed the election campaign until well on into 1935.

Baldwin was probably right to assume a direct link between the by-election swings and pacifist opinion – though not to the exclusion of local circumstances.[23] He certainly inserted in his speeches regular denials of the charge of warmongering, mixed, however, with mordant phrases such as 'the bomber will always get through', which were

---

*The private arms trade alone inspired a genre of literature which included Fenner Brockway's *The Bloody Traffic*, Gollancz, 1933 and *Zaharoff, the Armaments King* by Robert Neumann, trs. R. T. Clark, Allen & Unwin, 1935.

†6.5 million for and 2.2 million against on 5b, the crucial question of using military means to enforce sanctions against an aggressor.

intended as a form of vivid political education.[24] For nearly two years until the election result in November 1935 gave the necessary mandate, the government pursued a dual policy of gradual public awakening, combined with rearmament in the shadows, as discreetly as possible building up its air capacity, in particular a deterrent bomber capability against Germany, though without disturbing the balance between the Services or the priority of home defence.

Meanwhile, under the acrid stimulus of Nazi rule in Germany, and influenced by the TUC's success in weaning Labour away from pacifism, public opinion seems to have accommodated itself quite rapidly to the new, malevolent world picture, so that by 1936 (and the Spanish Civil War) the majority of Labour supporters were prepared to accept the need for war preparations against Fascism, if not yet in all circumstances. By the time of Munich, in September 1938, the transformation was self-evident:[25] pacifism had ceased to hold the public stage. Instead it had become the badge of dissent, often of hermetic, revolutionary groups like Dick Sheppard's Peace Pledge Union or the National Peace Council, while the League of Nations Union, unable to renew its ageing leadership, failed to defend the citadel of collective security against the reasoned criticisms of a new generation of experts like E. H. Carr and Arnold Toynbee. Although 600,000 registered as conscientious objectors in 1939–45, they had virtually no political support among the public, in contrast to the influence of a quarter that number in 1914–18.

Government was not, however, freed to rearm as it might wish. Quite apart from the leverage exercised by the City, the Society of Aircraft Constructors, or informed opinion (by which Fisher meant 'the opinion of the people who are going to lend us money'),[26] older ghosts haunted policy-makers, fearful of renewed financial instability. Commenting in 1935, on a proposed defence loan, to meet the requirements of the second DRC Report, the head of the Treasury, Warren Fisher, told Sir Richard Hopkins:

So little are they [the public] conscious, in my opinion, of the dangers which are looming everywhere that the one hope is to educate them in every way. This will take time, but if the first stage takes the form of the tax-collector running his hand still further into their pockets, may not the result of such sound finance be that we shall be forced to go unarmed?[27]

Preoccupied by public reactions to cuts in social services, if these were required to pay for rearmament in 1937, and fretting about inflation 'which would lead to continuous pressure for increased wages, and produce conditions in which subversive ideas flourish',[28] Fisher and Hopkins – and their intellectual acolyte, Chamberlain, now Prime Minister, prejudged on financial rather than strategic grounds the system of rationing the Services, which then undermined the policy of deterrence towards Germany, and helped replace it by carefully considered schemes of appeasement in 1937–8.[29] Yet in those years the Treasury took every precaution to prevent the public realizing that financial considerations were governing the pace of rearmament[30] – as Hopkins pointed out in a particularly candid memorandum in January 1939:

If and when it comes to be realised, in addition to the anxiety in men's minds about impending war, how completely we are snowed under by mounting expenditure, and it comes to be thought that this country is coming to the end of its tether, and is prepared to let things slide, the foreign influx will be swollen by an internal movement away from sterling. The foreigner, after all, can take away no more than he possesses here, but there is no limit to what our own people might try to send abroad. It seems to me that we should make whatever effort we can to preserve the confidence of our own people in the continuing value of our currency.[31]

As 1940 showed, such fears were illusionary, spawned by blindly orthodox assumptions about the free movement of capital and the choices open to a government in peacetime. Plainly, in 1938–9, government lacked the courage, or confidence in public tolerance, to impose controls. Yet the authorities had a virtual monopoly of information about rearmament, and Chamberlain frequently derided the parliamentary and pacifist opposition for its ignorance. It is not easy to answer the question why the Chamberlain government failed to capitalise on the change in public opinion or to prolong its predecessor's attempts at political education. Perhaps the simplest explanation comes from the history of aircraft procurement (see Chapter 9); in the search for institutional compromise, Ministers ignored the public, out of fear and ignorance of the trade union movement. Their misgivings about industrial unrest which, as late as March 1939, induced them to reject compulsory National Service, masked a more general – and deeply pusillanimous – disquiet about the working-class electorate as a whole.[32]

Government made itself aware of public opinion through so many channels that only a study of a great variety of instances can reveal particular patterns. Immigration and public order were questions where sectional pressures tended always to disrupt the apparatus of control, carefully constructed over long periods of time to hold community opinion and national political interests in balance. In drafting the original Aliens Act in 1905, the government had steered with great caution between the violent clamour of local factions and the populist appeals made by the Conservative Opposition;[33] and its response to the arrival of Jewish and other refugees from the Third Reich in the 1930s suggests a similar care to balance public hostility to Nazi methods against the understandable fears of professional bodies or trade unions about the effects of immigration on British employment.[34] Their dilemma was that the anti-semitism of the 1900s had been largely dissipated by the outrageous behaviour of the British Union of Fascists, and the publicity given to organised persecution in Germany; yet against a background of one million unemployed, individual trade unions refused to allow the integration of particular craftsmen or government retraining schemes not already available to their own members.[35] The British Medical Association, for example, opposed the entry of more than a tiny quota of doctors.

As A. J. Sherman points out in *Island Refuge*, the continued inflow of refugees, particularly in the later stages when the Nazi régime allowed them to take out of Germany virtually no possessions or assets, raised difficult questions of moral and practical politics, at a time when the government was seeking to avoid an out-and-out breach with Germany.* By emphasising that they were only 'birds of passage', by regulating entry, and seeking a 'home' in inhospitable regions of the Empire, like Northern Rhodesia or British Guiana (and blaming Americans for *their* quota restrictions), the government succeeded in getting a favourable response at home. The TUC was able to give positive help during 1938, on the basis of a strict quota,[36] and as immigration slowed to a trickle of the mainly young and adaptable, after the Evian Conference, organised opposition faded away.[37]

The story is not a particularly flattering one to a British audience, and few Ministers came out of it with much credit for humanity towards the refugees themselves; but in so far as government attempted to balance its foreign policy towards Germany against domestic pressures and League of Nations opinion, its policy must be counted successful. The social tensions explicit in the East End of London during the 1900s were not revived. The Home Office played a skilful part, ensuring that institutions' interests were fully represented by trade union general secretaries or employers' federations, while making it clear that they were not to raise the issue on the party political level. They were fortunate in that the Board of Deputies of British Jews wisely refrained from making excessive demands on behalf of German Jews; to avoid racial prejudice, the government also emphasised the fact that many of

---

*Even though the Board of Deputies of British Jews took great care to prevent their dispossessed co-religionists becoming a burden on the rates.

the refugees were not Jewish at all. And in this respect, crisis avoidance became public policy, in a kind of tacit conspiracy to eliminate the questions of race and immigration as far as possible from political debate.

In a similar fashion, the Cabinet dealt with the problem of political violence in the mid-1930s endangering as little as possible the harmony between parties and institutions so carefully built up in the preceding decade. Most of the organised protests of the twenties, the early hunger marches, for example, or the Cook–Maxton campaign of 1928, had taken place without real support from the Labour party or TUC, because of their association with the Communist party and their extra-parliamentary taint. But by the time of the 1934 Incitement to Disaffection Act, the violence and arrests which had occurred during the 1932 Hunger March, together with the use of the 'Moscow conspiracy' theme by Conservative party and national press, had won back much Labour sympathy.

The harsh provisions of the Act itself directly influenced the early growth of the National Council for Civil Liberties, just at the time when the Communist Party's abandonment of revolutionary tactics and its new battle-cry of the 'war against Fascism' made it politically respectable. Radical protest broke out of its long isolation: the 1936 Hunger March attracted more general support (and consequently won more concessions from government) than any of its predecessors. This made it doubly difficult for the government to respond to the political violence caused by the BUF's inflammatory programme, and the tactics Fascists adopted in the East End of London, without either enraging respectable Labour by another Disaffection Act, or proving itself to Conservatives too supine to maintain law and order.

A whole series of balances therefore affected the genesis of the Public Order Act – between condemning the BUF and, by implication, justifying the CPGB,[38] between Tory and Labour sympathisers for either or both, between the poles of excessive force and the infringement of 'ancient liberties' – vigorously defended, not only by the NCCL, but by the Liberal and Labour parties. Despite public outrage at the brutality of BUF stewards, revealed at the Olympia meeting in 1934, and a number of police requests for powers to limit the wearing of uniforms, to enter meetings and to control processions, the Cabinet delayed, preferring to consult the Labour Party and even ILP MPs, in order to avoid implication in an offensive against the hunger marchers ('which would not be popular owing to the general sympathy with the plight of the unemployed'), or the right to hold open-air meetings,

348

since these were the resort 'of poor people who could not afford the hire of halls'.[39]

In the event, Labour, Liberal and trade union leaders were prepared to ban private armies, but not to interfere with the right of demonstrations; and plans were pigeon-holed until, in 1936, the BUF's physical attacks on Jewish communities in the East End brought fear of Nazi-style atrocities. Sir John Simon, the Home Secretary, proposed a bill to meet 'sustained public demand', citing evidence 'that the Jewish element is tending to throw itself into the arms of the Opposition, and the strain on the Metropolitan Police . . . is deplorable'.[40] Armed with evidence of a security threat from actual Nazis,* and only too aware that the Communist Party was taking on the mantle of ensuring community safety,[41] the Cabinet brought in the Public Order Act. Yet even so they limited its powers to what the public considered the greatest offence, the wearing of military style uniforms ('people are very much alive to the fact that in Germany, the wearing of black or brown uniforms led to the overthrow of popular liberties'), scarcely touching on the rights of demonstrators and then only in agreement with the parliamentary opposition.[42] Throughout, public opinion, as perceived through the different lenses of police reports, secret intelligence, the Board of Deputies, or the Opposition parties, governed the shape not only of the final Act but its subsequent operation. In October 1937 for example, Lord Trenchard, the Metropolitan Police Commissioner, requested a blanket prohibition for three months of all marches, after a flagrant BUF demonstration in Bermondsey: Hoare, the new Home Secretary, refused to proceed without formal agreement from each Party leader, and House of Commons approval.[43]

Political education is one thing, manipulation another. In classical democratic theory, an elected government has every right, indeed a duty, to inform and educate an often ignorant public; but to seek to coerce, bribe or suborn the public smacks of dictatorship. Yet the line between is so faint as to be imperceptible, and its position changes according to the circumstances of the time: what was legitimate (or corrupt) in the days of Lloyd George no longer applied even ten years later when the revolutionary bogy had been laid. Moreover, the widest

---

*CP 206/36 cited Special Branch evidence that the London and Dalston branches of the British Nazi Party counted 288 members with 1,500 affiliates. MI5 strongly advised counter measures to prevent propaganda, sabotage and espionage; but for fear of revealing this security element in the Commons, Simon preferred to ask the German and Italian embassies to close these branches down, rather than take powers to prohibit them individually and in public.

349

categories, such as the function of education and literature in forming early understanding of, and compliance with the political system simply cannot be assessed in the present state of historical knowledge.[44]

The education system, and its stratification on predominantly class lines, changed little between 1911 and implementation of the 1944 Education Act, which itself only restructured the old apparatus on sound bureaucratic principles, derived from Balfour's original statute in 1902. The numbers of children in state secondary education (almost by definition members of the working class) rose from 161,000 in 1911 to 470,000 in 1938; but as a proportion of the total attending primary school, only from 2·6 per cent to 8·4 per cent.[45] It is true that as a result of the patient work of the school inspectorate, something approaching a common, examinable core was inserted into the curriculum; but as far as induction to citizenship was concerned, the weight of inertia and lack of resources was so great that even R. H. Tawney, life-long crusader for working-class education, was occasionally constrained to argue that the advantages of raising the school-leaving age lay mainly in improving conditions of work and preserving the morale of the young from the bitterness of unemployment.[46] A contemporary Conservative report proclaimed that the 'primary duty of national education is to develop a strong sense of national obligation in the individual citizen, to encourage in him an ardent understanding of the state's needs, and to render him capable of serving those needs.'[47]

The impression given by literary evidence from the inter-war period is that, with a small number of exceptions, working-class horizons remained bounded by stereotyped images of political behaviour and the role of the state and institutions.[48] Even in higher education, the inquisitive mind was as rare as it had been in 1911; the hackneyed impression of fevered Socialist and Communist activity at Cambridge and Oxford when analysed is reduced to a handful of radicals bubbling among the total undergraduate body – hence the private languages, and self-consciously élitist behaviour of the 'Macspaunday' writers, who in their later political writing barely scratched the surface of middle England complacency and (with the exception of one or two brilliant but idiosyncratic books, like Christopher Caudwell's *Studies in a Dying Culture*, tended to vituperate a class and political structure of which their knowledge was slight, to a minority, narcissistic audience, as uncritical of Communist *agitprop* as high Tory readers were of the productions of the Right Book Club.

If prevailing values in Britain had not reflected consensus about the political system, then it is unlikely that apathy would have been so widespread, even in the Depressed Areas, or that the unusually radical feelings noticed during the second half of World War II could so easily have been mollified by social reform rather than social transformation. Nothing similar to the prolonged crisis of values between 1911 and 1921 occurred; nothing which demanded reappraisal or rejection of existing patterns of political behaviour. The relative prosperity of all those in work in the 1930s and the phenomenon of socialisation in individuals to the blunt facts of the economic and political order, are only partial explanations; to understand the appearance of apathetic consent, it is necessary to ask how the practice of opinion management developed and how effective a form of control it had become.

After its inception in the Great War the management of opinion by government developed on two levels, the open, unashamed one of anti-German, anti-Bolshevik and finally anti-Nazi propaganda, which embodied a traditional, intensely nationalistic concept of British values – with only slight influence outside the sphere of foreign relations; and the secretive side which, in and immediately after the war, was intended to mobilise support for the existing political order – and in particular for Lloyd George's Coalition – against dissident or revolutionary groups (see above pp. 131–2). It is the second that is of more interest, being directed against criticism from within rather than easily count-tered threats from overseas. By 1920, it had developed into such a dense network that it can almost be called a system in itself.

Attention has usually focused on the 'normal' manipulation of the Lloyd George era, his attempts to buy control of newspapers (he failed with *The Times* but succeeded with the *News Chronicle*), or his assi-duous cultivation of the mass daily papers and their proprietors, Lords Northcliffe, Rothermere and Beaverbrook, whom he wooed unashamedly with ministerial preferment and access to privileged or secret informa-tion. Far more important than that volatile and ultimately unsatisfactory means of access to the public mind was the attempt to set up an organisa-tion under his own control, with almost unlimited funds, like a philoso-pher's stone to turn public hostility into uncritical adulation.

The search may be dated from January 1917 when Steel-Maitland drafted for him a memorandum on press liaison, on the unpopular sub-jects of war loans and conscription. '*An atmosphere should be created* which would make people ready to take up such a loan – or in the case of industrial compulsion *which would make them accept* what would other-wise be a most unpalatable measure'[49] [my italics]. In due course, trans-cending the use of the patriotic appeal and the crude, 1915–16 methods

351

of suppression, Lloyd George proceeded to the lavish use of Coalition funds, public money, secret information and Intelligence personnel, and blurred almost beyond retrieval the distinction between government and party propaganda or public and private morality.

The lineage of Sidney Walton's network, flanked by that of Admiral Hall, formerly head of Naval Intelligence, staffed by ex-members of the Secret Intelligence Service, primed with its techniques and store of nformation, and financed jointly by government, joint party funds, and prominent employers, has already been traced (see above p. 132). The octopus they created may, not unfairly, be compared with the Nixon apparatus at the time of Watergate, without the dénouement of exposure. At first it operated informally, relying for house-room on the publicity branch of the Ministry of Labour, and the existing organisation left over from Beaverbrook's defunct Ministry of Information. Later, in 1919, it became the Supply and Transport Sub-Committee; and whereas Hall, dispensing government funds, concerned himself with public relations on behalf of the Coalition, Walton with his £100,000 from industrial sources, created the machine for press penetration which he called 'Industrial Information'[50] – specifically directed against the spread of militant trade unionism and socialist influence. Walton's vision of a captive press acting as 'a vast college of simple economics' (in so far as it actually existed beyond his imagination) was achieved by bribery on a substantial scale, for the 'signed, authoritative' articles he put out in over 1,200 newspapers and magazines were not spontaneous or reimbursed in the normal way, nor were they submitted, in a free market, for editorial acceptance.

The golden years of corruption ended in 1922 with Lloyd George's fall; there is no reason to suppose that any British government or Minister since has dealt as Lloyd George did by handing over to Sir Vincent Caillard (Chairman of Vickers Engineering), a private individual, secret intelligence material on 'agitators' for use against shop stewards in his own factories.[51] Walton and his unpleasant crew survived, partly because of the reluctance of the Carlton Club rebels to pursue their case against corruption to the full (another parallel with the early days of Watergate behaviour). In private, Baldwin declared that Lloyd George had 'sucked the morality' out of his colleagues, and Eric Geddes admitted 'we had lost all sense of proportion and I did things of which I am now thoroughly ashamed';[52] but it was only the sale of honours and the Maundy Gregory scandal that they referred to, in public, for Bonar Law had been far too close to the secret propaganda machine since 1916 for him not to have known, or for them to dare uncover the whole appalling truth.

In any case, the machinery was too valuable to be entirely destroyed. Walton's organisation was merged with the Industrial League, headed by Lord Burnham, the newspaper proprietor, and G. H. Roberts, MP. Although Law cut back the amounts of public and party money spent on 'publicity'[53] – admitting for the first time in public that such things existed – he appointed the egregious Admiral Hall as Principal Agent at Central Office in 1923; and Conservative Party managers in due course wiped Lloyd George's eye by hiring Walton themselves two years later to run the 'Information Fund' and their campaign against the General Strike with a float of £10,000.[54]

It is almost impossible to gauge how effective this propaganda barrage was. Ministers believed it to be essential and measured success by the degree to which they kept the Opposition case out of public view, either in the press or in party campaigns,* and by public response to the epithets 'revolutionary' and 'unpatriotic' which they continually pinned on minority groups. But unlike the corruption of the Nixon years, the British system of manipulation can be explained in terms of its context, the revolutionary atmosphere of the period and the real revolutions which had occurred in Europe. As the Supply and Transport publicity committee argued in 1922, their work was necessary 'to ensure that the government's position . . . is kept permanently before the public with a view to securing the support and maintaining the morale of the nation'.[55] Such reasoning probably enabled the 1924 Labour Government to quiet its conscience and retain the organisation in being, albeit without the deliberate use of strike-breaking.

But the Carlton Club rebels did achieve something by their revulsion from Lloyd George's unrestrained use of methods more usually associated with Mussolini's Italy: they rebuilt the boundary wall between party and government propaganda, largely (though in the 1920s not entirely) restraining private and institutional funds for party use, and government money for organisations serving the 'national' interest. At times, with the Conservative response to the Zinoviev letter,[56] or during the General Strike, the lines became blurred again: Walton worked for Conservative Central Office but frequently overstepped into government public relations work, in matters like the despatch of a band of

*See, for example, Davidson papers, correspondence with Robert Donald and Hall Caine, for attempts to forestall the Labour Party in setting up a new London evening paper, 1924–6. Walton claimed to have distributed 10 million leaflets in factories and schools during the years 1919–22 – an effort far beyond the resources of the Labour Party.

M

fact-finding American journalists to South Wales in the care of Evan Williams, spokesman for the Coal Owners Association![57] But by this time, black propaganda and undercover attempts to denigrate left-wing groups had largely been discontinued, and the publicity department's role reduced to one of general advertisement of government policy on industrial questions. Walton spent £25,306 in the five months of the 1926 miners' strike, not – and the point is worth making – on bribery of journalists, but on press advertising (£21,450), payment to speakers (£1,947) and postage (£1,900). The contrast is clear: the age of the advertising men had begun.

As a result, government and party propaganda developed along steadily more formal lines. The manipulators began to understand both the limits of their now sanitised trade, and the need for substantial resources and continuity of persuasion. The lesson of the Lloyd George era was that there was no simple relationship between propaganda and public consent. Of a suggestion by Chamberlain in 1926 to use the Industrial Court to prevent strikes, Steel-Maitland wrote: 'the only sanction behind its findings is public opinion – which is in fact of very little weight in any but the most important disputes, and even then *most uncertain* in its operation.'[58]

During these years, the Conservative Party made most of the running, learning quickly to introduce new techniques. After all, it possessed the financial resources and organisation to make best use of advertising techniques, broadcasting and film. Much was learnt from America: in the 1930s, Conservative 'psychological' propaganda relied heavily on the analysis of social and economic groups, which stemmed from the Hawthorne Experiment, conducted in 1928 at Western Electric, Chicago.[59] As part of the post-mortem on the 1929 election, a place was made, if not for the personnel, at least for the language of the social sciences.[60] Emphasising the inter-action of opinion research and propaganda (shortly after the formation of the Publicity Department), Davidson wrote, in 1929:

It is in the devising of an intensive propaganda campaign, based on scientific records, and directed to the special classes that must be reached, that the Chief Intelligence Officers' work mainly lies. The pamphlet is very valuable if properly drawn up dealing with a 'line' subject. . . . The very great value of propaganda agents in factories, public houses, at football matches and indeed wherever large numbers of the 'unconverted' may congregate, is incontestable; while the use of the cinema and the dance and lantern lecture requires much fostering.[61]

The belief that a properly skilled and well-financed organisation mechanically transmuted itself into votes lasted for many years in the Conservative Party. Lacking funds, Transport House never aspired to these levels of triumphalism. But this did not necessarily work to their long-term detriment, since the Labour Party could rely on unpaid local militants and trade unionists to a far wider degree than its opponents, whose organisation sometimes tended to stagnate in the trough between elections.* But although Labour could run press campaigns almost on the proverbial shoestring, their methods came increasingly to resemble those of the Conservatives.[62] For both, professional skills, higher salaries, and modern techniques became essential components of party propaganda organisation. Commenting on the takeover of the Conservative St Stephens News Agency by a commercial group, Editorial Services, in 1930, Hoare declared 'that the improvement [in the number of papers using the services] is probably due to the fact that they are now prepared by expert outside journalists, writing from the Conservative standpoint'.†

In an almost self-conscious reaction to the excesses of the Coalition period, the Civil Service reasserted both its established status, against the hybrid growths created by Lloyd George after 1916, such as the 'Garden Suburb', and the canons of public service morality which, like Treasury control, had been temporarily eroded by the emergency. Whitehall departments created during the inter-war years a procedure for control of access to information (see below p. 362) and for formal instruction and persuasion of the electorate, as if taking as their text the mordant observation of the insurance companies about public consent to conscription in 1916: 'No system of legal obligation and penalties, even if the individual were aware of them, will induce or compel the general population to take steps which from their point of view are difficult and complicated, and the importance of which they cannot realise.'[63]

In an apparently anodyne way, each Ministry developed its own information service, and sought access openly to the press and to radio

*As Hoare shrewdly observed, Labour Party propaganda was often far better sustained, despite its organisational inadequacy 'because they can rely on the continued activity of trade union workers to act as permanent agents in factories up and down the country' (Templewood VI 3).

†In the 1930s the Conservatives published a whole range of periodicals: *Notes for Speakers, The Elector, The Popular View, Gleanings and Memoranda* and *Home and Empire*. Nevertheless, they still fell short of perfection: the Mansell Committee in 1937 criticised the Publicity Department's work, especially its old-fashioned attitude to films, a view confirmed by the Butler-Topping Committee in 1941 and Topping's Organisation Review in 1944.

broadcasting. As Thomas Jones told the Institute of Public Administration in 1936:

Governments dispense information and advice and assistance, and in turn
they themselves seek information and advice and assistance. Governments
actively supply information by letter and leaflet to individual enquirers; by
communications to organisations for the use of their central office, their
branches or their individual members; by books and pamphlets; by articles
in the press sometimes signed by a Minister, sometimes inspired and anonymous; by broadcasts; by cinema films. Work of this type is increasingly in
the hands of Public Relations or Press Officers of the various Ministries.
Even Downing Street has now a trained journalist, a full-time officer, who
maintains daily contact with the Press and does the work which used to fall
to one of the Private Secretaries. In addition there are more systematic
bodies whose business is not only to carry on directed or free research but
to advise the public.[64]

But at the same time Whitehall also developed the doctrine that all
this work, being in the national interest, was politically and ideologically
neutral. Rebutting his offer of public relations assistance, Wilfred
Eady, Secretary of the UAB, wrote to Tom Jones in 1934:

Handling the Press is one of the things that in these days every civil servant
thinks he can do perfectly, though by handling the Press he has not in mind
the kind of subtleties to which in the past *you* have reverted [a sardonic
reference to Jones' work for Lloyd George, particularly during the Irish
Treaty negotiations in 1921].[65]

Eady set out the doctrine with ponderous clarity, two years later:

In the extension of public relations work in Government Departments
there is a risk of these Departments being drawn into activities of a purely
propagandist character. That is they might become (and be known to have
become) publishers of purely tendentious information. Such a development
would endanger the character and reputation of these Departments for
impartiality. In proportion as public opinion proved susceptible to the dope
of government propaganda it would lose those characteristics which are
most to be desired. With the Fascist, Nazi and Soviet examples abroad,
one is justified in looking askance at any proposal which might have the
effect of intensifying the grip of the state on the intellectual and spiritual
life of the people.
[But] under present day conditions when administration touches individual
and community life at so many points, administrative and legislative responsiveness to public opinion is of fundamental importance; and it can scarcely
be regarded as less desirable that public opinion should be fertilised by the

most intimate possible contact with all the facts. [Hence] the policy of preserving the purity, etc., of Government Departments by the maintenance
of a monastic isolation becomes untenable.

For many years this has been recognised in practice. Today no important
piece of economic or social legislation is introduced into parliament or
embodied in regulations with the force of law, without first having been the
subject of consultation – and perhaps negotiations – between the departments
and the organised interests concerned. . . .

The problem thus becomes how to consolidate the gains and at the same
time reduce or eliminate the risks. The temptations to propaganda which
are inherent in newspaper work can, I believe, be corrected by active cooperation with those who lead opinion in the leisure and educational institutions of this country. The variety of outlook and the sensitiveness of these
leaders to any infringement of their intellectual freedom would, I assert, be
a considerable deterrent to propaganda. These wider contacts would also
provide the departments with a more sensitive index of public opinion.[66]

Quite apart from the derogation of ministerial responsibility to the
electorate through the parliamentary medium that this implied, it was
manifestly absurd to declare that such public relations work could be
value-free, as if the civil servants involved existed in a vacuum. The
process undoubtedly was necessary to the furtherance of modern
government; but the pretence of non-political activity could last only so
long as the party propaganda machines themselves and the institutions
accepted it. By the early 1940s, with an election in sight, on highly contentious issues of social reform, neither was prepared to do so any longer.

It is possible that the employers' institutions were the first to realise
that if they could capture the allegiance of the government's newly
extended publicity apparatus, then they could more effectively than
ever before cloak sectional interest behind the appearance of official
neutrality. Sir Joseph Ball, head of the Press Section in 10 Downing
Street (and another graduate of the Intelligence Service) reported to
Baldwin in 1935 that funds for the forthcoming election would be freely
available from industry – but for a National Publicity Bureau, in the
service of the National Government, rather than for Conservative
Central Office.[67] Weir had, of course, urged the formation of a National
Party in the preceding year (see above p. 221); and by this time the
BEC had carefully distanced itself from its former fund-raising operations in support of the Lloyd George manœuvres.[68] But it was the
setting up of a huge government propaganda apparatus in wartime, and
the advent of Labour to a share of power in 1940, which finally precipitated party rivalry for control of the means of manipulation.

Inhibited by the devotion of individual ministers to the organisations

357

each had built-up in the preceding twenty years, Neville Chamberlain's government attempted in 1939 to duplicate the aims of the 1918 Ministry of Information without at first creating a central propaganda department.* When they did, the Ministry of Information proved for a time slipshod, hampered by lack of continuity and the fact that press censorship remained with the Home Office. Sir John Reith was given no clear brief when appointed Minister of Information in January 1940. Indeed, in spite of Chamberlain's former reliance on Ball and the Conservative publicity machinery, the Prime Minister seemed to have no clear concept of the role of a state rather than a party organisation in raising national morale: his conversations with Reith reveal a curious reluctance to divert resources from one to the other.[69] In contrast, Churchill at the Admiralty revelled in publicity, as though he was once more in charge of the *British Gazette*, feeding semi-secret titbits to the press and often painting 'a rosy picture that had no connexion with reality', to the horror of the Director of Naval Intelligence.[70]

But the Ministry of Information, finally endowed with what Sir Stafford Cripps called 'unlimited funds', in 1941, and its subsequent vast and pertinacious inquiries into opinion, provided at last the official mechanism for assessing public opinion towards which government had groped since 1916; and if some of its productions, especially the early films,[71] seem jejune, they did touch on the unresolved question of 1914–18 – for whose country and for whose future were the people to fight? On 18 June 1940, the day after the fall of France, the Director-General raised the question whether the Coalition Government should there and then make its promises about social reform after the war. Backed by his colleagues, the 'political warfare section' of the Foreign Office, and Attlee himself, this proposal led on towards the establishment of the War Aims Committee in August 1940, 'the first of an unbroken relay of committees, each of which handed on the baton of reconstruction to the next, all the way through to the last meeting of the Reconstruction Committee in May 1945'.[72]

In spite of the appearance of all-party government, the Ministry of Information soon became an ideological battle-ground. It was all right perhaps for Henry Watt to make the film *Squadron 992*, conscious of

*The earliest plans, dating from 1935, envisaged a single government service to control the supply of information, distribution of news and censorship. Against the opposition of the Service Ministers, Foreign Office and Home Office, Hankey and Fisher argued that World War I had proved the uselessness of divided control, with five departments vying against Beaverbrook's Ministry of Information (Hoare XI 4: memorandum by A. P. Waterfield, 8 October 1939; also Hankey 7/9). Nevertheless, in 1939, the Services refused to be bound by such limits and the Cabinet gave way.

the need 'to make films to win the war, to make the ordinary people strong and proud in themselves';[73] but not for Michael Powell to make a 1942 film of the life of 'Colonel Blimp' with the intention of showing that modern warfare could not be conducted by an obsolete élite, hidebound by class prejudice. Churchill told Brendan Bracken, by then Minister of Information, 'I am not prepared to allow propaganda detrimental to the morale of the Army, and I am sure the Cabinet will take all necessary action.'[74] The bitter message was toned down; but such productions, surveyed uneasily by Special Branch, may have encouraged the beginning, not of outright political opposition, but of personal dissidence and widespread withdrawal of allegiance from the established order.

Access to the medium of information became a matter of suspicion as early as June 1940 when Churchill's overwhelming command of BBC audience ratings was suddenly challenged by a series of Sunday evening talks by J. B. Priestley called 'Postscript'.[75] 'As Priestley got into his stride, he introduced into his vignettes of wartime life a new and idealistic theme: the idea that there could be no going back to the social conditions of the 1930s.'[76] At once the Tories complained: David Margesson, the Government Chief Whip, told the BBC that the talks were 'Leftish'. A much more important battle developed over the future of the Ministry of Political Warfare, with its brief to stimulate resistance in Nazi-occupied Europe. After an epic Whitehall battle, the prize went to Dalton; Attlee having argued with great persistence that this was a task best accomplished 'from the Left'.[77]

What in modern terms ought to be called the struggle to establish future hegemony, by outlining the values and programmes of peacetime before the post-war Election decided party balances, replaced the banned struggle between the parties in Coalition. Instead, they sought to use the 'neutral' state apparatus to instil their own ideological preconceptions into the public mind. During 1941–2, radical populists insisted on their right to set out different interpretations of political questions, even on BBC programmes like the 'Brains Trust'; and Conservatives (by no means all of them diehards) countered the trend as best they could, sensing already that it would be hard for the party to rival Labour's popularity in the next election.[78] Best-known is the case of the Ministry of Information's handling of the Beveridge Report: Bracken at first refused all official facilities, deciding only at the last moment to give it full publicity, in answer, perhaps, to Goebbels' promises of a new European order. But the long battle of ABCA (the Army Bureau of Current Affairs) against War Office directives limiting the subjects suitable for troops to discuss, illustrates most clearly the clash between government's and the radicals' approach to war aims, against the same need as in 1914–18 to retain the allegiance and maintain the fighting capacity of a wholly conscript army.

Even civilian morale and industrial harmony scarcely produced such problems for the Coalition Government as the question of the conscript soldier's freedom of thought. Between the rights of the 'citizen soldier', advocated by veterans of the Spanish Civil War like Tom Wintringham, and the traditional hierarchical view of the soldier's obligation propounded by the War Office, there emerged a hybrid portrait of a warrior serving in a sort of New Model Army, defending British ideals, and, by implication, the British system against Fascism.*

But what should this soldier be taught: and what should he be encouraged to discuss? Only at the very end of the First World War had the War Office begun to extend the bounds of army education to include some mention of national war aims; and the scope had not increased greatly in the inter-war years, despite the formation of the Army Education Corps. Faced with the ambiguities of the 'phoney war', and well-documented evidence of dissatisfaction and boredom in 1939–40, the War Office acted on the recommendations of the Hayning Report in May 1940. But Army education promptly became a double-edged weapon, for expansion of the Education Corps brought in large numbers of radical teachers who insisted on opening up troop discussions to include criticism of the nature of the society which had engendered war. Deeply anxious about where this activity would lead, even given its capacity to monitor instruction and censor letters home, the War Office hesitated between strict control and the recommendations of General Willand, the Director-General of Welfare, in June 1941, to set up the Army Bureau of Current Affairs (ABCA).[79]

The mere existence of ABCA exacerbated the political tensions between those who argued that morale and fighting capacity depended on unthinking obedience, and those who demanded conscious dedication and intelligent consent in the struggle against Fascism.†

All through the war, the War Office tried repeatedly to censor or restrict ABCA's work, and in particular its attempt to instil in soldiers the rudiments of political analysis. In the summer of 1943 Churchill

---

*The War Office introductory pamphlet made a comparison with the New Model Army 'who know what they fight for and love what they know', (though not with its sequel, the Putney Debates and the mutiny at Burford Church!)

†The introductory pamphlet for officers gave instructions on how to conduct ABCA discussions and declared roundly that morale was more important than discipline – 'it can even be asked whether really effective discipline can exist without morale.'

even considered closing down the Bureau. Labour Cabinet Ministers seem to have opposed open political discussion, but they did argue that the war must be justified to the troops if it was worth winning at all. Hence the skirmishing over the Army Council's right to censor ABCA material concerning Russia and, above all, the ABCA summary of the Beveridge Report in December 1942. In spite of the fact that the liberals were usually in a minority, the 'Winter Scheme' of 1942–3, which included discussions on citizenship and the British way of life, was made permanent; and the scope of what was permissible widened constantly, leading in due course to remarkable manifestations of freethinking, such as the Cairo 'parliament', and the debate on what was virtually a motion of no-confidence in the government, among troops of the Rhine Army in January 1945.

In the end, convinced by opinion-testing that the majority of the troops enjoyed ABCA groups, the Government permitted popular discussion, even at the price of political polarisation. There was probably no alternative. The Conservatives' own party reorganisation committee tardily recommended in 1944 an appeal to youth and future reform if the party was to win the election. Topping at least was aware of the swing towards radicalism, the extent of enthusiasm for the 'Russian experiment', and popular determination not to be plunged back into the misery of the 1930s.[80]

It is unlikely that, in their discussions, ABCA groups did more than cover traditional Labour Party subjects; the exigencies of war and inevitable troop movements prevented any continuity for a group.[81] Radicalisation probably progressed no faster than among the civilian population, whose desires were summed up by the Postal Censor in January 1941, in his report on lower-middle and working-class assumptions about the future ('they are looking forward confidently to a post-war levelling of class distinction and a redistribution of wealth'[82]). Government wisely let the War Office carry the unpopularity of censorship, with the minimum of actual intervention. What was awakened, and sharpened by memory of the 1930s, was overwhelming support for moderate reform, to which the Labour Party appeared natural heir. In many constituencies in the post-war election, 90 per cent of the Service vote was cast for Labour, and the promises of *Labour's Immediate Programme*. This was sufficient to obliterate that dangerous radicalism noted by Mass Observation in 1940, and the deep scepticism about propaganda newsreels and 'participation groups', which in other circumstances might have led, as it did in Cromwell's New Model Army, to the Putney Debates.

ABCA did not 'turn the world upside down', and may indeed have contributed to the illusion of sloughing off the past in 1945. The state still retained its powers of manipulation, censorship and supply of information, virtually unimpaired by the success of radical teachers in getting soldiers in the desert to discuss the future of capitalism. William Morris's warning to Fabian Socialists on the vast cunning and residual power of 'the system' held good.

Government had succeeded in vitiating public discussion on a number of notable occasions in the previous thirty years, either by direct coercion (the suppression of *Forward* in 1916, of news about the Liverpool police strike in 1919, of the Archbishop of Canterbury's broadcast during the General Strike)[83] or personal interference (Chamberlain with the BBC's reporting of Eden's resignation,[84] and Halifax's suppression of a projected correspondence in *The Times*, unwelcome to the government, at the time of Munich.[85]) Often this had been achieved with the press's own consent, as in the voluntary self-censorship employed by the Newspaper Proprietors' Association during the Abdication crisis in 1936.

Editorial restraint about politically embarrassing subjects was not much impaired by journalists' free-ranging search for news in wartime:* the *Daily Mirror*'s 'War to win the war' campaign remains the only significant exception during the critical stage before 1943, and the D-notices scheme was observed almost without question in wartime and down to 1950. In contrast with the view propounded by newspapers themselves, criticism of the government and the political order lagged behind public opinion, thus confirming the deprecatory estimate of its capacity to initiate change by the *Mirror*'s own gifted editor, Hugh Cudlipp.[86] The real onslaught came from free-ranging intellectuals, attacking, in a private capacity, pre-war leaders and the political misdeeds of the 1930s.[87]

In the nature of things, access to official archives is the least productive method of tracing the lineaments of government control of information, although the inefficiency or generosity of early 'weeders' has in the past left a number of fruitful pointers.[88] Yet in theory it should provide one of the best measures of how opinion was managed. The only coherent case, that of access to information about the process of

---

*Among many cases, it is worth mentioning that the press never raised the awkward question of the miners' wage settlement in October 1939 (above, p. 265), nor questioned the bland dissimulation put out by Ministers to disguise their capitulation to NUM strength.

government and Cabinet and Ministerial archives, does allow a limited analysis of what governments wished to reveal about themselves, and the ways they used 'conventions' to modify original 'constitutional' assumptions in order to meet changing circumstances.[89]

Before 1914, Cabinet secrecy was absolute (though at this stage it did not extend to the categories of advice given by civil servants to Ministers, nor to Ministers' proceedings in Cabinet committees), and the onus of restraint fell on the Crown, which was regarded, in constitutional terms, as 'concerned with the good repute of public life, and with the long and impartial view of ministerial authority, as distinct from party and personal views'.[90] During the 1914–18 war, the modern system of Cabinet papers and minuting (showing the part taken by individual Ministers) was instituted, vastly increasing the quantity and accuracy of records available about central government.[91] At the same time, the Sovereign's control over disclosure fell into desuetude and was replaced by the authority of the Prime Minister, assisted by the Cabinet Secretary. But the formal obligations on Ministers, which had in most cases been honoured before 1914, were rapidly discredited by a flood of revelations, as Generals and Ministers sought to capitalise on their knowledge of the inner history of the war, in what Sir Rupert Howarth called 'much unauthorised and mischievous publication by persons of great eminence'.[92]

To cope with this unwelcome development, the Cabinet Office evolved a convention that war memoirs represented a 'dying class' of revelation, and that the real ban should start in 1919 – a threshold that was, with few exceptions, accepted by Ministers and (for lack of access to *any* Cabinet records) by historians down to 1934. But then, after a mass of leaks about the climactic debates of the Labour Cabinet in August 1931, George Lansbury's son was prosecuted and convicted under the Official Secrets Act. A sharp tightening up of existing procedures followed,[93] as Hankey, the Cabinet Secretary, and his staff set out to bring Ministers into line with the restricted position of civil servants.[94] Meanwhile, a whole new range of 'conventions' was evolved, most of which remained binding until the celebrated court case of the Crossman Diaries in 1975.

The details do not matter here: but Ministers' freedom to retain Cabinet papers or use them in their memoirs was substantially restricted,[95] and the scope of secrecy was extended to civil servants' transactions with Ministers. Cabinet Office authority steadily increased, despite a vague pledge by Churchill (as an historian, an interested party) to liberalise after the Second World War. Three notable wartime cases indicated that government would not allow historians to revive recent controversies over appeasement and rearmament.[96] By 1945, something like a doctrine of the 'public interest' in secrecy had emerged; and until the introduction of the Fifty-year Rule in 1958, historians and political scientists were left without any form of documentary evidence for studying government since the formation of the modern Cabinet system in 1916, apart from individual memoirs and the carefully vetted official histories of certain (chiefly wartime) topics.

Headed by Hugh Dalton, Ministers themselves began to challenge the conventions in the early 1960s. But even then their emphasis was on the entertaining, often malicious, delineation of personality, rather than critical analysis of the political system, the documentary basis for which had remained the responsibility of officials writing, for the sole use of other civil servants, studies of particular departments and procedures whose prototype had been Hankey's 1919 'War Book' – an activity that suffered from many of the genetic disadvantages of incest.

Quite apart from the danger of perpetuating inefficiency or complacency, this growth in the apparatus of secrecy, and the consequent lack of hard fact, encouraged that trivial, personalised view of political activity, which since the 1930s has been the bane of British journalism, and which compares unfavourably with the level of press and public comment about government in almost every other European country. It prevented the induction of MPs as future Ministers into the real functions of high office, thus weakening their capacity *vis-à-vis* the Civil Service, and leaving them, while in opposition, more than ever dependent on inadequate Party research departments. Moreover, the conventions themselves allowed no scope for debate about the nature and value of secrecy itself, or the question as to whether any body of law sustained these modifications of the old formalities.*

Cabinet secrecy is a microcosm of the political values developed in the inter-war years, revealing one part of the process by which the dignified version of the system was maintained before the public eye. It was essential to the system of corporate bias, the diminution of party effectiveness and the elevation of the state apparatus. Without Cabinet secrecy, and the consequent facility for abolishing the custom of presenting defence estimates in detailed form, for example, concealment from Parliament of the later development of the atomic bomb, during the Attlee government in 1946–7, would have been impossible;[97] its existence and the supine behaviour of a generation of House of Com-

---

*The later extension of these conventions, their high tide in the 1950s, and the Crossman case, are considered in Chapter 14.

mons' Select Committees made it equally impossible to mount any wide examination of the government machine from *outside* Whitehall, such as Haldane had attempted in 1918.

Yet if the consequences were so serious, why did so little complaint come from those institutions, whose function it was to educate the public and comment on the principles of political activity? How is one to account for the inadequacy of the press or radio, and the decay of ancient voices of authority such as the churches, when confronted with government power in all its bureaucratic and legal forms?

The churches, it is true, attempted in the early 1930s to reassert their right to pronounce on deep moral and political issues, notably on the evils of unemployment, armaments and bombing. The disarmament resolution passed by the Convocation of Canterbury in January 1932 showed that the Church of England had abandoned much of the fervid nationalism and defence of official strategy that had offended many of its members in the trenches in World War One. The day before the Disarmament Conference opened in 1933, Archbishop Lang preached in the Cathedral at Geneva, and spoke out firmly against Nazi militarism. Very many Quakers associated themselves with the League of Nations Union and pacifist groups, and Methodists and Presbyterians joined Anglicans in an anti-war deputation to MacDonald in October 1932. But after 1935, as if in response to the change in popular mood, the churches grew silent, and only a handful of clerics, notably Bishop Bell of Chichester, continued after the war had begun to protest against the horrors of strategic bombing; while the vigorous dissent of the Peace Pledge Union and the Peace Army, led by Dick Sheppard, turned into sectarian by-ways, losing the mass support the anti-war movement had once attracted.

On social conditions, the Anglican Church seems to have taken its tone from its members, rather than giving a lead. The Church Assembly took issue with government over the inadequate financing of the Special Areas scheme in 1936; but only Archbishop Temple attacked the miseries of the dole in the language of the radicals, castigating the government so severely that Chamberlain issued a public reproof.* Power to affect government policy – as the temperance movement had still been able to do before 1914, or the nonconformist churches had done over the Balfour Education Act of 1902 – had evaporated. The

*At the Albert Hall, in November 1936, Temple called for 'a revolt against malnutrition, bad housing, and the economic system which tolerates the degradation of unemployment. Give no rest to your conscience or to the consciences of your neighbours. Constitute yourselves a public nuisance until these and other far greater nuisances are remedied.'

'visible colleges', the BMA and the Law Society, retained of course their negative power to lobby government, but only in the relatively unorganised scientific profession can there be found evidence of a politically hostile current of opinion, among scientists appalled either at the destructive power of modern weapons or the technical inefficiencies of British industry and management.[98]

Press, cinema and radio generally failed to crack the carapace of public acquiescence in attitudes inculcated by official propaganda. The BBC's anodyne role had been instilled at its very inception, and Reith, its first Director-General, while not avoiding the charge of indoctrination, probably did no more than perpetuate conformity to a set of values derived from the prosperous middle-class culture of the inter-war years.* Conscious of its enormous power in education – particularly adult education – the BBC showed itself anxious to probe the dismal conditions of the depressed areas; yet its comprehensive series of talks on the problems of unemployment, staged in the first six months of 1934, did so in a dense but curiously superficial way: the seven chosen experts tended to emphasise the national nature of the economic struggle and no one described the actual conditions of the unemployed.†

The factual basis of the BBC's talks was impeccable: yet, inevitably, in their selection and presentation of facts, and their use of imagery, speakers alienated themselves (as Mass Observation often noticed) from the 'man in the street'. Controversy – from which the ban was only lifted in 1928 – remained too often artificial where the 'condition of England' argument was concerned, and even when the battle for public hearing opened up between conservatives and radicals in the Second World War, Reith and his colleagues continued to act as standard-bearers of the higher interests of the nation, serving the long-term interests of the state, even if not of particular parties or governments.

The byzantine mentality of the Corporation reinforced Reith's own concept of balance, making it almost impossible for minority opinion to gain broadcasting time. Political discussions produced invitations to Conservative, Labour and Liberal speakers, not to representatives of the CPGB or BUF. Because the marginalised Left and Right had no access to the air, to proclaim Mosley's Manifesto or the United Front,

---

*To Beatrice Webb's complaint that the BBC tended to standardise its audiences and reinforce the values of liberal capitalism, Reith replied that it expressed British mentality at its best. (Beatrice Webb, *Diaries*, vol. 2, p. 297.) In defence of a palpably middle-class code of values, Harold Nicolson was refused permission even to refer to Joyce's *Ulysses*. (H. Nicolson, ed. N, Nicolson, *Diaries*, Collins, 1966–8, Vol. 2, p. 99.)

†William Fervis was asked to do this, but the BBC censored his script, and he refused to give the talk unless the cuts were restored. (C. Day Lewis, ed., *The Mind in Chains: Socialism and the cultural revolution*, (Muller, 1937), p. 147.)

'politics' remained synonymous with the nineteenth-century parliamentary constitution; and during the Abdication crisis, all references to the deeper issues of the King's pro-German sympathies and his desire to revive the political powers of the Crown were carefully excised.

Changes in the economics of newspapers and the structure of their ownership contributed to a similar decline in the range and presentation of dissenting viewpoints, one clear instance being the timid attitude towards Nazi Germany reflected, almost universally, by the 'quality' papers.[99] In so far as the main dailies took up positions in the 1930s, they tended towards regular support of the main political parties, abandoning the earlier, freebooting relationship with government characteristic of Lords Northcliffe, Rothermere and Beaverbrook. Meanwhile the market forces which had killed off the radical press in the later nineteenth century, continued to confine left- or extreme right-wing opinion to dailies with minute circulation, and to emasculate or trivialise criticism of the existing order. The clash of political opinion took place elsewhere, among periodicals or book publishers, and it is significant that when Conservative Central Office discussed extension of their propaganda in the thirties, they concentrated on founding a new right-wing weekly (to counter the *New Statesman*) and on the formation of a group of young writers to challenge Victor Gollancz's Left Book Club; this emerged, as the Right Book Club, in 1936.[100]

It was probably already anachronistic for Beaverbrook to tell H. A. Gwynne, editor of the *Morning Post*, in 1925: 'You have the authority and he [Churchill, Chancellor of the Exchequer] *must* listen because of your enormous power over the central body of Conservative opinion.'[101] In the decade of unrestrained competition between national dailies which followed, Fleet Street's influence over Downing Street, inherited from the Lloyd George period, was largely dissipated. In 1932, Chamberlain could thank Beaverbrook for his assistance with the conversion of $5\frac{1}{2}$ per cent War Loan, cordially but without any compromise.[102] Press organisation and the extremely high capital sums involved were beginning to create a pattern of mass communication conforming much more closely than in the early part of the century to the balance of forces in society, contriving consensus and restricting choice, and excluding from public notice minority groups like farmworkers, whose plight failed either to attract trade union assistance in the inter-war years, or the sort of emotional response from reporters bestowed on the industrial depressed areas.[103]

The evidence does not suggest that dissent was deliberately ignored, but that variety and divergence existed – and can exist – only within limits set by the serried inconsistencies of dominant interests – in other words, the appearance of greater plurality than actually exists, which only the theory of hegemony can fully explain.[104] In turn, in so far as it portrayed the condition of Britain rather than contemporary America, the cinema tended to reinforce existing imperial and political codes,[105] and in wartime took on the propagandist role which, in endless revivals of the 1939–45 experience, it has sustained to the present day.

By comparison with the late nineteenth century, Britain was becoming a less violent, more law-abiding society,[106] and a decisive increase was taking place in the number of those who had a property stake in the social order. The number of those with disposable wealth (taken at the level of the assets bequeathed when they died) increased; house-ownership extended into wholly new areas as, for the first time, the upper working class became potential buyers, aided by the reduced interest rates of the 1930s, and the willingness of building societies to lend to lower social groups.[107] The new *employed* middle class and white-collar workers now aspired to buy the two million houses built by private firms for sale in the 1930s, in the process becoming ratepayers and acquiring, with the furniture and electrical goods and mass production cars, the outlook of propertied men and women.

This changing social and economic context created an almost impenetrable attitude compounded of complacency and self-sufficiency which, more than almost any other factor, reinforced the characteristic distinctions of the 1930s between educated and ill-educated, those in work and the unemployed, between prosperous and depressed areas, and between aspirants to higher status and those whose 'poverty of desire' led automatically into the trap diagnosed in the 1950s by John Newsom as

A form of socialisation that comes to terms with the facts of poverty early on, by blunting individual feeling and aspiration, and turning children away from their parents towards the support of their peer groups, [which] may in fact act as a sadly realistic preparation for the hard life to come.

In such circumstances, it is hardly surprising that Conservative governments' effective rallying cries were not those of 1914 – patriotism or loyalty – so much as the bogymen of financial insecurity: inflation and devaluation in the 1931 election campaign, Bolshevism (1919, 1924, 1927, 1939) and the threat of air bombardment.

Behind the formal doctrine, with its bland projection of the virtues of party and parliamentary politics and its tacit avoidance of discussion about the influence of pressure groups and institutions, lay the real and important process of opinion-testing and assimilation, accompanied by political education, and propaganda designed to distinguish, among other things, between legitimate and deviant forms of political protest and participation. It can, of course, be argued that this diagnosis is old-fashioned conspiracy theory: a version of history open to the objection that

The public is seen as an atomised mass, passive receptacles of messages originating from a monolithic and powerful source. In the left-wing political version of this model, the source is controlled by and represents the interests of the ruling class. . . . In some right-wing versions, the media are also seen as powerful, but their influence is in the direction of lowering cultural standards and propagating values of permissiveness.[108]

Yet every case examined reveals a constant element. From the days of Lloyd George, continually improved agencies transmitted to central government an ever-widening range of information about public opinion. At the same time, a series of filters was evolved to reduce this torrent to a form manageable by, and palatable to, Ministers, thus enhancing the residual power of civil servants and the Cabinet Office, and tempering or diminishing the flow of party opinion in the majority of policy decisions. The tightening of public secrecy, and security over Ministers' own freedom to reveal, must be seen as complementary to the creation, from an originally corrupt series of essays in opinion manipulation, of a formal system of opinion management.

Awareness of the need to take public opinion into consideration did not lead politicians and civil servants on to acceptance of popular democracy, but rather the reverse, as the political élite superimposed on the traditional cycle of general elections and party warfare something which can be called *continuous contract*. Continuous contract means, simply, the fine measurement of opinion and its careful management by propaganda, together with the creation of a degree of mystification*

*I have in mind here not so much the formalities and fictions surrounding modern government, the orotund images of 'government objectives', 'national interest', etc., or the due processes by which citizens, individually or collectively, must approach government if they are to be heard, which are common to all modern societies, but their acceptance by the public. To take the case of the hunger marchers: government, as the CPGB saw very clearly, could not concede their demands for direct represent-ation, except at the risk of overwhelming the party electoral system. In February 1934 MacDonald told representatives of the NUWM that they would not be received in Downing Street: 'This deputation can do no service to the unemployed. The Com-munist purpose of these marches is well-known. The Government is responsible for a Bill which, when in operation, will facilitate the more satisfactory treatment of the whole question of unemployment, and that Bill is now receiving consideration in the House of Commons *whose knowledge and experience enable it to discuss the best way to achieve the object of Government.*' [my italics] What is curious, given the conditions

about the political process, in the interests of harmonious government. What governments considered to be their worst failures were precisely those where they got their estimates wrong, in highly contentious fields such as demobilisation after 1918, immigration, unemployment benefit, or rearmament. These taught them that conformity could not be enforced. Authority existed only where it rested on consent: as Steel-Maitland warned of OMS recruiting before the General Strike, 'Let it be remembered that it would be disastrous to attempt it and fail.'[109] Wisdom about the tolerance of the public that governments claimed to represent prevented opinion management from slipping back into manipulation, like precious metal transmuted downwards into dross; and this helps to explain why it survived unchecked into the brief golden age after 1945.

---

of the depressed areas in the thirties, is that such dicta were not widely repudiated. Bagehot's theory of deference has to be modified to fit twentieth-century circumstances: only a theory of submission to the dominant political ethic, encouraged by opinion management and institutional collaboration, suffices.

13 CORPORATE BIAS

The year 1945 marked the point at which the electorate gave the Labour Party, for the first time, an overall parliamentary majority, validating in public the claim to be the natural alternative to the Conservatives which had already been substantiated in 1940. So began a period of twenty years when nearly all the deep objectives of the state – and of most governments since the mid-1920s – in economic planning, social welfare, harmony and the avoidance of crisis seemed to have been achieved. And, in a more artificial sense, it is the effective moment where access to primary sources in government archives ceases.*

An attempt should therefore be made to answer the questions asked in the Introduction, before going on to an historically more speculative period. The course of political relationships since 1911 between government and industrial organisations – the central issue in a modern industrial society – shows that the long secular change which followed the crisis of the nineteenth-century political system ended in establishment of a new order, even though remnants of the old remained, to confuse the superficial observer. Like most previous systems in Britain, what was created was never precise, nor contractual in the sense ascribed by Maine or Dicey to the law of the constitution, but existed as a code among those groups admitted to the process of government – a sort of *outillage mental* acquired by the leaders of institutions as part of their political apprenticeship, or a passport into the state domain.

During the crisis of political values and the state itself which afflicted all industrial nations in Europe in the 1900s and 1910s, and culminated in the manpower and production crises of the First World War, British governments stimulated institutional growth among bodies representing business and labour interests, in order to maintain public consent.

---

*Under the thirty-year rule, access rolls forward each year, so that at the time of writing the archives for 1947 had become available. But any substantive comment on the Labour Government's performance, 1945–51, must wait for some years to come.

Afterwards, these institutions continued to grow, acquiring new representative functions on behalf of their members, among employers and trade unions, and as intermediaries of central government. In spite of the failure of the National Industrial Conference in 1919, and of subsequent attempts to create a formal 'parliament of industry' or to impose a corporative system, the political relationship between increasingly powerful and legitimate interests developed into a complicated ritual, where earlier, simplistic ideas about collective bargaining and class representation were modified under the influence of the search for public consent by party governments, and the 'higher interests' of the nation-state.

Under the double stimulus of government's needs and the changing economic and social conditions of their membership, what had once been interest groups outside the formal constitution – what Hobbes called 'lesser Common-wealths in the bowels of a greater, like worms in the entrayles of a naturale man'[1] – became governing institutions, existing thereafter as estates of the realm, committed to cooperation with the state, even if they retained the customary habit of opposition to specific party governments. As a necessary condition of their transformation, other institutions which had once shared these functions, voluntary societies, churches, the press and to some extent parties themselves, declined in political significance.

Yet the governing institutions failed to become wholly representative of their various constituencies, remaining exposed to popular discontent and members' rights of recall. For the purpose of central government they could not be relied on as if they had been estates in the classic corporatist model of the state, largely because they did not supersede the political parties or, indeed, come to resemble them. They did not, for example, develop ideologies, claiming only to represent the sum of members' individual wills. Hence the slow, tentative, often secretive patterns chronicled above, informal, flexible and highly sensitive to changes in the balance of power.

Before attempting to generalise, therefore, it is necessary to emphasise again the tentative, even fragile character of the system. Physical growth of an institution does not by any means result in an increase in its political power. Progress towards institutional collaboration, and the avoidance of economic competition and class conflict is a tendency, not an irreversible trend.[2] Schematically, the process may be described as a series of interactions of declining importance: first, the triangular cooperation between government and governing institutions (in this case employers and trade unions); secondly, between these institutions and their constituents (TUC and unions, BEC or FBI and federations of particular industries); thirdly, between individual members (federations and firms, unions and branch officials or shop stewards).

In a different, but intersecting plane lie the relationships between government and party, government and state bureaucracy (of which local government is an extension); and in yet another those between all three and the public or, in parliamentary terms, the mass electorate. In direct contrast to the rigid linkages laid down – though not necessarily implemented – in the Fascist constitutions of Italy or Portugal, or the totalitarian systems of Hitler's Germany and Stalin's Russia, the British system in the half-century after 1916 depended on a multiple bargaining process at all levels – the first being the most important – even though its aims of social harmony, economic well-being and the avoidance of crisis were not dissimilar.

The phrase 'governing institution' is to be understood as a description of a body which assumes functions devolved on it by government, shares some or all of the assumptions about national interests held by government, and accepts aims similar to those laid down by government; with the fundamental qualification that this form of association is not compulsory, but voluntary to the extent that it takes place within general limits derived, negatively, from the evidence of what the institution's constituent members will or will not accept. Prevailing economic and social circumstances, like the conditions which led to the shop stewards' movement in the First World War, or to the employers' volte-face on state intervention in the late 1920s, rather than theoretical considerations of where collaboration conflicted with their natural or primordial interests, governed the speed with which institutions succumbed to government's desires.

To put it simply, what had been merely interest groups crossed the political threshold and became part of the extended state: a position from which other groups, even if they too held political power, were still excluded. Because recognition by government meant so much, and since classical theory did not allow for it, it follows naturally, that attempts were made, often in a partisan way, to define at law the legitimacy of such an association. Certain governments sought to define the constitutional status of trade unions (1906, 1927), or employers' organisations (cartels and monopoly legislation, or Ministry of Labour's delegated powers, after 1940). These often disruptive attempts to circumscribe governing institutions were, of course, distinct from, and supplementary to, the permanent process of brokerage between them and government which continued virtually unchecked, since both *normally* preferred to legal definition something much closer to the concept of free collective bargaining, as understood between employers and union leaders, albeit on a more complex, national scale.

In order to sustain their new role, the governing institutions acquired administrative trappings; and BEC/FBI and TUC began to resemble each other and also the governments with which they associated. Yet, as their variable performance over fifty years suggests, their role was not governed by the size and density of their bureaucracies; the TUC remained until the 1960s (and perhaps still remains) poor and ill-staffed compared, say, with the TGWU or AUEW, the CBI by comparison with the Engineering Employers' Federation. A theory of bureaucratisation cannot explain more than the *appearance* of certain administrative habits, and the outlook these engendered towards their own constituencies; the institutions' place in relation to the state was dictated almost entirely by the needs of governments and by their own representative function. The weaknesses which came from their lack of power to enforce discipline on their own members was not necessarily to governments' advantage; but their strengths, where they existed, remedied the weaknesses of the state, complementing in time of crisis its ability to persuade or coerce the mass of the population or impose its requirements on the industrial, business or financial communities.

This system is not corporatism, but one where *corporate bias* predominates. The association of governing institutions, committed ultimately to a consensual view of the national interest, reduced sharply and permanently the power of interests and organisations still outside the threshold: and the harmony which was achieved, as a result, enabled governments of the 1930s and 40s to maintain order and consent and to survive the Second World War as no other European state did. Corporate bias can be detected at all levels of political activity,* as pervasive a phenomenon as the oligarchic tendencies which led Michels to elaborate his iron law of oligarchy. It is, of course, inseparable from the decline of party and parliamentary politics and is, necessarily, sustained by continuous opinion management. By 1945 it had replaced, for all *practical* purposes, classical democratic theory as that had been understood in 1911.

But that was not the only change. Corporate bias tended to negate

---

*It can be seen, for example, in the relationships between government departments concerned with trade and agriculture, the National Farmers' Union and the Agricultural Workers', 1930–9, especially where questions of Empire trade, quotas and tariffs were concerned; or, to take a very different case, in the process through which lower deck unofficial political activity in the Royal Navy was transmuted by the creation of 'representative' bodies in the early 1920s.

more obvious manifestations of class conflict, blurring what had been seen in the 1900s as sharp lines of social and economic cleavage. The relatively simple class structure of Edwardian England was replaced by a denser, overlapping and sometimes contradictory set of alignments, often apparently dissociated from economic causes and lacking articulation. In seeking to explain this phenomenon, Ralf Dahrendorf has argued that class conflict over the distribution of authority in society declines in intensity and violence as it shifts from the economic or industrial sphere to the political one, and as institutions bargain over the allocation of tangible rewards.[3] More recently, Anthony Giddens has suggested that the new élites who run the institutions, at different levels in the class structure, should be seen as ruling groups, each imposing its own hegemony, stabilising the system by evolving, out of the old forms of parliamentary activity, an acceptable social-democratic mode to cover the still 'illegitimate' functions of the governing institutions.[4]

Similar insights into the consequences of corporate bias derive from studies of modern Western states in the tradition of Adorno and Horkheimer in the 1960s – at a time when the British system had already begun to decay. Jürgen Habermas and others of the Frankfurt school[5] have pointed to how, especially in Germany and the United States, the lineaments of class struggle became confused in the post-war era of prosperity.

In the planned capitalist state, the dominance of man over man (or of one class over another) has largely given way to the dominance of a few spheres of social formation over others. . . . The gap that ran *between* the great position groups in the early stages of capitalism has shifted, as it were, to within individuals themselves.[6]

Contradictions in the political order were transposed to a broader sphere; and when political equilibrium between power groups had been achieved, 'the state was primarily responsive to group interests, leaving no one group to press for the national interest or general good'.[7]

In such conditions, the state bureaucracy operates in a vacuum, defining the general good by default; and control over public opinion reaches a point at which, 'from the perspective of scientific research, which is making great strides in this area, there are neither factual nor normative limits to manipulation'.[8] Consequently, legitimate rule tends to be maintained, not through traditional free-market economics, nor economic management (the 'neutral' state asserting a sort of collective capitalist will) but through the political system, in which avoidance of

375

crisis is made the highest priority. The class struggle is diffused and transposed, as 'concrete constellations' (rather than parliamentary-democratic parties, which have become merely filtering devices for popular opinion or agencies for government propaganda) bargain over the distribution of social and economic rewards. The state itself becomes enmeshed with the institutions out of which the system is now constituted, its tasks becoming primarily managerial – what Offe calls 'the logic of compensatory plugging of functional holes'.[9]

At the same time, however, the state cannot allow those excluded from political bargaining to become too large or hostile a group, and it develops methods to compensate for politically intolerable consequences, either by paying perpetual Danegeld, or incorporating them as new power groups. The problem occurs if and when marginal groups like the unemployed or immigrants cannot be accommodated; for a return to the politics of class, whether from Right or Left, would be inherently destructive of the compromises already achieved – as it proved to be across Europe in the 1900s. In Britain, at least until the late 1960s, it was solved with remarkable cunning: governing institutions and parties combined to take issue with the excluded, not on the question of the threat to their own role in the composition of the state, but of the threat to the already obsolescent parliamentary system – forcing them, almost by definition, to attack from outside the confines of what the great mass of the electorate still accepted as the legitimate centre of political activity.

Pursuing the argument empirically through half a century of history makes it clear that corporate bias in the British state ensured a uniquely low level of class conflict, compared with the countries of comparable social and economic development in Western Europe. Britain was the one society to survive the collapse of political values in the 1900s, the First World War, and the depression of the 1930s, without lapsing into authoritarian rule like Italy and Germany, or political decay like France.* It is reasonable to assume a relationship between internal political harmony and national survival, if only to explain the absence in the 1930s of effective revolutionary discontent, and in the 1940s of opposition to the rigours of war: Dunkirk, after all, was the symbol of national reconciliation, not its cause.

In the circumstances after the great European 'civil war' of 1914–18, corporate bias offered the only practical alternative to fascism or totali-

---

*Hence its apparent value as a model in the rebuilding of Europe in the 1950s: a model based, however, on nineteenth-century premises about classical democracy, rather than an understanding of what corporate bias involved.

tarianism and, given the possibly ephemeral nature of the war settlement of 1945, may perhaps still do so. But if the argument is prolonged, it leads to the conclusion that while a balance sheet taken in 1945 would have shown on the credit side the accomplishment of a 'British Revolution' in economic and social life (for which the parliamentary democratic system received the credit), the debit should have been the admission that there still existed an innate conservatism, almost unchanged since the greater crisis of 1915–22.* Backward-looking in its aims, gradual in method, revisionistic in theory, the new system accommodated itself to change by moving at the least speed commensurate with the interests of each governing institution, while each vied with the rest to ostracise dissent and manage, or accommodate, mass opinion. Only in this sense did it cope with the stresses imposed on it, as if in response to Marx's own dictum that 'men do not pose questions which they cannot answer.' The price, as C. Wright Mills observed more than a decade ago, was that the countervailing power of the public to control government† diminished grievously – a development which had gone a long way in Britain before 1939.

But if the system failed the individual, or the minority group, lacking the means 'to articulate the inarticulate cry', it is also true to say that it put the state in perpetual pawn: on occasions when institutional compromise broke down, government broke down also. After fifty years in which the state's organisation and functions had been extended on the basis of corporate harmony, withdrawal of consent by any one of the participants necessarily impaired the most vital functions of government, a situation which could not be remedied by the law and all the paraphernalia of coercion, either in imposing conscription on Ireland in 1917, or enforcing the UAB scales in February 1935 – or for that matter industrial relations legislation in 1968 or 1971. Government and institutions had grown up, like Siamese twins, displaying two separate bodies and heads to the world outside but sharing the heart of power.

In summing up the present state of debate among political scientists on the nature of corporatism and its relationship to the modern state, Alan Cawson has written:

*In particular the powerful effect of the past and its long-delayed, haphazard metamorphosis – what Maitland called the 'long troughs and hollows of history' – in areas remote from febrile activity over the distribution of wealth, wages and political power.

†What John C. Calhoun, a defender of the autonomy of the Southern States, called, in 1850: 'a power on the part of the ruled to prevent rulers from abusing their authority, by compelling them to be faithful to their constituents.'

A full understanding of the significance of pressure-group activity and the distribution of power in capitalist society needs to be derived, not on the basis of abstracted empiricist theories of pluralism, nor ideologically based assumptions of class rule, but on an historical and materialist analysis of the changing political structures which correspond to different stages of capitalist development.[10]

The evidence I have given in earlier chapters does, in that sense, permit a certain degree of historical theorising.

First, it is necessary to distinguish corporate bias from theories of the corporate state, as expounded on the Fascist model, in practice most clearly in Italy in the 1920s, and Portugal under Salazar, or by neo-Fascists and quasi-corporatists in Britain and elsewhere.[11] Even if the military verdict of 1944 and the Portuguese revolution of 1974 are not to be taken as final comments on the value of Fascist, as opposed to totalitarian systems, as far as Britain was concerned their schemes were inapplicable, because, as Lloyd George discovered in 1919, the real system, in all its density, remained resistant to their imposition. The aim of a system 'where competition, class conflict, and political disunity were *structurally* rendered impossible'[12] was too alien to the flexible practice of institutional cooperation; and while the governing institutions may have talked of reducing the power of governments of opposite political colour, they desired less and less any modifications in the anatomy of the state to whose power they now had access.

Secondly, corporate bias should be seen as having political substance in its own right, rather than being simply a matter of economic practice, or 'redistributive corporatism' as it is sometimes called. Several recent commentators have related modern corporatism primarily to government control of economic planning, and to centripetal tendencies in the economic thinking of both major parties in Britain.[13] J. T. Winkler writes: 'Corporatism is an economic system in which the state directs and controls predominantly privately-owned business according to four principles: unity, order, nationalism, and success'[14] and he argues that in Britain government is already moving into a directive phase. This is a presentation which, when applied historically, tends to ignore both the political element in economic decision-making and the power of governing institutions strongly evident at least forty years ago.

Other historians have divided between explanations of corporatism as a result of increasing state power in the 1930s,[15] and the alternative of state power diminishing in the face of autonomous growth by large, monopolistic industrial and banking enterprises.[16] The antithesis, like that between corporatist political systems and government economic control, is surely misconceived. It is true, in a limited sense, to argue as Hannah does, that governments since the 1930s have neither encouraged nor discouraged the vast increases in industrial combination in Britain, the predominance of large firms, and, later, of multinational corporations; but this is to forget the supportive, indeed essential, framework of political harmony and employer-union understanding which made possible the mergers and company corporate structures of the inter-war and post-war years.

Hannah concedes that 'an assessment of the impact of the corporate economy which focuses solely on the economic costs and benefits is . . . inevitably incomplete, for corporations exercise a pervasive influence not only on economic but on political and social life also'.[17] But he goes no further than suggesting a purely functional theory of institutional growth: the legitimation of employers' associations and trade unions as a consequence of their economic size, and propensity to collaborate in collectivist planning. A declaration almost of political neutralism, such as 'the relationship is neither one of business pressure groups dictating to government nor of government agencies planning the activities of business',[18] cannot easily be squared with the historical pattern of industrial politics.

Hobsbawm's conception of the dynamic role of the state, and Nigel Harris's analysis of *étatiste* corporatism and the state's attempt to foster collectivism, in so far as they can be attributed to pre-1945 conditions, both err in the other direction by granting governments more power than they ever in practice possessed. Vested with emergency powers and majority popular support, British cabinets still could not achieve all their aims in two world wars without the consent of trade unions and employers, and in peacetime they were forced to abrogate their understanding of the national interest, even in a case as important as the delivery of fighter aircraft, where its implementation would have conflicted with established power relations.

Between 1911 and the present day, central government has undeniably moved from a position of facilitating to one of supporting economic change, and finally to direction – but only with the agreement of the governing institutions, whose formal, representative structures have consistently relieved government of the impossible task of dealing with, and harmonising the clash of wills of, large numbers of heterogeneous interest groups at all levels of political life. Indeed, from the late 1920s until about 1965, the trend was for governments to try to ensure public compliance in the process rather than to seek to drum up – as they could easily have done – popular protest against 'blackmail' by the institutions. Because the system of government was created as the sum of separate forces, each motivated by its component parts, operating in growing equilibrium within the matrix of the state itself, the question whether change occurred as a result of state neutrality or dynamism should be rephrased. It occurred in the form described here because the existing pluralist system no longer worked, and because the divergent interests could no longer be harmonised without bringing the more powerfully based ones into the orbit of government.

Thirdly, corporate bias, as it is presented here, is not an ideology, even when it encompasses the nature of the state. Too great variety of behaviour patterns existed, and the system of the 1940s was still too unstable, to allow the title 'corporatism'. Corporate bias which, like the bias of a wood at bowls, is in itself no more than a tendency always to run to one side, must suffice, rather than the typology of aims, unity, order, nationalism, and success, suggested by Winkler when analysing British government in the late 1970s. Admittedly, a great deal of research needs to be done to develop a convincing historical analysis of the underlying patterns of behaviour of trade unions or employers' organisations, and their leadership or cadres; but the result is unlikely to reveal a coherent ideology for either. The usual example chosen to suggest the existence of ideology is the industrial parliament concept.[19] But merely to string together a list of its advocates from Lloyd George onwards, including the 'Tory corporatists' and trade unionists like Arthur Henderson, proves nothing. The 'alternative to parliament' even when put forward collectively by the TUC Research Department or the NCEO Council was a purely mechanical device for embodying practices which the authors knew already existed, or which they believed could be introduced to promote harmony and crisis avoidance. It was not an assertion of the role of institutions within a coherent intellectual system*.

In spite of these qualifications, analysis of corporate bias does reveal much about the nature of the British political system and of the state that developed after the first major twentieth-century crisis. The central

---

*See, for example, the formulation given by the Balfour Committee on Trade and Industry (Final Report, March 1929, pp. 126–9, Cmd.3282). When Churchill revived the idea in his Romanes Lecture in 1931, he referred to the industrial parliament in terms simply of economic management, calling it 'a deliberative assembly which would also serve as an advisory channel to the government on all matters affecting industrial relations as well as the wider issues of industrial and economic policy'. (Quoted in Susan Howson and Donald Winch, *The EAC 1930–39* (1977, p. 5.) This would not have been a body capable of dealing with power-bargaining between *political* bodies, which Lloyd George, at the Criccieth meeting in 1917, evidently hoped to create, and which emerged from the struggles of the early 1920s.

tenet of classical democratic theory, that choices were made through the electoral system utilising the mechanisms of party and parliament was, of course, modified by Joseph Schumpeter more than thirty years ago, when he pointed out that electors were actually restricted to infrequent acts of choice between opposing and stylised party presentations; policy was made continuously by party governments, in between elections, virtually independent of any general will.[20] But the concept of democracy needs to be modified much further to account for participation by institutions in the governing process, and for the phenomenon of opinion management by the state in its bureaucratic aspect. As institutions crossed the threshold separating pressure groups from a share of the state's powers and authority, they enhanced the tendency already present among governments to categorise political choices in terms of the national interest, over and above class or sectional interests, and to accept as necessary an interdependence almost as binding as the medieval doctrine of organic society.[21] Even by the 1930s it had become impossible to argue, as Baldwin did at the time of the General Strike, that the role of government was simply to hold the ring, protecting alike the interest of the state and the public at large against the evil consequences of sectional rivalry.

Yet until very recently, the proposition that governments were responsible primarily to the electorate for the protection of the state-held firm, as a universal truth about liberal democracy, even when the state, in Dahrendorf's formulation, was seen as a neutral switchboard, responding passively to the pressures of competing interest groups; because it had ceased to be all-powerful and had to acquiesce in bargaining as the only way to win the social harmony which it, and the public, sought. This view has been challenged:[22] but not unravelled to the point where an alternative typology of pressure groups and their legitimacy, and relationships to the state, can easily be constructed. For this reason I have used the term 'governing institution' to differentiate between mere pressure groups, however powerful in a single plane, and bodies which have been recognised by government as bargaining partners, granted permanent rights of access and accorded devolved powers by the state.

It may be too much to assert that the governing institutions became *part* of the state in the sense that government departments are a part, or the armed services. Yet political parties whose function is to mediate between state and society are part of the state only in so far as their leaders form the personnel of Cabinets. Without in any way asserting that the governing institutions resembled parties, their leaders, at given times, took up similar positions in the expanded state. For, in response to the crisis of the 1900s and the First World War (which was in essence a crisis of the state*), and in contrast to the narrowing of the area of the state which authoritarian rule in Germany and in Italy implied, British governments gave way to, or actually encouraged, corporate bias in order to overcome problems which the classical democratic system could not solve. As a result, their effective power was steadily circumscribed by that of the institutions they admitted, even in periods of wartime emergency, when they appeared to exercise unlimited control. As a recent historian of the employers' movement suggests, 'it is less the accretion of state power than the growth of shared or indeterminate power that is central to our understanding of the nature of recent change in society.'[23]

If this is accepted, classical theory about parties needs also to be modified. As I suggested earlier, parties were subordinated within the expanded political system, and lost some of their primordial rights as mediators between state and society, in spite of the continued functioning of the electoral system. Hence Beer's pertinent observation that the trend towards corporatism involves diminution of the status of party yet also that 'corporatism cannot constitute a complete polity and must be supplemented by some other course of will and direction such as has come in the past from party government.'[24]

Theory about competition between pressure groups must also be re-examined. What was created resembled not a free market but a political cartel, valid so long as the participants accepted the advantages of the whole (that is, the national interest) as greater than those to be obtained from breaking out. Competition was gradually restricted to those groups left in the pluralist sector outside, who had not crossed, and perhaps never could cross, the state threshold. Otherwise competition existed only in a customary sense, at a lower level, such as collective bargaining over wages and conditions, subject to rules determined elsewhere, and increasingly confined within limits acceptable to the state. A reversion, like companies abandoning a cartel to undercut its prices, came to be seen as abnormal as well as undesirable since it necessarily harmed the cartel's objectives, order, cooperation, and

---

*It is not coincidental that the breakdown of the nineteenth-century party-parliamentary system occurred at the same time as did the legal redefinition of trade unions as 'unincorporated corporations'; and as farsighted political analysts such as F. W. Maitland, Figgis, Laski and G. D. H. Cole began to argue in favour of the 'pluralism' of representative institutions other than parliament; at the same time, other groups introduced into the debate the themes of syndicalism, guild socialism and industrial self-government.

stability.[25] But, of course, the more institutions penetrated the state the more the power which they still retained to contract out, in defence of their members' interests, weakened its totality.[26]

To define corporate bias fully, it is necessary to clarify three other terms used in relation to it in current debate. By *incorporation*, I mean the adoption of major interest groups in the governing process, not their subordination and conversion into agencies of state control; by *corporatism*, the institutional growth, recognition and self-regulation of institutions, not a hierarchical system of estates with government at the top; and by *corporate state*, a system of politics in which the parliamentary constitution is modified to permit the organisation of functional groups on a national scale, not a system of central control of all aspects of national life. It follows that the historical delineation of *corporate bias* given above comes quite close to the definition of an 'ideal type' of corporatism put forward by Philippe Schmitter:

A system of interest representation in which the constituent units are organised into a limited number of singular, compulsory, non-competitive, hierarchically ordered and functionally differentiated categories, recognised or licensed (if not created) by the state and granted a deliberate representational monopoly within their respective categories in exchange for observing certain controls on their selection of leaders and articulation of demands and supports.[27]

There are two important distinctions: monopolistic the governing institutions may have been in their own sphere, but in the sphere of the state they shared power with government; and government rarely achieved the deliberate control over them suggested above. *Corporate bias* is better put as a system which encourages the development of corporate structures to the point at which their power, divergent aims, and class characteristics can be harmonised, even if that harmony involves a partial loss of class distinction, individuality, and internal coherence. An element of representativeness remains, however, permitting constituents, whether on the shop floor or company boardrooms, to revoke consent; totalitarianism is logically impossible.

Traditional distinctions between capitalism and socialism are no longer particularly valuable in describing such a system, because the spread of corporate bias involves the development not only of new institutions and ancillary organisations, but also of new functions and concepts of legitimacy: the state is product of historical circumstances, as are the governing institutions which evolve both independently and at governments' volition. Traditional Marxist theory that the state is merely the agency of the governing class can only be applied to the multiple forms of interlocking representation inherent in corporate bias if the institutions on *both* sides of the class struggle are defined as fractions of the ruling class (which means that the TUC and trade union leaderships have to be designated as collaborators), or if the state can be abstracted and depicted as supreme manipulator, playing off each section against the others. Although this may have occurred at times between 1911 and 1965, any such activity should surely be seen as an aberration from the principal trend towards interdependence.

A more serious problem occurs when analysing the dynamism of such a system. Does it lie in the continued, mechanically perfect, harmonising of competing wills, so that the result, in Engels' famous phrase 'may be viewed as the product of a power which works as a whole unconsciously and without volition. For what each individual wills is obstructed by everyone else, and what emerges is something that no one willed'?[28] Or does the motive power come from one or more specific areas, perhaps from the government bureaucracy, as Beer suggests?[29] Like the question of ideology, that must be considered later; there existed in Britain in 1945 nothing comparable to the concept of 'mega-bureaucracy' put forward by Robin Marris,[30] and the evidence suggests the existence of only a minimum level, or lowest common denominator of agreement among the political cartel, on aims naturally suited to the pursuit of compromise, absence of disorder and avoidance of crisis – the supportive, rather than the directive stage which supervened when the state entered its second great crisis in the 1960s.

What follows is a survey of the period 1945–65, intended to follow up such fundamental questions as the economic context altered, and as the wages and prices structure, productivity, the supply of credit, technology and other services became politicised, following government action, and the full employment policy accepted as a necessary corollary of wartime popular consent. Although inevitably truncated, it gives a basis on which to ask questions about the legitimacy of the system and how it was challenged by marginal groups or those who had once fulfilled a role within it and had subsequently been deprived. Where was the line drawn between the corporate sector of the state and the vestiges of pluralism in political life? How was the practice of liberal democracy able to survive, given the mordant prediction that:

Capitalist development itself essentially modifies the nature of the state, widening its sphere of action, constantly imposing new functions on it (especially those affecting economic life) making more and more necessary its intervention and control in society.[31]

384

How, even with their resources of manipulation, were the state and governing institutions able to satisfy demands without either invoking new powers (which previous experience had shown to be unpopular), or imperilling existing bargains and understandings? Finally, what was the nature of the crisis that followed, and still envelops British political life?

PART THREE

14 THE CULT OF
EQUILIBRIUM, 1945–65

The greatest danger for a contemporary historian is not that his sources are limited by the varied restrictions on access to the records of public and private bodies, nor that the closer he comes to the present the more obviously the questions he asks are couched in the language of current prejudice. If his training has been of any value, he will know how to unravel the circumlocutions of Royal Commissions and White Papers, orotund phrases recorded at party conferences, and the febrile concentration of the Press on personalities. He may perhaps be able to discern, behind the whitewash, outlines of monstrous things done by men and corporations shielded by official secrecy and the law of libel; and he will know very well that in research into any period of the past, no matter how remote, his own ideological preconceptions will intrude, transmuting his work, in Goethe's phrase, into the rewriting of history by his own generation. No; the real danger is to apply to the present deductions from a past reduced to order by the arbitrary processes of minuting, filing and selecting; to go beyond the function of telling society where it is and, with far greater arbitrariness, to shut off or encompass the infinite possibilities still latent in the future.

Nevertheless it is not unreasonable to apply deductions drawn from the first half-century to the two post-war decades, given the existence today of a much more incisive literature about the period since 1945 than was available in 1950, say, about the inter-war years; nor to try and match them to the period 1965–75, so long as one remembers that the evidence becomes increasingly suspect. (The study of institutions' *negative* power, for example, becomes extremely hard to pursue without access to state archives showing what Cabinet decisions were not taken and why, although a mass of useful material can be found in private sources such as the diaries of the late Hugh Dalton and Richard Crossman.)

What follows needs, however, to be qualified. Except at enormous length and repetitiveness, it is hardly possible to examine each facet: parties, Cabinet, the state apparatus, the new public sector of industry and the governing institutions, against the backcloth of huge increase in the scope and complexity of the modern industrial state. Nevertheless the whole must be kept in view, because individual studies of the past can never establish the relative weighting of each,[1] the balance of power between them on any given issue of economic or social policy, or their respective contributions to the pursuit of harmony and the avoidance of crisis. Secondly, the problem of distinguishing between governing institutions and groups outside the sphere of the state becomes more difficult as single massive trade unions like the TGWU, or employers' groups such as car manufacturers, take up political roles based on an adventitious power to affect or deflect government policy which raise them for much of the time from one rank to the other. This problem always existed (see Chapter 9) and can still be resolved by allowing for the special circumstances of such encroachments* without necessarily modifying the central distinction, based on assessment of their share in the functioning of the state.

Thirdly, one cannot do more than ask questions about the role of civil servants in the state apparatus. If the history of government departments in the inter-war years is fragmentary (apart from the dense, official war histories), after 1945 it is non-existent. To ask whether the charges against the bureaucracy made in the 1968 Fulton Report on the Civil Service were accurate at the time, or whether they still stand, is the unfulfilled duty of Parliamentary committees for which the often misconceived diatribes in Ministers' posthumously published diaries are a poor substitute.

It is possible only to hint at the continued dominance of the Treasury in economic management, at least down to the abortive defence of the pound in the years 1965–7, by pointing, say, to Cabinet acquiescence in the circumscription of the unfortunate Department of Economic Affairs and to the increased emphasis on wages policy as an antidote to inflation. It also appears that other departments lost a measure of influence. After manpower budgeting had been abandoned, and, later, physical controls as weapons of economic management (both Treasury

---

*A good early case can be found in the interaction between Bevan, Minister of Health in Attlee's government and the BMA, during the formation of the National Health Service in 1946–8, when the need to coopt doctors' and specialists' expertise was recognised (even more explicitly than in the case of managers' skills in the coal or iron and steel industries) in the enabling nature of legislation which permitted details to be settled by bargaining between Ministry officials and the BMA. The special circumstances, urgency of the measure, and acceptance by the Cabinet that such skills were irreplaceable, explain the phenomenon, without raising the BMA to 'governing institution' status. (*Vide* Harry Eckstein, *Pressure Group Politics: the case of the British Medical Association*, Allen & Unwin 1960.)

'victories'), Ministry of Labour influence declined. The trade union movement no longer needed its support against entrenched employers, and began to find it an unnecessary filter, hindering access to Cabinet, while successive Labour and Conservative leaders in the forties and fifties appointed as Ministers men unlikely to try to recover the policy-making role once held by Ernest Bevin.[2]

Finally, an earlier qualification needs to be restated: corporate bias was never a static system but subject to continual tension and flux, exposed not only to centrifugal tendencies, caused by opposition from the membership of governing institutions and the actions of governments (moved at times by apparently greater *raisons d'état*, to do with external threats in the 1930s, or fear of the subversion of civil society by inflation, thirty years later), but also to a continual harassment from the discontented political parties and the press. It never acquired the patina of legitimacy which hallowed the nineteenth-century parliamentary constitution; no political economist provided it with the sort of justification Bagehot or Dicey had conferred on changes in the forms of party democracy after the 1860s. Prophets of corporatism, as it was understood in the inter-war years, were instead almost wholly discredited by the military extinction of Fascism in Germany and Italy in 1944–5, while corporate bias itself – though quite distinct – remained too politically embarrassing to be admitted publicly to an electorate schooled in nineteenth-century dogma by parliamentary and party ceremonial. It existed in the twilight, the dark side of the double standard of political morality known to consenting participants but publicly deprecated if not actually denied. Essential as triangular collaboration of institutions had become to the growth of the state, its constitutional acceptance was therefore indefinitely postponed.

In spite of a reaffirmation in 1943 of the Bridlington agreement, structural reforms in the trade union movement occurred only slowly in the post-war years. Competition and overlapping survived almost unchecked and although two major amalgamations took place, with the formation of the NUM and NUSDAW, these only enhanced the dominance of the biggest unions. The 'big six' now included over 50 per cent of trade unionists affiliated to the TUC.* They had become

* *TUC Membership* (millions)	*1944*	*1948*	*1951*	*1954*	*1957*	*1960*	*1963*	*1966*
male	6·2	7·6	7·7	7·7	7·9	7·9	7·8	7·9
female	1·6	1·7	1·8	1·8	1·9	1·9	2·1	2·2
total	7·8	9·3	9·5	9·5	9·8	9·8	9·9	10·1

(continued overleaf)

bureaucratic conglomerates with undue weight on the General Council, hampering the growth of new unions more attuned to changes in the pattern of industry and employment in the tertiary sector, like NUPE; and poaching busily on the province of white-collar workers. The movement's aims seemed to be to create huge monopolies, based on the doctrine of the closed shop, run by domineering bosses like Arthur Deakin (TGWU), Will Lowther (NUM), Tom Williamson (GMWU) or Harry Douglass (iron and steel trades), backed by obscure rule-books and disciplinary powers,[3] whose style may have been modelled on that of Bevin, but without his managerial skills.

The cult of size for its own sake turned what had once been manageable institutions into sprawling, precarious empires vulnerable both to unofficial shop-floor revolt and employers' counter-attack. It became difficult to discern the movement's political will, or its ideological sensibilities. The General Council remained content, after its report to the 1944 Congress, to take a passive attitude, until the freeze on wages in 1947; while the Economic Committee seems to have requested no more than that the nationalised industries be brought up to the standards of efficiency set by private enterprise. In default of individual unions' initiative, no change could take place so long as the oligarchy held their seats; despite Aneurin Bevan's angry remonstrances on behalf of what he saw as a suppressed radical minority: 'Do not let the trade union leaders think that they alone speak for their members.'[4]

By the late 1950s, after Deakin's death, a left-wing group began to emerge: Jim Campbell (NUR) was joined by Frank Cousins (TGWU), and in 1959 George Woodcock replaced the stereotyped figure of Vincent Tewson as General Secretary of the TUC. The monolithic face of the big six on the General Council and the bloc votes at Conferences suffered, affecting the Labour Party in opposition and the lineaments of cooperation with government and management, just at the time of economic downturn and post-Suez political humiliation. For all Williamson's discipline, the GMWU broke ranks in June 1959 to support CND against Gaitskell, a change of mood related not only to the nuclear issue but to growing radicalism at the base.

Changes in personalities and policies reflected belatedly new patterns

	1945	*1948*	*1951*	*1954*	*1957*	*1960*	*1963*	*1966*
Density (%) (working population)								
male	45.1	55.8	55.7	54.9	54.8	53.6	51.9	51.9
female	25.0	24.0	24.6	24.0	24.1	24.1	24.7	25.1
total	38.6	45.2	45.0	44.2	44.0	43.1	42.2	42.1

(Source: Halsey: *Trends in British Society*, table 4.12.)

of industry: the boom in cars, petro-chemicals, man-made fibres, aerospace. A combination of narrowing differentials,* and awareness of the importance to the economy of car exports, encouraged aggressive wage claims throughout the motor industry, and the emergence of white-collar unions like ASSET and DATA (ASTMS and TASS) whose loyalties often cut across those of traditional unionism. Yet the trade union movement's perceptions of its role in political society took a very long time to develop beyond the tentative positions occupied in the past. After the 1944 Labour Party Conference, workers' participation attracted no support (as late as 1953 the General Council moved against a resolution on the question, proposed by the NUR) and the TUC remained faithful to Herbert Morrison's doctrine – 'public control of industry, rather than workers' control as such'.[5]

The majority of trade union leaders accepted the superior capacity of management, provided management used it with the sort of responsibility pledged at the Nuffield Conference in 1943, and did not even challenge Stafford Cripps' sardonic description of joint consultation,† nor Morrison's refusal to the Union of Bank Employees of a voice in choosing the new Court of the nationalised Bank of England. Instead, members of the General Council, acting in their individual capacity, took office on the new State industry boards; only to find that they were too often given charge of 'Labour' questions, which tested their dual loyalties without giving them substantive power over investment and managerial decisions.[6]

More important than the triumphalism which led Citrine in 1946 to inaugurate 'a new era of responsibility' was the General Council's attempt, in its 1944 *Report on Reconstruction*, to tie future governments to an explicit industrial contract, and to create a forum through which to advise on and participate in, state economic policy. But this essay in formalising the triangle won little support from the Attlee Cabinet and the TUC had to wait until 1961 when the National Economic Development Council (NEDC) was set up. Rather than insist, or expose the underlying contradiction involved in Attlee's assumption that it would cooperate, without recognition of its constitutional pretensions, the General Council reverted to the concept of a steady

---

*The average differential (unskilled wage in relation to the skilled) in engineering had fallen from 71 per cent in 1914 to 19 per cent in 1946, and declined to 16 per cent in 1956.

†'There is not yet a very large number of workers in Britain capable of taking over large enterprises . . . until there has been more experience by the workers of the managerial side of industry, I think it would be almost impossible to have worker-controlled industry in Britain, even it if was on the whole desirable.' (*The Times*, 28 October 1946.)

return to normal activity and free collective bargaining; with an eye on a future Conservative government and the need to rebut any charge that corporate membership of the Labour Party made it a 'political' body, to be treated thereafter as part of the Opposition.

'We expect of this [Conservative] government,' the General Council declared in 1951, 'that they will maintain to the full the practice of consultation. On our part, we shall continue to examine every question in the light of the economic and industrial implications.'[7] Conservative reciprocation, at least until 1957, marked a substantial gain over the 1930s, and there seemed no need to pursue the formal implications of being a governing institution further, except in moments of defence against a government's unilateral breach of the conventions, as in 1957, in asking for sacrifices unmatched by the other side. Nor did the TUC apparently try to prune the employers' right to manage: indeed in 1949 a group of officials, studying in America under the auspices of Marshall Aid, returned convinced of the need for 'scientific management' – no more than a step away from endorsing sophisticated Taylorism. Instead of inviting industrial conflict, the General Council sought to consolidate wartime gains, and in formal terms achieved parity of representation on some 850 committees by 1958, including the National Production Advisory Council and all the Economic Planning Boards.[8]

Yet equal status no longer stood for substantive power: with the demise of Joint Production Committees, the erosion of Ministry of Labour and Board of Trade influence in Whitehall, and government's own assumption of economic management by Keynesian methods rather than by physical planning and controls, the centre of activity reverted to the informal sphere of contacts between TUC, BEC and government. This change showed itself in the genesis of the wages freeze of 1948–50. With Labour in office, the TUC had not until then exercised its undoubted hold over the Party and Cabinet,* although it can be presumed that Labour Party managers had noted evidence that the unions, rather than the Party, had made the wartime gains: fewer individual trade union members now bothered to affiliate to the Party than had done in the 1930s.† After 1948, however, the General

---

*In 1945 120 MPs carried trade union nomination: 20 members of the Cabinet had trade union backgrounds; and the TUC had 12 members out of 22 on the NEC, half of the NCL, and provided the greater part of the Labour Party's finance, after repeal of the Trades Disputes Act in 1947. (Only 10 per cent of members, on average in the decade after 1945, contracted out of the political levy.)

†GMWU, 70% in 1937, 30% in 1946; TGWU, 57%, 37%. D. F. MacDonald, *The Trade Unions and The State* 2nd ed., (Macmillan 1976), p. 143.

Council discovered that it could hold the TUC membership's allegiance only so long as the terms of the tacit compact were observed.

By 1950, the oligarchy's hold on the bloc vote had been seriously undermined and the wages freeze became inoperable a year later. Facing a steady drift to the Left, Deakin found it necessary to instruct the Party Conference in the facts of life: 'You know you would listen if you wanted to get money from trade unions.'[9] He even requested the dissolution of the Tribune Group. General Council influence on the Party's 1952 report on nationalisation (reducing it to a faint cry for a state water supply) indicated that loyalty to an ageing party leadership had become one aspect of the big six's defence against the opposition from within the unions not just to party policy but to continued cooperation in industrial politics.

TUC radicalism in the years after Attlee's retirement in 1955 is often seen in terms of a renewed campaign for socialism; the offensive against rearming Germany, manufacture of nuclear weapons, and revision of Clause 4, giving rise to deductions about the unions' capacity for mobilising working-class consciousness against a leadership imbued with social-democratic tendencies. Without denying the emotional repercussions of these issues on members, only ten years after the war's end, it is better described as a response, first, to changes in working-class living standards, and secondly, to the prospect of a future Labour government implementing policies of which individual trade unions (under the new dispensation, freer from the oligarchy's constraints) might disapprove. After all, in the crucial vote for Party Treasurer in 1954, which could be seen to determine Attlee's successor, the 4 million votes given to Hugh Gaitskell (against Aneurin Bevan's 2 million) made him as much the TUC nominee as Attlee had been in 1936. What followed Gaitskell's elevation as leader was not so much an attack on him, personally, as resolution of the tensions in the movement, which were also reflected in personal clashes on the General Council.

This presentation makes it easier to explain periods of temporary harmony, such as preceded the 1959 Election, when the TUC feared perpetuation of a Toryism linked to an employers' counter-attack and deflationary economic policy. But afterwards, particularly in 1960, when the bloc vote was used against Gaitskell, on unilateral disarmament, with all the big six except the GMWU in opposition, a certain rupture did take place. Hugh Gaitskell affirmed the independence and the separate identity of the Party (disingenuously stigmatising the bloc vote on which he and Clement Attlee had previously relied), as Arthur

Henderson had done in 1913, Ramsay MacDonald in 1924, and as Harold Wilson was to do in 1967.

This lapse allowed the Conservatives, fearful of a left-oriented TUC, the threat to NATO implied by the Campaign for Nuclear Disarmament, and the likelihood of wage-inflation and unofficial action, to describe union influence as illegitimate – something which the General Council had avoided with considerable success in the previous twenty years. Accused of Tammany Hall practices and susceptibility to Communist Party infiltration – in the notorious ETU ballot-rigging case – the TUC found itself confronted by press and public hostility. Being loyal to the leadership on party and trade union matters, and aware of the threat to their influence in industrial politics, *vis-à-vis* government and management, the bigger unions swung back one by one, USDAW in May 1961, the NUR in July; leaving only Frank Cousins and the TGWU, in isolation.

The means were thus created to restore harmony in the Labour movement by 1964, and to reaffirm that the TUC was a stable body, no longer swayed by the ideologues of the Left. Having briefly prevented the parliamentary opposition to Gaitskell from being ostracised, like the ILP in 1931 or the Tribunites in 1951, the unions put an end to their hopes of Socialist policy in the TUC's own greater interest – a quietus symbolised by Cousins' acceptance of Cabinet rank in the new government. But the compromise, embodied in Harold Wilson's attempt to break out of the old vicious circle of debate about socialism, into the new painless world of technology and intervention via industrial regeneration, was not completed in time for the return of a Labour Government in 1964. Wilson presided over a party less committed than in 1945 or 1940 to the General Council's *weltanschaung*, while the TUC had only modified, not conquered, the dissent springing from a membership more motivated by class feelings than at any time since the end of the war.

Like the unions, and for much the same reasons, employers' organisations adjusted only very slowly to the changes which transformed industrial organisation after 1945. In most large companies management had effectively slipped out of shareholders' control. The new state sector aggregated a quarter of the industrial workforce and half of total investment in the late 1940s; the tertiary sector grew rapidly; and from the mid-1950s developed a formidable concentration of large and multinational companies which ran on unchecked through the sixties, reinforcing the existing divergence between them and small and

medium-sized business.* But although in several cases these developments owed something to government policy, and at worst were not
uncongenial (given the qualified success of the Monopolies Commission
after 1948), they were not reflected in the power relationship between
governments and industry in any simple fashion.

After their great wartime gamble, when BEC and FBI had accepted
the challenge implied in Labour's manifesto in order to prove that
management could be humane, responsible and efficient, the majority
of larger companies met trade unions' demands for amelioration of
conditions, at least to the extent of arranging for better leisure facilities,
personnel departments, and compensation for injury or redundancy.
But at the same time, to keep production lines active and sustain
export orders, they tended to pay high wage increases in areas such as
engineering, where labour was scarce, and to hoard labour by over-
manning, in order to even out the peaks and troughs of the annual
cycle. From 1945 to 1957 wages ran continually ahead of productivity
and Britain's share of world trade fell steadily to 21 per cent in 1953,
and a mere 13·7 per cent in 1964.[10] The Engineering Employers'
Federation found itself in the front line, both by tradition and circumstances, defending management against wage inflation and what it
regarded as the threat posed by the tendency of white-collar unions
to join the supposedly militant TGWU and GMWU. For a decade
they succeeded in preventing this conjunction – keeping alive the
pretence that foremen ranked as lower management (with incalculable
results in the motor industry, in the later efflorescence of DATA and
ASSET) – but failed to hold wages, partly from fear of loss of member
companies, unwilling to endure damaging strikes, and partly from the
reluctance of Conservative governments of the 1950s to upset industrial
harmony.

Consequently, what had been the most aggressive section of employers
began to sound a curiously muted note, and C. A. R. Crosland, writing
in 1956, suggested that, as Beveridge had forecast, labour power in
conditions of full employment had weighted the balance in favour of
the unions.[11] Even in the immediate post-war years, the TUC's inability
to hold back wage demands presaged reduced profits unless managers
could keep pace with wage rates, and with competition overseas, by
creating a high-wage, high-technology industrial revival. Their failure
to do so, as much as that of the TUC, invalidated the terms of the tacit

*The hundred largest firms, which had controlled 15 per cent of national output
in 1900, controlled 42 per cent by 1974, compared with 32 per cent in the USA and
22 per cent in West Germany.

compact of the White Paper of 1944, as far as government was concerned. But the assumption that wages could be held in some relationship with productivity was perhaps as unreal as governments' other assumption that full employment, stable prices and rising standards and profits could all be maintained without reference to external factors. Given government's own failure of economic management, and the lack of support from Westminster (or from Whitehall until the Treasury reverted to incomes policy after 1961), the incapacity of employers' organisations to prevent their members drifting towards plant bargaining and local accommodation to unions is understandable. But, cumulatively, these deficiencies made it impossible to develop the wartime practice and understandings into forms of central bargaining like those of Germany or Sweden; and, at the same time, they inevitably diminished BEC and FBI's *political* power.

The political parties woke up late to the implications, even though employers' organisations suffered much more noticeably than the TUC. At first, the Labour Government's trust was not vitiated, even by its experience over the Iron and Steel Bill,* and the Cabinet, with the exception of Aneurin Bevan and John Strachey, remained susceptible to the cult of good management to the extent of giving way to lobbying and lighting the 'bonfire of controls' after 1949.

Industry and Society (1947) had stated that 'under increasingly professional managements, large firms are, on the whole, serving the nation well'. The BEC, led by Sir Greville Maginnis, had persuaded TUC and government representatives on the NJAC in 1945 to set up a new Joint Consultative Committee on a voluntary basis, thus committing both to a nebulous venture whose terms of reference excluded wages and conditions and whose weight rested entirely on industry-by-industry cooperation – thus deterring Labour from more radical industrial relations legislation. Employers' judicious attitudes over such questions as credit control, and wages and prices control in 1948–9, enhanced the appearance of cooperation. Employers were able, therefore, without undue trouble, to defend the right to manage which Weir and the NCEO had thought endangered by socialism; and the managerial élite facilitated nationalisation in all cases but iron and steel, even if

---

*The nationalisation debates showed vestiges of the trust put in good management ever since the Labour Party Committee on Industry in 1934 had acknowledged the need for 'people who are experts in the industry, not mere politicians. . . . If you do not recognise industry, your industry will go out of existence, and the men and women who are dependent for their livelihood on the industry are not going to thank you because you think that by pure phrase-making you are going to make industry effective.' (LPAC 1934, p. 165.) For 1948 comment, see *Parliamentary Debates*, Commons, vol. 458, col. 60.

within a few years they deserted key but unprepossessing boards like coal and transport. Their opposition to steel nationalisation, on the other hand, showed how necessary their knowledge was to the government: for when the Cabinet finally went ahead, after weakening in the face of the Iron and Steel Federation's threat to withhold all staff and records,[12] the Federation's total lack of cooperation nearly paralysed the new Board, and made easy the Conservative's 1952 denationalisation.[13]

Political survival was not matched by internal reorganisation. Talk of a merger between BEC and FBI began as early as 1942 and continued for seven years. Yet, in spite of the need to show a less conspiratorial façade, the vested political interests of the BEC and the incompatibility between EEF and FBI prevented union.[14] The torpid appearance of the TUC in these years probably lessened what urgency existed. For lack of a more open, unified presence, the employers' organisations failed to obtain the devolved powers they might otherwise have been conceded; and trusting in their implicit understandings with the Conservative Party* they did not attempt to develop a theory of private enterprise within the mixed economy. On both counts they suffered severely later on.

Instead, mistrustful of the Labour government, the BEC responded grudgingly to dividend restraint in 1948, and argued for relaxation of price controls – even though the TUC was seen to be successful in holding back wages. Swayed by its most vocal component, the EEF, it clung to the doctrine of the 'right to manage' and, except in hard times, tended to regard political collaboration with government and TUC as an extraneous and possibly damaging activity. Indeed, right through the 1950s, the BEC retained traces of its pre-war attitudes, subscribing to and utilising heavily the propaganda resources of Aims of Industry and the Economic League. Yet, except in the one case of iron and steel, it was unwilling to fight either side openly. It preferred, for example, after 1945, to let the Joint Production Committees die of disuse, rather than challenge their existence,[15] and the refusal of its members, in the good years before 1957, to face up to national strikes, in default of government support, materially helped their gloomy prognostications about union power and inflation to come true.

The EEF could make a good case for saying that governments had betrayed them on the issue of wage restraint in the whole post-war

---

*BEC and FBI were closely associated in the late 1940s with Tory reformers and industrialist MPs like Oliver Lyttelton, Chairman of AEI, keen to show them in the most favourable light.

399

period, starting with the Foster Committee's adjudication of ship-building union demands in 1945 and the huge AEU wage claim of 1949.[16] The Ministry of Labour's refusal to help them resist during the Korean War crisis (1950–51) could be related to the subsequent success of shop floor activity and the steady increase in plant bargaining that followed. Conservative governments of the fifties did nothing to halt the drift towards the regular 'annual round', nor did the practice of comparisons with other unions' earnings and the cost of living, which appeared to institutionalise the gap between wages and productivity.

But post-war Cabinets worried more about production and the balance of payments, and pressed for settlements rather than strikes, whether in the softer days of Sir Walter Monckton (1954) or Iain Macleod (1956). In the latter case, the EEF spokesman put the issues very plainly: 'We should make it clear to the unions, the government, and to the country, that the union demands are wholly irresponsible and *must be rejected.*'[17] In spite of Harold Macmillan's promise, as Chancellor, to stand by them, twelve months of sparring with the AEU took the EEF to the post-Suez period when Macmillan, as Prime Minister, had to save both the pound and the Conservative Party by dissociating the new Cabinet from its earlier stance. 'In the long run, and for the common good, the umpire is better than the duel,' he declared at Leicester in March 1957. The Cabinet could not face a national engineering strike: British Railways caved in: Macleod worried about a financial panic, and Macmillan, soon to go to Nassau to restore Anglo-American relations, virtually ordered the EEF to settle on the best terms it could.[18]

Whatever the case employers put up, as a matter of practical politics it became clear that even a Conservative Government would listen to the TUC, when talking of the national interest, rather than to its erstwhile mentors, the BEC. Members of the EEF had been divided on the merits of resistance even before the engineering strike threatened in March 1957; at the climactic meeting after Macmillan's démarche the Board split 42 to 18 in favour of a settlement. Whatever guarantees they were subsequently able to get from Sir William Carron and the AEU, their political status had been cut down, and their relationship with government, as it had been understood since 1927, undermined.*

*Not least because the government blandly denied that any pressure had been exercised, knowing well that the Board would not tell the tale. Few of the EEF's member companies knew the full details of the meeting between Macmillan, Macleod, Sir Colin Anderson (BEC), Sir W. Robertson (BTC) and Sir Ellis Hunter (Ship-building Engineers' Federation) on 23 March. Not until 1958 did they respond, in a pamphlet, casting themselves in the position of the Czechs betrayed at Munich twenty years before, by being prevented from fighting the necessary battle.

Economic circumstances afterwards made it impossible again to screw up so much courage: although the big motor companies agreed in 1957 to be bound by EEF rules, rather than set up the separate federation which freebooters like Leonard Lord had wished for, the change only enlarged the Board without greatly increasing its common fund of agreement; and the trend towards local wages agreements, the annual round, and unofficial stoppages increased without serious check.*

Only after 1960, as Carron (AEU) and the TUC became alarmed at the impact on union prestige of unofficial strikes in the motor industry, did the EEF acquire allies;† and even then, there was no actual recourse until the government itself turned to wage restraint and legal curbs. Instead, the EEF evolved the notion of the 'package deal' on wages (1964 and 1968) and, with government connivance, tended to separate the rest of engineering from the peculiar circumstances of the motor manufacturers. Content to survive as an entity, the EEF lost its former position as protagonist for the employers; but because it covered so many important industrial sectors, and confronted so many of the major unions (TGWU, GMWU, AEU, ETU), its more passive stance influenced the whole range of employers and management.

Other manufacturers' organisations now had little influence:‡ even the FBI, never a habitual or successful lobbyist, had lost much of its political significance, except on questions like the EEC application.[19] Management may have earned its public plaudits after 1944,[20] but by its failure to defend its share of the political triangle, in the changing conditions of the 1950s, it contributed substantially to its own demise.

Some recovery took place after 1960, but at government's volition,

	1954	1959	1960
*Unofficial stoppages in engineering trades	110	280	400
Days lost per 1,000 employees	49	173	291

(Wigham, *The Power to Manage*, p. 299.)

†The EEF spokesman then blamed 'Communist agitation' and found Carron 'on the right side' (Wigham, p. 203) much as Lloyd George had found J. H. Thomas in 1919–21.

‡The National Union of Manufacturers (mostly small firms) served only as a conservative brake on the FBI (Kipping, p. 50). The Association of British Chambers of Commerce had grown by the 1950s to 100 Chambers, with 60,000 members, but like the NUM, represented a congeries of local interests, united only in opposition to 'big government' and the corporate tendencies of the BEC. The BEC's own density of membership had grown substantially since the 1930s: 90 per cent of large firms, 76 per cent of small, in the trade associations, with 270 affiliated groups, covering 70 per cent of the employed population – or 1½ times the total of the TUC (Wigham, *The EEF*, p. 333). The FBI counted 283 associations in 1957, of 7,537 firms, but its membership largely overlapped with the BEC whose primacy on 'political' questions had not then been challenged (Kipping, p. 23).

not unconnected with the revival of the free market tradition of the Conservative Party and the ideological quarrels among the Opposition. Having accepted that planning was necessary, to restore wages, productivity and investment to harmony, leaders of the business and industrial communities like Lord Chandos (the former Oliver Lyttelton) saw that it was no longer possible to retain the old unofficial link with government, if management's world-view was to prevail, since the BEC's negative power had largely been discounted by the government's concessions to trade unions. Their conversion coincided with Conservatives' acceptance of *The Next Five Years* (the so-called 'Brighton Revolution'), with its schedule of government planning to overcome balance of payments problems, and its open invitation to collaboration by industrialists. With FBI support, a formal framework was inaugurated, of which NEDC was the obvious industrial and economic focus, while the discussions between FBI, BEC and National Association of British Manufacturers (NABM) for a new 'national industrial organisation' represented the political dimension.

Government still gave the lead: after Labour's 1964 victory, George Brown deliberately sought to create one single employers' organisation, corresponding to the TUC, with which his Department of Economic Affairs could deal.[21] Yet the BEC remained suspicious, smarting from the EEF's experience of Cabinet vacillation in the previous decade, and arguing that a single body would debilitate the old Federations even more than the separatist tendencies of individual firms. A very old monopoly was at stake, defending itself against intervention by small, non-federated firms, and against erosion of a system which had preserved its authority, *vis-à-vis* government, for half a century. Yet in the end it backed down, 'not wishing to be made a scapegoat' by the rest;[22] recognising that the TUC had become so powerful that, as in 1919, they had to readjust, or abandon all pretensions to a share in political power. NABM remained outside NEDC, thus emphasising a significant and growing divergence between large and small firms, which had its political repercussions inside the Conservative Party;[23] and the new CBI, confident, even triumphant in its publicity, but with its internal contradictions barely resolved, resumed the ancient dance.

In the years immediately after the war, there was little obvious resistance from trade unions to the government's desire to prolong controls. (The government, of course, could count on BEC support for any form of wages policy, throughout its tenure of office). But though until 1951 the TUC acquiesced in the extension of Order 1305, the assumption that they would continue to work for 'a unified wage policy'[24] soon became untenable. It is perhaps too facile to state simply that union opposition forced the government to abandon physical planning of the economy in favour of Keynesian methods of demand management: Attlee's Cabinet was unprepared for the post-war wages spiral, and Ministers' simplistic distinction between planning in free and totalitarian societies provided no satisfactory concept of the role of unions in a democratic socialist society. If a way had to be found to incorporate them as representative institutions, Attlee and his colleagues in the first majority Labour Government were not prepared at first to seek it.

Bevin's influence, even from the post of Foreign Secretary, ensured survival of the wartime concept of maximum freedom within a few, broadly acceptable controls. Wages had been exempted from the discussions at the meeting of trade union executives in March 1946 which endorsed continued manpower controls; in theory, therefore, the TUC remained committed to further planning, a National Investment Board, and, if necessary, some form of wages control.[25] But in fact the TUC did nothing to prevent its members unions from defending the positions won in wartime, or pressing wage claims which, at a time of labour shortage, employers seemed ready enough to concede. Only the more radical, like the miners and ETU, stood by the idea of wage restraint as a component part of planned socialism, while the remainder of the big six, led by Deakin, advanced in the direction of raising the wages of low-paid manual workers, with Bevin's tacit approval.

Despite the plaintive protests of the 'Keep Left Group', the Cabinet never tried to plan wages before the financial crisis of 1947–9; and indeed, if the contrast between the targets of output and manpower allocation given in the 1947 *Economic Survey* and the out-turn, (when controls were not tightened but the figures of the *Survey* merely adjusted) is considered, the Cabinet may never have been seriously committed to physical controls.* Much of the explanation for the defeat of controls can also be assigned to opposition from bankers and bureaucrats, to say nothing of the constraints inflicted by the United States.

Once they had accepted the build-up of wage inflation in 1947–8 as detrimental to price stability in the uncontrolled industries and to the export drive, the government was faced with the problem of

*By 1950 the unsympathetic *Economist* could refer to the Survey as 'a humble document, meek almost to the point of being meaningless'. W. Rogow even suggests that, but for the post-war shortages, Labour Party planning would not have gone further than indications on the lines of the National Plan of 1964–5.

choosing between imposing controls (which had been resisted even in wartime) or trading on the accumulated capital of union goodwill. Exhortation at the level of the National Production Board Advisory Council had shown some returns – fewer days had been lost than in the last year of the war;* and trade unions had accepted the Control of Engagements Order, reintroduced to meet the 1947 winter shortages. But the general unions were now bent on consolidating wartime earnings into basic rates; a development which was the precursor of narrowing differentials, and inflation in conditions of full employment, yet was, nevertheless, hard to resist on theoretical grounds, and virtually impossible to check, for fear of renewed Communist Party infiltration.† Moreover the gap between controlled, essential industry and the uncontrolled sector was widening all the time, leaving the former desperately short of labour.

Deflation offered no alternative to an administration dedicated to sustaining full employment. Yet Attlee's Government was not exactly prisoner of the triangle of forces, especially since the employers supported restraint. Attlee issued the 'Statement on Economic Considerations affecting relations between Employers and Workers' after a consultation with the NJAC so cursory as to move Deakin to accuse the Cabinet of subordinating the unions to the state; and a measure of how the interests of the TUC were, in fact, linked can be seen when Deakin then turned on left-wing MPs and trade unionist objectors, and with help from Bevin and Morgan Phillips, labelled them as 'agitators'.

But when it came to *implementing* a wages policy, the government was in irons without trade union assent. They lacked the means to

*	1944	1945	1946	1947	1948	1949	1950	1951	1952
Money wages									
Weekly wage rates	153	159	172	178	187	193	196	212·5	230
Weekly wage earnings	198	196	207	221	239	244	263	289·5	312
Cost of living	140·6	145·7	150·8	159	169·8	174·9	180·5	197·1	215
Working days lost by strikes	3·7m	2·8m	2·1m	2·4m	1·9m	1·8m	1·4m	1·7m	1·8m

Source: Halsey *Trends in British Society*, tables 4.10, 4.11, 4.14. Note the stability of wage rates, 1947–50, followed by a substantial jump 1950–1 and a corresponding real fall in the standard of living 1949–50.

†Order 1305 had borne hardest on the general unions, especially in the 'controlled' industries, and was usually believed to have encouraged shop floor discontent. The CPGB made wide gains among dockworkers (led by Jack Dash), gasworkers and London busmen. (One-third of the 2·8 million working days lost in 1945 were due to unofficial strikes in the docks.) In spite of expulsion of many unofficial leaders, trouble continued, and was exacerbated by wage restraint in 1949–51. A prosecution of gas and dockworkers in 1951 led, after a failure similar to those of 1915 or 1943, to abandonment of Order 1305.

attract men to underpaid essential work, or the will to interfere with 'normal' machinery. Bevin had condemned the idea of wages policy as an affront to trade unionism as early as 1946; Attlee admitted in 1950 that the Cabinet had never given overriding directions to those arbitrating on wage claims.[26] In that sense, although the General Council did not shape the February 1948 White Paper, *Personal Incomes, Costs and Prices*, their endorsement made it work. But endorsement also meant that the TUC accepted as correct the deduction that rising wages caused inflation, and its practical corollary, the 1949 devaluation and the consequent check to rising living standards.

Member unions could be convinced of these unpalatable conclusions in a prevailing climate of austerity, when sacrifices appeared to be asked of all classes by a Chancellor with the bearing and moral authority of Stafford Cripps, so long as the state maintained its welfare programme, and so long as prices were held within a narrow band – 6 to 18 per cent above the level of 1945. Even on a temporary basis, wage restraint proved acceptable only as part of a clearly determined bargain; the impact on prices of the Korean War, ineffective price controls, continuing shortages of labour and rising wage earnings (even when wage rates remained stable) caused too much relative deprivation – to use W. G. Runciman's phrase – after the first two years.

In any case, the government also gave way, to preserve industrial peace and sustain exports and the needs of the war: the shipbuilders' case in 1948, and the engineers' in 1949, set a bad precedent, crowned by the British Transport Commission's surrender, overriding its own Court of Inquiry, in 1951. At the Trade Union Executive Conference in January 1950, the big six's loyalty just held, but in September, by 3·9 million to 3·7 million, the TUC threw out a General Council directive on continued wage control.

Ministers, tired after being in office since 1940, made no attempt to bring in statutory controls; and the General Council learned never again to be trapped between the requirements of government and the feelings of member unions facing a vigorous shop floor movement. Their opposition, even to Gaitskell's mild formulation of a National Wages Board, in November 1950, lasted for fifteen years. Watching from the other side, the Conservatives also learned, and prepared their appeal to an industrial prosperity, free of controls, based on high earnings and high profits. In 1951, after six years in opposition, and with a weak majority, the newcomers were not inclined to challenge the deduction that to manage the economy successfully required the consent of both sides of industry. R. A. Butler, the new Chancellor, still upheld the ideals of the Industrial Charter, and the General Council's public statements (see above, p. 394) seemed sufficient reciprocal guarantee for the Cabinet. Churchill appointed Walter Monckton as Minister of Labour, a man almost without party affiliation, whose nature inclined to compromise, and who rarely acted without the prior consent of the General Council. Monckton reversed a wages award once, in the summer of 1952 – only to have his decision annulled by the Cabinet, after protests from the TUC Economic Committee about interference with 'normal procedures'.

In return, the big six unions restrained left-wing and Communist Party demands for a precipitate return to free collective bargaining. (Regulation 1376 lasted another seven years, until the government succumbed, not to the TUC, but to BEC recrimination.) Nationalisation, apart from the anodyne issue of water supply, disappeared from the immediate agenda, and the TUC offered only token opposition to the return of iron and steel to private companies.

But such political harmony depended on economic prosperity. Although the cost of living remained stable, with falling import prices, low unemployment, and steadily rising money earnings,[27] by the mid-fifties the 'annual round' had become habitual, accompanied by ingrained resistance to any form of effective interference by outside bodies, however 'impartial'. In spite of the fears of inflation, leap-frogging and changing differentials, which Ministers occasionally voiced, no serious attempt to relate these money wages to productivity occurred. Instead the government began to bail out nationalised industries: in 1953 Monckton overrode the British Transport Commission to buy peace on the railways, and the Morris Committee conceded most of what the shipbuilding unions demanded, without in return obtaining TUC consent to permanent arbitration machinery. Cumulatively, crisis avoidance took precedence over economic management. Just as trade unions' negative power had assisted in the defeat of physical controls in the late 1940s, so, under a Conservative Government, it encouraged the shift from concentration on wage policy toward monetary controls, which unions could less easily counter, and the search for some authoritative, impartial body whose overview of wages in the national interest might somehow remedy the deficiencies of government itself.

These were the years in which the employers' side lost much of its political influence, partly because the BEC, in tune with its 1944 position, shunned too close identification with a Conservative administration,[28] and partly because Churchill and his senior colleagues, never intrinsically concerned with industry, found a closer affinity with the City, and sometimes, in their anxiety to keep on terms with the TUC, played on the evident divisions between BEC and FBI.[29] But it remained a non-interventionist Cabinet as far as the governing institutions were concerned. When the downturn and the credit squeeze came after 1955, it relied on hints to industry and the banks rather than coercion.[30] Beer noted:

> The extreme hesitation of departments and governments . . . to confront an open and public break with producer groups. It is the attitude (one detects it not only among officials and ministers, but also among MPs and members of the general public) that such organised groups have a 'right' to take part in making policy, relative to their sector of activity; indeed that their approval of a relevant policy or programme is a substantial reason for public confidence in it. . . . If forced into a sharp and systematic formulation that attitude would be in conflict with . . . the sovereignty of Parliament.[31]

For just that reason, it was in the interests of none of the three partners to force a sharp formulation during the brief golden age, 1951–6. Days lost by strikes rose a little from the low 1·4 million in 1950 but averaged only 2 million before 1957. Shop-floor acerbities diminished, as did Communist Party influence in most unions, largely because of the stern attitude taken by the TUC General Council after 1947. But in the election year 1955 strikers raised a number of important issues which broke the fifteen-year cycle of Conservative Party and press favour towards the trade union movement.* Dock strikes revealed the existence of widespread inter-union poaching, the aggressive expansionism of the TGWU, and the inability of the TUC to act quickly under the Bridlington rules; trouble in the newspaper industry exposed the struggle between printing unions for monopoly, and the encroachments of the Communist Party on the Electrical Trades Union; and finally action on the railways showed the consequences of changes in differentials. To remedy structural faults, the Genera Council initiated a series of modest reforms, insufficient, however, to give it more than a policing role, without touching on the question of unofficial strikes, to which government and press were now busily directing public attention.

How much effect the campaign for union reform, with its old 1920s nostrums of secret ballot or compulsory arbitration had on the 1955 election result is hard to assess. The Conservatives' majority of sixty

*A Gallup poll early in 1955, showed that the majority of respondents thought that the Government was weak in its dealings with trade unions.

seats may have owed something to fears of wage-push inflation, fears later accentuated by the balance of payments crisis in 1957, and external factors such as EEC countries' faster growth, narrowing Commonwealth markets, and loss of foreign confidence in sterling. But, short of reversing the direction of the previous decade, the new government could do little about the rise in imports, following the 1954–5 investment boom, nor could it stop creating credit (despite the mild squeeze on the banks, 1956–7) because of its commitment to full employment, and the dangers of antagonising organised labour. When in 1957 Peter Thorneycroft, the new Chancellor, challenged these assumptions, in the hope of breaking the spiral of inflation and restoring the real value of the pound,* the majority of his Cabinet colleagues took issue on price stability and employment, and in effect, forced him to resign, together with Enoch Powell and Nigel Birch.

The dilemma of a Tory government weighed down by Labour's negative power can be gauged from its subsequent disillusion with the returns to be obtained from monetary policy, expressed in the Radcliffe Report in 1959. But if fiscal methods were inadequate, the actual credit squeeze of 1956–7 in turn hit small businesses and started a long political alienation of old Conservative supporters without significantly affecting the upward drift of wages. So began the dismal saga of wage restraint, stretching out from the 1958 White Paper – *The Economic Implications of Full Employment* – and exemplifying, at every turn, why a tripartite bargain like that of 1948 could no longer be achieved.

The TUC refused to carry the odium of policing a wages policy and, disingenuously accusing government of having dismantled the apparatus of control and raised the cost of living by withdrawing food subsidies, declared that it would only bargain if these were restored, and the lowest level of income tax raised.[32] For their part, BEC and FBI united behind the slogan: 'the cure of inflation lay primarily in HMG's hands'.[33] Government should reduce public expenditure, ameliorate the top level of taxation and impose on nationalised industries profit requirements appropriate to private enterprise. With such *non possumus* arguments, both governing institutions put the onus back on government.

Clearly, both could not be satisfied. The Budget, in April 1956, shaded towards the BEC/FBI programme, but in July, after the TUC had refused to collaborate, cuts in public spending were partially offset by economies in defence and a promise of a 'price plateau' in

*Professor Paish's calculations, presented to the Cohen Committee in 1957, suggested that deflation could be used as a weapon to control wages.

nationalised industries' products. This limited appeasement of union sentiment proved acceptable to the employers' side (apart from protests about the 'exceptional risk' to profits);* but the General Council, caught between the BEC's unwise trumpeting of the need for firm restraint of wages, and opposition within the trade unions, prevaricated until the September TUC. There they thought it expedient to have a wide debate, during which whatever goodwill for the bargain had existed, vanished in massive opposition.

The price plateau was achieved, suggesting that the employers fulfilled their part; but the wages' rise continued, with only a slight diminution in 1957–9. Weakened by the Suez débâcle, and smarting under criticism from a General Council which appeared incapable of delivering the response Conservatives believed they had earned over the previous decade, that section of the party which may be called, variously, 'right wing', 'free-market oriented', or 'anti-corporatist', questioned the price of crisis avoidance and buoyed up Thorneycroft's assault. They lost; and Macmillan and Macleod completed their defeat by coercing the EEF into submission (see above, p. 400) in the higher interests of Government survival. But the result only demonstrated the decline in capacity of governments to achieve their desiderata. Ingenious though later essays in escape were, they too failed, increasing the frustration of those Tories not committed to centrist policies; and all the while the favourable economic conditions which had permitted the five good years before 1956 melted away, as Britain fell steadily behind her competitors in investment, productivity and real wages.

Because of the significance of the motor car and other related industries, where strikes had risen by 1958 to seven times the national average, unofficial strikes were soon added to wage inflation by those seeking to diagnose the causes of relative decline.† From then on, methods of wage restraint, and reform of trade unions to curb the supposed anarchy of shop stewards' militancy, combined to form a double panacea, increasingly attractive to politicians avid to restore the primacy of party and Cabinet in actually running the economy. There is no need to recount the wearisome search for the philosopher's stone of a new economic miracle, which always seemed to be impeded by the counter-vailing power of unions (witness the Cohen Council in 1957) or the

*BEC, FBI, NUM and ABCC combined to 'urge upon industry the wisdom and desirability of exercising restraint on price policy'. (FBI Report 1956, p. 4.) Profits did actually decline in 1956–7, for the first time since 1950 (*National Income Expenditure* 1963, table 16 and 17).

†These sentiments were clearly expressed in the Ministry of Labour inquiry into strikes at the Briggs Motor Bodies Factory, Dagenham, in 1957.

government's increasing sensitivity to the risk of being seen by public opinion to fail. The harm done by short-term or stop-go policies was incalculable. Dow comments:

The major fluctuations in the rate of growth of demand in the years after 1952 were thus chiefly due to Government policy. This was not the intended effect: in each phase, it must be supposed, policy went further than intended, as in turn did correction of those effects. As far as internal conditions are concerned, budgetary and monetary policy failed to be stabilising, and must on the contrary be regarded as having been positively destabilising.[34]

After 1957 the attempt to re-establish consensus also eroded the foundations of triangular harmony, however great the sacrifices (in difficult choices *not* being made) offered to its appeasement. Macmillan's government abandoned the vestiges of control over prices, capital issues and export quotas; as Minister of Labour, Macleod vitiated the judgments of wages councils in harsh cases like National Health Service nurses; finally, institution of the National Incomes Commission in June 1962 appeared to break the existing conventions by reserving the right of reference to the Commission to government alone.

The Conservatives did not actually assault trade union positions head on: Macmillan's government remained content with wage restraint in the public sector, monetary policy, and propaganda, while Macleod's succession to Selwyn Lloyd as Chancellor in 1962 seemed to indicate some sensitivity to the need to ameliorate TUC hostility. 'It was the central, guiding need to sustain that alliance which determined how far the Conservative Government made changes in all fields of policy.'[35] Yet the symptoms of serious lesions in the system of corporate bias began to appear. The concept of trade union reform by statute was encouraged by the celebrated ETU ballot-rigging affair and by a number of victimisation and closed-shop cases[36] which seemed to vindicate demands for embodying individual rights in legal form against corporate power. But, at the same time, the radicalisation of quite large areas of the trade union movement precluded the General Council, now led by George Woodcock, from acceding readily to the wages restraint which the Conservatives' not unfavourable overtures in the years 1962–4 demanded; this, in spite of the Chancellor's invitation to join NEDC and acquire formally what the General Council called 'access to the corridors of power'.[37]

The General Council's response, in undertaking its own structural inquiry in September 1962 and in drafting its own wages policy, may have justified the Government's assumption that a basis of accord existed and that Cousins and the Left might be out-manoeuvred. But in spite of evidence, in the 1958 *Plan for Progress*, that the Labour Party (with Harold Wilson as Shadow Chancellor) was being converted to propositions on wages policy, and to a claim for the status of party within the Labour movement likely to be detrimental to the role played by unions since the 1930s, the General Council evidently sensed a deterioration in Conservative popularity; and in January 1964 refused decisively to be associated with the Government's wages policy.

Since wages policy was by then central to any future government's success in economic management, this must be interpreted as a declaration that the old triangular arrangements had become inadequate. As leader of the combined Labour movement, restored at the 1963 Conference, after twelve years' wrangling, Wilson appeared to offer an alternative, which it is important to note in order to understand subsequent events and the nature of the disillusion which set in subsequently.

In 1963 the TUC had endorsed a resolution on economic planning which covered salaries, wages, profits and the 'social wage': led by Cousins and Ted Hill the Left voted in favour. This confluence of party and TUC was not simply a tactical preparation, suited to middle-class voters in the forthcoming election, but a reiteration of Labour's 'integrative role' (to use Panitch's description) inaugurated by Gaitskell, James Callaghan, Wilson and Brown two years earlier, the economic aspect of which (drafted with the German example of rapid growth, high wages and technological progress in mind) virtually guaranteed the TUC right of access to a future Labour government's decision-making. This, at any rate, was how the General Council interpreted it,[38] to the dismay of the BEC. No Conservative offer to the unions could compare. But it was not then clear* how little Wilson's skilful presentation had actually conceded, or how strong was his determination to institute trade union reform; and contradictions remained to be exposed when circumstances forced his government to change course in 1965–6. It would be unfair to dismiss the mood of heroic unity as a mere conjuring trick; rather, those who put their names to it did so with different themes at heart. Cousins, for example, believed that it would lead to changes in the whole system, with the trade unions in the vanguard of vast planning and nationalisation; few of his colleagues understood that the minimum price would be wage restraint and statutory controls.

*Only Len Murray (then head of the Economic Department) remained sceptical about the commitment to incomes policy rather than to industrial change, and warned of balance of payment problems and the dilemma for the TUC (Panitch, p. 57).

Insofar as Labour Party programmes in the 1940s envisaged interference with the free market in wages, they had concentrated on planning and further nationalisation, rather than restraint. But the state of the nationalised sector belied hopes that it could become the model of good industrial relations and scientific management. In spite of attracting a proportionately larger share of investment than privately-owned industry in the first ten years after the war, especially in such fields as housing* and atomic energy, the state industries failed – for many complex reasons – to become profitable, and their wage increases, reflected in the prices charged for basic services, added cumulatively to the phenomenon of inflation. Instead of exemplars of participation, they became the cockpit of white-collar unions' demands for status (electricity and gas) or manual workers' attempts to upgrade basic scales (British Transport Commission), while their 'separate' existence led to campaigns for comparability with private industry, and in due course to the Conservative Government's attempts to control wages nationally through them alone.

As early as 1947, the *Economic Survey* had acknowledged the near impossibility of coordinated planning.† Instead, the 1950s brought a heterogeneous series of compromises, state directives about the profitability of different sectors, and variable use of financial constraints and pricing policy. 'Scientific' coal-mining management in the pits, for example, came down in the end to a skilful balance between pit closures and manpower shedding on one hand and improved conditions on the other – a poor precedent when pit wages were caught up in successive freezes and profound discontent built up to the strikes of 1971 and 1974.

Instead of a home for full, sustained collaboration between unions, management and government, freed by public ownership from impediments of wage or class struggle, the nationalised industries became an element apart, subjected to arbitrary government interference, either to enforce pay restraint in the politically least painful field, or to override wages arbitration and forestall damaging national strikes. Their boards, staffed with officials and professional managers handling enormous capital sums, came under a long-range and rather disingenuous fire from BEC and FBI (who had done little to prevent the

*Where, for example, the incoming Conservative Government in 1951 set a target of 300,000 houses a year; whose fulfilment deprived other sectors of badly-needed investment. Overall, housing absorbed one-quarter of all fixed capital investment in the UK, 1945–54. (Dow, *Management of the British Economy*, pp. 214–219.)

†'The task of directing by democratic methods an economic system as large and complex as ours is far beyond the power of any government machine.'

managerial élite from deserting them in the early fifties). Insofar as the British Transport Commission was broken up under Beeching, their accusations of incompetence and financial indiscipline found a Conservative response. But whereas that side of the triangle withdrew from the positions promised in 1944, the trade union movement, still caught up in the uneasy compromises of the Morrison era and their confusing consequences,* failed to offer an alternative interpretation of the role of state industry attuned to the changed circumstances of the 1960s.

Meanwhile, for far too long, the parties confronted each other with dogmatic declarations on principles originally adumbrated in the 1930s, if not earlier; a sterile confrontation only slightly modified by the painstaking work of the Nationalised Industries Committee and by the Conservatives' attempt (in the 1961 White Paper, *Financial and Economic Obligations*) to resolve managerial contradictions which had by then become endemic. The Labour movement was divided between the protagonists of extending nationalisation, often quite uncritically, as the means to replace capitalism, and those who, with Wilson, advanced proto-Keynesian arguments about humane state intervention to rescue its casualties.

This inability to adapt practice to new conditions, despite the ingenious formulations of Antony Crosland and his successors, on one side, or the bleak machinations of the Beeching era on the other, touch on the nature of both political parties' evolution within the system of corporate bias. Committed to the continued existence of a large private industrial ownership, the defence of the pound, and a measure of wage restraint, albeit combined with price control, the Labour Party of 1963 seemed already to have abandoned pretensions to the class struggle and adopted an ideology suitable to such an economy.[39] As Leo Panitch indicates, it had become an 'integrative' party as a result of its own practice,[40] imbued with a concern for national unity remarkably similar to that of the Conservatives under Macmillan or Baldwin. Consequently, doctrines of the national interest were injected into the Labour Party's public teaching, substantially affecting its predominantly working-class supporters' attitudes towards wage restraint, inflation, and unofficial strikes.[41]

The choice of political imagery which this entailed may provide a better explanation of working-class attitudes to government's economic

---

*In most nationalised industries, the three tiers of joint committees became otiose. Joint consultative committees seemed useless parallel structures when real negotiations took place only at the top level.

practice in the fifties and early sixties than any theory of embourgeoisement or the dominance of political oligarchy. The Labour Party had become 'an independent factor in inculcating the working class in general and the trade union leadership in particular with national values consistent with consensus',[42] a metamorphosis not unlike that projected by MacDonald in the 1920s but achieved four decades later because of post-war electoral success, and because trade union leaders' acquiescence enabled the leadership, under Attlee and Gaitskell, to confine the left of the Party to a scope as narrow as that of the ILP after 1926 – the notable exception of the uneasy years 1957–62 being explained largely by the temporary change in attitude of the TUC.

After the brief radical upsurge of 1943–4, and the contrasts between speeches of leaders and the wishes of the rank and file demonstrated during the 1945 Election,[43] the party had settled down to a modest implementation of *Let Us Face the Future* and Morrison's 'need to argue each case' in state ownership. Avoidance of the barbed arguments of Harold Laski on one side and any sympathy for the Communist Party on the other* seemed to indicate that Baldwin had judged correctly Labour's essential attributes. In style indistinguishable from 'middle opinion' of the 1930s, utilising the Liaison Committee as an extension of central authority, rather than as mediator with the rank and file, Labour leaders 'thought they saw around them an efficiency-oriented managerial capitalism which had come to understand the evils of the unrestrained market and the need for cooperation with the state and with the unions'.[44] In spite of the party's recurrent concessions

*Despite its peak in 1944–5, when it achieved 55,570 members, 100,000 votes and two MPs, the CPGB lost political influence rapidly, as a result of identification with Russia in the cold war era, and Labour Party and TUC hostility. Any warmth from Labour MPs was repressed by the NEC: Konnie Zilliacus was expelled and his constituency, Gateshead, 'reformed'. But, as in the 1930s, the main work of marginalisation fell to the General Council, confronted with substantial CP influence in the ETU, foundry workers, AEU and the NUM, especially in Fife and South Wales. At one point, 9 CP members sat on the 34-man Executive Council of the TGWU. But the Communist Party's intemperate opposition to NATO, Marshall Aid, and wage restraint, gave the majority the advantage, and from October 1948 Vincent Tewson and Vic Feather moved to the offensive, denouncing CP 'sabotage' of European recovery and issuing to all unions *Defend Democracy* – an updated version of the 'Black Circular', without the sanctions. The big six took issue as well on wage restraint and succeeded in defining the CP as 'contrary to the whole conception of our movement, foreign to its traditions, and fatal to its prestige', *The Tactics of Disruption: Communist Methods Exposed* (TUC March 1949). In July 1949, Deakin persuaded the TGWU to forbid any Communist to hold union office: subsequently the 9 were forced off the Council and Bert Papworth was removed from the TUC General Council. Although the CP transferred its activity to the shop floor, achieving some success in the strikes of 1949–50, further penetration of the Labour movement became extremely difficult. The London Trades Council, older than the TUC itself, was expelled in 1952.

to the latter, in 1947 and 1950, its strength held in the lobbies, and at by-elections, till 1951.

Meanwhile, on matters of principle such as external strategy, NATO, the atom bomb, decolonisation and Empire, economic policy, and individual freedom,[45] its leaders took up positions not unwelcome to Conservatives of the post-war generation, adding substantially to the numbers of issues on which bipartisan agreement was possible in the fifties. Fewer questions debated in ideological terms in turn meant the further enfeebling of party as a means of presenting the electorate with choice. In opposition, Labour seemed unable to develop a theoretical challenge to the Conservative hold of the middle ground, yet eschewed a more socialist line (even though freed of the Communist taint) for fear of abrogating its future way to power. From *Labour Believes in Britain* (1948) onwards, the Party's propaganda was aimed at the white-collar rather than the manual worker. Subdued fanfares for the mixed economy predominated: 'the activist saw the welfare state and the nationalisation measures of 1945–8 as the beginning of the social revolution to which he believed the Labour Party was dedicated; while his leaders took these achievements to *be* the social revolution.'[46]

The Left grew strong enough to complain of its leaders' pusillanimity in the face of the Iron and Steel Federation's countermeasures, Conservative intransigence in 1950–1, the social costs of the Korean War, and their precipitate and ill-judged choice of a General Election in 1951. But with only a few points of strength in the unions to match its hold in the constituencies,* it could not yet bind the leadership, a fact which lent an air of unreality to the Bevanites' opposition. The issue was not one simply of socialism versus social democracy at parliamentary level. Conflict also occurred on the shop floor, in Trades Councils, and in constituency parties – and not always between the same sets of opponents. Left-wing trade unionists and local party workers were able during these years to develop a base from which to criticise both Gaitskell and what they considered an unrepresentative General Council;[47] and this movement, drawing fire from the grievances of lower-paid workers and skilled men suffering from changes in differentials, helped to accomplish the change in outlook of key unions in the middle fifties which in turn impaired the stubborn loyalty of the General Council itself.

*The Left drew its power in the PLP from the once divided constituency parties, as a result of the 1935 reforms. Bevan, Barbara Castle, Tom Driberg and Ian Mikardo held 4 of the 7 constituency seats on the NEC in 1951. Wilson and Crossman won 2 more in 1952.

Such a conflict could not have been avoided by hanging on in 1951; but nor could the Left have gained anything of substance without the consequent shift in trade union attitudes, and the worsening of Britain's economic position, which forced government to consider wage restraint as a prime means to control inflation and restore the prosperity on which electoral success was deemed to depend. But even with these advantages, the Left failed to establish permanent hegemony over party policy. As if to vindicate Anthony Downs' well-known prescription that competition drives political parties towards the ideological centre, Gaitskell won the war, well in advance of Wilson's ingenious peace.

The Party's managers, of course, and the solid mass of backbenchers, looking at the 1·5 million votes lost in 1955 (for the first time since 1931) tended to assume that progress towards socialism must wait on gaining power in a pluralistic society. Fundamentalism threatened the party's precarious centrist status. Also, the Left in the PLP, whether led by Bevan himself or his more disingenuous and no less ambitious heir, Harold Wilson, had never really embodied the radicalism of the party's base: the *Tribune* group, though committed to changing the party line, only challenged it on important *votes* twice, (on the extension of conscription in 1947 and on the hydrogen bomb in 1955). The TUC's volte-face occurred almost too late to affect the political balance, in the wake of Suez and Conservative turmoil, because Bevan, scenting a recapture of power at the forthcoming election, was already preparing to abandon unilateral disarmament. From the subsequent, unsuccessful, campaign, in 1959, it was possible to deduce how important non-aligned opinion had become, and hence the appeal to the centre: as the post-mortem showed, nearly twice as many people as in 1951 thought that it did not signify which party was in power.[48]

Finally, Gaitskell remained strong enough to defeat opposition on the issues he had chosen. On unilateral disarmament he overturned one conference decision, and if he conceded something on the revision of Clause 4 of the Party's Constitution, it was in deference, not to the PLP, but to the 1960 TUC (which refused to ratify the approval of the various delegates' conferences, given earlier, in March). Wiser than his successor seven years later, Gaitskell chose not to set the Party against the trade union movement on a doctrinal matter. Instead, he obtained the gloss he needed in order to change the emphasis of *Signposts for the Sixties* away from increased public ownership to the attack on wealth and oligarchic power.*

*'These men are not only wealthy; they are also powerful – a small and compact oligarchy. In private industry, the directors of a few hundred great combines determine

That the diatribe was directed at one side of the triangle, at a time when the increase in trade unions' *political* power, however negative, had become pre-eminent, seemed to matter less than the fact that the Labour movement rediscovered its coherence, sufficiently far in advance of the 1964 election. Nor did it seem to matter that the Party had evolved in a different way from those European socialist parties with whom it had shared many assumptions in the fifties. By 1964, Wilson appeared to have transmuted the dross of discontent by an alchemy based on the application of technology to industry, and opinion research to the electorate.

What had really occurred, however, resembled the dosing of a malarial patient with quinine: the symptoms disappeared, but the Party was not really strengthened, nor were its ideological fevers cured. Wilson's tragedy was that he reached the top fifteen years too late. His compromise might have transformed the Party and the trade union movement if it had been applied in 1951 or even 1955. By 1964, it was no more than many intelligent Conservatives judged necessary. And the Left, new or old, was not stifled by a leader who deprecated talk of Clause 4 as 'theology'. The dismal logic of 'integration', that class harmony could only be achieved if government maintained the incompatible aims of full employment, stable prices and rising living standards, resisted the facile claim made at the 1966 Conference that Labour – more than in 1945 – had become the 'party of government'.

In contrast, the Conservative Party began the period with its old wounds open, its dissident voices made coherent at the 1945 election only in a bravura defence of the past which defied the warnings of Topping's organisation review. Afterwards, this could be depicted as a sort of widom which had kept the Party free from over-hasty commitments, leaving it able both to explore the ambiguous desires of its membership and yet to avoid the archaic slogans, ranging from what Macmillan used to call 'Waldron Smithers and Co.' on one side to Leo Amery, plaintively reviving 1930's corporatism with his proposal for a 'House of Industry' on the other.[49]

That the inquest took place in relative tranquillity, before the Party again succumbed to the influence of its 'collective pursuit of power' (in Robert McKenzie's phrase) was due at least partly to the Labour

between them what Britain should produce. As their power increases, these men, together with the directors of leading insurance companies, are usurping the functions of a Government which is theoretically responsible to the whole people.' (*Signposts*, pp. 9–10.)

Party's cautious withdrawal on fundamental issues of power and individual privilege like the future of private education or the conception of private property rights implied by the Utthwatt Report on land usage. It also coincided with the 'liberal' attitude shown by the employers' organisations after about 1943: at the time of the Conservative motion of censure in November 1945, the Chairman of the FBI stated clearly that leaders of industry were ready to cooperate with the Labour Government and fit private enterprise into the new patterns.[50] The Conservative 'Industrial Charter' in fact owed much to the FBI, though less to the EEF-dominated BEC.

The one great survival of the inter-war years, whose history and personality might have obstructed the change, facilitated his own circumnavigation by holding the international stage. 'Deeply distressed at the prospect of sinking from a national to a party leader',[51] Churchill ran his Shadow Cabinet with the loosest possible rein; and in spite of diehard opposition from the managers in Central Office, Butler and his colleagues of the Industrial Policy Committee were able to draft the Charter and launch it with astonishing success.* The document accepted, in principle, the state ownership of coal, railways and the Bank of England; the welfare state; and central *indicative* planning, while all the time paying tribute to the Party's household gods:

Our abiding objective is to free industry from unnecessary controls and restrictions. We wish to substitute for the present paralysis a system of free enterprise which is on terms with authority and which reconciles the need for central direction with the encouragement of individual effort.[52]

These were sentiments which the hundred signatories of *A New Policy for Industry* could heartily endorse, though they might not have approved earlier hints of legislative controls over industrial practice.[53] But they were declaratory, not party dogma *tout court*, forming only part of a complex process of organisational readjustment stretching out from Topping's 1944 review to the prolonged consultation with constituencies which preceded the 1949 Maxwell-Fyffe Report.† As with all previous reviews, certain contradictions remained. Local autonomy still seemed threatened by the concept of a mass party – 'an

---

*2½ million copies were sold in the first three months. Butler, Macmillan, Oliver Lyttelton, Oliver Stanley and David Maxwell-Fyffe formed the Committee.

†Maxwell-Fyffe's inquiries, Macmillan later declared, 'started from the assumption that it was we who were at fault, and not the people of this country.' (CPAC 1962 p. 124.) He recommended three principal reforms, aimed at renewing the party's organisation and propaganda; at transforming its local organisations with the attributes of a mass party while at the same time increasing the responsiveness of central direction; and at eliminating, finally, the moneyed element among candidates.

educative political force and a machine for winning elections,'[54] while reorganisation ensured compliance in centrally-determined strategy, with only limited safeguards for democracy. But in fact central direction was much less powerful than it appeared to be, as the debate over the Industrial Charter revealed. Butler and the young Turks of the Research Department confronted a Central Office owing allegiance to Waldron Smithers and Co.; and although the names of Churchill and Eden sufficed to carry the Industrial Charter through the 1948 Conference, Butler's freedom in policy-making was subsequently curtailed, in the wake of the Maxwell-Fyffe report, which restored control to the leader – even if Churchill remained remote and, on fundamental issues, almost inarticulate.

In spite of the Charter, in the late forties the Conservatives displayed elements of ambiguity in many aspects of domestic and industrial politics. But they had succeeded, by implication, in repudiating much of the bleak legacy of the 1930s without dividing the Shadow Cabinet along historic lines. In public, and in party literature, the change was blazoned as 'reform by renewal', with Quintin Hogg searching for a new Tamworth Manifesto and the Butler Committee invoking Disraeli at every turn. 'As strategy, the principle was to withdraw from the position that the Socialist government was preparing to attack, leaving only a parliamentary force of skirmishers to occupy their attention, and to reform the party in prepared positions to resist the next wave.'[55] As a result, diehard opposition to the Charter and to contingent views about the role of trade unions could be sloughed off. Anti-union, anti-socialist propaganda suffered from the patent archaism of Smithers, Beaverbrook's *Daily Express*, and the small, doctrinaire right-wing papers, while the by-elections of 1949–50 (especially the loss of Hammersmith South) served to dampen premature triumphalism. As Churchill admitted, the narrow victory of 1951 enforced a caution which coloured the priorities of resource allocation in Butler's 1952 Budget.

Conservative refusal to stomach unemployment higher than the (historically unnatural) level of 1·5 to 1·7 per cent ensured trade union goodwill for the next five years. The diehards lost their voice: the 'free marketeers' seemed satisfied by the substantial modifications that *The Right Road for Britain* (1949) made to the Industrial Charter's stance on state intervention. In that climate, it was possible to absorb the National Liberals in December 1947 (though Clement Davies rejected Churchill's offer of alliance to the remaining Liberals in 1951). Central Office and Conference remained almost free from dissent until 1956, and contentious issues like African decolonisation or immigration, on which the right-wing made its challenge, were skilfully defused, usually by Macleod, at least until the Cabinet accepted the need for Commonwealth immigrants' legislation in 1961-2.[56]

Complete disavowal of the views of Lord Salisbury on Africa or the anti-immigrant lobby in the fifties, indicate how a party competing for the centre tacitly agreed to eliminate such questions from the national political agenda. It is not surprising that political observers at the time believed ideological principles to be a serious handicap to a governing party, nor that they pointed to the Labour Party's internal divisions as proof. R. T. MacKenzie saw pressure groups as being 'far more important channels of communication than parties for the transmission of political ideas from the mass of citizenry to their rulers',[57] and S. H. Beer confirmed that the Conservatives had accommodated their party to the realities of a triangular system of functional representation of producer groups, conceding a substantial degree of state management of the economy.[58]

With longer hindsight, it seems that the Conservative Party had, rather, fudged up a compromise, not between 'right' and 'left' but – to use Nigel Harris's terminology[59] – between statists and free marketeers, by settling, like Wilson after 1963, for an alternative strategy, based on the indirect management of an apparently open economy, where wages could rise as a result of collective bargaining because of increased productivity arising from technological change.

That conflict could be avoided was, of course, an illusion – but one based on belief in the prior responsiveness of management and unions to the requirements of government. Party ideology had been subordinated to the pursuit of votes. These were the years of 'situational control', of economic management by 'neutral' techniques, with obvious appeals, like the housing programmes of 1951-4, to consumer groups, even at the cost of crippling public investment in less electorally rewarding fields.[60] Competition at election time, over questions like pensions, reinforced the illusion of party differences, even though the policies themselves were characterised by their appeal to the middle range and the skilled industrial worker towards whom Eden deliberately directed the 1955 election campaign. In turn, the research apparatus measured the fifties' decline of the old, committed vote, and confirmed, in a neat circle, that these were indeed voters' preferences, thus ensuring that the Party would tie itself tighter to the criteria of performance.

At no time did the Conservative Party attack trade unions' negative power, by questioning the practicalities of full employment or the

420

principle of unfettered collective bargaining. Although the 'free marketeers' accumulated evidence that Monckton's concessions were merely Danegeld to insatiable trade union leaders, the Whips and the dense phalanx of lifelong backbenchers repelled criticism and ensured the exclusion of rebels, as they did during the far more serious crisis after Suez, when the Party split three ways at once. But a price *was* paid, by indefinite deferment of the debate begun in 1947 over the ideal role of the state in Tory cosmology. It could not be redeemed by conscious archaisms such as Churchill's espousal of the 1952 Budget as lineal heir to his father's Tory Democracy. Other great issues were also evaded in the period of Churchill's old age when the Cabinet creaked under an unworkable system of 'overlords'. Evolution towards European unity (despite the expressed views of BEC and FBI) was stifled, somewhere between Churchill's own largely emotional position and the party managers' factious attempts to cut Labour off from the development of European socialism.

Thus when the bad years began, after the balance of payments crisis in 1955 and failure to get wage and price restraint in 1956, attacks on wage inflation, the sanctity of full employment, and the negative power of the trade unions soon become acceptable, among a large sector of the Party, rather than a handful of diehards. At first, Eden refused to consider deflation. Unemployment was 'politically not tolerable',[61] whatever the effect of inflation on consumer expectations and his own election promises. Unfortunately, the Party got no credit for this altruism. Unable to reverse the expectations of union members, and habituated over ten years to consensus policies, the TUC could not deliver their side of the bargain demanded by the Cabinet; who in turn, in the aftermath of Suez, found themselves compelled to intervene in order to prevent the EEF from holding the line on wages.

Suez only aggravated the existing deep tensions in the Party, already revealed by the so-called 'middle class revolt' (which began in 1956 and called out Macleod's well-known defence of trade unionism at that year's Party Conference), which Eden's indecisive leadership would have been hard put to subdue. As it was, the struggle expressed itself in terms of personalities and Macmillan's search for harmony, stability and the avoidance of industrial conflict culminated, not in a public debate, but in a modified defence of the welfare state by Macmillan and Butler, against the Thorneycroft group who, in due course, resigned.

In a celebrated phrase, Macmillan made light of this dispute, as 'a little local difficulty'; but by retaining the cuts in public expenditure and the credit freeze which Thorneycroft, on Treasury advice, had initiated, and by not trying to check the slow rise in unemployment during Derick Heathcote-Amory's Chancellorship, Macmillan went some way to reconcile his party opponents. Control of inflation was declared necessary. But because prices stayed relatively stable in 1957–8, and Thorneycroft's resignation appeared to purge the Party of what Andrew Shonfield called 'worship of its primitive idols',[62] the TUC refrained from designating the figure of 621,000 out of work in January 1959 as a betrayal of the political contract.

By most standards, the government acted in this period with great skill, not only in sloughing off the Suez associations, but in discreetly encouraging management to shed labour and reduce overmanning, and achieving a modest decline in the rate of wage increases, without serious repercussions. But the cost of this compromise was much greater than in previous years. The TUC's belief, that the ratio of wages and prices counted for more than unemployment, lasted a shorter time than the business community's hope that affiliation to the EEC would rescue Britain from its structural economic malaise. Secondly, the free marketeers had not, like the Right wing, been marginalised after Suez. Party unity was sustained more and more by mechanical means, as Macmillan sought to manipulate men and policies through the secret Steering Committee,* and thus stifle wider debate. The setting of performance criteria, in publications like *This is what we have done* (1960) soon redounded to the Party's discredit with the onset of adverse economic circumstances. Wage drift began in 1961; the economy overheated and suffered from industrial discontent and unrewarding battles over wages in the public sector. Including the severe winter months, 1962–3 brought more days lost than in any year since 1926; in 1962 the Orpington by-election led the prophets of Liberal revival to conclude that the earlier middle-class revolt had only been temporarily suppressed and, at the same time, that the long years of affluence had weakened the Conservative allegiance of once-secure working-class groups.[63]

Worst of all, in the short-term, came a series of disasters: Macmillan's dismissal of a third of his Cabinet in July 1962; then the understandable but grave miscalculation over the Profumo affair; and the later personal attacks, reinforced by middle-of-the-road backbench MPs, which detracted from the Prime Minister's claims to have achieved 'the silent, the Conservative revolution'.[64] His latter-day defence of Con-

*An addition to the Liaison Committee, consisting of the Prime Minister, Butler, Hogg, Macleod and Edward Heath, the Chief Whip, with Michael Fraser as Secretary.

servatism, resting on a very abstract concept of individual freedom, which allotted policy to a pragmatic and undogmatic statism – pure Jean Monnet, a decade out of date – could scarcely contain the volume of protests, and while his legacy, the exclusion of Butler from the succession, helped to determine the form in which they afterwards emerged, it also saddled the Party with a leader 'who was hardly anybody's first choice',[65] without reconciling the now very divergent factions represented by Macleod and Enoch Powell – neither of whom would serve under Sir Alec Douglas-Home.

That division remained, unhealed by the vanishing dream of Europe, 'the last ace trumped by de Gaulle',[66] or the ascendancy of Edward Heath, cast as a liberal for his part in putting through the Resale Price Maintenance Bill – at the price of alienating most small businesses and shopkeepers. Heath attempted to reimpose the genial statism of the fifties but had to concede to his opponents the so-called 'Selsdon doctrine' in 1969 – at immense cost to the support of his subsequent government from both sides of industry. In spite of appearances, the business backgrounds of many Conservative MPs, and the continued preponderance of business groups in policy-making in the sixties,[67] the party which had instituted NEDC in 1961 (and in some eyes canonised the primacy of the governing institutions that sat on it[68]) had moved away by 1969 from statism and consensus policy, as a result of widening attacks from constituency parties which, appalled at the drift of voters, were reverting to attitudes abandoned twenty, if not forty, years before.

Although this tendency was checked, as it had been in the Labour Party, the strain on unspoken linkages and understandings began to undermine Conservative acceptance of corporate bias, revealing the system to be less monolithic, more susceptible to influence from below, and less in the control of party and institution leaders than had been imagined. What Beer, writing in 1964, called 'pre-modern' feelings threatened the authority created by half a century of continuous contract, even before the political leaders, Labour and Conservative in turn, set out to re-establish the primacy of party over institutions.

Symptoms of excessive formalism and lack of flexibility began to appear in all the component parts of the system during the sixties. Enthusiasm for sheer size and economics of scale began, sporadically, to be replaced by calls for devolution, disaggregation, participation, albeit without the enthusiasm which lent colour to the dramatic events in France and in Italy in 1968. In a very general way, the supposed benefits of consensus came to be seen, not as high aspirations as in 1940, but as the lowest common denominator of policies designed to avoid trouble. The growing complexity of the state apparatus, the real if unadmitted power of bureaucrats and technocrats over government, and the heavy-handed attitude of institutions towards dissent contrasted unfavourably with the actual inability of the state (compared with its European competitors) to accomplish its declared job of delivering a consistently better future. There is no lack of evidence (though inevitably, in the absence of official archives, superficial) to suggest that the parties to the triangular system had become formal, professional organisations to a degree unforeseen in the 1940s. Max Weber's rule of 'universal bureaucratisation' applied even to their constituent members, white-collar unions or industrial Federations. But the secular constraints which had ensured compliance to government and governing institutions' authority became jaded – appeals to the Dunkirk spirit succumbing, like patriotic calls of an earlier period, to sheer over-use.

The area in which popular consent had to be upheld had widened constantly since the 1930s, as matters such as supply of capital or wage bargaining, once regarded as outside the scope of government, became politicised. But since governments' performance could now be measured more easily against their own pretensions to manage the economy, the returns from official propaganda in a more sceptical, open society, steadily diminished. The trouble was not that the demands of those excluded from rewards impinged too harshly on the formulation of compromise, as Habermas forecast in the late sixties,[69] but that very much larger and better organised groups than before had to be appeased. This demanded a constantly rising level of activity, deleterious to the larger balance – witness, for example, the difficulties of Conservative and Labour governments after 1961 in placating at one and the same time immigrants and the anti-immigration lobby, while attempting to keep the whole issue out of national political life.

According to analysts of public opinion, deference voting, the numbers of those consistently supporting one party, and the turn-out in General Elections, declined after the mid-fifties.[70] Against a background of Liberal revival, a very widespread feeling accumulated that the parties were ceasing to be 'mass organisations' as that term had been understood in the uncomplicated post-war years, when youth and women's organisations attracted hordes of well-disciplined recruits. According to parliamentary party officials, the values of consensus politics made less impact, especially since politicians themselves seemed to sense, and at once appeal to, the lines of class cleavage which new age cohorts of voters imported as a prevailing characteristic of the sixties.[71] Yet the parties' mutual competitiveness, behind exaggerated election slogans based on a whole geography of market research and public relations work, brought them no nearer to discovering a golden key to unlock the public mind. It is quite possible that as early as the mid-sixties, electoral popularity had ceased to run concurrently with the economic cycle, though the supposed link between economic manipulation and voters' preferences remained part of conventional wisdom.

Several very general remarks can be made about the scepticism of this period when, for the first time in a century, a homogeneous, working-class, youthful culture broke out of the dreary confines of John Burns' pre-1914 truism – 'the tragedy of the working man is the poverty of his desires'. Changes in sexual habits, almost by definition, became a solvent of deferential attitudes. At a quite different level, the breach in the BBC's monopoly of radio and television altered the limits within which political variations and understandings had been aligned;[72] while the 1960 electorate 'more habituated to the printed medium than the electorate of any other large democracy' had, ten years later, turned to television as its prime source of political information.[73]

Cabinets had to readjust to the political implications of cultural change, as their predecessors had done after 1909. They still held substantial powers to inform and persuade; and the survival of continuous contract (see Chapter 11) can be gauged, if only in a negative sense, from successive governments' control over information which they deemed should not become public. The fact that the Official Secrets Act was used no more than once a year on average[74] indicates conformity, not lax judgment – the stark truth about repatriation of the Russians who had fought in the war for Vlasov against Stalin, and the pitiful remnant of pre-1920 refugees, who were handed back, unrequested, to imprisonment or death, has only recently surfaced,[75] while in 1945–8 the Labour Party was allowed to know very little about development of the atom bomb or the preparations Attlee's Cabinet made to use troops for industrial emergencies like the winter of 1947 – which took a form not unlike that of the old Supply and Transport Committee.[76] Ten years later it was still as easy to conceal the fact of collusion with the French government at the time of Suez, and to restrain the dissenting Anthony Nutting from publication of some of the facts until a safe eleven years had passed.

Continuous contract is not a question of protecting top secrets like the decoding work at Bletchley Park, with its unpalatable evidence of spying on other nations' communications in peace-time, but of the institutionalisation of secretiveness at all levels in the state apparatus. Of this, the extension of earlier conventions about Cabinet and civil service proceedings is a good instance. When the Select Committee of inquiry into the Civil Service in 1942 made far-reaching criticisms of bureaucratic rigidity, narrow, élitist composition, and Treasury inefficiency – much as Lord Fulton was to do twenty-six years later – the heads of departments met to concoct a reply; and not only rejected criticism outright, but warded off a dangerous proposal to keep the Service under review by a House of Commons Committee. Sir Richard Hopkins, for the Treasury, suggested that 'it would be the thin end of the wedge for introducing a system of Congressional Committees for sharing in the work of the executive government'. Edward Bridges, the Cabinet Secretary, feared that 'Gestapo-like bands' of MPs, quite unqualified, might entrench on the work of the Civil Service, and noted with relief that 'the Estimates Committee before the war had been prevented from asking policy questions, and had worked satisfactorily'.[77]

Twenty years later, however, both Estimates and Nationalised Industries Committees had skilfully widened their terms of reference to include policy, even before Richard Crossman, apostle of 'open government', initiated more specialised Commons' committees of inquiry. Meanwhile, confronted with the absurdity of having no formal access to Cabinet documents since the Secretariat started work in 1916, government itself brought in the Public Records Act, 1958 and the 'fifty-year rule'. Historians ground forward year by year (while private collections and memoirs from the 'forbidden' period held a premium for serialisation in Sunday newspapers) until rewarded with the prize of a thirty-year rule in 1967.

In itself, this amendment charted the shift in political climate: having pursued for years the lost private papers of Ministers who had escaped the net in 1934, and harassed former civil servants like Hankey and Thomas Jones,[78] the Cabinet Office suffered a series of reverses from the growing indiscretions of serving Ministers. As late as 1952, Attlee could still castigate Bevan for claiming that Cabinet collective responsibility did not outlast the fall of a particular government.[79] The old tradition was followed in their memoirs by Eden and Macmillan. But after 1960, the pace of revelation quickened. Dalton's third volume of memoirs, *High Tide and After*, gave detailed instances of Cabinet and other private discussions and was followed by a number of lesser indiscretions, all breaking the old conventions.

A trend began in which Ministers and Civil Service officials gave verbally the substance of Cabinet secrets, while avoiding open responsibility, to the authors of books like *The Battle of Downing Street*, and *Denis Healey and the Policies of Power*, and in 1965 Richard Crossman embarked on the diary in which he set out, quite openly, to challenge the whole corpus of information control.

The reaction of a prurient readership, avid for disclosures of personal foibles, vanities and betrayals, probably mattered less than the exposure of procedures and conventions created within a closed political environment to a public that had been kept politically illiterate. Crossman's 'revelations' about the role of the Civil Service may have done enormous harm not, as he intended, to stuffy, obstructive bureaucrats, but to the harmonious working of a finely calibrated machine whose values at first he simply failed to comprehend. However it was done, letting in the daylight on mystery – to use Bagehot's phrase – heightened rather than healed the breach between the real workings of the system and its formal presentation, weakening a major element in its coherence.

It is harder to discuss opinion manipulation in the very modern period. Looking at the fifties and sixties, Butler and Stokes commented on the increase in scepticism: 'A lengthening series of electoral studies might simply give repeated evidence of how very limited is the influence which political leaders are able to exercise over the mass electorate.'[80] It seems, on very limited evidence, that the post-war Labour Government felt uneasy about using the propaganda machine which it had inherited,* and that this curious altruism contributed to the increasing detachment of government information services from Party control, down at least to the mid-1950s. Labour responded to the anti-nationalisation campaign mounted by the Iron and Steel Federation, Aims of Industry and Tate & Lyle, with diffidence and a reluctance to drum up a populist campaign, that can only be explained by its belief in the prior need the government had for employers' goodwill.

The constraints which bound the 1951 Conservative Government in turn can be seen in their restraint from anti-union propaganda before the downturn in 1955 – the year in which Eden concluded: 'I knew that if we were to improve our position [in the election], I must in particular get my message to the better-paid, skilled industrial worker who could be expected to benefit from the kind of society we

---

*The Conservative Opposition and the press conducted a skilful campaign against 'excessive expenditure' in the information service to such effect that in 1948 cuts were made; the Central Office of Information remained careful to stay on neutral ground during the whole debate over nationalisation.

wanted to create.'[81] But circumstances and Nasser soon compelled him to revive the practice of manipulation to neutralise hostile comment in a manner reminiscent of Chamberlain at the time of Munich.*

This work, accompanied by evidence of governments' morbid sensitivity to public discussion of the briefing and lobby system,† suggest that possession of, and control of access to, technical and secret information continued to be a valuable weapon of control in political society. Indeed some of those who analysed the system in the sixties revived Ostrogorski's old fears in a new context, suggesting that access to the apparatus of advertising and opinion-testing would enable parties to manipulate mass opinion, causing it to demand rewards which, when in government, they could satisfy.[82] But a change was occurring even before 1964. For nearly five years of Wilson's administration, Downing Street was at loggerheads with Fleet Street, a condition only partly due to the suspicions of Wilson himself, a Prime Minister unnaturally preoccupied with his personal popularity. Macmillan and Home had already suffered similar exposure and, if the attacks were mild by American standards, and on the whole, superficial, they penetrated deeply enough to impair the appearance of magisterial authority of which, in his earlier years, Macmillan had been the outstanding exponent.

These twenty years saw the apogee of political stability, industrial equilibrium and economic prosperity, fortified by prolonged absence of ideological or class cleavages in society or the political parties. At any point before 1956, and generally until the mid-sixties, commentators could have been forgiven for concluding that conflict had been institutionalised through a pluralist system of representation. Britain seemed a model of the harmonious relations of governing institutions; and corporate bias a necessary component of a political system in which

---

*William Clark, Press Secretary at 10 Downing Street during the Suez crisis, recorded battering the parliamentary lobby, BBC and television with a 'well-orchestrated campaign of sabre-rattling', followed by the Prime Minister's off-the-record briefings with editors, not journalists, and Eden's preparations to control a hostile BBC, and to use secret funds to set up an alternative to its foreign news service – 'a ludicrous black propaganda station . . . to pour into Egypt the Goebbels-like stuff the BBC would not accept.' ('Ten Years after Suez', *Observer*, 3 October 1976.)

†As late as 1965 an *Observer* article 'The Prime Minister and the Press', which revealed some of its workings, brought a preemptory demand from 10 Downing Street to the editor for assurances of future good conduct. One aspect of the departmental briefing industry which deserves notice was the activity of professional diplomats in the Foreign Service who, largely at journalists' own request, dictated the substance of many diplomatic correspondents' reports during the post-war years, wherever in the world they happened to be.

intelligent economic management ensured that there was no need to defer gratification, and where social change could be achieved without undue distress to any group.

Whether the turndown related to economic, imperial or domestic political decline, or to social and cultural transformation, a sort of hardening of the arteries of communication set in during the late 1950s. Corporate bias continued to operate as a precondition of triangular harmony; but the messages between the parties, on which equilibrium depended, grew indistinct or distorted. However, governments possessed no other model. They could not intensify the process of 'creeping corporatism', even if they had wished to, because they were afraid of reviving objections from below, in particular from shop stewards and trade union rank and file, nor could they revive the supremacy of parliament because of the power of governing institutions. As the system decayed, therefore, the capacity of government to fulfil its over-extended obligations diminished, while, for lack of power to coerce, the state itself became slowly paralysed.

Faced with inflation, unofficial strikes, rising unemployment and falling productivity, it is hardly surprising that a new generation of political leaders tried to reimpose party order. After 1965, earnings and unemployment, which had held a close inverse relationship, diverged, suggesting that the old assumptions about the efficacy of Keynesian economic intervention no longer applied.[83] Such factors did not, automatically, produce a breakdown of the system and a reversion to traditional class or party antagonisms. But dissent, in the institutional constituencies, in small businesses or on the factory floor, was, noticeably, ceasing to be a mere marginal force operating imperceptibly against a massive citadel of economic and political power; while the majority of voters, who still eschewed radical change, could no longer avoid the conclusion that two decades of crisis avoidance had led to stagnant mediocrity.

Discontent could not easily be appeased by the fervid journeys of Ministers in search of EEC affiliation, nor the competition of governing institutions in what looked more and more like a 'zero-sum' game. After thirteen years' exclusion from power, optimistic Labour leaders, pursuing goals of economic rather than political management, over-confident in their capacity to halt decay, tried to reform the system from within; and, in the process, to use an appropriately scientific image, almost carelessly removed the protective ozone layer, exposing the system beneath to the excoriating rays of the sun.

15 A CRISIS OF THE STATE?

In comparison with the threats to the state's stability in the violent decade after 1911, the disturbances of 1964–75 hardly rate as more than a breakdown, followed by a sort of remission as yet too recent to assess. But even against that standard, the evidence of political change is not inconsiderable. Available electoral data, though not wholly satisfactory suggest that the arrival of cohorts of new voters, for example, in whom social class represented a dominant line of cleavage, may have been a powerful factor in weakening the parties' appeal to the centre for much of the sixties and in encouraging dissenting elements' appeal to fundamentalist dogma. The chronology, however, resists simple alignment: the electorate had become volatile, reflecting rapid but transient currents of opinion on such emotive issues as race or welfare benefits, and detaching itself from traditional party alignments. Yet after a period of exceptional Labour strength, followed by a swing to the Conservatives in 1969–70, subsequent evidence suggests that the support for the parties differed less between classes than it had in the early 60s, 'and a new cohort had entered the electorate in which the polarisation of party support was very weak'.*

Lacking a decisive mandate, governments of this decade slipped with apparent ease from centrist to dogmatic positions and back. The rapid rise in standards of living, housing and home environment of the previous decade made it hard to sustain further expectations, and symptoms of what in the United States was termed 'party decomposition' appeared, encouraging a certain revival of the House of Commons as forum of interest, and greater success for backbenchers' tilting against the windmills of Civil Service and Whips' offices.† Select Committees

---

*Butler and Stokes, *Political Change* 2nd ed., p. 411. The total vote cast at general elections dropped steadily to 72 per cent in October 1974; and the total number of votes cast for the two main parties fell from 85–90 per cent in 1950–55 to a mere 75 per cent in October 1974.

†In this category, Enoch Powell and Michael Foot revived the lost art of private members' obstruction to stifle House of Lords' reform in 1968–9; more recently

delivered a series of more pungent reports and showed greater ingenuity at penetrating the veils of official secrecy on matters such as Concorde costs, North Sea oil, and the PESC system of public expenditure.

On a more theoretical level, a demand developed for control of overweening Cabinet authority – Hailsham's 'elective dictatorship' – first through an Ombudsman and then in the search for a Bill of Rights; to say nothing of the slow-burning hostility to local government reform after 1972, and the explosion of Scots and Welsh nationalism. Yet these may only have been marginal events. In 1974 Lord Devlin found that 'all executive policy and most legislation is conceived, drafted and all but enacted in Whitehall';[1] while Parliament remained manifestly incapable of controlling current expenditure. In 1975, a Labour Government found it expedient to resort to referendum to validate a decision previously taken by both Houses of Parliament.

Perhaps the most significant phenomenon of the decade was disillusion with hung parliaments, electoral promises, and all the sterile show by the gladiators performing on a narrow stage. Government's opinion manipulation weaponry grew increasingly obsolete as the practice of information control suffered a whole succession of defeats, ranging from the highest Ministerial leaks which fuelled Peter Jenkins' *The Battle of Downing Street* (1970) to the Attorney-General's unsuccessful prosecution of *The Sunday Times* for publishing extracts from Richard Crossman's Diaries, which represented, in fact, a deliberate offensive directed against what Crossman had seen as an organised hypocrisy preventing not only public discussion of the rights and wrongs of any given Cabinet policy but any reasoned debate about the nature and value of secrecy itself.

The Government's defence against Crossman rested on what the Cabinet Secretary termed 'the requirements of good government and the proper functioning of the public service'[2] – matters of judgment which were never satisfactorily elaborated beyond the claim that 'a public right in the public interest' existed, even if a specific term of restriction could not be agreed. Yet, although the Diaries were published, Crossman did not achieve complete posthumous victory, for the state retained indirect sanctions, not least through the power of prosecution, and publishers' natural timidity about the appalling cost of litigation. To the present day, reform of the Official Secrets Act has been resisted, safeguarding Britain's record as one of the most secretive political

---

George Cunningham neatly saddled the Scottish Devolution Bill with near-unworkable conditions and John Mackintosh and Brian Walden emasculated the Dock Work Bill, 1976.

societies of the Western world; tart comment on a system which, informally, can permit copious ministerial revelations, within two years, of the most secret Cabinet debates such as those concerning the financial crisis of November 1976.*

The pervasive influence on press and public feeling of government and Treasury thinking about inflation and unofficial strikes since the appointment of the Donovan Commission on industrial relations in 1965, for example, scarcely needs emphasis – public opinion turned against 'shop stewards' militancy' as if that alone had been responsible for the country's failure of economic achievement.† Inculcating the mass electorate with fears of balance of payments and inflationary crisis to the exclusion of unemployment, and finding in the 'unconstitutional' pretensions of management or trade unions a scapegoat for government's own failings, may, in the tradition of Lloyd George, have represented a triumph of propaganda over public interest between 1965 and 1974. Only in the latter year did public odium against the Heath administration, after the three-day week, provide evidence of a temporary but substantial revulsion against the hegemony of political leaders and their use of communication skills.[3]

In another way, however, governments themselves prejudiced the state's residual authority. Suspicion of the theoretical right of judges, in Lord Simmond's words, 'to enforce the supreme and fundamental purpose, to ensure not only the safety and order but also the moral welfare of the state', was nothing new, nor the speculation that judges, like other men, tended to reflect assumptions absorbed from their background and upbringing.‡ But a corrosive hostility to the judiciary,

---

*It is worth adding, however, that the capacity of the State apparatus to conceal the reasons for important changes of policy survives virtually unchecked. The history of cut-backs in teacher training colleges since 1971 offers a significant recent example. (See David Hencke: *Colleges in Crisis: The reorganisation of teacher training 1971–77*, 1978.)

†Butler and Stokes, *Political Change*, 2nd ed., p. 199. 'Politicians, ably assisted by the mass media, successfully created the impression that if only strikes could be made to go away, they would take with them most of Britain's ills . . .' (Tony Lane and K. Roberts, *Strike at Pilkingtons*, Collins, 1971, pp. 235–7.)

‡Fifty years earlier, in 1920, Mr Justice Scrutton had declared: 'The habits you are trained in, the people with whom you mix, lead to your having a certain class of ideas of such a nature that, when you have to deal with your own ideas, you do not give as sound and accurate judgment as you would wish . . . Labour says "Where are your impartial judges?" They all move in the same circle of employers, and they are all educated and nursed in the same ideas as the employers. It is very difficult sometimes to be sure that you have put yourself into a thoroughly impartial position between the disputants, one of your own class, and one not of your class.' (Quoted in CIR Report no. 69, HMSO 1974); and it was a judge, Lord Atkins, who observed that some of his colleagues in the sixties became 'more executive-minded than the executive' in their urgency to check the decline of political conformity and the failure of Parliament to provide redress.

reflected at the level of academic discussion, seems to have been encouraged by organised opposition to the Industrial Relations Act and Court, after 1971, and by both parties' transparent surrenders to outside pressures in cases like the 'Pentonville Five' or the surcharge imposed on Clay Cross councillors. A real, constitutional danger grew, not simply of discrediting the legal system in public estimation, but of governments using the law for fundamentally incompatible political ends – as the Donovan Commission well understood. The law could regulate the balance between individuals but not between bodies whose power rested on extra-legal assumptions.

The common law knows nothing of a balance of collective forces. It is (and this is its strength and its weakness) inspired by the belief in the equality (real or fictitious) of individuals, it operates between individuals and not otherwise. . . . This, and not only the personal background of the judiciary explains the inescapable fact that the contributions which the courts have made to the orderly development of collective labour relations have been infinitesimal.[4]

Governments' attempts to circumscribe the trade unions' political power by statute brought about a dissociation between legally-prescribed activity and activity legitimised by a form of mass popular democracy, a clear enough cause of class tension and civil disorder, exposing as it did for fiction the theory that parliament is sovereign and showing, for the first time since February 1935, that governance rests ultimately on public tolerance of its authority. Beside this lesion, other more general evidence, like the shift in balance of advantage between different groups of workers, to the benefit of white-collar groups and most lower-paid manual workers, or the weakening of moral constraints which had formerly militated against immediate gratification in the form of demands for cash in hand, is too vague to serve as more than a hint that industrial conflict was outgrowing its habitual boundaries.[5]

As if in defiance of political instability, industrial concentration took place with remarkable speed, creating an oligopoly of giant firms in most sectors between 1967 and 1973, in the largest continuous series of mergers, amalgamations and takeovers ever seen in Britain.* Whatever the demands of socialists or free marketeers, governments hastened to bail out these giant concerns when the world recession and their own economic policies put their liquidity or production at risk. This could be depicted as a gain in the negative power of corporate management;

*In twenty major industries surveyed in 1969, three firms on average controlled between 50% and 90% of each market. (M. A. Utton, *Industrial Concentration*, Penguin, 1970.)

433

as true, in the *economic* (though not the political) dimension, as the continued influence over Labour or Conservative Party, even during the Selsdon period, of trade union leaders' fear of compulsory wages policy or deflation. The Labour Party's first devaluation debate, in November 1964, for example, was aborted out of regard for the impact on employment, and when devaluation could no longer be resisted, in November 1967, a wage freeze was rejected as impractical, in the face of union opposition.[6]

Economists will, no doubt, argue a long time over whether the rise in industrial productivity, coming on top of the technical improvement of industry in the mid-sixties, could have sustained the ambitious target of the 1965 National Plan, and if so, whether it was sabotaged by a failure of industry to invest (leading to redundancy, shorter working hours, and unplanned growth in the tertiary sector) or whether it was sacrificed to government's assumptions about the balance of payments and defence of the pound. But, cumulatively, the effect of changes of direction, as Chancellor succeeded discredited Chancellor, Reginald Maudling, George Brown, Roy Jenkins, and Anthony Barber, manifested itself in profound disillusion with the Treasury's role *vis-à-vis* inexpert Cabinets and with the very concept of Keynesian demand management. Most clearly, the period of 1965–8, strewn with signposts to the abandonment of *any* national plan, and the appearance of surrender to union expectations on wages, destroyed what confidence employers and managers retained. Subsequently, governments' lasting break with the old commitment to full employment completed the alienation of the TUC.

It is not the economic aspects of Labour's attack on wage inflation and the three bleak years that followed 1966 which matter here. Labour leaders had reunited the various parts of their movement and sold the result to the electorate on their capacity to heal growing class divisions. George Brown even heralded 'the end of the class war'.[7] Labour's integrative philosophy, however, had not changed. Regeneration applied to what already existed, based on an endorsement (implicit in policy documents since 1958) that wages and unofficial strikes and personal consumption all needed to be controlled to achieve economic growth.[8] Such tenets led to head-on conflict with trade unionists' alternative understanding of how policy should be made, without any corresponding gain in trust from management, who took the government's conversion merely to be the beginning of wisdom. To have achieved the voluntary cooperation of both parties would have required much more goodwill than this.

434

In the first stage, however, when it still seemed as if the Department of Economic Affairs might fulfil Haldane's 1918 requirements of a Ministry of Planning, private discussion between the General Council's Economic Committee and BEC/FBI (soon to become the CBI) and government aroused greater expectations than had existed since 1961. Management, of course, hoping to lower unit costs, favoured wage control, and Brown unwisely failed to insist on price control as a *quid pro quo* for the other side. But George Woodcock and the General Council, though looking for a positive contract, believed the Cabinet spoke their language and took Cousins' presence there as a guarantee of responsible behaviour. All three parties collaborated, from the Joint Statement of Intent, December 1964, to the drafting of *Prices and Incomes Policy* in the following April. Each then interpreted the sequel differently. The General Council imagined that NEDC would have a directive function – a transfer of power to the triangular forum which Wilson's Cabinet had no intention of making. Instead, they were left with a sop – 'the national interest, as defined by government, after consultation with management and unions'.[9] Even if the subsequent White Paper had not failed to satisfy trade unions' more egalitarian requirements, that assertion of where power lay would probably have prevented agreement.

Thereafter, opposition coalesced among trade union rank and file and in the TGWU and white-collar unions of which Jack Jones became the spokesman, while George Woodcock, John Cooper (GMWU), Sir William Carron (AEU) and Les Cannon (ETU) held to the Party line. Fatally, the Cabinet let the last-named group think that wage restraint would only hurt in extreme cases, while it allowed time for a sustained defence of the principle of collective bargaining and for restoring the purchasing power of manual workers, who had done relatively badly in the late fifties. But in any case, Harold Wilson and his Cabinet began to assert their primacy not only in the Labour movement, but in the management of the economy, as a necessary precondition to solving Britain's endemic problems. Whether they considered the depth of trade union feeling, or the degree to which their policy involved putting the clock back, is not clear: how far they took General Council assent for granted, however, can be gauged from their proposal that unions should implement the prices and incomes scheme at the same time as the Prime Minister was appointing the Donovan Commission to reform them and cure the 'disease' of unofficial strikes.

However justified their intention (and contemporary comparisons with other European countries suggest that unofficial strikes caused

435

fewer stoppages than inadequate maintenance, absenteeism, etc.), the Cabinet's conversion to the idea of statutory control preceded by several months the economic strains which destroyed the National Plan; and it prevented anything like full consultation with the TUC, the institution most nearly concerned. Wilson may, personally, have allowed the Cabinet to become overwhelmed with legislation to the exclusion of industrial strategy,* and the financial panic and expenditure cuts of July 1965 undoubtedly alienated his supporters on the General Council; but the decision to legislate and to use George Brown's gifts of persuasion to cajole the TUC, cannot be seen as anything but intemperate and destructive.

On 2 September 1965, Brown's skilful presentation won the accord of a General Council flattered to be asked to take part in rescue on such a grand scale. As in 1915–16, they preferred to work with the DEA and Ministry of Labour, as agents for an unpopular policy, rather than let government override them altogether.† Like Arthur Henderson in the First World War, Woodcock won over the majority. But at the Party Conference, the constituency associations demanded in return price controls and fresh nationalisation – a trend accentuated when the CBI was seen not to be collaborating fully in the 'early warning system'.‡ Further trouble was postponed by skilful handling of the Prices and Incomes Bill in Parliament while the Cabinet waited to increase its majority at the General Election. 'But the next Labour government was to learn to its cost that when phrases inevitably take form as policy instruments, meanings become less obscure and divisions bite deep'.[10]

Afterwards, the Labour government was freed from constraints of a narrow parliamentary margin. But during the previous twelve months, hourly wages had been rising at nearly 10 per cent a year, while company profits fell. Clearly, the cooperation of the CBI could no longer be taken for granted. While the Bill went through its stages, the government fought what looked like a test case against the Seamen's Union, in May and June 1967, with a deal of lurid language about the Communist menace, uncorroborated by evidence. When Cousins finally resigned,

---

*Crossman commented: 'As for the PM, he is economically trained, God knows, but he is incapable of imposing a strategy. . . . He has not insisted on a steady, controlled, concerted central purpose which would dynamise the whole machine of Whitehall.' (*Diaries*, vol. 1, p. 277.)

†The TUC asked for a concession that the government would only legislate if they failed to enforce restraint – very close to their behaviour over the Derby scheme on conscription.

‡A position justified by the CBI chairman, John Davies, on the ground that it was a voluntary body, unable to dictate to its members (CBI evidence to Donovan Commission, 23 November 1965, p. 323).

in July, to declare that the Bill terminated any 'understanding between employers and employed on what wages should be',[11] the General Council ignored the omen. Nevertheless, over the next few months a number of portents of discontent appeared, among trade union-sponsored MPs and on the General Council, with Hugh Scanlon's election to the presidency of the AEUW in 1967, and Laurence Daly's as secretary of the NUM. Given the opposition of Cousins and Jack Jones of the TGWU, the Cabinet could only now count on Cooper of the GMWU for absolute loyalty, as it switched, under Treasury influence, to deflation, pushed the Prices and Incomes Bill through, and tacitly abandoned the principle of full employment.*

The custom of triangular discussions seemed to have been abrogated: neither General Council nor CBI was consulted about compulsory restraint of wages and dividends. But this reassertion of party hegemony on the pretext of Britain's international difficulties may explain why the parliamentary party acquiesced. The Left as yet lacked TUC support. Woodcock pushed opposition to a vote but lost by 12 to 20 on the General Council, which then knuckled under, enabling George Brown to announce their surrender 'for the good of the country'.[12] Although government supporters' majority had lessened since 1965, rank-and-file protests were also defeated (by 3·9 million to 5 million votes at the TUC in September 1966) – both results due to a vestigial belief that the Labour government would return to economic growth after the 'temporary' crisis, and an understandable fear of precipitating its fall and repeating 1931.[13]

In contrast, the CBI was able to extract concessions from government on price rules; and their openly expressed wish for legal sanctions[14] may have been a substantial stimulus to the Cabinet's decision to make wages policy permanent – which was endorsed, ironically, by the Party's intellectuals (who knew little of trade unionism and who, like Crossman, had long been contemptuous of its leaders) on the ground that it would destroy the free market system and facilitate the introduction of socialism. Slowly the Labour movement was being polarised, the Cabinet, with the majority of NEC and General Council, running, however unhappily, against trade union rank and file, while the Left of the parliamentary party stood uneasily to one side.

The triangular consultations in September 1967 showed the Government dictating to the TUC and whispering softly to the CBI. But the

---

*Unemployment rose from 260,000 (1·1%) in July 1966 to 600,000 (2·6%) in February 1967 – a level not far beyond the previous post-war limit, but psychologically disturbing. The trend was not reversed.

Prices and Incomes Board was already making decisions piecemeal, opening the way to a whole series of inter-industry comparisons and to 'collective bargaining' in a novel form, most unwelcome to the Cabinet. Real earnings fell 1 per cent that year, reversing a decade of rising expectations, and a sudden if slight fall in union membership[15] suggested that the limit of tolerance had been reached. 'This resentment is building up,' Woodcock declared in March. 'Perhaps to the government it remains hidden below the surface, but to me and the General Council it is hitting very hard, frequently'.[16] Alienation symptoms ramified within the constituency parties, and Labour lost control of the Greater London Council after thirty-three years. But the Government, convinced that the unions could be made agents of social control, refused to take advice, either to forget legislation, or to accept the TUC's own (TGWU-inspired) alternative scheme.

Although the Prices and Incomes Bill was limited to one year, the Cabinet, fully supported by the Treasury, determined that there should be no return to voluntary wage-bargaining. Ray Gunter, Minister of Labour, was already urging the Donovan Commission to produce stringent recommendations on the legal framework. At last, trade union dissent burst out. Woodcock was arraigned by the rank and file at the September 1967 Trade Union Congress in a debate where the whole relationship of TUC and government came into question, and the dissident white-collar unions' *Plan for Progress* was passed by 4·8 million to 3·5 million. Although a bare majority was also obtained for the Prices and Incomes Bill, the meeting declared that, 'The mistake should not be made of assuming unquestioning and indefinite support of trade unionists, irrespective of the policies being followed',[17] a démarche followed by Scanlon's victory in the AEUW on a poll which united CPGB and the Left against 'Carron's law' and incomes policy.

The Cabinet responded, not to the TUC but to external circumstances. The Prime Minister tried to hold the redoubt against economic failure, taking personal control of the DEA from the supine Michael Stewart. But devaluation, which could have been beneficial in the summer, came, bodged in November, as a result of the Six-Day War in the Middle East, accompanied by austerity and deflation in order to secure the mass of foreign borrowing and, after the cuts of January 1967, the IMF conditions. These, in turn, vitiated trade unions' respect for the Labour Cabinet. The 'temporary crisis' had run on too long and the Economic Committee, in its review for 1968, charted its own alternative, and made a devastating comparison with 1931. Once again, a Labour Cabinet was betraying the movement for 'national' reasons;

worse, it was downgrading the role of the TUC within the state. NEDC 'no longer appeared to be fulfilling its original functions and was being used more and more as a sounding board for government policies'.[18]

As in 1931, the TUC could expect no support on this front from the CBI, riding high on expectations of permanent wage controls and post-Donovan legislation against restrictive practices. Paradoxically, however, the closer the TUC came to a break with the Cabinet, the more vital seemed its forty-year-old position *vis-à-vis* the state. Unable to take on, simultaneously, Cabinet, Treasury and CBI on the two fronts of wages policy and the survival of the corporate bias system, the General Council began to see that it had to fight two quite separate engagements, neither of which could be allowed to end in total victory or defeat. The need to wean Wilson and his colleagues away from their misguided attempt to impose Party supremacy was not, Jack Jones wrote in February 1968, reason 'to put the political clock back a hundred years'.[19]

Meanwhile, in spite of the dampening effect of the Prices and Incomes Bill on money incomes during 1968, an increasing number of unofficial strikes succeeded.* Their impact on the economic state and political composition of industry frightened the CBI.† Led, as usual, by the EEF, particularly the motor manufacturers, Ford, Rootes, British Leyland and Vauxhall, and with considerable support from the Conservative pamphlet *Fair Deal at Work* (April 1968), the CBI demanded a curb on the shop stewards' challenge to managerial authority.

Unfortunately for the Government, the Minister of Labour and the CBI, the Donovan Commission found for the defendants, in the sense that it made an important distinction between the formal and the informal but no less real aspects of trade unionism, and recommended incorporation of the latter, while deprecating statutory interference either with wages or procedures. What the Cabinet now sought differed from Donovan's findings on almost all counts; and to counter their effect Wilson took care not only to insert in the Prices and Incomes Bill the

---

*James Callaghan let slip a phrase about that being the last year of statutory restraint, and although he was disavowed by Wilson, his words seemed to indicate a change in outlook on the Labour NEC.

†Plenty of evidence existed of the disruption of integrated production, especially in the car industry and shipbuilding; also of wage drift, and the spread of plant bargaining, in which, thanks to the habitual complaisance of many employers, national rates were seen merely as the starting-point. Employers were not the only ones to suggest that union hierarchies had lost control: the Minister of Labour gave evidence to Donovan that 'if trade union leaders accept [the P and I Bill] there is a risk that they will cease to be regarded by their membership as representative of their interests, and their influence and authority may be transferred to unofficial leaders.'

blandishment of statutory recognition of the TUC, as against the unofficial movement, but also to place Barbara Castle, an acknowledged figure of the Left, at the restyled Department of Employment and Productivity (which succeeded the Ministry of Labour). Ignoring trade union lack of cooperation, Wilson and Castle took a high line at the Party Conference in autumn 1968 and, spurred by a fresh wave of strikes in the engineering industry and the appearance of a Conservative revival based on anti-union sentiment, moved rapidly towards *In Place of Strife*.

As a declaration of the primacy of party, using the power of the state, in the pluralist system, the Wilson–Castle White Paper was probably in tune with much contemporary political thinking, even of members of the Donovan Commission.[20] It envisaged wide government powers to intervene, not only in unofficial strikes but in inter-union disputes. But whatever the formal recognition conferred by the White Paper, the trade union movement could not stomach legislative control. Its negative power has never been better demonstrated than in what followed: for the General Council ingeniously resolved the problem of confronting the government and endangering its role in state activity by declaring, in effect, that on the Labour movement level *this* Labour government no longer represented working-class interests. On this issue the three groups, minority right, Woodcock-led centre, and the Jones–Scanlon wing could agree.

But in any case, the anger of the rank and file could hardly have been contained by compromise, even if Woodcock, who joined the Commission on Industrial Relations in March 1969, had not been replaced by Vic Feather. A month before, a strike at Fords (where the engineering shop stewards took a line as hard as that of their EEF employers) revealed the extent and density of resistance, when, contrary to previous practice, the TGWU and AEUW rallied to the shop stewards by making the dispute official. Having long assumed implicit support from the official leadership, the management was demoralised as well as infuriated by Jones's and Scanlon's response to the radical sentiments of manual and skilled workers. This strike also accelerated the publication of *In Place of Strife* since it seemed to put the Cabinet's authority at risk – one of many matters which Wilson took as a personal affront to his premiership.

Feather sympathised more openly than Woodcock with the rank and file. Nominee MPs in the Commons were mobilised: 53 voted against *In Place of Strife*, 40 abstained in the largest rebellion of the Parliament. The old claim to have 'created the Labour Party' was heard again, and, in a divided Cabinet, Callaghan emerged as the defender of trade union rights. Time being vital, Ministers settled for a quick Bill, which the Prime Minister, in apocalyptic mood, declared essential to economic victory, 'essential to the government's continuance in office'.[21] But the more he dramatised events, the worse the division grew. If 63 MPs pledged themselves to vote against the Bill, would the Government pass it with Tory votes? In the last resort 'the majority in the party was still chiefly concerned with avoiding a disastrous split on the question and still hopeful that Harold Wilson would reach an accommodation with the TUC.'[22]

This search for accommodation to avoid another 1931 inspired the General Council to handle tactfully the Special Conference summoned to reject *In Place of Strife* and endorse its own counter-proposals, *Programme of Action*. If the Cabinet paid the price and let the Bill fall, the TUC would do its part, as it had in 1965–6 (or in 1915–16). And however much Wilson and Castle manoeuvred, during the six meetings with the Council, 12 May–18 June, they were shifted remorselessly away from attempts to modify the Bill, to find something on which pride could survive but which the TUC would endorse. It was not simply a face-saving exercise: Ministers genuinely doubted whether, after so much backsliding, the General Council could without the statutory powers discipline its member unions as the state expected of a privileged institution.[23] No such guarantee was forthcoming, however, and, in the end, Wilson had to concede the substance, in return for much less than the TUC had given Attlee in 1949. The 'solemn and binding' undertaking, based on nothing more tangible than the thirty-year-old Bridlington agreement, showed that even with the support of one side of the triangle, a Cabinet which had totally committed itself could still not exert state power against the other, if that had dug in its defences.

The sequel showed that nothing of value had been gained, apart from this demonstration. Unofficial strikes continued, and a crescendo of wage inflation produced conditions in which the British economy almost foundered in the next seven years. The government, admittedly, tried to activate part II of the Prices and Incomes Bill in 1969 with modest success, since the parliamentary Left and the TUC both baulked at another confrontation shortly before a General Election. But prices and incomes policy succumbed in any case in a mass of inflationary settlements, following the strikes of 1969.* Economic disorder set in

---

*Days lost in strikes: 1967 2·8m, 1968 4·8m, 1969 6·8m, 1970 11m (Panitch, p. 214). Meanwhile profits declined, and exports tapered off, with no rise in investment and little in consumption – hence a lack of demand, and no improvement in *(con.)*

long before the June 1970 election transferred the damnable inheritance to a Conservative administration, unwilling, in its first phase, to check the operation of the 'free market'. Although the General Council did try to restrain demand (at least until February 1970, when government abandoned all pretences, against the flood of claims, particularly from lower-paid public service workers, aiming for higher minimum standards rather than the percentages of the statutory period*), those unions that cooperated suffered decline in membership or, like the GMWU, debilitating battles with rank and file such as the strike at Pilkingtons in April–May 1970.

Although the Heath Government was not committed to wage control, it was as disinclined as its predecessor to submit to institutions' negative power, and sought instead to re-assert the notion of party mandate (even if the verdict of June 1970 was unexpected and far from decisive) much as Baldwin had conceived it after the fall of Lloyd George. There was to be no more talk of a 'house of industry', but instead – as if Donovan had never reported or *In Place of Strife* been withdrawn – 'a fresh, clear comprehensive framework of civil law to make a more favourable environment for change, to buttress responsible action and to provide some deterrent to the small, irresponsible minority.'[24]

Deriving originally from proposals put forward by the Inns of Court Conservative Society in 1958, the Industrial Relations Act rejected,

---

productivity. In the four years after the demise of the DEA, the Treasury policy merely shifted emphasis from industrial investment to exports. Later trends in the Barber period (1970–4) speak for themselves: there is no need to emphasise the disastrous shifts, allied as they were to bounding inflation and unrestrained increase in money supply.

		Consumption outside industry	Net investment outside industry	Consumption by industrial workers
1967–70	As percentage of industrial	48·5 – 48·3	15·6 – 15·9	19·4 – 20·3
1970–74	production	48·3 – 52·0	15·9 – 18·3	20·3 – 21·6

		Net investment in industry	Net exports	
1967–70	As percentage of industrial	7·8 – 5·7	8·7 – 9·8	
1970–74	production	5·7 – 3·2	9·8 – 4·9	

Source: R. Bacon and W. Eltis, 'Declining Britain', *Sunday Times*, 9 November 1975.

*As H. A. Turner and Frank Williams suggest ('The Wage Tax Spiral and Labour Militancy' in D. Jackson, H. A. Turner, and F. Wilkinson, *Do Trade Unions Cause Inflation?*, Dept of Applied Economics, Cambridge University, 1972) the government's fiscal policy, tax levels, etc., affected *disposable* income and was a major factor in causing the lower paid to reject wages policy.

much more comprehensively than *In Place of Strife*, the triangular system which had obtained in British politics since the late 1920s, and reverted instead to the state of mind exemplified by the Churchill–Cave proposals for union reform of 1925–7. Privilege and legitimate authority were seen to derive from the state, in return for which institutions owed a duty to cooperate in achieving national aims set by governments in fulfilment of their party's mandate. The theory had, of course, been implicit in the Wilson–Castle Bill: but now it was declared, unequivocally, that, as befitted a large corporation, contracts would be legally binding – as if to recover the ground lost in 1906; and this position was backed up with penalties, governing not just trade unions' official actions but the actions of their members, however unrecognised or unofficial.

Quite apart from the very short time allowed for consultation, and the hints that amendments to the Bill in advance of Second Reading would be inadmissible, the TUC could hardly have accepted such a reversal of the terms of politics as they had been understood for a generation. Any doubts about the dangers of 'political' opposition to a newly-elected Tory government, such as the TUC had had in 1951, were soon removed by the effect on the attitudes of militant rank and file of price inflation and of well-publicised evidence of speculative gains in secondary banking or property. The General Council contested the Bill, letting the TGWU take the brunt, and brought it to a standstill in February 1972, three months after its introduction.

However passive the resistance, however divided the TUC on the question of civil disobedience, anti-government strikes or expulsions of unions which registered under the terms of the Act, it created the first deliberate breach with a party administration since 1926. But the General Council, though driven from below, could rely absolutely on a Labour Party only too keen to bury all memory of *In Place of Strife*; and on the distrust of the whole scheme shown by many members of the CBI, in particular the large companies who, almost universally, refused to use the new powers, leaving it to small firms (Con-Mech, Heatons) or individual eccentrics to bring them, by factious usage or special pleading, into more disrepute than need have occurred.

Fines on the TGWU failed to deter dockers from boycotting container depots, in precisely the sort of intra-union dispute least amenable to legal resolution; and when the Industrial Relations Court jailed five of them (the so-called 'Pentonville Five') the rank and file leadership, fortified by the effect of the miners' victory, after the Wilberforce Report in February 1972, advanced demands for a general strike. Taking the chance of the Law Lords' reversal of the Court of Appeal's

443

verdict, the Official Solicitor intervened to free the five, giving the Act, in practical terms, its quietus. A Conservative government, unprepared for the disruption of a general strike, and unsure of the attitude of the CBI, had learned again the lessons of May 1915, February 1935, and November 1941, that the law could not be enforced against organised mass objection.

They had come, however, much nearer than their predecessors to destroying the conventions on which the tripartite system rested. The *Financial Times'* hyperbole, that the Act 'might divide the nation more deeply than at any time since, perhaps, 1688, and that, whoever won, it might take generations to clear up the mess',[25] was not wholly unmerited. When the Government changed course, seeking to restrain wages in concert with the TUC (though not to the extent of giving up the Industrial Relations Act) and then, in the 'Chequers period', July to November 1972, wooing both sides by an attempt to recreate a sort of quasi-corporate harmony, it proved almost impossible to rediscover the bases of the system which corporate bias had helped to institute.

In any case, Heath failed to convince TUC or CBI of the Government's conversion; he seemed not to listen to the TUC's warnings of the effect of unemployment, nor those of the CBI about the dangers of class warfare. Too much instability had accumulated for Britain suddenly to emulate German or Swedish patterns of behaviour, created in years of economic growth.

Instead, against the sombre backcloth of a world recession – the years 1973–4 which, in John Cornwall's phrase, marked 'closing time in the gardens of the West' – wholly unprecedented inflation,* and a liquidity crisis right across industry, not only in the over-stretched, speculative fields, the Cabinet was forced into its own statutory wages and prices policy, stretching through three stages down to the fall of the government in 1974. In contrast with their compliance after victory in 1969–70, the TUC refused to collaborate with the Pay Board or Price Commission, their remaining feelings of responsibility† to the state succumbing to the rank-and-file pressure demonstrated only too clearly by the one-day

---

*In 1971–2 real earnings rose 7·4 per cent compared with money earnings of 15·4 per cent. In 1972–3 the position was reversed, money earnings standing at 13·9 per cent, real earnings a mere 1·1 per cent. Inflation reached 20 per cent on an upward curve, and by 1974 only wage demands of 30 or 40 per cent could bring real improvement. Meanwhile unemployment had risen sharply to one million, the fateful level of inter-war memory, while profit margins declined precipitately. The balance of payments deficit for 1974 was nearly £4,000 million after a year in which public expenditure had risen 40 per cent.

†550 settlements, covering 4 million workers were actually made in 1973 under Phase 1.

national strike decided on in March 1973 by a Special Congress, against General Council advice, and by the intransigence of the AEUW against the Industrial Court's sequestration of its assets, and other alarmingly violent manifestions of 1973 – the behaviour of pickets at Shrewsbury, and the feelings expressed by the miners' wage claim and subsequent most effective strike.

True to the end to the view of his Government's national mandate, and in a profound sense, to the traditional view of the two-party system, Heath let the logic of antagonism lead his Government (undermined by the cataclysmic effects of the 1973 Arab–Israeli war, coming on top of world recession), into its last, impossible battle against what were seen as direct challenges to government by miners, railwaymen and power workers. Even if the alarmist language on both sides is discounted,* an irreconcilable conflict had developed. But the appeal to the electorate in February 1974 presumed that voters alone, and not the governing institutions, could deliver a mandate commanding universal assent. Even if that had been true, the voters, assailed by anxiety and doubt, in the middle of a state of emergency and the three-day week, were not able to give a decisive answer, and settled for a Labour Party irretrievably committed to crisis avoidance.

Class divisions had opened up to such a point that moderate Conservatives may well have been happy to see a Labour Government returned. As in 1944–5, employers and managers in a sense detached themselves from the dangerous appeal to the nation, over the heads of the nine million voters who were also affiliated to the TUC. They had already won from the government the entry to the EEC through which they hoped to break out of Britain's economic straitjacket. The majority of the CBI were not prepared to contest the supremacy of party over trade unions any longer, since, manifestly, legal restrictions did not work; and the stage was set for Labour to abandon the doctrine that they and the TUC were subordinate, albeit privileged, institutions. But the reaction, like the cause, exceeded anything that had happened before: Labour's penance, in the early stages of the 'social contract', appeared to involve such submission to TUC dictates as to make the old balance of forces irrecoverable.

For the TUC offered no guarantees, but instead required government's performance on a series of weighty demands: abolition of most of the Industrial Relations Act and creation of the Advisory Conciliation and Arbitration Service (ACAS) out of the remnants; substantial

*M. McGahey declared the Scottish miners' intention of bringing down the government (*The Times*, 27 January 1974).

changes in the laws of picketing and tort; the very wide and contentious powers contained in the Employment Protection Bill; and commitment to the economic policy (permanent price controls, a wealth tax, government controls on large and multi-national companies, etc.) enshrined in *Economic Policy and the Cost of Living*, the statement issued jointly by Harold Wilson and Vic Feather in December 1973, which marked the Labour Party's act of contrition for *In Place of Strife*. In addition, the General Council took a share on the Liaison Committee which gave it greater influence over the Party, as a whole, than at any point since 1932.* This in turn bolstered the Left in the parliamentary party, giving rise to exaggerated fears in the press and Opposition of a capitalist *Götterdammerung*.† There is no doubt that the price of the Labour Party's peace with the TUC involved legislative measures which substantially increased the special status of trade unions at law, first recognised in 1906. The balance of power in industry shifted further – to the detriment of employers and management. Although no formal change took place in the relationship between the government and the TUC, the terms represented the most complete capitulation by the Labour Party to the industrial movement.

But in office, the deadly combination of unemployment, inflation and industrial stagnation forced the new Cabinet into another rescue operation, doing the work of which the Heath Government had been incapable. Faced with runaway wage demands in 1974, Wilson's Cabinet had to ask the TUC for restraint, as part of the 'social contract'; and the General Council accommodated them. Over three years, haltingly and reluctantly, the TUC helped to achieve wage restraint, and the predicted revolt from the shop floor evaporated, not simply because, as Conservatives claimed, sanity returned, nor, as the Left deduced, because of a reversion from class-based consciousness to the mish-mash of social democracy, but also because very many trade unionists came to understand that the political principle at the heart of debate in the previous seven years had been won, and was being implemented in labour and industrial legislation more far-reaching than any since the late 1940s. On this understanding, it was possible to accept a pay policy previously inadmissible, at a time when unemployment was still rising, far beyond the million, and public expenditure was being cut back; and

*The Liaison Committee was composed of 9 PLP, 10 NEC, 7 General Council; but its actual membership, and the effective position given to Jack Jones and his colleagues, gave the TUC more than numerical parity.

†Wedgwood Benn declared: 'The crisis we inherit when we come to power will be the occasion for fundamental change, not the excuse for postponing it'. (LPAC, 1972, p. 187.)

in the autumn of 1976, despite mordant predictions from the pessimists,* to acquiesce in the conditions for salvation imposed by the IMF.

Having defeated the attempts to reassert party over institutional power, the trade union movement felt able to withdraw to a less political stage. Secure in the leadership of Callaghan, erstwhile opponent of *In Place of Strife* and a far better guarantor of the future than Cousins had been in 1964, the TUC renewed the 'social contract' for three years, on terms which looked like a reversion to a very old division of political life. 'It is an elementary requirement of our basic purpose that we should do everything possible to contribute towards maximising the revenue of a firm or industry to increase the prospects of obtaining better wages and conditions,' Lord Cooper had told Donovan eight years earlier. 'We consider that industrial relations would be significantly improved if more firms regarded trade unions and collective bargaining as valuable institutions in promoting the objectives of the firm, to everyone's benefit.'[26] In the Employment Protection Act and ACAS, the means now existed to make that claim hold as far as employers were concerned; and the TUC forebore, even when supporting measures to reduce unemployment in 1976, to *insist* on a *quid pro quo* from government for stage III of pay restraint. Many of the General Council accepted the validity of the 1976 economic diagnosis, even if they did not couch it in the terms of IMF or CBI; and the progression back to the centre of former economic radicals, led by Jack Jones, seemed to complete the cycle began in 1964.

Without in any way suggesting that history had repeated itself, it does appear that some of the patterns of the period of equilibrium had been restored. But if there is not much evidence of permanent breakdown, comparable to the 1911–21 crisis of the state, changes different in kind as well as quantity had taken place since 1964. Shop-floor trade unionism had survived attempts at assimilation and control by the General Council and, having dissociated itself from the old stigma of Communist association, had received the accolade of the Donovan Commission's analysis that plant bargaining could be 'richer in content' than the old national agreements.[27] The clear breach which occurred between the first shop stewards' movement and the union hierarchies after 1917 did not recur in any simple fashion, although it was true to suggest that its

---

*"The performance of the economy since 1964 had been worse than most observers would have thought possible: and the situation in 1976 was so bad that it was reasonable to wonder whether the sacrifices that would be needed to get the economy back into internal and external balance could really be exacted by a government which had to rule by consent.' (Stewart, *The Jekyll and Hyde Years*, p. 234).

edge of class-antagonism often reflected the functional inability of the TUC to represent a heterogeneous membership.[28] Time and again militant rank and file opinion – of which shop stewards themselves were often only a reflection – stimulated changes in General Council policy, not only because leaders like Jones and Scanlon naturally responded, but because in many areas of industry, particularly the most advanced, technologically and structurally, union officials were being promoted 'with long experience of shop floor "unofficial" unionism behind them, men whose political base lay not within the official lay committees of the unions but rather on the shop floor with the rank and file.'[29]

Changes in the social composition of trade unions combined with the economic position of many firms suffering attrition during the world recession to create a certain common ground between shop stewards and middle management. Development was haphazard, often inconsistent, (as can be seen from a notable series of cases that suggest the reverse, stretching from the 1966 seamen's strike and that of 1967 in the London docks, through Pilkingtons in 1970 to the British Leyland toolmakers, from 1976 onwards, in which plant activists found themselves opposed by an overwhelming combination of employers, government and General Council). But during the political battle, after 1967, the General Council (which was far less oligarchic than in the 1950s) could not ignore this local level nor treat its representatives as 'agitators', diverting attention from its own failings in the style hallowed by Bevin and Deakin.[30] In February 1967 the Ford strike shattered comfortable illusions among union leaders as well as employers, forcing them to accept the existence of a form of workplace representation which had not been able to challenge that of political parties for more than forty years.

That the General Council did respond to the political requirements of its mass membership, however reluctantly, is suggested not only by its action against *In Place of Strife* and the Industrial Relations Act but by the notable decline in shop stewards' separatist activity after 1969. Officials, needing no lessons in mass democracy, carried the banners against the Industrial Relations Act.[31] Local organisations still suffered from the defects shown after 1919: apart from a handful of special cases such as the Cowley plant at British Leyland, there is little evidence to support David Coates' theory that a shop stewards' movement could *by itself* have gone on to mobilise a fiery and effective working-class consciousness; indeed in some industries, where bargaining called for a high level of technical skills, shop stewards seem to have become divorced from the factory floor and identified themselves with lower management – a factor which supports Alan Fox's recent revision of his evidence to Donovan, in the view that trade unions tend to operate on the margins of the structure of economic power, within the curtilage of given assumptions about national aims, rather than in contradistinction to government or management.[32]

Caution on economic questions in the mid-seventies, and diffidence about pressing for measures to create employment or to limit managerial prerogatives, or even campaign *à l'outrance* against confirmation of EEC membership in the 1975 referendum, should not, however, be seen as evidence of TUC political pusillanimity. It was no easier for the General Council publicly to trumpet its influence over government than it had been for the NCEO in the 1920s.[33] Still, it existed. So also did the General Council's own concept of the direction of the Labour movement. If the majority of trade unionists opposed the EEC on the grounds that joining a 'capitalist club' enhanced management's inherent advantages, that did not prevent Jack Jones and others from making contact with European socialists or Communist trade union federations and urging the sluggish British movement to accept their conclusions that the crisis of the Western world would be more likely to paralyse the 'club' in other countries. And that long-delayed awareness of European change, allied to the power demonstrated at home in 1967–74, tended in the long run to separate them from the little-England parliamentary Left, wrapped in its cocoon of nostrums derived from a vanished economic past.

Formal parity with the CBI or NEDC, on 'quangos' or other government bodies, which the press tended to group together under the pejorative heading of the 'new corporatism', mattered much less than the fact that a claim had been established to speak not merely on industrial policy, but on areas which in the past the TUC had recognised as the sphere of government: fiscal policy, investment, monopolies and the location and stature of public and private industry.*

This is not to say that trade unions' claims were substantiated for all time. The dissent of several individual unions from the 'social contract' after 1975, and divisions in the TUC about the Bullock recommendations on industrial democracy in 1976, indicate continued diversity in the movement. In the matter of short-term results, the TUC did badly out of the 'social contract'. In terms of organisational strength, actual

---

*A development foreshadowed by Hugh Scanlon in 1969: 'Conventional collective bargaining techniques are not appropriate for dealing with technological changes, particularly when the time in regard for planning has been reduced from decades to months . . . Those decisions may threaten technological unemployment, disappearance of trades and industries and geographical displacement of the workers themselves.'

P

control over its numbers, it is still weaker than the CBI,* though vastly more influential within the ambit of government policy. What Lloyd George deplored in an institution aspiring to governmental status – the inability to strike bargains and then make them binding on the great mass of trade unionists – remains the major factor preventing a revival of corporate bias (as the history of wage negotiations in very recent days, since 1976, has shown); although it is fair to add that that weakness was heavily accentuated by the appeasement of particular groups of well-organised workers in key industries by the Labour government after 1974.

The majority of recent commentators stress the convergence of *fundamental* interests with management, as union membership extends to the majority of all workers (having passed 50 per cent in 1974) and the increasingly careful demarcation of areas of 'acceptable' conflict. But to say that trade unions 'tend to treat as irrelevant to their [industrial] strategy whatever commitment they may have to another social order',[34] or that trade unions 'cannot transform society because their very nature and the character of their aims requires them to work within it'[35] does not mean that they never respond in defence of class positions. Class antagonism, as Dahrendorf suggested twenty years ago,† may have been avoided, but only when the political status of the movement, as understood by its mass membership, was not endangered. When it was, after 1967, a class tension reappeared. A similar deduction applies to the CBI and employers' response to the Bullock Report; and this dialectic would have been impossible, if both bodies had not retained their power within the state to redress the ambitions of the political parties and of each other.

It is impossible to say whether the system of corporate bias, destabilised, apparently deliberately, by parties trying to regain their lost dominion between 1966 and 1974, can be restored, since that depends on too many variable factors and on the doubtful ability of Cabinets to plan and achieve economic success commensurate both with the demands of public opinion and the constraints imposed by governing institutions. But even if it were to be restored, it could not be in the old form of creeping corporatism, because it is hard to see trade unions'

---

*Its finances depreciated rapidly from a peak of £1 million reserves in 1974 to £300,000 in 1976, and an overdraft in 1977, thanks to the refusal by larger unions to raise their subscriptions.

†'Industrial conflict has become less violent because its existence has been accepted and its manifestations have been socially regulated . . . By collective bargaining, the frozen forests of industrial conflict have been thawed.' (R. Dahrendorf, *Class and Class Conflict in Industrial Society*, p. 257.)

collective political power confined to the old, negative formulation. Even if trade union leaders remain diffident about claiming the full political potential of their movement, for fear of public recrimination, the movement's representative function has increased, over a wider area of state policy, as a result of the 'social contract' and the powers granted by legislation after 1974; and it is unlikely that a future government will make the mistake of treating the TUC as a mere agent. But it is equally unlikely that the General Council could so far forget the power of shop stewards and the mass membership, particularly of manual workers, ('factory-consciousness' to use Benyon's description), and unions' own locally-bred officials' experience, as to try and recapture the old oligarchic style. This, too, has affected the behaviour of the leadership and must, in due course, produce changes in their conception of the role of trade unions within the state.

In comparing 1929 with 1911 an enormous shift of political power could be seen to have taken place, benefitting in different but roughly equivalent ways the two parts of the Labour movement in Britain. Contrasting the later 1970s with the 1960s, a change has also taken place, but of unequal dimensions. Trade unionism, in its widest, non-sectarian sense, has become a more immediate, responsive vehicle for the representation of working people (by which I mean the actual membership, including very many members of what in other terms would be designated lower-middle or middle class). The lineaments of class struggle remain, but not in the sense utilised by Marxists in the past – though that is still useful for an understanding of pre-1940 history. Conflicts now tend to run within, rather than between, classes and this, rather than 'false consciousness' explanations, or an arbitrary assumption that, over forty years, working-class interests were best served by mere tactical compromise with government and employers, must be the answer to the problem posed earlier: of how to equate corporate bias with the existence of class consciousness. The transformation *vis-à-vis* the two mass parties – both of which, of course, retain immense working-class memberships – has had little to do with the conscious actions, sectarian ambitions or public pronouncements of trade union leaders or General Council, but much to do with the changing nature of civil society, the industrial economy, and the actual events of the decade.

As a result the political *potential* of the trade union movement (which resembles, in Masterman's famous phrase, the thing as yet powerless to be born) has transcended the relationships of the system characterised by corporate bias. Whatever may be true in the sphere of wage bargaining and specifically industrial activity, it overshadows the potential

451

of employers, owners and management to influence the organisation of the state; and however negatively the General Council may transmit the inchoate political will of its membership, trade union hegemony has broadened out further than in any comparable Western nation, profoundly to alter the nature of the state. This has, of course, no more to do with the present *formal* organisation of trade unions, their old-fashioned constitutions and archaic rule-books or their oligarchic behaviour, than had the appearance of political parties in the 1850s to the age of mass politics which followed. It is their potential as representatives of mass opinion collectively expressed on non-party lines which presents a challenge to the essence, and not simply the form, of political parties which cannot for very long be postponed.

The long process of political attrition suffered by the CBI in its first decade of existence was due partly to inherent structural failings, and partly to a pervasive feeling among its member companies that the attempt to re-establish party supremacy over trade unions, though bad for industrial relations, might lead in the long run to economic growth. A Labour government set on the course pledged in 1964 needed a CBI with an organisation and representative quality on NEDC comparable to that of the TUC. Hence the acquiescence of a reluctant EEF in the FBI/BEC merger in 1965,[36] and the support of the CBI for the National Plan, wages policy and finally *In Place of Strife*. But the Wilson and Heath governments failed, and the consequences reduced much of private and public industry to a ruinous pitch. The CBI in effect withdrew to prepared positions, safeguarding itself until order should be re-established. But the industrial climate deteriorated so far, that individual companies, disoriented by the *sauve qui peut* of Confederations and CBI, took their own remedial courses, making wage settlements as best they could against the inflationary tide – some of which, in extreme areas like the Coventry toolroom agreement or the Newspaper Proprietors' Association's dealings with the printing unions, surpassed the proverbial Danegeld.

Battered by protests from below, the CBI reasserted itself after 1974, first against the Employment Protection Bill, and secondly against the recommendations of the Bullock Report, 1976, on worker participation in management. Indeed, a Marxist analyst might suggest its role expanded as a consequence of an awareness among the capitalist class as a whole that its position was becoming increasingly insecure, not least because of the declining significance of the parliamentary system in general and the Conservative Party in particular.

On its own, however, the CBI had a poor record, dating back to the Pyrrhic victories of the sixties (such as the struggle to bring the motor manufacturers back into the EEF) which had not prepared the organisation for confrontations like that with the AEUW in 1967–8. Many Confederations evaded collective action against unions for fear of losing more members. But the CBI had concerted policy in its recommendations to the Donovan Commission with panache and success – *In Place of Strife* appears to have drawn heavily on Andrew Shonfield's 'Note of Dissent' to the Donovan Report. Moreover the lead taken by the EEF in setting up a long-range research and planning group to assess contemporary trends in industry, and its renunciation of the old secretive aspect by issuing a host of glossy publications intended to humanise managements' appearance, had some long-term effect.

In political terms, the CBI could not hope to rival the TUC during the lifetime of the Labour Government 1964–70. But after 1970, in spite of its record of support for wage restraint, *In Place of Strife* and industrial relations legislation, and its identification with the Heath Government's declared aims to hold down prices in nationalized industries, abandon price control, and recognise the 'right to profit' (which inspired the EEF to launch its ill-judged attack on the power of engineering unions in October 1971), the CBI found itself largely ignored by a Conservative Cabinet bent, like its Labour predecessor, on party primacy. No consultation took place on the abrupt change in policy towards large companies at financial risk, nor the 1972 Industry Bill which extended to Rolls-Royce, Chrysler and the rest the blanket support previously afforded only to nationalised industries. Instead, after its 1971 offensive had been undermined, the EEF found itself facing £50 million losses in production, chaos in the motor industry, and the old engineering trades Procedure torn to shreds.

Management recoiled from the effects of political preconceptions illogically changed after being carried to extremes. In 1971, the EEF had deduced that 'the balance of long-term power has shifted in some ways which suggest that the cost of resisting, or risking industrial action, has increased, and in a short-term calculation of least-cost, firms found it easier to concede'.[37] But after the subsequent carnage, which weakened militant white-collar sections like TASS as well as themselves, and showed that in fact government would intervene at almost any cost, the EEF turned again to collaborate with government – with some unacknowledged assistance even from the AUEW.

The CBI membership as a whole took up a similar position. Reluctance to use the Industrial Relations Act,* and acknowledgment, in the light of post-Donovan analysis, that in many cases bad conditions (such as failure to implement health safeguards, for example, in the asbestos industry) had been responsible for shop-floor discontent, improved their public face. Many companies showed themselves not unfavorable to the closed shop, even to the Employment Protection Bill,[38] on the assumption that trade unions would become allies in rationalising the scope of conflict within individual firms. The CBI recommended cautious overtures, starting at the base: 'Participation should begin at the shop floor – some agreed form of top-level machinery is only likely to work if a suitable "infrastructure" has been established and is operating successfully.'[39]

Reassessment on the part of major companies did nothing, however, to check the drift away of smaller firms, alienated first by the period of conflict and then by the political compromises after 1974. These gave the CBI only marginal support in the fight against what industrialists often called the 'Doomsday Machine' in 1973–5, and their political animus entered at a different level, into the 'free market' sector of the Conservative Party. And if *The Road to Recovery* (1976) represented the larger companies' conversion, it was aimed at recreating something less than the system of the sixties, just as *The Future of Pay Determination* (1976) threw the onus back on government, trusting in a battered Labour Cabinet to define the national interest in a sufficiently congenial way. Proposals for joint determination of fiscal targets echoed rather than rebutted the more pungent claims of the TUC, leading the CBI inevitably towards acceptance of a subordinate role in state planning.

Rather than take issue with the great companies, as the heirs of Crosland argued,[40] the Labour Government conceded a more favourable interpretation of profit after the 1976 financial crisis, eased cash flow problems, and allowed more sway to NEDC. Most important, on the fundamental political questions raised by the Bullock Report, it responded to CBI negative power (as skilfully and bluntly deployed as the TUC's response to *In Place of Strife*) with a recent White Paper bearing substantial concessions drawn from German and Swedish models, so that participation seemed likely to be relegated (as many

---

*Of a sample of 60 large and 21 smaller companies investigated in 1973–4, only 2 of the large, and none of the others, had made legally binding agreements. (B. Weekes, *Industrial relations and the Limits of Law: the industrial effects of the Industrial Relations Act*, 1971, Blackwell, 1975, pp. 58–60.)

trade unionists also wished*) to supervisory rather than main boards. But while the Bullock proposals antagonised management on political grounds (quite apart from any anxiety, in industry, Cabinet, Treasury or the rest of the Civil Service, about renewed ideological conflict) and stimulated their most cogent collective activity for thirty years, it in no way restored the CBI's overall influence, when set against the institutional hegemony of the TUC.

Ideological and factional strife inside the parties continued to evolve on asymmetrical patterns, as it had done since 1956, but with far greater real fervour than the stylised contests between Labour and Conservatives. In the Labour Party, the fundamental incompatibility between socialist aims and integrative practice had been deep-frozen by the accord of 1963, only to be thawed out and revived as a by-product of the struggle for supremacy in the movement five years later. So far as ideological positions were concerned, until 1968, or perhaps the early 1970s, the 'illegitimate' Left scarcely counted as a danger; but within the Party, Crosland's heirs had refurbished the decayed Marxist intellectual tradition and provided a fresh stimulus to the leftish majority which had developed, largely as a result of the 1967–9 struggle, on the NEC. As a whole, the parliamentary left benefited from the derogation of Wilson's authority, not so greatly as to dominate Cabinet or Shadow Cabinet, but so as to permit considerable influence over policy and the choice of personnel, perhaps for the first time since defeat of the ILP's programme, *Socialism in Our Time*, in 1928–9.[41]

In itself, this change hardly solved the ancient dilemma of a party commitment to goals whose support from militants tended to undermine the managerial confidence on which the 1974 Cabinet relied to stave off collapse of the mixed economy. But the accord between Party and TUC, consummated in the Wilson–Feather declaration of December 1973, provided a moral foundation on which the Left could accept, however unwillingly, the rescue operations which transformed the 'social contract' later, and which, after 1975, sustained a sort of party unity notably lacking in Wilson's later years. Paradoxically, opposition

*The 1977 TUC divided on Bullock, the AUEW, GMWU and ETU, *inter alia*, expressing wide reservations. The AUEW went further – declaring that 'In the context of rejecting Works Councils the TUC does so because either they will duplicate existing structures at plant level and, therefore, be superfluous or, even worse, supersede them. We concur with this view but maintain that such an argument is equally true of Supervisory Boards' stunting the possible further growth of collective bargaining ... their greatest danger is that the boards would create the illusion of power without the reality.' (*An Investigation into the Scope of Industrial Democracy*, AUEW, June 1976.)

came from the old centre-right of the party who were suddenly exposed as the tide of anti-union sentiment turned. Figures like Reg Prentice and Ray Gunter suffered as a result.

Although the Party appeared to march to the left of Wilson's 'broad church', notably at the 1972 Conference, which saw the apotheosis of Wedgwood Benn, and although it afflicted Wilson himself in the terrible years 1974–5, the change lacked depth when set against the political advances made by the TUC. Wilson's last service may have been to keep the parliamentary party's Left quiescent when drafting the 1974 Election manifesto. By 1976–7, especially after the Chancellor, Denis Healey, had reverted to economic orthodoxy and monetarism, Labour's 'integrative function' looked uncommonly secure.

But there was no longer any place for the social democrats' old antipathy to trade unions, despite the much-heralded secession of a handful of intellectuals. With the decline of individual membership,* the trade unions established practical as well as policy-making hegemony – counting 5·7 million of the party's 6·5 million members, sponsoring 127 of the 319 MPs successful in the October 1974 election, providing £3 million to the election fund, and the subscriptions of 7·1 million trade unionists – in all, 80 per cent of the party's total income.[42] As Jack Jones had pointed out at the 1971 Conference, 'in the past we have not had the dialogue necessary. The unions and the party leadership perhaps have both been unsure of their own ground; but we can make this policy with a great campaign to open up the approach to genuine industrial democracy based on the unions.' Since then the Labour Party has looked primarily to the Liaison Committee rather than NEC or PLP. The intellectual Left has lacked weight without TUC sanction – the real brunt of Paul Johnson's diatribes[43] – and the explicit socialism of *Labour's Programme* (1976) seems written on water when compared with the Liaison Committee's three-year plan.[44]

The Conservatives had been scorched by the flames of ideological fury long before their return to office in 1970.[45] Though held in check at

---

*A steady decline in the vitality, size and financial resources of constituency parties occurred after 1969, especially in inner cities; it was largely ignored by the leadership, but seized on by Benn, who, with unerring acuteness, used it in his populist arguments: 'Much of the present wave of anxiety, disenchantment and discontent', he told the Welsh Council of Labour in 1972, 'is actually directed at the party structure. Many people do not think that it is responding quickly enough to the mounting pressure of events or the individual or collective aspirations of the community. . . . It would be foolish to assume that people will be satisfied for much longer with a system which confines their national political role to the marking of a ballot paper once every five years.'

Shadow Cabinet level, the traditional Right accommodated to extreme positions, and attracted the support of Enoch Powell, on the very issues such as civil rights (especially in Ulster), immigration and sovereignty, which had previously been subordinated. It was not a question of direct support for, or cross-membership with the National Front (which reached its peak of 13,000 members in the mid-seventies, supported by no more than 100,000 voters[46]), nor even the stance of groups like the Monday Club and the National Association for Freedom, but of multiple examples of constituency dissent which developed in the late 1960s.

Edward Heath's attempt to maintain party unity by retaining the symbols of opposing forces, Macleod and Powell, in his Shadow Cabinet, may, as in Gaitskell's case, have ensured that the divisions did not become factions. But avoiding open disputation enhanced the tendency towards feverish and secretive policy-making in immense and often otiose detail in the years 1964–70. In complete contrast to the analysis after 1945, no consultation with the Party took place. Instead sheaves of detailed verbiage were launched on an uncomprehending and often resentful membership, in the strongest exercise of leadership theory since the days of Peel. The result, contrary to conventional wisdom, suggested that the leader was not the only, perhaps not even the dominant force in the Party. Propaganda did not exactly fail (though Central Office paid the usual price after 1974, as it had in 1945 and 1929); but the leadership moved too fast and too obscurely for a party genuinely and deeply divided, even if in tactical terms it successfully avoided asking questions about the nature of conservatism, facing the challenge posed by Labour's early success.*

Unexpected projection into office in 1970 exposed many contradictions, especially in the Party's industrial policy, between its commitment to the 'free market' orthodoxy of the Selsdon programme, and its 1972 second thoughts as the government abandoned harsh commercial logic to rescue the over-mighty industrial casualties. The Party lost the allegiance of management and the banking world generally. On the other hand, after Heath had been replaced by Margaret Thatcher, it seemed to have regained what in electoral terms may have been a more tangible asset, that of small businesses and shopkeepers, ratepayers' associations and all the paraphernalia of the *petit bourgeois* vote – a very old element in party strength, though lacking influence since the 1920s, which Heath himself had done much to antagonise at the time of the Retail

---

*'*How* we do things, rather than what needs to be done' provided the ambiguous keynote to *Putting Britain Right Ahead* (1965).

Price Maintenance Bill in 1962. Above all, the anti-trade union, anti-corporate, anti-bureaucratic element in the Party was strengthened, far more than at earlier times such as Powell's ill-directed campaign on immigration or the anti-EEC movement.[47] It mattered little to this sector that they looked back to a golden age, somewhere before 1914, which was a sheer archaism, given intellectual coherence only by the fashion for monetarism with which it happened to coincide.

At constituency level, the nature of Conservative support also changed in class and geographical terms, to make it more recognisably an English, rather than a Scottish or Welsh party, even when looking for new adherents among groups of skilled workers and the under-25s. That these trends have in no way diminished tensions between the two wings is suggested by the prevailing confusion of voices on industrial policy; with James Prior on one side instructing the party that it tried too much, too soon, and without proper consultation with trade unions,* and on the other the 'free marketeers', led by Sir Keith Joseph, who still avoids the hard question posed by Sir Otto Kahn-Freund: 'What I cannot see is that any government (outside of a totalitarian dictatorship) can, by threat of legal sanctions impose upon both sides of industry an incomes policy which they both reject.'[48] Yet the antithesis is not clear or simple; one side cannot be called corporatist, nor the other anti-socialist.† Very recent studies suggest that crisis avoidance has not been rejected in favour of ideological purity,‡ and perhaps the recent tensions arise more specifically (and superficially) from the need to harness two horses, and the fear that a dual policy of appeasing both anti-union sentiment in public, and union power in private, cannot logically be sustained.

In spite of the appearance of ideological polarisation in the political parties, the integrative function of both has survived; and the dramatic events of the last ten years may have prevented them from becoming cadre parties, as was sometimes suggested in the late sixties.[49] The

*In particular, see Prior's interview with John Torode, *Guardian*, 15 September 1977; and the conclusions of the party inquiry, after taking evidence from ex-civil servants and industrialists, that any future anti-union policy must fail (*The Times*, 18 April 1978).

†Sir Keith Joseph may have moved to the Right as early as 1969, but he has also written, more recently, 'any social arrangements for our epoch must contain, harmonise, and harness individual and corporate egotisms if they are to succeed.' (*New Statesman*, 13 June 1975, p. 769.)

‡'The fundamental concern of Toryism is the preservation of the nation's unity, of the national institutions, of political and civil liberty, and not the achievement of some ideological victory.' (Ian Gilmour, *Inside Right: a study of Conservatism*, Hutchinson, 1977, p. 6.)

effects of ideological disputes, however, had a deeply disturbing effect on the assumptions and understandings which had formerly supported triangular collaboration. Like an overloaded electrical circuit, the system began to blow more fuses than electricians could cope with in that dismal decade. Many of the symptoms of breakdown after 1965 were class-based – extra-parliamentary action, civil disobedience and disregard of constitutional authority, resentment of power 'inherent in anonymous social mechanisms and assumptions'.[50] But it would be unwise to predict either a renewal of class warfare, threatening the linkages created by corporate bias, or its diminution.

A breakdown on the scale of 1911–21 would have involved not just the 'dissociation effect' of a clash between theoretical and actual formulations of the system, but a prolonged failure to amend the former, to bring it up to date, or to incorporate the aspirations of major interest groups excluded from power, or to prevent the erosion of those secondary, intermediate forms of political culture which Durkheim characterised as essential to the prevention of anomie in the modern world. All these occurred in the earlier crisis, none of any scale in the second which should, rather, be defined as a period of prolonged instability, different in kind from the more dramatic events of 1968 in France or Italy, a peculiarly British cycle or Kondratieff 'long wave' bringing after forty years a slump in political confidence of very complex form.

Unlike the post-1918 case, this slump was characterised by the speed and success with which all the participants in the system attempted afterwards to retrieve their former positions, leaving nothing so clear-cut as the class divisions in contemporary France or Italy but instead 'the ambivalence of the British working-class imagery of society, the co-existence of active dissent and grudging acceptance of routine',[51] as key to public acquiescence in the continued manifestations of corporate bias. Whether this is good can be contested. To many minds, the system had become barren long before 1965. The crisis may have jolted a sufficient number of the political class out of accumulated lethargy and the belief that, whatever her economic failings, Britain had been endowed by the mandate of Heaven with natural political harmony. Had that happened, had the formal constitution been brought up to date, to make it possible to discuss without anachronistic polemic the future of politics, it would all have been worth it.

But it is by no means certain that this is so. Parties and institutions show few signs of careful introspection about their recent history or the way in which government has only been sustained by concessions to the institutions, weakening the very nature of the state. Corporate bias remains; but modern analysts tend to concentrate on the extension of corporatism in the purely economic field, or an irreversible drift towards Caesarism based on technocratic management keeping the planned economy moving.[52] While government in the future may well choose between progress towards socialism and reversion to the market order by taking some middle way in which 'the state directs and controls predominately private-owned business according to four principles: unity, order, nationalism and success',[53] it makes better sense to argue that the extension of economic management in post-war years on which this line of argument is based has only been possible because of the existing nature of the triangular system, and the power, inherent in corporate bias, of governing institutions to convey popular consent by means other than those of political parties. To imagine power as only positive is an illusion; without assessing negative power, the equation is incomplete.*

In the light of the thirty years since 1945, it is reasonable to retain the hypothesis advanced earlier, that the nineteenth-century concept of the state is wholly outdated, even when the modifications of early pluralist theory are taken into account. The modern state is composed not only of government and the state apparatus but includes the governing institutions; the degree of their inclusion serves as a means of distinguishing them from other institutions and interest groups merely contiguous to the state.† The function of governments in seeking crisis avoidance and the preservation of political harmony between class and interest groups can indeed only be achieved by that incorporation, since governing institutions both respond to and control their membership, as do the parties (albeit in a different mode) with the electorate.

Existing definitions of pluralism and corporatism need to be expanded to cope with this sharing of the state, because the governing institutions are not subsumed into a pyramid of authority, within fixed limits of activity, exercising power only in so far as it has been delegated by the state. The state exists effectively in these fields only because they have associated themselves with it; yet they retain on the one hand freedom always to respond to their own membership (a factor which vitiates, in

*Replying to criticisms of *Legitimation Crisis*, J. Habermas defined the role of government in late-capitalist society as having been limited to maintenance of the system, facilitation of institutional participation, guidance and reform along consensually agreed lines, and compensation for dysfunctional side-effects. (*Telos*, January 1976, p. 37.)

†A distinction which may be compared with that of Galbraith between large companies in the 'planning system' and small ones in the market system (J. K. Galbraith, *The New Industrial State* (Hamish Hamilton 1967), Chapter 1).

advance, the 'corporate state') and on the other, the power to utilise their part in the state to justify themselves to their membership, as functional organisations, distinct from and for that purpose of greater value than political parties.

This thesis depends on a study of the totality of the system, not of its component parts according to prior definitions of each one's functions; I do not deny that, in terms of those individual, non-political, functions, the behaviour of governing institutions and the balance of forces between them – say between management and unions in the purely industrial field – might look different. Nor do I deny the existence of distinctive class interests in those spheres, rising in times of general political crisis to colour, and perhaps determine temporarily the workings of the political system. But *normally* the system has worked otherwise, according to the harmonising activity of government and the governing institutions and political parties, each in their own way mediating between state and nation.*

It would be foolish to predict the absolute dominance of institutional or party power, since, on the evidence given here, neither could any longer constitute a complete system, unless its very nature was changed to an authoritarian construction, to the detriment of modified or late-capitalist organisation – in whose continuance *both* governing institutions have a vested interest. Yet corporate bias does evolve, and has changed since 1965, even if the set of relationships which will modify further the concept of democracy is as yet unknown. Before 1911, the greatest problem was how to assimilate working-class power into the forms of the political nation; in the inter-war years, how to incorporate the institutions of working-class industrial life. Now, there are no more organisations or classes to incorporate (unless the concept of class is strained to include categories such as the unemployed, women or youths) and the problem is to satisfy individual, multiple aspirations, and remedy the structural rigidities of traditional parties and of traditional trade unions. There is something in the British example still of value to countries where the relations between government and institutions have not reached this point, such as France, Italy and Spain; and those where they have been consolidated at an intermediate level, such as Germany, Belgium, Holland and Sweden. The question is, or will be,

---

*To use Claus Offe's formula: 'In the planned capitalist welfare state, dominance of man over man, or of one class over another, has largely given way to the dominance of a few spheres of social function over others. . . . The gap that ran between the great position groups in the early stages of capitalism has shifted, as it were, to within individuals themselves.' (Claus Offe, 'Political Authority and Class Structures', *International Journal of Sociology*, Spring 1972, pp. 95–6.)

fundamental to concepts of democracy in advanced states, and to the future relationship between state and individual; and it is difficult, on the evidence of the British case, to avoid the conclusion that trade unions' potential power will eventually predominate over that of management. Whether the tension between trade unions as vehicles of political activity and traditional political parties can be resolved is another question which in many European countries already threatens long established assumptions, especially on the left; for that, too, the British example is instructive.

To recognise that the trade union movement has played an original and distinctive part in modifying the nature of the state in Britain is to touch on a very sensitive area of myth and propaganda. At present, the political class, like Maynard Keynes in 1919,[54] still looks back to a marvellous age before the holocaust, unwilling, even after the decade of crisis, to accept that the future may lie in multiple forms of participation rather than in the sovereignty of party.

Political conservatism extends far beyond the British Conservative party to include all who believe that the political power of institutions is illegitimate, who deny that organisations other than parliament can ever fulfil a representative, democratic function separate from but complementary to the existing electoral process. In this context it is worth adapting the distinction made by Werner Hoffmann[55] between 'rule' – the fundamental underlying condition of a society – and 'power' – the organisation of its political and social relationships. For more than fifty years after the First World War, the British industrial and political system combined the two in relative harmony. Now, the appearance of disruption in power relations with which we have lived for a decade marks a much deeper conflict about the nature of rule. The short-term economic and political crisis may be over, the long-term one is not.

In the past, the system has been wonderfully flexible: if not, it could hardly have survived 1916–21, when other Western systems, exposed to similar strains, collapsed. New forms may evolve, to defer indefinitely an authoritarian alternative. But the weight of the past and fear of the future remains. It is difficult to know, in an ancient, densely organised polity, whether the actors resemble participants at the Congress of Vienna, seeking to restore the exiled kings, or whether they are conducting the traditional pursuit of reform by reference to ancient, but fictional liberties. The ways are obscure: devolution perhaps – but not the Devolution Bill; a revival of spirit – but not the crude nationalism of the Press; workplace organisation – but not of archaic trade union structures; Europe – but not of the EEC. Democracy may be more than one man one vote, every four or five years, but the form it will take cannot be seen.

William Morris once described the process: 'how men fight and lose the battle, and the thing they fought for comes about in spite of their defeat, and when it comes, it turns out not to be what they meant and other men have to fight for what they meant, under another name'. Only if that struggle is abandoned is there need to fear the thing which was not buried by the military verdict of 1945, renewed, under another name by governments whose skill at harmonising clashing wills would ignore or subordinate the institutions' responsiveness to membership which, in the last resort, as much as that of parties, sustains democracy.

But the earlier crisis of the state, after 1911, lasted more than a decade and there is no reason to suppose that the aftermath of the last will be any easier. The nightmare predicted by Habermas in *Legitimation Crisis* remains, in the existence of those categories left outside. Faced with a choice of abandoning at least one of the three desiderata of post-war equilibrium, full employment, rising living standards and stable prices, governments since 1969 have chosen the first. Though alienation of the unemployed may not yet be as serious a threat to political stability as it already is in several European countries, it is unlikely to decrease. The most serious thing would be to abort the crisis, to be content to rummage around the detritus of the past, seeing in the shadows on the cave wall only reflections of old triumphs, devouring the children and hesitating to bury the dead.

SOURCES AND REFERENCES

p. (vi).
MLWR 21/5/19 GT 7313 Cab 24/80.

INTRODUCTION

1 *University of Leeds Review*, March 1976.
2 Marx to Engels, March 1852. 'Long before me, bourgeois historians have described the historical development of this struggle.'
3 Thomas Jones, *Whitehall Diary*, R. K. Middlemas, ed., vol. 3, Ireland 1918–25 (Oxford University Press 1971), p. 103.

I THE EDWARDIAN STRUCTURE

1 C. F. G. Masterman, *The Condition of England* (Methuen 1909), p. 32.
2 *Vide* A. V. Dicey, *Lectures on the Relation between Law and Public Opinion in England during the nineteenth century* (Macmillan 1905), the summary of his American lectures.
3 G. M. Young, *Victorian England*, 2nd ed. (Oxford University Press 1953), p. 165.
4 R. C. Snelling and T. J. Barron, 'The Colonial Office' in *Studies in the Growth of nineteenth-century government*, G. Sutherland, ed., (Routledge & Kegan Paul 1972), p. 165.
5 Zara Steiner and V. Cromwell, 'The Foreign Office before 1914' in Sutherland, op. cit., pp. 187–8.
6 M. Wright, 'Treasury Control 1854–1914' in Sutherland, op. cit., p. 226.
7 *Vide* Thomas Jones, *Whitehall Diary*, R. K. Middlemas, ed., vol. 1, 1916–25 (Oxford University Press 1969), pp. 1–40.
8 See in particular, Alan J. Lee, *The Origins of the popular press in England 1855–1914* (Croom Helm 1976).
9 Beatrice Webb, *Diaries 1912–24*, M. I. Cole, ed., (Longmans 1952), p. 146.
10 F. G. d'Aeth, 'Present Tendencies of Class Differentiation', *Sociological Review*, February 1910.
11 For example, M. Loane, *The Queen's Poor: life as they find it in town and country* (Edward Arnold 1906); S. Reynolds, *A Poor Man's House*, 2nd ed. (John Lane 1909); M. Loane, *Neighbours and Friends* (Edward Arnold 1910); S. Reynolds and B. and T. Woolley, *Seems So! a working-class view of politics* (Macmillan 1911); and Robert Tressall's inchoate novel, *The ragged-trousered philanthropists*, written 1908–12 but not published until 1926 (Richards Press).
12 B. A. Waites, 'The effects of World War I on class and status in England 1910–20', *Journal of Contemporary History*, 11, 1976, p. 29.

Sources and references

13 P. Descamps, *La formation sociale de l'anglais moderne* (Paris 1914), pp. 60–61.

14 Quoted in Waites, op. cit., p. 29.

15 John Burnett, ed., *Useful Toil: autobiographies of working people from the 1820s to the 1920s* (Allen Lane 1974), p. 35.

16 G. Sutherland, ed., *Arnold on the education of the New Order* (1973).

17 See the account given by Flora Thompson in *Lark Rise to Candleford* (Oxford University Press 1939).

18 Quoted in Harold Silver, 'Nothing but the past or nothing but the present', *The Times Higher Educational Supplement*, 1 January 1977.

19 'Some dangers ahead', *The Times Educational Supplement*, September 1910.

20 A. H. Halsey, *Trends in British Society since 1900: a guide to the changing social structure of Britain* (Macmillan 1972), table 6.2. Only 1 per cent of the children of semi-skilled and unskilled workers born before 1910 received secondary education of grammar-school type (table 6.21).

21 E. R. Norman, *Church and society in England 1770–1970: a historical study* (Clarendon Press 1976).

22 CP Registry files: Chilston Committee Report, April 1928.

23 National Union Minutes of Council 1909, p. 16.

24 National Union Minutes 1911, p. 24.

25 CP Registry files, 1906 Reorganisation (in Sir Robert Topping's memorandum, 23 October 1930).

26 CP Registry files, Unionist Organisation Committee Report.

27 *Conservative Agents' Journal*, 1900–14, especially the 1912 volume, recording Steel-Maitland's retirement. Between 1909 and 1914 expenditure on Central Office rose from £23,414 to £45,525, on Agents from £6,150 to £11,414, and on grants to constituencies from £10,311 to £25,209 (SM GD 193/108/3).

28 H. V. Emy, *Liberals, Radicals and Social Politics, 1892–1912* (Cambridge University Press 1973), p. 276.

29 William Morris, *Signs of Change: seven lectures* (Reeves & Turner 1888, p. 46).

30 R. Price, *An Imperial War and the British working class: working-class attitudes and reactions to the Boer War 1899–1902* (Routledge & Kegan Paul 1972).

31 RA/A76/28–30.

32 B. Gainer, *The Alien Invasion: the origins of the Aliens Act of 1905* (Heinemann Educational 1972).

33 RA/R34/50.

34 RA GV/K2553/1–5.

35 H. M. Pelling, *A History of British Trade Unionism* (Penguin 1963), p. 112.

36 The EEF demanded recognition of the right to employ non-union labour, to allocate piecework, job description and the extent of overtime (EEF Minutes 1897).

37 Eric Wigham, *The Power to Manage: a history of the Engineering Employers' Federation* (Macmillan 1973), p. 61.

38 Wigham, p. 75.

39 See the file, Private Meetings of Secretaries of Employers' Organisations, 1898–1916, (EEF archives).

40 Pelling, *History of British Trade Unionism*, p. 148.

466

2 INDUSTRIAL CRISIS, 1911–14

1 G. Dangerfield, *The Strange Death of Liberal England* (Constable 1936).

2 R. J. Scally, *The Origins of the Lloyd George Coalition: the politics of social imperialism 1900–18* (Princeton University Press 1976).

3 Quoted in G. Abrahams, *Trade Unions and the Law* (Cassell 1968), p. 110.

4 Baldwin papers, D 3, vol. 2.

5 Not simply Taff Vale and the Osborne case but the widespread judicial interpretation, following a series of less significant cases; and the revival of statutes from disuse, such as the 1835 Highways Act, as a means to limit picketing.

6 K. D. Brown, *Essays in Anti-Labour History: responses to the rise of Labour in Britain* (Macmillan 1974), pp. 224–5.

7 Brown, pp. 240–1.

8 Cf. S. Meadows, 'The sense of an impending clash: English working-class unrest before World War I, *American Political Science Review*, December 1972. Overall unemployment figures (Halsey, 4.8).

1900	1905	1906	1907	1908	1909	1910	1911	1912	1913
2·5%	5%	3·6%	3·7%	7·8%	7·7%	4·7%	3%	3·2%	2·1%

9 *Parliamentary Debates*, Commons, 15 February 1912, vol. 34, col. 53.

10 G. R. Askwith, *Industrial Problems and Disputes* (John Murray 1920), p. 177.

11 R. J. Holton, *British syndicalism 1900–14: myths and realities* (Pluto Press 1976).

12 B. Pribicevic, *The Shop Stewards' Movement and Workers' Control 1910–22* (Blackwell 1959), pp. 25–32.

13 HO/45/OS/6965. Quoted by Carolyn Steedman in 'The Police in the English local community 1856–80' (unpublished Cambridge Ph.D. thesis 1976).

14 GV B246/1, 5 August 1911, Knollys to Asquith.

15 Quoted in W. Milne-Bailey, *Trade Union Documents* (Bell 1929), pp. 380–1.

16 L. Davidson, 'The Board of Trade and the Labour Department' in *Studies in the growth of nineteenth-century government*, G. Sutherland, ed., p. 25.

17 Master of Elibank (Liberal Chief Whip) to the King, 18 August 1911 (GV B246/7).

18 GV B348/51.

19 'Value of Ministers = o!' he had written after the dock strike (GV B348/25–27).

20 GV B348/7.

21 LPAC 1913, pp. 69–73.

22 J. Ramsay MacDonald, *The Social Unrest: its cause and solution* (T. N. Foulis, 1913).

23 LPAC 1914, p. 103.

24 LPAC 1914, pp. 78–9.

25 PC Minutes, June 1913.

26 Fitzherbert Wright, MP, urged Law to win the trade unions over, and to encourage them to organise and enter the political arena, where they would gain their objects better than by striking; and to encourage the Labour Party to become independent of the Liberals (Bonar Law Papers 29/1/3 (January 1913)). See also, for example, Baldwin's speeches on industrial relations before 1914, R. K. Middlemas and A. J. L. Barnes, *Baldwin: a biography* (Weidenfeld 1969), pp. 48–9.

27 Sir Arthur Steel-Maitland, the retiring chairman, and Sir Felix Cassell put forward proposals similar to Fitzherbert Wright's, (BL 30/1/24, 22 August 1913) (although Steel-Maitland had been in favour of compulsory arbitration in 1912).

28 BL 33/5/65, 2 October 1913.

29 EEF Minutes and circulars 1913–14.

30 'Personally I do not believe in introducing party politics into business. . . . My predecessors have kept party politics out of the administration of trade and business of the nation. That is the only way to succeed.' Quoted in C. Wrigley, *David Lloyd George and the British Labour Movement : peace and war* (Harvester Press 1976), p. 48.

31 Lord Riddell, *War Diary 1914–18* (Nicholson & Watson 1933), p. 76.

32 Wrigley, p. 86.

3 THE NECESSITIES OF WAR, 1914–16

1 G. D. Feldman, *Army, Industry and Labour in Germany 1914–18* (Princeton University Press 1966), p. 17.

2 208 Associations of employers were formed between 1890 and 1902; on the broader level, the Central Association founded the Central Agency of German Employers Associations, and the League, the Association of German Employers' Organisations.

3 The Free Trade Union movement numbered 2·5 million members by 1910—only twenty years after emerging from clandestinity. The Christian Trade Unions counted 343,000 members in 1913, the Hirsch-Dunker Workers' Associations 107,000. Generally, both the latter were less radical and more inclined to collaboration with employers and government than the FTU.

4 It had long been advocated by the *Kathedersozialisten* (Gustav Schmoller, Lujo Brentano and Adolf Wagner) who envisaged unions as collaborators with the state, if only they behaved respectably.

5 *Vide* E. L. Shorter and C. Tilley, *Strikes in France 1830–1968* (Cambridge University Press 1974).

6 Askwith, *Industrial problems and disputes*, p. 356.

7 Quoted in R. Miliband, *Parliamentary Socialism : a study in the politics of Labour*, 2nd ed., (Merlin 1973), p. 44.

8 WENC 35/6/8.

9 See, generally, Minutes of the Federation of Engineering Employers 1914.

10 G. D. H. Cole, *Trade Unionism and Munitions* (Oxford University Press 1923), p. 54.

11 C. Addison, *Four and a Half Years : a personal diary 1914–19* (Hutchinson 1934) vol. I, p. 85.

12 R. Page Arnot, *The Miners : years of struggle* (Allen & Unwin 1953) pp. 159–60.

13 Wrigley, *David Lloyd George*, p. 86.

14 RA GV B742/2.

15 *History of the Ministry of Munitions* (HMSO 1924–6), vol. 1, part 2, pp. 37–43.

16 GV B742/16.

17 D. Lloyd George, *War Memoirs*, vol. 1, pp. 177–9.

18 GV B742/23 and 27.

19 Beveridge Papers 1915, I, 6.

20 CAB 37/129/33, Appendices A and B.

21 WENC 29/9 (30 August 1916) J. S. Middleton to H. Gosling, showing how few records had been kept on the trade union side, and prophesying trouble post-war.

22 Taking 1930 as 100: 1911–14 roughly stable at 62–63; 1915 79·5; 1916 91·3; 1917 113·9; 1918 130·1; (Halsey, table 4:11).

23 LG D3/3/1.

24 *History of Ministry of Munitions*, vol. 4, part 1, p. 85. The words in italics are omitted from the printed version. I am grateful to Mr P. McGuire for pointing out the significance of the missing phrase.

25 *Munitions*, vol. 4, part 1, p. 1. 'The Government consented to try the policy urged by the trade unions first, holding dilution in reserve, and if that should not be accepted, industrial conscription.'

26 C. Addison, *Politics from Within, 1911–18* (Herbert Jenkins 1924) pp. 249–52.

27 BL papers 81/1/19.

28 SM GD 193/73/6. Memorandum of August 1915.

29 GV B742/83, Runciman to the King, 27 July.

30 J. H. Thomas, *My Story* (Hutchinson 1937), p. 40.

31 Askwith, p. 395.

32 GV B742/48.

33 GV B742/48.

34 WENC 35/6/8; PC minutes 11 February and 11 March 1915.

35 Generally, see J. Hinton, *The First Shop Stewards' Movement* (Allen & Unwin 1977, and Pribicevic, *The Shop Stewards' Movement*; also R. K. Middlemas, *The Clydesiders: a left-wing struggle for parliamentary power* (Hutchinson 1965).

36 *History of the Ministry of Munitions*, vol. 4, part 1, p. 79.

37 CAB 37/144/77.

38 *Munitions*, vol. 4, part 1, p. 1.

39 Wrigley, *Lloyd George*, p. 115.

40 LG D/17/4/1, 21 June 1915, Lloyd George to Henderson.

41 TUC Conference Minutes 1915, p. 35.

42 W. J. Reader, *Architect of air power: the life of the first Viscount Weir of Eastwood, 1877–1959* (Collins 1968), pp. 51–2.

43 Hinton, *Shop Stewards*, pp. 216–20; Min. Labour (1916), Industrial Reports No. 2.

44 Beveridge Papers III, 12–16.

45 Beveridge, III, 44, 21 February 1916.

46 Beveridge III, 43.

47 See, for example, M. R. D. Foot, 'Conscription and Society in Europe before 1914' in *War and Society: a yearbook of military history*, B. Bond and I. Roy, eds., (Croom Helm 1975).

48 Viscount Grey of Fallodon, *Twenty-five Years, 1892–1916*, vol. 2 (Hodder & Stoughton 1925), p. 72.

49 CAB 37/129/30, 9 June 1915.

50 CAB 31/129/33, 8 June 1915.

51 CAB 37/130/1.

52 GV 724/24–45.

53 Quoted in Wrigley, *Lloyd George*, p. 165.

54 War Policy Committee, 24 August.
55 Wrigley, *Lloyd George*, p. 166.
56 TUC PC Minutes, 7 September 1915.
57 PC Minutes, 28 September 1915.
58 A. J. B. Marwick, *The Deluge: British Society and the First World War* (Bodley Head 1965), p. 77.
59 CAB 37/139/26.
60 WENC 5/3/3, 18 January 1916.
61 CAB 41/37/2.
62 CAB 37/140/7, 10 January.
63 PC Minutes, 27 April.
64 CAB 37/146/24.
65 BL 53/6/73, 13 April 1916.
66 WENC 35/6 and WENC ADD/26.
67 BL 53/1/11, 1 April 1916.
68 BL 53/6/73.
69 Sidney and Beatrice Webb, *The History of Trade Unionism*, rev. ed. (Longmans 1920), pp. 637 and 646.
70 CAB 37/138/4, 23 November 1915.
71 LG D/11/2/23, September 1915.
72 WENC 5/2/3/8, January 1916.
73 *Vide The Wipers Times: a complete facsimile of the famous World War I trench newspaper* (P. Davies 1973), P. Beaver. ed.
74 GV Q 724/24, April 1915.
75 LG D/11/1/4.
76 GV B742/48 and 55, August 1915.
77 P. McGuire, 'Unofficial Trade Union Movements and Industrial Politics 1915–22' (D.Phil. thesis, Sussex University 1978).
78 TUC Conference resolution, June 1916.
79 McGuire, *op. cit.*
80 *History of the Ministry of Munitions*, vol. 6, part I, p. 116.
81 War Cab. 451, 24 July 1918.
82 Haldane 5911, 17 May 1915.
83 LG D/18/2/11, 30 May 1916.

4 NATIONAL DISUNITY, 1916–18

1 Cameron Hazlehurst, *The Triumph of Lloyd George* (forthcoming).
2 GV Q74/75.
3 GV B862/1/7–9.
4 *History of the Ministry of Munitions*, vol. 6, part 2, p. 43.
5 Beatrice Webb, *Diaries*, vol. I, p. 43.
6 WC7 (14 December).
7 WC12 (19 December).
8 See, for example, the memorandum on the need for a new spirit in government and in the conduct of the war, drafted by Tom Jones, R. H. Tawney, A. Zimmern, J. J. Mallon and Lionel Hitchins for Lloyd George's use, December 1916. (Jones, *Whitehall Diary*, I, pp. 3–5.)
9 PC Minutes, 6 December 1916.
10 LPAC 1917, p. 43.
11 PC Minutes, 19 April 1917.

12 GV B862/2/2.
13 D. Shackleton to Allan Smith, 20 April 1917 (EEF archives).
14 WC 39/1 (19 January 1917) and WC 55/8 (5 February).
15 WC 21/23, 13 February 1917.
16 WC 103/2, Appendix II.
17 LG F/217/1.
18 LG F/217/2.
19 WC 103/2.
20 WC 127/1.
21 After the refusal by one employer (Tweeddales) to recognise the ASE or to operate the appeals procedure.
22 GV B862/2/8.
23 *History of the Ministry of Munitions*, vol. 6, part I, pp. 102–4. Tweeddale himself was forced to resign.
24 LG F38/2/5, 26 May.
25 WC 188/11 and 190/1.
26 WC 240/14.
27 WC 310/1, 1 January 1918.
28 WC 437/18.
29 See also M. B. Hammond, *British Labor Conditions and Legislation during the War* (Oxford University Press, New York 1919), p. 221.
30 WC 252/2, 18 October 1917; WC 398/13, 24 March 1918. Maclean was said to be in touch with a revolutionary group in St Etienne and to represent a threat to French morale.
31 MDAOC minutes, 25 July 1917 (McGuire, *op. cit*).
32 WC 446/7, 16 July 1918.
33 WC 451/11, 24 July.
34 WC 476/10, 24 September.
35 WPC, 19 June 1917.
36 Hankey papers 8/2.
37 G174, WC 289/12, 3 December.
38 CAB 27/14, 8 December 1917.
39 CAB 27/14 (G185).
40 WC 300, 17 December 1917.
41 WC 336/11, 1 February 1918.
42 WC 373/12–13.
43 General Byrne, H. Duke, Mark Sykes, Dublin Castle officials, the Irish Lord Chief Justice, Attorney-General, etc. (GV 2790/23–25).
44 GT 4129.
45 Jones, I, p. 58.
46 LG F/30/2/8/31.
47 WC 421/6.
48 WC 453/7.
49 WC 385, 6 April.
50 WC 395/12.
51 WC 451.
52 WC 449/16.
53 Quoted in McGuire, *op. cit*.
54 Quoted in McGuire, *op. cit*.
55 Pribicevic, p. 43.
56 LG F/6/10 and F/215/3.

57 FBI/C/84.

58 FBI/C/84. Labour Report.

59 S. Blank, *Industry and Government in Britain: The Federation of British Industries in politics 1945–65* (Saxon House 1973), p. 14.

60 Wrigley, *Lloyd George*, p. 132.

61 FBI C/19.

62 EEF questionnaire on post-war problems, I/1/7.

63 Allan Smith forced the FBI to accept a very restrictive formula in August 1917; which he later held the FBI's 'Report on Capital and Labour after the War' to have infringed. (E. Wigham, *The Power to Manage*, p. 103–4, Blank *The FBI*, p. 16.)

64 McGuire, *op. cit.*; MDAOC records.

65 Jones, I, p. 36.

66 PC Minutes, 25 July 1917.

67 Jones, I, p. 37.

68 WC 212.

69 *Vide* Trevor Wilson, *The Downfall of the Liberal Party 1914–35* (Collins 1966), pp. 140–9.

70 SM GD 193/99/2/4, January 1917.

71 National Union Minutes, November 1917; Bayford (R. A. Sanders, MP) Diary, December 1917.

72 National Union Minutes, November 1917.

73 LG F23/2/1, 2 January 1918.

5 LLOYD GEORGE'S CONTRACT, 1917–20

1 D. Feldman, *Army, Industry and Labour in Germany*, p. 25.

2 Martin Kitchen, *The Silent Dictatorship: the politics of the German High Command under Hindenburg and Ludendorff 1916–18* (Croom Helm 1976).

3 Modern historians have been less certain: Branko Pribicevic corroborated C. L. Goodrich's view of the SSM as 'a genuine movement towards control of industry . . .' *The Frontier of Control: a study in British workshop politics* (Bell 1920), p. 10; against this, Hinton argues that this is true only of the ideologically committed leaders. So do Wrigley and McGuire, who point out complex geographical distribution and variations in behaviour in different industries and on different issues.

4 *Railway Review*, 1 March 1918 (I am grateful to Mr P. McGuire for this reference).

5 Jones, *Whitehall Diary*, I, *passim*.

6 Quoted in B. A. Waites, 'Effect of the First World War on Class and Status in England', *Journal of Contemporary History*, January 1976, p. 37.

7 Waites, p. 36. The National Union of Clerks was represented on many shop stewards' committees after 1917.

8 J. C. C. Davidson, *Memoirs of a Conservative: Memoirs and Papers 1910–37*, R. Rhodes James, ed. (Weidenfeld 1969), p. 106.

9 'In wartime it was our duty to listen to lots of things and to submit to lots of things that we are not in the habit of submitting to; and very frankly, we do not propose to submit to them in the future.' (Conference with Trade Unions 9 January 1919 EEF/H(3)15. I am grateful to Mr P. McGuire for this reference.)

10 EEF/CL/18/222, 23 November 1918 (quoted in McGuire, *op. cit.*).

11 H. Dubery in *The National Association of Employers and Employed* (1918) claimed an altruistic role for this body, but it declined in 1919 after the EEF began to withdraw support, and in 1922 Allan Smith advised his colleagues to withdraw completely.

12 In *Workshop Committees* (1917), p. 7, Charles Reynolds, a Manchester employer, wrote: 'During the past four or five years there has been a remarkable growth throughout industry of the idea of consultation, discussion, joint responsibility and joint working between employers and labour. The right of labour to concern itself with the general conduct, aims, methods and results of an industry has now been conceded and is now a commonplace of everyday thought.'

13 FBI Report: Nationalisation Committee – see A. Gleason, *What the Workers Want: a study of British labour* (Allen & Unwin 1920).

14 For an early instance, see Garton Foundation: *Memorandum on the Industrial Situation after the War* (1916), p. 8.

15 Jones, *Whitehall Diary*, I, p. 75.

16 Together with notes on 'leading rebels' such as J. T. Murphy, A. McManus and Robert Williams. LG F/6/1/23.

17 LG F/78/20.

18 G. N. Barnes' summary – Cd. 8663.

19 See, in particular, P. Abrams, 'The Failure of Social Reform', *Past and Present*, 25, 1961.

20 CAB 1/27/17 *passim*. See also chapter 12.

21 WC 328/18, 22 January 1918.

22 WC 476/10.

23 SM GD 194/396.

24 SM GD 193/109/5, Walton to Lloyd George, 3 April 1922; and LG F21/4/10, 2 August 1919; EEF Papers, Allan Smith Correspondence P/13/3. The original budget envisaged £45,000 for posters, £64,000 for press advertisements, £60,000 for leaflets, and £27,000 for a school for speakers; with expenses allowed for assistance from Conservative Central Office.

25 LG F1/4/8; Weir 4/1–3; TSC (PT) (CAB 27/811) gives the Supply and Transport Committee's own version.

26 Jones, I, p. 73.

27 B. S. Rowntree, *The Human Needs of Labour* (Nelson 1919), pp. 9–10.

28 Jones, I, p. 80.

29 LG F/217/2.

30 TJ C3/21.

31 Hankey 8/18, especially Part III.

32 *Parliamentary Debates*, Commons, vol. 85, col. 1906.

33 Abrams, *op. cit.*; P. B. Johnson, *Land fit for Heroes: the planning of British reconstruction 1916–19* (University of Chicago Press 1968).

34 C. Addison, *The Betrayal of the Slums: an attack on the government's housing policy* (Jenkins 1922, Chapter 1).

35 CAB 24/75, GT 6787 and 6887.

36 CAB 24/75, GT 6881.

37 SM GD 193/394.

38 WC 310/1, 1 January 1918. Geddes declared 'the sentiment regarding excess profits now prevailing amongst wage-earners was profound and vitally affected the reception that would be given to the government's proposals regarding recruiting.'

473

39 WC 533/2.
40 WC 535/1.
41 TJ C4/5.
42 EDDC 33, 15 August 1918.
43 LG F27/6/6, 9 February 1919, Horne to Lloyd George.
44 Whitley Committee, 5th Report, Trade Union representatives' Addendum.
45 First Interim Report, June 1917.
46 LG F27/6/25, September 1919.
47 LG F27/6 *passim*.
48 WC 208/11.
49 SM GD 193/395/1.
50 GT 6779 and SM GD 193/395/1. Memo by Horace Wilson, 25 November 1918.
51 WC 553/5 and Horne to Bonar Law, 13 February, advising him to rest the government's case on the NIC, BL 94/18.
52 Interview with the author, September 1966.
53 EEF/C/8/2, Brief Notes for the NIC.
54 LP WENC 29/9/16, Middleton to Gosling.
55 WC 482/13, 3 October 1918.
56 WC 487/17, 16 October.
57 GT 5617, and 5992, p. 1.
58 WC 491/2, 499/8.
59 WC 463/8.
60 WC 510/1, 6 December 1918.
61 GV B1412/1, 28 January 1919.
62 WC 521/2, 28 January 1919.
63 WC 525/1, 4 February 1919. In the event, they decided to recognise the Railway Clerks, trusting to union leaders like J. H. Thomas to deliver a *quid pro quo*. (LG F/2/6/5, Stanley to Lloyd George 2 December 1918.)
64 Ibid.
65 LG F30/3/32, 20 March 1919.
66 Jones, *Whitehall Diary*, I, p. 73; also RA GVB1412/5, where Horace Wilson suggested that the TUC had been ready to oppose government intervention in the Forty-hour Strike.
67 WC 525/1, 4 February 1919.
68 WC 529/3, 7 February 1919.
69 CAB 27/59, 14th meeting.
70 ADM/8667/162, 23 January 1919. I am grateful to Mr A. Carew for this reference.
71 Nevertheless, MI5 reported that public opinion would endorse the use of troops, (WC 526/1).
72 LG F30/3/31.
73 JCCD 745, Lloyd George to E. Shortt.
74 LG F30/3/32, 20 March 1919.
75 WC 529/3, 7 February 1919.
76 LG F30/3/31, 19 March 1919.
77 CAB 27/59/UC10; CAB 636/A/2.
78 EEF Papers, Management Committee C/8/2, 22 February 1919. EEF/I/1/12, February 1918, refers to earlier attempts to create a similar organisation and sets out detailed aims, covering co-operation between Federations, surveillance of government legislation, pooling of information and access to

government departments, supply of information and statistics and mutual defence against strikes. I am most grateful to Mr P. McGuire for these references. (See also E. W. Wigham, *The Power to Manage*, pp. 104–13.)

79 Ibid.
80 EEF C/8/2 (NIC brief).
81 TJ C5/51, 19 February 1919.
82 LG F27/6/21.
83 Wigham, p. 52.
84 WC 606A.
85 On Lloyd George's support for nationalisation, see Kirby, *The British Coalmining Industry*, Chapter 2, especially pp. 47–8.
86 On 7 August, for example, he argued that Sankey had failed to carry public opinion and that the Commons would never pass a nationalisation bill (WC 608A).
87 CAB 21/416/1, 27 September.
88 Lloyd George to the King, GVB 1528/1, 14 October 1919.

6 LLOYD GEORGE'S PYRRHIC VICTORY, 1920–2

1 R. H. Ullman, *Anglo-Soviet Relations, 1917–21* (Oxford University Press 1972), vol. 3, The Anglo-Soviet Accord, p. 25.
2 Jones, *Whitehall Diary*, I, p. 97.
3 Jones, I, p. 99. The whole discussion (pp. 89–103) is instructive.
4 LG F46/9/11, August 1920.
5 BL 101/4/84, 3 August 1920.
6 CAB 27/60 *passim*.
7 CP 97, 11 November 1919.
8 CAB 27/64.
9 CAB 27/84, 9 March 1920.
10 CAB 18/21, 12 April 1921.
11 CAB 27/83/21.
12

	1918	1919	1920	1921	1922
Cost of living	130·1	140·8	170·9	126·8	115·0
Money wages	93·0	121·0	162·0	130·0	101·0
(1930 = 100)					

Halsey, *Trends in British Society*, table 4.8.

13 JCCD H26, 22 September 1920.
14 'The average railwayman is only capable of thinking in very simple terms where figures are concerned,' the general manager of Eastern Railway reported, after a talk with Thomas in January 1920 (GV B1518/9).
15 GV B1518/9.
16 CAB 56/20/1, 15 October 1920.
17 CAB 57/20/2.
18 Jones, I, p. 133.
19 Jones, I, pp. 132–54.
20 Meeting of Lloyd George with Bevin, Williams and Thomas, 11 April (Jones, I, p. 140).
21 Jones, I, p. 133.
22 CAB 23/21/6, 13 April.
23 M. W. Kirby, *The British Coalmining Industry, 1870–1946: a political and economic history* (Macmillan 1977), p. 61.

24 CP 2851, 19 April.

25 CAB 30/12/2, 28 April.

26 Jones, I, p. 153.

27 Reynolds, *Workshop Committees*, p. 5. See also LG F/222/11 confirming that government regarded the struggle over the right to manage as a purely industrial matter.

28 CAB 21/197.

29 MUN 5/53, 300/99/32. I am grateful to Mr Andrew Hardman for this reference.

30 Jones, I, pp. 160–2.

31 Jones, I, p. 153.

32 'The FBI was regarded by us all as a body dwelling on lofty industrial heights and dictating policy to their member employers. The NCEO struck me as being as belligerent and uncompromising as one of our trade unions.' Walter Citrine, *Men and Work: an autobiography* (Hutchinson 1964), p. 87.

33 NCEO Annual Reports and Minutes of Council, 1919 et seq.

34 BEC/CON/1–4, NC93.

35 NC 156, 27 October 1921.

36 See, for example, Bridgeman, *Political Notes*, II (unpublished).

37 JG C6/53.

38 Represented by Allan Smith (Engineering Federation), Sir James Lithgow (Shipbuilding), Evan Williams (Coalmining) and Sir Andrew Duncan (Iron and Steel).

39 Presidential Address, NCEO/AR/1924.

40 Weir 4/2, 25 April 1921.

41 NCEO GPC Minutes, 21 December 1922.

42 V. L. Allan, 'The Reorganisation of the TUC', *British Journal of Sociology*, 1960.

43 PCM 19 November 1918, 8 October 1919.

44 PCM 27 October 1920.

45 PCM 13 May 1921.

46 PCM 1921–2, especially 21 March 1922.

47 Miliband, *Parliamentary Socialism*, p. 62.

48 TUC F & GP committee, 5 November 1923.

49 CP 1112, 21 April 1920.

50 PCM 21/22 September 1921 and LG F218/5.

51 LG F218/1, 5 October 1920.

52 LPAC 1919, p. 175.

53 Stephen White, 'The Councils of Action', *Journal of Contemporary History*, 4, 1974.

54 LP/CA/ADM 29. Generally, see, CA/GEN/1–1132 and LP/CA/ADM 1–42.

55 LP/GEN/1013, 12 January 1921.

56 LP/GEN/1113.

57 Correspondence between Robert Williams and Henderson. JSM/STR/55.

58 *Vide* CP1885 and CP1997 (21 October 1920) where the South Wales Councils are described as 'almost frankly Soviets' taking over local Trades Councils, for revolutionary purposes, led by Noah Ablett, S. O. Davies and the staff of the *Merthyr Pioneer*.

59 CA/MEM/6, 10 August 1920.

60 LG F217/9, 22 July 1920.

61 M. Cowling, *The Advent of Labour 1920–4: the beginning of modern British politics* (Cambridge University Press 1971).

62 CAB 57/20/2, 12 October 1920.

63 As early as March 1918, R. A. Sanders wrote from Central Office to Law, to express concern about Lloyd George's use of the British Workers' League, and its potential damage to Conservative voters. Neville Chamberlain, W. A. S. Hewins and the Conservative Agents, all concurred, and pleaded with Law not to let the party machinery be subjected to running BWL candidates (BL 83/1/15) (Bayford Papers).

64 Middlemas and Barnes, *Baldwin*, pp. 95–100.

65 W. A. S. Hewins, *The Apologia of an Imperialist: forty years of Empire policy*, vol. 2 (Constable 1929), p. 247.

66 L. C. M. S. Amery, *My Political Life*, vol. 2, (Hutchinson 1954), p. 233.

67 Bridgeman, *Political Notes*, vol. 2.

68 Ullman, *Anglo-Soviet Relations*, vol. 3, p. 278.

69 *Agents' Journal 1919–22 passim*, especially November 1919 and October 1922.

70 CNU 1920. In 1921, Central Office developed a labour sub-committee, and injected new attitudes into the summer school for MPs.

71 Labour Committee June 1921 report to CNU Executive.

72 CNU 1922 Report of Conference.

73 Davidson, *Memoirs of a Conservative*, p. 120.

74 M. Kinnear, *The fall of Lloyd George and the political crisis of 1922* (Macmillan 1973).

7 JOURNEY TO THE CENTRE, 1923–31

1 H. Finer, *Representative Government and a Parliament of Industry: a study of the German Federal Economic Council* (Fabian Society 1923); R. Picard, 'Economic Councils in France and Germany', *International Labour Review*, June 1925.

2 326, comprising 120 employers' representatives, 120 of trade unions and 86 others, chiefly government officials and consumers.

3 James Joll, *Europe since 1870: an international history* (Weidenfeld 1973), p. 256.

4 G. Scelle, 'Le conseil national économique', *Revue Politique*, October 1924.

5 W. Milne-Bailey, *The Industrial Parliament Project*, TUC General Council Research Department (December 1926).

6 Templewood, VI; Chamberlain to Wood, 25 January 1924.

7 Miliband, *Parliamentary Socialism*, p. 115.

8 D. Marquand, *Ramsay MacDonald* (Cape 1977), p. 429.

9 J. Scanlon, *Very Foreign Affairs* (Allen & Unwin 1938), p. 89.

10 *New Leader*, 4 January 1924.

11 CP 67/27, Appendix II.

12 Milne-Bailey, *Trade Union Documents*, pp. 24–25.

13 Jones, *Whitehall Diary*, I, p. 319.

14 Jones, II, p. 219.

15 W. J. Reader, *Imperial Chemical Industries: a history*, vol. 2 (Oxford University Press 1975).

16 See, generally, Jones, *Whitehall Diary*, vols. I and II, and S. Howson and

Sources and references

D. Winch, *The Economic Advisory Council 1930–39: a study in economic advice during depression and recovery* (Cambridge University Press 1977).

17 TJ B3 CCR/10.

18 TJ B4/61.

19 TJ C4/73. Conference at New College, Oxford, 12 July 1931.

20 If the staple industries are considered as a special case, British performance in the 1920s compares favourably with Western Europe, with an annual growth of industrial production of 2·8% as against 1·6% between 1900–14. Aldcroft and Richardson consider the late 1920s to mark 'the watershed between the old industrial régime of the pre-1914 era and the new industrial economy of the post-1945 period' (*The British Economy*, p. 220) – a return almost to the high growth of the mid-nineteenth century. Despite low capital investment, productivity grew rapidly, because of rationalisation of production methods, concentration on high growth areas (chemicals, electricity) and mass production, investment *replacement* (e.g., electricity for steam) and the long-term effects of wartime standardisation.

21 Raphael Samuel, ed., *Miners, quarrymen and saltworkers* (Routledge 1976).

22 L. Hannah, *The Rise of the Corporate Economy* (Methuen 1976); also E. J. Hobsbawm, *Industry and Empire: from 1750 to the present day* (Weidenfeld 1968) and S. H. Beer, *Modern British Politics: a study of party and pressure groups*, 2nd ed., (Faber 1969). For an early view, see A. F. Lucas, *Industry, reconstruction and the control of competition: the British experiment* (Longmans 1937).

23 The 62,762 limited liability concerns of 1914 grew to 95,055 in 1925.

24 NCEO 1927 Recruiting Campaign; also NC 2203, 2204.

25 NCEO Governing Council Membership

	1922	1924	1932
	Weir	Weir	Weir
	Smith	Milne-Watson	Gainford
	Lithgow	Moir	H. B. Shackleton
	Williams	Ralph Wedgwood	F. Holroyd
	Robinson	A. Dorman	A. L. Ayre
		Sir A. Ross	W. Burton-Jones

By 1928 the NCEO General Purposes Committee comprised seventy members, representing, *inter alia*, chemicals, mining and quarries, electricals, construction, milling, iron and steel, coke, cotton, jute spinning, gas, railways, newspapers, woollen trade and glass (NC 3000).

26 NC 2204.

27 BEC/CON1/259 (4).

28 NC 1690.

29 'The country will come to see from our statements that we do know what we want, and will begin to respect our opinion, and will look for it on all general labour questions.' NC 886 (1924).

30 SM GD 193/85/5; TUC Economic Committee C9/1; 16 April 1931.

31 1925 had shown an export decline, compared with 1924, despite a 7·8 per cent rise in world import demand. (FBI Economic Survey 1926).

32 As early as July 1925 (before Red Friday) Balfour pointed out to the Cabinet the advantage to industry of cheap coal in the home market. (CAB 58/9 (CCR 3rd meeting).)

33 NC 2435, April 1928.

34 Such as the use of naval stokers to maintain power stations (R. W. Lyman, *The First Labour Government* (1963), pp. 29 and 217–23; A. L. C. Bullock, *The*

Life and Times of Ernest Bevin, vol. I (Hodder & Stoughton 1960), pp. 237–47, and Davidson, *Memoirs of a Conservative*, p. 180, on Wedgwood's complacent attitude to the Supply and Transport organisation.) Bevin in particular, took issue, writing, as early as March 1924, 'It is not fair that only one union should be put in the position of having to decide whether to withdraw a strike because the government was embarrassed. The Government should be made to understand that, in matters of this kind, the General Council was the right body to be approached.' (PC Minutes, 9 April 1924.)

35 TUC Congress Report 1925. Also CP 36/24, 'In industrial matters, the Labour Party does not, or at any rate did not in its term of office, sufficiently represent the unions.'

36 W. Milne-Bailey, *The Industrial Parliament Project*, (TUC 1926), p. 9.

37 TUC F and GP Committee, 2 January 1925.

38 Tariff, land reform and industrial research were declared to be 'industrial' – hence TUC – questions: Parliamentary Committee Minutes, 25 March 1925. See also Milne-Bailey, *The Industrial Parliament Project* (TUC December 1926), p. 24.

39 Shackleton to Baldwin, September 1925. (SB D 3.1, vol. 2.)

40 GC Minutes, 25 June 1930.

41 JSM/TU, 14 December 1923. PREM 1/41, TUC deputation to MacDonald, June 1924.

42 Milne-Bailey, p. 23.

43 A. Clinton, *The Trade Union Rank and File: Trades Councils in Britain* (Manchester University Press 1977).

44 NC 2204.

45 NCEO 1925 Annual Report.

46 BEF MISC 1/7, March 1926; SM GD 193/348 (Washington Hours).

47 CAB 15/27/4, March 1927.

48 SM GD 193/346.

49 Ibid. 346, 11 April 1929.

50 Cf. *The Times*, 24 November 1925.

51 TJ C7/56. Mond had established works committees in all plants at ICI, based chiefly on the GMUW, and gave them full facilities for trade union work, even allowing union officials to collect dues at an office on the site – a degree of tolerance almost unmatched in Europe. The Quaker families, like Cadbury, also encouraged trade union affiliation, while leaving the choice of union open to individuals.

52 NC 2204.

53 NC 1578; JSM/UNE/6-50; PC Minutes 24 May 1925; SB D 2·3.

54 SB, vol. 6, D 2·3; NC 1430.

55 NC 3511 (1931).

56 The NCEO formed a Publicity Committee in 1922: four years later they considered hiring W. R. Cranfield, a 'publicist' with a 'staff of competent writers' experienced in supporting or opposing legislation, who had worked for several of the Federations before (BEF MISC 1/7).

57 NC 2204.

58 Milne-Bailey, p. 8.

59 Templewood VI. Cunliffe-Lister to Hoare, 1 November 1924, explaining Baldwin's hesitancy about appointing the supposedly anti-Labour Churchill. 'He wants a side, and a policy, that will attract sound trade unionists.'

60 CAB 24/24, 2 April.

61 Jones, II, p. 12.
62 SM GD 193/348.
63 Including Dudley Docker, Andrew Duncan, D. W. Ritchie, Sir William Larke, Lord Weir, Hugo Hirst (GEC), Arthur Pybus (English Electric); J. H. Thomas (NUR), J. T. Brownlie and R. Smithers (AEW), Herbert Smith (MFGB), John Bromley (ASLEF); SM GD 193/348.
64 CP 420/25.
65 SM GD 193/415.
66 SB vol. 6, D 2.3, Steel-Maitland to Baldwin, 16 April 1925.
67 SM GD 193/434.
68 Ibid.
69 Ibid.
70 SM GD 193/348.
71 B. Webb, *Diaries*, vol. 2, 1924–32, p. 73.
72 H.C. Deb., 6 August. Also Conservative National Union Report, October 1925.
73 Jones, II, p. 18.
74 Min. Lab. 27/3, meeting with Baldwin, 31 July 1925.
75 Indeed the NCEO claimed later that Weir's proposal to Baldwin of a compromise on the eight-hour day had been intended to ward off a settlement detrimental to the owners (Weir 4/11, 23 April 1926).
76 GC/SIC file 13/6/12. The members of the SIC were F. Bramley, A. Hayday, G. Hicks, B. Tillett and W. Citrine, to whom were added A. Pugh and J. H. Thomas in March 1926; a body of moderates if ever there was one.
77 SIC 13/6/8A, p. 9.
78 SIC 13/6/*passim*.
79 Jones, II, pp. 22–4.
80 H.C. Deb., vol. 195, col. 865, 11 May.
81 LAB 27/4–6; CAB 26/316; Rec/26, 14th and 15th meetings.
82 LAB 27/4, Bond to Baldwin, 27 September 1926; Middlemas and Barnes, *Baldwin*, pp. 435–8.
83 BP vol. 20, Weir to Baldwin, 24 September 1926; NCEO GPC Minutes, 5 October 1926.
84 CAB 25/53, CP 52/26.
85 Cf. Patrick Duff to Lord Stamfordham, GVK 2073/15.
86 See Chapter 1, 'Non-political unionism', *Essays in Labour History*, vol. 3 (London, 1977).
87 SB D 3.2, Notts Non-political Union file.
88 SB D4, Pol. 6, correspondence with Davidson.
89 Miliband, *Parliamentary Socialism*, p. 143.
90 GC Minutes, 17 May 1927.
91 Quoted in P. Renshaw, 'Anti-Labour Politics in Britain 1918–27', *Journal of Contemporary History*, October 1977, p. 709.
92 Labour Committee Executive reports to Council 1921–7.
93 Jones, II, p. 47.
94 See, generally, Allan Anderson, 'Labour legislation as a political symbol?' *Bulletin of Social and Labour History*, 1971–2.
95 Jones, II, p. 101.
96 CAB 237/36.
97 SB D 3.1, 11 October 1926.
98 SM GD 193/432 L(26)8.

99 Weir 4/11, SM GD 193/348.
100 1925 11·3%; 1926 12·5%; 1927 9·7%; 1928 10·8%; 1929 10·4%.
101 Wigham, *The Power to Manage*, pp. 133–4.
102 *Vide* John Foster in J. Skelley ed., *The General Strike: 1926* (Lawrence & Wishart 1976, pp. 389–93). Certain banks looked to direct investment in industry on the pattern adopted in the late nineteenth century by German and French banks.
103 SM GD 193/119/2.
104 TUC 1926, AR, p. 70.
105 Milne-Bailey, *Industrial Parliament Project*, p. 26.
106 CP 208/28 and 255/28.
107 SB D 3·1, Weir 4/14.
108 Cf. Steel-Maitland's paper 'Some Tendencies of Trade Union Opinion', January 1927 (CP 28/27).
109 See MacDonald and Gospel, 'The Mond-Turner Talks, 1927–33', *Historical Journal* xvi, 4 (1973).
110 SM GD 193/84/2.
111 GC Minutes June 1928. The NCEO interpreted in the same sense the answers to a questionnaire sent out to 200 members (NC 2666).
112 GC Minutes, 26 February 1929.
113 Minutes of Meeting, GC/12, 1928–9; see also SB D 3.1.
114 TUC Archives, Box 310, File 263.
115 TUC AR 1929, p. 29.
116 CP 28/27: Steel-Maitland 'Some Tendencies of Trade Union Opinion'; Weir 4/14.
117 CP 67/27.
118 M. W. Kirby, *The British Coalmining Industry*, p. 121.
119 SB D 3.2, Coal 4E.
120 Weir 4/20.
121 Weir 12/1.
122 Weir 12/1.
123 TUC, Box 310, File 263.
124 GC Minutes, 20 August 1931.
125 R. McKibbin, 'The Economic Policy of the 1929–31 Labour Government', *Past and Present*, No. 18.
126 I am grateful to Miss Paula McDiarmid for this reference.
127 TUC Box 310, File 263.
128 Milne-Bailey, p. 5.

8 COMPROMISE AND HARMONY, 1931–9

1 E. L. Wigham, *The Power to Manage*, pp. 135–6. Smith was succeeded by the more co-operative Alexander Ramsey.
2 NC 4374 contains a rebuke to Oliver Stanley, Minister of Labour, for sending out a list of employers whom he considered 'suitable' to give advice to the Unemployment Assistance Board in 1934.
3 NC 3750.
4 TJ C, *passim*. Jones, *Whitehall Diary*, vol. II, p. 274, which gives some justification to J. C. C. Davidson's view that the attacks on Baldwin (and on himself as Party chairman) originated in the old divisions between 'true party men' and coalitionists in 1922.

5 S. H. Beer, *Modern British Politics*, p. 297, for a discussion of the case of the Iron and Steel cartel.

6 B. W. E. Alford, *Depression and Recovery: British Economic Growth 1918–39* (Macmillan 1972, p. 79).

7 See, for example, the work of the General Council's Scientific Advisory Committee (Bullock, *Bevin*, vol. I, pp. 603–4) and the TUC's contribution to the Labour Party's 1937 Manifesto.

8 See, for example, Ernest Bevin's explanation to the Cabinet in February 1933 of the workings of the Coal Mines Act, 1931, (Kirby, *The British Coal-mining Industry*), p. 146.

9 Kirby, pp. 150–1.

10 A. Clinton, *The Trade Union Rank and File*, pp. 155–68.

11 Like W. S. Lewis, Midlands Area Secretary of the ETU, 1935–47, and Richard Coppock, Secretary of the Building Trade Workers, 1920–60. *Vide Dictionary of Labour Biography*, (Macmillan 1972–78) vols. 1–4 for similar examples of this cross-fertilisation.

12 Bullock, *Bevin*, p. 621.

13 *Public Control and the Regulation of Industry and Trade*, September 1932.

14 LPAC 1933, p. 14.

15 Milne-Bailey, *Trade Union Documents*, p. 2.

16 Bullock, *Bevin*, vol. I, p. 600.

17 NC 4320, 1933–4 recruiting campaign.

18 Weir, 12/4–48.

19 Ibid.

20 LPAC 1937, p. 146.

21 *Vide* W. J. Reader, *Imperial Chemical Industries: a history* (Oxford University Press 1975), vol. 2. The first quarter-century 1926–52.

22 Weir 12/1, 12/6.

23 W. M. Citrine, *Men and Work: an autobiography* (Hutchinson 1964), p. 250.

24 A. J. B. Marwick, 'Middle Opinion in the 1930s', *English Historical Review*, 1964, pp. 285–98.

25 See, in particular, L. P. Carpenter, 'Corporatism in Britain 1930–50', *Journal of Contemporary History*, I, 1976, pp. 3–25.

26 *Parliamentary Debates*, Commons, 5th Series, vol. 300, col. 432.

27 H. W. Richardson, *Economic Recovery in Britain 1932–9* (Weidenfeld 1967), Chapter 8.

28 *Parliamentary Debates*, 5th series, vol. 277, col. 60.

29 Third Report, 1936, Cmd. 5303.

30 NC 4585.

31 NC 6480.

32 TUC FGP 103.

33 PREM 1/217, March 1936.

34 PREM 1/218, February 1937.

35 S. H. Beer, *Modern British Politics* (2nd ed.), p. 297; for Duncan's work, see TJ A6: Comments on Lloyd George's memorandum, 14 March 1935, pp. 36–40.

36 Bullock, *Bevin*, vol. I, p. 543.

37 PREM 1/129.

38 PREM 1/365.

39 E. L. Wigham, *Strikes and the Government 1893–1974* (Macmillan 1976), pp. 76–80.

40 General Council Minutes, September 1934.

41 D. C. Watt, *Personalities and Politics* (Longmans 1965), Chapter 5; R. K. Middlemas, *Diplomacy of Illusion* (Weidenfeld 1972), pp. 80–81.

42 *Vide* R. Flood, *The British Machine Tool Industry 1850–1914* (1976). for a good analysis of government contract-rigging among arms manufacturers in the 1890s. No similar analysis exists for the inter-war years, but the government contract to build Singapore docks, 1928–9, provides an astonishing example of bribery and price-rigging (R. K. Middlemas, *The Master Builders* (Hutchinson 1963), pp. 298 and 301, and Davidson Papers). More recent examples in the aircraft industry abound.

43 See Chapter 9.

44 D. N. Winch's phrase. See his *Economics and Policy: a historical study* (Hodder & Stoughton 1969) for a general discussion of the question.

45 CP 26/32; CAB 8/32/6.

46 CAB 27/575.

47 PREM 1/141, 6 October 1933. See also CP 10/33.

48 CP 134/34.

49 The Rotherham and Durham PACs had even been superseded by Commissioners under Ministry of Labour powers. (R. C. Davidson, *British Unemployment Policy* (1938), p. 22.)

50 CAB 29/34, 18 July 1934.

51 CAB 44/34, 30 November 1934.

52 The BBC ran a six-week series of lectures on unemployment in the autumn of 1934.

53 JSM/MT/1.

54 Bullock, *Bevin*, p. 541.

55 NC 4585.

56 CAB 8/35 (6). The Committee files are CAB 27/575–576.

57 UAR 34/8, 4 May 1936.

58 *Vide* Frederic Miller, The British Unemployment Assistance Crisis 1935, *Journal of Contemporary History*, vol. 14, no. 2, 1979.

59 CAB 8/35.

60 SB D 2.3 Unemployment; 1935 Conservative Party Conference Report.

61 In July 1936, when the final scales were published, the General Council set up a deputation to the Prime Minister and a nation-wide campaign of protest which effectively precluded any renewal of NUWM action. (General Council Minutes, 22 July 1936.)

62 CP 26/32; CAB 8/32/6.

63 See, in particular, GC Minutes, April 1933, following Citrine's interview with the German Ambassador in London (GC 145). The General Council published Citrine's memorandum, *Fascism at Home and Abroad*, in February 1934.

64 G. D. H. and M. I. Cole, *The Condition of Britain* (Gollancz 1937), pp. 440–3; George Orwell, *The Road to Wigan Pier* (Gollancz 1937), pp. 187–9.

65 FAS/33/4–6.

66 GC 37, 24 October 1934.

67 SB D 4.3/Labour Government 2.

68 R. Skidelsky, *Oswald Mosley* (Macmillan 1976), p. 330.

69 One may exempt the Kibbokift Kindred (Greenshirts) who espoused

ideas of Social Credit; but they never aspired to the political role of Mosley's Blackshirts or the Irish Blueshirts.

70 Jones, *Whitehall Diary*, II, p. 275.

71 *Vide* GC Minutes 344 (3 September 1928), and F and GP 22 (4 February 1929) setting up questionnaires to all unions on 'CP and Disruptive Elements'.

72 Bevin 1/4, 24 May 1933.

73 Miliband, *Parliamentary Socialism*, p. 225.

74 Miliband, p. 206.

75 Ben Pimlott, *Labour and the Left in the 1930s* (Cambridge University Press 1977), p. 198.

76 JSM/UM/13.

77 GC Minutes, 4 September 1936.

78 Bullock, *Bevin*, vol. 1, p. 596.

79 'All comrades should realise that the TGWU is now the spearhead in this country of the drive against working-class unity' ran a CP newsletter in 1936. 'Bevin's power depends on his position in his own union. A decisive change in the TGWU would result in the establishment of the United Front in this country. The whole Party has a special responsibility for work against this section.' (TGWU Minutes 1937, Bullock, p. 607.)

80 Bullock, pp. 612–14.

81 R. Benewick, *The Fascist Movement*, pp. 225ff.

82 LP/FAS/33/6, p. 18.

83 CAB 68/32 (10).

84 CAB 24/251 for Baldwin's decision, p. 13; also SB D 2·9, 19 July.

85 CP 189/34.

86 CAB 23/86, 4 November 1936. Significantly, Northern Ireland was to be omitted, because of direct government responsibility for law and order.

87 CAB 26/37 (6); LP/FAS/33/16.

88 CAB 37/37 (11).

89 Quoted in Carpenter, *JCH*, 1976, p. 3.

9 EMERGENCY, 1935–40

1 *Parliamentary Debates*, Commons, 19 March 1934, vol. 299, cols. 1049–63.

2 CAB 50/21.

3 Cmd. 5107, p. 14.

4 Cmd. 5107.

5 E.g., CP 316/37 and CAB 22 December – 23/90A.

6 R. P. Shay, *British Rearmament in the Thirties: politics and profits* (Princeton University Press 1977), pp. 286–8.

7 Baldwin, D 2.3.

8 Middlemas and Barnes, *Baldwin*, p. 969; Weir 19/2, 6 October 1936.

9 CAB 16/112; DRC 38, 17 October 1935.

10 He pointed specifically to the recent rises in price of steel and textiles, despite the tariff granted to both industries.

11 CAB 16/123; DPRC 7, 1 August 1936.

12 CAB 16/136; DPRC 22nd meeting.

13 *Parliamentary Debates*, Commons, 5th series, vol. 309, cols. 1843–4.

14 CAB 16/139; DPR 56, 30 November 1935.

15 PREM 1/236.

16 E. H. J. N. Dalton, *The Fateful Years: Memoirs 1931–45* (Muller 1957), p. 44; Bullock, *Bevin*, vol. 1, p. 550.

17 G. D. H. Cole, *The People's Front* (Gollancz 1937), p. 293.

18 D. Butler, 'Trends in British by-elections', *Journal of Politics*, XI, 1949.

19 Miliband, *Parliamentary Socialism*, p. 236.

20 *Parliamentary Debates*, 29 May 1936.

21 CAB 16/14; DPR 85, 18 May 1936.

22 *Vide* Shay, *British Rearmament*, Chapter 2; AIR 19/9, 18 March 1936.

23 Weir, 19/16, 26 March 1936.

24 Weir 19/24.

25 CAB 57/27, NS (CM) 8.

26 T/161/1033/41460/1 et seq.

27 PREM 1/25, 21 March 1938.

28 GC 175, June 1936.

29 GC 168, May 1936.

30 Bullock, *Bevin*, vol. 1, p. 558.

31 Bullock, vol. 1, p. 626.

32 CP 57/36.

33 CP 96/36.

34 LAB 25/79.

35 CP 297/36.

36 CP 229/36.

37 CAB 13/38 (3), 14 March 1938.

38 PREM 1/236 and 1/251, 14 and 21 March 1938.

39 PREM 1/251.

40 GC Minutes, 24 March, 25 May 1938.

41 Cf. CP 27/37.

42 Shay, *British Rearmament*, pp. 288–9.

43 GC Minutes 153 et seq.

44 PREM 1/251; Memorandum from Sir Joseph Ball, n.d.; Bullock, *Bevin*, vol. 1, p. 626.

45 PREM 1/251.

46 P. Addison, *The Road to 1945: British politics and the Second World War* (Quartet 1976), p. 55.

47 Middlemas, *Diplomacy of Illusion*, pp. 414–19.

48 Hoare also wanted Bevin and Morrison, not just as Ministers but in the Cabinet (Templewood X 5).

49 Collin Brooks' diary, quoted by Addison, p. 56.

50 PREM 1/430, 1939.

51 Shay, *British Rearmament*, p. 253, citing T/161/855/44933, 10 June 1938.

52 Shay, T/161/922/40730/04.

53 T/161/922/40730/94.

54 T/161/949/49094/2, 4 November 1938.

55 CAB 23/97, 2 January 1939.

56 Middlemas, *Diplomacy of Illusion*, pp. 422–3.

57 Templewood X 5, 1937–9.

58 NC 6020.

59 PREM 1/336, October 1938.

60 R. A. C. Parker, *Economics, Rearmament and Foreign Policy* (1970), p. 265.

61 Addison, *The Road to 1945*, p. 55.

62 NC 6020.

63 Bullock, *Bevin*, 1, p. 636.
64 CAB 12/39(2).
65 CAB 15/39(3), 29 March.
66 CP 91/39; CAB 22/39(3).
67 CAB 22/39(3).
68 Bullock, 1, pp. 633–4.
69 PREM 1/365.
70 Templewood X 5.
71 Ibid.; NC 6480.
72 PREM 1/430, 15 September.
73 PREM 1/430.
74 GC Minutes, May 1939; Bullock, *Bevin*, 1, p. 638.
75 Quoted in Addison, *Road to 1945*, p. 59.
76 PREM 1/431, 7 March 1940. The Railway Clerks' Union complained that Chamberlain treated them like children.
77 Bullock, *Bevin*, 1, p. 642.
78 H. M. D. Parker, *Manpower* (HMSO 1954), pp. 62–3, 67–8.
79 CAB 45/39, 18 October.
80 As is argued by Maurice Cowling in *The Impact of Hitler : British Politics and British Policy 1933–40* (Cambridge University Press 1975).

10 THE WARTIME TRIANGLE, 1941–5

1 A. S. Milward, *War, Economy and Society 1939–45* (Allen Lane 1977).
2 H. M. D. Parker, *Manpower: a study of wartime policy and administration* (History of the Second World War), (HMSO and Longmans 1954).
3 E. H. J. N. Dalton, *Diary*; quoted in Addison, p. 60.
4 Dalton, *The Fateful Years*, p. 282.
5 PREM 1/359, 5 December.
6 Dalton, p. 305; Addison, pp. 95–6.
7 Not 33 and 60 as in most accounts. See Addison, p. 53, p. 98, and Jorgen S. Rasmussen, *Journal of Politics*, 32, 1970, p. 385.
8 Addison, p. 99.
9 Margesson to Baldwin, 4 March 1941, Margesson Papers.
10 NEC Minutes EC 16, 1939–40, 10 May 1940.
11 Bullock, *Bevin*, vol. 2, p. 339.
12 W. S. Churchill, *The Second World War*, vol. 2, 'Their Finest Hour' (Cassell 1949), p. 287.
13 Bullock, vol. 2, p. 4.
14 Bullock, vol. 1, p. 653.
15 PREM 4/100/5.
16 H. G. Wells, '*42 to '44: a contemporary memoir upon human behaviour during the crisis of the world revolution* (Secker & Warburg 1944), p. 163.
17 *Vide* Janet Beveridge, *Beveridge and his Plan* (Hodder & Stoughton 1954), pp. 106–11.
18 *Parliamentary Debates*, Commons, 5th Series, vol. 392, cols. 921–32.
19 Addison, pp. 171–2, citing Churchill's instructions to Greenwood, January 1941.
20 H. J. Laski, *The Old World and the New Society* (Labour Party 1942).
21 Addison, p. 94.
22 *Conservative Agents' Journal*, October 1941.

23 INF 1/292, Appendix to weekly report 22–29 September 1941, quoted Addison, p. 185.

24 TUC Special Conference Report, 25 May 1940, p. 18.

25 *Daily Herald*, 30 March 1940.

26 Bullock, 2, pp. 60–62. It became necessary to threaten conscription during the engineering apprentices' strike in 1941. D. F. Macdonald, *The State and the Trade Unions*, 2nd ed. (Macmillan 1976), p. 125.

27 H. M. D. Parker, *Manpower*, pp. 95–6.

28 E. S. Wigham, *Strikes and the Government*, p. 88.

29 S. Pollard, *The Development of the British Economy 1914–50* (Edward Arnold 1962), pp. 344–5.

30 Bullock, *Bevin*, vol. 2, p. 118.

31 Bullock, *Bevin*, vol. 2, p. 30.

32 Wigham, *Strikes and the Government*, p. 90.

33 Cf. Memo of 24 March 1943, Bevin 2/4.

34 Quoted in Wigham, *Strikes and the Government*, p. 90.

35 See, generally, W. H. B. Court, *Coal*, History of the Second World War, UK Civil Series (HMSO and Longmans 1951); R. Page Arnot, *The Miners in Crisis and War* (Allen & Unwin 1961); and M. W. Kirby, *The British Coal-mining Industry*.

36 Kirby, pp. 170–2.

37 Power 22/144 P2139/96/1: Manpower in the Coal Mining Industry, 10 April 1942.

38 Bevin 2/3; 2 May 1942.

39 CAB 71/9 LP 134(42), 28 May 1942.

40 Hancock and Gowing, *British War Production*, p. 471.

41 Kirby, p. 179.

42 Bullock, 2, pp. 298–9.

43 Bullock deprecates their assessment, but see Wigham, pp. 92–3.

44 Cf. Paul Addison ed., *The British People and World War II : Home Intelligence Reports on Opinion and Morale 1940–4* (1978).

45 H. M. Pelling, *British Trade Unionism*, p. 215. Citrine, for example, was serving on thirty public or industrial bodies, *Two Careers*, vol. 2 of the autobiography of Lord Citrine (Hutchinson 1967), p. 28.

46 For the history of their quarrel, and its patching up on Attlee's mediation, see Bevin 3/1, and Bullock, 2, pp. 132–6.

47 Forbes-Watson, Secretary of the BEC, declared: 'We did not start this war with Germany in order to improve our social services . . .' P. Addison, *The Road to 1945*, p. 214.

48 J. Harris, *William Beveridge* (Oxford University Press 1977), p. 311.

49 Addison, p. 218.

50 Addison, p. 223.

51 Addison, p. 233, quoting WP 43/255.

52 WP 43/140.

53 Bevin 2/4. Policy as Minister of Labour (24 March 1943), Industrial Relations (7 June 1943) and Reconstruction and Demobilization (21 June 1943).

54 WM (43) 140, 14 October 1943.

55 Dalton Diary, 22–26 March 1943, 24 May, 6 and 16 September.

56 Hickleton Papers, 18 August, 3 September 1943.

57 Attlee to Bevin, 30 September 1941, Bevin 2/4.

58 Addison, *Road to 1945*, p. 216.

59 Ibid., p. 256.

60 Bullock, 2, p. 315.

61 R. A. Eden, 'The Reckoning', *Memoirs* (Cassell 1960), pp. 453–4.

62 Bevin to Churchill, 21 March 1944, Bevin 3/1, suggesting that civil service unions might be allowed to affiliate to the TUC 'for industrial purposes only'.

63 Addison, *Road to 1945*, pp. 243–6.

64 *Parliamentary Debates*, Commons, vol. 401, col. 527.

65 NEC Campaign sub-committee, March–April 1945, Dalton, *Fateful Years*, pp. 432–3.

66 B. Donoughue and G. W. Jones, *Herbert Morrison : a portrait of a politician* (Weidenfeld 1973), p. 332.

67 LPAC, 1931, p. 172; also Snowden's speech, LPAC, 1928, p. 232.

68 Lord Wavell, *The Viceroy's Journal*, Penderel Moon ed. (Oxford University Press 1973), p. 131.

69 Courtauld's speeches were later collected in *Ideals and Industry : Wartime Papers* (Cambridge University Press 1949) and published with support from Conservative Party and the Industrial Christian Fellowship.

70 A recommendation reiterated in the Associated Chambers of Commerce pamphlet, *Postwar Reconstruction* (May 1943).

71 Eighth Conference, April 1943 (TJ C22).

72 TJ C22, p. 9.

73 TJ C22, p. 3.

74 TJ C22, p. 9.

75 Ministry of Fuel and Power, *Coal Mining*, Cmd. 6610 (1945). For a list of the members of the Committee, see Kirby, *The Coal Industry*, p. 189.

76 Quoted in Kirby, p. 191.

77 *Parliamentary Debates*, Commons, 5th series, vol. 411, cols. 87–8, 29 May 1945.

78 Kirby, p. 197.

79 Shinwell admitted that: see Sir Norman Chester, *The Nationalisation of British Industry 1945–51* (HMSO 1975), p. 8.

80 Kirby, p. 200; Chester, pp. 550–8.

81 Addison, p. 219, quoting Min Info 1/292; and Nuffield Conference Reports, TJ C22 *passim*.

82 PREM 4/21/3, 22 August 1941.

83 Addison, *Road to 1945*, p. 139.

84 H. M. Pelling, *The British Communist Party* (Black 1958), pp. 120–9.

85 Among textile workers in Lancashire, for example (see above, p. 212).

86 Bevin 2/4, memo of 21 June 1943, p. 2.

87 Addison, pp. 120–3.

88 Bullock, 2, p. 137.

89 S. H. Beer, *Modern British Politics*, 1st ed., p. 215.

90 Joan Robinson, quoted in José Harris, *William Beveridge*, p. 437.

II PARTY AND THE PARLIAMENTARY ILLUSION

1 Thomson to Hoare, 2 March 1927, Templewood V 2.

2 W. Milne-Bailey, *The Industrial Parliament Project* (December 1926), p. 5.

3 H. H. Asquith, *On Coalition* (1925), p. 40.

4 Templewood V 1, 25 January 1924. Perhaps the clearest index of anti-coalition feeling was the widespread revolt among constituency parties, during the 1922 election, against Bonar Law's decision not to atack too hard the ex-coalition Tories. Several local associations put up independent candidates, as did Lord Beaverbrook; these had an appreciable effect on the campaign.

5 Templewood VI 1.

6 CAB 305/26, 2 August 1926. Report by Blain.

7 J. C. C. Davidson papers, *passim*; Beaverbrook papers C111 (2 May 1928).

8 CNU Council Minutes 1933.

9 Memo by Younger, 13 April 1925, quoted in the Chilston Report on Organisation, April 1928.

10 The Chilston Report recommended revision of the Central Office-National Union 1906 Concordat, to the detriment of the National Union.

11 CNU Council Minutes 1928.

12 CNU Council Minutes, July 1930.

13 SM GD 193/121/5.

14 *Conservative Agents' Journal*, *passim*, especially July 1921, November 1923, 1927 and August 1930.

15 CNU Minutes 1933.

16 The 1933 Conference voted 344 to 737 against the platform on India. But since only 65 per cent of the 1,834 acceptances attended, the diehards claimed it to have been unrepresentative. A year later, at Bristol, the vote was 520 to 543 – a majority of only 23, with only 59 per cent attendance, which suggests that the diehards found it easier to attract delegates. But at the Queens' Hall meeting in December 1934, they mustered only 320 to 1,102.

17 J. Scanlon, *Very Foreign Affairs*, p. 89.

18 D. Marquand, *Ramsay MacDonald* (Cape 1977), pp. 764–5.

19 Ross McKibbin, *The Evolution of the Labour Party 1910–24* (Oxford University Press 1974), p. 246.

20 J. C. C. Davidson, *Memoirs of a Conservative*, pp. 264–5.

21 SM GD 193/120/1. (Trust C, the anti-socialist 'special election fund' of which Davidson, Steel-Maitland and Lord Queensbrough were trustees, had reached £265,432 by December 1926.)

22 Templewood VI 1. Davidson to Hoare, 30 December 1929.

23 Especially over the Washington Hours legislation (SM GD 193/348, January–April 1930). After a House of Commons struggle, the Labour Party Bill eventually excluded the railways, thus conceding one of the NCEO's main demands.

24 W. Milne-Bailey, *The Industrial Parliament Project*, p. 5, p. 27 (December 1926).

25 Miliband, *Parliamentary Socialism*, p. 161. The genesis of the Economic General Staff is to be found in MacDonald's 1924 proposal; it was revised in 1929, as the Economic Advisory Council, but as S. Howson and D. Winch argue (in *The Economic Advisory Council 1930–39*) the EAC 'arose out of the experience of a wide spectrum of serious observers of the economic scene throughout the 1920s' (p. 24).

26 'I want Labour, Capital and Economics, to unite in operating an administrative organ to spur all our industries.' R. MacDonald in Jones, *Whitehall Diary*, II, p. 220.

27 Templewood VI 2; R. Bassett, *Nineteen Thirty-one: Political Crisis* (Macmillan 1958), p. 41.

489

28 CAB 23/64, 4 June; SB D 4.3, Labour Government 2.

29 Templewood VI 2; Swinton 2/1.

30 Waldron Smithers' correspondence (Baldwin D 4·3, Labour Government 2).

31 Templewood VI 2.

32 Neville Chamberlain papers, 15 August 1931.

33 *Inter alia* H. Nicolson, *King George V : his life and reign* (Constable 1952), p. 461.

34 Davidson Papers, August–October 1931.

35 Bassett, *Nineteen Thirty-one*, p. 293.

36 Baldwin D 4.2, vols. 45/46; also MacDonald to Baldwin 2 October 1931.

37 Margesson MRGN 1/1 MacDonald-Margesson correspondence July–September 1932; Davidson papers; Stonehaven correspondence 1932–4.

38 SB D 4.2, vol. 46; memo by Stonehaven 12 December 1933.

39 Weir 12/4/48, memorandum on 'Britain's political situation as it appears to me', n.d. 1934.

40 SB D 4.2, vol. 46, Stonehaven memo 1, August 1934.

41 SB D 4.4 Propaganda; Baldwin's correspondence with Sir Joseph Ball.

42 Miliband, *Parliamentary Socialism*, p. 236.

43 Quoted in Addison, *Road to 1945*, p. 56.

44 Q. Hogg, C. Lancaster and P. Thorneycroft *Forward by the Right: A National Policy for Coal* (1944).

45 Miliband, *Parliamentary Socialism*, p. 183.

46 General Council Minutes, 10 November 1931.

47 Bevin papers, TUC/NEC meeting, 10 November 1931.

48 Bullock, *Bevin*, vol. 1, p. 503.

49 H. M. Pelling, *History of the Labour Party*, p. 195.

50 Labour 8·3 million votes, 154 seats: Conservatives 11·8 million, 532 seats.

51 LP/UN/18/47–53.

52 Miliband, *Parliamentary Socialism*, p. 236.

53 *The Nation*, 2 October 1937; TUC Conference Report 1937.

54 Bullock, *Bevin*, vol. 1, p. 598.

55 Henderson told the 1932 Conference: 'My view of the situation is that nothing has happened either to the Party or to our electoral position to warrant scrapping of our programme or policy, or the revolutionising of our methods.' LPAC 1932.

56 See, for example, the questionnaire and policy documents organised on the Distressed Areas (1936–7) (LP/DAC/1–12) and Fascism (1934) (LP/FAS/34/103).

57 Miliband, *Parliamentary Socialism*, p. 193.

58 SB D4 Adm. 5, vol. 47; TJ 4.6, 14 March 1935. Jones referred particularly to developments in the cotton industry, iron and steel, and the work of the Coal Mines Reorganisation Commission.

59 See, in particular, Carpenter, 'Corporatism in Britain', *JCH* 1976, I, pp. 1–16.

60 For a summary and list of signatories, see Harold Macmillan's memoirs, *Winds of Change*, vol. 1, 1914–39 (Macmillan 1966), appendix D.

61 See, for example, D. C. Watt, *Personalities and Politics*, R. K. Middlemas, *Diplomacy of Illusion*, R. P. Shay, *British Rearmament in the Thirties*, and especially D. N. Winch, *Economics and Policies*.

62 Middlemas and Barnes, *Baldwin*, p. 775.

63 Cf. D. H. E. Butler and D. E. Stokes, *Political Change in Britain: the evolution of electoral choice*, 2nd ed. (Macmillan 1974).

64 LPAC 1928, p. 225.

65 But see T. D. Burridge, *British Labour and Hitler's War* (Deutsch 1976), where it is argued that, as chairman of various important Cabinet committees, Attlee and Bevin had the chance to influence policy-making, while Churchill's attention was distracted by grand strategy.

66 N. Mansergh and E. R. W. Lumby, eds., *The Transfer of Power 1942–47* (HMSO 1970), vol. I, The Cripps Mission, January to April 1942, Doc. 60.

67 LPAC 1944, p. 161.

68 Miliband, *Parliamentary Socialism*, p. 278.

69 R. H. Tawney, 'British Socialism Today' in *The Radical Tradition: twelve essays on politics, education and literature*, R. Hinden, ed. (Allen & Unwin 1964).

70 TJ C22, Nuffield Conference, pp. 3–4.

71 MRGNL/4, Margesson to Baldwin, 4 March 1941.

72 Final Report 1949 (CP Organisation files).

73 Address to the Multiple Shops' Federation, 9 March 1945.

74 Cf. Addison, *Road to 1945*, chapter 3.

12   CONTINUOUS CONTRACT

1 TJ B7, IPA No. 80, 1st Memorandum 1931.

2 John Hilton, for example, author of the brilliant vignette of life on the dole, *Rich Man, Poor Man* (Allen & Unwin 1944), wrote for the Ministry of Health a series of perceptive analyses of the long-term social effects of mass unemployment in 1933–4. (TJ C21.)

3 TJ B5, November 1936, Lecture on 'Advisory Bodies in Government Service'. Jones cited in particular the Board of Trade Advisory Council, whose reports were currently circulated to Cabinet, the bodies set up under the Agricultural Marketing Act of 1933, state corporations like the Central Electricity Board, and the Ministry of Labour's National Joint Council of 1930.

4 *Vide* Steel-Maitland's files of press cuttings on industrial questions (SM GD 193/*passim*).

5 Davidson papers, Central Office Organisation, n.d., 1928.

6 'They are just the case which will attract the greatest amount of public sympathy, and for whom it is the hardest to do anything under the transference scheme.' SM GD 193/326. Cf. also E. Grigg to Baldwin (SB, vol. 6, D 2.3, Unemployment 1933).

7 CAB 44/34, 30 November 1934.

8 CAB 27/575, 29 October 1934. Nevertheless Chamberlain 'made all the running with his centralised scheme', as Horace Wilson wrote to MacDonald (PREM 1/141, 6 October 1933).

9 TJ C15–16, 1 November 1934, W. Eady to T. Jones.

10 TJ C16/44. Eady to Lord Rushcliffe, 18 February 1937.

11 CP 196/35.

12 UAR 34/10th meeting, 16 October 1935.

13 See p. 233 above.

14 CP 172/36, 22 June 1936, and CAB 44/36, 25 June 1936.

15 CAB 47/36, 29 June 1936.

16 Barnes and Middlemas, *Baldwin*, pp. 892–4.

17 The 1933 Conference actually pledged itself to call a general strike against British involvement in war in any circumstances.

18 For a comprehensive list see J. P. Kyba, 'British Attitudes Towards Disarmament and Rearmament 1932–5' (unpublished thesis, London 1967).

19 See, for example, David Butler, 'By-elections and their interpretation' in C. P. Cook and J. A. Ramsden, eds., *By-elections in British politics* (Macmillan 1973), pp. 5–12.

20 Labour polled 6·5 million votes in 1931 (gaining only 52 seats) and although this represented a fall of nearly 2 million from the 1929 peak of 8·3 million, it has been argued (by J. Stevenson and C. P. Cook in *The Slump: society and politics during the depression* (Cape 1977)) that 1929 was artificial. What is certain is that the *core* of Labour's working-class vote held steady.

21 Barnes and Middlemas, *Baldwin*, p. 746.

22 Ibid., p. 753.

23 Martin Ceadel, 'Interpreting East Fulham' in Cook and Ramsden, *By-elections*, pp. 137–8; also Barnes and Middlemas, pp. 745–7, and Kyba, *passim*.

24 For a discussion of the *imagery* of fear, see Uri Bialer, 'The Danger of Air Bombardment' in Brian Bond, ed., *War and Society; a year book of military history 1975* (Croom Helm 1976).

25 C. Madge and T. Harrisson, *Britain by Mass Observation* (Penguin 1939), pp. 87–96.

26 T 161/783/48431/02/1, January 1937; quoted in R. P. Shay, *British Rearmament in the Thirties*.

27 T 171/324, 12 February 1935; quoted in Shay, *op. cit.*

28 T 161/783/48431/3, 11 January 1937.

29 Middlemas, *Diplomacy of Illusion*, chapters 3 and 4; Shay, *op. cit.*

30 CAB 24/280; CP 247/38, Appendix I.

31 T 171/341, 11 January 1939; quoted in Shay, *op. cit.*

32 As is indicated by the careful soundings taken by Sir Joseph Ball, Chamberlain's Press Advisor in 10 Downing Street; CAB 15/39(3), 29 March 1939.

33 See Bernard Gainer, *The Alien Invasion; the origins of the Aliens Act of 1905* (Heinemann Educational 1972).

34 A. J. Sherman, *Island Refuge; Jewish Refugees from the Third Reich* (1975).

35 TUC GC and FGP Minutes, December 1935–March 1936. Also Hoare X5, 1938, May 21. 'Refugees from Austria, MPs in general humane [but] in particular hostile to immigrants, e.g. also doctors.'

36 Sherman, pp. 183–90.

37 JSM/REF/28/7.

38 CP 189/34 Annexe; CAB 24/251, 11 July 1934.

39 CAB 23/79, 29/34(2), 18 July 1934.

40 CAB 24/264; CP 261/36.

41 CAB 55/36(2), 29 July 1936.

42 CAB 27/610 *passim*.

43 CAB 23/89, 30/37(11).

44 Nothing as yet exists in British historiography comparable to Michel Foucault's huge project of analysing the control institutions in society and the human sciences linked with them, in, for example, *Discipline and Punish: The birth of the prison*, trs. A. Sheridan (Allen Lane 1976).

45 Halsey, *Trends in British Society*, table 6.2. The great increase took place after the 1944 Act had provided the means: the total in 1951 (direct grant and aided grammar schools, and secondary modern) was 2,049,000 or 33·6 per cent.

46 TJ C/59 – Memorandum of 1924.

47 Quoted in N. Middleton and S. Weitzman, *A Place for Everyone : a history of state education from the end of the eighteenth century to the 1970s* (Gollancz 1976), p. 340. For a discussion of education and the continuing phenomenon of deference, see also A. P. Thornton, *The Habit of Authority : paternalism in British history* (Allen & Unwin 1966).

48 In so far as state education became the almost universal source of literacy by the 1840s, an element of independent, self-taught literacy began to disappear – of which a poignant symbol was the decline in the great working-class libraries, particularly in mining communities in South Wales, which, by the 1950s, were little used, and in the 60s were broken up and sold.

49 BL B 1, memorandum of January 1917.

50 SM GD 193/109/5. Walton's memorandum of 3 April 1922.

51 LG F/6/1/23. See also LG F/1/4/8, and Weir 4/1–3 for Walton's access to secret government information.

52 Barnes and Middlemas, p. 110; Jones, *A diary with letters*, p. 45.

53 CP 314/23.

54 SM GD 193/389.

55 CP 314/23.

56 J. C. C. Davidson, *Memoirs of a Conservative*, pp. 203–4.

57 Davidson papers, Propaganda, 26 August 1926.

58 SM GD 193/432, 18 March 1927.

59 *Conservative Agents' Journal*, 1935.

60 SM GD 193/121/5. Hoare Organisation Report 1929–30. Templewood VI 3.

61 Davidson papers, CO Organisation, n.d., 1929. By this time, 'Political Education' rated a separate heading in the CNU Annual Report. Political education classes were being held in 300 constituencies in 1927. (See also JCCD 226, 8 December 1929, Davidson to Hall Caine, in which the Party Chairman defined the main groups involved: local 'elementary' political education in the constituencies, professional work by agents and women's groups, and the 'higher' schools in Provincial Areas and at Ashridge.) A further development of political education took place in 1930 (Templewood VI 3) in which, despite the débâcle of the 1929 election, the advertising agents, Bensons, were drawn in closer as advisors; but some of the centralisation of Davidson's period was done away with in favour of Area control.

62 Such as War Resistance (JSM WR 1–37) and the campaign against the UAB scales after the Standstill Act (JSM/MT/5–42); and NCL *Appeal to the Public Conscience*, February 1935.

63 CAB 37/131/1, 1 July 1916.

64 TJ B6 November 1936, 'Advisory Bodies in Government': Lecture to the IPA.

65 TJ C15, Eady to Jones, 1 November 1934.

66 TJ C15, Eady to Jones, 12 November 1936.

67 Baldwin D 2.3, Ball to Baldwin, 12 June 1935.

68 Its publicity files show that in the 1930s it avoided self-styled publicists like W. T. Cranfield and Stanley Jay, both cast in the Sydney Walton mould,

leaving public relations work to individual Confederations (NCEO Publicity BEC/MISC/1/7).

69 Sir John Reith, *Into the Wind* (Hodder & Stoughton 1949), pp. 352–3.

70 P. Addison, *Road to 1945*, p. 79.

71 *The heart of Britain* (1941); *Yesterday is over your shoulder* (1942).

72 Addison, p. 117.

73 Lecture at the Imperial War Museum Conference on War Propaganda, July 1973.

74 Quoted in Addison, p. 132.

75 Asa Briggs, *The history of broadcasting in the United Kingdom* (Oxford University Press 1970), vol. 2, The war of words, p. 210.

76 Addison, p. 118.

77 Dalton, *Diary*, 9–16 July; quoted in Addison, p. 113.

78 Addison, p. 162, citing Mass Observation polls of 1942.

79 This section is based on the work of Penny Summerfield, whose forthcoming book discusses in detail the ABCA controversy and the significance of army education and propaganda in World War Two.

80 April 1944 Organisation Review. Great stress was laid on the introduction of younger candidates: 'As the present trend of public opinion is so definite, it will be extremely difficult to secure the return of Members of advanced years.'

81 As Summerfield notes, even the post-D-Day electoral registration campaign was only 60 per cent effective.

82 Addison, p. 162. Quoting INF 1/292 Home Intelligence Weekly Report No. 15.

83 CAB 26/26(2) and CAB 28/26(1).

84 *The diplomatic diaries of Oliver Harvey 1937–40*, John Harvey, ed. (Collins 1970), p. 102.

85 A. Duff Cooper, *Old Men Forget* (Hart-Davis 1953), p. 227.

86 Hugh Cudlipp, *Publish and be damned: the astonishing story of the Daily Mirror* (Dakers 1953), pp. 221–5. See also A. C. H. Smith et al., *The Popular Press and Social Change* (Birmingham University 1970), and S. Briggs, *Keep Smiling Through: the Home Front 1939–45* (Weidenfeld 1975), and Angus Calder, *The People's War: Britain 1939–45* (Cape 1969).

87 'Cato' (M. M. Foot et al.), *Guilty Men* (Gollancz 1940), T. H. Wintringham, *People's War* (Penguin 1942). See also A. L. Rowse, *All Souls and Appeasement: a contribution to contemporary history* (Macmillan 1961).

88 See, for example, C. Andrew, 'Can the truth about the Zinoviev Letter ever be written?' *The Times Higher Educational Supplement*, 14 October 1977.

89 For a fuller discussion, see R. K. Middlemas, 'Cabinet secrecy and the Crossman Diaries', *Political Quarterly*, 47, 1, 1976, pp. 39–58. See also D. R. Hopkin, 'Propaganda and censorship in twentieth-century history' (unpublished thesis, Aberystwyth 1972).

90 PREM 1/171.

91 As noted earlier, the system was not designed to record everything that took place, but to summarise discussion and present formal conclusions in a manner which facilitated future reference and executive action; nothing concerning party political discussion was (or is) minuted, even when those considerations were central to the evolution of policy.

92 PREM 1/171.

93 CAB 21/391 (1934).

94 CAB 21/443.

95 PREM 1/171, 8 November 1934; CAB 35/34/4.

96 PREM 4/6/14. Churchill himself commented: 'While controversy is no doubt inevitable, it is a consideration whether it should be allowed to start so soon.'

97 M. M. Gowing assisted by L. Arnold, *Independence and Deterrence: Britain and atomic energy 1945–52* (Macmillan 1970), Chapter 16.

98 P. G. Wersky, 'The Visible College', in *Nature*, vol. 233, p. 529.

99 F. R. Gannon, *The British press and Germany 1936–9* (Clarendon Press, 1971).

100 Baldwin, Propaganda D 4.4.

101 Beaverbrook Papers, Box C148, Press.

102 Ibid., Box 80. Yet only two years earlier, Davidson, a graduate of the old school, had been talking of the need for 'complete co-operation in the campaign of education and propaganda'. (Ibid., Box C111, Press.)

103 Cf. James Curran et al., eds., *Mass Communication and Society* (Edward Arnold for Open University Press 1977); P. Beharrell and G. Philo, *Trade Unions and the Media* (Macmillan 1977).

104 Cf. Stuart Hall, 'Culture, the Media and the "Ideological Effect" ', in Curran, *Mass Communication*.

105 J. Richards, *Visions of Yesterday* (Routledge 1973); Colin Seymour-Ure, *The Political Impact of Mass Media* (Constable 1964).

106 The basis of criminal statistics varies over time and between different police forces, and a change in practice such as occurred with the Criminal Justice Act of 1914 may give the impression of a sudden fall in numbers of offenders sentenced to prison for serious offences. Nevertheless, the numbers sentenced fell steadily from 149,397 in 1901 to 35,439 in 1920, 24,870 in 1940. (Halsey, *Trends in British Society*, p. 531, table 15.4.)

107 The building societies advanced £9·3m in 1910, £29·1m in 1920, £88·7m in 1930 and £137m in 1938, while the number of mortgages increased from 159,348 in 1930 to 232,294 in 1938. (Halsey, *Trends*, table 10.34.) As a percentage of the population, house ownership rose from 25 per cent in 1900 to 31 per cent in 1940.

108 S. Cohen and J. Young, eds., *The Manufacture of News: Social problems, deviance and the mass media* (Constable 1973), p. 10.

109 SM GD 193/434, 6 November 1925.

13 CORPORATE BIAS

1 Thomas Hobbes, *Leviathan* (Dent, Everyman ed. 1914), p. 177.

2 As is argued, for example, by W. P. Grant and D. Marsh, 'The Parties: Reality or Myth?', *Government and Opinion*, 12, 2 (1977), pp. 205–6.

3 R. Dahrendorf, *Class and Class Conflict in Industrial Society* (Routledge & Kegan Paul 1959).

4 Anthony Giddens, *The Class Structure of the advanced societies* (Hutchinson 1973), p. 107.

5 Jurgen Habermas, *Legitimation Crisis*, trs. Thomas McCarthy (Beacon Press, Boston 1975); Claus Offe, *Strukturprobleme des Kapitalistischen Staates* (Frankfurt 1972); G. Agnoli, *Transformazion der Democratie* (1969).

6 Claus Offe, 'Political Authority and Class Structures', *International Journal of Sociology* II, 1 (Spring 1972), pp. 95–96.

Sources and references

7 Ibid.

8 R. Altmann, *Spate Nachricht vom Staat* (Stuttgart 1969), p. 51.

9 C. Offe, 'Political Authority', p. 116.

10 Alan Cawson, 'Pluralism, Corporatism and the Role of the State', *Government and Opinion*, 13, 2 (1978), p. 194.

11 See, generally, L. Carpenter, 'Corporatism in Britain'. The distinction between liberal and authoritarian models of corporatism is taken up by L. C. O. Panitch in 'The Development of Corporatism in Liberal Democracies', *Comparative Political Studies*, 10, 1 (1977), pp. 61–90.

12 Carpenter, p. 25.

13 R. E. Pahl and J. T. Winkler, 'The coming corporatism', *Challenge*, March/April 1975, pp. 28–35; S. Brittan, 'Towards a corporate state', *Encounter* 44 (1975), pp. 58–63; and, earlier, A. Shonfield, *Modern Capitalism: the changing balance of public and private power* (Oxford University Press 1966); Nigel Harris, *Competition and the Corporate Society: British Conservatives, the state and industry 1954–64* (Methuen 1972).

14 J. T. Winkler, 'Corporatism', *Archives Européene de Sociologie* (1976), p. 103.

15 E. J. Hobsbawm, *Industry and Empire* (Weidenfeld 1969).

16 L. Hannah, *The Rise of the Corporate Economy* (Methuen 1976).

17 Hannah, p. 197.

18 Hannah, p. 297.

19 S. H. Beer, *Modern British Politics* (2nd ed.), pp. 74–7.

20 J. Schumpeter, *Capitalism, Socialism and Democracy* (Allen & Unwin 1975), 2nd ed., pp. 256–69.

21 As is argued by G. Ionescu in *Centripetal Politics: Government and the new centres of power* (Hart-Davis, MacGibbon 1975).

22 R. Benewick, 'Politics without ideology: the perimeters of pluralism' in R. Benewick et al., *Knowledge and Belief in Politics: the problem of ideology* (St Martin's Press, New York 1973), pp. 130–50.

23 S. Black, *Industry and Government in Britain: the FBI in Politics 1945–65* (Saxon House 1973), p. 3.

24 Beer, *Modern British Politics*, 2nd ed., pp. 427–8.

25 This is put in a different form by Poulantzas when he describes the state as 'the factor of cohesion in a social formation, and the factor of the reproduction of the conditions of production of a system'. Nicos Poulantzas 'The Problem of the Capitalist State' in J. Urry and J. Wakeford, eds., *Power in Britain: sociological readings* (Heinemann Educational 1973), p. 298.

26 'The more society tends to be corporate, the less authoritative is the state,' G. Ionescu, *Centripetal Politics*, p. 20.

27 Philippe C. Schmitter, 'Still the Century of Corporatism?', *Review of Politics* 36 (1974), pp. 93–4. I am grateful to Alan Cawson for bringing this definition to my notice.

28 Engels to J. Bloch, 21 September 1890.

29 Beer, *Modern British Politics*, 2nd ed., pp. 427–8.

30 Robin Marris, 'Is the Corporate Economy the Corporate State?', *American Political Science Review*, 1972.

31 Rosa Luxemburg's supposition that only an 'ideal collective capitalist' could avoid the suicidal anarchy of capitalist society. 'Social Reform or Revolution' in D. Howard, ed., *Selected Political Writings of Rosa Luxemburg* (Monthly Review Press, New York 1971), p. 79.

14 THE CULT OF EQUILIBRIUM, 1945–65

1 Especially for the employers, since the only major study is partial, the FBI being a less significant subject than the BEC, whose archives have only recently been opened. Eric Wigham's book on the Engineering Employers' Federation is valuable, but inevitably invests one part of the BEC with greater significance.

2 There exists, also, a handful of studies, to suggest that the crucial role of a few men like Hankey, Warren Fisher or Horace Wilson was perpetuated – witness the part played by Sir Richard Way (Minister of Aviation) during the formative stage of the Concorde project, and the effect of changes among them, c. 1960, on the decision to apply for membership of the European Economic Community. (J. Bruce-Gardyne and Nigel Lawson *The Power Game, an examination of decision-making in government* (Macmillan 1977).)

3 F. P. Graham, 'A Legal Analysis of Trade Union Discipline in the United Kingdom' (Oxford D.Litt thesis, 1960) showed that of 80 unions studied (94 per cent of the TUC membership) 64 had powers of expulsion on general grounds.

4 29 September 1954, quoted in G. M. Harrison, *Trade Unions and the Labour Party since 1945* (Allen & Unwin 1960), p. 129.

5 TUCAR, General Council Report 1945.

6 C. Jenkins, *Power at the top: a critical survey of the nationalized industries* (MacGibbon & Kee 1959), *passim*. Only Citrine became a chairman of the CEGB.

7 Quoted in Pelling, *History of British Trade Unionism*, p. 234. The TUCAR 1952 referred to 'long-standing practice to seek to work amicably with whatever government is in power' (p. 300).

8 S. H. Beer, *Modern British Politics*, 1st ed., 1965, p. 337.

9 LPAC 1952, p. 245.

10 J. C. R. Dow, *The Management of the British Economy 1945–60* (Cambridge University Press 1964), p. 247.

11 C. A. R. Crosland, *The Future of British Socialism* (Cape 1956).

12 E. H. J. N. Dalton, *High tide and after: Memoirs 1945–60* (Muller 1962), pp. 248–9.

13 S. E. Finer, *Private Industry and Political Power* (Pall Mall 1958), pp. 16–19; Iron and Steel Council, First Report (September 1951), para. 45.

14 Sir Norman Kipping, *Summing Up* (Hutchinson 1972), p. 49.

15 Wigham, *The Power to Manage*, p. 158.

16 Wigham, pp. 164–92.

17 Wigham, p. 178.

18 Wigham, pp. 180–6.

19 R. J. Lieber, *British Politics and European Unity: parties, élites and pressure groups* (University of California Press 1971), p. 104.

20 S. Blank, *History of the FBI*, pp. 220–4, shows how the image of the businessman had improved since the early days of wartime.

21 W. Grant and D. Marsh, *The Confederation of British Industry* (Hodder & Stoughton 1977) pp. 25–6.

22 Kipping, p. 228.

23 In March 1965 they formed the Society of Independent Manufacturers, which by the mid-seventies, under the title of Smaller Business Association, possessed 20,000 members.

Sources and references

24 M. Polanyi, *Full Employment and Free Trade* (Cambridge University Press), p. 200.

25 Harrison, *Trade Unions and the Labour Party*, p. 224; TUC Reconstruction Report 1944.

26 MacDonald, *Trade Unions and the Government*, p. 150. Order 1376, which replaced 1305 in 1951, was brought in only after consultation with the NJAC; and, to meet General Council requirements, exempted inter-union disputes from the ban on strikes, whilst in practice denying recognition to shop stewards' action.

27	*1947*	*1948*	*1949*	*1950*	*1951*	*1952*	*1953*
Unemployment rate	3·1	1·8	1·6	1·5	1·2	2·1	1·8
Weekly wage earnings	221	239	249	263	289	312	331
Cost of living	159	169	174	180	197	215	221
1930 = 100							
	1954	*1955*	*1956*	*1957*	*1958*	*1959*	*1960*
	1·5	1·2	1·3	1·6	2·2	2·2	1·7
	335	386	417	436	451	471	502
	225	236	247	257	264	266	268

Source: Halsey, *Trends in British Society*, tables 4.8, 4.10, 4.11.

28 Kipping, pp. 84–5, 90.

29 E.g., over price stabilisation in 1955. S. Blank, *The FBI*, pp. 131–2.

30 R. Anthony Eden, *Memoirs, part 2, 1951–7,* 'Full Circle' (Cassell 1960), p. 358; H. G. Johnson, 'The Revival of Monetary Policy in Britain', *Three Banks' Review*, June 1956, p. 11.

31 S. H. Beer, *Modern British Politics* (2nd ed.), p. 329.

32 TUCAR 1956, p. 262.

33 FBI Report 1956, p. 3.

34 Dow, *Management of the British Economy*, p. 384.

35 N. Harris, *Competition and the corporate society*, p. 270.

36 *Spring vs. the TGWU*, 1955; *Bonsor vs. Musicians' Union*, 1956; *Huntley vs. Thornton et al.*, 1957.

37 TUCAR 1963, p. 390.

38 TUCAR 1964, p. 384.

39 At least if one takes R. H. S. Crossman et al., *New Fabian Essays* (Turnstile Press 1952), *Twentieth Century Socialism* (Penguin 1956), and Crosland, *The Future of British Socialism*, as representing main-line thinking.

40 L. Panitch, *Social Democracy and Industrial Militancy: the Labour Party, the trade unions and incomes policy 1945–7* (Cambridge University Press 1976), pp. 233–6.

41 What one commentator, in a different context, has called 'the attempt to obtain working-class consent to more exploitation by means of a communitarian conception, defining a community of interests between capital and labour in the name of a supposed interest transcending social classes'. (Vittorio Foá, 'Incomes Policy: a Crucial Problem for the Unions', *International Sociological Journal*, January 1964, p. 264.)

42 Panitch, *Social Democracy*, p. 236.

43 R. B. McCullum and A. Redman, *The British General Election of 1945*, p. 129.

44 Panitch, p. 240.

45 A democratic government must plan 'in a manner which preserves the

498

maximum possible freedom of action to the individual citizen', *Economic Survey 1947*, Cmnd. 7046.

46 Miliband, *Parliamentary Socialism*, p. 307.

47 H. A. Turner, *Trade Union growth, structure and policy : a comparative study of the cotton unions* (Allen & Unwin 1962), pp. 270–1.

48 D. H. E. Butler and R. Rose, *The British General Election of 1959* (Macmillan 1960), pp. 199–200.

49 L. S. Amery, *Thoughts on the Constitution* (Oxford University Press 1947).

50 *Annual Register*, 1945, p. 100.

51 J. D. Hoffman, *The Conservative Party in Opposition 1945–51* (1964), p. 23.

52 The Industrial Charter (Conservative Party 1947), p. 62.

53 In R. A. Butler, *Fundamental Issues : a statement on the future work of the Conservative Education Movement* (Conservative Political Centre 1946).

54 Maxwell-Fyffe Report, p. 12.

55 J. Ramsden, 'From Churchill to Heath' in R. A. Butler, ed., *The Conservatives : a history from their origins to 1965* (Allen & Unwin 1977), p. 417.

56 For a careful documentation of Conservative reluctance to legislate, despite local pressures in the late fifties, see N. Deakin, *The Immigration Issue in British Politics 1948–64* (Sussex Univ. D.Phil. thesis 1972).

57 R. T. Mackenzie, *British Political Parties : the distribution of power within the Conservative and Labour Parties* (Heinemann 1955), p. 303.

58 Beer, *Modern British Politics*, 1st ed. (1965), pp. 319–25.

59 Harris, *Competition and the corporate society*, pp. 1–3.

60 For a study of the housing pledges and their consequences, see M. Pinto-Duschinsky 'Bread and Circuses' in V. Bogdanor and R. Skidelsky, eds., *The Age of Affluence 1951–64* (Macmillan 1970), pp. 53–63.

61 Eden, *Memoirs 'Full Circle'*, pp. 262–3.

62 Andrew Shonfield, *British Economic Policy since the War*, 2nd ed. (Penguin 1959), p. 248.

63 *Vide* J. H. Goldthorpe et al., *The Affluent Worker : political attitudes and behaviour* (Cambridge University Press 1968).

64 CPAC 1962, p. 140.

65 M. Proudfoot, *British Politics and Government 1951–70 : a study of an affluent society* (Faber 1974), p. 118.

66 D. H. E. Butler and A. S. King, *The British General Election of 1964* (Macmillan 1965), p. 74.

67 A. Roth, *The Business Background of MPs* (Parliamentary Profile series 1961); W. L. Guttsman, *The British Political Elite* (MacGibbon & Kee 1963), Chapter 10.

68 See the quotation from Lord Bridges (Beer, p. 390).

69 Jürgen Habermas, *Legitimation Crisis* (Boston 1976).

70 D. H. E. Butler and D. E. Stokes, *Political Change in Britain : the evolution of electoral choice*, 2nd ed. (Macmillan 1974), pp. 409–13.

71 Butler and Stokes, pp. 9–10, 409–11.

72 'The structure of mass communications in Britain permits certain sorts of variations [but] they also contain the variations that are possible within quite narrow limits, set by the inconsistencies within a cluster of dominant interests.' P. Abrams, 'Mass Communication', *The Times Higher Educational Supplement*, 2 September 1977. See also Tom Burns, *The BBC : Public Institution and Private World* (Macmillan 1977).

73 Butler and Stokes, *Political Change*, p. 419.

74 B. Drewey, 'The Official Secrets Act', *Political Quarterly*, January 1973, pp. 88–93.

75 N. Bethell, *The Last Secret: forcible repatriation to Russia 1944–7* (Futura 1977). Nikolai Tolstoy, *Victims of Yalta* (Hodder & Stoughton 1978) gives in detail the way Eden and Foreign Office officials concealed the truth even from Churchill.

76 Cabinet, 8 March 1946 et seq.

77 Note of a meeting, Treasury Papers, 11 November 1942.

78 Hankey's memoirs – *The Supreme Command 1914–18* – were ready in 1946 but their clearance was held up until, in the end, he published, without consent but in bowdlerised form, in 1961. (S. W. Roskill, *Hankey, man of secrets*, vol. 2, 1919–31 (Collins 1972), pp. 335, 532–4.) Jones was allowed only to publish *Diary with Letters* (1956) containing material after 1930 when he had already left government service, and his full *Whitehall Diary* did not appear until after 1969.

79 *The Times*, 20–21 August 1952.

80 Butler and Stokes, *Political Change* (2nd ed.), p. 480.

81 Eden, *Memoirs*, 'Full Circle', p. 299.

82 Beer, *Modern British Politics*, pp. 347–8.

83 Harris, *Competition*, p. 319.

15 A CRISIS OF THE STATE?

1 Report of the Royal Commission on Industrial Representation, 1974, p. 5. For a much more apocalyptic conclusion see Tom Nairn, *The Break-up of Britain: Crisis and neo-nationalism* (NLB 1977).

2 Sir John Hunt's affidavit, pp. 3, 18. See generally, R. K. Middlemas, 'The Crossman Diaries Case', *Political Quarterly*, 1976.

3 Butler and Stokes, *Political Change*, p. 424.

4 Otto Kahn-Freund, *Labour and the Law* (Stevens 1972), p. 2.

5 For a fuller consideration of these and other aspects, see A. Touraine, *The Post-Industrial Society*, trs. L. F. X. Mayhew (Wildwood 1974), and D. Bell, *The Coming of Post-Industrial Society: a venture in social forecasting* (Heinemann Educational 1974).

6 R. H. S. Crossman, *The Diaries of a Cabinet Minister*, vol. 1, Minister of Housing 1964–6 (Cape/Hamilton 1975), p. 71; M. Stewart, *The Jekyll and Hyde years: politics and economics since 1964* (Dent 1976), p. 82.

7 In a speech at Lancaster House, *The Times*, 17 December 1964.

8 L. Panitch, *Social Democracy and Industrial Militancy* provides the most lucid survey for the years 1964–70.

9 *Statement of Intent*, quoted in Panitch, p. 73.

10 Panitch, *Social Democracy*, p. 105.

11 *Parliamentary Debates*, Commons, vol. 731, cols. 1789–94.

12 *Parliamentary Debates*, Commons, vol. 732, col. 1852.

13 TUCAR 1966, pp. 395–400. The fact that some of the opposition to the Prices and Incomes Bill came from the CPGB-led 'Committee for the Defence of Trade Unions' may be another explanation.

14 CBI AR 1966, pp. 3, 12.

15 Total union membership fell by 1.4 per cent in 1967 (Panitch, p. 150).

16 TU Conference of Executives, 2 March 1967, quoted in Panitch, p. 138.

17 TUCAR 1967, p. 507.

18 TUCAR 1968, p. 374.
19 *Tribune*, 9 February 1968.
20 Cf. Alan Fox's research paper for the Commission, *Industrial Sociology and Industrial Relations* (1966) and Andrew Shonfield's *Note of Dissent*.
21 *The Times*, 18 April 1969.
22 P. Jenkins, *The Battle of Downing Street* (C. Knight 1970), p. 117.
23 Panitch, *Social Democracy*, p. 192.
24 *Parliamentary Debates*, Commons, 3 July 1969, speech by Robert Carr, spokesman on labour and industry.
25 Quoted in Panitch, p. 225, note 67. See also *The Times*, 23 July 1972.
26 Evidence to the Donovan Commission 1966, p. 54.
27 J. F. B. Goodman and T. G. Whittington, *Shop Stewards in British Industry* (McGraw Hill 1969), p. 38. 'In most well-organised industries it is the national agreements which are of minor significance: the worker relies primarily on shop-floor bargaining to win acceptable terms.' (R. Hyman, *Strikes* (Fontana 1972), p. 44.)
28 'Informal trade unionism occurring because formal unions are incapable of fulfilling their functions satisfactorily.' V. L. Allen, *Militant Trade Unionism: a re-analysis of industrial action in an inflationary situation* (Merlin Press 1966), p. 115.
29 H. Beynon, *Working for Ford* (Allen Lane 1972; reissued EP Publishing 1975), pp. 267–8.
30 A. D. Flanders and H. A. Clegg, *The System of Industrial Relations in Great Britain* (Blackwell Oxford 1964), p. 334; Lane and Roberts, *Strike at Pilkingtons, passim*.
31 Goodman and Whittington, *Shop Stewards*, Chapter 4.
32 Alan Fox, *Beyond Contract: Work Power and Trust Relations* (Faber 1974). David Coates, *The Labour Party and the struggle for Socialism* (Cambridge University Press 1975). I. Boraston, H. Clegg and M. Rimmer emphasise the *diversity* of shop-floor organisation and the importance of assessing whether local trade union officials or elected shop-floor representatives predominate in political cases, *Workplace and Unions: a study of local relationships in fourteen unions* (Heinemann Educational 1975).
33 *Vide* Len Murray's interview in *The Times*, 22 August 1977, in which he emphasised the traditional distinction of view between trade unions and political parties.
34 R. Miliband, *The State in Capitalist Society* (Weidenfeld 1972), p. 160.
35 Tony Lane, *The Union makes us strong*, p. 266.
36 W. Grant and D. Marsh, *The Confederation of British Industry*, pp. 12–20.
37 *Wage Inflation and the Employer* (1971) quoted in Wigham, *The Power to Manage*, pp. 271–2.
38 B. Weekes, *Industrial Relations and the Limits of the Law: the industrial effects of the Industrial Relations Act 1971* (Blackwell 1975), pp. 58–61. Guest Keen & Nettlefold encouraged unionisation, much as Mond had done forty years before.
39 CBI, *The Road to Recovery* (October 1976).
40 Stuart Holland, *The Socialist Challenge* (Quartet 1975).
41 M. Hatfield, *The House the Left Built: Inside Labour Policy-making 1970–5* (Gollancz 1978).
42 R. Taylor, 'The Uneasy Alliance, Labour and the Unions', *Political Quarterly*, October 1976.

Sources and references

43 Paul Johnson, 'A Brotherhood of National Misery', *New Statesman,* 16 May 1975, et seq.

44 'The next three years: the problem of priorities' (Liaison Committee Document, July 1976).

45 For a good analysis of the state of the party in the late 60s, see R. Rhodes James, *Ambitions and Realities: British Politics 1964–70* (Weidenfeld 1972).

46 Martin Walker, *The National Front* (Fontana 1977), pp. 9, 149–50, 158–68.

47 Philip Norton, *Conservative Dissidents, 1970–74* (Temple Smith 1978).

48 O. Kahn-Freund, *Labour and the Law* (Stevens 1972), pp. 54–5.

49 Beer, p. 419.

50 J. Westergaard and H. Resler, *Class in a Capitalist Society: a study of contemporary Britain* (Heinemann Educational 1976), p. 16.

51 Westergaard and Resler, p. 26.

52 J. T. Winkler, 'Corporatism', *Archives européenes de sociologie,* 1976; J. T. Winkler and R. Pahl, 'The coming corporatism', *Challenge,* March–April 1975.

53 Winkler and Pahl, pp. 132–3.

54 J. M. Keynes, *The Economic Consequences of the Peace* (Macmillan 1919), pp. 1–3.

55 *Stalinismus und Antikommunismus* (Frankfurt 1967), pp 13–14.

INDEX

LIST OF ACRONYMS

ABCA	Army Bureau of Current Affairs
ACAS	Advisory Conciliation and Arbitration Service
AEU/AUEW	Amalgamated Engineering Union
ASE	Amalgamated Society of Engineers
ASLEF	Amalgamated Society of Locomotive Engineers and Firemen
ASRS	Amalgamated Society of Railway Servants
BEC	British Employers' Confederation
BSP	British Socialist Party
BUF	British Union of Fascists
CBI	Confederation of British Industries
CCR	Committee of Civil Research
CID	Committee of Imperial Defence
CND	Campaign for Nuclear Disarmament
CPGB	Communist Party of Great Britain

CWC	Clyde Workers' Committee
DEA	Department of Economic Affairs
DORA	Defence of the Realm Act
DRC	Defence Requirements Committee
DSIR	Department of Scientific and Industrial Research
EAC	Economic Advisory Council
EEF	Engineering Employers' Federation
ETU	Electrical Trades Union
FBI	Federation of British Industries
GFTU	General Federation of Trade Unions
GMWU	General and Municipal Workers Union
ILO	International Labour Organisation
ILP	Independent Labour Party
IMF	International Monetary Fund
IWW	International Workers of the World
JCC	Joint Consultative Committee
LRC	Labour Representation Committee
MFGB	Miners' Federation of Great Britain
NABM	National Association of British Manufacturers
NAEE	National Association of Employers and Employed
NCEO	National Confederation of Employers' Organisations
NCCL	National Council for Civil Liberties
NCL	National Council of Labour
NEC	National Executive Council
NEDC	National Economic Development Council
NIC	National Industrial Council/Conference
NJC	National Joint Council
NTWF	National Transport Workers' Federation
NUM	National Union of Mineworkers
NUPE	National Union of Public Employees
NUR	National Union of Railwaymen
NUWM	National Unemployed Workers' Movement
PEP	Political and Economic Planning
PLP	Parliamentary Labour Party
SBAC	Society of British Aircraft Constructors
SDF	Social Democratic Federation
SFIO	French Socialist Party
SLP	Socialist Labour Party
SPD	German Socialist Party
SSM	Shop Stewards' Movement
TGWU	Transport and General Workers' Union
TUC	Trades Union Congress
UAB	Unemployment Assistance Board
USDAW	Union of Shop Distributive and Allied Workers
WENC	War Emergency National Council
WSPU	Women's Social and Political Union

512